MAURICE MORGANN

SHAKESPEARIAN CRITICISM

MAURICE MORGANN

SHAKESPEARIAN CRITICISM

COMPRISING

1. An Essay on the Dramatic Character
of Sir John Falstaff
2. Extensive Revisions of the Essay
3. A Commentary on *The Tempest*
4. Miscellaneous Comments

EDITED WITH INTRODUCTIONS
AND NOTES BY
DANIEL A. FINEMAN

OXFORD
AT THE CLARENDON PRESS
1972

Oxford University Press, Ely House, London W.1

GLASGOW NEW YORK TORONTO MELBOURNE WELLINGTON
CAPE TOWN IBADAN NAIROBI DAR ES SALAAM LUSAKA ADDIS ABABA
DELHI BOMBAY CALCUTTA MADRAS KARACHI LAHORE DACCA
KUALA LUMPUR SINGAPORE HONG KONG TOKYO

PRINTED IN GREAT BRITAIN
AT THE UNIVERSITY PRESS, OXFORD
BY VIVIAN RIDLER
PRINTER TO THE UNIVERSITY

FOR NAOMI

PREFACE

'THE better we know it', wrote D. Nichol Smith of Morgann's *Essay on Falstaff* in 1903, 'the more we shall regret that it is the only critical work he allowed to survive.' Morgann's other admirers have often had the same thought as they reflected upon the tradition that at his death his executrix carried out his behest to destroy all his literary papers. It is therefore with a fair expectation of pleasing those who have taken delight in the *Essay*, and wished for more, that I here partly disprove the legend of the lost manuscripts. The following pages contain two hitherto unpublished pieces of Shakespeare criticism by Morgann—his Revisions of his *Essay* and his Commentary for an edition of *The Tempest*. In bulk the two manuscripts more than double the Morgann canon of critical writing, till now limited to the *Essay*; and though not left in a state that can be described as ready for the press, their contents are sufficiently elaborated to deepen and extend significantly our knowledge of the working of Morgann's mind. To make the Revisions immediately comprehensible, as well as to make the volume complete, I have also re-edited the *Essay*.

It gives me pleasure to express my gratitude to the many who have helped me in my study of Morgann and his texts. I feel a deep sense of obligation to the Director and staff of that scholars' paradise, the Folger Shakespeare Library at Washington, D.C. It was while enjoying the benefits of a Fellowship there that, under the expert guidance of Dr. James G. McManaway, I came upon the new Morgann materials reproduced in this volume. The manuscripts are printed by permission of the former Director of the Folger Library, Dr. Louis B. Wright. The present Director, Dr. O. B. Hardison, Jr., has authorized the printing of quotations from Arthur Murphy's Commonplace Book. Miss Dorothy Mason of the Folger staff has given me valued help on several points. The cost of photo-copying the manuscript materials was covered by a timely grant-in-aid from the Modern Language Association of America. In England I was enabled to proceed with the first stage of my work on Morgann by a scholarship from the Anglo-Jewish Association of London. A grant from the Penrose Fund of the American Philosophical Society,

Philadelphia, Pa., made it possible for me to complete my basic research at Cambridge, Oxford, and London. The Hebrew University of Jerusalem and the Research Authority of Tel Aviv University provided grants for typing the Morgann materials.

The late D. Nichol Smith encouraged me to carry on my study of Morgann and kindly put at my disposal a memorandum by Morgann which has since been deposited in the Bodleian Library. I quote from the Shelburne Papers by permission of Dr. Howard H. Peckham, Director of the William L. Clements Library, University of Michigan, at Ann Arbor. Mr. William S. Ewing, formerly Curator of Manuscripts at the Clements Library, has been very helpful. Courteous and indispensable aid in pursuing my researches has also been extended by officials of the Library of Congress, the New York Public Library, the Henry E. Huntington Library at San Marino, California, the Newberry Library at Chicago, Illinois, the Harvard University Library, the Yale University Library, the Duke University Library, the Public Archives of Canada at Ottawa, the British Museum, the Royal Mint, the National Library of Wales at Aberystwyth, the Pembrokeshire County Library, Shakespeare's Birthplace Library at Stratford-upon-Avon, the Cambridge University Library, and the Bodleian. Father John Britton, S.J., drew my attention to Morgann's autograph corrections in the copy of the *Essay on Falstaff* at the Newberry Library. The Reverend E. G. Jones of Capel Colman, Boncath, Pemb., was my gracious host on a genealogical visit to Morgann's birthplace in Wales. Finally, I am happy to record my debt to Professor Adam A. Mendilow, sometime Head of the Department of English at the Hebrew University of Jerusalem. He drew my attention to the mention of Morgann by Percival Stockdale and has spent innumerable hours with me, bringing his extensive knowledge of Western literary theory and critical practice to bear upon some of the problems raised by Morgann's thought. To the stimulus of these conversations this book owes much of whatever merit it may possess. For its defects, of course, I alone am responsible. As for its interest, its proper public must now decide.

D. A. F.

Tel Aviv University
April 1971

CONTENTS

ABBREVIATIONS, SYMBOLS, ETC.

1. ABBREVIATIONS

app. crit.	*apparatus criticus.*
Com.	Morgann's Commentary on *The Tempest.*
Com. I. ii. 229	Morgann's comment on *The Tempest*, Act I, Scene ii, line 229, as reproduced in the present edition.
ED	Early or Earlier Draft(s).
Es.	the *Essay on Falstaff* (1777), or the copy in the manuscript book, or the present edition of the *Essay.*
fol.	followed.
Intro.	Introduction to the present edition.
LR	Longer Revision(s) of *Es.*
par(s).	paragraph(s).
prec.	preceded, preceding.
ref(s).	reference(s).
SR	Shorter Revision(s) of *Es.*

2. PAGE REFERENCES

N.B. The pagination of the *Essay* of 1777 is inserted in the present edition of the *Essay*, and is used for all page references. (See the sixth and last items in this list.)

T	printed page in *Es.* or in manuscript book containing *Com.*
PT	printed page of Preface in *Es.*
TMS (PTMS)	part of T (PT) containing manuscript comment.
I	interleaf page of a manuscript book.
PI	interleaf page facing PT page in *Es.* manuscript book or preliminary interleaf page in *Com.* manuscript book.
T10	p. 10 of *Es.* or of copy of Vol. I of Theobald's *Shakespeare* (1733) in *Com.* manuscript book.
T10MS (PT5MS)	part of T10 (PT5) containing manuscript annotation.
T62n	part of T62 containing footnote(s).
I10	interleaf page facing printed page 10.
I10:2 (T10:2, P18:2, PT8:2, T89MS:2, T62n:2)	second sentence on I10 (T10, P18, PT8, T89MS, T62n).[1]

[1] A sentence is considered as terminated by a full stop, an exclamation point, or a question mark—*not* by a colon. Incomplete MS. sentences count as full sentences. The count begins afresh on each page (e.g. T5:6 and T6:1 refer to the same sentence); it excludes MS. sentences not reproduced in this edition. A speech-prefix is counted as part of the next sentence; a lemma is counted as a single sentence.

I10:2a (I10:2b,   first (second, third) part of second sentence on I10.[1]
I10:2c)

I15a:1 (I15b:1)   first sentence of earlier (later) layer of writing on I15.[1]

[T5], [I113:2]   the following materials begin with T5:1 (I113:2) and continue, unless otherwise indicated, with T5:2 etc. (I113:3 etc.).

3. SYMBOLS REPRESENTING THE STATE AND RELATION OF MANUSCRIPT MATERIALS

A symbol in this group applies to the materials following it [exclusive of any in square brackets] either to the end of a paragraph or to the point where another symbol intervenes. (For further details, see below, pp. 136–7).

(C)   cancelled.

(CM)   cancelled by mistake.

(U)   uncancelled.

(UM)   uncancelled by mistake.

(R)   element(s) in an ED retained in later version(s).

Materials not prec. by a symbol are uncancelled.

4. OTHER SYMBOLS

[ ] encloses material inserted by the editor.

⟨ ⟩ encloses material actually or implicitly cancelled.

ʌ indicates point at which revision is to be inserted or footnote is to be subjoined.

]* = bracket for lemma supplied by editor.

*lemma] = lemma and bracket supplied by editor.

/ separates a later from a following earlier ED in *app. crit.*

—?— = undecipherable word.

—?— —?— = two or more undecipherable words.

5. PLACE OF PUBLICATION

Unless otherwise indicated, books cited have London as their place of publication.

6. REFERENCES TO SHAKESPEARE'S PLAYS

Act, scene, and line numbers are those of the Globe edition.

7. SHORT TITLES USED IN NOTES

See List, pp. 355 ff.

[1] See footnote on previous page.

a biography of Milton which includes a long appreciative footnote about Morgann.[1]

Nothing is known of his education. He seems to have been estab-lished in London by 17 November 1756, when he was appointed Deputy Weigher and Teller at the Royal Mint. On 7 June 1758 he was made Weigher and Teller, a sinecure worth £130 a year, not counting emoluments, which he retained to his death.[2] Sixteen months earlier, in February 1757, he had published *An Enquiry Concerning the Nature and End of a National Militia*. Issued anonymously, like the other four publications later to come from his pen, the sixty-page pamphlet was intended to promote support for Pitt's militia bill, which was soon afterwards passed by both Houses. The skill at grounding an argument on general principles, the cogency of thought, and the adroitness in exposition displayed in the tract were abilities calculated to recommend him a few years later to the young Earl of Shelburne, then at the outset of his political career.

He began to serve Shelburne in the capacity of personal secretary and political adviser about 1762,[3] and in this role he found the vocation he was to follow for the next quarter of a century. His special province was American affairs. At first, as is shown in memoranda he drafted for his patron during the latter's short term as President of the Board of Trade in April–September 1763, he approached American questions with a mixture of doctrinaire authoritarianism and shrewd perceptiveness. Holding to the mer-cantilist dogma that 'the colonists are merely Factors for the purpose of Trade', he advocated compelling the Americans to subserve England's commercial interests by ringing them in with bayonets and tomahawks. But he also proposed new settlements in the north-west, and, still more significantly, warned that the only tax which could rightly be imposed on the Americans was one intended in the first instance to regulate trade rather than to raise a revenue.[4] Two years later, when the Stamp Act was passed for purely revenue purposes (22 March 1765), and not even Benjamin Franklin, then

[1] 'The Life of Milton' in *The Prose Works of John Milton*, ed. Charles Symmons, vii. 81–4.
[2] Royal Mint, 'Record Book 1752–1764', pp. 59 and 117, and ibid., '1797–1804', 5–6.
[3] Morgann to Shelburne, 17 June 1782 and 4 Oct. 1782, Shelburne Papers, W. L. Clements Library, University of Michigan, Ann Arbor, vol. 68, pp. 389 ff.
[4] Ibid., vol. 67, pp. 107–10, and vol. 85, ff. 26–34.

INTRODUCTIONS

I. LIFE

MAURICE MORGANN was born *c.* 1725, most proba
bylan in the parish of Clydey, Pembrokeshire, where
resided since the sixteenth century.[1] He came of forebe
in Welsh history, among them Llywelyn ap Gwilyn
Newcastle Emlyn and uncle and patron to the p
Gwilym (*fl.* 1340–70). Going still further back, th
which Morgann and his brother were the last
claimed unbroken descent from the first marri
Fychan, the thirteenth-century Welsh magnate fro
union the house of Tudor was descended. His
derived from princes of South Wales, from Ferdina
of the Spanish monarchy, and from Thomas Ph
Virgil and author of *The Regiment of Life* (1544)

He was perhaps the son of the homonymous
Blaenbylan who provided in his will, signed 25
future of his wife, Hannah, his daughter, Sarah, a
Sons', David and Morris.[3] The affiliation
Morgann's known brother was named Willia
certain, however, that he and his brother
Blaenbylan, and that they lived at the family
of age (*c.* 1745–50).[4] During this period the
connection with the Symmonses of near-
Symmons the elder, M.P. for Cardigan fr
his two sons, John Symmons the younger, l
ton House', and Dr. Charles Symmons, ch

[1] Morgann is usually said to have been born in Lond
Blaenbylan has, however, been repeatedly noted by
with Richard Fenton, *A Historical Tour through Pembr*
The likelihood that he was born before 1726, based c
paragraph, is suggested by Dr. B. G. Charles in his art
of Welsh Biography, eds. J. E. Lloyd and R. T. Jenk

[2] Pedigree of Morgan family, comp. William Lew
Library of Wales, Aberystwyth.

[3] Will deposited in National Library of Wales. (*M*
of *Morris Morgan.*)

[4] Fenton, pp. 490–1.

B

in London, anticipated serious trouble across the Atlantic, Morgann predicted the riots which in fact ensued.[1]

On his patron's return to office as Secretary of State for the South in the ill-fated Chatham administration (1766–8), Morgann became Under-Secretary of State in charge of Shelburne's 'American desk'.[2] In this position, though remaining a confirmed mercantilist, he mitigated his former dogmatism and enlarged on his earlier insight. 'Bodies of Men', he now argued, '. . . are not influenced by Reason but by Passion, and the peculiar Mode and Colour of Those Passions they derive from peculiar Customs, Manners, Laws and Situations.' From this maxim it followed that to deal with the recalcitrant colonists successfully, England would have to cater for the feelings and prejudices induced by their circumstances. The repeal of the Stamp Act, carried out by the Rockingham administration early in 1766, was therefore not enough. If America was to be saved, he advised Shelburne, the new ministry must go further: it must openly disavow the Rockinghams' Declaratory Act, which affirmed Parliament's theoretical right to tax the Americans in all cases whatsoever, and it must rescind the Mutiny Act, which in effect levied a revenue tax on the colonists. Based on principles so far acceptable to Americans, this sweeping programme of appeasement would, he claimed, allay the justified resentment of the moderate colonists; and in the more harmonious atmosphere thus created, England should clinch the matter by turning the 'Face of Authority' to American extremists and jolt them to their senses through the punishment of a single man and a single province for clear-cut violations of the Trade Laws.[3]

The conciliatory tendency in this bifold scheme found no echo in high policy, which moved fatally in the opposite direction of provoking the Declaration of Independence. With his advice regarding the newly won province of Canada, however, Morgann had better luck. Rejecting the commonly held belief that the French Canadians ought ultimately to be anglicized, he urged instead that they be allowed to maintain their distinctive mode of life;[4] and before long he was in a position to help make his ideas prevail. When in December 1767 the new office of Secretary of State for America was created and Shelburne ceased to be responsible for transatlantic affairs,

[1] Ibid., vol. 85, ff. 71–7.
[2] P.R.O. SP 44/141, pp. 119–20. Shelburne Papers, vol. 134, pp. 143–4.
[3] Shelburne Papers, vol. 49, pp. 711–22, vol. 58, pp. 243–7, and vol. 85, ff. 81–8.
[4] Ibid., vol. 85, ff. 26–34, and vol. 64, pp. 525–51.

Morgann, released from his employment as Under-Secretary, was appointed special envoy of the Privy Council to Canada. His mission was to conduct a thorough investigation of the state of the judicature in Canada and to confer with local officials and obtain a report from them on the subject; on his return he was to submit all the data he had collected to the Council and so provide them with a basis for instituting a system of law appropriate to the country's needs.[1] He arrived in Quebec on 22 August 1768 and remained for over a year. Francis Maseres, the local Attorney-General, observed that Morgann, 'the legislator, as we use to call him, . . . is a well-bred agreeable man, but not a lawyer; and he has a pompous way of talking that seems borrowed from the house of commons cant about the constitution, &c, without having precise Ideas of what he would say'.[2] But the governor, Sir Guy Carleton, was more favourably impressed. Convinced no less than Morgann that the *habitants* ought to be allowed to maintain their own culture, he eventually asked him to draft the official report required by the Privy Council on the state of the judicature. This document, vigorously setting forth the view shared by the two men that French law must be substantially retained in Canada, helped to pave the way for the Quebec Act of 1774, which laid a foundation for civil and religious liberty in Canada.[3]

On 13 November 1766 Morgann had been made secretary of the province of New Jersey with a salary of £300 a year, paid by the deputy out of the perquisites of office. In late October 1769, on his return journey from Canada, he stopped in New Jersey in order to designate a new deputy. He was back in England by 18 January 1770.[4]

During the following twelve years his patron continued in opposition and Morgann held no post in the public service. The principal records of his activities during this period of relative leisure are three publications. In 1772 he brought out a remarkable *Plan for the*

---

[1] W. P. M. Kennedy and G. Lanctot, *Reports on the Laws of Quebec, 1767-1770* (Ottawa, 1931), pp. 10-12.

[2] Ibid., pp. 12-13. The story of the jocular nickname Morgann was given in Canada may have something to do with Symmons's describing him as 'the intended legislator of Canada' ('Life of Milton', p. 82).

[3] Kennedy and Lanctot, pp. 13, 47-8, and 51-73 (a copy of the long-lost report, as discovered by Kennedy in British Museum Kings MS. 207).

[4] *Documents relating to the Colonial History of the State of New Jersey*, Archives of the State of New Jersey, First Series, eds. Frederick W. Ricord and William Nelson, x (Newark, 1886), 1-4 and 132-5. British Museum Additional MSS. 22, 129, ff. 11-12. Kennedy and Lanctot, pp. 84-5.

Abolition of Slavery in the West Indies, which presented in brief compass, a good fifteen years before anyone else, virtually the entire case against the slave-trade as it was later to be brought before Parliament and the public by the organized abolition movement. Asserting the absolute mental equality of Negroes and whites, claiming that antipathies between the two races derive from economic rather than natural causes, and foreseeing that the exploitation of Negroes would lead one day to 'terror and destruction' in America (p. 15), Morgann placed the blame for evils present and to come not on profiteering individuals but on the 'imbecility' of the state (p. 10) that countenances and fosters social injustice.

In 1777, turning from the vindication of a socially depressed race to the rehabilitation of a victim of the theatre, he published his defence of Falstaff against the charge of cowardice—*An Essay on the Dramatic Character of Sir John Falstaff*. In 1779 appeared his *Letter to my Lords the Bishops*, a curious piece of opposition propaganda in which, via some interesting theorizing on the superiority of preventive to punitive law, he traced the current spread of profligacy to the decay of the constitution under the North regime. Britain's moral health, he concluded, could be restored solely through 'more frequent elections by more numerous electors' (p. 26); and until the time grew ripe for parliamentary reform, outstanding individuals might hold things together by setting personal examples of probity. Privately, he took a more despairing view. The one chance the country had of being saved, he informed Shelburne, lay in the possibility that the horrors of a Franco-Spanish invasion, adjudged imminent in 1779, might touch off a revolution. In the course of this upheaval, he predicted, rank and status would go by the board and a new group of men, surging to the fore by virtue of their 'great Boldness & ability', might re-establish a liberal social order. Nothing short of a cataclysm of this kind, he declared, could defeat the invaders, impel the revolted colonies to reunite with the mother country, and by thus preserving the Empire maintain England's greatness.[1]

Even after the invasion scare had subsided and American victory became increasingly certain, he encouraged Shelburne in his belief that reunion with the colonies was possible and necessary.[2] Entertaining this hope, he embarked on 8 April 1782 for New York, to

[1] Shelburne Papers, vol. 165, pp. 201-9 and 213-23.
[2] Ibid., vol. 87, ff. 147-56.

serve as secretary to his old friend, Sir Guy Carleton, who had lately
been appointed Commander-in-Chief of His Majesty's forces in
North America as well as one of the two Royal Commissioners for
restoring peace to the colonies and plantations in America. Morgann
and his new chief arrived on 5 May.[1] Congress's prompt and brusque
refusal on 14 May to receive him as Carleton's representative[2] failed
to shake his conviction that despite all difficulties, the Royal Commissioners in New York should and could re-associate America with
England. It was, of course, not to be. While he pleaded for his dream
in Manhattan, matters were taking a different turn in London and
Paris. Back in power as Secretary of State (March 1782) and then
as Prime Minister (July 1782–February 1783), Shelburne eventually
concluded the historic treaty with the American Commissioners in
Paris which committed Britain to recognizing the absolute independence of the former colonies. Yet ironically enough, the treaty may
owe something to a long, realistic report which Morgann sent his
patron from New York.[3] Contrary to his intention, his frank on-the-
spot appraisal of the formidable obstacles to reunion may have
helped to persuade Shelburne that outright independence was the
only practical basis on which peace could be achieved. Still more
definitely, the treaty reflects Morgann's earlier interest in developing
the north-west, a proposal also advanced by others, which now
formed part of Shelburne's imaginative vision of a vigorously expanding and free America co-operating with England as an equal
partner in commerce.

   While in New York Morgann helped the local advocates of reunion
with his advice and his pen and forwarded several analyses of the
army's financial operations to his patron, who had long been deeply
interested in the subject of economic reform.[4] Chiefly, however, he
was occupied as Carleton's secretary with a host of administrative

   [1] Departure: *London Chronicle*, 11 Apr. 1782. Morgann's employment: Carleton to
Rockingham, 3 Apr. 1782, *bis*, P.R.O. T. 1/578, ff. 250–3. Carleton's commissions:
P.R.O. 30/55/101 (10429) and 104 (10435). Arrival: William Smith, 'Memoirs', New
York Public Library, vol. 7, 5 May 1782. It is sometimes mistakenly said that Morgann
was secretary to the embassy for ratifying the peace with America. The error may arise
from the fact that Carleton, to whom he was secretary, held a royal commission for
restoring peace in America.
   [2] *Journals of the Continental Congress* (Washington, 1914), xxii. 263.
   [3] Morgann to Shelburne, New York, 12 June 1782, Shelburne Papers, vol. 68,
pp. 373–87.
   [4] William Smith, 'Memoirs', vol. 7, 23 May, 20 July, and 4 Aug. 1782. Shelburne
Papers, vol. 69, pp. 9–70; see also John Norris, *Shelburne and Reform* (1963).

details connected at first with maintaining the military establishment and later with dismantling the last British bastions on American territory. The main records of his activities under Carleton are in the British Headquarter Papers, 1775–83, a collection of documents which Morgann retained in his personal possession until 1789, when he gave them to his friend John Symmons of Paddington House, who in 1804 deposited them at the Royal Institution.[1]

Morgann was back in London by 11 August 1783.[2] It may have been shortly afterwards that in his patron's absence he acted as host to Dr. Johnson at Shelburne's home at Wycombe. Boswell records under the year 1783 the two verbal encounters between Morgann and Johnson which give the episode its place in literary annals. The first, as Boswell notes, 'is not a little to the credit of Johnson's candour'. Having argued the wrong side of a question with Morgann till the small hours, Johnson accosted him the next morning at breakfast with the avowal: 'Sir, I have been thinking on our dispute last night—*You were in the right.*' In the second anecdote, Morgann comes out the victor in similar fashion. Unable to make Johnson yield in his perverse defence of an inferior versifier, Morgann tried to gain his point indirectly by inquiring which was the better poet, the one in question or another of equal insignificance. 'Johnson at once felt himself rouzed; and answered, "Sir, there is no settling the point of precedency between a louse and a flea".'[3]

Before leaving New York, Morgann had been notified by the Treasury that, conformably with the promise earlier made to him, he had been granted a life pension of £250.[4] In 1784, to compensate him for the loss of his place as Secretary of New Jersey, he was made Provincial Agent for New Brunswick. He gave up this post in 1786, on being appointed one of the Commissioners of the Hackney Coach Office, at £200 a year.[5]

---

[1] Known today as the Carleton Papers, they are now, after a brief sojourn in America, housed in the P.R.O. (series 30/55). Before their peregrination they were admirably calendared in *Great Britain, Historical Manuscripts Commission, Report on American Manuscripts in the Royal Institution*, 4 vols., 1904–9 (H.M.C. 59).

[2] Endorsement on Carleton to North, 11 July 1783, P.R.O. C.O. 5/110, f. 79ᵛ.

[3] Boswell, *Life of Johnson*, ed. G. B. Hill, rev. L. F. Powell (Oxford, 1934), iv. 192–3. (According to Boswell, the two poets were Derrick and Smart, but the *European Magazine*, xxx (1796), 160, says more plausibly that they were Derrick and Boyce.)

[4] George Rose to Carleton, 6 Sept. 1782, P.R.O. 30/55/48 (5543). Morgann to Shelburne, 29 Oct. 1782, Shelburne Papers, vol. 68, pp. 427–30.

[5] William Rees Williams (ed.), *Old Wales* (Talybout, Breconshire, 1905–7), ii. 134. T. R. Roberts, *Eminent Welshmen*, i (Cardiff, 1908), 384.

The security attained in this way seems to have enabled him to withdraw from active duty under Shelburne. What appear to be the last reports he wrote for his patron date from 1786.¹ He did not, however, give up his interest in public affairs. As late as 1795 he published his *Considerations on the Present Internal and External Condition of France*, sixty trenchant and closely reasoned pages indicting the Jacobin terror as a uniquely dangerous form of anarchy—'not a mere negation of order, but positive disorder organized' (p. 16)—which might destroy Europe unless extirpated by the allies. In R. B. Sheridan's opinion, the author of the pamphlet was 'qualified to think for a whole nation, and to direct its conduct'.²

This foray against the French Revolution apart, he seems to have spent his autumn days in private literary pursuits and sociable leisure. William Cooke remembered him as a delightful companion, 'the charm of every society he mixed with; particularly as his conversation was enriched by the greatest urbanity of manners, and the happiest arts of *badinage* and pleasantry'.³ To this period probably belong the 'many pleasant hours' which Percival Stockdale spent with him 'at Mr. Fitzmaurice's in the Isle of Wight'.⁴ In London he continued to make his home for some years at 84 St. Martin's Lane, where, apparently, he wrote the epilogue to Arthur Murphy's *Three Weeks After Marriage* spoken by Mrs. Abington on her benefit night (10 February 1786),⁵ drafted his revisions to his *Essay on Falstaff*, and worked up his Commentary on *The Tempest*. From the same address he sent to Sir Joseph Banks, President of the Royal Society, a paper he had once written on the subject of naval signals.⁶ After 1790 he moved into a house at No. 2 High Row, Knightsbridge. Here he entertained such friends as the Symmons brothers, Cooke,

---

¹ Shelburne Papers, vol. 87, ff. 389–95, and Bodleian Western MSS., Eng. lett. d. 219, ff. 25–33.

² *Monthly Review*, xcvi (1794), 457. Sheridan is identified as the author by Christie Nangle, comp., *The Monthly Review, Second Series, 1790–1815: Index of Contributors and Articles* (Oxford, 1955).

³ *Conversation*, 2nd edn. (1807), p. vii. In the first edition of his poem (1796) Cooke included some lines, later dropped, in which he inscribed his work to Morgann under the name of 'Eugenio', described as a winning, knowledgeable, vivid conversationalist (pp. 3–4).

⁴ *Memoirs* (1809), ii. 158.

⁵ Folger Shakespeare Library MS. W. b. 480, f. 146. Morgann had done this sort of thing before: Stockdale, loc. cit., mentions an 'excellent Prologue' Morgann provided for a production in 1773 of Susannah Centlivre's *The Busy Body*.

⁶ 3 Mar. [17]89, Add. MSS. 33, 978, ff. 231–2.

Murphy, and Oliver Humphry, the painter; and here, on 28 March 1802, serenely and 'without alarm', he died.[1] He appears never to have married. In his will, drawn up on 28 April 1795, he bequeathed all his property in Wales and elsewhere to Lucy Kingston 'who now lives with me', 'to whom I have great obligations'.[2] He also appointed her his executrix. Obedient to his repeated injunctions, Charles Symmons reports, she destroyed his numerous manuscripts on literary, political, and philosophical subjects, 'some of which . . . would have planted a permanent laurel on his grave'.[3] Fortunately, the revisions of his *Essay on Falstaff* and his Commentary on *The Tempest* escaped the fate that apparently befell his other unpublished writings at his death. But even without the benefit of these two literary manuscripts, long lost from view, his fame has survived. If his social and political thought has never had justice done to it, either for its intrinsic interest or for its very modest influence on British policy during the later eighteenth century, his critical essay, with its thesis that Falstaff is a man of courage, has kept his name alive.

II. REPUTATION AND INFLUENCE

The idea that Falstaff is a charmer began attracting adherents at least by 1709, when Nicholas Rowe remarked that out of gratitude for the 'diversion' afforded by the fat knight's agreeable wit, some people might be 'sorry to see his Friend *Hal* use him so scurvily' on becoming king.[4] However, though one could throughout the eighteenth century confess affection for Falstaff without exciting scandal,[5] it was quite unheard of to assert, as Morgann did in his *Essay*, that 'he was intended to be drawn as a character of much Natural courage

---

[1] Jesse Foot, *Life of Arthur Murphy* (London, 1811), pp. 420-1. Morgann to O. Humphry, Bodleian Western MSS. 25, 434, ff. 365-9. Symmons, p. 84.

[2] Somerset House, Kenyon, sig. 295, ff. 1-2. The will was witnessed by John Symmons of Paddington House, John Lowes, Rector of Whippingham, Isle of Wight, and Eliza Brown of Whippingham. The will was proved on 7 Apr. 1802.

[3] Symmons, p. 83.

[4] 'Some Account of the Life &c. of Mr. William Shakespeare', prefixed to Rowe's six-volume edition of Shakespeare's *Works* (1709), reprinted in *Eighteenth Century Essays on Shakespeare*, ed. D. Nichol Smith, 2nd edn. (Oxford, 1963), p. 10.

[5] Among those who did so were Corbyn Morris, *An Essay towards Fixing the True Standards of Wit, Humour, Raillery, Satire and Ridicule* (1744), p. 29, John Upton, *Critical Observations on Shakespeare* (1746), p. 85, Samuel Foote, *The Roman and English Comedy* (1747), p. 41, William Guthrie, *An Essay on English Tragedy* (1757), p. 12, Arthur Murphy, 'The Theatre', *London Chronicle*, 25-7 Jan. 1757, p. 96, and Francis Gentleman, *The Dramatic Censor* (1770), ii. 396.

and resolution' (T15). This was heresy absolute and unmitigated; it flouted the seemingly self-evident fact, unanimously reported by a round score of commentators from 1625 to 1777, that cowardice is a basic and inalienable ingredient in Falstaff's composition.[1]

It is understandable, therefore, that not a few contemporary readers were put off by Morgann's little volume when it appeared in 1777. 'Here is an odd Book come out to prove Falstaff was no Coward', Mrs. Thrale scribbled in her diary, and added: 'when says Johnson will one come forth to prove Iago an honest man?'[2] Thomas Davies, the publisher of the *Essay*, was soon circulating the same quip in print: 'I should as soon believe Roderigo to be a man of sense, and Iago a man of virtue, as suspect Falstaff to have any spark of bravery in him.'[3] Taking an equally dour view, George Colman the elder rebuked the talented author of the *Essay* in the pages of the *Monthly Review* for engaging in false refinement and sophistry. 'In dramatic writings, especially', he observed, 'the obvious meaning is most probably the true one; and it is surely no great compliment to Shakespeare's admirable delineation of the character of Falstaff, to suppose that it has hitherto been generally misunderstood.'[4]

Seven years later, Davies returned to the charge: 'if the knight is proved to be a man of courage', he protested, 'half the mirth he

---

[1] For the score of commentators see below, note to *Es.*, T2. The sole exception seems to be an anonymous ballad on the Duke of Monmouth (1681), which refers to Falstaff as a generally bold fighter: see *The Shakspere Allusion-Book*, reissued by E. K. Chambers (Oxford, 1932), ii. 275.

[2] *Thraliana*, ed. Katherine C. Balderston, 2nd edn. (Oxford, 1951), i. 35: entry for 28 May 1777. Boswell records a more polished version of Johnson's sally, *Life of Johnson*, ed. G. B. Hill, rev. L. F. Powell (Oxford, 1934), iv. 192: 'Why, Sir, we shall have the man come forth again; and as he has proved Falstaff to be no coward, he may prove Iago to be a very good character.'

[3] *A Genuine Narrative of the Life and Theatrical Transactions of Mr. John Henderson* (1777), pp. 51–2. S. M. Tave, 'Notes on the Influence of Morgann's *Essay on Falstaff*', *R.E.S.* n.s. iii (1952), 374, has plausibly wondered 'whether Davies had been present when Dr. Johnson delivered his opinion of Morgann's essay'. In *The Amiable Humorist* (Chicago, 1960), p. 269, Tave repeats the conjecture and notes that Davies's 'other comments on Falstaff . . . indicate that he had read Morgann more seriously than he would admit'. Tave's book, along with his *R.E.S.* article (pp. 371–5) and his 'Corbyn Morris: Falstaff, Humour, and Comic Theory in the Eighteenth Century', *M.P.* 1 (1952/3), 102–15, provide a valuable account, to which I am indebted, of Morgann's reputation and position in his own and the next generation.

[4] *Monthly Review*, lvii (1777), 79–80. See also below, p. 39. Colman is identified as the author by B. C. Nangle, comp., *The Monthly Review, First Series, 1749–1789: Indexes of Contributors and Articles* (Oxford, 1934). In the following pages, identification of *Monthly Review* contributors derives from this volume or from Nangle's similarly titled Index to the *Second Series, 1790–1815* (Oxford, 1955).

raises [in the tavern scene] is quite lost and misplaced'; while the
fact that he is a coward is irrefragably established when 'not satisfied
with seeing the dead body of Percy before him, to make all sure, [he]
wounds the corpse in the thigh'. The 'man of genius' who wrote the
Essay, Davies concluded, could not have intended anything more
than to convince the public of his competence 'to support any
hypothesis by brilliancy of wit'.[1]

The Revd. Richard Stack of Dublin, however, did not think that
the *Essay* could be dismissed simply by objecting to the obvious
disparity between its thesis and the common view of Falstaff. Its
author, he observed, had 'managed his subject with so much ability
and address' that in his own words it had become a real 'question,
whether *Falstaff* is, or is not a man of courage' (cf. *Es.*, T12). To
re-establish the common view, it was necessary to meet Morgann on
his own ground, and Stack undertook to do this in the 'Examination'
of the *Essay* which he read before his fellow members of the Royal
Irish Academy on 11 February 1788. His 'expert antagonist', he
pointed out, regards Falstaff as a character that appeals to the feelings
independently of the understanding. The distinction is valid, Stack
agreed, and for this very reason he claimed the *Essay* was fallacious
in arguing that Falstaff misleads the understanding into taking him
for a coward while rightly persuading the heart that he is courageous.
With a character designed to affect the sensibility, Stack insisted,
a playwright must conform to a faculty which, unlike the reason,
does not take time to sift and compare and so arrive at conclusions;
its apprehensions are 'instantaneous and strong'. The dramatist must
therefore make forcible and unequivocal impressions from the start
and he must avoid inconsistent ones later on, since they could not
'easily make their way to the heart, already predisposed'. Accordingly, in the opening scenes of *Henry IV*, Shakespeare has Falstaff
produce an initial impression of cowardice and so sets up strong
expectations with regard to his future behaviour, which are fulfilled;
any subsequent appearances which seem contradictory are errors of
the understanding. The very way in which the author of the *Essay*
argues the reverse, Stack claimed, denies the nature of the sensibility
on which he professes to base his case. He deliberately has to put off

---

[1] *Dramatic Miscellanies*, i (1784), 272-3. In iii (1784), 130, he applauds Morgann's
idea that Aristotle would have worshipped at Shakespeare's feet, if he had known him
(*Es.*, T70). (Davies's work is spelled *Micellanies* on the title-pages, but *Miscellanies* in
the half-titles and running titles.)

considering the early determinative Gadshill and Eastcheap episodes
to the end; and in attempting to prove Falstaff's alleged valour, he
persistently subtilizes and refines. Inevitably, the semblances of
courage he arrives at in this fashion are not intuitions of the sensibility but products of the understanding, and therefore, on the
Essay's own principles, ill founded.

Supporting these contentions with a detailed analysis of scene and
situation, Stack tried to show how the *Essay* can pretend to demonstrate Falstaff's valour only by laboriously discrediting Poins's and
Lancaster's contrary views of the knight, by going to ludicrous
lengths to whitewash his palpable acts of cowardice, and by so
stretching the obvious sense of many episodes as to drain them of
their incomparable humour. Such strenuous intellectual efforts, he
urged, necessarily misrepresent Falstaff's impact on the feelings.
'Dramatic characters are not drawn for speculative ingenious men
in their closets, but for mankind at large.'[1]

This was the high-water mark though not the last of the adverse
criticism. Morgann himself was so impressed that he took Stack's
observations very much into account in the manuscript revisions he
drafted for the *Essay* (see below, pp. 39–40). The *Analytical Review*
was not just impressed, it was convinced. Applauding Stack's performance, the magazine informed its readers that the *Essay* had
attracted notice only because its 'congruity of language' had blinded
readers to its 'incongruity of argument'. Percival Stockdale was of
like mind. Morgann's treatise, he later recalled, 'was fraught . . . with
much fine criticism . . . [and] read with curiosity, and avidity, for
awhile;—but the absurdity of it's plan inevitably prevented it's long
life'. After Morgann's death, Malone jotted down in his copy of the
Essay both his own belief that it was a 'fanciful and absurd' piece of
work and a variant version of Johnson's initial response: 'When this
pamphlet first appeared, Dr Johnson being asked his opinion of it,
replied, "all he sh^d say, was, that if Falstaff was not a coward,
Shakespeare knew nothing of his art".'[2] The same point, made

---

[1] 'An Examination of an Essay on the Dramatic Character of Sir John Falstaff',
Transactions of the Royal Irish Academy, [ii,] *1788* (Dublin [1789]), 'Polite Literature',
3–37. (For publication date see below, p. 39.) The passages quoted are on pp. 3, 3, 6,
15, and 25. Stack concludes with something of a *non sequitur*. Having argued at length
that Falstaff produces an ineffaceable impression of cowardice upon us, he ends by
claiming that 'in the gay wit we forget the contemptible coward' (p. 37).

[2] *Analytical Review*, vii (1790), 406. Stockdale, *Memoirs* (1807), ii. 159. Malone's
copy is in the Bodleian. The MS. note here cited is printed by Hill, ed. Boswell, *Life*

earlier by Colman, was also emphasized in the *British Critic* review in 1797 of Richard Hole's apologies for Iago and Shylock—two papers which defended the kind of view that Johnson and Davies had scouted in advance as self-evidently absurd. To the reviewer it was plain that Morgann's pernicious influence lay at the bottom of these new 'idle efforts'—the 'bane of true criticism'—to demonstrate the goodness of Shakespearian characters that all the world had 'felt to be detestable'.[1]

But if the censorious spoke up with asperity, there were others who had but to read to be delighted. On the book's appearance the *Critical Review* recommended it 'with an unusual degree of zeal and approbation . . . in its entire state, to our readers'. The *Scots Magazine* presently reprinted in part the same notice of a sagacious, novel, and elegant performance intended 'to stem the tide of ancient prejudice'.[2] With equal alacrity William Kenrick lauded the *Essay* in his *London Review*. An enthusiastic lecturer on Falstaff who had of late reprimanded a critic for charging him with representing Falstaff as a harmless, inoffensive creature when in fact he had 'left him in full possession of his character for gluttony, lying, cowardice and theft', Kenrick now adopted the *Essay*'s thesis and quoted approvingly from the introductory section (*Es.*, T1–T3, T15:4–T16:3, and T17:3–T20:1), from the argument to prove that in playing dead Falstaff evinced courage (T22:6–T26:4), from the eloquent 'Eulogium of Shakespeare' (T65:3–T70:1), and from the crucial passage on how the 'whole' Falstaff is rendered jovial by 'grouping' (T172:6–T178:1).[3] So entirely converted was Kenrick that a few months later in the same periodical he was reproaching the actor, John Henderson, for two main defects in his portrayal of Falstaff, both illuminated

---

of Johnson, iv. 515. Garrick's opinion of the *Essay* is unknown: he owned a presentation copy, now in the Folger Shakespeare Library.

[1] *The British Critic*, ix (1797), 362–3: review of *Essays by a Society of Gentlemen at Exeter* (1796). Richard Hole is identified as the author of the apologies for Iago and Shylock contained in Exeter *Essays*, pp. 395–409 and 552–73, by the *Gentleman's Magazine*, lxix (1799), 272, and by Nathan Drake, *Mornings in Spring* (London, 1828), ii. 140. Both regard the apologies as ironical *jeux d'esprit*. Not so John Aikin in the *Monthly Review*, 2nd Ser., xxii (1797), 7–9, and the *British Critic* reviewer, who fail to note Hole's explicit assertion that he is discussing Shylock not as Shakespeare presents him but as he might appear to someone who reinterprets in his favour the bare facts used by the playwright. In his treatment of Iago, however, Hole provides the reviewers with fairer game.   [2] *Critical Review*, xliii (May 1777), 397. *Scots Magazine*, xxxix (1777), 261.

[3] *Introduction to the School of Shakespear . . . [and] A Retort Courteous on the Criticks* (1774), p. 28. *The London Review of English and Foreign Literature*, ed. William Kenrick *et al.*, v (May 1777), 366–73.

by the recent work of 'a very masterly critic'. The first was the inordinately fat physique he gave the knight, based on too literal an interpretation of the humorous exaggerations in the play (cf. *Es.*, T127–T129), the second the symptoms of fear he displayed 'from the vulgar notion of the Knight's rank cowardice'. Meanwhile, the *London Magazine* and the *Universal Magazine* reproduced passages from what Kenrick had called the 'Eulogium of Shakespeare' under the titles, respectively, of 'A New Character of the celebrated Shakespeare', and 'A Rhapsody on the Genius and Writings of Shakespeare'.[1]

Before the decade was out, the *Essay* had become an influence on critics of greater significance. Of the three best-known contemporary studies of Falstaff—those by Richard Cumberland, Henry Mackenzie, and William Richardson—the first possibly and the last two definitely drew on Morgann. Cumberland, who regarded Falstaff as a gross, swaggering coward, may have been affected by the *Essay* in two striking incidental observations. He suggests that if Shakespeare had extended Falstaff's existence in *Henry V*, he 'might have furnished scenes of admirable comedy by exhibiting him in his disgrace'. Morgann too speculates that had Shakespeare chosen to prolong Falstaff's life, 'the *Fleet* might be no bad scene of further amusement' (T183)—a remark recently praised by Robert Langbaum as 'the best explanation I have seen of Falstaff's "disgrace"'. Cumberland further notes that because all Falstaff's 'failings, which should have raised contempt, have only provoked laughter', the grateful reader or spectator 'begins to think they are not natural to his character, but assumed for his amusement'. Though this is an obvious refinement on Rowe (see above, p. 11), it also recalls Morgann's remark that, when the sport of girding at Falstaff is over, 'we give him . . . undeserved credit for the pleasure we enjoyed' (*Es.*, T175).[2]

The debt of the other two critics is both more certain and more central to their interpretations. Mackenzie found in Falstaff a delightfully witty and coldly sagacious sensualist, none of whose passions ever rise beyond the 'control of reason, of self-interest, or of indulgence'. In this conception of the character, ordinary cowardice—the tendency to give way to fear at the slightest threat—could have no

---

[1] *London Review*, vi (Nov. 1777), 397–9. *The London Magazine*, xlvi (June 1777), 313–14. *The Universal Magazine of Knowledge and Pleasure*, lxi (July 1777), 5–6.

[2] 'On the Characters of Falstaff and his Group', *The Observer*, No. 86 (1786). Robert Langbaum, *The Poetry of Experience* (1957), pp. 174–5.

place, and Mackenzie explicitly took his cue from Morgann: 'Though I will not go so far as a paradoxical critic has done', he observed, 'and ascribe valour to Falstaff; yet if his cowardice is fairly examined, it will be found not so much a weakness as a principle.' Exhibiting 'the sense of danger', he went on, 'but not the discomposure of fear', Falstaff deliberately proportions his recreancy to the degree of peril he encounters rather than displays the terror of the natural born craven; his presence of mind saves him from Douglas's sword. In thus delicately harmonizing Morgann's thought with his own, Mackenzie also modulated his predecessor's benevolent idea of Falstaff as a realistic veteran who renounces 'the Vanities and Superstitions of honour' (*Es.*, T100) into the less flattering conception of a man who is 'wise' but lacks 'the sense of honour'.[1]

William Richardson, Professor of Humanity at the University of Glasgow, is under even greater obligation to Morgann. In the *Monthly Review*, with a stern back-reference to Colman's strictures, Christopher Moody noted that Richardson in his study of Falstaff cited Morgann in describing the knight's cowardice as 'the result of deliberation, rather than the effect of constitution'. But Moody failed to remark, as Professor Babcock has done more recently, though without going into detail, that Morgann's influence goes a good deal beyond this idea.[2] It appears even in so peripheral a matter as Richardson's observation that Shakespeare wished in Falstaff 'to display the magic of his skill by rendering a mean character highly interesting', which recalls Morgann's comment that Shakespeare, who 'delighted in difficulties', resolved to convert the coarse, cheap stage fool of tradition into a subtle and richly drawn buffoon

---

[1] 'Critical Remarks on the Character of Falstaff Concluded', *The Lounger*, No. 69 (27 May 1786). The first half of the paper appeared in No. 68 (20 May 1786). Mackenzie may also have found the hint for his linking of Falstaff with Caliban in *Es.*, T25. Again, his remark that Falstaff's wit, even when it causes us to laugh with rather than at him, 'still partakes in him' of his essential and characteristic 'Epicurean grossness', may owe something to *Es.*, T168.

[2] *Monthly Review*, lxxxi (1789), 54, rev. of Richardson's *Essays on Shakespeare's Dramatic Character of Sir John Falstaff and on His Imitation of Female Characters* (1788; reissued, 1789). R. W. Babcock, 'William Richardson's Criticism of Shakespeare', *J.E.G.P.* xxviii (1929), 128–30. Richardson credits the idea to Morgann in a footnote, p. 14, which reads 'Essay on Shakespeare's Falstaff', the half-title of the *Essay*; he omits the acknowledgement in all later editions (see next note). He may also have been thinking of Mackenzie, to whom he seems to owe both his conception of Falstaff as a gross Epicurean with extraordinary insight into the motives of mankind and the analogy, later a favourite with Coleridge, between the fascinating vicious knight and the equally fascinating and vicious Richard III.

(*Es.*, T148). Far more important, however, is Richardson's indebtedness to the *Essay* for the pivot of his interpretation of Falstaff, that while 'our feelings' approve of the knight, 'our reason' condemns his 'real character'. This theory is a cruder and differently oriented version of Morgann's fundamental distinction between the stage Falstaff who strikes our sensibility as jovial and good-natured and the real Falstaff who is recognized by our critical reason as a vicious and disgusting person. Taken in by Falstaff's social gifts and power to amuse, Richardson says, our sensibility conceives an 'improper attachment' for him, but our wiser understanding, recognizing that he consecrates all his attractive abilities to the basest purposes, perceives that he is 'irretrievably lost; totally and for ever depraved. An important and awful lesson!' Except, of course, for the monitory whiff of hell-fire at the end, this is essentially the analysis found in the *Essay* of the two lights in which Falstaff may be viewed. Richardson seems even to grasp the distinction between 'dramatic' and 'whole' character by which the *Essay* accounts for Falstaff's power to charm despite his viciousness. He not only follows Morgann in using the phrase *dramatic character* in the title of his essay, but introducing the phrase into his text he observes that Falstaff's 'agreeable qualities . . . can be said to prevail in his character' only in the sense that they 'are brought more into view'. This comment, particularly in the proximity of the tell-tale phrase, sounds like a clear echo of Morgann's explanation of how Shakespeare conceals Falstaff's turpitude from the audience and so enables him to charm as a dramatic character where in real life he would repel.[1]

---

[1] *Essays on Shakespeare's Dramatic Character of Sir John Falstaff*, etc. (1788), pp. 11, 17, 19, 55–6. Smith (ed.), *Eighteenth Century Essays*, pp. lxi–lxii, notes that Richardson reproduces Morgann's title. Of Richardson's three often-reprinted series of essays on Shakespeare, the first, *A Philosophical Analysis and Illustration of Some of Shakespeare's Remarkable Characters*, came out in 1774. The phrase 'Dramatic Characters' appeared for the first time in the title of the second series, *Essays on Shakespeare's Dramatic Characters of Richard III, King Lear and Timon of Athens*, which was published in 1784 (reissued, 1785), seven years after Morgann's *Essay*. Thereafter the phrase appeared in all title-pages of the series—the 4th edition of the first series, retitled *Essays on Shakespeare's Dramatic Characters of Macbeth, Hamlet, Jacques, and Imogen* (1785; reissued, 1786); the 2nd edition of the second series (1786); the first edition of the third series, containing the study of Falstaff (1788; reissued 1789); and the two collected editions of the three series, *Essays on Some of Shakespeare's Dramatic Characters* (1797; reissued 1798) and *Essays on Shakespeare's Dramatic Characters* (1812; reissued posthumously, 1818). The Advertisement by the Author prefaced to the collected editions erroneously gives the original title of the first series as '*Dramatic*' rather than '*Remarkable Characters*'. The mistake supports the inference that Richardson saw a special significance in the phrase.

Morgann's influence on the Falstaff studies of others went hand in hand with growing respect for his own achievement. Some of Richardson's reviewers improved the occasion by making favourable references to the *Essay*. The *English Review* observed that 'the ingenious and acute apologist of *valiant* Jack' saw the seamy side of Falstaff's character no less clearly than Richardson. The *European Magazine*, in an article reprinted in the *Hibernian Magazine*, advised those truly interested in discovering why they love Falstaff to close their Richardson and open their Morgann: 'we are fond of his company on a principle something better than merely the amusement he affords us'. Though unable to make up his mind about the hypothesis regarding the knight's courage ('*si non e vero e bon* [sic] *trovato*'), the reviewer, after quoting a passage from Richardson and another from the *Essay*, capped the latter with the cry: 'Such is the Falstaff of Mr. Morgan, of Shakespeare, of Nature!'[1]

A little later, completely won over to Morgann's conception of Falstaff, Henry James Pye observed that critics like Davies who could find nothing but specious paradox in the *Essay* were, as Morgann said, either blind pedants or slavish minds too timid to think for themselves (*Es.*, T108–9). Pye delivered this opinion in his *Commentary* on Aristotle, where he quoted or referred to the *Essay* in eight places. Drawing public attention for the first time to the long notes on Shakespeare's art of characterization and on his 'Poetic magic' (*Es.*, T58n–T62n and T71n–T77n), Pye declared that the first places the playwright's 'superiority in the delineation of manners in the clearest light', and the second goes into its subject 'as far as it is capable of being investigated'. But the *Essay*, he said, had to be read in its entirety, 'since every part is replete with elegance of taste and accurate and impartial judgment'.[2]

Belatedly reviewing Stack in the hitherto antagonistic *Monthly Review*, Thomas Ogle now observed that the truth might lie with both parties to the controversy. Shakespeare, Ogle suggested, may well have presented Falstaff inconsistently now as a coward and now as showing a semblance of courage, depending on the humorous

---

[1] *English Review*, xiv (1789), 97–8. *European Magazine*, xiv (1788), 422–5. *Walker's Hibernian Magazine* (Jan. 1789), 24–6.

[2] *A Commentary Illustrating the Poetic of Aristotle* (1792), pp. 307–9 and 274. Pye also quotes Morgann on pp. xii, 123 (see note to *Es.*, T150), 175, and 486, and refers to him on pp. 101 and 325. Did Pye discover Morgann late? In the first edition of the *Poetik of Aristotle* (1788) the occasional references in the notes to contemporary criticism ignore the *Essay*.

effect he wished to achieve.¹ Five years later, Thomas James
Mathias, alluding in a friendly, jocular way to Morgann's expertise
in 'courage and finesse', explained in a note that he was referring
to his 'pleasant *Extravaganza* on the *Courage* of Sir John Falstaff',
and added the titbit that 'Mr. Morgan is known to his friends by the
name of Sir John'; in later editions he went on to recommend that
the *Essay* be reprinted.² More warmly appreciative, William Seward
described Morgann's word-picture of Shakespeare's poetic character
as 'the portrait of Homer painted by Apelles', and—the first of a long
line—regretted that 'Mr. Morgan has given us no more illustrations
of Shakespeare in his own refined and delicate manner'.³

All in all, whether friendly, unfriendly, or somewhere in between,
the contemporary reception accorded Morgann's *Essay* shows not
only that he had 'at least a thin line of readers',⁴ but that through
them he had succeeded in putting the question of whether Falstaff
is brave or craven on the agenda of Shakespeare criticism. This
moderate fame, and the interest of the question of Falstaff's courage,
not yet 'threshed over till there is nothing but chaff left',⁵ ought, it
should seem, to have attracted the attention of Coleridge, Hazlitt, and Lamb to a book in which they would have encountered

¹ *Monthly Review*, 2nd Ser., vii (1792), 61–3.
² *The Pursuits of Literature, Part the Fourth and Last* (1797), p. 41. Reprinted in the
Annual Register, xxxviii (1797), 512. The recommendation that the *Essay* be reprinted
does not appear in any edition up to and including the 'ninth' of 1799. It is found in
the 'eleventh' edition (1801), pp. 353–4, just before the date '1797', which was first
added to the end of the note in the 'ninth' edition, p. 345. The note including the
recommendation recurs unchanged in the 'thirteenth' edition (1805), pp. 353–4 and the
'sixteenth' edition (1812), p. 296, and presumably in the intermediate editions as well.
³ *Supplement to the Anecdotes of Some Distinguished Persons* (1797), p. 151, and in
four subsequent editions of which the last appeared in 1804.
In *Poems on Several Occasions* (Edinburgh, 1811), p. 52, John Taylor, a member of
Morgann's circle, applauded Stephen Kemble's performance of Falstaff in terms suggesting that ideas in the *Essay* may have had some effect on the stage. In contrast to the
coarse ruffianly Falstaff familiar in the theatre, Taylor wrote

> Kemble, to *Shakespeare's* meaning right,
> Exhibits a degen'rate knight,
> Who seems to make no empty vaunt,
> That erst he jok'd with *John of Gaunt*.

Kemble began appearing as Falstaff in the late eighteenth century.
⁴ Tave, *R.E.S.* N.S. iii (1952), 374. Among his readers, as Tave notes (*The Amiable
Humorist*, p. 270), must also be included William Belsham; see his *Essays, Philosophical,
Historical and Literary* (1789), p. 33, where he quotes a passage from the *Essay*, referring
to Morgann not by name but as 'an animated writer'. Belsham may owe something of
his idea of Shakespearian characterization to Morgann: see below, p. 102.
⁵ M. R. Ridley, *Shakespeare's Plays* (1937), p. 101.

a response to Shakespeare as dynamic as their own. Depending on how they understood it, they might have found it suggestive of their own approach or almost diametrically opposed. Yet not one of them appears really to have known the *Essay*. Wide and curious readers all, they nowhere mention Morgann's name or otherwise show clear signs of the interest in him one might anticipate. Instead of the expected continuity, whether linear or dialectic, there is hiatus.

Hazlitt well exemplifies the situation. In the Preface of his *Characters of Shakespeare's Plays* (1817), he recorded his impression that his only English predecessors in character analysis were Richardson and Thomas Whately.[1] The distinction he went on to make in his chapter on *Henry VI* between Falstaff's 'sensual and philosophic cowardice' and Parolles's 'pitiful and cringing cowardice' smacks of Mackenzie; and his statement in the chapter on *Henry IV* that Falstaff 'openly assumes' the character of a coward, even if interpreted as meaning he is not one by constitution, seems rather a modification of Cumberland than a borrowing from Morgann.[2] More directly reminiscent of the *Essay* is his point in the same chapter on *Henry IV* that we are not shocked at Falstaff's violations of the 'restraints of society' because 'no mischievous consequences do result'. Also in the Morgann vein is his description in the *English Comic Writers* (1819) of Falstaff as a tumbling leviathan and as a humorist who exhibits his own absurdities purposely. But these parallels, as Professor Tave has observed of the last of them, are too slight, in the absence of other evidence, to warrant a theory of influence; and the Morgannian phrases Hazlitt later used in a review of Spence's *Anecdotes*—'the butt and the wit, the jester and the jest' (cf. *Es.*, T20)—were probably culled, as Tave has also argued, from the *London Magazine* review of the 1820 edition of the *Essay* rather than from the *Essay* itself.[3]

---

[1] *Complete Works of William Hazlitt*, ed. P. P. Howe (1931), iv. 171. Hazlitt names George Mason, but he means Whately.

[2] *Works*, ed. Howe, iv. 293 and 279. For Cumberland see above, p. 16.

[3] *Works of Hazlitt*, ed. Howe, iv. 279 (chapter on *Henry IV*): cf. *Es.*, T158. Howe, vi. 32 and 22 (*Lectures on the English Comic Writers*, II and I): cf. *Es.*, T170 and T174. Review of Spence's *Anecdotes* in the *Edinburgh Review*, xxx (May 1820), 328. P. L. Carver, 'The Influence of Maurice Morgann', *R.E.S.* vi (1930), 320–2, suggested that the passages in the *Edinburgh Review* and the first *Comic Writers* lecture show Hazlitt's knowledge of Morgann; Tave's convincing refutation is in his *R.E.S.* article (cited above, p. 12 n.), p. 372. Herschel Baker, *William Hazlitt* (Cambridge, Mass., 1962), p. 303, seems to imply that Hazlitt was acquainted with Morgann, but as evidence he cites the Preface to Shakespeare's *Characters*, where Hazlitt refers only to Richardson and Whately.

Equally tenuous is Morgann's relation to Coleridge, who said explicitly that 'Falstaff was no coward, but pretended to be one merely for the sake of trying experiments on the credulity of mankind'.[1] It is possible, of course, as Professor Babcock has suggested, that Coleridge and Hazlitt were alerted to Morgann through the references to him in the April and May issues of the *Monthly Magazine* for 1811,[2] the second of which summed up the case made out in the *Essay* against the conception of Falstaff as a poltroon. But if the articles did not send the critics to the *Essay* itself, the question of meaningful influence does not arise. Not the bare idea that Falstaff is no coward, already in general circulation, but the complex argument Morgann presented and his bold, original analysis of Shakespeare's aesthetic strategies, made up the subject-matter on which he had something challenging to say to Coleridge and Hazlitt. The same holds true for Lamb, who might as readily as his friends have seen the *Monthly Magazine* in the spring of 1811. Had Lamb been thus stimulated into seeking out the *Essay*, he would have discovered he had there been preceded both in his contention that the actors make us see what we should be left to conceive and in his belief that Shakespeare's characters are in their substance '*essentially . . . different*' from those of all other authors (cf. *Es.*, T128 and T58n). Lamb's public enunciation of these opinions, like Coleridge's pronouncement on Falstaff's cowardice, post-dates the *Monthly Magazine* notices.[3] But the balance of probabilities tips against the

[1] *Coleridge's Shakespearean Criticism*, ed. T. M. Raysor (1930), ii. 29. See also ii. 210.

[2] Vol. xxxi, pp. 211 and 325-6. See R. W. Babcock, *The Genesis of Shakespeare Idolatry, 1766-1799* (Chapel Hill, 1931), pp. 229-30. The three further proofs of Coleridge's knowledge of Morgann advanced by Babcock, p. 235, are even less persuasive: (1) Coleridge's use of the term 'passive impressions' in his *Essay on Method* is not particularly Morgannian. (2) His reference to Shakespeare's 'magic characters' (ed. Raysor, ii. 84) clearly alludes to Dryden's 'magic circle' and *not* to the close of Morgann's note on Shakespeare's supernatural: see *Es.*, T77n and note. (Incidentally, it is not Raysor, as Babcock suggests, but J. D. Campbell who is 'puzzled' by Coleridge's comment.) (3) Finally, Coleridge's statement that Shakespeare's characters are to be inferred by the reader, below, as is argued pp. 105-6, is too inherently a part of his differently oriented critical approach to imply Morgann's influence. So too with the other 'parallel passages' cited below, notes to T16, T59, T61.

[3] Lamb's 'On the Tragedies of Shakspeare, considered with reference to their fitness for Stage Representation' appeared in *The Reflector*, No. iv, in 1812: see E. V. Lucas (ed.), *The Work of Charles and Mary Lamb* (1903), i. 414. Collier records Coleridge's account of Falstaff as no coward, quoted above, under the date of 13 Oct. 1811; the conversation took place, he writes, 'a little while since'. (Coleridge's slightly earlier remark that Falstaff is 'content to be thought both a liar and a coward'—not quite the same as saying he is no coward—is recorded by H. C. Robinson under the date of 23 Dec. 1810.) See Raysor, ii. 210.

hypothesis that the articles induced Lamb, Coleridge, or Hazlitt to look up the *Essay*. 'Had they known it', as Nichol Smith said, 'they must have responded somehow to its fervid subtlety'—and responded in a way that would be unmistakable.[1]

As it happens, just when the creators of the new Romantic criticism in England were getting down to the business of propounding their views on Shakespeare, Morgann's posthumous fame, such as it was, disappeared almost entirely from Shakespearian contexts. Brief notices of his death in two periodicals[2] were followed at first only by reprints of Seward's and Mathias's favourable but hasty and out-of-the-way mentions of him, which continued to appear in later editions until 1804 and 1812 respectively (see above, p. 20). Nor was his claim to be recognized as a Shakespearian critic much advanced by the appearance in 1806 and 1807 of the laudatory and subsequently reprinted memorials composed by his friends Charles Symmons and William Cooke. Symmons's tribute, which held the *Essay* to form 'a more honourable monument to the memory of Shakespeare than any which had been reared to him by the united labours of his commentators', appeared in a footnote to his *Life of Milton*, while Cooke's recollections, which found in Morgann's account of Shakespeare 'the spirit of the poet himself breathing through his commentator', formed part of the Dedication to John Symmons of the second edition of his didactic poem entitled *Conversation*.[3] Except for a bare listing of the *Essay* in the bibliography of critical works in standard current editions of Shakespeare, for two references in a dull book by the ever-faithful Pye, and perhaps for the *Monthly Magazine* articles in 1811, the few other allusions to Morgann in the

---

[1] Smith, *Shakespeare in the Eighteenth Century* (Oxford, 1928), pp. 87–8. The closest contact a major Romantic critic had with Morgann's thought is apparently recorded in a brief review (1791) by A. W. Schlegel of Stack's 'Examination'. On the strength of what he finds in the 'Examination', Schlegel confidently declares the thesis of the *Essay* to be 'unbegreiflich' and says that Stack displays 'eine etwas zweideutige Bescheidenheit wenn er im Eingange seiner Gegner als beinahe unüberwindlich schildert' (*Sämmtliche Werke*, ed. Eduard Böcking, x [Leipzig, 1846], 54–5). In his Vienna *Lectures on Dramatic Art and Poetry* (1st Ger. edn., 1809–11), Eng. trans., rev. edn. (1846), p. 426, Schlegel continues to regard Falstaff as 'a cowardly soldier'.

[2] *Gentleman's Magazine*, lxii. 1 (1802), 470 and 582. *European Magazine*, xli (1802), 334.

[3] On Symmons see above, p. 4. His footnote was reproduced in a separate edition of the *Life of Milton* (1810), pp. 122–5, and in abridged form in S. E. Brydges, *Censura Literaria*, iv (1807), 178–81. Cooke, *Conversation* (1807), pp. v–xiii. (See also above, p. 10.) Further editions containing the 'Dedication' appeared in 1815 (the 'fourth' edition) and in 1822. The 'Dedication' also appeared in the *Gentleman's Magazine*, lxxvii (1807), 643–4.

fifteen years following his death are also in places fairly remote from contemporary interest in Shakespeare. Percival Stockdale recalled him as a pleasant companion, talented author, and paradoxical critic in a volume of *Memoirs*; quoting Symmons on his character, Richard Fenton noted his association with Wales in *A Historical Tour Through Pembrokeshire*; Samuel Foot mentioned him and his Falstaffian paradox at the close of his *Life of Arthur Murphy*; and Nicholas Carlisle twice noted his 'admirable Essay' in connection with Stack's 'Examination' in an *Index to the Transactions of the Royal Irish Academy*.[1]

Once the Romantic critics had completed their task, however, he began to come back into the view of those concerned with Shakespeare. In the very year that Hazlitt declared Whately and Richardson to be his sole worthwhile English forerunners in character analysis, Nathan Drake found space in a solid two-volume study of Shakespeare to praise and quote at some length Morgann's spirited defence of the English bard calumniated by Rymer and Voltaire.[2] And three years later, heralded by pre-publication announcements in several periodicals,[3] a second edition of the *Essay* appeared. The brief preface lauded the 'acuteness' Morgann displayed in discussing 'the principles on which the dramatic characters of Shakespeare are formed'.[4] Certain reviews concurred. Observing that the allegation of Falstaff's valour was the book's 'original sin', the *New Monthly Magazine* heartily approved of its 'general tenour'. Going still further, John Scott, in the *London Magazine*, not only avowed himself convinced by the Falstaffian argument but—seemingly the first after Richardson fully to understand Morgann's concern with Shakespeare's concealment of Falstaff's viciousness—declared that the author's 'deep, intense, and unequivocal feeling' for the playwright qualified him 'to enter within the veil, to adore his genius in its most retired and sacred seats'.[5]

---

[1] H. J. Pye, *Comments on the Commentators on Shakespeare* (1807), pp. ix and 179. Stockdale (1809), ii. 159. Fenton (1810), pp. 483 and 490–4. Foot (1811), pp. 420–1. Carlisle (1813), pp. 59 and 76.

[2] *Shakespeare and His Times* (1817), ii. 553–4.

[3] e.g. *The British Critic*, N.S. xii (Oct. 1819), 448, and *The Repository of Arts, Literature, Fashions, Manufactures &c.*, Ser. 2, viii (1 Nov. 1819), 308. References from Tave, *R.E.S.* N.S. iii. 372.   [4] See below, Textual Introduction, pp. 127–8.

[5] *The New Monthly Magazine and Universal Register*, xiii (1820), 90. *The London Magazine*, i (1820), 194–8. John Scott is identified as the reviewer by Josephine Bauer, *The London Magazine 1820–1829*, Anglistica, i (Copenhagen, 1953), 216 and 255. The book was also listed under 'New Publications' in the *Quarterly Review*, xxii (1820), 562.

Though an insight of this kind into Morgann's thought would not recur for almost a century, and though the edition of 1820 was hardly snapped up by the public—the unsold sheets were reissued as a 'new edition' five years later—the reappearance of the *Essay* marked its establishment in the nineteenth-century Shakespearian consciousness. Formerly an isolated voice, Charles Symmons now reflected current critical opinion when in his *Life of Shakespeare*, prefixed to S. W. Singer's edition of Shakespeare's *Dramatic Works* (1826), he referred to his old friend's *Essay* as an 'eloquent' work by 'a man of genius'. Henceforward, 'Morgann on *Falstaff*', as Henry Crabb Robinson called it, was a volume known to the *cognoscenti*, the sort of book a bibliophile might grangerize with fine plates and a Phillips discreetly pillage, using quotation marks but without identifying his source, for a sounding peroration to a study of Falstaff.[1]

The historical significance later to be attributed to the *Essay* was soon foreshadowed. Coleridge's avowed disciple, Charles Knight, described it in 1839 as 'a remarkable specimen of genial criticism upon Shakespere' by an author who in his day 'stood almost alone in the endeavour to understand the poet'. Over a decade earlier, in an admirable anthology of English and continental Shakespeare criticism, Drake appended to an excerpt from Morgann the observation that it 'rivals in its tone and manner what has since been so eloquently expressed by Schlegel and other German critics on the [poetic] character of Shakespeare'.[2] In the main, however, Morgann was at first more narrowly recognized by Victorians as the author of the best 'single disquisition' on Falstaff.[3] Thriving in a literary atmosphere favourable to contrasting a man's outer actions with his true inner being, his paradoxical theory that despite cowardly appearances Falstaff is really a man of courage obtained ever wider assent. Drake and Hackett might think the view untenable, but the trend was against them. Beginning with Maginn, Knight, and Verplanck, though sometimes as with the last two subject to Mackenzie's

[1] Symmons in Singer, i. 71. *Henry Crabb Robinson on Books and their Writers*, ed. Edith J. Morley (1938), i. 316. A copy of the 1777 edition of the *Essay*, grangerized with 38 plates and bound in a nineteenth-century binding, is in the Folger Shakespeare Library. James Orchard Phillips, *On the Character of Sir John Falstaff* (1841), p. 55. (A copy of the 1777 edition of the *Essay* appears in the *Catalogue of the Shakespeare-Study Books in the Immediate Library of J. O. Halliwell-Phillips* [1876], p. 18.)

[2] Knight, *Pictorial Edition of the Works of Shakspere, Histories*, i (1839), 297; cf. his 'Shakspere's Critics' (1847), in *Studies in Shakspere* (1849), p. 555. Drake, *Memorials of Shakespeare* (1828), pp. 35–43; see also p. 251.

[3] Charles Armitage Brown, *Shakespeare's Autobiographical Poems* (1838), p. 274.

reservations, the idea that Falstaff is no coward won increasing acceptance; and those who adopted it usually knew they were indebted to Morgann and cited his arguments, even if, like the anonymous author of an article in *Fraser's Magazine*, they had not actually read his book. During the second half of the century, among others, Reed, Lloyd, Brough, Foster, Hudson, Dowden, Jacox, Swinburne, and Randolph all spoke up for the new orthodoxy. Randolph's pleasant Shakespearian diversion with its several appreciative references to Morgann seems scarcely conceivable except against the background of the reversal in established opinion; and the shift is nowhere better illustrated than in Swinburne's verdict that Morgann's 'able essay', while eliciting 'from Dr. Johnson as good a jest and as bad a criticism as might have been expected', had proved its point so thoroughly as not 'to require or even to admit of corroboration'.[1]

In the measure that Morgann's view of Falstaff entrenched itself, the larger merits of the *Essay* also won more general esteem. The owner in private of Morgann's manuscript Commentary on *The Tempest*, Dowden announced in public not only his acceptance of the *Essay*'s Falstaffian thesis but also his belief that 'no piece of eighteenth-century Shakespeare criticism is more intelligently and warmly appreciative'. In his *D.N.B.* article on Morgann (1894) Thomas Seccombe declared the 'very generally praised' *Essay* unsurpassed for 'profound appreciation of Shakespeare'. Then, in 1895, picking up the idea adumbrated by Drake and Knight over fifty years previously, Walder said that 'the philosophical criticism of Shakspere' began in Morgann; and in 1901, Lounsbury remarked more cautiously that, on surveying eighteenth-century criticism, only in

[1] Drake, *Memorials*, p. 35. James H. Hackett, *Notes and Comments* (New York, 1864), p. 349. William Maginn, 'Sir John Falstaff' (1837), in *Shakespeare Papers* (New York, 1856), pp. 26–7. Knight, *Pictorial Shakspere*, *Histories*, i. 295, 297, 299, and 302. Gulian C. Verplanck (ed.), *Shakespeare's Plays* (New York, 1847), i. 61–2. Anon., 'On the Character of Sir John Falstaff', *Fraser's Magazine*, xlvi (Oct. 1852), 403–10. Henry Reed, *Lectures on English History and Tragic Poetry* (Philadelphia, 1857), p. 206. William Watkiss Lloyd, *Essays on the Life and Plays of Shakespeare* (1858), sig. BB4. B. Brough, *The Life of Sir John Falstaff* (1858), p. 86. Charles J. Foster (1862) in Hackett, *Notes and Comments*, p. 342. H. N. Hudson, *Shakespeare: His Life, Art, and Characters*, 4th edn. (Boston, 1872), ii. 84. Edward Dowden, *Shakspere: A Critical Study of his Mind and Art*, 13th edn. (1906: 1st edn., 1875), pp. 365–6. Francis Jacox, *Shakspeare Diversions* (1875), pp. [349]–53. A. C. Swinburne, *A Study of Shakespeare* (1880), p. 111. A. M. F. Randolph, *The Trial of Sir John Falstaff* (New York and London, 1893), pp. viii, 7–8, 13, and 138. The pressure of the new orthodoxy also appears in G. H. Radford's 'Falstaff', included by Augustine Birrell among his own *Obiter Dicta* [*First Series*] (1884), pp. 201–34: Radford doubts that Falstaff ever really performed services in battle (p. 222), but avoids calling him a coward.

the *Essay* did he 'seem to see indicated dimly the view of Shakespeare which was developed in the nineteenth century, and which reigns triumphant today'.[1]

Morgann was now on the verge of coming into his present-day fame. The signal was given in 1903 by David Nichol Smith, who, in his collection of *Eighteenth Century Essays on Shakespeare*, republished Morgann's work for the first time since 1825. It was, he declared, an important book that had met with 'unaccountable neglect'. Distinguishing Morgann firmly from Warton, Whately, and Richardson, he found him to be

the true forerunner of the romantic criticism of Shakespeare. Morgann's attitude to the characters is the same as Coleridge's and Hazlitt's; his criticism, neglecting all formal matters, resolves itself into a study of human nature. It was he who first said that Shakespeare's creations should be treated as historic rather than as dramatic beings. And the keynote of his criticism is that 'the impression is the fact'. He states what he *feels*, and he explains the reason in language which is barely on this side idolatry.[2]

Nichol Smith's judgement was at once endorsed by A. C. Bradley, who had already been taken with Morgann because he believed him to interpret the workings of Shakespeare's imagination from within in the fashion of Goethe, Coleridge, Lamb, and Hazlitt. In a lecture avowedly affected by Morgann's influence he had adopted his view of Falstaff as a man of courage, and, following H. T. Roetscher, refined on his conception of the knight as a military free-thinker.[3] Now, reviewing Smith's anthology, Bradley declared it would deserve a warm welcome if it contained nothing but Morgann's *Essay*, so long out of print, 'for there is no better piece of Shakespearian criticism in the world'. Morgann, Bradley continued, 'reached *in principle* the whole position in which criticism has rested from the days of Schlegel and Coleridge'. In him the earlier superstitions have disappeared—all the talk about the rules, poetic justice, and Shakespeare's want of art; and the habit of judging Shakespeare from the outside

---

[1] Dowden, *Shakspere*, p. 366. E. Walder, *Shaksperian Criticism* (Bradford, 1895), pp. 18-19. Thomas R. Lounsbury, *Shakespeare as a Dramatic Artist* (New York and London), p. 376.

[2] pp. xxxvii-xxxviii; 2nd edn., pp. xxxvi-xxxvii.

[3] 'The Rejection of Falstaff', *Oxford Lectures on Poetry* (1909), pp. 247-75 (see especially pp. 266 and 274-5).

has given place to the use of a sympathetic imagination which follows the dramatist into the minutest details of his composition, conscious that, whether the informing spirit of his work be called 'art' or 'nature', it carries life and meaning into every atom of its creation, and that, where it seems to us to fail, we should doubt more than once before we conclude that the error lies with Shakespeare. Something of this spirit is quite visible in Richardson; in Morgann it is full grown, and has for its instrument a mind not less poetical than acute. . . . But Morgann would have been an exceptional critic in any age, and in his own his *Essay* stands almost as much alone as do the Songs of Blake. It appears for long to have had scarcely any influence on criticism. Its time was not yet. Indeed, its time is only now . . .[1]

These words ushered Morgann into his present reputation. To this day, the *Essay* is esteemed largely because it is supposed that in it the spirit of Schlegel and Coleridge appears full grown. Nichol Smith in a later pronouncement and other students of Shakespeare criticism from C. F. Johnson to A. M. Eastman have consolidated the image of Morgann as the first major Romantic critic of Shakespeare.[2] The specific basis for the consensus is epitomized in an authoritative handbook as follows: 'Morgann, in proving that Falstaff was no coward, believed in Shakespeare's characters "rather as historic than dramatic beings".'[3] The doctrine of historic beings is understood to present the theory behind the Romantic system of

[1] *Scottish Historical Review*, i (1904), 291 and 294–5.

[2] D. Nichol Smith (ed.), *Shakespeare Criticism: A Selection* (1916), pp. xvi–xvii and xxi. Charles F. Johnson, *Shakespeare and His Critics* (Boston, 1909), pp. 156–63. George Stuart Gordon, 'Morgann on Falstaff', rev. of Gill's edition of the *Essay*, *T.L.S.* 15 Nov. 1912, reprinted in *The Lives of Authors* (1950), pp. 23–32. Raysor (ed.), *Coleridge's Shakespearean Criticism* (1930), vol. i, p. xxiii. Babcock, *Genesis of Shakespeare Idolatry* (1931), pp. xxv and 242. Herbert Spencer Robinson, *English Shakespearian Criticism in the Eighteenth Century* (New York, 1932), pp. 198–205. Augustus Ralli, *A History of Shakespeare Criticism* (Oxford, 1932), i. 73–81, 88, 107, 142, and 197. David Lovett, *Shakespeare's Characters in Eighteenth Century Criticism* (Baltimore, 1935), pp. 282 and 288. J. Dover Wilson, *The Fortunes of Falstaff* (Cambridge, 1943), p. 2. F. E. Halliday, *Shakespeare and His Critics* (1949), pp. 246–7. J. W. H. Atkins, *English Literary Criticism: 17th and 18th Centuries* (1951), pp. 261–7. William Empson, 'Falstaff and Mr. Dover Wilson', *Kenyon Review*, xv (1953), 223. Aisso Bosker, *Literary Criticism in the Age of Johnson*, 2nd edn. (Groningen, 1953; 1st edn., 1930), p. 286. Arthur Sewell, 'The Concept of Character in the Eighteenth Century', *Litera*, iv (1957), 18–19. Oscar James Campbell and Edward G. Quinn, *A Shakespeare Encyclopaedia* (1966), s.v. Morgann. Arthur M. Eastman, *A Short History of Shakespearean Criticism* (New York, 1968), pp. 52–62.

[3] J. Isaacs, 'Shakespearian Criticism: II, From Coleridge to the Present Day', in *A Companion to Shakespeare Studies*, ed. Harley Granville-Barker and G. B. Harrison (Cambridge, 1934), p. 302.

character-study, the argument concerning Falstaff is held to provide a detailed application of that theory, and the two together are regarded as the heart of the *Essay*. Thus interpreted, Morgann is recognized above all as the first who on an impressive scale and with large insight discussed a Shakespearian character as not a mere dramatis persona but a living person, as complex, as familiar, and as mysterious as our most intimate friends or ourselves. And just as it is commonly accepted that the Romantic tradition culminated superbly in Bradley, so the concept of a Morgann–Bradley school of criticism passes as current coin among students of Shakespeare.

This is the view taken of Morgann's achievement not only by those who, like Ridley, L. P. Smith, and Atkins, praise it as his glory,[1] but also by the increasing numbers who impugn it as his fallacy. In the hue and cry against Bradley which has been raised by critics of varying tendencies during the past forty years, Morgann has been attacked precisely because he is regarded as providing the archetype for the Bradleyan confusion of Shakespeare's characters with living human beings. A. B. Walkley, the earliest of Morgann's systematic assailants, singled out the passage in the *Essay* on historic beings as the 'first appearance' of the 'heresy'.[2] Developing Walkley's preliminary skirmish into what has been called a 'thirty-years war against the whole Morgann–Bradley tradition',[3] E. E. Stoll pursued Morgann over many a polemic page as the man who had set the bad example for the over-refined psychologizing of dramatic characters which had seduced and dominated Shakespeare criticism for well nigh a hundred and fifty years. Morgann, he charged, did not know how to read dramatic score; he failed to realize that not latent impressions but only obtrusively emphasized details tell in the theatre, and he distorted matters hopelessly by considering episodes without reference to the chronological order of their impact on the audience.[4] In pressing these points home, some of them made long

---

[1] M. R. Ridley, *Shakespeare's Plays* (1937), pp. 4–6. Logan Pearsall Smith, *On Reading Shakespeare* (1933), pp. 48, 101–4, and 179. Atkins, *English Literary Criticism: 17th and 18th Centuries*, p. 266.

[2] 'Professor Bradley's Hamlet', *Drama and Life* (1907), p. 148.

[3] Harold Jenkins, in *Shakespeare Survey*, vi (1953), 13.

[4] Stoll's attack on Morgann begins with 'Falstaff', *M.P.* xii (1914), 65–108, and ranges through *Shakespeare Studies*, rev. edn. (New York, 1942; 1st edn., 1927), pp. 117, 119, 140, and 402–90; 'Recent Shakespeare Studies', *Shakespeare-Jahrbuch*, lxxiv (1938), 58–63 and 80–1; *Shakespeare and Other Masters* (Cambridge, Mass., 1940), pp. 349–81 *passim*; and *From Shakespeare to Joyce* (Garden City, N.Y., 1946), ch. XII.

before by Stack,[1] Stoll constantly related them to his basic accusation that Morgann is the original practitioner of what Benedetto Croce has denominated 'objectivist criticism' of Shakespeare—the kind of criticism that detaches the playwright's characters 'from the creative centre of the play and [transfers] them into a pretended objective field, as though they were made of flesh and blood'.[2] Taking up the cudgels from a different point of vantage, L. C. Knights has presented essentially the same indictment: 'more than any other man, it seems to me, Morgann has deflected Shakespeare criticism from the proper objects of attention by his preposterous references to the aspects of a "character" that Shakespeare did not wish to show'.[3]

In reinforcing the standard image of Morgann, the anti-Bradleyite movement has also, of course, had certain damaging effects on his position as critic. In particular, as the tendency has prevailed to find in Shakespeare's characters not living people but symbolic embodiments of complex attitudes or thematic elements contributing to a total imaginative effect, Morgann's influence upon the interpretation of Falstaff has waned. Earlier in the present era, Brandes, Raleigh, Brook, A. E. Morgan, and Quiller-Couch could all discuss Falstaff's character without referring to any other critic but not without quoting approvingly from the *Essay*.[4] And into the mid-1940s, Charlton, Kittredge, Spencer, Palmer, and Neilson and Hill employed Morgann's arguments to prove the knight no coward, while Harbage pricked out a Falstaff avowedly dependent on the *Essay*, and Dover Wilson, though repudiating the idea of Falstaff as a man of courage, impressed a specialist in the criticism of *Henry IV* as having his head

---

[1] Discovering Stack after he published his early study of Falstaff, Stoll interspersed the revised version (in his *Shakespeare Studies*) with frequent quotations from and references to the 'Examination'.

[2] *Ariosto, Shakespeare and Corneille*, trans. Douglas Ainslie (New York, 1920), pp. 312–13. Cf. F. E. Halliday, *Shakespeare and his Critics*, p. 248.

[3] 'How Many Children Had Lady Macbeth?' (1933), in *Explorations* (Harmondsworth, 1964; 1st edn., London, 1946), p. 24.

[4] George Brandes, *William Shakespeare*, trans. William Archer (New York, 1935; orig. edn., Copenhagen, 1898), p. 184. Walter Raleigh, *Shakespeare* (1907), p. 189. Stopford A. Brook, *Ten More Plays of Shakespeare* (1913), pp. 286–9. A. E. Morgan, *Works of Shakespeare, The First Part of King Henry the Fourth*, eds. R. P. Cowl and A. E. Morgan (1914), pp. xxxii–xxxiv. Arthur Quiller-Couch, *Shakespeare's Workmanship* (1918), p. 149. Others of the same era who follow Morgann for their interpretation of Falstaff are J. A. R. Marriott, *English History in Shakespeare* (1918), pp. 117–28, and J. B. Priestley, *The English Comic Characters* (1925), pp. 92–5. R. R. Simpson, *Shakespeare and Medicine* (Edinburgh and London, 1959), still depends on Morgann in his chapter on 'The Medical History of Sir John Falstaff'.

with Stoll but his heart with Morgann.[1] Today, however, with the
dominance of the new attitude towards Shakespeare's characters,
most critics in one way or another agree with Brooks and Heilman
that Morgann's questioning of the knight's cowardice, which is
supposed to assume that we are to take him as a human being, is
irrelevant to the play.[2] The change is reflected in a comparison of
S. B. Hemingway's New Variorum Edition of *Henry the Fourth,
Part I*, published in 1936, with A. R. Humphreys's revised Arden
Edition of the play, published in 1960. Hemingway devoted more
space—eight and a half pages of small print—to summarizing Morgann's arguments against Falstaff's cowardice than to digesting the
views of any other critic.[3] In contrast, Humphreys mentions him but
hurriedly in his Introduction, and then chiefly to point out that the
'tiresome question' of the knight's cowardice 'would have been
quickly settled had not Falstaff's vitality confused critics as to the
difference between dramatic and real persons'.[4] So spent a rocket,

[1] H. B. Charlton, *Falstaff*, reprinted from *Bulletin of the John Rylands Library*, xix
(1935), 19 (cf. p. 15 for dependence on Morgann). George Lyman Kittredge (ed.), *Complete Works of Shakespeare* (Boston, 1936), p. 544, and *Sixteen Plays of Shakespeare* (Boston, 1946), pp. 508–9. Hazelton Spencer, *The Art and Life of William Shakespeare*
(New York, 1940), pp. 183–4 and 401. John Palmer, *Political Characters of Shakespeare*
(1945), pp. 183–4. William Allan Neilson and Charles Jarvis Hill (eds.), *The Complete
Plays and Poems of William Shakespeare* (Boston, 1942), p. 633. Alfred Harbage, *As
They Liked It* (New York, 1961; 1st edn., 1947), pp. 74–8. Samuel B. Hemingway, 'On
Behalf of that Falstaff', *Shakespeare Quarterly*, iii (1952), 310 (referring to J. Dover
Wilson, *Fortunes of Falstaff* [1943]).

[2] Cleanth Brooks and Robert B. Heilman, *Understanding Drama* (New York, 1945),
p. 345. Cf. H. M. McLuhan, '*Henry IV*, A Mirror for Magistrates', *University of
Toronto Quarterly*, xvii (1948), 152; Muriel Bradbrook, *Shakespeare and Elizabethan
Poetry* (1951), pp. 198 and 269; C. L. Barber, *Shakespeare's Festive Comedy* (Princeton,
1959), p. 198; and I. Scott-Kilvert, *Shakespeare: Henry IV Parts I and II*, [British
Council] Notes on Literature, No. 96 (July 1969), pp. 7–8.

[3] (Philadelphia), pp. 406–14. Matthias Shaaber, the editor of the New Variorum
Second Part of Henry the Fourth (Philadelphia, 1940) pays less attention to Morgann,
partly because, as he indicates on p. 606, Hemingway had already covered much of the
ground, and partly because he is often more amused than impressed by the kind of
evidence Morgann finds in the play to prove Falstaff's reputation for valour: see particularly pp. 63, 106, and 324.

[4] *The First Part of King Henry IV*, pp. xliii–xliv. Humphreys also names Morgann
on p. xlii, apropos of the *miles gloriosus* elements in Falstaff, and on pp. xliii–xliv, without mentioning him, he describes Falstaff as 'unified of paradoxical opposites . . . butt
and wit together'—observations which savour strongly of *Es.*, T20 and T146. (Cf.
F. P. Wilson, *Shakespearian and Other Studies*, ed. H. Gardner (Oxford, 1969), p. 39:
'As Maurice Morgann saw, [Falstaff's] character is compounded of many paradoxes.')
In spite of himself, moreover, Humphreys appears unable to let the tiresome, settled ques-
tion alone: 'Falstaff may be a physical coward but he is not a moral one' (pp. lvii–lviii).
Morgann's decline as an authority on Falstaff is also reflected in James L. Sanderson's

indeed, is the once dazzling idea of Falstaff as a man of valour that some of Morgann's admirers prefer to follow A. W. Gill, who in 1912 brought Davies and the *Analytical Review* up to date, and take the defence of Falstaff's courage in a Pickwickian sense. Gill's phrase for that part of the *Essay*, in the Preface to his edition, is 'a critical *jeu d'esprit*' (p. xiv). Echoing him, one more recent critic tells us that Morgann only half-believed in his thesis; he was being playful, says another, perhaps only amusing himself, hazards a third, working a fanciful, charming, and ingenious vein of *bagatelle*, explains a fourth.[1]

Morgann has also suffered from the anti-Bradleyite movement in another way. Stoll, who in some ways studied the *Essay* carefully, differentiated: 'Morgann', he wrote, 'subtilized Falstaff, people since have sentimentalized him.'[2] Less observant, others have blurred the distinction and described Morgann as a sentimentalist who wishes to explain away Falstaff's vices and to see in him 'essentially a harmless, loveable person'.[3] On 'any close reading of the text', a recent critic avows, he is puzzled to understand how 'the final open rejection of Falstaff should have so disturbed romantic critics of Shakespeare from Morgann to Bradley'.[4] A reasonably close reading

students' edition of *Henry the Fourth Part I* (New York, 1962), where in 125 pages taken up by critiques of the play, Morgann is represented by a two-page snippet and his supposed point of view by a further three pages from Bradley, as compared with six by Stoll and seventeen and a half by A. C. Sprague devoted to refuting the 'Morgann–Bradley thesis'. (Sprague's article, 'Gadshill Revisited', appeared originally in *Shakespeare Quarterly*, iv (1953), 125–37.) On the other hand, R. J. Dorius (ed.), *Discussions of Shakespeare's Histories* (Boston, 1964), gives Morgann eight out of a total of 149 pages, buttresses him with eleven more by Bradley, and presents him as a persistent seminal influence on the criticism of *Henry IV*. Still more recently, in his Casebook, *Shakespeare: King Henry IV, Parts I and II* (1970), G. K. Hunter allots thirty-one pages to Morgann, more than to Bradley or to any of the eleven other critics he includes.

[1] Wellek, *History of Modern Criticism*, i. 118. Harbage, *As They Liked It*, p. 77. Allan Gilbert, *The Principles and Practice of Criticism* (Detroit, 1959), p. 67. J. I. M. Stewart, *Character and Motive in Shakespeare* (1949), p. 117. For a consideration of this view see below, pp. 44 ff.

[2] *Shakespeare Studies*, p. xi.

[3] *John W. Shirley*, 'Falstaff, an Elizabethan Glutton', *P.Q.* xvii (1938), 271. Shirley is not alone. According to W. Jaggard, *Shakespeare Bibliography* (Stratford-upon-Avon, 1911), p. 222, the *Essay* is 'an effort to whitewash Falstaff's character'. Of like mind are John Bailey, 'A Note on Falstaff', in *A Book of Homage to Shakespeare*, ed. Israel Gollancz (1916), pp. 149–52; R. M. Alden, *Shakespeare* (New York, 1922), pp. 177 and 217; and Peter J. Seng, 'Songs, Time, and the Rejection of Falstaff', *Shakespeare Survey*, xv (1962), 33.

[4] Irving Ribner, *The English History Play* (Princeton, 1957), pp. 172–3. (In the revised edition of his book, 1965, p. 171, Professor Ribner claims it is impossible not to feel 'sadness and regret' at the way Falstaff is treated, and dropping the 'Morgann

of Morgann's text will, of course, disclose that if he says 'we curse' the 'poetic justice' which consigns Falstaff to the Fleet, he also, as was long ago noted in the *English Review*, holds that the corrupt knight deserves a yet 'severer doom'.[1] The oversimplification of his view seems to arise in part from the too hurried reading which the dashing style of the *Essay* invites and in part from accepting the stereotype of Morgann as an ur-Bradley.

Nevertheless, even though by and large he continues to be associated with Bradley, Morgann seems to have come through the controversy over the Romantic approach to Shakespeare with enhanced prestige. No longer 'the chief accepted expositor' of Falstaff,[2] he is more usually regarded, in T. S. Eliot's phrase, as the author of 'a remarkable piece of writing which deserves meditation and commands our respect whether we agree with its conclusions or not'.[3] Even those anti-Bradleyites who are sternest in denouncing Morgann as the founder of a bad tradition respect his intellectual powers. He is 'subtle' and 'brilliant', they say, 'a gifted man'; if his influence has been unfortunate, at least his incidental insights are 'admirable' and 'profound'.[4] Less rigorous opponents of Bradley, not to mention those who remain sealed of his tribe, are still more deeply convinced of the *Essay*'s abiding value. Although books dealing with the sector of literary history to which he belongs sometimes omit to mention him, they more often tell us that the *Essay* is 'justly famous', 'most remarkable', 'exhilarating', 'one of the best books on Shakespeare ever published', a work '*aureus ac auro magis aureus*'.[5] Even a cursory survey of English literature in the

to Bradley' reference, he rebukes 'romantic critics' only for failing to see that the rejection of the knight is essential to Shakespeare's design.)

[1] In point of fact, not 'Romantic' Morgann but 'Neoclassical' Johnson (note to *2 Henry IV*, V. v. 97) is Bradley's predecessor in holding that the consignment of Falstaff to the warden and the Fleet is morally indefensible. Another Romantic who justified 'the final contempt . . . [Falstaff] received from the young king' is Coleridge (*Shakespearean Criticism*, ed. Raysor, i. 238). In 1838, C. A. Brown, *Shakespeare's Autobiographical Poems*, p. 273, observed that Morgann and Richardson provide the proper corrective to Johnson and Hazlitt on this matter. Cf. *Es.*, T154 and T179.

[2] Stoll, *Shakespeare Studies*, p. 416.

[3] 'Shakespearian Criticism from Dryden to Coleridge', in *A Companion to Shakespeare Studies* (1934), eds. Granville-Barker and Harrison, p. 297.

[4] Stoll, *Shakespeare Studies*, p. 416. L. C. Knights, *Explorations*, p. 24. Kenneth Muir, 'Changing Interpretations of Shakespeare', *The Age of Shakespeare*, A Guide to English Literature, ii, ed. Boris Ford (Harmondsworth, 1955), p. 289.

[5] C. J. Sisson, *Shakespeare* (1955), p. 16. Wilson, *Fortunes of Falstaff*, p. 2. (Cf. also Wilson's praise, in his New Shakespeare edition of *Macbeth* (Cambridge, 1947), pp. xlv–xlvi, of the intelligence Morgann displays in his response to the weird sisters,

eighteenth century will find space to observe that his 'brilliant study
... showed later critics how to discuss a Shakespearian character as
a human being'.[1] As the smoke of battle clears, indeed, Morgann
seems to be emerging as something like a classic. It is with no sense
of special pleading that J. I. M. Stewart and W. M. T. Nowottny
assign him the place before Coleridge in the 'great line' of Shakespeare's English critics, while Harbage names him as a matter of
course with Johnson, Goethe, Hazlitt, and Coleridge as one of those
'who head the roster of perceptive commentators'.[2]

No less significant, as formerly with Mackenzie, Richardson, and
Bradley, the *Essay* is once again, after the fashion of a living classic,
being absorbed and integrated by some modern critics into the substance of their own thought. Arthur Sewell adapts Morgann to an
aesthetic rather than psychological interpretation of Falstaff. According to Una Ellis-Fermor, Morgann gave us the 'unforgettable sentence' that 'Shakespeare contrives to make secret impressions upon
us' (*Es.*, T13); and taken to signify the means 'whereby we come into
imaginative possession of realities beyond the reach of our conscious understanding', the phrase 'secret impressions' recurs like a
leitmotive through her regrettably unfinished book.[3] Following a
different tack, J. I. M. Stewart finds the *Essay* remarkable for the
light it throws upon artistic creation rather than aesthetic experience.
Morgann, he suggests, perceived that Shakespeare incorporated a
latent personality of his own in Falstaff.[4] And adopting a historical

---

Es., T69.) Harold C. Goddard, *The Meaning of Shakespeare* (Chicago, 1951), p. v.
Bernard M. Wagner, *The Appreciation of Shakespeare* (Georgetown, 1949), p. x. Atkins,
English Literary Criticism: 17th and 18th Centuries, p. 266.

[1] Roger P. McCutcheon, *Eighteenth-Century English Literature* (New York, 1949),
pp. 97–8. Morgann also has his place in Alan Dugald McKillop, *English Literature from
Dryden to Burns* (New York, 1948), p. 312, and A. R. Humphreys, *The Augustan World*
(1954), p. 216.

[2] Stewart, *Character and Motive in Shakespeare*, p. 120. Nowottny, 'Editors, Editions
and Critics', in *William Shakespeare: The Complete Works*, ed. C. J. Sisson (1953),
p. xxvii. Alfred Harbage, *Conceptions of Shakespeare* (Cambridge, Mass., 1966), p. 54
(cf. Harbage's Introduction to Terence Hawkes (ed.), *Coleridge on Shakespeare* (Harmondsworth, 1969; orig. pub. New York, 1959), pp. 25–7). Cf. G. M. C. Orsini,
'Coleridge and Schlegel Reconsidered', *Comparative Literature*, xvi (1964), 116:
'Morgann . . . makes a brilliant aesthetic interpretation of the character of Falstaff,
which remains a classic.'

[3] Sewell, *Character and Society in Shakespeare* (1951), pp. 13–14. Ellis-Fermor
Shakespeare the Dramatist (1961), pp. 37, 51, 56, 59, 60, 74, 76, 81 ('secret impressions'
in conjunction with 'grouping': see *Es.*, T58n, T155, and T172–T173), and 87.

[4] *Character and Motive*, p. 122. Stewart declares that, in calling Shakespeare's
characters different modifications of the poet's thought (*Es.*, T16), Morgann means

perspective, Ernest Lee Tuveson and Robert Langbaum discern in Morgann a noteworthy contributor to the development of the modern consciousness. According to the first, he extended the theory of the unconscious mind implicit in Locke, while for the second, by applying to Falstaff an 'existential rather than moral judgment of character', he introduced into Shakespeare criticism one of the seminal ideas which mark 'the difference between the mind of Europe before and after the Enlightenment'.[1]

Attesting to the *Essay*'s continuing vitality, these readings of Morgann develop rather than fundamentally change the established conception of him as the archetypal Romantic critic. Five scholars, however, have entered variously dissenting opinions. Protesting against the notion that Morgann was 'the prophet and founder of a new school of criticism', S. M. Tave sees in him primarily a contributor to the developing eighteenth-century enthusiasm for amiable humour.[2] The other four, struck in varying degrees by the importance in the *Essay* of the idea glimpsed by Richardson in 1788 and by Scott in 1820, and then lost from sight, have suggested each in his own way that the received view of Morgann underestimates the intricacy and misses the purport of his thought. Though formerly disposed to run down the *Essay* as a 'much overrated' and 'absurdly overpraised' performance, remarkable chiefly for its silly objectivistic speculations about Falstaff's youth, Professor René Wellek has of late corrected himself handsomely. He has deleted a disdainful reference that appeared in the first edition of *Theory of Literature* and hails Morgann, in his *History of Modern Criticism*, as the author of 'the most self-conscious and original of eighteenth-century essays on Shakespeare'. More discriminating in his account of the *Essay*'s objectivist tendencies, he writes that Morgann 'constantly *runs the risk* of confusing fiction and reality'—a statement to be compared with his remark on a later page that Coleridge and Bradley actually do mistake the one for the other.[3] Professor Harbage,

---

that 'Shakespeare from the vast heaven of his mind, expresses whole constellations of emotion in personative form'.

[1] Tuveson, *The Imagination as a Means of Grace* (Berkeley and Los Angeles, 1960), p. 39, where Morgann's conception of the mind is expounded with the aid of a quotation from E. S. Dallas's *The Gay Science* (1866). Langbaum, *The Poetry of Experience* (1957), pp. 177 and 160.

[2] Tave, *R.E.S.* N.S. iii (1952), 374 and *The Amiable Humorist*, pp. 127–34.

[3] *The Rise of English Literary History* (Chapel Hill, 1941), p. 98. *Theory of Literature*, in collab. with Austin Warren (New York, 1949), p. 15, 2nd edn. (New York, 1956),

who ranks the *Essay* 'high above the usual treatise in aesthetics or any subsequent discussion of Falstaff', has observed that although 'Morgann has been accused of confusing art and reality . . . no critic has had a finer perception of their distinction'. Mrs. Nowottny has astutely remarked that the 'very confusions' of the *Essay* 'focus' the 'real critical dilemma', to this day unresolved, of finding 'a method which can elucidate what is real without straying out of the world of the play'. And as long ago as 1912, A. W. Gill declared that because they are indifferent to Falstaff's 'artificial condition', as described by Morgann, both Johnson and Hazlitt 'seem to be fumbling at a lock with keys that do not quite fit it'; Morgann, in contrast, takes us so deep 'into the *technique* and creative efforts of the dramatist that a reverent spectator might almost feel . . . as if he were trespassing on sacred mysteries'.[1]

As will be seen in the sequel, such views not only offer a surer guide to his thought than the common opinion which brackets him with Coleridge and Bradley; they also provide a firmer foundation for his continuing fame as a Shakespearian critic of extraordinary interest and power.

p. 14. *History of Modern Criticism* (1955), i. 117–18 (on Morgann, italics added) and ii. 182 (on Coleridge and Bradley).

[1] Harbage, *As They Liked It*, p. 77. Nowottny, in Shakespeare's *Complete Works*, ed. Sisson, p. xxvii. A. W. Gill (ed.), Morgann, *Essay on the Dramatic Character of Sir John Falstaff* (1912), pp. xv–xvi. With Gill cf. Scott as quoted above, p. 24.

CRITICAL INTRODUCTION

I. THE *ESSAY ON FALSTAFF* AND ITS REVISIONS

i. *Authorship and Date*

ALTHOUGH published in 1777 under a mask of anonymity, the *Essay on Falstaff* quickly became known as Morgann's and, as we have seen, was widely referred to as his during the last twenty years of his life. This circumstance along with the absence both of any other claimant and of any disclaimer by Morgann leaves no doubt that, as is universally held, he was the author. It is equally certain that he wrote the revisions of the *Essay* which are printed in the present volume for the first time. They are found in an interleaved copy of the *Essay*, which is fully described in the Textual Introduction to the Revisions, below. On the title-page, beneath the words 'Sir *JOHN FALSTAFF*' and above the printer's rule, an unknown hand has written: 'by Mr Morgan with M.S. notes *by the Author*'. The anonymous ascription is borne out on both chirographic and substantive grounds. By its general appearance as well as by certain idiosyncrasies of letter formation, capitalization, and spelling, the hand in which all the annotation in the book is written is clearly identifiable as the one found in holograph manuscripts signed by Morgann. Furthermore, the handwritten materials enter so intimately into the thought of the *Essay*, expanding, clarifying, and correcting dozens of major and minor points, that any other authorship seems inconceivable.

The date at which he composed the main part of the printed *Essay* may be readily inferred from the information he supplies about its genesis. Reminded by an 'accidental Conversation', he reports in LR 2, of the impressions he had taken of Falstaff before seeing the knight on the stage, he recognized that these earlier feelings, which he had hitherto tended to dismiss as flouting the common opinion, were in fact 'well founded'. The rest of the story is told in the Preface. To his listener's amazement, he thereupon put forward his view of Falstaff as a man of courage. His interlocutor promptly invited him to 'deliver and support [his] Opinion from the Press', promising him that if he did so, he would 'be answered thro' the same channel'. Accepting the challenge, Morgann tells us, he wrote up most of the *Essay* in a short space of time, but then laid his manuscript aside, almost forgetting it till three years later he was persuaded by some friends that his efforts deserved to be published. Thus encouraged, he revised the *Essay* and sent it to press.

Since the book, which is dated 1777, was in circulation by the end of May of that year,[1] the hurried writing of the first draft must have taken place in early 1774. This year, which Nichol Smith and others accept as the date of composition of the *Essay*, is confirmed by two passing allusions. One, in T93, is to the mild notoriety enjoyed by Dr. William Cadogan a little earlier (see note to T93). The other, on T112, is to current difficulties of the Nabobry, apparently a reference to the circumstances under which the Indian Regulation Act of 1773 was passed. It seems not to have been sufficiently noted, however, that a very important part of the *Essay* was written later. While the book was printing, he observes in the Preface, he added 'some considerations on the *Whole* Character of FALSTAFF' which do not altogether square with the more 'favourable . . . representation of his Morals' found on earlier pages. He must have composed this added material, roughly the concluding fifth of the *Essay*, in early 1777.

Morgann thus revised the original *Essay* fairly extensively while it was going through the press; and as the reference in his Preface to a possible second impression shows, he clearly had further revising in mind before the sheets of his book were sent to the binders. He may have entered the few minor corrections in the Newberry copy of the *Essay* (see below, p. 132 n.) soon after the *Essay*'s appearance. He may also about the same time have written in a number of emendations on printed pages in the manuscript book, presumably before it was interleaved. These early revisions would most likely be corrected errata (see below, pp. 132–3) and changes of the type found in SR 1, SR 2a and 2b, and SR 3, though they might also include all the SR written on T pages, i.e. all except for 5a, 5b, 6, 9a, 9b, 12, 27, 31, and 32b. But even if he wrote many SR soon after publishing the *Essay*, a dozen years were to elapse before he settled down in earnest to the task of revision in the now interleaved copy. He clearly did not begin till after his return from New York in 1783. So much is indicated by his reference to the American war as an event recently

[1] See Mrs. Thrale's record of its appearance, p. 12, above, and the early notices in the *Critical Review* and the *London Review*, p. 15, above.

concluded (LR 1b, I40–I41). The *terminus a quo* may be further advanced to 1785 on the strength of his notation 'Henry 8th 291' just above his criticism of Johnson's note to Act IV, Scene ii of that play (LR 7, I15:1, *app. crit.*). The note in question occurs on p. 290 in vol. vii of Johns. 1785. If one turns to the only other sources where Morgann might have found the note, the relevant page numbers are all quite different.[1] It seems therefore a plausible inference that he used Johns. 1785 and with characteristic careless-ness jotted down '291', the number of the page facing Johnson's note rather than, as accuracy required, '290'.[2]

A somewhat later date of composition is implied by the resentment he expressed in LR 10—ED at the charges of 'Singularity Caprice false Refinement Paradox & Subtlety' which had been brought against him. Admittedly, all except the fourth appear in the brief notice in the *Monthly Review* with which George Colman the elder castigated the *Essay* on its appearance in 1777 (see above, p. 12): 'his taste seems . . . vitiated by *singularity* and *caprice*; and his ingenuity betrays him into *false refinement*. The plainest propositions may be controverted by *subtle* disputants . . .' (italics added). But this need not necessarily argue an early date for the revisions. Since in the main the entries on later pages of the manuscript book were written after those on earlier pages, it is probable that the list of charges, which appears on I129, post-dates the references to John-son's note and to the recently concluded American war, which are found on I15 and I141 respectively. If, therefore, Morgann was reply-ing specifically to Colman, it would appear that he was doing so some years after the wounding review came out.

This inference is reinforced by the likelihood that he was reacting, or also reacting, to the almost identical bill of indictment which Richard Stack presented in his 'Examination' of the *Essay* (see above, pp. 13–14), presumably published in the second half of 1789. This date may be deduced from the fact that papers read on 13 March 1789 were the latest included in the '1788' volume of *Transactions of the Royal Irish Academy*, which contains Stack's critique. In his first three pages Stack accuses the *Essay* of engaging in 'paradox'

---

[1] Johns. 1765 and 1768, v. 462; Johns. 1773, vii. 253–4; Johns. 1778, viii. 283; Malone, 1790, vii. 100; Johns. 1793, xi. 146. (For the short titles here and in the text see List of Short Titles used in the Notes, pp. 355 ff., below.)

[2] A *terminus a quo* of 1785 is further suggested by the list of publishers Morgann jotted down in the *Essay* MS. book: see LR 11a, *app. crit.* to I189:7 and note thereto.

(p. 3), 'singularity and refinement' (p. 4), and subtlety (p. 5)—all the charges in Morgann's list except caprice; and through the rest of his paper Stack rings the changes on the theme of ingenious, subtle, excessive refinement. That Morgann may well have had the 'Examination' in mind is further suggested by the frequency with which, although never mentioning Stack by name, he reformulates ideas in such a way as to obviate his criticisms. He is in effect cutting the ground from under Stack's charge that he contradicts himself (see above, pp. 13–14) when in LR 10 he explains why a critic who proposes to unravel Shakespeare's art must necessarily exercise much subtlety and when in his revised introductory section (LR 1, 2, and 3) he clarifies his theory of how stage characters and particularly Falstaff affect audiences.[1] In the same revised introduction he seems still to be forestalling Stack's criticisms when he eliminates the misleading implication that Falstaff's courage compensates for and so discharges the disgust arising from his vicious manners and when he deletes his explicit announcement that he will defer consideration of the transactions at Gadshill to a later page.[2] Elsewhere he presents less vulnerably a number of other details which had drawn some of Stack's most damaging fire. Thus he provides a more elaborate discrediting of Lancaster, drafts anew his report of the scene with Mistress Quickly and the officers, retouches his account of the routing of Pistol, rehandles three significant points in the Gadshill episode, allows for a psychological foundation other than cowardice for Falstaff's monstrous lies, and insists that his thesis does not in any way belittle the hilarity at Eastcheap.[3]

To be sure, his attention to the last point is less conclusive for a composition date of 1789 or after, since the argument that he detracts from Falstaff's humour in the tavern scene was also put forward by Davies in his *Dramatic Miscellanies* of 1784 (see above, pp. 12–13). A period near the latter date may seem to receive further support from Davies's observation that 'Falstaff was, till very lately, an unique in dress as well as character' (op. cit. iii. 83). Morgann apparently ignores this recent change in theatrical practice when he denounces the outlandish rig worn by the stage Falstaff (LR 11a, I135 ff.). But this evidence for a slightly earlier date is too meagre to weaken the much stronger probability, based on the frequency

---

[1] See note to LR 10 and below, pp. 77 ff.
[2] *Es.*, T12 and T17; see also below, pp. 94 ff. and 87.
[3] See LR 8, SR 5a and 5b, SR 6, LR 10, and LR 12, and notes thereto.

with which in effect he replies to Stack, that he worked on his revisions after the appearance of the 'Examination'. Not many months after its appearance, however, since a *terminus ad quem* is suggested by his whimsical proposal to ban the teaching of Greek and Latin 'after the year 1800 or perhaps in better Wisdom after 1790' (LR 6a, I117:2). He would scarcely have penned these words either after New Year's Day 1791, or very much before. This appears to fix the date by which the anterior pages in the manuscript book were filled in, and there is no reason to suppose that revisions on subsequent pages were composed at a significantly later period. The absence of any allusions whatsoever to Malone's 1790 edition of Shakespeare falls in with, if it does not actually confirm, the inference regarding the *terminus ad quem*. In all likelihood, therefore, Morgann wrote his revisions *c*. 1789–90.

ii. *The Bearing of the Revisions on the* Essay

As his concern for meeting the objections of his critics indicates, when Morgann came back to his *Essay* over a dozen years after it had appeared, he was no longer content with the modest plan for revision outlined in his Preface. He had there spoken of reducing certain passages of too grave a tone, 'particularly near the commencement', to the status of footnotes, and of reforming others which carried playfulness of discussion 'even to levity'. Presumably he would also have wished to eliminate the discrepancy he referred to between his earlier and later accounts of Falstaff's morals. But by the time he took the task in hand he was intent upon readjustments of another nature. He quite forgot his earlier wish to reform his occasional levity, letting stand, for instance, his spoofing speculations about the quantity of base metal in Falstaff's seal ring (T51). And although in revising materials 'near the commencement' he did indeed remove inconsistencies about Falstaff's morals (see below, pp. 91–2) and sink certain weighty matters to the foot of his page (LR 1b and 3b), these changes were incidental to a far more sweeping revision which affected almost the entire introductory section of the *Essay*. In the revisions designed for later points in the book there were not even by-products of this kind: he concentrated either on improving his style or, by far his major preoccupation, on coping with difficulties in his arguments which had earlier gone unmentioned and presumably unnoticed. In confronting the difficulties, moreover, as in rewriting the introductory section, he often went a good deal beyond what was needed to reply to the specific objections of his critics.

Altogether he composed thirty-five SR affecting a word, a phrase, or a sentence or two, and fourteen LR, each of them running to a paragraph or more and, taken together in their final drafts, filling about one-third as many pages as the original *Essay*. Of the SR nineteen are merely stylistic: they enhance clarity or elegance of expression without modifying the thought. Six more of the SR (4, 11, 12, 16, 24, and 35), however, introduce significant deletions, as do the same number of LR (1, 2, 3, 10, 11, and 13); and the remaining ten SR (5, 6, 9, 15, 21, 22, 27, 28, 29, and 33) make substantive changes in the sense that they replace, qualify, or add to ideas presented in the original, as do all the LR to an even greater degree.

The cumulative effect is to place the *Essay* in a new light. This may not at once be obvious because of the character of the revisions. The manuscript book, to begin with, does not project any radical recasting of the work as a whole. Proposing to retain over seven-eighths of his original text without change, Morgann kept the same basic division of his discourse into two unequal parts, the first and by far the longer one dealing with Falstaff as a man of courage (T1–T146:1) and the second, added as we have noted while the book was being printed, dealing with Falstaff considered as a real-life or whole character (T146:2–T185). All the revisions which he completed were to fall into place under one or the other of the two headings without altering the *ordonnance* within each division beyond the occasional intercalation of new material. More than this, he did not put fully into effect even the limited scheme of revisal he was working on. Not only did he fail to align his printed text at all points with the new material, but in more than one revision, in passages over which he worked the hardest, writing, rewriting, lining out, and recasting yet again, he seems still to have been bearing down on his idea rather than couching it in a form he was entirely satisfied with. Yet more teasingly, he often failed to indicate precisely where his revisions were to dovetail with his text, and he did not go through the printed *Essay* systematically to indicate exactly which passages were to be cancelled.

But however incomplete he left his revisal, he carried it far enough forward to furnish a gloss that is invaluable for the full understanding of the *Essay*. Morgann, we have seen, is almost universally regarded as the first major critic to expound and demonstrate the Romantic method of analysing a Shakespearian character as if it were a living human being. It has less often been acknowledged that, when one examines the *Essay* rigorously, the precise nature of his thinking often seems doubtful and obscure. It is not clearly proto-Romantic or anything else. Perspicuity, brilliance, and intellectual power stand out on every page, so much so that he can justly boast of his readers' admitting they 'gallop with him' in his headlong course (LR 3— ED 5, *app. crit.* to I55:2). Arrest the gallop for a moment, however, seek the exact interconnection between ideas, look for the underlying logical structure of the whole, and the outcome is likely to be frustration. G. S. Gordon remarked, 'there is no end to the breeding of ideas in such a mind as his; what he wants is readers to work them out'. Yet when the effort is made to work them out, the result seems often to prove how right his friend, William Cooke, was to say of him that 'the luxuriousness of a fine imagination . . . made it sometimes difficult for him to settle on the close point'.[1] There emerge evident fallacies, concepts that fail to harmonize with their apparent congeners, propositions that puzzle because they are insufficiently explicit or because they seem to lead nowhere. In the Preface to his edition of the *Essay*, A. W. Gill noted the difficulty with a certain wryness. Putting the best face on the matter, he could honestly say only that 'the observant reader . . . who is prepared for some confusion, will probably find clues enough scattered about to save him from being often at a loss'.[2]

The great importance of the revisions is that they allow the observant reader to proceed with greater assurance, and so to make out the true nature and significance of Morgann's critical position. Cutting down greatly on the confusion, they permit a far more confident spotting of the clues and do away with most of the moments when one need feel at a loss. Sometimes at a stroke and sometimes after much casting about, they sweep away the main inconsistencies and fallacies which bedevil the text of 1777; here and there they bring out implications earlier left obscure or uncertain; often they give a new clarity of meaning to other passages left untouched in the original. As a result one can for the first time fully

[1] Gordon, rev. of Gill (see above, p. 28 n.), p. 31. Cooke, *Conversation*, 2nd edn. (1807), p. x.
[2] p. xv. Cf. Gordon, op. cit., p. 30, who describes the *Essay* as 'a scene of admirable disorder'.

unfold his ideas as they deserve without having the thought fray or snap; and on this foundation it becomes possible to see that his theory of Shakespearian characterization, as exemplified by his analysis of Falstaff, is consistent, systematic, and different from the Romantic view commonly attributed to him.

In using the revisions to help clarify Morgann's thought it is convenient to consider them in relation to the following topics: his attitude towards his argument for Falstaff's courage; his conception of the dramatic function of the cowardice commonly found in Falstaff; his explanation of the consensus that Falstaff is a coward; his intent in distinguishing between historic and dramatic beings; and his theory of characterization compared with that of the Romantics.

iii. *Morgann's Attitude towards his Falstaffian Thesis*

Both in his own day and in ours so many perceptive readers have queried Morgann's seriousness in vindicating Falstaff's soldierly character (see above, pp. 31–2) that the question cannot be side-stepped by anyone undertaking to discuss the *Essay* as a significant and valuable piece of criticism. In the long run, no doubt, the answer depends on the view taken of the work as a whole. If, as I shall argue, Morgann propounds a substantial, coherent theory of Shakespeare's art, and if, as I shall also argue, that theory is illus-trated in part by his thesis concerning Falstaff's courage, then the thesis, though not infallible, can hardly be intended as a leg-pull. This consideration apart, however, there are two other more direct clues to his intentions—his occasional comments on his literary purposes and his deliberately provocative ascription of courage to Falstaff. Both have been interpreted by some readers as indicating that in his defence of Falstaff he knowingly plays a game with truth.

Mr. J. I. M. Stewart, for example, a staunch present-day admirer of Morgann, has taken this view of his avowed intentions. Mor-gann's idea of the knight's character, he claims, is almost necessarily 'fanciful . . . since he sets out frankly in quest of literary diversion'.[1] Nor can there be any doubt about the frankness or general tenor of his professions. Straight off in his Preface he announces that he has made his Falstaffian argument 'subservient to Critical amusement'

---

[1] *Character and Motive in Shakespeare* (1949), p. 117.

(PT3). But whether this necessarily implies fancifulness is less clear. The comparison to the morning's ride which follows in the Preface says no more than that the 'real object' of the *Essay* is not to prove Falstaff courageous but chiefly to afford 'Exercise' and 'the Delight' which a rich Shakespearian landscape may excite. This need not mean that the Falstaffian thesis is to be taken with a grain of salt. On the other hand, something of the sort may well seem to be hinted at in another more vivid passage which has caught many a reader's eye. About to make some 'minute observations' on Shakespeare's handling of Falstaff, Morgann justifies his procedure by declaring that his argument concerning the knight, 'like the tales of our Novelists, is a *vehicle* only; *theirs*, as they profess, of moral instruction; and *mine* of critical amusement. The vindication of *Falstaff*'s Courage', he continues, 'deserves not for its own sake the least sober discussion; *Falstaff* is the word only, *Shakespeare* is the *Theme*: And if thro' this channel', he goes on to say, he furnishes the rational amusement in question, perhaps the reader will not everywhere expect of him 'the strict severity of logical investigation' (T47).

What is one to make of this? 'Deserves not for its own sake the least sober discussion'—has ever a critic before or since spoken so slightingly of what he presents as a major literary discovery? May it not be, then, that despite his protests to the contrary elsewhere (cf. T28), he offers his 'discovery' with tongue visibly in cheek, suggesting that it is a kind of fiction, incompatible with strict logical investigation? Is he not saying that what really counts in the *Essay* is the theory of Shakespeare's art and that the rest should be taken, and dismissed, as diversion? It is in this sense at any rate that the oft-quoted declaration, '*Falstaff* is the word only, *Shakespeare* is the *Theme*', seems often to be understood. Yet the interpretation is borne out neither by other comments of a like nature elsewhere in the *Essay* nor in the language actually employed in the passage under consideration. The parallel he draws with the novelist's serious lesson is not any overriding concern with Shakespeare's art in the *Essay* but the entertainment it purveys. No less curious, the stirring antithesis of Shakespeare as theme to Falstaff as word not only runs counter to the flat statement a few pages earlier that 'The Courage of *Falstaff* is my Theme' (T27) but in the present passage seems on close examination to make a distinction without an operative difference. Putting the two on much the same level, he calls Falstaff the vehicle and Shakespeare the channel through which he furnishes the amusement which he says is his primary aim. The equation of the two, moreover, is consistent with his avowed purpose, which he carries out, of avoiding 'general criticism' as 'easy' and 'uninstructive' in favour of investigating Shakespeare's arts concretely by examining the 'single point' of Falstaff's valour in microscopic detail (T16). As for the repudiation of strict logic in his investigation, similar observations elsewhere in the *Essay* (T28 and T113) leave it an open question whether he may not be merely rejecting formal method rather than arrogating the right to be cavalier in the article of truth.

What the original *Essay* leaves doubtful, the revisions help to ascertain. Although Morgann alters none of the passages I have mentioned, he is at some pains to be more explicit about the questions they raise in revisions which affect other parts of the text. To start with, he clears up the puzzle of why he should disparage his discovery. Undertaking in his revision of the introductory section to elucidate the literary rationale of the *Essay*, he continues to think of the vindication of Falstaff's courage as 'nothing' or 'almost Nothing', a 'slight . . . Matter' that 'Might intitle its author to commiseration perhaps or indeed any Thing but a patient Hearing', 'for what is Falstaffe that we sho<u>d</u> think or care about Him?'[1] But in the remarkable apology for his subtle and refined critical method into which he digresses in LR 10, he reveals what lies behind his insistence. 'Enquiries & speculations' of the sort carried out in the *Essay*, he observes in the digression, are 'wholly unimportant to the Concerns of human Life'. Though the sentiment may sound like blasphemy to the modern critical ear, it reflects a scale of values which is understandable enough in a man who spent most of his adult life pondering the needs and desires of entire communities in a far-flung and storm-wracked empire. Compared to the aspirations and anxieties of nations, what indeed 'is Falstaffe that we sho<u>d</u> think or care about Him?' This perspective not only renders intelligible the apparent oddity of his belittling his discovery that Falstaff is courageous but also clears him of the suspicion that he wishes in this way to warn his readers against taking him too seriously.

The same point of view further accounts for his reiteration while clarifying his literary rationale of the idea earlier stressed in the printed text that 'critical Amusement' is his 'sole End tho' regulated & directed by a pretended one of another Sort' (LR 3c). By

[1] LR 2—ED 4a and c; LR 2 and 3c; LR 2—ED 4b; LR 2—ED 4d; LR 2—ED 4c.

amusement—rational, critical amusement, as he tends to say—he means, to judge from scattered passages in the *Essay* and in the revisions, a combination of things: for one, the numerous quotations from Shakespeare which he interweaves with his text—a mode of amusement which he at first overvalues in the revisions but finally reduces to its proper subordinate place (see notes, p. 387); for another, the challenge of 'Novelty' (LR 2—ED 4d); for a third, the cheerful, sometimes playful tone which he deliberately cultivates throughout (PT 5-6, T113). But more than all these, in the hunting image he finally hits upon, he means what he calls the 'Pleasures of the Chase' (LR 3c; cf. LR 2 and LR 2—ED 4d). This figure improves on the morning's ride analogy in the Preface—exercise amid a picturesque Shakespearian landscape—by making the nature of the exercise clear and focusing on it without giving equal weight to the delight of surveying a Shakespearian world. The 'Pleasures of the Chase' are the bracing intellectual exercise Morgann offers of following the sinuosities of his thought, as distinct from the seizing of the quarry or closing in on the substance of his argument. If he can make every page compensate in one or more of these ways, particularly the last, for his insignificant subject-matter, he feels, he may then have a proper claim upon an intelligent person's time and attention. Urbane recreation of this sort, so he implies, is after all a civilized and rational occupation, and therefore its own excuse for being.

However, he also makes it abundantly clear in his revisions that neither in disparaging his vindication of Falstaff's courage nor in setting out to entertain does he intend the slightest compromise with that 'attention to truth and candour which', as he observes in the *Essay*, 'ought to accompany even our lightest amusements' (T28). His defence of Falstaff, he insists, is 'real Truth' and no 'less a Reality for being unimportant' (LR 3—ED 5, *app. crit.*; LR 3c). Admitting that his proof of Falstaff's courage is 'nothing', he still means his 'nothing', every word of it; the very truth of his argument, he hopes, will compel adversaries to 'triumph even in their own Defeat' (LR 2 and LR 2—ED 4c). Similarly with his commitment to amuse. It is all-important but by no means a privilege to stretch the facts. On the contrary, he is perturbed by certain readers' reporting that they enjoyed the *Essay* hugely, 'but as for Truth it was what they did not look for or find' (LR 3c).

He puts into words the exact three-cornered relation he envisages between the nullity of his subject, his adherence to truth, and his primary goal of purveying amusement when in the final version of the digression in LR 10 he explains why he cannot avoid ingenuity in his argument. Irked by the charge of over-refinement brought against him by Stack and others, he has at first blurted out rancorously that his pedantic critics 'anathamize those Actions which they are in no Danger of Committing' and that though he genuinely seeks the truth, he would rather 'overshoot the Mark . . . than herd for ever however securely in the Faction of Fools' (LR 10—ED). After this indulgence in resentment, however, he presently controls his temper and, scratching out what he has written, composes a real reply to Stack which illuminates his double obligation to truth and entertainment when dealing with an inherently valueless subject. Stack, it will be recalled, accused him of self-contradiction on the grounds that he offered subtle and involved accounts of what were supposed to be direct, straightforward impressions on the feelings (above, pp. 13–14 and note to LR 10). Distinguishing between the plainness and simplicity of impressions which were never designed for rational scrutiny and the complex reasoning that may be necessary to uncover and explain them, Morgann observes that such subtlety is indispensable for the careful investigation he conducts into the 'hidden *Art*' by which Shakespeare produces his effects: 'No Refinement can be too much for the Reach & Artifice of Shakespear.' But this in itself, he adds, cannot justify his ingenuity, since the subject on which he expends it is inherently insignificant. On the other hand, he explains, so long as 'he shall consider Truth only as a secondary Object & Subservient to the Purposes of innocent Dissipation & Amusement', he considers himself entitled to develop his argument in all its complexity. If he does not let his intricate pursuit of truth get out of hand and overshadow the entertainment it conveys, he may, he asserts, be 'as ingenious, as subtle, as refined, as singular, and as Orriginal as He pleases'. Truth, in other words, is justified by amusement, not impaired or undermined by it. In disavowing strict logical severity in the *Essay*, therefore, he is rejecting procedures too solemn to sort with amusement rather than hinting an intention to draw the long-bow.

Another ambiguity of the *Essay* is clarified by the way in which, still in the digression in LR 10, he deals with a particular proof of the knight's courage as illustrating Shakespeare's 'hidden Art'. He treats these topics as the two faces of the same sincerely held truth which he makes subservient to amusement. The revision thus reinforces the indications in the printed *Essay* that in writing '*Falstaff* is the word only, *Shakespeare* is the *Theme*', he is not, as the rhetorical flourish suggests, opposing the trivial to the significant and so perhaps implying that his Falstaffian argument need not be taken in earnest. His thought is rather that, because he studies Falstaff as an example of Shakespeare's arts, he has available an admirable vehicle or channel for the rational, critical amusement which he offers the reader—rational by its level, critical in its substance. It is to bring out this idea, as also appears in the light of the revisions, that he employs the analogy of the novelist's tale. He does not, as we have noted, compare his Shakespearian theme to the novelist's moral; the point he wishes to make is rather in the nature of a chiasmus: whereas the novelist's amusing fiction conveys serious instruction, he says, his seriously advanced argument conveys amusement—though, as he adds elsewhere, he hopes 'of a kind more rational than the History of Miss *Betsy*, eked out with the Story of Miss *Lucy*, and the Tale of Mr. *Twankum*' (T113). More rational pastime than these vapidities is surely afforded by his using his thesis as an occasion for mental exercise, for the piquancy of paradoxical novelty (paradoxical in the sense of that which seems absurd but may be true), and for the urbanities of a skilled conversationalist, the whole artfully interwoven with quotations and echoes from Shakespeare.

His occasional ambiguous comments on his purposes thus yield no tenable grounds for believing him to be ironical in his defence of Falstaff; on the contrary, as illuminated by the revisions, they point in the opposite direction. The other clue to his intentions which has been similarly misunderstood is the teasing equivoque with which, as part of his programme of amusement, he informs his thesis. This ambiguity, unlike the others I have been considering, is deliberate. It arises in the first instance from the disparity between courage in the special sense he has in mind and the word as commonly understood. He is very careful to point out in the passages in which he discusses the quality he attributes to Falstaff—passages retained in revision without any material change (T23–T24, T99–T101, T165–T166)—that he is thinking of natural or constitutional courage, as he calls it, and not the derring-do in the face of danger that is commonly conveyed by the term *courage*. The Falstaffian virtue, as he describes it, is a capacity for positive, realistic behaviour to counter and control adverse circumstances; it may even 'avail itself of flight as well as of action' (T23). It can best be understood as a combination of resolution, enterprise, and ability, the words which he from time to time couples with *courage* or *boldness* in order to bring out his meaning (T11, T18, T168; cf. also LR 11a, I188:5). He uses similar collocations outside the *Essay* to describe the men who, so he fancied, would exploit the revolution he falsely prophesied for 1779. Amid the wreckage of an overthrown social order, he predicted, these freebooters of 'great Boldness & ability' would act on 'a new principle of Rank, that of Spirit and ability' (above, p. 7). Again, in 1782, he writes from New York to a friend in London that Lord Shelburne has the 'spirit & Ability' needed to restore order quickly to the disarranged state of England. What he has in mind here, as with the freebooters and Falstaff, is the tough-minded capability that can impose constructive system on any disorder which threatens its values.[1] In the *Essay* he further observes that natural or constitutional courage is as hereditary a quality as 'features and complexion' and is independent of opinion and of the prevailing modes of honour, though the latter may strengthen it and lift it up to heroism (T45, T23, T99). Referring to 'Courage and Ability' as 'first principles of Character' (T165), he makes it even clearer in the note on characterization (T59n) that courage in his sense is an ultimate element in the individual, less a finished part than a raw source of what we today normally perceive as personality. The 'energies of courage and activity', he explains in the note, along with 'different... sorts of sensibilities, and a capacity . . . of discernment and intelligence', form for Shakespeare the 'first principles of *being*' which are found in varying degrees in all human minds and which are rounded out in each person into a distinct individuality under the influence of the cultural environment. Professor Harbage seems to modernize Morgann's intention admirably when he suggests that the quality as manifested in Falstaff is 'vitality, life-force, the faculty of survival'.[2]

---

[1] Shelburne Papers, William L. Clements Library, University of Michigan, Ann Arbor, vol. 165, pp. 202 and 220 (cf. p. 7, above). Morgann to Evan Nepean, 10 Sept. 1782, P.R.O. C.O. 5/107, f. 79.

[2] Alfred Harbage, *As They Liked It* (New York, 1961), p. 77. William Winter, *Shakespeare on the Stage: Third Series* (New York, 1916), p. 325, refers to 'Falstaff's illimitable animal spirits'. The ghost of the old triune soul strangely modified in its lowest reaches seems to stir, if not walk, in Morgann's first principles. The vegetable soul, in control of nutrition, growth, and reproduction, appears to have appropriated the elemental, amoral, self-assertive life to which Morgann's principle of courage and activity refers. The parallel between his other two principles and the sensible and rational souls is more evident.

But although Morgann is clear enough on the matter, he is also deliberately provocative in flaunting the word *courage*. He knows that however fairly he may differentiate between the morally motivated and socially honoured behaviour usually called by that name and the conscienceless, visceral drive he is thinking of, all the explanation in the world cannot quite strip the term of the social approbation it connotes. He is equally provocative in his use of the term *cowardice*, which he introduces without warning as an antonym to constitutional courage in the full knowledge that it is the normal counter-term to the other kind of courage and that it carries overtones incongruous with his intent. As a result, when he offers to vindicate from all imputation of cowardice the highwayman who runs away from the men in buckram, or when he undertakes to demonstrate the valour of the soldier who plays dead at Shrewsbury, even if in one part of our minds we are prepared to weigh the possibility of Falstaff's being in a certain sense uncowardly and courageous, in another part we cannot escape the feeling of paradox.

This of course is exactly what Morgann intends. He is having his fun with a semantic situation which he has consciously produced and which he expects his reader to enjoy. However, there is fun and fun, and the kind he offers should not be mistaken. J. I. M. Stewart has suggested that it is *bagatelle* (above, p. 32). Not *bagatelle* but *badinage*, the term his friend Cooke applied to his conversation (above, p. 10), is the relevant gallicism. A much-laboured-over revision draft brings out the necessary distinction. Concerned to deny the charge of sophistry while keeping the paradox from which the accusation stems, he writes: 'I do not mean to trifle with the Reader. Amusement tis true [is] my Principal Aim but I expect no less than to produce full and ample Conviction that Shakespear meant to draw Falstaffe as a man of considerable Courage' (LR 2—ED 4a; cf. ED 4b). In propounding his thesis, *il badine*, he banters and teases if only by the very fact that he claims for Falstaff the 'considerable Courage' which is what he says it is, yet is not courage as commonly understood. But though he does this for the sake of amusement, of entertaining his reader, *bagatelle* forms no part of either his plan or his practice; as he insists, he does not trifle, he does not compromise the integrity of his argument.

On the contrary, the manuscript book reflects his renewed determination to win the assent he believes his thesis entitled to. He will not, he avers in a cancelled draft, 'give up one Iota of Argument in

behalf of Falstaff's Courage' (LR 12, *app. crit.* to 1142:5); and better
than his word he not only preserves every one of the proofs which
he had originally marshalled in order to vindicate Falstaff, but in
eight revisions he strengthens weak points and brings up various
reinforcements. At one point he traces a line through a phrase which
might seem carelessly to open up the possibility that the knight's
'natural Courage' can be impugned (SR 16). At another, he introduces a new detail which suggests fortitude on Falstaff's part during
the robbery at Gadshill (SR 15). Elsewhere, he sharpens an *'implied
negation'* of Falstaff's cowardice (SR 7) and substitutes for weaker
more telling details which show that the Hostess and Doll Tearsheet,
at least, regard Falstaff as a fighting man (SR 5 and 6). He even tries,
however inconclusively, to appropriate the results of the latest
available scholarship for his effort to link Falstaff with the brave
Oldcastle and to dissociate him from Fastolfe, whom he continues
to suppose a recreant in history as well as in *Henry VI* (SR 9).
He also seeks to stamp Lancaster even more inescapably than before
with perfidy, as part of his devaluation of the prince's sneers at
Falstaff (LR 8). And in LR 10, the most interesting of this group
of revisions, he reconsiders the ticklish moments at Gadshill which
culminate in Falstaff's saying to Prince Henry, 'I am not John of
Gaunt, indeed, your grandfather, but yet no coward, Hal.' The new
analysis he provides of this episode surpasses in acuteness all his
previous efforts to illustrate how Shakespeare's dialogues are 'a perfect Imitation of Nature . . . growing necessarily out of Character
Motive and Exigence'.

The first important point which the revisions help to make clear
is, then, that he proposes his paradox about Falstaff not ironically
but in good earnest. The revisions are even more necessary to clarify
a second aspect of his Falstaffian thesis—the dramatic function he
assigns to the knight's cowardice.

iv. *The Element of Cowardice in Falstaff*

It may appear at first blush an attempt to outdo Morgann in his own
preserve of paradox to claim that he finds a legitimate element of
cowardice in Falstaff. Yet find it he does and intended to from the
start, though perhaps only statements of his own such as are found
in the revisions can put the matter beyond doubt. In the original

Essay he is most misleading on the subject. Wholly engrossed in throwing his paradoxical bomb-shell, it appears, he so neglects and slurs over the real complexity of his view that he seems to deny rather than to attach any positive significance to Falstaff's cowardice. His grand aim emerges as simply and crudely to dissuade his readers from falling into the vulgar error of responding to Falstaff as a poltroon.

This erroneous interpretation of his intent is strongly supported not just by his omitting to say what he really means in peremptory terms but also by the way he formulates the theoretical foundation for his argument in his introductory section. He begins by laying down the axiom that 'In Dramatic composition, the *Impression* is the *Fact*' (T4). With an eye to Hume's division of all perceptions into impressions or feelings and ideas or thoughts, he defines impressions as 'certain feelings or sensations of mind which do not seem to have passed thro' the Understanding' (T5; see note thereto). In life, he further observes, 'the Understanding and . . . feelings are frequently at variance' (T5–T6), and in these conflicts the reason is wrong and sensibility right because the former takes a superficial delight 'in abstraction and general propositions' which are seldom if ever 'perfectly applicable to any particular case', while the feelings, cutting deep and true, 'often arise from the most minute circumstances, and frequently from such as the Understanding cannot estimate, or even recognize' (T6:2). In the specific matter of assessing character, he goes on, the generalizing reason judges ill because it grossly deduces motives from actions whereas the particularizing sensibility grasps the truth because 'it determines of *actions* from certain *first principles of character*, which seem wholly out of the reach of the Understanding . . . [and which are] distinct . . . in every distinct individual' (T6). It is through 'some secret reference to these *principles*' that in real life we 'love and hate at first sight' (T7) and that in the playhouse, despite contrary inferences by our reason, we feel Falstaff to be a man of courage. For Shakespeare 'could make a more perfect draught of real nature [than other authors], and steal such Impressions on his audience, without their special notice, as should keep their hold in spite of any error of their Understanding, and . . . [could] thereupon venture to introduce an apparent incongruity of character and action . . .' (T9). Constructed on this plan, Falstaff performs certain acts which the superficial reason, taken in by 'appearances' (T16; cf. T2), erroneously adjudges craven, but to the trustworthy feelings he comes home for what he really is, a man of constitutional courage.

Although he engages in 'actions of apparent Cowardice' (T13), his *'real* character', conveyed by accurate impressions, 'is different from his *apparent* one' (T14).

Granted its soundness, this explanation may well seem to proscribe cowardice from the proper apprehension of Falstaff. If, as Morgann reiterates, cowardice is false appearance and courage true reality, the intelligent reader will surely refuse to be bamboozled. More than this, the appearance is said to be the figment of a faculty inherently given to error especially in assessing character while the reality is truth perceived by the faculty which is by nature accurate in such matters—so much so that 'a little reflection may . . . unite our Understandings to our Instinct' and leave us obliged 'to repeal those decisions' which the generalizing reason has imposed (T15). And even more categorically: if cowardice 'mingle[s] in our mirth . . . we are . . . the dupes of our own wisdom' (T132). No wonder readers have gathered that Morgann is advising them not to be dupes, not to be distracted by Falstaff's seeming cowardice, that bubble of a deceived and deceiving faculty, if they wish to enjoy the knight consistently with Shakespeare's intentions.

And yet he nowhere actually and outright gives such counsel, except perhaps in the passage last quoted, which would presumably for that reason not have survived a complete revision of the *Essay*. For despite misleading phraseology, the thought is at bottom alien to his conception of how Falstaff is to be apprehended, as appears though faintly even in the text of 1777. If one collates his remark about Shakespeare's 'perfect draught of real nature' with his claim that the understanding and the feelings are often at odds in life, one may infer that he considers it not an incidental by-product but a central part of Shakespeare's purpose to induce such a variance in the spectator with regard to Falstaff. The inference finds an echo when he says that the 'difference between reality and appearance' in Falstaff's character 'may be . . . the source of all our laughter and delight' (T14). If this remark too is considered in relation to Shakespeare's purposes, it implies that the playwright intends in Falstaff an incongruity which can yield its proper pleasure only in so far as the spectator at once feels and fails to resolve it. The idea is again insinuated when he says that the reader 'will find that he has by no means decided . . . even for himself' the question of whether Falstaff be craven or courageous and that the 'difficulty' may arise 'out of the Art of *Shakespeare*' (T12–T13).

In all three passages, admittedly, if the thought comes through at all, it is by little more than subaudition. Never rising above an obscure whisper, it is drowned in the dominant contrary emphasis on cowardice as a fallacious appearance, a corrigible error of the stupid reason, and in the strong suggestion thus conveyed that the reader ought to root out the aberration from his response. But one of Morgann's main objects in revising his introductory section is precisely to avoid being misconstrued in this way. Systematically, he modifies or deletes every strain of thought which helps to create the wrong impression in the original *Essay*. In presenting his theoretical background, for example, while retaining the Humean distinction between impressions and the understanding, instead of merely saying it is one 'which we all comprehend' (T5:3), he now develops it in such a fashion as to bring out the importance of the spectator's reason side by side with his sensibility in his response to plays. In ordinary life, he points out in LR 1a, we relate to the world at times through one faculty and at times through the other, 'and our Minds are made up of both'. A good play, he goes on in an early draft, 'just as the World itself does', should open 'many Things to our Understanding' as well as 'impress others on our Sensibility' (LR 1—ED 1a). Although at a late stage he cancels the entire fragment in which the passage just cited appears, in the definitive version of LR 1a and in its complement LR 2 he not only continues to find the understanding positively involved in aesthetic response but sees it as indispensable even when it jumps to wrong conclusions. In LR 2, after contrasting the bad playwright who addresses only the intellect with the good one who appeals exclusively to the feelings, he distinguishes two superior types of dramatist which, since Shakespeare can be identified with all three, in effect represent two more highly artistic ways in which a single gifted playwright may handle the understanding of the audience. In one he intersperses impressions on the sensibility with consonant appeals to the reason, and in the other, as happens with Falstaff, he may set the reason and feelings

at Variance with each other in the Theatre as they often are in real Life and steal such Impressions on his Audience without their Special Notice as shall keep their Hold in spite of any Errour into which He may chuse to lead their understanding, and . . . may thereupon venture to introduce an apparent Incongruity of Character and Action either for Purposes of Mirth or any other worthy the attainment. This wo.d be . . . a perfect Draught of human Nature . . .

Though the phrasing is very close to that of the parallel passage in the text of 1777 (T9), the new context and the slight differences rule out the misapprehension fostered by the earlier version that proper response should be purged of errors of the reason. Bringing together ideas which in the *Essay* are separated and interrelated only by implication, he now states in so many words that the variance between reason and feeling which Shakespeare sets up in the theatre is not an incidental consequence of his drawing a deeply lifelike character but a deliberate contribution to a considered dramatic strategy. The playwright *chooses* to mislead the spectator's understanding; and in so electing he has his 'purposes' (cf. LR 2—ED 2, where the idea appears for the first time: the understanding is, we are there told, 'on purpose Misled'). For his purposes to succeed the spectator must therefore not only feel but think as Shakespeare wishes him to. And this, Morgann claims in LR 1a, is exactly what takes place. In reacting to a character like Falstaff, he says, the spectator finds 'in Himself a Disagreement of Judgment and Sensibility' because 'a mixed Effect was intended to be produced'. With this statement and its development in LR 2 the strangled whisper of the printed *Essay* becomes a full-voiced declaration that Shakespeare designs and requires an ambivalence in the audience's response to Falstaff. We are made to feel strongly that the knight is a man of courage; but the idea simultaneously entertained by our reason of his cowardice has no less integral a part in the 'whole Effect', as he puts it in LR 1a, which the playwright 'looks to'.

In other words, although the reason errs in taking Falstaff for a coward, it is right and necessary that it should so err. Certain cancellations in the revisions reflect his new alertness to the danger of obscuring this point. Casting his eye back over the 'Disagreement of Judgment and Sensibility' induced in the spectator, he momentarily considers inserting 'supposed' (or perhaps 'suppositious') before 'Disagreement'; and of course the disagreement could be called 'supposed' in that, as he continues to believe, one party to it, the sensibility, is right and the other, the reason, is wrong. But the adjective might mislead because in another sense which he now wishes to emphasize, the disagreement is not 'supposed' at all but very real: it takes place and should take place in the spectator's mind. So his pen gets no further than 'suppos', at which point he scratches out the word before completing it (LR 1a, I31:2, *app. crit.*). The cancellation of the whole of LR 1—ED 1b also reflects his desire to

avoid the same possible ambiguity. His object in the draft is to build
up the contrary-to-fact proposition, perfectly legitimate in itself, that
if the antithetical reactions excited by Falstaff are 'irreconcielable'
in the sense of having an equal claim to register the truth, Shakespeare 'is an Author undeserving of Notice or Regard'. But he is also
concerned to praise Shakespeare for inducing precisely an irreconcilable conflict of reason and feeling, irreconcilable in the sense that
the perceptions of the two faculties are antithetical to one another.
There is therefore a fair chance of being misunderstood. He draws
a line down the entire passage.

Not content with affirming unequivocally his view of how the
variance of judgement and sensibility functions and with safe-
guarding it from new misapprehension, he also carefully removes
three old sources of misunderstanding. One is the appearance–reality
contrast between cowardice and courage which, however sound in
itself, suggests strongly that cowardice has no place in the response
to Falstaff. Through his blanket cancellation of T6:4–T22:5 he
discards his repeated references to the contrast, and though he keeps
the early allusion on T2 to Falstaff's supposedly craven acts as
'appearances', he now has the idea fade by degrees into another
which overtly harmonizes with his desire to stress the 'mixed Effect'.
No longer attributing the delight caused by Falstaff to the 'difference
between reality and appearance' in his character, he derives it in
LR 1a from the 'apparent opposition' and in the first paragraph of
LR 2 from the 'apparent Incongruity' of action and character in the
knight, being careful to point out in both places that the conflict is
part of Shakespeare's design.[1] By the new formulation he not only
gives substance to the earlier shadowy and elusive hint that Falstaff's
cowardice is an indispensable component of the aesthetic experience;
he also submerges the distinction between the knight's cowardice
and courage in terms of appearance and reality: one must take the
trouble to inquire on what grounds the opposition or incongruity is
apparent in order to uncover the idea that it is because the cowardice
is apparent and the courage real. In the sequel he drops even this
implication at two removes. In the second paragraph of LR 2 he
speaks of the incongruity without the compromising adjective

---

[1] Intent on stressing the last idea as he works over LR 1a, he carets in the word
'intended' between 'was' and 'to' in the clause 'from the apparent opposition of which
that Delight was to be drawn' (*app. crit.* to I32:1) even though he does not need it
to make his meaning clear and in so doing he awkwardly repeats an early occurrence
of 'intended' in the same sentence (I31:3).

'apparent', and in the third he refers to 'what there *realy* is of Incongruity' in Falstaff (italics added). At this point no trace remains of the former potentially deceptive contrast; instead he now associates reality with the 'mixed Effect' by which Shakespeare excites the 'Disagreement'. Presumably, had he completed his revised text, he would also have removed the reference later in the *Essay* to Falstaff as 'cowardly in appearance and brave in reality' (T146:2).[1]

The second source of misunderstanding he eliminates by deleting T6:4–T22:5 is the extraordinary idea that we can know Falstaff or anyone else for what he really is only through the action of our sensibility intuiting first principles of character which are both peculiar to him and 'wholly out of the reach of the Understanding'. It would seem likely that he dropped this idea not merely because it suggests that we ought not to recognize the cowardice our reason deduces in Falstaff but because it has a more elementary, more glaringly obvious defect. First principles of character, unique in each individual and various as the variety of men, are a plain contradiction in terms. We have seen on an earlier page that following the normal usage he elsewhere defines such principles as a relatively small number of elements varying in degree but not in kind which are common to all men (T59n; cf. T165). The moment they become unique in every individual, whatever else they may be, they cease to be first principles in any but a Humpty-Dumpty sense. It seems a plausible surmise, therefore, that the thick expunging line he traces down through the middle of the passage in question on T6—it is the only rejected passage actually lined through in the original introductory section—reflects in the first instance a recognition of his gaffe. So sensitive, indeed hypersensitive, does he apparently remain to its possible recurrence that in an early revision draft he stops short and cancels before going on when he finds himself referring to 'first Principles of Character'—not necessarily unique first principles—as immediate perceptions of the sensibility (LR 1—ED 3a, *app. crit.* to I22:3; cf. below, p. 60).

Yet another defect in the concept of unique first principles of character also marks the third potentially misleading idea eliminated in the blanket cancellation of the original introductory section—the finding that, in conflicts between head and heart, head is wrong and

---

[1] A subsidiary reason for dropping the contrast between cowardly appearance and courageous reality may have been a desire to avoid confusion with another, more fundamental appearance–reality contrast later on in the *Essay*: see below, pp. 89–90.

heart is right because the former can only generalize while the latter comes to grips with concrete particulars. In addition to invalidating the 'mixed Effect', this idea shares with the obviously derivative notion of unique first principles the irremediable flaw that if they are well founded, if it is true that such minute circumstances as first principles of character peculiar to each individual lie beyond the reach of the understanding, Morgann is stopped before he starts. All through his book he not only deals professedly in circumstances of this kind but does so on the manifest assumption that his understanding and that of his reader are perfectly capable of recognizing and appraising them. The moment when he realizes that his theoretical statement to the contrary cuts athwart his practice in the *Essay* seems to be clearly marked in the manuscript book. In LR 1—ED 1a, a segment written early and cancelled late (see notes, pp. 380–1), he transcribes the distinction between generalizing reason and particularizing sensibility from the *Essay* with no material change except for his now saying explicitly that generalizing is an 'Errour' ingrained in the understanding. And so the passage stands till on subsequently rereading what he has written his eye is arrested by the statement 'the sensibility is excited by circumstances the most minute and such as the understanding can frequently neither estimate nor recognize'. 'Recognize'? One can almost hear his mind click as he draws two wavy lines through the word: how can the reason be said not to recognize the details it deals with throughout the *Essay*? In this state the sentence remains, broken and ineffectual by the deletion of 'recognize', until it is discarded in the cancelling of the entire ED of which it forms part.

This, of course, shelves rather than resolves the problem of how the reason can be right about Falstaff if it also can and should be wrong about him. Morgann moves towards an answer in the final version of LR 1. In the main body of the revision, LR 1a, he makes the positive role of the reason clearer when he transforms the statement in the *Essay* that a little reflection can 'unite our Understandings to our instinct' (T15) to 'the understanding will detect its own Errours'. And he brings out the aesthetic significance of the errors when he replaces the associated notion in the original that we ought to 'repeal' the erroneous decisions of the reason with the indication that the mistake concerning Falstaff's cowardice is deliberately induced by Shakespeare and must therefore not be foiled.

As for his earlier devaluation of the reason, he eventually relegates it to a footnote (LR 1b; cf. ED 3) where he remodels it into a form consistent with his new clarity on the subject. The point he now wishes to make, as he remarks in the earliest draft, is not that the reason has no 'use in the world' but only that 'it has not those particular uses . . . which it is supposed to possess' (LR 1—ED 3a). Working along these fresh lines, he disconnects the short clause about love and hate at first sight from the unique first principles with which it is linked in the *Essay* (T7:4) and spins it out into an entirely new and witty expatiation on the idea that not the reason but the sensibility really directs and controls human affairs. Referring finally not to the sudden intuition of love at first sight but to the more persistent feeling of love *tout court* (cf. LR 1—ED 3a with 3b), and instancing further what happens over periods of time in the making of languages, governments, and wars, he observes that in such matters the human reason has little to contribute: 'without knowing the first Principles of any one Thing in Nature she compares a little finds out a few Relations and for the rest amuses herself with weaving general Propositions which will never apply to any particular case whatever.' The words are reminiscent of the text of 1777 but not the thought. In the delicate matter of first principles,[1] it will be noted, he not only is far from suggesting that they are unique in each individual but extends their reference far beyond the earlier specific association with character to everything that exists. This fits in with the new turn he gives the old phrasing. Where earlier he had contrasted the generalizing reason with the particularizing sensibility in order to explain how the understanding errs when it conflicts with the feelings in judging character, he now mentions only the generalizing reason without drawing the contrast in mode of operation with the feelings and his aim is to make the different point that, just as in all other areas of life so in the accurate appraisal of character, the reason unlike the sensibility is not of any immediate importance or value. Further, he now glances at the special situation in which the reason is of value. Though the understanding cannot make a language, he says, 'she comes in with her Boast that after Some Ages she has been able to find out the Principles of the Work. We form Governments and when it is too late for use she makes grammars perhaps of those

---

[1] At an earlier stage, hypersensitive still, he temporarily corrects 'without knowing . . . the first Principles of any one Thing' to the more non-committal 'first Principle': see LR 1—ED 3b, *app. crit.* to I28:1.

too. . . . We make Peace & War whilst Reason only writes a History of Events.' In other words, the reason is ineffectual in the press of human affairs and is reliable only in retrospective analysis.

This idea underlies a distinction nowhere expressly articulated by Morgann but so fundamental to his theory as a whole that conceptualizing it puts his position in a yet clearer light. The distinction is that between what we may call for short the aesthetic and the critical reason. The former is the reason of daily life transferred to the theatre where, subdued to the playwright's will and purposes, it is immersed in the aesthetic experience. The critical reason is the same faculty in its autonomous, retrospective function analysing what happens in the theatre. In interpreting Morgann's dealings with the understanding it is often most helpful to ask which of these two functions he has at the back of his mind. The distinction explains, for example, how he can permit the reason both to affirm and to deny that Falstaff is a poltroon. It is the playwright-bound aesthetic reason which sincerely though mistakenly adjudges the knight a coward and the autonomous critical reason which can expose the fallacy. Not, of course, that the critical reason invariably judges correctly. Autonomy is not infallibility. In its critical capacity, the reason may sluggishly take over false conclusions it arrived at in its aesthetic role. But it also has the power to rise above such mistakes, and when it does, 'the understanding will detect its own Errours', that is, the critical reason will detect the errors of the aesthetic. The latter on the other hand should, as happens when we respond to *Macbeth*, submit entirely to a master dramatist, even though in the process 'the laws of nature give way' and 'we never once wake to the truth of things, or recognize the laws of existence' (T69); while the dramatist, for his part, proves that he is indeed a master by his ability to exercise as required such dominion and control.

This is precisely the assumption underlying Morgann's account of Falstaff's cowardice. If the reason could not function otherwise in aesthetic response than it can in critical analysis, if the playwright was not therefore able to bind the reason entirely to his will, the spectator, exercising the autonomous critical powers of the faculty, might realize that he is being inveigled into an unsound opinion of Falstaff, reject the fallacy, and so collapse the 'mixed Effect' into the single and unqualified perception of Falstaff as a man of courage. This, of course, would disarrange the entire Shakespearian design. It is the opposition between Falstaff's cowardice and courage which is intended to affect us, and unless we experience the opposition, so Morgann claims, we shall not have the Falstaff Shakespeare conceived for our delight.

And there the matter of his essential view of Falstaff's cowardice and the theory underlying it might be left, were it not for LR 3a, in which at a very late stage of revisal he recasts and amends a part of LR 2. A question arises because these afterthoughts may seem to cancel out the idea of Falstaff's cowardice brought forward in LR 1 and 2. Designed to continue from the passage in LR 2 quoted above which says that a playwright may create 'a perfect Draught of human Nature' by pitting feeling against (aesthetic) reason in the spectator, LR 3a begins: 'Now Reason I am afraid has very little to do in this Case and had better perhaps take a Nap, least it sho͡d fall as it is very apt to do into great Errours, till the play is over.' So far, perhaps, there is no necessary dissonance with the 'Case' referred to, since he may have in mind not the aesthetic but the critical reason. As he proceeds, however, this interpretation seems to be retroactively called into doubt. 'A dramatic Writer', he goes on, 'has very seldom occasion to consider his Audience as rational Beings unless it be indeed to keep out of the Way of a very troublesome Faculty.' And then, in the next sentence, he allows the occasion which the playwright seldom has, precisely the occasion exemplified by Falstaff, to melt away in the generalization that for the dramatist 'an Audience is *only* an animated Mass compounded of certain Feelings & Passions' (italics added; cf. also the cancelled false start in LR 3a, *app. crit.* to I152:1). By this 'only', if he is aware of its full significance and means it, he puts paid to the possibility of having the reason called into play in aesthetic response and so revokes the view he has been at such pains to bring to the fore in LR 2 and LR 1.

But does he really mean to reverse himself? It hardly seems likely. Far from indicating an intention to cancel materials which the 'only' would invalidate, the evidence runs the other way. In its final form, the opening of LR 3a is jointed with LR 2 far more securely than as first drafted (cf. ED in *app. crit.*); and a sentence in LR 3b, which he composed after LR 3a (see notes, pp. 388–9), seems yet more decisive. The passage in question, particularly as originally worded (see *app. crit.* to I165:1), parallels very closely a remarkable statement in the problematic section of LR 3a that when we witness a play 'we become . . . both the Instrument and the Hearers attending with delight to a very interesting Tune skillfully played on our own Sensibilities'

(I153:2). There is no hint here that the reason might also be some-how involved. But in LR 3b both as he first sets down the thought and as he revises it, no doubt to avoid awkwardly repeating LR 3a, he uses phrasing aligned with LR 2. The drama, according to the final version in LR 3b, is 'little more than an Exercise of Sensibility whilst the Intellect not being offended is almost passive in the Case'. This approximates to the opening of LR 2 where, on this occasion with a significantly qualified 'only', 'a Play in Representation' is described as 'for the most Part . . . an Action on our sensibilities only, the understanding being little more than a mere looker on'. The phrases 'for the most Part' and 'little more than' prepare for the more refined ways, as described in the succeeding sentence in LR 2, in which a gifted playwright may appeal to the understanding of the auditors. The language used in LR 3b, which as a whole elaborates on certain ideas in LR 3a, shows a similar awareness of the position developed in LR 2 and 1a. The description of the reason as 'almost passive' would cover even appeals to the aesthetic reason which are at variance with impressions stolen on the sensibility.

The most probable explanation of the discrepancy in LR 3a is, therefore, carelessness, a momentary failure to keep in the air all the billiard-balls he is juggling. The ninety interleaf pages laden with other materials that intervene between the two revisions show that he com-posed LR 3a some time after finishing LR 2; and at this later stage other considerations press upon him, among them, as we shall see in the next section, the need to excise a fallacious view of impressions as dumb, and, what is more to the present purpose, a desire to bring out the idea that there is no room in the theatre for any independent exercise of the understanding by the spectator. In this connection, his imagination working as usual luxuriantly, he weaves in a theory, originally recorded at greater length to serve as a footnote to another passage (LR 3—ED 1), about how the Greek drama originated and developed and why the three unities are irrelevant to Shakespeare. At this point he stops, without leading back into the text of LR 2—a task which in the event he never carried out. Under these circum-stances he might well in the heat of composition fall into language which is at odds with his starting-point in LR 2 many pages earlier in the manuscript book. The conflict is not frontal but by implication only; and the implication is by no means logically required by the topic at hand—the total submission of auditors to the playwright, who plays upon them as does a musician upon an instrument.

Perhaps if he had actually formulated his implicit distinction between the aesthetic and critical reason and so had it present in his mind he might have avoided the slip. It seems even more likely that if he had completed working LR 3a into his text, he would have spotted and ironed out the discrepancy along the lines of the parallel passage in the later-written LR 3b. At all events, it is easy enough to resolve the discord and bring out in full the position implied by what he says in LR 1a and LR 2 about the role of reason in aesthetic response. The necessary strokes of the pen are inserted in square brackets in the following transcript of the relevant passages in LR 3a:

Now Reason I am afraid has very little to do in this Case and [except for following the dramatist blindly] had better perhaps take a Nap. . . . A dramatic Writer has very seldom occasion to consider his Audience as rational Beings unless it be indeed [to achieve a very special effect; otherwise he prefers] to keep out of the Way of a very troublesome Faculty. To Him an Audience is only an animated Mass compounded of certain Feelings & Passions [and on occasion of their reason, all of] which it is his Business to Excite and to play upon. . . . We become by this Means in the course of the Process to be in Fact both the Instruments and the Hearers attending with delight to a very interesting Tune skillfully played on our own Sensibilities [and at times even on our own understandings].

The essential point to be conveyed by these or the like changes is that in the theatre, as he implies in LR 1a and LR 2, the reason is assimilated to the status of the feelings for purposes of response; it reacts automatically to stimuli, it does not judge them.

There remains a last question posed by his treatment of Falstaff's cowardice. Granted that the spectator's delight depends in part on his going along with his errant aesthetic reason, what is the consequence of true knowledge? If by reading the *Essay*, say, his eyes are opened to the fallacy which underpins the 'mixed Effect', how is he to take Falstaff when next he visits the theatre? On this subject Morgann says nothing in the printed text of 1777, a silence which, like his other early ambiguities, encourages the belief that the *Essay*'s arguments are to be carried into the playhouse. In revising the introductory section, however, he notices the problem, and after some characteristic groping, arrives at a solution consistent with his other views. Observing in LR 1a that on the error of the reason being exposed 'the Charm will be dissolved', he at first writes flatly and carelessly—one of his billiard-balls falling to the ground again—that the critic, and presumably along with him anyone he persuades, '*will* defraud Himself of some Delight *by* having united' the reason and the sensibility (LR 1a, *app. crit.*; italics added). In the final text, however, he tempers the categorical assertion into 'He *may* have . . . defrauded Himself of some Delight *in* having united' the two faculties (italics added). The critic may avoid doing himself out of delight, of course, only if his critical knowledge does not impede the working of the aesthetic reason; and whereas '*by* having united' implies that a unification has been brought into being which is henceforward in force everywhere, '*in* having united' delimits the unification more narrowly to the realm of critical activity. In composing LR 2 Morgann carries the thought further. When enlightened by the critic's truth about Falstaff, he says, 'we are all right again in our Discourse', i.e. in our talk about the knight after the play is over; and in regard to what may happen in the theatre, there is once again an instructive difference between early and later drafts. Writing first that if the 'Rectitude' given us by the critic 'diminishes our pleasure, [it is] perhaps not worth the Purchase' (*app. crit.*), he presently eliminates the 'perhaps' and puts it that if our pleasure is lessened, the rectitude is definitely 'not worth the gaining'. Finally, on revising LR 2 in LR 3a, he rules out the necessity that the critic's activity be a threat. Critical researches, he now claims, are 'a Matter of mere curiosity producing . . . nothing as to the Force and Influence of the Play'. In other words, they need not diminish our delight. Being 'all right . . . in our Discourse' need not inhibit the disagreement of sensibility and reason Shakespeare intends to excite in our minds whenever Falstaff stands before us on the boards. Once the curtain rises, the poet's spell can always come into its own, sweeping away all impertinent memories of rational critical hours.

In thus putting it beyond doubt that Morgann assigns a positive and necessary function to cowardice in the effect Falstaff is designed to produce on the spectator, the revisions reverse an impression carelessly conveyed in the original *Essay*. With regard to an allied question, the consensus obtaining in Morgann's day, and increasingly restored in our own, that Falstaff is a thoroughgoing poltroon, the revisions go even further: they correct outright misstatements in the *Essay*.

v. *The Consensus that Falstaff is a Coward*

In attempting to account in the *Essay* for the consensus that Falstaff is a coward, Morgann commits the fundamental error of putting the question in the wrong terms. Maintaining as he does that the understanding of a properly responsive spectator is misled into taking Falstaff for a coward while his feelings rightly apprehend him as a man of courage, he over-hastily infers that the problem raised by the consensus is psychological, that what he has to explain is why reason should completely cut out sensibility to dominate current opinion about Falstaff. Some of the most interesting pages in the manuscript book show the circuitous process by which he gradually extricates himself from the web of fallacy and contradiction in which this initial misconception entangled him.

The terms of the question as he asks it allow him to answer along one or the other of two lines: people either do not know or do not own up to what they feel when they respond to Falstaff. He tries both approaches, and in each one ends in disaster. His experiment with the first consists chiefly in an attempt to float the notion that impressions can be subliminal. To the reader who may claim to be 'unconscious of ever having received' an impression of Falstaff as a man of courage, he replies that it is because his true feelings are 'concealed and covered over perhaps, but not erased, by time, reasoning, and authority' (T13). Two closely related difficulties beset this suggestion. First, in his opening account of impressions he asks the reader to identify them as familiar phenomena of consciousness: 'there are none of us unconscious', he says confidently, of these 'sensations of mind' which do not pass through the understanding but are felt as strongly 'as if we could compare and assort them in a syllogism' (T5, T7). Further, he states that Shakespeare contrives not only 'to make' but 'to preserve' impressions of Falstaff's courage (T13). It is puzzling, therefore, that a few lines lower on the same page we should find these impressions presented as 'covered over . . . but not erased', flitting spectre-like through a dim twilight zone of consciousness. This is hardly to preserve them, to keep them intact and unimpaired. What has happened to their syllogistic clarity and pristine vividness? The three factors mentioned as causes of the obfuscation—'time, reasoning, and authority'—do not really bear examination. The first, the passage of time, might perhaps account for the obscuring of our original impression of Falstaff if we saw him but once on the stage and were thereafter led under the influence of the second and third factors to forget what we had experienced. But we see Falstaff repeatedly, we saw him last night. For the argument to hold, the influence of authority and reasoning must operate on our impressions in the theatre, making them subliminal as they are received, which is contrary to their nature as first defined. Furthermore, authority itself is only the consolidation of reasoning, and the opposition between reasoning and the impression cannot cover over the latter since the very conflict between the two is initially represented as no less conscious a phenomenon than the impression itself. The variance can be as he says a 'fact which every man's experience may avouch' only if the warring constituents remain in awareness— a presupposition, incidentally, of his view of the way Falstaff's cowardice functions.

The second difficulty is that neither he nor anyone else can square the notion of major impressions of a dramatic character reduced to a subliminal state in the spectator's mind with his premises that 'In Dramatic composition the *Impression* is the *Fact*; and the Writer, who, meaning to impress one thing, has impressed another, is unworthy of observation' (T4). A dramatist can scarcely be said to succeed in the grand object of impressing if his spectator is unconscious or only barely conscious of what has supposedly been impressed upon him. More particularly, it seems incredible that Shakespeare could have meant his audience to be so unaware of the impressions he communicates as to ignore them in their avowed response. Yet if he wished them to be aware of Falstaff's courage, he failed, it would appear from the consensus, to achieve his aim, and so on Morgann's own premises he must be written down an incompetent writer. This of course is the last thing in the world he really wants to say, but as a matter of logic the inference seems inescapable and justifies Johnson's 'splendidly comprehensive'[1] rebuke that in effect he declares 'Shakespeare knew nothing of his art' (above, p. 14).

The two difficulties suffice to explain why on revising his introductory section he goes no further than a brief flirtation in an early draft with the idea that the reader might be 'plagued . . . with some intrusive Impression' of a courageous Falstaff (LR 2—ED 2, I10:2). He soon cancels this refinement on T12:3 in the rejected introduction and thereafter finds impressions plainly and abidingly conscious, as required by their definition and by the premises about

[1] A. C. Sprague, 'Gadshill Revisited', *Shakespeare Quarterly*, iv (1953), 137.

their importance for dramatic composition. He retains the passages setting forth the premisses in the *Essay* and continues to be mindful of their purport, observing in LR 9, for example, that 'however it may be in real Life, from the Impression in the Drama there is no appeal'. It is as if he has realized that, with regard to the system of dramatic effects he describes, to say that people do not know what they feel is tantamount to the antilogy of saying that they do not feel what they feel.

On getting rid of the idea and along with it the first type of answer to his misconceived question, however, he is still far from out of the wood. There remains his equally bootless development of the second line of approach to his question according to which people do not own up to what they feel about Falstaff; and this proves more difficult to surmount. His involvement is more intricate and ridden by more fallacies and has a proportionately more tenacious hold on him. He begins with the brisk assertion that there is really nothing extraordinary in the fact that people deny the sense they have of Falstaff as a man of courage. In life too, he says, 'we often condemn or applaud characters and actions on the credit of some logical process, while our hearts revolt and would fain lead us to a very different conclusion' (T6). Perhaps behind this observation there lies some fugitive unexpressed glimpse into a dark corner of the mind, but what is expressed flies in the face of all experience, not least Morgann's own. Almost a decade before writing the *Essay* he had warned against the danger of forgetting that men openly take their stand on vital issues under the influence not of reason but of passion (see above, p. 5); and in the *Essay* itself, immediately after propounding the curious dictum of the masterful intellect silencing the rebellious heart, he goes on to argue for two pages, apparently without perceiving the contradiction, that 'we are greatly swayed by . . . feelings, and are by no means so *rational* in all points as we could wish'. This is surely the sounder view. Not a rational but a rationalizing animal, man normally reflects a dominance of feeling in his opinions. The reverse situation is not the usual but the special one, for example, the kind he alludes to when later in the *Essay* he argues that men of 'very nice honour' will quell whatever sense they may have that Falstaff is no coward for the same reason that they would repudiate his analogue in life. They will behave in this way, he says, in order not to appear before the world as brooking 'any composition in the very nice article of Courage' (T109). Here, as is further shown by the gallant comparison he adduces—the 'virgin or matron' who dares not openly 'pity or palliate the soft failing of some unguarded friend' (T110)— the censure springs from the fear that to do otherwise would reflect on their honour and not from a suppositional inherent tendency in men to condemn on logical grounds while the heart vainly revolts.

But even in ages punctilious to a fault about the appearances of honour, how many theatre-goers would hold back from admitting Falstaff's courage, if they really felt the quality in him, out of concern for the *qu'en dira-t-on?* The special case, obviously, cannot account for everybody's saying that the knight is a coward. For this purpose he needs a universal pattern of behaviour; and so he insists on his illusory generalization about the logical head and the rebellious heart. Still more, error begetting error, he seeks to found the specious behaviour pattern on an equally specious psychological law. If in a conflict between the feelings and the understanding we voice only the judgement of the latter, he declares, it is because our minds are incapable of doing otherwise. We cannot transfer a mental impression to another 'by *words*'; it is 'an imperfect sort of instinct and propor- tionably dumb', in its very nature incommunicable (T7–T8). Nor is he wrong to claim that the impression as such cannot be imparted to another. I am unable 'by words' or in any other way to produce in your sensibility a perception of the impression in mine. But this logical truism is one thing; it is something else again to contend on these grounds that I cannot report an impression intelligibly and render at least its approximate significance and force in words. The *Essay* itself proves how possible it is to do so. Furthermore, even if it were not possible, I should still be sharply aware of my impressions and strongly influenced by them in articulating any judgement to which they might be relevant. There is in the admittedly incom- municable nature of impressions no foundation for claiming as he does that the understanding is the absolute sole lord of opinion.

Error still begets error. A few pages back we watched him dispose of the allied concepts that the reason can neither recognize minute circumstances nor grasp first principles of character peculiar to each individual. Over and above the other flaws they exhibit, both con- cepts surreptitiously undermine the *Essay* since they intimate that the critical reason cannot know the fine and highly specific particu- lars which give rise to impressions of courage in Falstaff. In the passage in the *Essay* now under scrutiny, so eager is he to erect an impenetrable wall between mute feeling and articulate reason that he goes further and denies outright that 'we can . . . account for Impressions' (T7). This impetuous declaration, of course, cuts the ground even more openly from under the *Essay*. It must be added that two pages after making such extreme claims he moderates them a little when, referring back expressly to the idea that 'the Impression . . . has no Tongue', he adds: 'nor is its operation and influence *likely* to be made the subject of conference and communication' (T10; italics added). This 'likely' makes the *Essay* logically possible again since what is unlikely is not impossible; but letting the earlier claims stand, he seems to have no inkling that he is correcting them; and though he here stresses probability rather than necessity, he still speciously describes the impression as tongueless in order to uphold the spurious notion, now reiterated, that in calling Falstaff coward we talk 'the language of the Understanding only . . . how much soever our hearts and affections might secretly revolt' (T9–T10).

On completing LR 2 and thereby cancelling T6:4–T22:5 he eliminates the statements that we are unable or unlikely to account for impressions. The obliteration of these ideas reflects his growing alertness as he revises to the desirability of according what he says about the relation between the reason and the feelings with his own rational analysis of impressions in the *Essay*. But he still does not see that the same consideration applies to his illusory behaviour pattern and its accompanying psychological law, both of which he keeps as supposedly necessary to explain the consensus. He maintains unchanged the sentence in the *Essay* describing the pattern (T6:3; see notes, pp. 384–5); and although the reference to the psychological law disappears in the cancellation of T6:4–T22:5, it reappears in yet stronger form in LR2–ED2, in which he for the first time says explicitly that Shakespeare misleads the spectator's reason 'on purpose'. Linking the law with this idea, he observes that under such circumstances he cannot expect the reader to admit that Falstaff is brave, 'for it is the Understanding . . . which forms our opinion and governs our Discourse'; and he goes on to transcribe the scattered phrases in the *Essay* which describe the impression as a mute. Polishing the thought for the final version of LR 2, he gives it a slight further twist. Since Shakespeare has produced a 'mixed Effect' in Falstaff, he writes, the playwright 'must be content with that Erroneous Judgment of his Play which He himself has excited for it is the understanding which governs our Discourse—the poor Impression has no Tongue: It is an imperfect sort of Instinct only and proportionably dumb.' Granted his starting-point, the logic is impeccable; but what a staggering idea it is that Shakespeare's mastery should resolve itself into his having constructed Falstaff so perfectly that everyone necessarily misjudges him. We have seen how in discarding the notion of subliminal impressions he scotches the suggestion that Shakespeare is a bad playwright. Here, obviously without attracting his notice, the same wretched implication has once again crept to the fore.

Perhaps the actual setting down of the passage just quoted and the opportunity thus offered of looking squarely at its contents helped to break the hypnotic spell which the semi-personification of the impression as a wistful, tongueless instinct seems to have exercised over him. Perhaps, too, the process was aided by his having shifted back and forth from the one to the other as he worked over the materials of LR 2 and LR 1b (see notes, p. 382). While in the former he was reiterating his groundless psychological law that the understanding shunts aside the feelings to hold absolute sway over discourse, in the latter he was scratching out the thought that the reason 'affects to repeal our Sensibilities and set up a standard of its *own*' in order to develop just the opposite view that, even in the weighty deliberations of a council of state, the reason can do no more than sanction the 'foregone Compulsions' (LR 1—ED 3a) or, as he finally phrased it, 'foregone Conclusions of Sensibility'. He was also advancing the idea in LR 1b that whatever skill reason might show in belatedly composing grammars, the actual creation of a language is 'so far beyond her ability that she might as well make a world'. The force that really shapes language, as it does other human institutions, he suggested, is the sensibility; and in the light of what he was saying about councils of state, it might seem that the feelings, the formative influence upon language to begin with, would remain deeply implicated in its use.

Whether or not swayed by such considerations, he at last recognized where he had gone wrong. He could safely assume, he finally realized, that, other things being equal, Shakespeare with his 'unbounded ability . . . to obtain his own ends' (T125) must impart impressions so vivid that a properly responsive and reasonably intelligent spectator would have no difficulty in saying what they were. It was a blind alley, therefore, to inquire what quirk in human psychology leads people to ignore the impressions of courage conveyed by Falstaff. The proper question to ask was rather what external force might prevent the impressions from being communicated as intended by the playwright. Once the question is couched in these terms, the answer is clear: the actors.

Those incompetent, misguided actors. They are, he had said it all along, 'the very worst judges of *Shakespeare*' (T127). Yet although he speaks of them in this style in the original *Essay*, they play but a minor role in his speculations of the time, appearing only in two places where he objects to the gratuitous signs of terror and cowardice they introduce into Falstaff's behaviour (T24–T25 and T127–T129). They put in things not mentioned in the text, he complains, and when they rely on it, they fail to distinguish between 'humourous exaggeration and necessary truth', bolstering out Falstaff's body with masses of 'stuffing' and having him emit strident bull-calf roars as he flees the men in buckram. But he strikes these blows at the actors almost in passing; it is their vulgar 'mummery' and 'low buffoonery' which he emphasizes rather than any deep connection between their 'idle tricks' and his main argument. In revisal, on the other hand, he very early sees a connection of this kind. In LR 2— ED 2, where other explanations of the consensus tumble confusedly over one another—subliminal impressions, dumb impressions, the misled understanding—he also for the first time singles out the players as a distinct, 'accidental', or external force which prevents the proper understanding of the play; and by the time he writes LR 2—ED 3 he recognizes that in attempting to vindicate Falstaff's courage he will have to take into full account 'the errours of the stage from whence We have taken Impressions Never intended by the Author'. Alluding again in the definitive version of LR 1a to the dangers of 'an improper & Erroneous Representation on the Stage', he explains in the final text of LR 2 how it has come about that in their playing of Falstaff the actors circumvent Shakespeare and 'pervert his Designs & excite feelings & Passions opposite to his purpose'.

Their inherent power to subvert an author's intentions is great, he points out—he has even seen them, he notes in an afterthought (*app. crit.* to I36:2), turn Othello's sublime suicide into a piece of vainglorious posturing. Curiously piquant today in view of the espousal by many modern critics of exactly the same reductive and aberrant notion of Othello which he claims actors conveyed (see note to LR 2, I36), the illustration helps to explain how, because built on an 'Incongruity of Character & Action', Falstaff was at a decisive moment in his stage history even more vulnerable than Othello to the players' capacity for ignorant misrepresentation. The original Shakespearian acting tradition was disrupted by the Civil War, Morgann notes, and on reviving the play at the Restoration the actors in their limited way tended to miss the point about Falstaff and 'bring down the Character to the Action and involve them both in the same indistinguishable glare'. Once this mistake was established, the cause was lost, for, as he tries to explain more fully in LR 2—ED 2, though with some characteristic difficulty in settling on the close point, actors regard themselves as professionally bound by the traditions set up by their predecessors. 'It was acted so before my Time' is the player's perennial answer to doubts cast on his judgement (LR 11a).

This situation, he observes, inevitably gives rise to difficulties of a special kind with Falstaff. The spectators normally have no reason to question the actor's performance. It is the most natural thing in the world for them to 'give all the Force of Truth' (LR 1a, *app. crit.* to I29:1) to the stage representation of a play, to take it as a faithful embodiment of its author's intentions. In this way, so runs his argument in LR 2, a received public opinion is set up; and in the case of Falstaff, owing to his ambiguity, 'there is certainly Enough in the Play to confirm Prejudice once obtained or Even Excuse any careless surrender of Judgment where there was none'. Hence if a sceptical critic should impugn the common opinion of Falstaff, he can hardly expect anyone to agree with him merely on the strength of consulting the book as originally written, since playhouse memories and 'the common Concurrence & Consent' would make the reader 'bend' the text 'in spite of Himself' to the accepted view (cf. note to LR 11a, I181).

While writing LR 2 he still does not perceive that the actors are all the solution his theory needs for the problem of the consensus. Side by side with the tale of their deplorable influence he maintains his original reference to the behaviour pattern (T6:3) and his account of the dubious psychological law, the latter wrought up as we have seen to a higher pitch than in the *Essay*. As a result, in the context of LR 2 the players are only an immediate and aggravating cause of the common misconception of Falstaff; the real grounds are still alleged to lie in the nature of the human mind. Even if the players were to amend their crudities and transmit impressions of courage as Shakespeare intends them to, we would, on the principles expounded in LR 2, continue to say that Falstaff is a coward, while our hearts vainly revolt against the judgement. The difference is that we would then necessarily misjudge the knight as part of a rich experience rather than as the whole of an impoverished one.

But the shaky principles supporting this tortuous analysis are henceforward doomed. The actors are increasingly in his thoughts as he proceeds with his revision. When immediately after completing the last paragraph of LR 2 he turns back to improve the section dealing with his literary rationale, he points out that they are the real obstacle to the acceptance of his vindication of Falstaff. Many readers, he notes, have told him

that if I held out sometimes a Semblance of Truth it was but looking to the Playhouse and the Illusion instantly vanished. There as in his own Home Falstaffe was to be substantially seen and heard & felt; There he had doffed the Lion's skin in which I had phantastically accoutred Him and stood forth once more a wretched Coward & a genuine Poltroon. (LR 3c.)

Taking up the challenge, he defies 'the whole Theatric State to bloody Battle & to bruising Arms'. He has, in fact, already launched the campaign with a witty stricture on the actors' transformation of the Royal Presence scene into slapstick (LR 4), and he now carries on with his scornful reference in LR 10 to the 'Player Falstaff' who during the robbery at Gadshill 'saws the Air at a Distance with all the Manifestations of Cowardice'. In this way the actors obtain the guffaws they seek, though 'People of that Sort', he hopes, 'will make No Difference between the Reader and Me'. In other forays against the enemy he denounces the players for their seemingly malicious determination to degrade Falstaff 'by every sort of Injury Within their Power': they trick him out in 'Singular . . . Slovenly' garb as if he were a 'Captain of Banditti', they exaggerate his fatness so immoderately as to incapacitate him for physical exertion at the robbery, and when confronted with the need to have him carry off the dead Percy on his back they 'take care . . . not to let [the episode] pass off with! Marks of infinite Labour accompanyed with the most Enormous Indecency' (LR 11, passages from early A, B, and C stages: see note to LR 11).

A few interleaf pages later in the manuscript book he finally gives the foe his natural and preordained place in his theory as the sole cause of the consensus. He composes LR 3a, a revision of part of LR 2, in such a way as to delete the sentences explaining why the playwright 'must be content with that Erroneous Judgment of his

Play which He himself has excited'. In their place he says only that 'The Author must abide by the Impressions He has made'. Thus at a stroke he clears his reformed text of the fallacious psychological law that the impression cannot enter opinion. He presumably also intends to excise the brash declaration in T6:3 that we often condemn or applaud on logical grounds while our hearts secretly revolt —the similar statement in T10:1 is in the cancelled introductory section—for like the cashiered psychological law, the specious behaviour pattern is irrelevant to the explanation of the consensus as it now stands and therefore has ceased to have a *raison d'être*. Under the new dispensation those who call Falstaff coward no longer suppress the secret inclinations of their hearts; on the contrary, expressing exactly what they feel, they illustrate the sounder theory in LR 1b that discourse puts the conclusions of sensibility into words. Nor does their opinion in any way suggest incompetence in Shakespeare, who intended them to feel something quite different. This unhappy implication of earlier explanations also vanishes at long last, to be replaced by the idea that owing to special conditions in the theatre the spectators are unable to react as Shakespeare wishes them to. It is the business of the playwright, it is true, to manipulate the minds of his spectators, but he does so through the instrumentality of 'those Organs on the Stage which he has artificially inspired'; and if, as happens with Falstaff, they betray his inspiration and 'practise Tricks & Tones & Grimaces contrary to [his] Ends & Designs', the spectators can only respond accordingly, for the actors call, though they do not write, the tune.

At this stage he has rid this part of his theory of the worst of the confusion embrangling it in the original *Essay*; and in LR 11 he draws up the specification of actors' distortions foreshadowed by the new wisdom of LR 3a. Piecing together the scattered passages in which he has earlier attacked the players for injuring Falstaff (LR 11, A, B, and C stages), he adds to them to work up a comprehensive and lively arraignment of 'that Vassal Soul that trembling Coward that greasy slovenly Compound of Dirt & Meaness which we meet occasionally in Drury Lane and Covent Garden'. He stresses anew that by their literal-minded simplifying of the exaggerations of the text, the players 'spoil all the Mirth & Humour of the Peice'. Specific comments on their grotesque portrayal of Falstaff's running away at Gadshill and on their obscene representation of his treatment of Percy's corpse (LR 11b and c) help to explain why Morgann refuses to take seriously either the roaring like a bull-calf on the one occasion or the stabbing of Percy on the other (T124, T128, T43, and T103–T104). Although avouched in the book, roaring and stabbing alike seem to him to be essentially part of the players' debased caricature of Falstaff; and adducing other evidence, he leaves no doubt that degradation there was, beyond any warrant in the text. In particular he observes that 'in every Scene upon the stage almost in every Speech there is some Intimation of Cowardice in Falstaffe—A Wink a Tone a Shrug or Something or other which indicates the Poltroon'. Several of the instances he cites are mentioned by other critics of the day, but the one which he analyses more particularly seems not to be recorded elsewhere. When in the early scene in the prince's chamber Falstaff calls Hal 'the most comparative rascalliest sweet young prince', he reports, there was a significant piece of business: 'the Prince touches his sword in act to draw & Falstaffe shrinks & shrugs and fawns for safety.' Setting the tone and example for the part of Falstaff as acted through the rest of the play, the little episode substantiates his claim that the actors brought a degraded cowardly Falstaff on to the contemporary stage.

In LR 11, apparently the last revision he wrote, as in LR 3a, he adduces no other cause of Falstaff's being misapprehended. The sole hindrance to grasping Shakespeare's intentions that he now mentions is 'Action . . . Emphasis or Tone of Voice' on the stage; he says that 'any Reader . . . who has given Credit' to what he 'has seen or heard there or has referred to any Thing but his own genuine Taste & Feelings . . . is already in another Party and I neither sollicit or wish his Concurrence'. Had he completed the revisal of LR 2 begun in LR 3 he would perhaps have stated expressly that on his final view, were it not for the actors' misrepresentations, there would be no consensus that Falstaff is a coward. The point is clearly inferred, however, as is also its converse that if the players were to transmit Shakespeare's intentions faithfully, theatre-goers would sense the constitutional courage in Falstaff as well as believe they have grounds for doubting it, and the resultant popular opinion would reflect their ambivalence.

'I must explain what there realy is of Incongruity [in Falstaff's character] and refer it to its true source, and I must discharge all those Errours which the Ignorance of the Players has mingled with the real Principles of the Play.' Deprived by LR 3a of its original contextual reference to the now abandoned spurious psychological law and all that it entails, this statement in LR 2 applies perfectly to Morgann's purposes as amended and clarified by the revisions we have considered in the last and present sections. It does not, however, take into account his doctrine of historic and dramatic beings, which lies at the centre of his theory of Shakespeare's art of characterization. In this matter, to which we turn next, the revisions again provide helpful guidance, though we must obtain basic orientation chiefly by reading the text of 1777 more rigorously than seems to have been usual.

vi. *Rather as Historic than Dramatic Beings*

If the characters of *Shakespeare* are thus *whole*, and as it were original, while those of almost all other writers are mere imitation, it may be fit to consider them rather as Historic than Dramatic beings; and, when occasion requires, to account for their conduct from the *whole* of character, from general principles, from latent motives, and from policies not avowed. (T62n.)

No sentence in the *Essay* is better known or more often quoted in part or in whole than the conclusion to the note on characterization, and no sentence has been in part or in whole more frequently or more fundamentally misconstrued. It is commonly understood to sum up Morgann's critical position, which is taken to be that he proves Falstaff no coward by analysing him as if he were a historic being and thus provides the archetype for the Romantic study of Shakespeare's characters as living people. But although, as we have seen, almost unanimously adopted by critics of all shades for the past sixty years, this view cannot stand up to careful examination. Morgann's method of proving his thesis is not what it is alleged to be and he is in any event referring in the note to other aspects of his theory of Shakespearian characterization. Further, in his method of proof as in the other matters he has in mind in the note and discusses elsewhere in the *Essay*, he thinks in critical categories which far from being prototypical of Romantic notions are often at cross purposes with them. The present section will consider the first of these points, the next the second.

To begin with, a purely accidental factor appears to have fostered the widespread mistaken belief that what he says in the note relates to his method in proving Falstaff no coward. He subjoins the note to a discussion of Shakespeare's art in which he digresses for a few pages while in the midst of demonstrating Falstaff's courage, and as a result many readers seem to have assumed that he must still have his paradoxical argument in mind. Actually, however, there is no sign that he does. Not a word can be found in the note which expressly links historic beings or whole characters—the first is the human analogue for the second—with Falstaff, let alone with the Falstaffian thesis. It is another idea and another person in the drama that he talks about. Presenting the whole character as a concept by which to explain why Shakespearian characters are so extraordinarily lifelike, he says that he will apply it not to Falstaff but to Lancaster—a promise he duly keeps when twenty pages later he unfolds 'the general impulses and secret motives' of Lancaster's conduct (T82).

The negative evidence of the note becomes positive in the section on Falstaff's whole character, a late addition, it will be recalled, which Morgann drew up while the book was passing through the press. At the very outset of this section he dwells for three pages (T152–T154) on the fact that the whole character is a consideration not brought to bear in his earlier proof of the knight's courage. In all that has gone before, he claims, he has been concerned with Falstaff's 'Dramatic truth', with the 'impression' he produces as 'a stage character'. Now he proposes to 'change his position', 'to discover the hidden causes of such effects'. To this end, he says, he will examine Falstaff as he really is in his whole character, as if he were a living, historic person, and 'this is a very different matter'—so different that the familiar Falstaff hitherto surveyed will as a result in many of his aspects 'vanish like a dream'.

There are, it should be noted, no grounds for any suspicion that on composing the added section three years after completing the main body of the *Essay* he has shifted his key critical premises. On the contrary, he has been thinking all along in the same two basic and complementary categories of the dramatic and the whole character. His discrimination of the first is in fact brought out in a curious way as early as the opening sentence of the *Essay*, where he observes that his 'ideas . . . concerning the Courage and the Military Character of the Dramatic Sir *John Falstaff*' are not shared by the rest of the world. In this passage 'the Dramatic Sir *John Falstaff*' stands out as deviating from everyday English. Normally the phrase would signify the 'striking' or 'exciting' or 'vivid' Sir John, but this range of meaning does not fit. Wrenching accepted usage slightly, he is evidently employing the term *dramatic* as he generally does elsewhere in the *Essay*, including the title and the added section, in the special sense of referring to a character regarded as conterminous with the effects it produces on the stage.

Equally consistent in his idea of the whole character, he uses it in the added section exactly as in the note or the connected unfolding of Lancaster, even though with typical untidiness he does not refer back to these earlier written passages. (The note or the account of Lancaster could not of course refer forward to an added section still unwritten when they were submitted to the press.) The gist of the matter in the note is that Shakespeare's characters seem 'nature itself' because there is more to them than the effect they produce on the stage. Composed of 'first principles of *being*' which are found in nature (see above, p. 50), they can 'act and speak from those parts of the composition which are *inferred* only, and not distinctly shewn'. Hence they possess 'a certain roundness and integrity . . . which give them an independence' over and above the 'relation' they have to other characters they are 'grouped' with in the play. They are, in other words, 'whole' in that they have the complete psychologies of people in real life rather than just that portion of mental activity which they convey as dramatic characters through their relations with the other dramatis personae; and so it often happens that 'passages, which tho' perfectly felt [i.e. felt to be perfectly plausible], cannot be sufficiently explained in words, without unfolding the whole character of the speaker'. His detailed, searching analysis of Lancaster illustrates the doctrine admirably. On unfolding the prince's whole character he discovers that his chief motive for publicly censuring Falstaff is a mean, politic desire to disgrace his brother's favourite. This sufficiently explains the otherwise inexplicable, though 'perfectly felt', insidiously insulting tones in which Lancaster utters his rebuke. In the added section, though he now has Falstaff's viciousness rather than Lancaster's cold-blooded malice in view, he uses almost the same words earlier employed in the note. If we would explain the otherwise unaccountably natural behaviour of a character, he says, we must inquire 'if there be not something more in the character than is *shewn*; something inferred, which is not brought under our special notice' (T153). To do this we must refer to the 'principles of general nature' which animate Shakespeare's characters; and so considered Falstaff appears as an 'independent' figure rather than 'grouped' (T172).

The idea of the whole character set forth in the note and exemplified by the unfolding of Lancaster is thus repeated in the added section; and in now applying it for the first time, as he says, to Falstaff, he is not in the slightest concerned with advancing his paradoxical argument. True, he says in passing that he engages in the new line of investigation 'for further proofs of *Falstaff's* Courage, or for the sake of curious speculation' (T154), and the first of these objectives intimates that he will be exploring Falstaff's whole character in order to extend the earlier demonstration of his courage. But as is suggested by the alternative objective added in revision, 'or for the better Illustration of Shakespear' (SR 21), he actually does nothing of the sort. Having at this stage proved his paradox as well as he can, he devotes the remainder of the *Essay* to showing how Shakespeare by his art makes a character in reality vicious appear jovial and delightful. And as he canvasses this topic he does not turn up a single new proof of his thesis; whatever mention he makes of Falstaff's courage (see T165–T166, T168, and T178) presupposes his earlier demonstration rather than adds to it.

Conversely, an examination of the over one hundred pages devoted to that demonstration quite bears out his claim that he there analyses Falstaff as a dramatic rather than as a whole character. In other words, in proving Falstaff no coward he is not as is often alleged the trail-blazer for objectivism in Shakespeare criticism, that is to say for the system that extracts a character from its dramatic context and treats it as an independent human being (see above, p. 30). On the contrary it is precisely in his dramatic context that he studies Falstaff in working out the case for his courage: he seeks constantly to pin down the impressions he conveys or those other characters convey about him. The method is best described in the revisions. In the *Essay* as we have seen he commits himself to the hollow notion that a man's true character is known not by inference from his motives but by direct intuition of his unique first principles, which are wholly out of the reach of the understanding. Jettisoning this idea at an early stage of revisal, he finally in LR 3a formulates the theory that is really involved in his critical practice:

There are various Arts of impressing but the most general is that of giving Actions & Sentiments a Tone & Colouring which they can derive only from some specific Motive, which Motive however is never Exposed to our special Notice. This Motive however is not lost to us: it operates secretly on our Feelings . . .

Behind this statement lies the recognition that the sensibility judges of character just as the reason does, by referring to motivation. The difference is that the sensibility intuits motives through tones and attitudes while, unless they are stated explicitly, the reason comes to know them through the roundabout ways of logical analysis. But, as he makes clear in the sequel, these procedures though cumbersome can be equally effective in discovering the motive: 'or if we give ourselves the Trouble, [the sentence just cited continues] we may discover it by Inference & Deduction by which means it operates only on our Sensibilities and escapes the comment of our Understandings.' One could not ask for a plainer declaration that impressions are accessible to critical investigation. Unless the first 'it' should have been cancelled as belonging to a draft superseded when he added the words 'by which means it', etc., he even describes the secret process by which the sensibility intuits motives as in itself a concealed and presumably highly accelerated form of inference and deduction. But the important point is that the reason can in this way track down impressions, bring their operation into the open, and make them a subject of rational knowledge. The same view appears in another revision draft where he says of a passage in *Henry IV, Part II* that it is 'with other Reference to Falstaffe's Courage than as it may imply Discredit by the aid of logical Inference & Deduction but is yet of a Nature to strike directly on our Feelings and to make Impressions of the utmost Abasement & Dishonour' (LR 9—ED).

Although it is only in revisal that he adequately puts into words the theory of how impressions of character are produced and how they are to be investigated, he actually applies the theory throughout the demonstration of Falstaff's courage in the original *Essay*. Characteristically, his procedure there is to examine sentiment and action for their attitudinal and emotional connotations or, as he phrases it in LR 3a, for their 'Tone & Colouring', and on the strength of this analysis to infer the general motive or basic impulse which would normally be felt as integral to the connotations. Here, for example, is how he argues that Falstaff's soliloquy on honour at the battle of Shrewsbury is motivated by courage rather than by cowardice. The passage, he says, is one of those

that have impressed on the world an idea of Cowardice in *Falstaff*;—yet why? He is resolute to take his fate: if *Percy* do come in his way, *so*;—if not, he will not seek inevitable destruction; he is willing to save his life, but if that cannot be, why,—'honour comes unlook'd for, and there's an end.' This surely is not the language of Cowardice: It contains neither the Bounce or Whine of the character; he derides, it is true, and seems to renounce that grinning idol of Military zealots, *Honour*. But *Falstaff* was a kind of Military free-thinker . . . (T98–T99.)

The start is no doubt a little confused. Wishing to say that the soliloquy falsely suggests cowardice to the reason while conveying a true impression of courage to the feelings, he is careless in using the term 'impressed' for the appeals to the reason, as he himself recognizes in revisal when he substitutes the word 'imposed' (SR 12). But the slip does not detract from the force of the distinction he has in mind or from his primary interest in what the speech connotes. A soldier represented as repudiating honour on the field of battle we reasonably regard as a coward: the rational inference is in fact part of our aesthetic response to the episode. But the deduction, on Morgann's view, is contradicted by other feelings which enter even more strongly into our experience; and in pinning down these feelings he seeks their immediate and specific causes, the words and deeds that arouse them, rather than tries to ferret out their supposed psychological origins in the whole character. It is the associations evoked by Falstaff's language, he claims, which make us feel he is not a coward. As in his observation about 'neither the Bounce or Whine' he listens above all for tones of voice (cf. T120:4), these being, he says in LR 3b, 'the Natural and indeed only Language of sensibility' and therefore carriers of impressions *par excellence*. This mode of reasoning clearly does not probe into Falstaff as a historic being; *pace* Stoll, it does not argue him a man of courage by psychologizing him. Even the allusion to him as a kind of military free-thinker is not an argument derived from supposing him to be a particular kind of person but rather an inference from sentiment and action. The seemingly biographical comment actually epitomizes particular associations which may in principle be assumed to fall together for the audience in a certain pattern.

The handling of the soliloquy is typical. On page after page of the argument for Falstaff's valour, if one reduces the statements to their primary elements, one finds that Morgann is examining 'Tone & Colouring' and so proving himself, oddly enough, a devoted practitioner of precisely the close verbal analysis of texts which he is nowadays condemned for ignoring by some of those who accuse him of objectivism. In an influential essay Professor L. C. Knights quotes

the conclusion of the note on characterization and observes thereupon that, for all his recognizing 'what can be called the full-bodied
quality of Shakespeare's work', Morgann failed to realize 'that this
quality sprang from Shakespeare's use of words . . .'. The very
reverse would appear to be true. Turn from the passage in Knights's
essay to the last word of the note on characterization in the manuscript book and one discovers that immediately thereafter Morgann
has added in his own hand: 'To speak of Shakespeare and yet say
nothing of his Language and Power of Expression may seem strange
Especially as the peculiar & forcible Modes [of] Expression which
He has given to Falstaffe seems to demand it.'[1] The curiosity of the
anticipated reply to Professor Knights apart, the statement is not in
any way surprising. It simply shows that in revisal Morgann is far
more self-conscious than before about the fundamental concern he
has felt all along for the ways in which Shakespeare uses words.

He evinces the same critical concern even when deriving evidence
of Falstaff's courage from his standing as a military man. As he
analyses the impressions made by the knight on the other characters
of the play, he is as always ultimately ascertaining the impact of
sentiments on the spectators. True, while on this subject he gets into
terminological trouble by using the term 'impression' loosely,
saying that the evidence under consideration is 'weak and trifling'
and proves 'Impression only' (T29). The 'only' here may well seem
to deny the principle that 'In Dramatic composition the *Impression*
is the *Fact*'; and it is probably for this unintended implication as
well as because the passage is garbled that in revisal he deletes the
entire sentence (SR 4; see note). But what he has in mind is clear
enough. When he speaks of Falstaff's reputation among the other
characters of the play as 'Impression only', he is using the word to
signify 'vague belief of a character requiring additional confirmation

---

[1] LR 6a. Knights's observation occurs in 'How Many Children had Lady Macbeth?',
Explorations, 2nd edn. (Harmondsworth, 1964), pp. 23–4. On occasion Morgann employed verbal analysis on political pronouncements as well. Asked by Shelburne to
comment on the King's Speech of 8 July 1780, he noted that writings may 'make an
Impression on the Mind very different from what the *Letter* only would authorize .
This may be caused, he explained, either by 'some peculiar and unexpected Tone,
alien from the Matter which the *Letter* is supposed to express' or by the reader's attributing to the writer a coherency of thought not warranted by the text, the discrepancy
in both instances being chargeable 'either to the Incapacity or (if the Case requires it)
to the *Art* of the Writer'. He then went on to apply these principles in detail to the
speech in question. (Shelburne Papers, William L. Clements Library, University of
Michigan, Ann Arbor, vol. 165, pp. 225–6.)

before we can accept it'. His critical objective, however, is still to detect impressions in the sense more habitual in the *Essay* of 'effects on the feelings of the spectators'. From this point of view he understands the opinions others have of Falstaff to be merely ancillary to the more decisive impressions of courage which the knight conveys in his own person.

In the detailed argument he builds up for Falstaff's courage Morgann is thus no objectivist. The single passage which can properly be taken as erring in that direction is a whimsical speculation on Falstaff's gradual corruption from youth and is so unimportant for his thesis that in revisal he can and does delete it (T17:3–T20:1a). Elsewhere in the revisions he shows himself equally sensitive to the need for avoiding confusion of the dramatic Falstaff with a living person. In LR 11, on finding himself veering this way when he writes 'If there realy was such an existing Character', he lines through the incomplete sentence as a false start and gets back on his main track with a comment on how persuasively actors distort the impressions Shakespeare intended (I185, *app. crit.*). In LR 9, apropos of Falstaff's promise to marry Mistress Quickly as she nurses his broken head, he says that although in life we might be justified in appraising Falstaff's behaviour more favourably than Shakespeare does, 'if nothing of this Kind is expressed or insisted on, what have we to do [as spectators] with Colours which are not thrown on the Peice?' The observation is all the more to the point in that he makes it about what he calls the only episode in the play which truly conveys an impression of Falstaff's not being 'a gentleman or a Soldier'. But these revisions only confirm the awareness he shows earlier not just of the objectivist fallacy but also of the possibility that he might be thought to perpetrate it. He is in fact quite explicit in the original *Essay*. Having shown as part of his study of Falstaff's standing as a soldier that he derives 'from a noble or distinguished stock' and that in his period birth and 'natural courage' were closely connected, Morgann pauses to consider the objection that since the knight is 'in truth the child of invention only . . . a reference to the Feudal accidents of birth serves only to confound fiction with reality'. No, he replies:

Not altogether so. If the ideas of Courage and *birth* were strongly associated in the days of *Shakespeare*, then would the assignment of high birth to *Falstaff* carry, and be intended to carry along with it, to the minds of the audience the associated idea of Courage, if nothing should be specially interposed to dissolve the connection;—and the question is as concerning this intention, and this effect. (T46–T47.)

With few exceptions those of his readers who have put themselves on record have not noticed this express repudiation of objectivism any more than they have attended to his other assertions regarding his critical procedures or to the way he carries them out. Instead they say that he demonstrates Falstaff's courage through a close and detailed analysis of the knight's whole or real character, and they sometimes suggest, as a corollary, that he contrasts this courage with the appearance of cowardice to be found in Falstaff's merely dramatic being.[1] Why he should be so widely taken to make a distinction of this kind is perhaps to be explained as follows. Since the early nineteenth century it has appeared natural to discover the most authentic impulses and motives of fictional characters as with people in real life in their hidden inner depths. This expectation has doubtless seemed fulfilled by Morgann in the first instance because he professes to disclose essential valour in Falstaff, has a clear sense of the character as endowed with the psychology of a living person, and says that constitutional courage forms part of the character so considered. Corroboration might further be found in verbal similarities between some of his comments on how he goes about proving Falstaff courageous and certain of his references to the whole character. In order to vindicate the knight, he says early on in the *Essay*, he will be uncovering 'latent' and 'obscured' principles and using inference and deduction to disclose 'secret' and 'hidden' impressions which are not brought to our 'special notice' (T4, T9, T13, T37). Although he here has in mind what he calls the dramatic character, he may appear to be repeating much the same observations without any difference in denotation when apropos of the whole character he says that he uses inference and deduction to uncover 'latent' or 'secret' motives and 'hidden causes' which are 'withdrawn from our notice' (T62n, T82, T153). He may thus seem to be groping confusedly towards absorbing the dramatic into the whole character in so far as it is the *locus* of the courage to be apprehended by spectators. The whole character would in this way become the

---

[1] See, for example, J. Isaacs's summary of the theme of the *Essay* cited above, p. 28, and cf. J. I. M. Stewart's version of Morgann's view to the effect that 'the entire artistry in Shakespeare's creation of Falstaff consists in the disparity between the real or whole character (which is courageous) and the partial or apparent character (which is cowardly)'. *Character and Motive in Shakespeare*, p. 118.

sole bearer of truth, and the dramatic, by another rectification of what he actually says, the realm of illusions such as he finds Falstaff's cowardice to be. This correction might appear all the more warranted in the light of the parallel contrast in the introductory section (T2, T13, T14, T16) between the reality of his courage and the appearance of his cowardice. And final confirmation might seem to be provided in two other passages in the same section which, contrary to his later assertions, imply that the whole character conveys impressions of courage. In the first he says that 'Cowardice *is not* the *Impression*, which the *whole* character of *Falstaff* is calculated to make on the minds of an unprejudiced audience' (T5). In the second, as an aid to bringing out the knight's courage without having constantly to combat entrenched bias, he begs leave to reserve consideration of the Gadshill robbery and its aftermath 'till we are more fully acquainted with the whole character of *Falstaff*' (T17; cf. T35 and note for another, less misleading passage of this kind).

Based on some such reasoning as the foregoing, the common interpretation of the *Essay* thus has both a respectable internal logic and a certain claim to be grounded in Morgann's own words. It is not, however, sufficiently so grounded; its logic is not Morgann's but a scheme superimposed on and distorting his essential critical theory and practice. One of the basic distinctions he draws between the dramatic and the whole character is not the familiar contrast of illusion versus truth, as the common interpretation would have it, but the more unusual one of being apprehended as opposed to not being apprehended by the audience; and it can stand on its own without correction. He is in fact proceeding with a clear sense of this difference rather than groping confusedly towards something else when he applies the same notions—'secret', 'latent', withheld from notice—to both the dramatic and the whole character. Though he means that both can be made the subject of rational discourse only if uncovered and brought into the light by the critical reason, he also uses the same terms to point to quite different ways of functioning for the spectator. In regard to the dramatic character, he is referring to the impressions of personality and motive it conveys, and he calls them latent and secret in that they strike the spectator's sensibility directly without passing through the (aesthetic) reason.[1]

[1] He has this in mind when in a sometimes misunderstood passage he speaks of Shakespeare throwing circumstances advantageous to Falstaff 'in the *back ground*' while bringing 'nothing *out of the canvass* but his follies and buffoonery' (T44).

In regard to the whole character he is referring to the rich array of personality traits and motives of which it consists by virtue of possessing a total psychology, and he calls them latent and secret in that they are neither seen nor felt by the spectator.

From the point of view of direct effect on the audience, latent impressions conveyed by the dramatic character are thus diametrically opposed to hidden causes in the whole character; the former have such an effect, the latter do not. He brings out the same essential distinction when he observes that his earlier consideration of the dramatic character 'respected the Impression only, without regard to the Understanding' whereas the question of the whole character 'relates to the Understanding alone' (T153). Thinking here of the understanding primarily in its critical rather than in its aesthetic capacity,[1] he means that the various and varied facets of the dramatic character are immediately felt and so known by the spectator while the yet more complex, full-bodied reality of the whole character can be known only by extra-aesthetic, rational investigation and is therefore blanked out to the spectator while the play is being performed.

In revisal he accordingly purges the introductory section of most of the passages which seem to imply that it is the whole character which conveys impressions of courage. In addition to eliminating the misleading contrast between the knight's courage as reality and his cowardice as appearance, he also removes the proposal to postpone considering the robbery at Gadshill and its aftermath pending better knowledge of 'the whole character of *Falstaff*' (T17:1). What he probably meant was not the whole character in the special sense but rather the dramatic character of Falstaff in its entirety (cf. T129 and T181), and the inclusion of the passage in the cancelled introductory section effaces the muddle (as well as an impolitic allusion to a critical manœuvre denounced by Stack: see above, pp. 13–14). True, he leaves untouched the yet earlier passage which seems to imply that the spectator feels Falstaff's courage in his whole character (T4:6), but since here too he probably meant the dramatic

---

[1] He is probably thinking of the reason in its aesthetic capacity as well in what he says of the dramatic 'Impression'; as we have noted, particularly when contrasting the dramatic and the whole character, he tends to slight the role of the aesthetic reason in the former, which on such occasions he identifies exclusively with impressions on the sensibility. It is, however, clearly the critical reason alone to which he refers the question of the whole character. As will appear below, this blanket assignment of the whole to the exclusive jurisdiction of the critical reason requires a certain qualification, though not in such a way as to affect the account here given of his intention in making the statement.

character in its entirety, if he had completed revising the *Essay*, he would in all likelihood have corrected the original phrasing.[1] The emendation would have gone along with his evident effort to adumbrate the concept of the whole character in the revised introduction more clearly than he had in the original. At a very early stage of revisal, in fact, he begins LR 2 by distinguishing the character considered as referring 'to the general Principles of human Nature' from the character considered as a dramatic being (LR2— ED 1); and though he soon cancels the draft, he eventually concludes LR 2 by retouching his original inventory of Falstaff's incongruities (T20:1b) and having it culminate in the following statement:

> This is a singular Composition and if we trust to our Sensibilities we must add a Natural one; but by what Art those Qualities have been so mingled or what those Principles are in Nature to which under this Mixture they refer we have not enquired. . . . It was not Expected by Shakespeare that we sho.^d . . . whilst the Cause was with Him to his Auditors He never Meant to give more than the Effect.

The composition which strikes the sensibility as a natural if singular mixture of qualities is the dramatic character. So too is the *locus* of the art which mingles discordant qualities by producing impressions on the feelings which run counter to concurrent appeals to the reason. On the other hand, to seek out the principles in nature to which the mixed qualities refer is to look for the whole character, the hidden cause of those effects which alone Shakespeare meant to give us.

The difference between the whole and the dramatic character is further illuminated by an observation in LR 2—ED 1 which notes 'the double Relation' to spectators in which all dramatic characters stand: 'The optics seeing must be considered as well as the object shewn.' In other words, the dramatic character may be thought of either as the stage figure (the 'object shewn') caused by the underlying whole character or as the impression caused by that figure in the spectator's mind (the 'optics seeing'). These two aspects of the

---

[1] Unless, though this seems less likely, he decided that the phrasing would do, after all. His words are, it will be recalled: 'Cowardice *is not* the *Impression*, which the *whole* character of *Falstaff* is calculated to make.' If 'calculated' is taken in its stronger sense of 'designed' or 'planned' rather than in the weakened meaning of 'likely' or 'apt', the sentence *can* mean, consistently with his theory, that cowardice is not the impression which the whole character as deliberately handled by the playwright, i.e. in its dramatic form, is designed to produce.

dramatic character are, however, alike in content. The cause or stage
figure and the effect or dramatic impression stand in exact point-
to-point correspondence with one another: same physical appearance, same complement of qualities, same intellectual, moral, and
emotional nature. The whole and the dramatic characters, in contrast, though also related to one another as cause to effect, are by
no means identical in this way. On the contrary, they differ in
principle, the difference being caused by the process Morgann calls
'grouping'. By this he means the giving of a particular form to
characters by having them undergo, as he says in an early version of
LR 2—ED 1, 'the external Influence upon them of their companions
of the Drama and of the situations in which they stand'. To be so
shaped, he explains in the original *Essay*, is a condition of theatrical
representation: 'The characters of every Drama . . . must be grouped'
(T58n). He does not, however, make the converse claim that every
grouped character may be unfolded as an independent being.
Existing in the whole is a state which in 1777 he ascribes to Shakespeare's characters alone or to his characters as distinct from 'those
of almost all other writers' (T58n, T62n). In revision, though more
liberal, he still limits 'wholeness' to such characters in plays as are
what they ought to be or are 'worth Notice' (LR 13 and LR2—ED 1).
The important point, then, is not so much that all characters in plays
exist in the grouped state but that a great playwright like Shakespeare
who creates whole characters has no recourse but to group them
into the normal theatrical mode of existence if he would make them
dramatically negotiable. Even a character such as Falstaff who on his
view stands apart from the plot or main action of the drama must be
mediated to the audience in this way. Unlike the other characters who
are 'involved in the fortunes of the play', he claims, 'Falstaff passes
through it as a lawless meteor'; his position at the end of the play
is that 'he was engaged in no action, which, as to him, was to be
compleated; he had reference to no system, he was attracted to
no center' (T183). Yet Falstaff is his most interesting example of a
character made accessible to spectators by being grouped and so
converted under the 'external influence' of particular situations and
other characters into a stage 'appearance, which we are to take for a
reality' (T153).[1]

---

[1] In calling the dramatic impression at this point an appearance as compared with
the reality of Falstaff's whole character he of course runs the risk of puzzling a reader
who may recall that earlier in the book he contrasts the erroneous appearance of the

The conversion takes place on Morgann's theory even with regard to qualities that are not modified. Falstaff, for instance, has the same constitutional courage in both his whole and his dramatic character; but it is the attribute as it emerges in the latter rather than as it originates in the former which strikes the spectator's sensibility. This point has been missed (or ignored) by those supporters of the usual interpretation of the *Essay* who assign his courage exclusively to the whole character considered as the *locus* of truth. As we shall see, the fact that Falstaff's courage is an invisible reality as well as a sensible impression has a positive importance of its own in Morgann's analysis of the knight. But if Falstaff has qualitatively though not functionally identical courage in both modes of existence, in respect to other qualities the situation is quite different. His character as grouped differs from the whole not just by its accessibility to spectators but in contour and content as well. The idea is illuminated by his use of the term 'grouping' in a letter about a picture painted by his friend Oliver Humphry in which the artist portrayed himself surprised at his easel by a little girl and her young brother bringing him a gift of an egg. Professing himself greatly moved by the expression of tender feeling in this painting, Morgann undertook to ground his appreciation on critical principles. 'I would say', he wrote to Humphry, who had loaned him the painting, '. . . that the grouping was excellent, if by *grouping* is meant the proper relative positions of the persons delineated, comprehended within a certain waving Line, and if a certain *unity* of *action* and *Design* is applicable to pictures as well as to the Drama, I would call this Picture a perfect *unity*.'[1] This is instructive if one bears in mind both what Morgann is trying to do and the nature of the artistic medium he is talking

knight's cowardice with the true reality of the dramatic impression of his courage. If the reader does not perceive that the earlier appearance–reality contrast is quite different from the later one, he may well equate the two, link the appearance of cowardice with the dramatic character and the reality of courage with the whole, and so find additional confirmation here for the common reinterpretation of Morgann's position as discussed above, pp. 85–6. Perhaps Morgann revises the earlier appearance–reality contrast out of existence to avoid such confusions as well as for the more compelling reason mentioned above, p. 58. However, though the use of the same terms for different things is bothersome, and he is no doubt right to eliminate the flaw, there is no real inaccuracy of thought. Within his dramatic character, Falstaff's cowardice may be an appearance compared with the reality of his courage, while both qualities together may form part of his appearance as a dramatic character when the latter is compared with the reality of his whole character, in which, of the two qualities, only that of courage is to be found.

[1] 26 Aug. [1797], Bodleian Western MSS. 25434, f. 365.

about. Attempting to account for the expressive success of the picture, he finds it to depend upon the unity of action and design, which in turn depends upon the grouping, 'as comprehended within a certain waving Line'. Now, in a painting there can of course be no portrayal in the round; hence to group the persons delineated means to show some of their facets in certain lights and to conceal others. The effect of the picture is thus finally determined by a modifying process of selection and exclusion from the totalities of the real-life people represented.

When Morgann applies the term *grouping* to Shakespeare's drama, he has in mind a similar action of art upon nature. Holding that the playwright's characters must be grouped if they are to be dramatically viable at all, he further maintains that, as with their analogues in the picture, some parts of them will be obscured or not shown at all. This difference between the whole and the grouped character, however, is not merely the quantitative one brought on by selective subtraction; the more significant change wrought by art on nature is qualitative. It involves, as he says of the grouping of Falstaff, the 'disposition of light and shade and . . . the influence and compression of external things' (T172); and these can sometimes have far-reaching, even radical consequences. Thus it is by virtue of the way Falstaff is grouped that 'his ability . . . [is] disgraced by buffoonery, and his Courage by circumstances of imputation, and those qualities . . . [are] thereupon reduced into subjects of mirth and laughter' (T172–T173). Even more striking is the moral contrast between Falstaff in his real nature and 'the jovial delightful companion' (T172) we respond to in the theatre. The one is virtually the polar opposite of the other. If the knight's whole character is unfolded, he sums the matter up in the added section, he will be found 'most villainously unprincipled and debauched' on at least ten counts: he is 'a robber, a glutton, a cheat, a drunkard, and a lyar; lascivious, vain, insolent, profligate, and profane' (T171 and T156). In revisal he carefully withdraws inconsistent milder statements which, as noted in the Preface, occur near the beginning of the *Essay*. He there says that Falstaff owns 'a mind free of malice or any evil principle' (T18:4), appears more dissolute than he really is, possesses 'innocence as to purpose' (T20:1), has not 'much baseness to hide' (T21:1), and cannot be justly censured as 'a rascal upon principle' (T22:4). As part of his reform of the introductory section he gets rid of all these comments, which could apply well enough to Falstaff's dramatic character, but seem in context to refer to his true nature and so flatly contradict what is said in the added section. Had he completed the revision he would no doubt also have disposed of a like reference to Falstaff later on as 'a knave without malice, a lyar without deceit' (T146:2).

The phrase 'much baseness to hide', incidentally, occurs in the course of a rash argument that is instructive in the very fallaciousness because of which Morgann presumably included it among the materials cancelled in the original introduction. Rather confusedly he contends that Falstaff would pass everywhere for a highly respectable person if only he possessed the prudence of a certain politician who 'let himself out as the ready instrument and Zany of every successive Minister' (T21). Wit seems here to have overreached itself and lost touch with theory. If as a grouped character Falstaff exhibited the vile prudence in question, he would obviously evoke the same contempt Morgann arouses for people like the zany when he says with bitter sarcasm that they win 'the admiration . . . of mankind'. On the other hand, in his whole character Falstaff is on Morgann's showing not far from such prudence. Any merit there might be in his attachment to a single prince is outweighed by his improbity in pandering to his excesses. It appears clearly enough in the *Essay*, once his true self has been opened up, that he is generally on a moral par with the repulsive zany; and in revision Morgann makes the charge very specific by elaborating on his habitual 'Practice of the basest Accommodation' (SR 31; cf. T172). Into the inventory of Falstaff's ten vices he inserts an eleventh, 'Parasite' (SR 22), while in a longer addition (LR 14) he repeats the word and brings out all its ugly significance, putting the real Falstaff in the same class with pimps and pointing out that he 'knew his Condition perfectly and acted manifestly upon Plan and under all the arts of Management and Design'.[1]

But what, it may be asked, does Shakespeare gain by creating Falstaff as a whole that is distinct from his stage appearance? On

---

[1] These revisions highlight a further ineptitude in the 'zany' passage which would explain its cancellation. Because he lacks the zany's prudence, Morgann says, '*Shakespeare*, ever true to nature, has made *Harry* desert, and *Lancaster* censure him'. But Morgann later argues in effect that it is precisely owing to Falstaff's real vileness that Shakespeare, ever true to nature, has Harry desert him (see T179). As for the Shakespearian truth-to-nature motivating Lancaster's censure, as Morgann eventually sees it, it has nothing to do with Falstaff's allegedly being too decent to be a toady: the cold-blooded boy, according to the *Essay*, censures Falstaff out of a mean desire to sully the reputation of his brother's favourite (see T82–T84).

Morgann's view, a great deal; in fact, as he sees it, the playwright could scarcely have achieved his complex artistic ends in any other way. A first advantage, not peculiar to Falstaff but one which the knight shares with most other Shakespearian characters, is the quality of absolute lifelikeness. According to Morgann, this characteristic derives directly from the fact that Shakespeare conceives his characters as wholes. We feel them to be flesh-and-blood persons, he claims, because in every case we have a sense of the whole lying behind the grouped character. The point deserves special attention because Morgann does not explicitly note how it complements his other assertion that the concrete, multifaceted particularity of the whole is blanked out on the boards. Though he does not say so, his explanation of how Shakespeare's characters produce a completely lifelike effect on the stage qualifies his ascription of the whole character to the exclusive domain of the critical reason. The whole can affect spectators in the theatre in the way he claims only by making a direct impression on their feelings. It is, however, a severely limited impression. The spectators, he suggests, have no more than a general and indiscriminate awareness of the whole character. His revelatory phrase for the content of the awareness is 'relish of the whole'. There is, he says, a 'peculiarity . . . which conveys a relish of the whole' in any 'point of action or sentiment . . . held out for our special notice' in the dramatic character (T61n). The 'relish' can hardly consist of specific details since these might on Morgann's theory differ so radically from the dramatic effect as to undermine it rather than make it seem vibrantly real. The point is brought out by the tautology he falls into the second time he uses the phrase—'to give to every particular part a relish of the whole and of the whole to every particular part' (T146–T147). It is as if instinctively he jibs at concluding as his rhetorical pattern requires, 'and to the whole of every particular part', and thus disallows the possibility that the dramatic, at this stage in the *Essay* already copiously described as specific, enters into the general effect conveyed by the whole. (He also, of course, thus rejects any reciprocity in the cause–effect relation between the whole and the dramatic character.)

Other comments likewise bring out how indeterminate is the spectator's apprehension of the whole character. The whole character, he says, accounts for our feeling that there are 'certain sentiments or actions in a character, not derived from its apparent principles, yet appearing, we know not why, natural' (T153). 'We know not why' clearly indicates a general feeling the particular grounds of which remain obscure. The whole character, he observes elsewhere, gives 'an integrity and truth to facts and character, which they could not otherwise obtain' (T62n). This 'felt propriety and truth from causes unseen' (T62n), as he further describes it, can only be a directly perceived, undifferentiated human reality which gives the particularized dramatic behaviour on the stage the impress of absolute truth.

Falstaff thus strikes us as utterly lifelike because, as are other similarly real Shakespearian characters, he is conceived as a whole. But this, on Morgann's showing, is only the first and most general of the artistic benefits accruing to Shakespeare from the way he creates the knight. Other advantages, and such as are indispensable to Falstaff's dramatic effect, derive from his distinctive constitution; they have to do with the subterranean influence his whole character exerts as a hidden cause, particularly through the courage and villainy which predominate in its composition. To take his courage first, though it is of course the source of the qualitatively similar virtue we respond to directly in his dramatic character, it also serves another important purpose which seems to have gone un-noticed. Morgann adverts to this function in the following chain of reasoning which appears early in the *Essay*: (1) a character really felt to be as devoid of respectable qualities as Falstaff is often said to be could not win our affection by his wit and humour since the latter would necessarily reflect his obnoxiousness; but (2) 'if a Dramatic writer will but preserve to any character [of this kind] the qualities of a strong mind, particularly Courage and ability ... it will be afterwards no very difficult task (as I may have occasion to ex-plain) to discharge that *disgust* which arises from vicious manners'; and (3) the character's wit and humour will then easily endear him to us (T11:1–6; T11:8–T12:1). The passage is admittedly not of the clearest. Morgann's critics since Stack appear to have taken it to advance what might be called a theory of compensatory courage as opposed to their own theory of compensatory humour. Morgann, they believe, holds that the virtue of valour in Falstaff makes up for his turpitude and so inhibits the aversion he would otherwise excite, and they generally counter with the view that it is in fact Falstaff's humour which discharges the disgust arising from his vicious manners. Undertaking to refute Morgann along these lines,

Stack argues that it is unnecessary to postulate courage in Falstaff since cowardice is no meaner than fraud or lying and none of these base qualities are 'so detestable but that great endowments of mind, especially if they be such as universally charm, shall be able completely to discharge the disgust arising from them' ('Examination', p. 36). On this principle and by the 'contrivance' of having occasions of mirth arise from Falstaff's very vices, Stack concludes, Shakespeare 'has seduced judgment to the side of wit' (ibid., p. 37). But this theory of compensatory humour, though perhaps convincing enough as a disproof of the theory it rejects, fails to come to grips with the theory actually developed later in the *Essay*. As Morgann subsequently distinguishes the whole from the dramatic character, the latter is the impression received by the spectator. Hence, if viciousness formed part of Falstaff's dramatic being, it could not be dispelled by either humour or courage; it would necessarily be felt as part of the impression made by the character. This view, it may be noted, is quite consistent with the phrasing of the chain of reasoning early in the *Essay*. Morgann begins by suggesting precisely that Falstaff is not felt to be obnoxious. No less consistently, he then goes on to maintain that if a character otherwise vile is also endowed with courage, it may 'afterwards' be possible to discharge the disgust arising from vicious manners, whereupon any wit and humour the character possesses may endear him to us freely and without inhibition.

The point to be clarified then, is, how Falstaff's courage can lead to situations which 'afterwards' prevent his viciousness from entering into his dramatic character, and this Morgann cannot explain until he has gone into the different modes in which Shakespearian characters exist. Accordingly he has no recourse but to say, as he does, that he 'may have occasion to explain' the matter later in the *Essay*. For the same reason, presumably, on asserting a few pages farther on that if Falstaff were really a coward it would 'spoil all our mirth', he adds: 'But of that hereafter' (T41). The fact that he subsequently forgets these commitments and fails to supply the promised explanation leaves his position all the more open to misunderstanding—just how open Stack demonstrated. Certain hints in the added section of Falstaff's whole character can, however, be pieced together to reconstruct the missing theory. Devoting the added section chiefly to investigating how the odious Falstaff is transformed into a likeable stage figure, he claims that by grouping

him so as to neutralize his viciousness, a process which goes unper-
ceived by the audience, Shakespeare makes it possible for his
dramatic being to be liked 'afterwards', without *arrière pensée*, for
his humour, and, for that matter, for his courage as well. If, then,
taking this into account, we now inquire how his courage abets the
suppression of his viciousness, the idea of courage as compensation
is clearly ruled out. The only answer consistent with his theory and
with the language he uses in the chain of reasoning is that by virtue
of the quality as found in his whole character, Shakespeare throws
him into situations on the stage which prevent his hateful aspects
from being dramatically actualized. Were he not courageous, his
villainy would thus not be covered over and his attractive qualities
would not be free to charm without hindrance.

This hidden function of Falstaff's courage naturally raises the
question of why Shakespeare should create Falstaff vicious and then
go to lengths to veil his true moral nature. Why not create a Falstaff
essentially likeable throughout his whole as well as in his dramatic
character? Morgann's reply takes us to the heart of Shakespeare's
complex purposes in bringing Falstaff into being, as he sees them.
The playwright, he holds, intended Falstaff to get into disgraceful
scrapes while endearing himself to audiences as 'the life of humour,
the spirit of pleasantry, and the soul of Whim' (T172, SR 33); but
along with this he also proposed through such a character 'to furnish
out a Stage buffoon of a peculiar sort; a kind of Game-bull which
would stand the baiting' by the audience when he got into his
scrapes and 'rise, like another Antaeus, with recruited vigour from
every fall' (T176). To this end Falstaff had to have in his dramatic
character not only the likeability of wit and humour and the resiliency
of constitutional courage; despite these appealing qualities he had
also to provoke 'baiting' in the audience rather than arouse the
sympathy that would normally go out to a congenial character in
straits. Hence it was not enough to give him, as Morgann shrewdly
observes, 'every infirmity of body that is not likely to awaken our
compassion, and which is most proper to render both his better
qualities and vices ridiculous' (T149-T150); it was further necessary
to see that his vices were abundant and to fashion him out of
drastically different moral stuff from the 'perfect good nature,
pleasantry, mellowness, and hilarity of mind' (T174) he appears to
be made of. 'A character really possessing the qualities which are on
the stage imputed to *Falstaff*, would be best shewn by its own natural

energy; the least compression would disorder it, and make us feel for it all the pain of sympathy' (T175). On the other hand, by making Falstaff bad and contemptible and then grouping him in such a way as mainly to conceal his badness without, however, withdrawing the associated stimulus to contemn, Shakespeare has the spectators take Falstaff to their hearts through his positive qualities while at the same time, never realizing why or even being aware of inconsistency, they delight without compunction in his being put down. 'It is the artificial condition of *Falstaff* which is the source of our delight;[1] we enjoy his distresses, we *gird at him* ourselves, and urge the sport without the least alloy of compassion; and we give him, when the laugh is over, undeserved credit for the pleasure we enjoyed' (T175).

The general underlying principle seems to be that in modifying the whole character for dramatic effect Shakespeare can prevent unwanted constituent elements from affecting audiences while allowing others, even if closely associated with those he neutralizes, to evoke their proper responses. So in observing of one of Falstaff's victims that 'we feel no pain for *Shallow*, he being a very bad character, as would fully appear, if he were unfolded' (T179), Morgann implies that although Shallow's badness is veiled from the spectators, the associated repulsion of sympathy is not. With regard to Falstaff himself, the same principle accounts not just for his being eminently baitable but also, as Morgann sees it, for his inherent superiority as a comic character, 'the most perfect . . . that perhaps ever was exhibited' (T20). Half a dozen closely reasoned though ill-ordered pages in the added section on Falstaff's whole character are devoted to expounding the argument which, as clarified here and there in revision, may be sorted out briefly as follows. The highest comedy, he claims, is founded on incongruity, and philosophically considered, 'the greatest of all possible incongruity is vice', so that 'if we could preserve ourselves from sympathy, disgust and terror, the vices of mankind would be a source of perpetual entertainment' (T159–T160). Normally, of course, they are not. When we contemplate vice our sense of incongruity usually and properly intertwines with moral reactions like disgust and fear which are far removed from comic laughter. Now, if we analyse carefully, we shall

---

[1] It is not clear whether by 'artificial condition' Morgann means simply 'grouped' or more narrowly 'grouped so as to mask the true nature of the whole'. Either way, the source of delight in Falstaff's 'artificial condition' is of course quite distinct from that in his 'mixed Effect' of courage–cowardice (T15, LR 1a, and above, pp. 55–6).

see that these emotions are responses not to actions, which are in themselves morally 'indifferent or *neutral*' (T157, SR 23b), but rather to the intention of the agent, 'in which . . . consists all moral turpitude' (T158), and to the consequences of his actions for others. Accordingly, by the double device of concealing vile intentions and preventing pernicious consequences, Shakespeare divests Falstaff's vice of 'disgust and terror' (T162) and so has it impress us as 'mere *incongruity* and *humour*' (SR 24b and c)—the absolute incongruity of vice which can 'furnish the Comic with its highest laughter and delight' (T162–T163).

A comment in LR 14 further illuminates and is illuminated by the artistic process under consideration:

Let us suppose that [Shakespeare] sho^d open the base Designs of Falstaff and Accompany those Designs with Effects correspondent to the Cause. This might Disgust. Let Him then conceal the Design[s] and permit the Effects to remain in all the Colours which they derive from their Cause. This may impress the Cause on the Multitude with^t Disgust.

The 'Multitude' is the audience as opposed to the critic exercising his function, and the 'Effects' are Falstaff's actions as a dramatic character. Caused by his baseness but not reflecting it, since it is concealed, his actions can possess 'all the Colours they derive from their Cause', that is to say, the 'mere *incongruity* and *humour*' into which vice is transformed when stripped of disgust and terror; and thus modified they can be said to impress the cause (as neutralized by concealment) on the audience without exciting revulsion.

Perhaps the most interesting example of the secret workings of the whole character is suggested in a revision which is dominantly concerned with considering one of Stack's objections to the *Essay*. Morgann had maintained that Falstaff's cock-and-bull story in the tavern of having fought against superior numbers at Gadshill showed up not his cowardice but only his capacity for lying. To this he added that because the lies were too gross to be intended for credit they ought properly to be taken as '*humourous rhodomontades*' (T142). No, said Stack, content to disprove both statements by refuting the first, no, it is plainly not Falstaff's lies but his cowardice that is the principal object exposed in the scene: 'the lies could in fact have had no existence, unless we imagine some foundation on which they were raised'—viz., his cowardice ('Examination', p. 12). Agreeing in revisal that Falstaff's lies must have a sound psychological foundation, Morgann proceeds in LR 12 to focus on an aspect of the matter which both he and Stack had ignored and which has exercised many a critic since—the incredible nature of the lies and the seeming abandonment of all truth to life by Shakespeare in placing them in Falstaff's mouth. The difficulty has never been better pinpointed: 'If the Lies of Falstaff were Intended for Imposition How comes it about that they are so preposterous as to create a Doubt of that Intent? If for Humour & Rhodomontade only How come they to be detected as Lies and Imposition?' Either way, he points out, Shakespeare would appear to have 'deserted the ability of Falstaff'—to have made him behave with unbelievable stupidity; for the Falstaff is unbelievably stupid who, as it seems 'without any real Impulse from Nature and Passion and watched and cautioned by the Prince and Poins', keeps increasing the number of rogues in buckram whom he claims to have downed. 'The Charge goes against Shakespear Himself'; if he thus departs from 'Nature & Propriety in order to produce . . . [merely] farcical Incidents', he has ceased to be Shakespeare.

Morgann would be the first to concede that this is a problem discerned by the critic rather than a weakness which troubles the spectator. While awaiting the explanation of the difficulty which he says he will provide later, he observes in a discarded ED, readers may safely 'leave Shakespear to the Plaudit[s] of those honest Sensibilities which form his best and surest Fame' (LR 12, *app. crit.* to I148:4). But the problem is no less real for being posed by the critical reason. How is it, indeed, that Falstaff strikes us as so intensely alive precisely when on sober analysis he is behaving in a psychologically 'impossible' fashion? Unfortunately, Morgann does not keep the promise made in LR 12 to provide a full defence of the playwright after he has opened Falstaff's 'Character a little further when the whole Conduct of Shakespeare will appear Easy Natural & Plain'. But clues to the nature of the defence are many and through them it can be reconstructed with a fair degree of probability. To begin with, both by what he says about opening Falstaff's 'Character a little further' and the fact that he says it at the end of LR 12 which he inserts just before the section on Falstaff's whole character, he makes it clear that he proposes to find the plausible motive for the knight's apparent stupidity in the hardened reprobate who is disclosed when the character is fully unfolded. To what part of that Falstaff one should look is suggested by certain of his traits as described in the added section. He is, we are there told, 'supposed perfectly to comprehend' the Prince's delight in excess 'whatever was his pursuit' and 'thereupon not only to indulge himself in all kinds of incongruity, but to lend out his own superior wit and humour against himself, and to heighten the ridicule by all the tricks of buffoonery for which his corpulence, his age, and situation, furnish such excellent materials' (T174). These tendencies, we are further informed, are part of his pleasant dramatic character as fashioned through grouping out of his essentially despicable personality. If we then seek the particular area in his whole character from which they stem, we find it clearly enough in the repulsive parasitism mentioned in the *Essay* and brought out in LR 14, where the unfolded Falstaff is called a pimp-like butt and buffoon who deliberately 'Sacrifices his Integrity and lends Himself out to gratify the . . . unreasonable Passions of another for the End [of] Subsistence and Reward'. But what impels Falstaff to sacrifice his integrity exactly as he does in the tavern scene? Although Morgann does not explain in so many words, a motive that consists with his other relevant remarks is not far to seek. Falstaff realizes that his master, the Prince, expects him to utter monstrous lies on this occasion.[1] Such a perception on Falstaff's part appears to be a fair example of his perfect comprehension of, and willingness to cater to, the Prince's delight in excess whatever his pursuit. Indeed, if that generalization is to hold water, it surely must apply in this way to the tavern scene.

Morgann's account of Falstaff's whole character would thus provide as promised a defence of Shakespeare's perfect truth to nature in having the knight seem to abandon his own 'Wit & ability' by telling preposterous lies. Falstaff would not be suddenly stricken with an access of stupidity. In multiplying the men in buckram as in his other absurd vaunts he would be consciously and deliberately prostituting his own intelligence in order to pander to the expectations of the master on whom he depends. The lies would be intended not to be believed by the Prince but to be taken by him as if so designed, and therefore, though really mere humour and rodomontade, they would properly be detected as imposition. Nor is this all. Along with vindicating the playwright's truth to life, Morgann's theory would also account for the subtle blend of dramatic

---

[1] I do not, however, suggest that Morgann implies the theory that in the tavern scene Falstaff realizes he was attacked by the Prince and Poins at Gadshill and by humouring them turns the tables on them.

effects in the episode. First, as we have seen in earlier sections, Falstaff strikes the audience ambivalently both as the coward he is not and the man of spirit and ability he is. Second, by the principles considered in the present section, his real motive for lying, his contemptible parasitism, belongs exclusively to his hidden whole character and is therefore concealed from the spectators. They feel only that he lends out his wit against himself and, owing to the relish of the whole in the part thus brought to their notice, that his behaviour is right and natural. This indiscriminate sense of his being absolutely lifelike in turn interdicts their remarking any seemingly inconsistent stupidity on his part, such as the critic may puzzle over. Instead, affected by that part of the hidden whole actually entering into the visible dramatic character, they find the episode more highly comical for displaying the colours of vice purged of its normally attendant disgustfulness. Finally, in consequence of the same underlying art, they take Falstaff to their hearts, 'guts, lyes and all' (T132), and at the same time, for all the affection thus inspired and without feeling any contradiction, delight in his distresses as he enmeshes himself in lies.

Although not the basis for his proving Falstaff no coward, Morgann's doctrine that Shakespeare's characters may fitly be considered rather as historic than dramatic beings is thus a tool for probing deep into the mysteries of the playwright's art by distinguishing between the real and the dramatically effective and giving each its due. As will appear in the next section, this is a mode of analysis quite different from the Romantic system of character-study which is usually attributed to him.

vii. *The* Essay *and Romantic Criticism*

The widespread belief that Morgann is, as Nichol Smith declared, 'the true forerunner of the Romantic criticism of Shakespeare', unquestionably has more to go on than a misconception of how he demonstrates Falstaff's courage. As Smith also observed, his affinity with the Romantics 'is seen even in so minor a matter as his criticism of Johnson'. He speaks, for example, of 'a line of sober discretion' (T63), Hazlitt of a 'Procrustes' bed of genius', which Johnson set up for judging Shakespeare; and LR 7 holds up as proof of antipathy for Shakespeare's higher poetic flights exactly the same

comment by Johnson which that sophisticated inheritor of the
Romantic tradition, Walter Raleigh, would over a hundred years
later cite in order to show how 'in a certain sense Johnson was
antagonistic to Shakespeare'.[1] In the major and positive matter of
the concept of the whole character, a yet stronger case for kinship
with the Romantics might be made out. Morgann clearly has in
common with them the belief that Shakespeare's characters like
historic beings have partly hidden individual personalities which
can be discovered, sounded, and charted. Further, when he says
that Shakespeare avoids 'mere imitation' (T62n) to hew his characters 'whole . . . out of the general mass of things, from the *block* as it
were of nature' (T154, SR 20b), he is, like Coleridge, though in
different terminology, contradistinguishing Shakespeare's 'true
imitation of essential principles' from 'a blind copying of effects'.[2]
In Coleridge's vein, again, he observes that the characters are 'but
different modifications of *Shakespeare*'s thought' and that his 'comprehensive energy of mind' includes a 'wonderful facility of compressing, as it were, his own spirit into these images, and of giving
alternate animation to the forms' (T16 and note, T58n, and T61n).

In other words, he shares with the Romantics certain striking
features of their conception of what goes into the making of a Shakespearian character. Yet the common denominator, impressive though
it may be, no more makes him one of them than does his disparage-
ment of Johnson. For the latter to enlist him under their banner,
it would have to form part of a larger repudiation of eighteenth-
century criticism, including, one would suppose, censure of Warburton instead of the respectful statement that he 'seldom fails
on great Occasions' (*Com*. IV. i. 139; cf. *Com*. I. ii. 396, *Com*. II. ii.
149, and *Es*., T63). In the same way, to make him one of the
Romantics his concept of the whole character would have to be
integrated in a broader view of Shakespeare's art coinciding with

---

[1] D. Nichol Smith (ed.), *Eighteenth Century Essays on Shakespeare* (Oxford, 1963)
p. xxxvii. Hazlitt, as cited in note to *Es*., T59. Walter Raleigh (ed.), *Johnson on Shakespeare* (Oxford, 1908), p. xxiii. For further instances of Morgann's antagonism to
Johnson see note to *Es*., T63.

[2] *Coleridge's Shakespearean Criticism*, ed. T. M. Raysor (1930), i. 223. In this context Coleridge's 'blind copying' = Morgann's 'mere imitation', and Coleridge's 'true
imitation' = Morgann's 'mimic creation' (*Es*., T60), cf. 'Theatric forms' (*Es*., T154).
William Belsham, *Essays, Philosophical Historical and Literary* (1788), p. 20, makes
a similar distinction when he says that characters like Falstaff are 'not so much close
and exact copies of nature as bold imitations'. On Belsham's knowledge of Morgann
see above, p. 20.

theirs and used in their fashion to elucidate what happens in the plays. And this more fundamental similarity is precisely what one does not find. The undeniable resemblances turn out to be partial and peripheral, not central.

Considered in itself, the idea that Shakespeare's characters are extraordinarily true to life or even that they are so because the poet entered searchingly and entirely into every mind that he portrayed is not an innovation of the Romantics but by their day an eighteenth-century commonplace, which they inherit.[1] They differ from earlier critics not by their concern with the characters but by the perspective from which they view them. According to Professor M. H. Abrams, our best authority on the subject, the Romantic critics break new ground generally in that they regard 'the poet . . . himself as the predominant cause and even the end and test of art', while their predecessors in contrast consider a literary work as essentially 'something made in order to effect requisite responses in its readers'.[2] Referring to a difference of focus within a common range of interests, the generalization holds as true in the field of Shakespeare criticism as in any other. The controlling question the Romantic critics ask, the question that overtly or implicitly directs and motivates other queries, is, what does Shakespeare express in a given character? The parallel question posed by their predecessors is, what effect does the character produce on the spectators? Ultimately poet-centred in their approach, the Romantics treat the characters not simply as real-life people brought into being by a vitalizing power but as the expressions of a creativity and wisdom which, so embodied, are the primary value of the play. For Coleridge, what finally sets Shake-spearian imitation off from 'blind copying' is the 'quantum of difference' from the original caused by the presence in the imitation of the Proteus-like poet;[3] and to the manifestations of this presence, more generally understood as the working of the creative imagination, the Romantics subordinate such other interests as the imitation of essential principles or the impact of characters on audiences. Morgann, on the other hand, belongs to the older critical tradition

---

[1] On this point see Arthur Sewell, 'The Concept of Character in the Eighteenth Century', *Litera*, iv (1957), 1 ff. Sewell, p. 17, rightly objects to René Wellek's describing Morgann, in his *History of Modern Criticism*, i (New Haven, 1955), 117, as 'the first to argue that Shakespeare, in "unfolding" his characters from within, must himself have felt every varied situation'. See T61n and note.

[2] *The Mirror and the Lamp* (New York, 1953), pp. 21 and 15.

[3] *Shakespearean Criticism*, i. 128 and 218, ii. 87 and 201. See i. 200 n.

alluded to by Abrams, which focuses on the responses elicited from spectators. For him the characters are not primarily expressions of Shakespeare's genius but artefacts made by that genius to affect audiences. It is from this angle of vision that he approaches the problems we have discussed in earlier sections—the impression of courage and the effect of cowardice Falstaff conveys, the consensus regarding the knight's military character, and the way in which the dramatic and the whole character function. It is from this same angle of vision that he considers Shakespeare's ability to compress his spirit into the characters and the entire truth to nature of which they are compact. He is thus not ahead of but at the height of his age. Rather than with the poet-oriented psychological critics of the Schlegel–Coleridge school, he is allied with the audience-oriented psychological critics of his own day, with men like Burke, Hartley, Gerard, Beattie, and Alison, for whom 'the business of criticism is the understanding of emotional response'.[1] And this concern leads him to a view of Shakespeare's psychological realism which differs markedly from that later advanced by the Romantics. To be specific, he rejects the following four interrelated principles which are fundamental to their conception:

1. A Shakespearian character presents to the audience the fully rounded psychology of a person in real life.
2. In a Shakespearian character, the psychic levels that would be hidden in real life are revealed.
3. The revelation of the depths of souls is a climactic, aesthetic experience offered to the spectator or reader.
4. Conversely, the truthful laying bare of the concealed springs of action is a major objective and palmary triumph of Shakespeare's art.

Because Romantic views have been so long established or at least familiar, these principles may seem today to be the natural and inevitable components of any serious theory of psychological realism in Shakespeare. On these grounds, among others, it would appear, it has usually been taken for granted that Morgann, who obviously entertains such a theory, must of necessity apply the four principles and so bring into being the approach to Shakespeare which prevailed from the days of Goethe, Schlegel, and Coleridge to those of Bradley. There is, however, nothing inevitable about the

[1] Gordon McKenzie, *Critical Responsiveness* (Berkeley and Los Angeles, 1949), p. 117.

principles. They are corollaries not of the general proposition that Shakespeare is a psychological realist but of a particular nineteenth-century way of approaching and understanding his psychological realism. Looking at the matter from the different critical perspective of his own time, Morgann just as naturally adopts quite different though equally tenable principles.

1. Morgann's account of Shakespeare's art of characterization, as we have so far analysed it in the preceding section, clearly rejects the first Romantic principle. Flatly denying that a Shakespearian character presents its fully rounded real-life psychology to the spectators, he insists instead that it offers them only a qualitative transformation of its true personality. Growing out of his audience-oriented point of view, and keeping him clear of the Romantics' tendency to objectivism, which is fostered by their paramount concern with the poet's creativity, this initial difference leads him to diverge from their other principles as well.

2. In applying their second principle, that Shakespeare reveals the characters' true inner selves which in life would remain undisclosed, the Romantics differ among themselves as to the playwright's method. Goethe, Schlegel, and Lamb find that Shakespeare lays bare the inmost workings of the soul directly, side by side with outward behaviour; in Goethe's celebrated image, the characters are like transparent clocks. According to Coleridge, on the other hand, 'Shakespeare's characters are like those in life, to be *inferred* by the reader, not *told to him*'.[1] Morgann is at odds with both Romantic views. As opposed to that of Goethe, Schlegel, and Lamb, he so conceives of the whole character as to make it mandatory that key parts of the normally hidden clockwork remain invisible; the entire dramatic effect, as we shall see more fully when we come to the next principle, depends on such concealment. This also marks him off from Coleridge. Though he regards the whole character as knowable only by being inferred from the shown parts of the composition, he does not agree that the spectator—his equivalent of Coleridge's reader—should draw the inference. No less important, he does not equate what is shown with the outward manifestations of personality and what is concealed with the secret depths of souls.

[1] A. W. Schlegel, *Lectures on Dramatic Art and Poetry* (1809–11), Eng. trans., rev. edn. (1846), p. 362. (Schlegel mentions Goethe's image, which occurs in *Wilhelm Meister*, Bk. III, Chap. 11.) Lamb, 'On the Tragedies of Shakspeare, considered with reference to their fitness for Stage Representation' (1812). *Coleridge's Shakespearean Criticism*, i. 227.

On the contrary, when he analyses Falstaff's whole character 'in the very different appearances' it takes, as he phrases it in revisal, when 'seen externally and from without' and when seen 'from within' (LR 13), he puts it beyond doubt that he regards *both* aspects as hidden causes of the dramatic character. It is Falstaff's external, not his internal, character to which, he declares, 'many things which he does and says [as a dramatic being], and which appear unaccountably natural, are to be referred' (T171); and to this end he unfolds, however sketchily, some of the hidden *external* aspects of the knight's whole character. In revisal he is at some pains to heighten certain details in this hasty outline of the real Falstaff (SR 27, 28, and 29); and he rewrites the paragraph introducing the comments in order to specify, as he had not done in the original *Essay*, that he will now be inquiring 'into the real Composition of Falstaff's Character considered not as a dramatic Being merely but with Reference to the general Principles of his Frame and to that common Nature to which every dramatic Character ought ultimately to refer' (LR 13). The revisions thus bring out even more clearly the distinctive and non-Romantic light in which he sees the relation between shown and hidden parts. Since as visible entities the shown parts exclude the external whole character, they cannot be coextensive with it, and conversely, since the concealed parts include the external whole character, they cannot be coextensive with the inner.

This analysis holds true for the note on characterization as well. When he there proposes to account 'from latent motives, and from policies not avowed' for conduct which seems otherwise inexplicably natural, he is not, as seems usually to be assumed, making a perfect equation of the concealed parts of characters with their deep-lying springs of action. If carefully examined, the note will be found to express nothing incompatible with the division in the added section of Falstaff's internal aspects into those which are obscured and those which are disclosed. In the note he says only that certain secret motives and unavowed policies may be withheld from sight. He does not claim that all such are by their nature hidden; in fact he allows that some of them at least may form part of the grouped character when he observes a sentence or two earlier that 'the point . . . of sentiment, which we are most concerned in, is always held out for our special notice'. In LR 3a he goes further and declares that specific motives which are 'never Exposed to our special Notice' may be directly conveyed to the sensibility in the form of impressions.

In sum, although he differentiates between a character's outward fronting of the world and his inner impulses, he does not derive his basic idea of hidden and shown parts of the composition from this distinction. 'Shown' for him is what is tendered to the spectators for their apprehension and what they perceive: it is the content of the grouped character, including those traits and motives which are secretly conveyed to the feelings without attracting the notice of the reason. 'Hidden' is what is not so tendered and perceived: it is the content of the whole character. What is shown may be external or internal in the personality as transmitted to the audience; what is hidden may be external or internal in the personality as it really is in nature. The controlling principle in his classification is not the real-life psychology of characters but, harmoniously with the eighteenth-century critical tradition to which he belongs, the kind of effect they produce in the theatre. The Romantics, in contrast, though they may disagree among themselves as to Shakespeare's method, are at one in analysing his characters in terms of what is normally disclosed and undisclosed in living men and women. It is this difference at bottom which places his discussion of Shakespeare's art of concealment in another universe of discourse from both that of Coleridge and that of Goethe, Schlegel, and Lamb in their varying explanations of how the playwright reveals the innermost recesses of souls.

3. The clash with regard to the third principle is no less definite. Where the Romantics consider the laying bare of characters' inner depths in all their complexity to be a climactic, aesthetic experience offered by the playwright, Morgann claims on the contrary that it is precisely the deliberate concealment of important parts of the characters which makes for the audience's supreme delight. The principle is a general one with him. 'True Poesy', he writes, is 'an effect from causes hidden or unknown. . . . Means, whether apparent or hidden, are justified in Poesy by success; but then most perfect and most admirable when most concealed' (T71). Extending the idea to characterization, he observes: 'A felt propriety and truth from causes unseen, I take to be the highest point of Poetic composition' (T62n); and he develops accordingly his concept of the whole character abiding in aesthetic limbo except for the indiscriminate relish that is communicated. It is precisely because the whole character is thus dislimned from the spectators, he explains, that so potent an impression of its vitality is communicated. 'And this is in

reality that *art* in Shakespeare, which being withdrawn from our notice, we more emphatically call *nature*' (T62n). Were the cause of the felt truth of character to be brought into the open, the effect would dwindle sadly, if not entirely fade away. We can experience the mysterious sense of total life in Shakespeare's characters only on condition that the 'relish' remains undifferentiated. As he observes in LR 14, the curious may 'infer the Cause from the Effect at their Leizure by What logical Process they please. They are not [Shakespeare's] Subjects. They are for the most part their own Dupes and he does not trouble his Head about them.'

With the Romantics it is always just the opposite. For them, not the details concealed from the spectator but those revealed to him account for the abundant life animating Shakespeare's characters. According to Bradley, it is the pinnacle of the Shakespeare-lover's delight 'to realise fully and exactly the inner movements which produced these words and no other, these deeds and no other, at each particular moment'.[1] Morgann in contrast claims that precisely such awareness would destroy the true Shakespearian effect. Consistently with his view of the critic's role in relation to the 'mixed Effect' in Falstaff (above, pp. 64-5), he holds that those who seek the full and exact realization advocated by Bradley are 'for the most part their own Dupes'.

A gulf yawns between the Romantic position on the matter and Morgann's. With regard to the fourth and last principle, the gulf deepens to an abyss.

4. Morgann fully shares the Romantic critics' conviction that Shakespeare knows all the secret motions of the human heart. As they do, he believes that it would be easier 'to give a just draught of man' from Shakespeare's 'Theatric forms . . . than by drawing from real life'; as they do, again, he holds that Shakespeare is a better historian than 'any other of hi[g]her & more authentic Pretence' (T154 and LR 8—ED 2). But his high opinion of the playwright's knowledge of men leads him to very different conclusions from those which seem natural to the Romantics. They find it to be Shakespeare's genial achievement that he represents the true 'inner movements' of his characters' minds. Morgann, as appears from his account of Falstaff's viciousness, discovers Shakespeare's supremacy to lie in his unrivalled skill in manipulating and masking the characters' movements of mind to achieve his artistic ends.

---

[1] *Shakespearian Tragedy* (1905), p. 13.

The full significance of this view of Morgann's deserves closer consideration. From his own day to the present many have admired the digression in the *Essay* in which he extols Shakespeare's 'Magic hand' (T66–T73). In a widely disseminated preface Nichol Smith praised it as 'one of the great things in the whole range of English criticism. There is nothing greater', he declared, '—perhaps nothing so great—in Coleridge or Hazlitt.'[1] And there can be no question that the passage glows with enthusiasm and is alive with discernment. But Morgann's use of the word *magic* should not be misunderstood. He is not exalting the term as Coleridge does when he speaks of 'that synthetic and magical power, to which we have exclusively appropriated the term imagination'.[2] Coleridge is thinking of transcendental insight, coadunation, and the esemplastic power. Morgann has in mind the poetical prestidigitator whose marvels, though not the secret of his skill, can be explained by rational investigation; on his view, it is all as it were done with mirrors, a rare and infinitely difficult conjurer's trick played on an audience that is 'rapt in ignorant admiration'. Behind the idea lies the full weight of his theory. When he says that Shakespeare's 'characters not only act and speak in strict conformity to nature, but in strict relation to us', he does not mean that they are represented to us as in themselves they really are; he is thinking very precisely of the difference between the whole and the grouped character: 'just so much is shewn as is requisite, just so much is impressed'—and the rest is deliberately veiled. As the passage makes clear, it is in this sense that 'True Poesy is *magic* not *nature*'. The emphasis falls on the 'cunning' with which Shakespeare uses his power. He scatters 'the principles of character and action' not to open our minds but to bind us with spells. 'We discern not his course, we see no connection of cause and effect . . . he commands every passage to our heads and to our hearts, and moulds us as he pleases.'

The sole bound Morgann sets to the Shakespearian magic is that it cannot disguise first principles of character. The degrees of intelligence, sensibility, and courage and ability possessed by a whole character will appear in its dramatic counterpart no matter how it is grouped (T165). But otherwise Shakespeare may twist reality at will to his purposes. If in two places in the *Essay* Morgann inadvertently suggests other limitations, he makes the necessary correction

---

[1] *Shakespeare Criticism: A Selection* (1916), p. xvi.
[2] *Biographia Literaria*, Chap. XIV, ed. J. Shawcross (Oxford, 1907), ii. 12.

in revisal. A dramatic writer, he declares in the original, has only to obscure malicious intention and prevent evil consequences and he may pass off actions, 'without much ill impression, as mere *incongruities*, and the effect of *humour* only' (T158). On revising he deletes 'without much ill impression'. In the corrected version there need not be any such impression at all when the playwright chooses to pass off vicious actions as 'mere *incongruity* and *humour* only' (SR 24a, b, and c). A little later in the *Essay* he observes that if we stop short of loving Falstaff it is partly because 'there will be always found a difference between mere appearances and reality' (T174). In revisal he scratches out this careless suggestion that Shakespeare cannot when he wishes altogether conceal the repulsive reality of Falstaff's whole character. The new shortened sentence states that our attraction to Falstaff is kept within certain bounds only because the poet at times deliberately relaxes the influence of external pressures upon him and so allows his 'more unpleasing condition' to take dramatic effect (SR 35). Both emendations reinforce his basic contentions that Shakespeare is always in full command and that with Falstaff he means to falsify.

'Falsify' is not, of course, Morgann's word, and it may be asked whether it really is accurate. Perhaps he intends only the less provocative idea that an author reorganizes and reshapes the data of ordinary life to portray a deeper truth? One of his most discriminating admirers has in fact suggested that by 'artificial condition' (cf. above, p. 97) he 'means that the drama conveys reality by imposing upon it an artistic arrangement . . . which brings out the essentials'.[1] In support of this interpretation it might be urged that he speaks of the difference between comedy and tragedy as being that 'between suffering an evil effect to take place, and of preventing such effect, from actions precisely of the same nature' (T158); and that the kind of manipulation here referred to is perfectly consonant with the view that each of the two kinds of artistic vision has its own valid insight into reality. In what he says of Falstaff's whole character, however, he cannot be so construed. He claims indeed that Shakespeare reorganizes and reshapes, but not for a valid insight or a deeper truth. There is on his view no deeper truth than the knight's baseness. The essentials of reality in his case necessarily include his vicious qualities, and instead of their being brought out, they are

---

[1] W. M. T. Nowottny in *William Shakespeare: The Complete Works*, ed. C. J. Sisson [1954], p. xxvii.

more than concealed. They are, he says explicitly, 'obscured, and perverted to ends opposite to their nature', while other pleasanter attributes not his own are 'imputed' to him as Shakespeare 'passes off' his vice as mere humour (T175–T176 and T158). The language is blunt and unequivocal. Shakespeare 'passes off' evil, he 'imputes' what does not exist, and 'obscures' and 'perverts' what does. This is clearly to falsify. And if we recall how the relish of the whole character works, the playwright clinches the falsification by thus giving it the sanction of absolute 'integrity and truth'.

This view hardly foreshadows the Romantic doctrine that the creative imagination recasts and reorders actual objects, which '(as objects) are essentially fixed and dead',[1] in order to symbolize a living reality. Behind it lie rather the paramount concern of eighteenth-century critics with the audience, and, as a function of that concern, Burke's view that because designed 'to display rather the effect of things on the mind of the speaker, or of others, than to present a clear idea of the things themselves', poetry 'cannot with strict propriety be called an art of imitation'. The poet, Burke further points out, links up words in such a way as to arouse in the reader the associations which go with the correspondent ideas, but the 'assemblage of words' need not represent the actual arrangement of the ideas and their referents in nature; the words 'may be moulded together in any form and perfectly answer their end. The Picturesque connection is not demanded, because no real picture is formed; nor is the effect of the description at all the less on that account.'[2] Extending Burke, as Babcock has plausibly suggested, and, it may be added, perhaps with some recollection of Morgann as well, William Richardson observes: 'objects intended to please, and interest the heart, should produce their effect, by corresponding or consonant feelings. Now, this cannot be attained by representing objects as they appear. In every interesting representation, features and tints must be added to the reality; features and tints which it actually possesses must be concealed.'[3] If Richardson here partly

---

[1] Coleridge, *Biographia Literaria*, Chap. XIII, ed. cit. i. 202.

[2] Edmund Burke, *A Philosophical Inquiry into the Origins of Our Ideas of the Sublime and Beautiful*, 2nd edn. (1759), pp. 332, 333, and 330. The first and third observations do not appear in the first edition of 1757.

[3] *Essays on Shakespeare's Dramatic Characters of Richard III*, etc. (1784), pp. 145–6; cf. p. 136. R. W. Babcock calls this principle 'selective imitation' and derives it from Burke in 'William Richardson's Criticism of Shakespeare', *JEGP* xxviii (1929), 136, and *Genesis of Shakespeare Idolatry* (Chapel Hill, 1931), p. 178. Babcock also notes

echoes Morgann, he is inverting his source, since he faults Shakespeare for failing to apply the principle in question, whereas Morgann admires the poet's mastery in putting it into effect. But the important point about Richardson's possible obligation to Morgann, as about Belsham's (see above, p. 102), is not that Morgann leads them into radically new ways of thinking but that these essentially derivative minds rightly see his way of thinking to be harmonious with familiar assumptions. For the strength and interest of his thought lies not in his anticipating a later orientation but in the individual way in which, without breaking out of the frame of reference afforded by his time, he develops the idea that the poet adapts his imitation of nature to the effect he wishes to produce.

Not only does he claim, as we have seen, that Shakespeare convincingly falsifies reality but he holds that the poet makes evil acceptable. To quote Professor Harbage's fine epitome of Morgann's view of Falstaff: 'We fondle the viper and stroke the wolf. We laugh. It is Shakespeare's intention.'[1] That there might be a moral issue involved either in the nature of the playwright's 'arts and managements' or in their consequences seems not to cross Morgann's mind. A consideration of this kind crops up only in his two allusions to Voltaire. In the first, which occurs in a confused passage in the cancelled introductory section, he censures *Candide* on the ground that the titular hero is manifested only to our understanding. As a result, he says puzzlingly, Voltaire wins our approval for actions which any court of law would brand as criminal (T8:4–T9:2). The cause–effect relation he posits is hardly self-evident. In fact, of the tangle into which his thoughts knot at this point, the only strand of any substance is the notion that characters which appeal exclusively to the reason are so partially portrayed as to be 'ill pictures of human life'. Another plausible objection to them is, as he points out in LR 2 (cf. also LR 2—ED 1), that they are laboured and dull, though *Candide* hardly seems a persuasive illustration. But he errs when he asserts in the original introduction that characters exhibited only to the understanding are for that reason subversive of morality and 'wretched guides of conduct'; and he traps himself into inconsistency when as part of this attack on them he condemns Voltaire for

the relevance of an earlier article by Richardson, *The Mirror*, No. 24 (14 Apr. 1779). Richardson here speaks of the poet's treating nature in such a way as to achieve a 'consistency of . . . effects on the mind'.

[1] *As They Liked It*, 2nd edn. (New York, 1961), p. 78.

having employed his arts to make evil acceptable: a hundred pages later he will be praising Shakespeare for doing exactly the same thing. Once he deletes the passage he remains with his later reference to *Candide* in which he discusses more neutrally Voltaire's techniques for divesting crime of disgust and terror and condemns the book not for its literary method but because its 'moral purpose' is the 'enormously profane' one of 'satyrising Providence itself' (T162). From this it appears that he finally sees a moral question neither in managements which falsify nor in the fact that they make the immoral attractive but, consistently with the ethical considerations set forth in the *Essay* and refined on in revisal (T157–T158, SR 23 and 24), only in the ends for which such activities are carried on; and Shakespeare's ends, as he describes them, are to court artistic difficulty in rejuvenating and subtilizing a cliché of the stage and so give us the unforgettable mirthful experience of Falstaff (T148). These purposes are presumably as free of immoral tendency as they are of any commitment to confront us with the truth.

It hardly seems necessary to labour the point that the particular way in which Morgann conceives of Shakespeare as a practitioner of poetical magic, even though the magic is white, would be anathema to the Romantics. In their approach to Shakespeare's characters they believe with Coleridge that a great poet shows his supremacy by conveying 'truth, either moral or intellectual' as his '*ultimate* end'[1]—ultimate within the profound imaginative experience of which pleasure is the immediate object. In this matter as in his relation to the other principles, Morgann is not one of the Romantics. He does not think as they do; he comes at Shakespeare from a different point of the compass. Though he was the first to say that 'when occasion requires' the critic may fittingly consider Shakespeare's characters 'rather as Historic than Dramatic beings', and the Romantics do exactly that, his occasion is not theirs, and it makes all the difference. For them Shakespeare's psychological realism is a luminous end which embodies the poet's wisdom, for him it is a means manipulated by the poet to keep us 'the fools of amazement' (T69). He discovers Shakespeare's significant purposes not as they do by encountering the characters as creatures of flesh and blood but by discounting their substratum of reality. Just as the phrase about historic and dramatic beings does not serve him to describe his method in proving Falstaff no coward, so it does not import the

---

[1] *Biographia Literaria*, Chap. XIV, ed. cit. ii. 9.

Romantics' conception of how Shakespeare has his characters live and function in the plays and so reach out to engage us in their fortunes. Failing this, he does not in any meaningful sense inaugurate their school.

He is not, however, any the less impressive for not being a true herald of Romantic criticism. The high opinion in which he has generally been held for over half a century is still warranted, though on other grounds than usually alleged. If not really a forerunner of assumptions and practices belonging to a later age, he bases a remarkable and original critical system on the presuppositions of his own. Our discussion of the *Essay* in the light of the revisions indicates in fact that he works out not just a different but, as a small minority of his present-day critics have suggested (above, pp. 35–6), a finer and more sophisticated analysis of Falstaff than has commonly been realized. Instead of merely trying to prove Falstaff devoid of cowardice by considering him as a real-life person, as is usually supposed, he discovers a legitimate effect of pusillanimity in his ambiguous make-up, demonstrates his constitutional courage by studying his dramatic rather than his historic being, and investigates the latter in order to show how Shakespeare converts its natural ugliness into the pleasing dramatic appearance which delights audiences. He thus finds Shakespeare's principal arts and managements to be of two kinds: those involving a variance between appeals to the reason and impressions on the feelings and those involving a modification of the basic human reality out of which the playwright shapes his characters. Further, behind this differentiation of the whole from the dramatic character, as W. M. T. Nowottny has observed, is the seminal idea of allowing for the mode and degree in which an artistic fiction is related to life and so of sorting out whatever conflicting claims may exist between the work of art as an autonomous creation and the work of art as an imitation of reality. A second fruitful general idea underlying Morgann's subtle and complex analysis of Falstaff concerns the relation between the artist and the critic. Admittedly, he goes against the grain of modern criticism by his failure to find profound meanings in Shakespeare's handling of character and by his insistence on subordinating literary criticism to rational amusement. Such an approach cannot but disappoint present-day students of literature who are haunted by an Arnoldian faith in poetry as 'an ever surer and surer stay' and in right criticism as the sponsor and hierophant of poetry. But still significant in his view of poetical magic is the distinction he draws with exemplary clarity between critical analysis and aesthetic response. Granting full self-sufficiency to the artist in the domain of affecting audiences, he assigns criticism the unambiguous status of a real branch of knowledge. Finally, with regard to the premisses and implications of his position he evinces the self-consciousness which, as noted by Professor Wellek, characterizes the original *Essay* and which in the revisions, by enabling him to weed out fallacies, correct errors, and bring out obscured or neglected implications, reveals the substantial structure of thought into which coheres what might otherwise be taken for a catena of brilliant and sometimes erratic insights. The critic thus brought into view, though not archetypal for the Romantics, has, I suggest, an even stronger title to the place hitherto given him largely on mistaken grounds in the main line of Shakespeare criticism.

II. THE COMMENTARY ON *THE TEMPEST*

i. *Authorship and Date*

Morgann wrote his Commentary on *The Tempest* in an interleaved and re-bound first half of a bisected first volume of Theobald's edition of Shakespeare (1733). His authorship of the Commentary is established in the first instance by two considerations. One is the hand in which the annotation both on the interleaves and on the printed pages is written: it is as unmistakably Morgann's as that in the manuscript book containing the revisions of the *Essay on Falstaff*. The other consideration is the similarity between three comments on *The Tempest* and certain passages in the *Essay*. One such comment elaborates on the idea in the *Essay* that far from being temporary and local as in *Macbeth* the magic in *The Tempest* is universal: *Com.* I. ii. 250; *Es.*, T74n. Another comment defines magic as 'an Effect without any known cause', almost the very phrase used in the *Essay*: *Com.*, I. ii. 22 (cf. *Com.* IV. i. 139–63); *Es.*, T71. The third comment, which notes Shakespeare's 'Art of making *compendious Time* and *compendious Place*', recalls the 'compendious *nature*' independent of 'the relations of place' and 'continuity of time' which the poet is said to obtain in the *Essay*: *Com.* V. i. 4; *Es.*, T70. In addition to these resemblances, moreover, one finds more general parallels in wit, style, and cast of mind. For example, the critic who turned accepted opinion upside down to argue that Falstaff is constitutionally brave would seem to be just the man to propound the paradox, and defend it with subtlety and skill, that *The Tempest* was originally Shakespeare's *first* play.

The manuscript book also contains testimony by others to Morgann's authorship. Edward Dowden, who once owned the book, entered this note on the binder's leaf:

The MS. Notes are by Maurice Morgann author of the Essay on the 'Dramatic Character of Sir John Falstaff'. It appears from these Notes that he designed an Edition either of 'The Tempest' or of Shakespeare's Plays.[1] E. Dowden

Immediately below his signature Dowden wrote:

See p. of Dramatis Personae for authorship of notes, & leaf opposite printed p 7 as to the design of an Edition

And below this he added:

John Symmons whose name is on titlepage was probably John Symmons M.P. father of Dr Charles Symmons whose praise of M. Morgann's essay on Falstaff is quoted by Lowndes[2]

The owner's inscription referred to by Dowden reads 'John Symmons 7 vol's'. One might perhaps expect that this was written not by the M.P. but by his son, John Symmons of Paddington House, the close friend of many years' standing to whom Morgann entrusted the Carleton Papers and who witnessed his will (above, pp. 3, 9, and 11n). The possibility, however, is ruled out by a comparison of the signature on the title-page with that found in over three dozen signed autograph letters of the younger John Symmons deposited in the British Museum.[3] On these grounds,

---

[1] The six brief Miscellaneous Comments on other plays (below, pp. 351–2) offer little support for the idea that Morgann may have intended to bring out a complete Shakespeare rather than an edition of *The Tempest*. Dowden apparently thought the larger scheme might be suggested by what Morgann says in *Com.*, Introduction, 17; but although the few generalizations one finds there might in principle apply to a more sweeping editorial plan, they are in fact the peroration to a preface which, as Morgann himself declares on PI10 (below, p. 122), is designed to precede only the single play. The authenticity of Dowden's handwriting and signature is confirmed by specimens of Dowden's correspondence in the Folger Shakespeare Library.

[2] William Thomas Lowndes, *The Bibliographer's Manual of English Literature*, rev. edn. (1861), pt. vi, pp. 1612–13. R. L. Widmann, 'Morgann's Copy of Theobald', *N. & Q.* N.S. xvii (1970), 125, who prints the MS. material on the binder's leaf, errs in describing the notes below Dowden's signature as 'in another hand' and in saying that the MS. book has no notes on *Two Gentlemen of Verona* (see below, p. 352).

[3] Letters to C. Whitefoord, 1799–1809, Additional MSS. 36593. Letters to M. Whitefoord, 1810–15, Additional MSS. 36594. Letters to Sir J. Banks, 1798–1804, Additional MSS. 33980. Etc.

therefore, Dowden appears to be right in identifying the title-page signatory as the elder John Symmons, who was also Morgann's friend; and other considerations reinforce the inference. The notation '7 vol's' implies that the owner inscribed his name before Volume I was cut in half and the first part was interleaved and re-bound, since after the bisection the set presumably consisted of at least eight volumes. This accords with the likelihood that the elder John Symmons, who was born in 1701, obtained a first edition of Theobald's *Shakespeare* on its appearance in 1733 or soon thereafter. By the time Morgann became interested in such matters, if Malone's statistics are to be trusted,[1] copies must have been harder to procure.

More definite evidence of authorship is provided, as Dowden observed, by the jotting scrawled across the upper quarter of the Dramatis Personae page (T2), which claims the notes for Morgann in the following terms:

M^r. M. author of the Essay on the dram: character of Falstaff, attaching more value to certain notes, scribbl'd by himself on the margin of this unhappy book, than perhaps anyone besides, drew his pen peevishly thro' them [o]n some unmeant instance of [in]attention in a weary [a]uditor —*O Vatum irritabile genus*!

Unlike the signature on the title-page, this note, with its concluding tag from Horace (*Ep.* II. ii. 102), *is* written in the hand of John Symmons of Paddington House. His known intimacy with Morgann makes it more than likely that he wrote *en connaissance de cause*. Symmons, it may be added, demonstrably jotted down his little notice of Morgann's peevish moment before the book was made into its present form. He himself specifies that the notes he refers to were 'scribbl'd . . . on the margin', and Morgann records in PI10:3 that

(C) There are some notes in the margins and the Bottom of pages But those Notes were written before the Book was interleaved and are now wove into the interleavings.

The chronological relation to be inferred between Symmons's jotting and the two sets of notes, marginal and interleaf, is fully confirmed by the physical state of the copy. Obviously recut at the time of interleaving, the book has many printed pages on which bits of marginal annotation were sliced off in the process. But on not a single interleaf page is any writing thus mutilated, even in those places

[1] According to a MS. note by Malone ('Shakespeariana', i. 238: Bodleian, Malone 140), the first edition of Theobald ran to only 1,360 copies, and the text was sufficiently in demand to warrant an additional 10,000 copies in various editions from 1740 to 1774.

where, cramped for space, Morgann huddled his script at the bottom or the side of the page. Of the manuscript notes on the printed pages, therefore, at least those which have been partly cut off must have been written before the interleaving. And since three words in Symmons's jotting, all flush with an outer edge, have had their initial letters excised, it follows that his remark too must have been written before the book was interleaved.[1]

But this was not Symmons's sole contact with the book. His pen was busy in it again at a later stage, setting down and signing with his initials *Com.* IV. i. 55–6, the only manuscript note on Shakespeare which was not written by Morgann. To write the comment as he did on an interleaf, Symmons must again have had access to the book some time after he had recorded the misadventure with the inattentive auditor. It appears further that his comment was to be included in the edition: the corresponding passage in the Shakespearian text is marked in Morgann's hand with a circled 'a' (*app. crit.* to *Com.* IV. i. 55–6), the device he normally used to indicate that a comment is provided on an interleaf page.[2]

The date at which Morgann began annotating the margins cannot be determined with any certainty. If one assumes that the Theobald volume came into his possession after John Symmons the elder died, the earliest possible date of composition would be 1764.[3] If, however, he had already worked out his highly original views on the genesis of *The Tempest* by 1777, one may conjecture that he would have at least hinted at them in the *Essay*, perhaps in the thought-packed note much of which deals with the play (*Es.*, T74n–T77n). This supposition would assign the marginal notes to a period between 1777, when the *Essay* was published, and the indeterminate date thereafter when the Commentary manuscript book was interleaved.

Some comments at least must have been entered on the interleaves in or after 1785. The heading above *Com.* I. ii. 250 (see *app.*

---

[1] On the other hand, as is indicated by blots on I59 corresponding to the lines drawn through T59MS, not all the marginal notes were cancelled before the book was interleaved.

[2] Symmons's connection with the book suggests that it may have escaped Miss Kingston's destroying hand (above, p. 11) because it was in his possession when Morgann died or because he could claim it as a family keepsake.

[3] Francis Green, 'Symins of Martell and Llanstinan', *West Wales Historical Records*, xiv (1929), 229. (Symmons's death date is often erroneously given as 1771.) In the *Essay on Falstaff*, composed largely *c.* 1774, Morgann shows signs of having consulted a volume i of Theobald's 1733 edition of Shakespeare: see note to *Es.*, T64.

crit.) clearly refers to Johns. 1785[1] as the place in which Morgann studied Johnson's note on magic in *The Tempest* (see note to *Com.* I. ii. 250). Other indications strengthen the inference that he consulted the same edition of Johns. throughout. Apart from the allusion in *Com.* I. ii. 408 to an opinion of Pope's and Swift's which goes unmentioned in the eighteenth-century editions of Shakespeare, all the scholarly Shakespeariana not in Theobald which Morgann uses in his interleaf comments are found in Johns. 1785. In *Com.* IV. i. 14 he alludes to materials which made their initial appearance in the 1780 *Supplement* to Johns. 1778, and it is possible that for a part of his discussion of III. iii. 48 he may have been influenced by a note of Henley's which appeared only in the *Supplement* and Johns. 1785 (see note to III. iii. 48). In contrast, Johns. 1793 lacks some of the data he refers to in certain comments or else supplies additional information in which he would presumably have been interested: it deletes not only Henley's note but also an observation by Johnson on III. ii. 71 which Morgann knows and rejects; it omits Warburton's vindication of Ariel's song and his comment on Prospero's passion, to which Morgann refers in *Com.* I. ii. 396 and IV. i. 139; and it provides First Folio readings obviously unknown to him which are highly relevant to his discussion of I. ii. 301–2 and II. i. 250. In all these matters Malone 1790 resembles Johns. 1793.[2] The available evidence thus suggests that Morgann used Johns. 1785 extensively in writing his Commentary, a conclusion that receives yet further support from his recourse to the same edition in composing LR 7 (see above, p. 39).

A precise *terminus ad quem* for the interleaf notes is less easily settled, except, of course, for the unimpeachable one of 1802, the year of Morgann's death. The date can be moved back by a decade if one assumes that while writing his Commentary he would have had enough curiosity to examine the most recent edition of Shakespeare. On this supposition, his ignorance of pertinent information found in Johns. 1793 means that he ceased working on his manuscript before that edition appeared. If one draws the same conclusion from his ignorance of the same information in Malone, the latest date becomes 1790.

[1] For the short titles, e.g. Johns. 1785, used in this paragraph, see List of Short Titles, pp. 355 ff. below.

[2] Though Morgann apparently knew Capell's edition of 1768 (see *Es.*, T64 and note thereto), there is no sign that he consulted it or its companion set of *Notes* (1783) in composing the Commentary.

To sum up, one may tentatively say that he began scribbling on the margins after 1777, and a little more definitely that he brought his annotation on the interleaves to the most advanced stage it was to reach in 1785 or afterwards, though probably not after 1790.

ii. *Literary Purpose and Achievement*

Morgann did not begin serious work on his edition of *The Tempest* till after the manuscript book was interleaved. On the margins of the printed text he had earlier inscribed thirty-eight notes, eighteen relating to his theories about the revision of the play, fourteen touching on other details of interpretation, and six recording five emendations to the text. These jottings are almost all terse and sometimes take the form of cryptic hints which as they stand would be almost meaningless without the sort of oral elaboration which came to so abrupt an end in the incident recorded by Symmons. The interleaves, on the other hand, show him in the act of making a book, elaborating the hints in the margins into fifty comments in proper form, and complementing them with another forty-seven which present new materials. Developing and amplifying in thirty-four comments his theory that *The Tempest* is a revised early play, he worked up his other interpretative observations in the margins into eleven more, to which he added twenty-two new ones of the same kind. He also fetched eight glosses from the *Shakespeare*s of Johnson and Theobald, and included four more of his own; and to his earlier notes on five textual points, including the only observation not transferred to an interleaf (*Com.* II. i. 220), he added another thirteen.

'What the Plan of this Edition is', he wrote in his Introduction, 'will best appear from its Execution.' It was evidently no part of his plan to establish the text through his own efforts. Content to learn about First Folio readings from others (see *Com.* IV. i. 3), he seems in any event to have been unendowed with the spirit of exactitude required for textual criticism. In the *Essay* he scarcely ever quoted Shakespeare with entire fidelity to the original and in his *Tempest* Commentary he often failed to transcribe accurately from the printed text to the opposite interleaf page. Plainly, he proposed to graft his seven original textual conjectures as well as the eleven he gleaned from others onto a *Tempest* derived ready-made from Theobald. As for explaining obscure or difficult passages, for all the pains he now and then took to clarify some of them, there is no sign that he intended a systematic and complete treatment of the play from this point of view. The primary interest of his *Tempest* was obviously to lie somewhere other than in his text and his glosses. Though he had something to contribute in passing to each of these departments, his main claim to attention would be found rather in his interpretation of the play—his arguments to show that *The Tempest* is a *rifacimento* and his other critical observations. Feeling that on this ground he could dispute the palm with commentators otherwise more erudite than himself, he announced at the end of his Introduction that his policy would be to respect the learned men who had dealt with Shakespeare, 'yet always to remember that this Edition is not theirs but my own'.

In preparing the manuscript book he had arranged to insert six consecutive interleaves before the start of the play and single interleaves regularly thereafter (see below, Textual Introduction). In his impatience to get started, however, he wrote out his Introduction on I1–I8 instead of on the six preliminary leaves which had been designed for the purpose (PI1–PI12). He then realized that this might puzzle a reader of his manuscript and so added the following explanation in I7:3–I8:1:

(C) I did not imagine that this Introduction wo.ᵈ have exceeded a Page or two but I find it to have incroached too far on those Leaves designed to accompany the Text. I shall therefore in so far as the Case shall require Mark the Page with References [I8] to those Leaves which immediately follow Mr Theobald's Preface and which ought to have been employed in this introductory Use, and for this purpose I have numbered those Leaves.[1]

Further, having entered his notes to T3–T8 (I. i. 1–I. ii. 47) on PI1–PI7, he recorded beneath the last of them, in PI7:6:

(C) I have now reached the point which brings, in opposite pages the comment to the Text, and I hope, for the rest, to keep Them together.

This hope he did not quite succeed in fulfilling. Requiring space for revised versions of two comments originally written on I9 and I11 (*Com.* I. ii. 99–100 and 152–8) he again had recourse to the

---

[1] The leaves Morgann refers to follow not Theobald's Preface but the List of Subscribers (not d7ᵛ but e8ᵛ: see below, Textual Intro.). He numbered not only these leaves but also the following fourteen interleaf pages. His slipping into these minor inaccuracies just when he was trying to set matters straight is typical enough.

preliminary interleaves. But he was still as careful as ever to indicate cross-references (see *app. crit.* to *Com.* I. ii. 99–100 and 152–8) and just after the second revised comment he described the new state of affairs in PI9:6–PI10:1:

(C) NB These notes accompany the play to page 8 of the Book. To which are added two notes on passages in pages 20 and 22 of the Book But I have renewed the comment on the pages following page 8 of the play on the Leaves opposite to those pages expunging the two notes on page 20 and 22 as being given in a [PI10] more perfect state in page 7 & 8 [=PI7 and PI8] of the manuscript Leaves.[1]

As if concerned that he had not yet made everything quite clear, he added immediately thereunder (PI10:2):

(C) The general Observations made on the Play extending from its Commencement to page 7 of the printed Leaves have rendered it necessary to seperate the notes on the Text from the opposite Pages where they ought to have been found to the interleaved Pages preceding the play and which are differently numbered but I shall endeavour to place the notes subsequent to page 8 of the printed Play on the opposite Pages so that they may meet the Eye together.[2]

To this he subjoined the remark, already cited (above, p. 117), about having incorporated the marginal notes into those on the interleaves.

Although less lucid than he intended, these elaborate explanations stand in striking contrast to the absence of any such indications in

[1] More minor inaccuracy. By 'page 8 of the Book' in PI9:6 he means T8 but by 'pages 20 and 22 of the Book' in PI9:7 he means I9 and I11, which are numbered 20 and 22 in his original pagination of the first thirteen interleaves (see prec. note and Textual Intro.). The 'added two notes' mentioned in PI9:7 are 'on passages' on T9 and T11: it is the ED of these notes, as is more clearly explained in PI9:8–PI10:1, that are 'on page 20 and 22' (= I9 and I11). The reference in PI9: 8 to renewing the comment on interleaves opposite the Shakespearian text 'on the pages following page 8' (= T8) presumably antedates Morgann's entry on I8 of *Com.* I. ii. 53, which glosses a passage on T8.

[2] The minor inaccuracy continues. The Introduction or 'general Observations' are not on 'printed Leaves' but on the interleaf pages numbered 13–18 in Morgann's original pagination of the first thirteen interleaves (see prec. note). Within the same system of pagination these pages 13–18 (= I2–I7) can be described as 'differently numbered' from pages 1–7 (= PI1–PI7), which contain the comments on T3–T7— though how matters are made clearer by this description is not apparent. In the two references to 'opposite Pages' the meaning is 'opposite interleaf pages'. The statement that the comments 'subsequent to page 8' (= T8) will appear on interleaf pages opposite the relevant passages cannot apply to *Com.* I. ii. 53 (cf. prec. note on the same idea in PI9:8) and, of course, to *Com.* I. ii. 99–100 and *Com.* I. ii. 152–8.

the *Essay* manuscript book. They suggest that he had in mind and wished to avoid the possible confusion of a compositor. Other signs that he was consciously preparing for publication are his correction of 'If I were to give an Edition of this Play . . .' in his Introduction to 'I think it proper to . . .' (*app. crit.* to I6), and the relative fullness, compared to the *Essay* manuscript, with which he punctuated his comments. However, though he seems to have come closer to final copy than in his revisions of the *Essay*, here too he did not complete his task. He did not correct the text of *The Tempest* as *Com.* I. ii. 29 requires. He left *Com.* I. ii. 118 and 229 in a state that could only baffle a reader who did not have before him Theobald's commentary, which is, of course, serviceably at hand in the manuscript book, but would not have appeared in Morgann's edition. He marked six passages for comments which he did not provide (*Com.* II. i. 68, V. i. 48, 74–5, 88, 130, and 267). He also failed to make clear his intentions towards four of Theobald's notes with which he disagreed and towards fourteen more which he let stand without comment (see Appendix: Morgann's Treatment of Theobald's Notes). Further, he never supplied the information he undertook to provide concerning Portuguese superstitions about the Bermudas, the method of staging the second scene of *The Tempest*, and the system of magic adopted in the play (see *Com.*, Introduction, I. ii. 1 and 250). Finally, there is the matter of his deletions. Those in the margins, of course, raise no questions. Symmons's explanation suffices; and besides, as Morgann himself observes, all the ideas on the margins (except for *Com.* II. i. 220) are assimilated into the material on the interleaves. But why did he cancel a round two dozen interleaf notes? Twelve (*Com.* I. ii. 118, 146, 269, 373, II. i. 9, 246, 297, ii. 98, 103, 110, 134, and III. iii. 48) are scattered through the manuscript and twelve (*Com.* I. i. 10, 51, 63, ii. 3, 15, 22, 23, 27, 29, 67, 99, and 152) are on the preliminary interleaves, where he systematically lined through every page with writing on it, sparing only his comment on I. i. 1 on PI1. If several of these apparently discredited notes were perhaps rejected as unimportant or inaccurate, the balance seem no less valuable or pertinent than those which bear no stigma of having incurred his displeasure; and the cancelled comment on II. i. 297 is indispensable if the undeleted comments on I. ii. 180, II. i. 296, 306, 317, and III. ii. 124 are to make sense. A plausible explanation is that he intended not to discard most of the cancelled notes but to revise them into a more suitable form.

Before he did so, however, he for some reason set the project aside, never to return to it; and the deleted notes remain unreplaced, further evidence that the manuscript, as it stands, is a book still in process of being worked over, not copy ready for the press.

Yet however inadequate Morgann may have considered his efforts, and however incomplete he left them, if he had published his manuscript in its extant state, he would today be recognized as having made an early major contribution to the study of *The Tempest*. The notes on his Commentary at the end of the volume indicate, item by item, how the views he expresses fit in with contemporary and later opinion. Here it will suffice to summarize his achievement.

1. He not only contended that *The Tempest* is a revised play fifty years before the claim was put forward by anyone else but he worked out the theory on a scale and with a cogency that remained unrivalled till the present century. Anticipating several arguments that have since been advanced on the subject, he also offered others of perhaps equal merit which have not yet been brought forward (see the outline of his arguments in the note on *Com.*, Introduction).

2. In developing his revision theories, as in other comments, he made a number of striking observations on *The Tempest*, some later hit upon independently by a line of critics from Coleridge to Dover Wilson and Kermode, and others to this day not published elsewhere. Particularly noteworthy are (1) his discernment of the contrasting philosophic and spectacular modes combined in the play (see 'Spectacular Effects' in the outline, note on *Com.*, Introduction); (2) his sensitivity to the quality of Prospero's magic—a perception which cuts through both the narrow emphasis upon its Elizabethan origins and the attempt to subdue its effects to psychological realism (*Com.* I. ii. 250); (3) his observation that Miranda is kept wholly innocent of magic and his association of her with Milton's Eve (*Com.* I. ii. 188, 304, and III. i. 48); (4) his original and perceptive explanation of Prospero's 'passion' (*Com.* IV. i. 139–63); (5) his astute comments on the characters of the boatswain, Gonzalo, Trinculo, and Stephano (*Com.* I. i. 10, II. i. 297, and ii. 14); (6) his remark that Prospero's invocation of the elves, etc., seems irrelevant (*Com.* V. i. 33 and I. ii. 250); (7) his penetrating description of the opening of the storm scene as an Induction (*Com.* I. i. 1); and (8) his alert responses to stylistic texture (*Com.* I. ii. 146, 408, and II. i. 246).

3. He suggested three emendations (*Com.* I. ii. 3, 269, and II. i. 243) and a restoration (*Com.* V. i. 236) which, as since proposed by others, have a recognized place in the textual study of *The Tempest*; and he furnished an explanation of a significant piece of stage business which, as advanced by a more recent scholar, has become a permanent part of our understanding of the play (*Com.* I. ii. 23, 67, and 169).

4. He raised two questions of detail, one relating to Elizabethan financial practices (*Com.* III. iii. 48), the other to the scene of the play (*Com.*, Introduction and I. ii. 229), which to this day have not been squarely confronted by Shakespearian critics.

5. Finally, he recorded a view of dramatic time which has implications not just for *The Tempest* but for critical theory in general (*Com.* V. i. 4).

Surprisingly, perhaps, he makes no reference in the Commentary to the principles of interpretation worked out in the *Essay on Falstaff*. In commenting on the characters in *The Tempest* he considers their dramatic effects without ever invoking expressly or implicitly the concept of the whole character. The main overlap between the *Essay* and the Commentary is the view of how Shakespeare represents the supernatural which is common to both (cf. *Es.*, T71n–T77n and *Com.* I. ii. 250), and this is marginal to the system of criticism found in the *Essay*. As does the Commentary as a whole, it supplements rather than complements the impressive thought structure of the *Essay*, on which rests Morgann's claim to be considered a major Shakespearian critic. Yet the Commentary, as we have seen, has more than a touch of its author's characteristic brilliance. It seems fair to conclude that if it had been published towards the end of the eighteenth century, although not entitled to rank with the *Essay* as a significant critical work, it would have sensibly affected subsequent study of *The Tempest*. Not only would Morgann have left his mark on the received text but, far more important, he would have helped to shape the body of opinion which envelops the play and forms part of its meaning. Though there can be no profit in speculating about the success his revision theory might have attained, it is too carefully thought out to suppose that it could have been ignored, or that, unignored, it could have proved anything other than stimulating. As in working out his contention that Falstaff is a man of courage, he accompanies his argument with such a wealth of insight that, whatever the intrinsic merits of his thesis, he provides a remarkable concurrent apprehension of the vital depths of Shakespeare's art. For this reason, even at this late date, when much of what he had to say has since been said by others, his Commentary on *The Tempest* may justly make a claim upon those who are concerned with Shakespeare.

TEXTUAL INTRODUCTION

I. THE *ESSAY ON FALSTAFF*

i. *Previous Editions*

THE *Essay on Falstaff* has appeared in the following editions, of which only the first has authority.

1. AN | ESSAY | ON THE | DRAMATIC CHARACTER | OF | Sir *JOHN FALSTAFF.* | [rule] | I am not *John of Gaunt* your Grandfather, but yet | *no* COWARD, *Hal.* | *First Part of* HENRY IV. | [two rules] | *LONDON*: | PRINTED FOR T. DAVIES, IN RUSSEL-STREET, | COVENT GARDEN. | MDCCLXXVII.

Collation. 8°: π^2, a⁴, B–M⁸, N⁶; pages: [*4*] [1] 2–8, ²[1] 2–185 [186–8]; 28 lines + headline (page numbers) and signature and catchword line, 134 (145)×80 mm.

Contents. π1ʳ half-title (AN | ESSAY | ON | SHAKESPEARE'S *FALSTAFF.*), π1ᵛ blank, π2ʳ title, π2ᵛ blank, a1ʳ–a4ᵛ (pp. [1]–8) Preface, B1ʳ–N5ʳ (pp. [1]–185) text, N5ᵛ (p. [186]) errata (see pp. 132–3, below), N6 blank. $1–4 signed: M4, N3, and N4 unsigned.

Variants. a1 unsigned or signed A. a2 unsigned but with direction number 2. M6ᵛ (p. 172), l. 4, 'Is this' omitted (see last erratum, p. 133, below). N6 lacking.

2. Maurice Morgann, *An Essay on the Dramatic Character of Sir John Falstaff.* London: T. Boys, Ludgate Hill, 1820.

8°: 2 leaves, pp. [iii]–x Preface to the Present Edition, pp. xi–xv The Author's Preface, p. [xvi] blank, pp. [1]–189 text.

The edition silently and painstakingly refurbishes No. 1 for the contemporary reader. The errata and other misprints are corrected, and spelling, capitalization, and italics are consistently normalized according to early nineteenth-century conventions. So too is punctuation: occasional errors are corrected, the various quotation styles in the original are reduced to uniformity, and numerous commas are added. In the same spirit of modernization, supposed solecisms are schoolmastered into propriety, e.g., the subject 'he' is inserted before the predicate 'may have pushed' in PT7:1; and 'nor has his misfortunes' (T22), 'these kind of' (T57), and 'further expressions'

(T67) are corrected, respectively, to 'have', 'kinds', and 'farther'. Other changes: a new paragraph is begun at T69:8; and two critical emendations are introduced into the text—'proof of *impression*' instead of 'proof Impression' in T29:4 and 'attached to' instead of 'attached' in T145:1.

2A. ——, ——. 'New Edition', London: Wheatley and Adelard, 1825.
A reissue of No. 2, with new title-page.

3. Maurice Morgann, 'An Essay on the Dramatic Character of Sir John Falstaff 1777', in *Eighteenth Century Essays on Shakespeare*, ed. D. Nichol Smith. Glasgow: James Maclehose, 1903.
pp. xxxiii, xxxvii–xxxviii, and lxii–lxiii introductory comments on *Essay*; pp. [216]–218 [Author's] Preface, pp. 218–303 text; pp. 347–8 notes to *Essay*.

On the major importance of this edition, see above, p. 27. It retains many features of No. 1: standard eighteenth-century spellings, conventions of capitalization and italicization, the use of quotation marks at the head of lines in which quotations continue, the frequent use of a colon followed by a capital letter to separate main clauses which might stand as independent sentences. However, in addition to correcting the errata and other obvious misprints, the edition also occasionally and unsystematically standardizes variant and deviant spellings and italicizes proper names originally printed in roman. Further, it imposes a single convention for quotations, and alters other punctuation fairly extensively. Of about 250 punctuation changes, approximately 180 consist of commas omitted or added conformably with modern conventions of pointing to bring out seemingly logical features of grammatical structure. Morgann's masterfully articulated sentences seldom require such clarification and seem better served by the original punctuation of No. 1, which often indicates the presence or absence of pauses and particular emphases and intonations which cut across 'logical' grammatical relations: cf. No. 5.

As a note indicates, 'attached' in T145:1 is emended to 'attacked'. A misreading in T56:6—'secretly out of' for 'secretly on'—radically distorts the sense of the passage. Less serious slips are: 'with' omitted after 'both' in T19:1, 'the' omitted before '*degree*' in T59n:2, 'doth' instead of 'do' in T105n:3, 'a' inserted before 'habit' in

T141:2, 'nor' instead of 'or' in T150:2, and 'consists' instead of 'consist' in T161:2, and 'influence of' instead of 'influence and' in T172:5. Other errors: a note claims that in T45:1 No. 1 has 'who' instead of 'which'; on p. lxiii No. 2A is described as a 'third . . . edition'; and on the same page 'the first detailed criticism' of the *Essay* is said to have appeared in 'the *London Review* for February, 1820' (the date should be May 1777: see above, p. 15).

3A. ——, ——, ——, ——. 'Reissued', New York: Russel & Russel, 1962.

The Morgann materials are identical with those in No. 3.

3B. ——, ——, ——, ——. 'Second Edition', revised, Oxford: Clarendon Press, 1963.

pp. xxxii–xxxiii, xxxvi–xxxvii, and lxi–lxii introductory comments on *Essay*; pp. [203]–204 [Author's] Preface, pp. 205–83 text; pp. 331–2 notes to *Essay*.

The following substantive differences from No. 3 occur: the misreading in T56:6 is corrected; the error in the notes about T45:1 is omitted; the first detailed criticism of the *Essay* is now erroneously ascribed, p. lxii, to the *London Magazine* for February 1820, which contained an extended critique (see above, p. 24), but hardly the first; in T90:6 '*Fare ye*' is misprinted '*Far eye*'; in T77n:2 'He' is erroneously italicized; in T29:4 the emendation 'proof of *impression*' is adopted from No. 2. Otherwise No. 3B substantially reproduces No. 3 as described above. The radically revised policy regarding the text which the editor had adopted in No. 5 is not reflected in No. 3B.

4. Maurice Morgann, *An Essay on the Dramatic Character of Sir John Falstaff*, ed. William Arthur Gill. Oxford Library of Prose and Poetry. London: Frowde, 1912.

2 leaves, pp. iii–xvi Introduction, pp. [1]–8 [Author's] Preface, pp. [1]–185 text.

A type facsimile reprint of No. 1: 'follows its original by page and line'; reproduces long s's, signatures, and catchwords; corrects the errata and 'obvious misprints' including a very few punctuation marks and the spelling *Shakespear* in the catchword on T36 and in T125:4; otherwise lets stand all 'harmless irregularities' and even 'doubtful readings' (p. xvi).

5. Maurice Morgann, 'An Essay on the Dramatic Character of Sir John Falstaff. MDCCLXXVII', in *Shakespeare Criticism A Selection*, ed. D. Nichol Smith. World's Classics Series, No. 212. London: Oxford University Press, 1916.

Reprinted eight times; 2nd edition, without substantive changes, 1946, frequently reprinted.

pp. xvi–xvii and xx–xxi introductory comments on *Essay*; pp. 153–5 [Author's] Preface, pp. 155–89 text.

Reproduces 'representative passages' from No. 1, i.e. about one-third of the *Essay*. The omissions, indicated by ellipses on pp. 169, 180, and 185, are T28:2–T57:3, T78:3–T146:1, and T156:1–T175:3. The ellipsis in l. 16, p. 170, is an error for a dash composed of three hyphens in No. 1 (T58n:4): nothing has been omitted.

Except for suppressing quotation marks at the head of every line in which a quotation continues, the text resembles No. 4 in that it follows No. 1 very closely. In contrast to Nos. 3 and 3B, the slips in T19:1, T59n:2, and T150:2 do not occur, and although errata and obvious misprints are corrected, deviant spellings are preserved and the varieties of quotation style are allowed to stand, as is, in the main, the punctuation of No. 1.

6. Maurice Morgann, 'An Essay on the Dramatic Character of Sir John Falstaff', in *The Appreciation of Shakespeare: A Collection of Criticism*, ed. Bernard M. Wagner. Georgetown, 1949.

p. x, introductory comment; pp. 362–409 text.

A word-for-word photographic reproduction of No. 2A, with the pages redisposed and the Preface to the Present Edition omitted.

ii. *The Present Edition*

The copy-text for the present edition is the specimen of the 1777 edition of the *Essay* in the manuscript book containing Morgann's revisions, as described in the next section. The unfinished state of much of the manuscript material makes it impossible to print as a continuous text the revised version which he contemplated. A new edition of the *Essay* is therefore provided in the present volume, with the revisions printed separately and in such a way as to permit their being used as a gloss on the original. The LR are printed immediately after the *Essay*: see next section. The SR appear in the *apparatus criticus* to the *Essay* at their intended points of insertion. They are numbered consecutively and further sub-classified with letters of the alphabet (e.g., SR 7a and 7b) when separate changes are involved in a revision of the same sentence. Those introduced by *fol. by* or *prec. by* are to be added as indicated to the original text. In every instance, the latest version of the SR is reproduced, even if cancelled; and the few ED of critical interest are enclosed within square brackets in the *apparatus criticus* immediately after the word or words in the SR which supersede them. Unless otherwise indicated, an SR or ED is found on the same page in the manuscript book as the passage to which it is related.

The *apparatus criticus* also indicates which passages in the *Essay* are actually or implicitly cancelled and by which LR or SR, if any, they are superseded. It further records all signs and notations on T pages of the manuscript book relating to the insertion of revisions and all implied points of insertion, specifying in each case which revision is involved. The only alterations introduced into the manuscript materials reproduced in the *apparatus criticus* are (1) the italicizing of passages underlined in the original and (2) the emending [within square brackets] of an occasional verbal slip in the manuscript.

To facilitate the correlating of both SR and LR with the original *Essay*, passages in the latter which are to be cancelled are enclosed within angle brackets, points at which insertions are to be made are marked with carets, and the pagination of the copy-text (and thus of the edition of 1777), preceded by the letters PT or T, is entered in square brackets before the first word of every page of the original. For the system of describing the state of manuscript materials and referring to printed and interleaf pages of the manuscript book see List of Abbreviations, Symbols, etc., at the beginning of the present volume.

With regard to the *Essay* of 1777, the object has been an accurate representation of the text which Morgann presumably intended for contemporary readers and for which he composed his revisions. Deviations from the original have accordingly been kept to a minimum. Inconsistencies in the use of capitals and italics are allowed to stand as are the several conventions for quoting which are employed indiscriminately. Other punctuation, except where obviously erroneous, is also kept unchanged, thus preserving the associated suggestions regarding intonation and emphasis (see comment in preceding section under No. 3). While misprints are corrected, all deviant spellings are retained: 'refering' in T7:4, 'gaurded' in T36:1, '*Apalachian*' in T65:3, 'acquital' in T90:5, 'atchievment' in T144:2, and 'Zanys' in T148:4. Also retained are variant spellings, whether normal for the time, as 'unweildy' in T25:1, 'priviledge' in T89:2, and '*Shakespear*' in T125:4, or in varying degrees old-fashioned, as 'prophane' in T92:6 and 'falshoods' in T145:1. '*Shakespear*' occurs again in the catchword on T36, though not in the first word of T37. The spelling in this catchword (the only one of textual interest) and the other variant and deviant spellings are all of them characteristic of Morgann and may show through from the manuscript used by the compositor.

In addition to reproducing the original pagination in square brackets and using angle brackets and carets as mentioned above, the following alterations have been made in the text: the pagination and lineation have been revised, quotation marks have been placed as required before instead of after stops and have been eliminated at the head of lines of continuing quotation, all dashes made up of strung-together hyphens have been normalized, all 'long s's' have been converted into 'short s's', and index letters from 'a' to 'g' have been used for the seven footnotes in the *Essay* in place of the conventional symbols * and † in the original. The only other departures from the copy text are the following corrections of words and punctuation.

1. *Correction of Words*

  (1) The ten errata listed on p. [186] of the *Essay*

location	original reading	correction
T49n:2	Hen. VI.	Henry IV.
T50n:2	Hen. VI.	Henry IV.
T60n:3	Be *this*[1]	Be *thus*
T65:3	*Sciola*	[*Scioto*][2]
T78:3	as far	so far
T84:4	*minching malicho*	*miching malicho*
T105:1[3]	off the sickly[1]	off in the sickly
T108:7	bare[1]	base

[1] Also corrected in Morgann's hand in a presentation copy of the *Essay* of 1777 in the Newberry Library, Chicago. (The title-page is inscribed 'To Mr. —?— from the Author'. The recipient's name has been cut off by the binder.) Apart from the three corrected errata indicated by the present footnote and the corrected erratum recorded below, p. 133 n. 1, the Newberry copy has one other MS. correction in Morgann's hand: see *app. crit.* to *Es.*, PT4:2.

[2] So corrected in the MS. book: the errata list erroneously corrects to '*Sciota*'. For the only other erratum corrected in the MS. book see below, p. 133 n. 1.

[3] The errata list, *Es.*, T186, refers erroneously to T50.

T109:6 into circumstances into circumstance
T172:3 The jovial delightful[1] Is this the jovial delightful

(ii) Six misprints.

location	original reading	correction
T53:3	houses, and and	houses, and
T62n:4	others writers	other writers
T79:2	*bedt-ime*	*bed-time*
T87:1	he his supposed	he is supposed
T120:4	condered	considered
T179:6	*let*	*Let*

2. *Corrected Punctuation*

(i) Eighteen added stops: Cowardice. T16:4; *Mowbray*, T31:5 and T54:2; *Grandfather's*, T51:2; *find'*, T53:6; *here*, T86:6; Coleville, T90:3; *faith*,' T91:2; What, T104:4; *Jack*, T104:6 and T112:4; what, T105:3; indeed, T111:2; Prince, T116:2; *What*, T122:5; discovery; T136:3; principles, T180:3; convenient. T180:3.

(ii) Four altered punctuation marks: contents. [*vice* contents,] T53:5; influence; [*vice* influence,] T60n:3; Hangman, [*vice* Hangman;] T115:1; *Hal*, [*vice Hal*;] T144:2.

(iii) Twenty added quotation marks: *stab'*.—'*Alas* T30:1–2; *slave*,' T30:10; *broke'*, T31:5; Falstaff'. T36:5; '*Faith* T40:2; *night*.'— T40:2; '*Go*,' T40:6; *you?*' T90:2; *deserve*.' '*I would'*, T90:6–7; 'Poins T117:4; '*But* T117:6; '*These* T138:3; *lord*,' T169:1; *speak*,' T169:4; *born'*, T184:3; *shaked'* T184:4.

(iv) Four moved quotation marks: 'Ch. Just. *Well* [*vice* Ch. Just. '*Well*] T37:8; 'Fals. *I* [*vice* Fals. '*I*] T86:1; *I . . . spirit!* [*vice* '*I . . . spirit!*] T92:1; Again . . . 'Hear [*vice* 'Again . . . Hear] T139:4.

II. THE REVISIONS OF THE *ESSAY ON FALSTAFF*

Morgann set down the revisions of his *Essay on Falstaff* in an interleaved copy of the *Essay* of 1777 bound in marbled boards, which is owned today by the Folger Shakespeare Library, Washington, D.C. (Folger MS. S. a. 23). According to Henry C. Folger's records, the manuscript book was obtained from Maggs Bros.,

---

[1] According to the errata list, this mistake is found only 'in a few of the copies'. Both the Newberry copy and the MS. book copy are in this state, and both have Morgann's autograph correction of the error.

London, and put into temporary storage on 13 October 1914, presumably soon after its receipt. Maggs Bros. are unable to trace the provenience of the manuscript,[1] which is not listed in their catalogues.

A bibliographical description of the book in its normal condition, i.e. without interleaves and handwritten annotation, has been given above, p. 127. In the manuscript book a1 is signed A, a2 is unsigned but has the direction number 2, 'Is this' is omitted in l. 4, M6^v, and N6 is lacking. Ninety-one interleaves showing on each side a visible surface of c. 235 × 150 mm. are bound into the manuscript copy, in which the printed pages show a visible surface of c. 230 × 140 mm., with top and bottom margins c. 45 and 50 mm. high, and inner and outer margins c. 25 and 35 mm. wide, respectively. The edges of both the printed leaves and the interleaves are worn, but nowhere to the point of mutilating any writing beyond decipherment. Single interleaves are inserted at every opening from A1^v–A2^r (pp. 2–3 of the Preface) to E3^v–E4^r (pp. 54–5), from F2^v–F3^r (pp. 68–9) to M8^v–N1^r (pp. 176–7), and from N2^v–N3^r (pp. 180–1) to N4^v–N5^r (pp. 184–5); two consecutive interleaves are inserted at the end of the book, after N5. The seven interleaves one would expect to find at the openings from E4^v–E5^r (pp. 56–7) to F1^v–F2^r (pp. 66–7) and at N1^v–N2^r (pp. 178–9) appear to have been removed.

For the pagination of the manuscript book see List of Abbreviations, Symbols, etc., pp. xiii–xiv, above. The two final interleaves inserted after N5 are paginated I186, I187, I188, and I189.

Morgann's revisions cover all the interleaf pages, except as follows: I1 and I79 are blank; I87, I149, I157, and I168 have writing on about one-quarter of their surface, and I30, I50, I78, I99, I121, I159, I169, and I180 on about one-half. A compendious inventory of the contents of the interleaf pages may be compiled by piecing together the partial inventories in the notes to LR 1–2 (I1–150), LR 3 (I51–I78), LR 6 (I78–I86) and LR 11 (I86–I189). For the PI pages see LR 5 and 6a. The copious annotation overflows from the interleaves to the margins of the printed text on thirty pages: PT3–PT6, PT8, T15, T16, T38, T41, T42, T52, T53, T62, T74, T81, T88–T92, T108, T109, T111, T112, T120, T124, T126, T164, T185, T186. In addition, Morgann emends his printed text or marks it for emendation on forty-one pages: PT4, T4–T6, T10, T29–T31, T33, T48, T63, T65, T70, T73, T94, T98, T104, T122–

---

[1] Letter to the editor from Maggs Bros., Ltd., dated 11 June 1959.

T124, T128, T129, T130, T133, T141, T142, T146, T154, T156–T159, T161, T167, T169–T174, T176.

The annotated pages are on the whole as full of cancellations as the most exacting advocate of *limae labor* could desire. The present edition reproduces (1) all the uncancelled manuscript materials, except for a few passages which, as recorded in the notes, are repeated almost verbatim in later drafts, and (2) all the cancelled materials which are of any critical interest. The SR occur in the main in a single version only and for this reason as well as because of their relative brevity are reproduced, as explained in the preceding section, in the *apparatus criticus* to the *Essay*. The fourteen LR, which are collected with their ED immediately after the *Essay*, are so placed not only because of their relative length but also in order to exhibit properly the significant elements in the extensive re-working which they have often undergone.

The latest version of each LR even if cancelled in part or in whole is reproduced as the main text, disengaged from whatever ED or other extraneous materials or markings it may be interlined or intermingled with in the manuscript. Also reproduced with such materials and markings blanked out are (1) all signs and notations on I and T pages which indicate links between revision drafts or between them and the printed *Essay*; (2) most ED which should have been but are not cancelled (the few omissions are mentioned in the notes); and (3) all ED which even though cancelled seem in some way significant for tracing the development of Morgann's thought. The signs and notations are recorded with explanations of their significance in the *apparatus criticus*. The ED if extended are printed just after the relevant main text with an *apparatus criticus* of their own; if brief they are recorded in the *apparatus criticus* to the main text or the extended ED.

To present the LR materials intelligibly I have had first to sort out the various layers of composition and their links with the printed *Essay*, to piece together on each level separated passages which were intended to be continuous, and in this way to establish the several drafts of the revisions as well as the inner stratification of revisal in each draft. Though this reconstruction rests wherever possible on Morgann's signs and notations in the manuscript, as recorded in the *apparatus criticus*, it depends far more often on editorial inferences from the state of the manuscript. Where such inferences are complex, they are discussed in the notes, but where, as is more frequently the case, they seem uninvolved, I have silently used them as the basis for establishing the main text, its ED, and the relations between them and the printed text. For instance, only the results are normally given of the numerous investigations I have had to make of the order and texts of successive, intermingled, and at times imperfectly cancelled versions of parts of sentences.

For the symbols used to represent the state of and relations between manuscript materials see List, p. xiv, above. Where necessary, they are supplemented in the *apparatus criticus* and the notes. The *apparatus criticus* indicates relations between drafts by a set of conventions which depend on the fact that every passage transcribed in the *apparatus criticus* from the manuscript has its base text. The base text is determined as follows:

(i) For all passages, except those described in (ii) and (iii) below, the base text is the lemma.

(ii) If the passage is the second or third in a series of ED introduced by the heading *2ED* or *3ED*, the base text is the preceding ED. Such ED series are transcribed in inverse order of composition and are separated from one another by a diagonal stroke (/).

(iii) If the passage is enclosed within square brackets, the base text is one of the following:

    (*a*) normally, the word just before the brackets; or

    (*b*) if the passage is marked *ED* and its first word is marked (R), the entire preceding passage from the word(s) retained up to and including the word just before the brackets; or

    (*c*) if the passage is the second or third in a series of ED, as in (ii) above, the preceding ED.

A passage is related to its base text according to the following conventions:

1. Unless otherwise indicated, a passage is in the same state as its base text and is on the same page in the manuscript book.

2. A passage designated as an ED has been superseded by its base text.

3. A passage or part thereof marked (C) has been cancelled before the implicit or actual cancellation, if any, of its base text.

4. A passage or part thereof marked (UM) is in the same state as its base text or as any part of it marked (UM) and should have been cancelled on being superseded or rejected.

5. A passage marked (U) should have been cancelled later, along with the cancellation of its base text.

6. A passage introduced by *fol. by* or by *prec. by* forms no organic part of its base text or is intended to be deleted therefrom. Where appropriate, a passage so introduced is further designated *false start* or *afterthought*.

In the matter of style, my object has been, with due concern for readability, to use typography to represent the revisions in their manuscript state rather than to give them the normal outward appearance of pages in a printed book. Accordingly, the forms of words have not been tampered with: Morgann's abbreviations have not been expanded; his deviant and variant spellings, including occasional proper names beginning with minuscules, have been allowed to stand; and his inconsistent use of capital letters, some-times serving no apparent purpose and sometimes presumably intended for emphasis or for grouping items in series, has been scrupulously reproduced, though this has at times meant silently implementing a somewhat arbitrary editorial decision as to whether a given initial letter is majuscule or minuscule. In the interests of readability, however, apart of course from the stringent regularizing of letter size and form inherent in typographical transcription, I have admitted the following modifications of the original texts: (1) All materials underlined once in the manuscript are italicized in the transcript. (2) Verbal slips are emended within square brackets; where anything other than a pure editorial addition is involved, the actual manuscript reading or the manuscript source of the emendation, if any, is given in the *apparatus criticus*. (3) Minimal punctuation has been introduced where needed to forestall possible unintelligibility, viz., chiefly at the ends of sentences. To the same end, the punctuation of the original has occasionally been changed. The haphazard and scarce punctuation in the manuscript is recorded at the head of the *apparatus criticus* to each LR and extended ED; all additional or different punctuation is editorial.

Shakespeare quotations supplied by the editor are taken from Johns. 1785, the edition Morgann used (see above, p. 39; cf. pp. 118–19).

III. THE COMMENTARY ON *THE TEMPEST*

The manuscript book containing Morgann's Commentary on *The Tempest* is a specially interleaved and re-bound first half of a copy of

volume i of Theobald's *Works of Shakespeare* (1733). It was at one
time owned by Edward Dowden and is now held at the Folger
Shakespeare Library, Washington, D.C. (call-number: PR 2752
1733 c. 9 v. 1 Shakespeare Collection). So far as I know, the manuscript book is all that survives of the original seven-volume set of
Theobald's Shakespeare from which it came.

Before being altered for interleaving, the volume was presumably
identical with other copies of the same edition, as follows:

Title-page. THE | WORKS | OF | SHAKESPEARE | IN |
SEVEN VOLUMES. | [rule] | Collated with the Oldest Copies, and
Corrected; | With NOTES, Explanatory, and Critical: | By Mr.
THEOBALD. | [rule] | *I, Decus, i, nostrum: melioribus utere Fatis.*
Virg. | [rule] | *LONDON:* | Printed for A. BETTESWORTH and C.
HITCH, | J. TONSON, F. CLAY, W. FEALES, | and R. WELLINGTON. |
[rule] | MDCCXXXIII.

Collation. 8°: (engr. +) π^2, A^8, a–e^8, B–2H^8, 2I^6; pages:
(engr. +) [*14*] [i] ii–lxviii [*18*] [1–3] 4–75 [76–9] 80–149 [150–3]
154–219 [220–3] 224–308 [309–311] 312–99 [400–3] 404–87 [488];
40 lines + headline and signature and catchword line, 167
(177)×93 mm.

Contents. (Engr. facing $\pi 1^r$ bust of Shakespeare 'B. Arlaud del.'
'G Duchange scul.'), $\pi 1^r$ title-page, $\pi 1^v$ blank, $\pi 2^r$ title-page for
Volume the First. Containing, The TEMPEST. The MIDSUMMER-
NIGHT'S DREAM. The TWO GENTLEMEN of VERONA. MERRY WIVES of
WINDSOR. MEASURE for MEASURE. MUCH ADO about NOTHING.,
$\pi 2^v$ blank, A1^r–A5^r dedication to Orrery, A5^v blank, A6^r–d7^v
(pp. [i]–lxviii) Preface, d8^r–e2^r (unpaginated) Milton's Epitaph,
Davenant's Ode, Jonson's 'On the Effigies', Jonson's 'To the Memory
of . . . Shakespeare', e2^v–e8^v (unpaginated) Names of the Subscribers,
B1^r (p. [1]) title-page for *The Tempest*, B1^v (p. [2]) Dramatis
Personae, B2^r–F6^v (pp. [3]–[76]) text, F7^r (p. [77]) title-page for
Midsummer Night's Dream, F7^v (p. [78]) Dramatis Personae,
F8^r–L3^r (pp. [79]–149) text, L3^v (p. [150]) blank, L4^r (p. [151])
title-page for *Two Gentlemen of Verona*, L4^v (p. [152]) Dramatis
Personae, L5^r–P6^r (pp. [153]–219) text, P6^v (p. [220]) blank, P7^r
(p. [221]) title-page for *Merry Wives of Windsor*, P7^v (p. [222])
Dramatis Personae, P8^r–X2^v (pp. [223]–308) text, X3^r (p. [309])
title-page for *Measure for Measure*, X3^v (p. [310]) Dramatis Personae, X4^r–2C8^r (pp. [311]–399) text, 2C8^v (p. [400]) blank, 2D1^r
(p. [401]) title-page for *Much Ado About Nothing*, 2D1^v (p. 402])

Dramatis Personae, 2D2ʳ–2I4ʳ (pp. [403]–487 text, 2I4ᵛ–2I6ᵛ (pp. [488–492]) blank. $1–4 signed.

The manuscript book lacks the engraving facing π1ʳ and P7–2I6 (pp. [221]–[492]). The resultant half-volume has, however, been restored to approximately its original bulk by the insertion of (1) six consecutive preliminary interleaves at the opening between e8ᵛ and B1ʳ; (2) a single interleaf at every opening from B1ᵛ–B2ʳ to P5ᵛ–P6ʳ; and (3) two final interleaves after P6ᵛ. All the pages in the book, interleaf and printed, have been cut by the binder to the same visible surface size: 118 mm.×194 mm. On the printed pages, the top margins above the headlines are *c.* 5 mm., and the bottom, inner, and outer margins are *c.* 15 mm., *c.* 9 mm., and *c.* 16 mm., respectively.

Morgann marked the six consecutive interleaves between e8ᵛ and B1ʳ in their upper outer corners as pages 1 to 12 and then went on to number the fourteen following interleaf pages, beginning with the one facing B1ᵛ, from 13 to 26, at which point he abandoned the system. In the present volume, the manuscript book is paginated as indicated in the List of Abbreviations, Symbols, etc., pp. xiii–xiv, above.

The Commentary on *The Tempest* occupies eighty-five interleaf pages, as follows: (1) PI1–PI10; (2) sixty-three of the seventy-five pages interleaved in the text of *The Tempest*: I2–I31, I33–I39, I41–I47, I49–I57, I60, I63–I66, I69–I73; and (3) twelve pages interleaved in the text of *Two Gentlemen of Verona*: I154–I165. Manuscript materials pertaining to the Commentary also occur on sixty-five of the seventy-five pages on which *The Tempest* is printed: T2–T26, T29–T31, T33–T39, T41–T47, T49–T55, T59–T66, T68–T75. Thirty-four of these pages have both marginal annotation and cross-references. Of the remainder, nine have annotation only: T2, T4, T22, T24, T30, T59, T61, T62, T75; and twenty-two have cross-references only: T10, T18, T23, T26, T29, T31, T34, T36, T37, T38, T41, T42, T43, T45, T47, T49, T52, T54, T64, T68, T69, T70. A few manuscript notes on *Midsummer Night's Dream* are found on fourteen T pages and on one I page: T79–T86, T93, T131, T132, I132, T138, T139, T148. An observation on *Two Gentlemen of Verona* occurs on T153–T155. The words 'Edward Dowden Library' have been rubber-stamped near the upper edge of the side of the binder's leaf facing π1ʳ. A jotting by Dowden beneath the rubber stamp imprint and John Symmons's inscription of his name on the title-page for the set (see above,

p. 116) complete the account of the pages bearing handwritten material. All other pages in the manuscript book, whether interleaf or printed, are devoid of manuscript annotation.

The present edition reproduces Morgann's Commentary without the Theobald text of the play, which was intended to accompany it. However, each of Morgann's comments and, where necessary, early marginal notes is preceded by the relevant passage from Theobald's text, with 'long s's' changed to 'short s's', misprints corrected, and speech headings given in square brackets wherever the speech is not reproduced beginning with its first line. The act, scene, and line numbers are those of the Globe edition. Theobald's text is excerpted on the same principles as required for the few comments on *Midsummer Night's Dream* which, along with the introductory comment on *Two Gentlemen of Verona*, are reproduced in the section of Miscellaneous Comments following the Commentary.

Except for a few cancelled ED which are in themselves of no significance or are repeated almost verbatim in later drafts, all manuscript materials in the book have been reproduced either in the Critical Introduction or in the sections devoted to the Commentary and the Miscellaneous Comments. The latest version of every comment, even if cancelled, is reproduced as the main text. A few more extended ED are transcribed after the main text; briefer ED are reproduced in the *apparatus criticus*. The early marginal notes on T pages are reproduced immediately below the later written comments, or, when no specifically replacing comment exists, beneath the relevant passage excerpted from Theobald's text.

In addition to recording briefer ED, the *apparatus criticus* also reproduces all symbols and notations by which Morgann marks cross-references between a comment or marginal note and a passage in *The Tempest*. For the symbols describing the state of the manuscript materials see list, p. xiv, above. In the *apparatus criticus*, the same set of conventions regarding base texts apply as in the *apparatus criticus* to the *Essay on Falstaff*: see above, pp. 136–7. With one addition and one exception, the stylistic principles adopted in transcribing the revisions of the *Essay* (above, p. 137) also apply to the Commentary on *The Tempest*. The addition is that materials underlined twice are printed in small capitals. The exception is that the punctuation of the manuscript is normally transcribed without change and when supplied or altered is treated exactly as if it were a verbal slip emended by the editor.

AN ESSAY ON
THE DRAMATIC CHARACTER OF
SIR JOHN FALSTAFF
(1777)

With the Author's MS. Corrections
(*c.* 1789–90)
Comprising Cancellations, Shorter Revisions,
and Cross-References to Longer Revisions

AN ESSAY ON
THE DRAMATIC CHARACTER OF
SIR JOHN FALSTAFF

(With Shorter Revisions, etc.)

[PT1] PREFACE.

THE following sheets were written in consequence of a friendly conversation, turning by some chance upon the Character of FALSTAFF, wherein the Writer, maintaining contrary to the general Opinion, that, this Character was not intended to be shewn as a Coward, he was challenged to deliver and support that Opinion from the Press, with an engagement, now he fears forgotten, for it was ⟨three⟩ years ago, that he should be answered thro' the [PT2] same channel: Thus stimulated, these papers were almost wholly written in a very short time, but not without those attentions, whether successful or not, which seemed necessary to carry them beyond the Press into the hands of the Public. From the influence of the foregoing circumstances it is, that the Writer has generally assumed rather the character and tone of an Advocate than of an Inquirer;—though if he had not first *inquired* and been *convinced*, he should never have attempted to [PT3] have amused either himself or others with the subject.—The impulse of the occasion, however, being passed, the papers were thrown by, and almost forgotten: But having been looked into ⟨of late⟩ by some friends, who‿ observing that the Writer had not enlarged so far for the sake of FALSTAFF alone, but that the Argument was made subservient

ESSAY ON FALSTAFF. Text of *Es.* in MS. book: for emendations, see Textual Intro. to *Es.* The *app. crit.* records the revised state of the *Es.* projected in the MS. book, as follows: (1) all SR (they are numbered serially [in square brackets] and unless otherwise indicated are on the same T page as the part of *Es.* to which they refer): (2) indications of all insertions and cancellations in *Es.* marked or implied in the MS. book; (3) all handwritten symbols and notations on T pages in the MS. book indicating links and insertions. For (2) and (3), cross-references to LR are supplied as required.

For further details see Textual Intro. to Revisions of *Es.* For abbreviations and symbols used in the text and the *app. crit.* see pp. xiii–xiv.

Preface. PT1:1 three] *presumably to be modified: see note to PT1–PT9*

PT3:2 of late] *presumably to be modified: see note to PT1–PT9*   who] who, [SR 1]

to Critical amusement, persuaded him to revise and convey it to the Press. This has been accordingly done, ⟨though he fears something too hastily, as he found it proper [PT4] to add, while the papers were in the course of printing, some considerations on the *Whole* Character of FALSTAFF; which ought to have been accompanied by a slight reform of a few preceding passages, which may seem, in consequence of this addition, to contain too favourable a representation of his Morals.⟩

The vindication of FALSTAFF's Courage is truly no otherwise the object than, some old fantastic Oak, or grotesque Rock, may be the object of a morning's ride;, yet [PT5] being proposed as such, may serve to limit the distance, and shape the course: The real object is Exercise, and the Delight which a rich, beautiful, picturesque, and perhaps unknown Country, may excite from every side. Such an Exercise may admit of some little excursion, keeping however the Road in view; but seems to exclude every appearance of labour and of toil.—Under the impression of such Feelings, the Writer has endeavoured to preserve to his Text a certain lightness of air, and chear-[PT6]fulness of tone; ⟨but is sensible however that the manner of discussion does not *every where*, particularly near the commencement, sufficiently correspond with his design.—If the Book shall be fortunate enough to obtain another Impression, a separation may be made; and such of the heavier parts as cannot be wholly dispensed with, sink to their more proper station,—a Note.

He is fearful likewise that he may have erred in the other extreme; and that having thought [PT7] himself intitled, even in argument, to a certain degree of playful discussion, may have pushed it, in a few places, even to levity. This error might be yet more easily reformed than the other.⟩—The Book is perhaps, as it stands, too bulky for the subject; but if the Reader knew how many pressing considerations, as it grew into size, the Author resisted, which yet seemed intitled to be heard, he would the more readily excuse him.

The whole is a mere Experiment, and the Writer considers it as such: [PT8] It may have the advantages, but it is likewise attended with all the difficulties and dangers, of *Novelty*.

PT3:3–PT4:1 though he . . . his Morals] *presumably to be cancelled: see note to PT1–PT9*

PT4:2 than] *fol. by* as (*same revision in Newberrry copy*) [SR 2a]   ride;] *fol. by* which [SR 2b]

PT6:1–PT7:2 but is . . . the other.] *presumably to be cancelled: see note to PT1–PT9*

[T1] ON THE DRAMATIC CHARACTER OF SIR *JOHN FALSTAFF*.

THE ideas which I have formed concerning the Courage and Military Character of the Dramatic Sir *John Falstaff*, are so different from those which I find generally to prevail in the world, that I shall take the liberty of stating my sentiments on the subject; in hope that some person as unengaged as myself, will either correct and reform my error in this respect; or, joining himself to my opinion, redeem me from, what I may call, the reproach of singularity.

[T2] I am to avow then, that I do not clearly discern that Sir *John Falstaff* deserves to bear the character so generally given him of an absolute Coward; or, in other words, that I do not conceive *Shakespeare* ever meant to make Cowardice an essential part of his constitution.

I know how universally the contrary opinion prevails; and I know what respect and deference are due to the public voice. But if to the avowal of this singularity, I add all the reasons that have led me to it, and acknowledge myself to be wholly in the judgment of the public, I shall hope to avoid the censure of too much forwardness or indecorum.

It must, in the first place, be admitted that the appearances in this case are singularly strong and striking; and so they had need be, to become the ground of so general a censure. We see this extraordinary Character, almost in the first moment of our acquaintance with him, involved in cir-[T3]cumstances of apparent dishonour; and we hear him familiarly called *Coward* by his most intimate companions. We see him, on occasion of the robbery at *Gads-Hill*, in the very act of running away from the Prince and *Poins*; and we behold him, on another of more honourable obligation, in open day light, in battle, and acting in his profession as a Soldier, escaping from *Douglas* even out of the world as it were; counterfeiting death, and deserting his very existence; and we find him on the former occasion, betrayed into those *lies* and *braggadocioes*, which are the usual concomitants of Cowardice in Military men, and pretenders to valour. These are not only in themselves strong circumstances, but they are moreover thrust forward, prest upon our notice as the subject of our mirth, as the great business of the scene: No wonder, therefore, that the word should go forth that *Falstaff* is exhibited as a character of Cowardice and dishonour.

What there is to the contrary of this, it is my business to discover. Much, I think, will presently [T4] appear; but it lies so dispersed, is so latent, and so purposely obscured, that the reader must have some patience whilst I collect it into one body, and make it the object of a steady and regular contemplation.

But what have we to do, may my readers exclaim, with principles *so latent, so obscured?* In Dramatic composition the *Impression* is the *Fact*; and the Writer, who, meaning to impress one thing, has impressed another, is unworthy of observation.

It is a very unpleasant thing to have, in the first setting out, so many and so strong prejudices to contend with. All that one can do in such case, is, to pray the reader to have a little patience in the commencement; and to reserve his censure, if it must pass, for the conclusion. Under his gracious allowance, therefore, I presume to declare it, as my opinion, that Cowardice *is not* the *Impression*, which the ⟨*whole*⟩ character of *Falstaff* [T5] is calculated to make on the minds of an unprejudiced audience; tho' there be, I confess, a great deal of something in the *composition* likely enough to puzzle, and consequently to mislead the Understanding. ⟨—The reader will perceive that I distinguish between *mental Impressions*, and the *Understanding*.—I wish to avoid every thing that looks like subtlety and refinement; but this is a distinction, which we all comprehend.— There are none of us unconscious of certain feelings or sensations of mind, which do not seem to have passed thro' the Understanding;⟩ the effects, I suppose, of some secret influences from without, acting upon a certain mental sense, and producing feelings and passions in just correspondence to the force and variety of those influences on the one hand, and to the quickness of our sensibility on the other. ⟨Be the cause, however, what it may, the fact is undoubtedly so; which is all I am concerned in. And it is equally a fact, which every man's experience may avouch, that the Understanding and those feelings are frequently [T6] at variance. The latter often arise from the most minute circumstances, and frequently from such as the Understanding cannot estimate, or even recognize;

Essay. T4:3–4 observation. It] *notation between pars.*: (C) See 2 Manu[script] *superseded by notation at T5:2*

T4:6 *whole] probably requires reformulation: see Intro., pp. 87–8*

T5:2 The reader] X *above letters* he *in* The *and* See 2 Man[uscript] *in outer margin =* link with LR 1a

T5:2–T6: 2 The reader . . . particular case] *superseded by LR 1a and LR 1b, except for T5:4b, which concludes LR 1a*

whereas the Understanding delights in abstraction, and in general propositions; which, however true considered as such, are very seldom, I had like to have said *never*, perfectly applicable to any particular case.⟩⟨And hence, among other causes, it is, that we often condemn or applaud characters and actions on the credit of some logical process, while our hearts revolt, and would fain lead us to a very different conclusion.⟩

⟨The Understanding seems for the most part to take cognizance of *actions* only, and from these to infer *motives* and *character*; but the sense we have been speaking of proceeds in a contrary course; and determines of *actions* from certain *first principles of character*, which seem wholly out of the reach of the Understanding. We cannot indeed do otherwise than admit that there must⟩ [T7] ⟨be distinct principles of character in every distinct individual: The manifest variety even in the minds of infants will oblige us to this. But what *are* these first principles of character? Not the objects, I am persuaded, of the Understanding; and yet we take as strong Impressions of them as if we could compare and assort them in a syllogism. We often love or hate at first sight; and indeed, in general, dislike or approve by some secret reference to these *principles*; and we judge even of conduct, not from any idea of abstract good or evil in the nature of actions, but by refering those actions to a supposed original character in the man himself. I do not mean that we *talk* thus; we could not indeed, if we would, explain ourselves in detail on this head; we can neither account for Impressions and passions, nor communicate them to others by *words*: Tones and looks will sometimes convey the *passion* strangely, but the *Impression* is incommunicable. The same causes may produce it indeed at the same time in many, but it is the separate possession of [T8] each, and not in its nature transferable: It is an imperfect sort of instinct, and proportionably dumb.—We might indeed, if we chose it, candidly confess to one another, that we are greatly swayed by these feelings, and are by no means so *rational* in all points as we could wish; but this would be a betraying of the interests of that high

T6:3 And hence . . . different conclusion.] *cancellation implied by LR 3: see Intro.*, *p. 75*   different conclusion] *fol. by* X = *link with LR 2 (earlier with LR 2–ED 1; see notes, pp. 384–5)*

T6:4–5 The Understanding . . . there must] *cancelled*

T6:4–T22:5 The Understanding . . . *constitutional coward?*] *superseded by LR 2 and LR 3*

L

faculty, the Understanding, which we so value ourselves upon, and which we more peculiarly call our own. This, we think, must not be; and so we huddle up the matter, concealing it as much as possible, both from ourselves and others. In Books indeed, wherein character, motive, and action, are all alike subjected to the Understanding, it is generally a very clear case; and we make decisions compounded of them all: And thus we are willing to approve of *Candide*, tho' he kills m͵ Lord the Inquisitor, and runs thro' the body the Baron of *Thunder-ten-tronchk*, the son of his patron, and the brother of his beloved *Cunégonde*: But in real life, I believe, *my Lords the Judges* would be apt to inform the [T9] *Gentlemen of the Jury*, that my *Lord the Inquisitor* was *ill killed*; as *Candide* did not proceed on the urgency of the moment, but on the speculation only of future evil. And indeed this clear perception, in Novels and Plays, of the union of character and action not seen in nature, is the principal defect of such compositions, and what renders them but ill pictures of human life, and wretched guides of conduct.

But if there was *one man* in the world, who could make a more perfect draught of real nature, and steal such Impressions on his audience, without their special notice, as should keep their hold in spite of any error of their Understanding, and should thereupon venture to introduce an apparent incongruity of character and action, for ends which I shall presently endeavour to explain; such an imitation would be worth our nicest curiosity and attention. But in such a case as this, the reader might expect that he should find us all talking the language of the Under-[T10]standing only; that is, censuring the action with very little conscientious investigation even of *that*; and transferring the censure, in every odious colour, to the actor himself; how much soever our hearts and affections might secretly revolt: For as to the *Impression*, we have already observed that it has no tongue; nor is its operation and influence likely to be made the subject of conference and communication.

It is not to the *Courage* only of *Falstaff* that ⟨we⟩ think these observations will apply: No part whatever of his character seems to be fully settled in our minds; at least there is something strangely incongruous in our discourse and affections concerning him. We all like *Old Jack*; yet, by some strange perverse fate, we all abuse him, and deny him the possession of any one single good or respectable quality. There is something extraordinary in this: It must be a

T10:2 we] *cancelled; superseded by* I [SR 3] *see notes, p. 385* strange art in *Shakespeare* which can draw our liking and good will towards so offensive an object. He has wit, it will be said; chearfulness and humour of the most characteristic and captivating [T11] sort. And is this enough? Is the humour and gaiety of vice so very captivating? Is the wit, characteristic of baseness and every ill quality capable of attaching the heart and winning the affections? Or does not the apparency of such humour, and the flashes of such wit, by more strongly disclosing the deformity of character, but the more effectually excite our hatred and contempt of the man? And yet this is not our *feeling* of *Falstaff*'s character. When he has ceased to amuse us, we find no emotions of disgust; we can scarcely forgive the ingratitude of the Prince in the new-born virtue of the King, and we curse the severity of that poetic justice which consigns our old good-natured delightful companion to the custody of the *warden*, and the dishonours of the *Fleet*.

I am willing, however, to admit that if a Dramatic writer will but preserve to any character the qualities of a strong mind, particularly Courage and ability, that it will be afterwards no very difficult task (as I may have occasion to ex-[T12]plain) to discharge that *disgust* which arises from vicious manners; and even to attach us (if such character should contain any quality productive of chearfulness and laughter) to the cause and subject of our mirth with some degree of affection.

But the question which I am to consider is of a very different nature: It is a question of fact, and concerning a quality which forms the basis of every respectable character; a quality which is the very essence of a Military man; and which is held up to us, in almost every Comic incident of the Play, as the subject of our observation. It is strange then that it should now be a question, whether *Falstaff* is, or is not a man of Courage; and whether we do in fact contemn him for the want, or respect him for the possession of that quality: And yet I believe the reader will find that he has by no means decided this question, even for himself.—If then it should turn out, that this difficulty has arisen out of the Art of [T13] *Shakespeare*, who has contrived to make secret Impressions upon us of Courage, and to preserve those Impressions in favour of a character which was to be held up for sport and laughter on account of actions of apparent Cowardice and dishonour, we shall have less occasion to wonder, as *Shakespeare* is a Name which contains All of Dramatic artifice and genius.

If in this place the reader shall peevishly and prematurely object that the observations and distinctions I have laboured to establish, are wholly unapplicable; he being himself unconscious of ever having received any such Impression; what can be done in so nice a case, but to refer him to the following pages; by the number of which he may judge how very much I respect his objection, and by the variety of those proofs, which I shall employ to induce him to part with it; and to recognize in its stead certain feelings, concealed and covered over perhaps, but not erazed, by time, reasoning, and authority.

[T14] In the mean while, it may not perhaps be easy for him to resolve how it comes about, that, whilst we look upon *Falstaff* as a character of the like nature with that of *Parolles* or of *Bobadil*, we should preserve for him a great degree of respect and good-will, and yet feel the highest disdain and contempt of the others, tho' they are all involved in similar situations. The reader, I believe, would wonder extremely to find either *Parolles* or *Bobadil* possess himself in danger: What then can be the cause that we are not at all sur-prized at the gaiety and ease of *Falstaff* under the most trying circum-stances; and that we never think of charging *Shakespeare* with departing, on this account, from the truth and coherence of charac-ter? Perhaps, after all, the *real* character of *Falstaff* may be different from his *apparent* one; and possibly this difference between reality and appearance, whilst it accounts at once for our liking and our censure, may be the true point of humour in the character, and the source of all our laughter and delight. We [T15] may chance to find, if we will but examine a little into the nature of those circumstances which have accidentally involved him, that he was intended to be drawn as a character of much Natural courage and resolution; and be obliged thereupon to repeal those decisions, which may have been made upon the credit of some general tho' unapplicable propositions; the common source of error in other and higher matters. A little reflection may perhaps bring us round again to the point of our departure, and unite our Understandings to our instinct.—Let us then for a moment *suspend* at least our decisions, and candidly and coolly inquire if Sir *John Falstaff* be, indeed, what he has so often been called by critic and commentator, male and female,—a *Constitutional Coward.*

It will scarcely be possible to consider the Courage of *Falstaff* as wholly detached from his other qualities: But I write not professedly of any part of his character, but what is included under the [T16] term, *Courage*; however I may incidentally throw some lights on the whole.—The reader will not need to be told that this Inquiry will resolve itself of course into a Critique on the genius, the arts, and the conduct of *Shakespeare*: For what is *Falstaff*, what *Lear*, what *Hamlet*, or *Othello*, but different modifications of *Shakespeare*'s thought? It is true that this Inquiry is narrowed almost to a single point: But general criticism is as uninstructive as it is easy: *Shakespeare* deserves to be considered in detail;—a task hitherto unattempted.

It may be proper, in the first place, to take a short view of all the parts of *Falstaff*'s Character, and then proceed to discover, if we can, what *Impressions*, as to Courage or Cowardice, he had made on the persons of the Drama: After which we will examine, in course, such evidence, either of *persons* or *facts*, as are relative to the matter; and account as we may for those appearances, which seem to have led to the opinion of his Constitutional Cowardice.

[T17] The scene of the robbery, and the disgraces attending it, which stand first in the Play, and introduce us to the knowledge of *Falstaff*, I shall beg leave (as I think this scene to have been the source of much unreasonable prejudice) to *reserve* till we are more fully acquainted with the whole character of *Falstaff*; and I shall therefore hope that the reader will not for a time advert to it, or to the jests of the *Prince* or of *Poins* in consequence of that unlucky adventure.

In drawing out the parts of *Falstaff*'s character, with which I shall begin this Inquiry, I shall take the liberty of putting Constitutional bravery into his composition; but the reader will be pleased to consider what I shall say in that respect as spoken hypothetically for the present, to be retained, or discharged out of it, as he shall finally determine.

To me then it appears that the leading quality in *Falstaff*'s character, and that from which all the rest take their colour, is a high degree of wit [T18] and humour, accompanied with great natural vigour and alacrity of mind. This quality so accompanied, led him probably very early into life, and made him highly acceptable to society; so acceptable, as to make it seem unnecessary for him to acquire any other virtue. Hence, perhaps, his continued debaucheries and dissipations of every kind.—He seems, by nature, to have had a mind free of malice or any evil principle; but he never took the trouble of acquiring any good one. He found himself esteemed and beloved with all his faults; nay *for* his faults, which were all connected with humour, and for the most part, grew out of it. As he had, possibly, no vices but such as he thought might be openly professed, so he appeared more dissolute thro' ostentation. To the character of wit and humour, to which all his other qualities seem to have conformed themselves, he appears to have added a very necessary support, *that* of the profession of a *Soldier*. He had from nature, as I presume to say, a spirit of boldness and enterprise; which in a Military [T19] age, tho' employment was only occasional, kept him always above contempt, secured him an honourable reception among the Great, and suited best both with his particular mode of humour and of vice. Thus living continually in society, nay even in Taverns, and indulging himself, and being indulged by others, in every debauchery; drinking, whoring, gluttony, and ease; assuming a liberty of fiction, necessary perhaps to his wit, and often falling into falsity and lies, he seems to have set, by degrees, all sober reputation at defiance; and finding eternal resources in his wit, he borrows, shifts, defrauds, and even robs, without dishonour. —Laughter and approbation attend his greatest excesses; and being governed visibly by no settled bad principle or ill design, fun and humour account for and cover all. By degrees, however, and thro' indulgence, he acquires bad habits, becomes an humourist, grows enormously corpulent, and falls into the infirmities of age; yet never quits, all the time, one single levity or vice of youth, or loses any of that chearfulness of [T20] mind, which had enabled him to pass thro' this course with ease to himself and delight to others; and thus, at last, mixing youth and age, enterprize and corpulency, wit and folly, poverty and expence, title and buffoonery, innocence as to purpose, and wickedness as to practice; neither incurring hatred by bad principle, or contempt by Cowardice, yet involved in circumstances productive of imputation in both; a butt and a wit, a humourist and a man of humour, a touchstone and a laughing stock, a jester and a jest, has Sir *John Falstaff*, taken at that period of his life in which we see him, become the most perfect Comic character that perhaps ever was exhibited.

It may not possibly be wholly amiss to remark in this place, that if Sir *John Falstaff* had possessed any of that Cardinal quality, Prudence, alike the guardian of virtue and the protector of vice; that quality, from the possession or the absence of which, the character and fate of men in this life take, I think, their colour, and not from real vice or virtue; if he had considered his wit not as *principal* but *accessary* only; as the instrument of [T21] power, and not as power itself; if he had had much baseness to hide, if he had had less of what may be called mellowness or good humour, or less of health and spirit; if he had spurred and rode the world with his wit, instead of suffering the world, boys and all, to ride him;—he might, without any other essential change, have been the admiration and not the jest of mankind:—Or if he had lived in our day, and instead of attaching himself to one Prince, had renounced *all* friendship and *all* attachment, and had let himself out as the ready instrument and Zany of every successive Minister, he might possibly have acquired the high honour of marking his shroud or decorating his coffin with the living rays of an Irish at least, if not a British Coronet: Instead of which, tho' enforcing laughter from every disposition, he appears, now, as such a character which every wise man will pity and avoid, every knave will censure, and every fool will fear: And accordingly *Shakespeare*, ever true to nature, has made *Harry* desert, and Lancaster censure him:—He dies where he lived, in a Tavern, broken-[T22]hearted, without a friend; and his final exit is given up to the derision of fools. Nor has his misfortunes ended here; the scandal arising from the misapplication of his wit and talents seems immortal. He has met with as little justice or mercy from his final judges the critics, as from his companions of the Drama. With our cheeks still red with laughter, we ungratefully as unjustly censure him as a coward by nature, and a rascal upon principle: Tho', if this were so, it might be hoped, for our own credit, that we should behold him rather with disgust and disapprobation than with pleasure and delight.

But to remember our question—*Is Falstaff a constitutional coward?*⟩

With respect to every infirmity, except that of Cowardice, we must take him as at the period in which he is represented to us. If we see him dissipated, fat,—it is enough;—we have nothing to do with his youth, when he might perhaps [T23] have been modest, chaste, '*and not an Eagle's talon in the waist*'. But *Constitutional Courage* extends to a man's whole life, makes a part of his nature, and is not to be taken up or deserted like a mere Moral quality. It is true, there is a Courage founded upon *principle*, or rather a principle independent of Courage, which will sometimes operate in spite of nature;

T22:5 . . . *constitutional coward?*] *end of passage beginning T6:4 and superseded by* LR 2 *and* 3

a principle, which prefers death to shame, but which always refers itself, in conformity to its own nature, to the prevailing modes of honour, and the fashions of the age.—But Natural courage is another thing: It is independent of opinion; It adapts itself to occasions, preserves itself under every shape, and can avail itself of flight as well as of action.—In the last war, some Indians of America perceiving a line of Highlanders to keep their station under every disadvantage, and under a fire which they could not effectually return, were so miserably mistaken in our points of honour as to conjecture, from observation on the habit and [T24] stability of those troops, that they were indeed the women of England, who wanted courage to run away.—That Courage which is founded in nature and constitution, *Falstaff*, as I presume to say, possessed;—but I am ready to allow, that the principle already mentioned, so far as it refers to reputation only, began with every other Moral quality to lose its hold on him in his old age; that is, at the time of life in which he is represented to us; a period, as it should seem, approaching to *seventy*.—The truth is that he had drollery enough to support himself in credit without the point of honour, and had address enough to make even the preservation of his life a point of drollery. The reader knows I allude, tho' something prematurely, to his fictitious death in the battle of Shrewsbury. This incident is generally construed to the disadvantage of *Falstaff*: It is a transaction which bears the external marks of Cowardice: It is also aggravated to the spectators by the idle tricks of the Player, who practises [T25] on this occasion all the attitudes and wild apprehensions of fear; more ambitious, as it should seem, of representing a Caliban than a *Falstaff*; or indeed rather a poor unweildy miserable Tortoise than either.—The painful Comedian lies spread out on his belly, and not only covers himself all over with his robe as with a shell, but forms a kind of round Tortoise-back by I know not what stuffing or contrivance; in addition to which, he alternately lifts up, and depresses, and dodges his head, and looks to the one side and to the other, so much with the piteous aspect of that animal, that one would not be sorry to see the ambitious imitator calipashed in his robe, and served up for the entertainment of the gallery.—There is no hint for this mummery in the Play: Whatever there may be of dishonour in *Falstaff*'s conduct, he neither does or says any thing on this occasion which indicates terror or disorder of mind: On the contrary, this very act is a proof of his having all his wits about him, and is a stratagem, such as it is, not improper for a [T26] buffoon, whose fate would be singularly hard, if he should not be allowed to avail himself of his Character when it might serve him in most stead. We must remember, in extenuation, that the executive, the destroying hand of *Douglas* was over him: '*It was time to counterfeit, or that hot termagant Scot had paid him scot and lot too.*' He had but one choice; he was obliged to pass thro' the ceremony of dying either in jest or in earnest; and we shall not be surprized at the event, when we remember his propensities to the former.—Life (and especially the life of *Falstaff*)might be a jest; but he could see no joke whatever in dying: To be chopfallen was, with him, to lose both life and character together: He saw the point of honour, as well as every thing else, in ridiculous lights, and began to renounce its tyranny.

But I am too much in advance, and must retreat for more advantage. I should not forget how much opinion is against me, and that I am to make my way by the mere force and [T27] weight of evidence; without which I must not hope to possess myself of the reader: No address, no insinuation will avail. To this evidence, then, I now resort. The Courage of *Falstaff* is my Theme: And no passage will I spare from which any thing can be inferred as relative to this point. It would be as vain as injudicious to attempt concealment: How could I escape detection? The Play is in every one's memory, and a single passage remembered in detection would tell, in the mind of the partial observer, for fifty times its real weight. Indeed this argument would be void of all excuse if it declined any difficulty; if it did not meet, if it did not challenge opposition. Every passage then shall be produced from which, in my opinion, any inference, favourable or unfavourable, has or can be drawn;—but not methodically, not formally, as texts for comment, but as chance or convenience shall lead the way; but in what shape soever, they shall be always distinguishingly marked for notice. And so [T28] with that attention to truth and candour which ought to accompany even our lightest amusements I proceed to offer such proof as the case will admit, that *Courage* is a part of *Falstaff's Character*, that it belonged to his constitution, and was manifest in the conduct and practice of his whole life.

Let us then examine, as a source of very authentic information, what Impressions *Sir John Falstaff* had made on the characters of the Drama; and in what estimation he is supposed to stand with mankind in general as to the point of Personal Courage. But the quotations we make for this or other purposes, must, it is confessed, be lightly touched, and no particular passage strongly relied on, either in his favour or against him. Every thing which he himself says, or is said of him, is so phantastically discoloured by humour, or folly, or jest, that we must for the most part look to the spirit rather than the letter of what [T29] is uttered, and rely at last only on a combination of the whole.

We will begin then, if the reader pleases, by inquiring what Impression the very Vulgar had taken of *Falstaff*. If it is not that of Cowardice, be it what else it may, that of a man of violence, or *a Ruffian in years*, as Harry calls him, or any thing else, it answers my purpose; how insignificant soever the characters or incidents to be first produced may otherwise appear;—for these Impressions must have been taken either from personal knowledge and observation; or, what will do better for my purpose, from common fame.⟨Altho' I must admit some part of this evidence will appear so weak and trifling that it certainly ought not to be produced but in proof Impression only.⟩

The *Hostess Quickly* employs two officers to arrest *Falstaff*: On the mention of his name, one of them immediately observes, '*that it may chance to cost some* [T30] *of them their lives*,⟨*for that he will stab*'. —'*Alas a day*,' says the hostess, '*take heed of him, he cares not what mischief he doth; if his weapon be out, he will foin like any devil; He will spare neither man, woman, or child.*'⟩ Accordingly, we find that when they lay hold on him he resists to the utmost of his power,⟨and calls upon B⟩*ardolph*, whose arms are at liberty, to draw. '*Away, varlets, draw Bardolph, cut me off the villain's head, throw the quean in the kennel.*' The officers cry, *a rescue, a rescue!* But the Chief Justice comes in and the scuffle ceases. In another scene, his wench *Doll Tearsheet* asks him '*when he will leave fighting* ****** *and patch up his old body for heaven*'. ⟨This is occasioned by his drawing his

T29:4 Altho' I . . . Impression only] *cancelled* [SR 4] *see note*

T30:1–2 *for that . . . or child*] *first five words cancelled;* X *above dash preceding Alas and* X *below quotation mark following child* = *passage to be superseded by* [I30:1] Such is the Impression which these officers have taken and such the Sensations [*ED:* (C) Ideas] of the Hostess and [*last word overlaps with and written in above* Accordingly *in T30:3*] [SR 5a] *see note*

T30:3 and calls upon B] *apparently superseded by* [I30:2] The struggle is of some Duration as during this Period the Hostess says Wilt thou &c In the mean Time He calls upon B. [SR 5b] *see note*

T30:7b heaven'.] *fol. by* X *in inner margin* = *insert SR* 6

T30:8a This is . . . great provocation] *cancelled; superseded by* [I30:3] Fighting then was much his Practise according to Mrs Tearsheet This is said on occasion of his drawing his Rapier in Consequence of great Provocation [SR 6]

rapier, on great provocation⟩, and driving *Pistol*, who is drawn likewise, down stairs, and hurting him in the shoulder. To drive *Pistol* was no great feat; nor do I mention it as such; but upon this occasion it was necessary. '*A Rascal bragging slave,*' says he, '*the rogue fled from me like quicksilver.*' Expressions, which as they remember the cow-[T31]ardice of *Pistol*, seem to prove that *Falstaff* did not value himself on the adventure. Even something may be drawn from *Davy, Shallow*'s serving man, who calls *Falstaff*, in ignorant admiration, the *man of war*. I must observe here, and I beg the reader will notice it, that there is not a single expression dropt by these people, or either of *Falstaff*'s followers, from which may be inferred₍ₐ₎ the least suspicion of Cowardice in his character; and this is I think such an *implied negation*₍ₐ₎ as deserves considerable weight.

But to go a little higher, if, indeed, to consider *Shallow*'s opinion be to go *higher*: It is from him, however, that we get the earliest account of *Falstaff*. He *remembers him a Page to Thomas Mowbray, Duke of Norfolk:* '*He broke*', says he, '*Schoggan's head at the Court-Gate when he was but a crack thus high.*' *Shallow*, throughout, considers him as a great Leader and Soldier, and relates this fact as an early indication only of his future Prowess. *Shallow*, it is true, is a very ridi-[T32]culous character; but he picked up these Impressions somewhere; and he picked up none of a contrary tendency.—I want at present only to prove that *Falstaff* stood well in the report of common fame as to this point; and he was now near seventy years of age, and had passed in a Military line thro' the active part of his life. At this period common fame may be well considered as the *seal* of his character; a seal which ought not perhaps to be broke open on the evidence of any future transaction.

But to proceed. *Lord Bardolph* was a man of the world, and of sense and observation. He informs *Northumberland*, erroneously indeed, that *Percy* had beaten the King at Shrewsbury. '*The King*', according to him, '*was wounded; the Prince of Wales and the two Blunts slain, certain Nobles,* whom he names, *had escaped by flight; and the Brawn Sir John Falstaff was taken prisoner.*' But how came *Falstaff* into this list? Common fame had put him there. He is singularly obli-[T33]ged to Common fame.—But if he had not been a Soldier of repute, if he had not been brave as well as fat, if he had

T31:3 inferred] *fol. by* that either of them Entertained [SR 7a]   negation] *fol. by* of the Fact [SR 7b]

been *mere brawn*, it would have been more germane to the matter if
this lord had put him down among the baggage or the provender.
The fact seems to be, that there is a real consequence about Sir
John Falstaff which is not brought forward: We see him only in his
familiar hours; we enter the tavern with *Hal* and *Poins*; we join in
the laugh and *take a pride to gird at him*: But there may be a great
deal of truth in what he himself writes to the Prince, that tho' he be
'*Jack Falstaff with his Familiars, he is* Sir John *with the rest of Europe*'.
It has been remarked, and very truly I believe, that no man is a hero
in the eye of his valet-de-chambre; and *thus* it is, we are witnesses
only of *Falstaff*'s weakness and buffoonery; our acquaintance is with
Jack Falstaff, Plump Jack, and *Sir John Paunch*; but if we would
look for *Sir John ⟨Falstaff⟩*, we must put on, as *Bunyan* would have
expressed it, the spectacles of observation. With respect, for instance, [T34] to his Military command at Shrewsbury, nothing
appears on the surface but the Prince's familiarly saying, in the
tone usually assumed when speaking of *Falstaff*, '*I will procure
this fat rogue a Charge of foot;*' and in another place, '*I will procure
thee Jack a Charge of foot; meet me to-morrow in the Temple Hall.*'
Indeed we might venture to infer from this, that a Prince of so
great ability, whose wildness was only external and assumed, would
not have procured, in so nice and critical a conjuncture, a Charge of
foot for a known Coward. But there was more it seems in the case:
We now find from this report, to which *Lord Bardolph* had given
full credit, that the world had its eye upon *Falstaff* as an officer of
merit, whom it expected to find in the field, and whose fate in the
battle was an object of Public concern: His life was, it seems, very
material indeed; a thread of so much dependence, that *fiction*,
weaving the fates of Princes, did not think it unworthy, how coarse
soever, of being made a part of the tissue.

[T35] We shall next produce the evidence of the Chief Justice of
England. He inquires of his attendant, '*if the man who was then
passing him was* Falstaff; *he who was in question for the robbery*'. The
attendant answers affirmatively, but reminds his lord '*that he had
since done good service at Shrewsbury*'; and the Chief Justice, on this
occasion, rating him for his debaucheries, tells him '*that his day's
service at Shrewsbury had gilded over his night's exploit at Gads Hill*'.
This is surely more than Common fame: *The Chief Justice* must have
known his whole character taken together, and must have received

T33:4 Falstaff] *cancelled* [SR 8]

the most authentic information, and in the truest colours, of his behaviour in that action.

But, perhaps, after all, the Military men may be esteemed the best judges in points of this nature. Let us hear then *Coleville* of the dale, *a Soldier, in degree a Knight, a famous rebel, and 'whose betters, had they been ruled by him, would have sold themselves dearer'*: A man who is of consequence [T36] enough to be gaurded by *Blunt* and *led to present execution*. This man yields himself up even to the very Name and Reputation of *Falstaff*. *'I think'*, says he, *'you are Sir John Falstaff, and in that thought yield me.'* But this is but one only among the men of the sword; they shall be produced then by *dozens*, if that will satisfy. Upon the return of the King and Prince Henry from Wales, the Prince seeks out and finds *Falstaff* debauching in a tavern; where *Peto* presently brings an account of ill news from the North; and adds, *'that as he came along he met or overtook a dozen Captains, bare-headed, sweating, knocking at the taverns, and asking every one for* Sir John Falstaff'. He is followed by *Bardolph*, who informs *Falstaff* that *'He must away to the Court immediately; a dozen Captains stay at door for him.'* Here is Military evidence in abundance, and *Court evidence* too; for what are we to infer from *Falstaff's* being sent for to Court on this ill news, but that his opinion was to be asked, as a Military man of skill and experience, concerning the defences necessary to be taken. Nor is [T37] *Shakespeare* content, here, with leaving us to gather up *Falstaff's better character* from inference and deduction: He comments on the fact by making *Falstaff* observe that *'Men of merit are sought after: The undeserver may sleep when the man of action is called on.'* I do not wish to draw *Falstaff's* character out of his own mouth; but this observation refers to the fact, and is founded in reason. Nor ought we to reject, what in another place he says to the Chief Justice, as it is in the nature of an appeal to his knowledge. *'There is not a dangerous action'*, says he, *'can peep out his head but I am thrust upon it.'* The Chief Justice seems by his answer to admit the fact. *'Well, be honest, be honest, and heaven bless your expedition.'* But the whole passage may deserve transcribing.

'Ch. Just. *Well, the King has severed you and Prince Henry. I hear you are going with Lord John of Lancaster, against the Archbishop and the Earl of Northumberland.'*

[T38] 'Fals. *Yes, I thank your pretty sweet wit for it; but look you pray, all you that kiss my lady peace at home, that our armies join not in a hot day; for I take but two shirts out with me, and I mean not to sweat extraordinarily: If it be a hot day, if I brandish any thing but a bottle, would I might never spit white again. There is not a dangerous action can peep out his head but I am thrust upon it. Well I cannot last for ever.—But it was always the trick of our English nation, if they have a good thing to make it too common. If you will needs say I am an old man you should give me rest: I would to God my name were not so terrible to the enemy as it is. I were better to be eaten to death with a rust than to be scour'd to nothing with perpetual motion.'*

'*Ch. Just. Well be honest, be honest, and heaven bless your expedition.*'

Falstaff indulges himself here in humourous exaggeration;—these passages are not meant to be taken, nor are we to suppose that they were [T39] taken, literally;—but if there was not a ground of truth, if *Falstaff* had not had such a degree of Military reputation as was capable of being thus humourously amplified and exaggerated, the whole dialogue would have been highly preposterous and absurd, and the acquiescing answer of the *Lord Chief Justice* singularly improper.—But upon the supposition of *Falstaff*'s being considered, upon the whole, as a good and gallant Officer, the answer is just, and corresponds with the acknowledgment which had a little before been made, '*that his day's service at Shrewsbury had gilded over his night's exploit at Gads Hill.—You may thank the unquiet time*, says the Chief Justice, *for your quiet o'erposting of that action*'; agreeing with what *Falstaff* says in another place;—'*Well God be thanked for these Rebels, they offend none but the virtuous; I laud them, I praise them.*'—Whether this be said in the true spirit of a Soldier or not, I do not determine; it is surely not in that of a mere Coward and Poltroon.

[T40] It will be needless to shew, which might be done from a variety of particulars, that *Falstaff* was known, and had consideration at Court. *Shallow* cultivates him in the idea that *a friend at Court is better than a penny in purse*: *Westmorland* speaks to him in the tone of an equal: Upon *Falstaff*'s telling him, that he thought his lordship had been already at Shrewsbury, *Westmorland* replies,—'*Faith Sir John, 'tis more than time that I were there, and you too; the King I can tell you looks for us all; we must away all to night.*'—'*Tut*, says Falstaff, *never fear me, I am as vigilant as a cat to steal cream.*'—He desires, in another place, of my lord John of Lancaster, '*that when he goes to Court, he may stand in his good report.*' His intercourse and correspondence with both these lords seem easy and familiar. '*Go*,' says he to the page, '*bear this to my Lord of Lancaster, this to the Prince, this to the Earl of Westmorland, and this* (for he extended himself on all sides) *to old Mrs. Ursula'*, whom it seems, the rogue ought to have married many years before.—But these [T41] intimations are needless: We see him ourselves in the *Royal Presence*; where, certainly, his buffooneries never brought him; nor was the Prince of a character to commit so high an indecorum, as to thrust, upon a solemn occasion, a mere Tavern companion into his father's Presence, especially in a moment when he himself deserts his looser character, and takes up that of *a Prince indeed*.— In a very important scene, where *Worcester* is expected with proposals from *Percy*, and wherein he is received, is treated with, and carries back offers of accomodation from the King, the King's attendants upon the occasion are *the Prince of Wales, Lord John of Lancaster, the Earl of Westmorland, Sir Walter Blunt, and Sir John Falstaff*.—What shall be said to this? *Falstaff* is not surely introduced here in vicious indulgence to a mob audience;ʌ—he utters but one word, a buffoon one indeed, but aside and to the Prince only. Nothing, it should seem, is wanting, if decorum would here have permitted, but that he should have spoken one sober sentence in the [T42] Presence (which yet we are to suppose him ready and able to do if occasion should have required; or his wit was given him to little purpose) and Sir *John Falstaff* might be allowed to pass for an established Courtier and counsellor of state. '*If I do grow great*, says he, *I'll grow less, purge and leave sack, and live as a nobleman should do*.' Nobility did not then appear to him at an unmeasurable distance; it was, it seems, in his idea, the very next link in the chain.

But to return. I would now demand what could bring *Falstaff* into the Royal Presence upon such an occasion, or justify the Prince's so public acknowledgment of him, but an established fame and reputation of Military merit? In short, just the like merit as brought Sir *Walter Blunt* into the same circumstances of honour.

But it may be objected that his introduction into this scene is a piece of indecorum in the author. But upon what ground are we to sup-[T43]pose this? Upon the ground of his being a notorious Coward? Why this is the very point in question, and cannot be granted: Even the direct contrary I have affirmed, and am endeavouring to support. But if it be supposed upon any other ground, it does not concern me; I have nothing to do with *Shakespeare*'s indecorums in general. That there are indecorums in the Play I have no doubt:

T41:4 audience;] *LR 4 to be subjoined here as footnote; see note to LR 4*

The indecent treatment of *Percy*'s dead body is the greatest;—the familiarity of the insignificant, rude, and even ill disposed *Poins* with the Prince, is another;—but the admission of *Falstaff* into the Royal Presence (supposing, which I have a right to suppose, that his Military character was unimpeached) does not seem to be in any respect among the number. In camps there is but one virtue and one vice; Military merit swallows up or covers all. But, after all, what have we to do with indecorums? Indecorums respect the propriety or impropriety of exhibiting certain actions;—not their *truth* or *falshood* when exhibited. *Shakespeare* stands to us in the place [T44] of *truth* and *nature*: If we desert this principle we cut the turf from under us; I may then object to the robbery and other passages as indecorums, and as contrary to the truth of character. In short we may rend and tear the Play to pieces, and every man carry off what sentences he likes best.—But why this inveterate malice against poor *Falstaff*? He has faults enough in conscience without loading him with the infamy of Cowardice; a charge, which, if true, would, if I am not greatly mistaken, spoil all our mirth.—But of that hereafter.

It seems to me that, in our hasty judgment of some particular transactions, we forget the circumstances and condition of his whole life and character, which yet deserve our very particular attention. The author, it is true, has thrown the most advantageous of these circumstances into the *back ground*, as it were, and has brought nothing *out of the canvass* but his follies and buffoonery. We discover however, that in a very early period [T45] of his life he was familiar with *John* of *Gaunt*; which could hardly be, unless he had possessed much personal gallantry and accomplishment, and had derived his birth from a distinguished at least, if not from a Noble family.

It may seem very extravagant to insist upon *Falstaff*'s birth as a ground from which, by any inference, Personal courage may be derived, especially after having acknowledged that he seemed to have deserted those points of honour, which are more peculiarly the accompanyments of rank. But it may be observed that in the Feudal ages rank and wealth were not only connected with the point of honour, but with personal strength and natural courage. It is observable that Courage is a quality, which is at least as transmissible to one's posterity as features and complexion. In these periods men acquired and maintained their rank and possessions by personal prowess and gallantry; and their marriage alliances were made, of course, in families of the [T46] same character: And from hence, and from the exercises of their youth, we must account for the distinguished force and bravery of our antient Barons. It is not therefore beside my purpose to inquire what hints of the origin and birth of *Falstaff*, *Shakespeare* may have dropped in different parts of the Play; for tho' we may be disposed to allow that *Falstaff* in his old age might, under particular influences, desert the point of honour, we cannot give up that unalienable possession of Courage, which might have been derived to him from a noble or distinguished stock.

But it may be said that *Falstaff* was in truth the child of invention only, and that a reference to the Feudal accidents of birth serves only to confound fiction with reality: Not altogether so. If the ideas of Courage and *birth* were strongly associated in the days of *Shakespeare*, then would the assignment of high birth to *Falstaff* carry, and be intended to carry along with it, to the minds of the audience the associated idea of Courage, [T47] if nothing should be specially interposed to dissolve the connection;—and the question is as concerning this intention, and this effect.

I shall proceed yet farther to make a few very minute observations of the same nature: But if *Shakespeare* meant sometimes rather to *impress* than explain, no circumstances calculated to this end, either directly or by association, are too minute for notice. But however this may be, a more conciliating reason still remains: The argument itself, like the tales of our Novelists, is a *vehicle* only; *theirs*, as they profess, of moral instruction; and *mine* of critical amusement. The vindication of *Falstaff*'s Courage deserves not for its own sake the least sober discussion; *Falstaff* is the word only, *Shakespeare* is the *Theme*: And if thro' this channel, I can furnish no irrational amusement, the reader will not, perhaps, every where expect from me the strict severity of logical investigation.

Falstaff, then, it may be observed, was introduced into the world, —(at least we are told so) [T48] by the name of *Oldcastle*.[a] This was

[T48n][a] I believe the stage was in possession of some rude outline of *Falstaff* before the time of *Shakespeare*, under the name of *Sir John Oldcastle*; and ⟨I think it probable⟩ that this name was retained for a period in *Shakespeare*'s Hen. 4th. but changed to *Falstaff* before the play was printed. ⟨The expression of '*Old Lad of the Castle*', used by the Prince, does not however decidedly prove this; as it might have been only some known and familiar appellation too carelessly transferred from the old Play.⟩

T48n:1 I think it probable] *cancelled; superseded by* [I48] *it may be* [SR 9a]
T48n:2 The expression . . . old Play] *tentatively superseded by* [I48] (C) but if there

assigning him an origin of nobility; but the family of that name disclaiming any kindred with his vices, he was thereupon, as it is said, ingrafted into another stock[b] scarcely less distinguished, tho' fallen into indelible disgraces; and by this means [T49] he has been made, if the conjectures of certain critics are well founded, the Dramatic successor, tho', having respect to chronology, the natural *proavus* of another Sir *John*, who was no less than a Knight of the most noble order of the Garter, but a name for ever dishonoured by a frequent exposure in that Drum-and-trumpet Thing called *The first part of Henry VI.* written doubtless, or rather exhibited, long before *Shakespeare* was born,[c] tho' afterwards repaired, I think, and [T50] furbished up by him with here and there a little sentiment and diction. This family, if any [T51] branch of it remained in *Shakespeare*'s time, might have been proud of their Dramatic ally, if

[b] I doubt if *Shakespeare* had Sir *John Fastolfe* in his memory when he called the character under consideration *Falstaff*. The title and name of *Sir John* were transferred from *Oldcastle* not *Fastolfe*, and there is no kind of similarity in the characters. If he had *Fastolfe* in his thought at all, it was that while he approached the name, he might make such a departure from it as the difference of character seemed to require.

[T49n] [c] ⟨It would be no difficult matter I think to prove that all those Plays taken from the English chronicle, which are ascribed to *Shakespeare*, were on the stage before his time, and that he was employed by the Players only to refit and repair; taking due care to retain the names of the characters and to preserve all those incidents which were the most popular. Some of these Plays, particularly the two parts of Henry IV. have certainly received what may be called a *thorough repair*; that is, *Shakespeare* new-wrote them to the old names. In the latter part of Hen. V. some of the old materials remain; and in the Play which I have here censured (Hen. VI.) we see very little of the new. I should conceive it would not be very difficult to feel one's [T50n] way thro' these Plays, and distinguish every where the metal from the clay. Of the two Plays of Henry IV. there has been, I have admitted, a complete transmutation, preserving the old forms; but in the others, there is often no union or coalescence of parts, nor are any of them equal in merit to those Plays more peculiarly and emphatically *Shakespeare*'s *own*. The reader will be pleased to think that I do not reckon into the works of *Shakespeare* certain absurd productions which his editors have been so good as to compliment him with. I object, and strenuously too, even to *The Taming of the Shrew*; not that it wants merit, but that it does not bear the peculiar features and stamp of *Shakespeare*.⟩

The rhyming parts of the Historic plays are all, I think, of an older date than the times of *Shakespeare*.—There was a Play, I believe, of *the Acts of King John*, of which the bastard *Falconbridge* seems to have been the hero and the fool: He appears to have spoken altogether in rhyme. *Shakespeare* shews him to us in the latter part of the second scene in the first act of *King John* in this condition; tho' he afterwards, in the course of the Play, thought fit to adopt him, to give him language and manners, and to make him his own.

was a Character under the Name of oldcastle before the Time of Shakespear the Expression of old Lad of the Castle proves that it was an outline of Falstaff being [SR 9b] *see note*

T49n:1–T50n:3 It would . . . of *Shakespeare*.] *tentatively superseded by LR 5* indeed they could have any fair pretence to claim as such *him* whom *Shakespeare*, perhaps in contempt of Cowardice, wrote *Falstaff*, not *Fastolfe*, the true Historic name of the Gartered Craven.

In the age of Henry IV. a Family crest and arms were authentic proofs of gentility; and this proof, among others, *Shakespeare* has furnished us with: *Falstaff* always carried about him, it seems, *a Seal ring of his Grandfather's, worth*, as he says, *forty marks*: The Prince indeed affirms, but not seriously I think, that this ring was *copper*. As to the existence of the *bonds*, which were I suppose the negotiable securities or paper-money of the time, and which he pretended to have lost, I have nothing to say; but the ring, I believe, was really gold; tho' probably a little too much alloyed with baser metal. But this is not the point: The *arms* were doubtless genuine; they were borne by his Grandfather, and are proofs of an antient gentility; a gentility doubtless, in [T52] former periods, connected with wealth and possessions, tho' the gold of the family might have been transmuting by degrees, and perhaps, in the hands of *Falstaff*, converted into little better than copper. This observation is made on the supposition of *Falstaff*'s being considered as the head of the family, which I think however he ought not to be. It appears rather as if he ought to be taken in the light of a cadet or younger brother; which the familiar appellation of *John*, 'the only one (as he says) given him by his brothers and sisters', seems to indicate. Be this as it may, we find he is able, in spite of dissipation, to keep up a certain *state* and *dignity* of appearance; retaining no less than four, if not five, followers or men servants in his train. He appears also to have had apartments in town, and, by his invitations of *Master Gower* to dinner and to supper, a regular table: And one may infer farther from the Prince's question, on his return from Wales, to *Bardolph*, '*Is your master* here *in London*', that he had likewise a house in the country. Slight [T53] proofs it must be confessed, yet the inferences are so probable, so buoyant, in their own nature, that they may well rest on them. That he did not lodge at the Tavern is clear from the circumstances of the arrest. These various occasions of expence,— servants, taverns, houses, and whores,—necessarily imply that *Falstaff* must have had some funds which are not brought immediately under our notice. That these funds were not however adequate to his style of living is plain: Perhaps his train may be considered only as incumbrances, which the pride of family and the habit of former opulence might have brought upon his present poverty: I do not mean absolute poverty, but call it so as relative to his expence. To have *'but seven groats and two-pence in his purse'* and a page to bear it, is truly ridiculous; and it is for that reason we become so familiar with its contents. *'He can find'*, he says, *'no remedy for this consumption of the purse, borrowing does but linger and linger it out, but the disease is incurable.'* It might well be deemed so in his course of dissipation: But I [T54] shall presently suggest one source at least of his supply much more constant and honourable than that of borrowing. But the condition of *Falstaff* as to opulence or poverty is not very material to my purpose: It is enough if his birth was distinguished, and his youth noted for gallantry and accomplishments. To the first I have spoken, and as for the latter we shall not be at a loss when we remember that *'he was in his youth a page to Thomas Mowbray, Duke of Norfolk'*; a situation at that time sought for by young men of the best families and first fortune. The house of every great noble was at that period a kind of Military school; and it is probable that *Falstaff* was singularly adroit at his exercises: *'He broke Schoggan's head,'* (some boisterous fencer I suppose) *'when he was but a crack thus high.'* *Shallow* remembers him *as notedly skilful at backsword*; and he was at that period, according to his own humourous account, *'scarcely an eagle's talon in the waist, and could have crept thro' an alderman's thumb ring'*. Even at the age at which he is exhibited [T55] to us, we find him *foundering*, as he calls it, *nine score and odd miles*, with wonderful expedition, to join the army of Prince John of Lancaster; and declaring after the surrender of *Coleville*, that *'had he but a belly of any indifferency he were simply the most active fellow in Europe'*. Nor ought we here to pass over his Knighthood without notice. It was, I grant, intended by the author as a dignity which, like his Courage and his wit, was to be debased; his knighthood by low situations, his Courage by circumstances and imputations of cowardice, and his wit by buffoonery. But how are we to suppose this honour was acquired? By that very Courage, it should seem, which we so obstinately deny him. It was not certainly given him, like a modern City Knighthood, for his wealth or gravity: It was in these days a Military honour, and an authentic badge of Military merit.

But *Falstaff* was not only a Military Knight, he possess'd an honourable *pension* into the bargain; the reward as well as retainer of service, and which seems (besides the favours per-[T56]haps of Mrs. *Ursula*) to be the principal and only solid support of his present expences. But let us refer to the passage. '*A pox of this gout, or a gout of this pox; for one or the other plays the rogue with my great toe: It is no matter if I do halt, I have the wars for my colour and my pension shall seem the more reasonable.*' The mention *Falstaff* here makes of a pension, has I believe been generally construed to refer rather to *hope* than *possession*, yet I know not why: For the possessive MY, *my pension* (not *a* pension) requires a different construction. Is it that we cannot enjoy a wit, till we have stript him of every worldly advantage, and reduced him below the level of our envy? It may be perhaps for this reason among others that *Shakespeare* has so obscured the better parts of *Falstaff* and stolen them secretly on our feelings, instead of opening them fairly to the notice of our understandings. How carelessly, and thro' what bye-paths, as it were, of casual inference is this fact of a pension introduced! And how has he associated it with misfortune and infirmity! Yet [T57] I question, however, if, in this one place the *Impression* which was intended, be well and effectually made. It must be left to the reader to determine if in that mass of things out of which *Falstaff* is compounded, he ever considered a pension as any part of the composition: A pension however he appears to have had, one that halting could only seem to make more reasonable, not more honourable. The inference arising from the fact, I shall leave the reader. It is surely a circumstance highly advantageous to *Falstaff*, (I speak of the pensions of former days) whether he be considered in the light of a soldier or a gentleman.

I cannot foresee the temper of the reader, nor whether he be content to go along with me in these kind of observations. Some of the incidents which I have drawn out of the Play may appear too minute, whilst yet they refer to principles, which may seem too general. Many points require explanation; something should be said of the nature of *Shakespeare*'s Dramatic cha-[T58]racters;[d] by

[T58n] [d] The reader must be sensible of something in the composition of *Shakespeare*'s characters, which renders them essentially different from those drawn by other writers. The characters of every Drama must indeed be grouped; but in the groupes of other poets the parts which are not seen, do not in fact exist. But there is a certain roundness and integrity in the forms of *Shakespeare*, which give them an independence as well as a relation, insomuch that we often meet with passages, which tho' perfectly felt, cannot be sufficiently explained in words, without unfolding the whole character of the speaker: And this I may be obliged to do in respect to that of *Lancaster*, in order to account for some words spoken by him in censure of *Falstaff*.—Something which may be thought too heavy for the *text*, I shall add *here*, as a conjecture concerning the composition of *Shakespeare*'s characters: Not that they were the effect, I believe, so much of a minute and laborious attention, as of a certain comprehensive energy of mind, involving within itself all the effects of system and of labour.

what arts they were formed, and wherein they differ from those of other writers; something likewise more professedly of *Shake-* [T59]*speare* himself, and of the peculiar character of his genius. After such a review we may not perhaps think any consideration arising out of [T60] the Play, or out of general nature, either as too minute or too extensive.

Shakespeare is in truth, an author whose mimic creation agrees in general so perfectly with that [T61] of nature, that it is not only

[T59n] Bodies of all kinds, whether of metals, plants, or animals, are supposed to possess certain first principles of *being*, and to have an existence independent of the accidents, which form their magnitude or growth: Those accidents are supposed to be drawn in from the surrounding elements, but not indiscriminately; each plant and each animal, imbibes those things only, which are proper to its own distinct nature, and which have besides such a secret relation to each other as to be capable of forming a perfect union and coalescence: But so variously are the surrounding elements mingled and disposed, that each particular body, even of those under the same species, has yet some *peculiar* of its own. *Shakespeare* appears to have considered the being and growth of the human mind as analogous to this system: There are certain qualities and capacities, which he seems to have considered as first principles; the chief of which are certain energies of courage and activity, according to their degrees; together with different degrees and sorts of sensibilities, and a capacity, varying likewise in the *degree*, of discernment and intelligence. The rest of the composi-[T60n]tion is drawn in from an atmosphere of surrounding things; that is, from the various influences of the different laws, religions and governments in the world; and from those of the different ranks and inequalities in society; and from the different professions of men, encouraging or repressing passions of particular sorts, and inducing different modes of thinking and habits of life; and he seems to have known intuitively what those influences in particular were which this or that original constitution would most freely imbibe, and which would most easily associate and coalesce. But all these things being, in different situations, very differently disposed, and those differences exactly discerned by him, he found no difficulty in marking every individual, even among characters of the same sort, with something peculiar and distinct.—Climate and complexion demand their influence; '*Be thus when thou art dead, and I will kill thee, and love thee after*', is a sentiment characteristic of, and fit only to be uttered by a *Moor*.

[T61n] But it was not enough for *Shakespeare* to have formed his characters with the most perfect truth and coherence; it was further necessary that he should possess a wonderful facility of compressing, as it were, his own spirit into these images, and of giving alternate animation to the forms. This was not to be done *from without*; he must have *felt* every varied situation, and have spoken thro' the organ he had formed. Such an intuitive comprehension of things and such a facility, must unite to produce a *Shakespeare*. The reader will not now be surprised if I affirm that those characters in *Shakespeare*, which are seen only in part, are yet capable of being unfolded and understood in the whole; every part being in fact relative, and inferring all the rest. It is true that the point of action or sentiment, which we are most concerned in, is always held out for our special notice. But who does not perceive that there is a peculiarity about it, which conveys a relish of the whole? And very frequently, [T62n] when no particular point presses, he boldly makes a character act and speak from those parts of the composition, which are *inferred* only, and not distinctly shewn. This produces a wonderful effect; it seems to carry us beyond the poet to nature itself, and gives an integrity and truth to facts and character, which they could not otherwise obtain: And

wonderful in the great, but opens another scene of amazement to the discoveries of the microscope. We have been charged indeed by a Foreign writer with an overmuch admiring of this *Barbarian*: Whether we have [T62] admired with knowledge, or have blindly followed those feelings of affection which we could not resist, I cannot tell; but certain it is, that to the labours of his Editors he has not been overmuch obliged. They are however for the most part of the first rank in literary fame; but some [T63] of them had possessions of their own in Parnassus, of an extent too great and important to allow of a very diligent attention to the interests of others; and among those Critics more professionally so, the ablest and the best has unfortunately looked more to the praise of ingenious than of just conjecture. The character of his emendations are not so much that of *right* or *wrong*, as that, being in the extreme,ₐ they are always *Warburtonian*. Another has since undertaken the custody of our author, whom he seems to consider as a sort of wild Proteus or madman, and accordingly knocks him down with the butt-end of his critical staff, as often as he exceeds that line of sober discretion, which this learned Editor appears to have chalked out for him:ₐ Yet is this Editor notwithstanding 'a man take him for all in all', very highly respectable for his genius and his learning. What however may be chiefly complained of in these gentlemen is, that having erected themselves into the condition, as it were, of guardians and [T64] trustees of *Shakespeare*, they have never undertaken to discharge the disgraceful incumbrances of some wretched productions, which have long hung heavy on his fame. Besides the evidence of taste, which indeed is not communicable, there are yet other and more general proofs that these incumbrances were not incurred by *Shakespeare*: The *Latin* sentences dispersed thro' the imputed trash is, I think, of itself a decisive one. *Love's Labour lost* contains a very conclusive one of another kind; tho' the very last Editor has,

this is in reality that art in *Shakespeare*, which being withdrawn from our notice, we more emphatically call *nature*. A felt propriety and truth from causes unseen, I take to be the highest point of Poetic composition. If the characters of *Shakespeare* are thus *whole*, and as it were original, while those of almost all other writers are mere imitation, it may be fit to consider them rather as Historic than Dramatic beings; and, when occasion requires, to account for their conduct from the *whole* of character, from general principles, from latent motives, and from policies not avowed.ₐ

T63:2 extreme,] *fol. by* Either way [SR 10]
T63:3 him:] *see LR 7*
T62n:4 avowed.] *fol. by LR 6, at least in an early version; see Textual Note to LR 6a*

I believe, in his critical sagacity, suppressed the evidence, and with-drawn the record.

Yet whatever may be the neglect of some, or the censure of others, there are those, who firmly believe that this wild, this uncultivated Barbarian, has not yet obtained one half of his fame; and who trust that some new Stagyrite will arise, who instead of pecking at the surface of things will enter into the inward soul of his compositions, and expel by the force of congenial [T65] feelings, those foreign impurities which have stained and disgraced his page. And as to those *spots* which will still remain, they may perhaps become invisible to those who shall seek them thro' the medium of his beauties, instead of looking for those beauties, as is too frequently done, thro' the smoke of some real or imputed obscurity. When the hand of time shall have brushed off his present Editors and Commentators, and when the very name of *Voltaire*, and even the memory of the language in which he has written, shall be no more, the *Apalachian* mountains, the banks of the *Ohio*, and the plains of *Scioto* shall resound with the accents of this Barbarian: In his native tongue he shall roll the genuine passions of nature; nor shall the griefs of *Lear* be alleviated, or the charms and wit of *Rosalind* be abated by time. There is indeed nothing perishable about him, except that very learning which he is said so much to want. He had not, it is true, enough for the demands of the age in which he lived, but he had perhaps too much for the reach [T66] of his genius, and the interest of his fame. *Milton* and he will carry the decayed remnants and fripperies of antient mythology into more distant ages than they are by their own force intitled to extend; and the metamorphoses of *Ovid*, upheld by them, lay in a new claim to unmerited immortality.

Shakespeare is a name so interesting, that it is excusable to stop a moment, nay it would be indecent to pass him without the tribute of some admiration. He differs essentially from all other writers: Him we may profess rather to feel than to understand; and it is safer to say, on many occasions, that we are possessed by him, than that we possess him. And no wonder;—He scatters the seeds of things, the principles of character and action, with so cunning a hand yet with so careless an air, and, master of our feelings, submits himself so little to our judgment, that every thing seems superior. We discern not his course, we see no connection of cause and ef-[T67]fect, we are rapt in ignorant admiration, and claim no

T65:3 *Scioto*] *MS. corrects erratum (see Intro., p. 132) in outer margin* kindred with his abilities. All the incidents, all the parts, look like chance, whilst we feel and are sensible that the whole is design. His Characters not only act and speak in strict conformity to nature, but in strict relation to us; just so much is shewn as is requisite, just so much is impressed; he commands every passage to our heads and to our hearts, and moulds us as he pleases, and that with so much ease, that he never betrays his own exertions. We see these Characters act from the mingled motives of passion, reason, interest, habit and complection, in all their proportions, when they are supposed to know it not themselves; and we are made to acknowledge that their actions and sentiments are, from those motives, the necessary result. He at once blends and distinguishes every thing;—everything is complicated, every thing is plain. I restrain the further expressions of my admiration lest they should not seem applicable [T68] to man; but it is really astonishing that a mere human being, a part of human-ity only, should so perfectly comprehend the whole; and that he should possess such exquisite art, that whilst every woman and every child shall feel the whole effect, his learned Editors and Commenta-tors should yet so very frequently mistake or seem ignorant of the cause. A sceptre or a straw are in his hands of equal efficacy; he needs no selection; he converts every thing into excellence; nothing is too great, nothing is too base. Is a character efficient like *Richard*, it is every thing we can wish: Is it otherwise, like *Hamlet*, it is productive of equal admiration: Action produces one mode of excellence and inaction another: The Chronicle, the Novel, or the Ballad; the king, or the beggar, the hero, the madman, the sot or the fool; it is all one; —nothing is worse, nothing is better: The same genius pervades and is equally admirable in all. Or, is a character to be shewn in progressive change, and the events [T69] of years comprized within the hour;—with what a Magic hand does he prepare and scatter his spells! The Understanding must, in the first place, be subdued; and lo! how the rooted prejudices of the child spring up to confound the man! The Weird sisters rise, and order is extinguished. The laws of nature give way, and leave nothing in our minds but wildness and horror. No pause is allowed us for reflection: Horrid sentiment, furious guilt and compunction, airdrawn daggers, murders, ghosts, and inchantment, shake and *possess us wholly*. In the mean time the *process* is completed. *Macbeth* changes under our eye, *the milk of human kindness is converted to gall; he has supped full of horrors*, and his *May of life is fallen into the sear, the yellow leaf*; whilst we, the fools of amazement, are insensible to the shifting of place and the lapse of time, and till the curtain drops, never once wake to the truth of things, or recognize the laws of existence.—On such an occasion, a fellow, like *Rymer*, [T70] waking from his trance, shall lift up his Constable's staff, and charge this great Magician, this daring *practicer of arts inhibited*, in the name of *Aristotle*, to surrender; whilst *Aristotle* himself, disowning his wretched Officer, would fall prostrate at his feet and acknowledge his supremacy.—O supreme of Dramatic excellence! (*might he say,*) not to me be imputed the insolence of fools. The bards of *Greece* were confined within the narrow circle of the Chorus,ʌ and hence they found themselves constrained to practice, for the most part, the precision, and copy the details of nature. I followed them, and knew not that a larger circle might be drawn, and the Drama extended to the whole reach of human genius. Convinced, I see that a more compendious *nature* may be obtained; a nature of *effects* only, to which neither the relations of place, or continuity of time, are always essential. Nature, condescending to the faculties and apprehensions of man, has drawn [T71] through human life a regular chain of visible causes and effects: But Poetry delights in surprize, conceals her steps, seizes at once upon the heart, and obtains the Sublime of things without betraying the rounds of her ascent: True Poesy is *magic*, not *nature*; an effect from causes hidden or unknown. To the Magician I prescribed no laws; his law and his power are one; his power is his law. Him, who neither imitates, nor is within the reach of imitation, no precedent can or ought to bind, no limits to contain. If his end is obtained, who shall question his course? Means, whether apparent or hidden, are justified in Poesy by success; but then most perfect and most admirable when most concealed.ᵉ—But [T72] whither am

[T71n] *ᵉ* These observations have brought me so near to the regions of Poetic *magic*, (using the word here in its strict and proper sense, and not loosely as in the *text*) that tho' they lie not directly in my course, I yet may [T72n] be allowed in this place to point the reader that way. A felt propriety, or truth of art, from an unseen, tho' supposed adequate cause, we call *nature*. A like feeling of propriety and truth, supposed without a cause, or as seeming to be derived from causes inadequate, fantastic, and absurd,—such as wands, circles, incantations, and so forth,—we call by the general name *magic*, including all the train of superstition, witches, ghosts, fairies, and the rest.—*Reason* is confined to the line of visible existence; our *passions* and our *fancy* extend far beyond into the *obscure*; but however lawless their operations may seem, the

T70:3 confined within . . . the Chorus] ⋋ *inscribed in outside margin opposite this line = place at which LR 3—ED 1-3 was originally intended to be subjoined as footnote; see note to LR 3—ED 1-3*

I going! This copious and delightful topic has drawn me far beyond my design: I hasten back to my subject, and am guarded, for a time at least, against any further temptation to digress.

[T73] I was considering the dignity of *Falstaff* so far as it might seem connected with, or productive of military merit, and I have assigned him *reputation* at least, if not *fame*, noble connection, birth, attendants, title, and an ho-[T74]nourable pension; every one of them presumptive proofs of Military merit, and motives of action. What deduction is to be made on these articles, and why they are so much obscured may, perhaps, hereafter appear.

[T75] I have now gone through the examination of all the persons of the Drama from whose mouths any thing can be drawn relative to the Courage of *Falstaff*, excepting the *Prince* and *Poins*, whose images they so wildly form have yet a relation to truth, and are the shadows at least, however fantastic, of *reality*. I am not investigating but passing this subject, and must therefore leave behind me much curious speculation. Of Personifications however we should observe that those which are made out of abstract ideas are the creatures of the Understanding only: Thus, of the [T73n] mixed modes, virtue, beauty, wisdom and others,—what are they but very obscure ideas of *qualities* considered as abstracted from any *subject* whatever? The mind cannot steadily contemplate such an abstraction: What then does it do?—Invent or imagine a subject in order to support these qualities; and hence we get the Nymphs or Goddesses of virtue, of beauty, or of wisdom; the very obscurity of the ideas being the cause of their conversion into sensible objects, with precision both of feature and of form. But as reason has its personifications, so has *passion*.—Every passion has its Object, tho' often distant and obscure;—to be brought nearer then, and rendered more distinct, it is personified; and Fancy fantastically decks, or aggravates the *form*, ⟨and adds 'a local habitation and a name'.⟩ But passion is the *dupe* of its own artifice and *realises* the image it had formed. The Grecian theology was mixed of both these kinds of personification. Of the images produced by passion it must be observed that they are [T74n] the images, for the most part, not of the passions themselves, but of their remote effects. *Guilt* looks through the medium, and beholds a devil; *fear*, spectres of every sort; *hope*, a smiling cherub; *malice* and *envy* see hags, and witches, and inchanters dire; whilst the innocent and the young, behold with fearful delight the tripping fairy, whose shadowy form the moon gilds with its softest beams.—Extravagant as all this appears, it has its laws so precise that we are sensible both of a local and temporary, and of an universal magic; the first derived from the general nature of the human mind, influenced by particular habits, institutions, and climate; and the latter from the same general nature abstracted from those considerations: Of the first sort the *machinery* in *Macbeth* is a very striking instance; a machinery, which, however exquisite at the time, has already lost more than half its force; and the Gallery now laughs in some places where it ought to shudder:—But the magic of the *Tempest* is lasting and universal.

[T75n] There is besides a species of writing for which we have no term of art, and which holds a middle place between nature and magic; I mean where fancy either alone, or mingled with reason, or reason assuming the appearance of fancy, governs some real existence; but the whole of this art is pourtrayed in a single Play; in the real madness of *Lear*, in the assumed wildness of *Edgar*, and in the Professional *Fantasque* of the *Fool*,

---

T73n:5b and adds . . . a name.'] *cancelled* [SR 11]

evidence I have begged leave to *reserve*, [T76] and excepting a very severe censure passed on him by Lord *John* of *Lancaster*, which I shall presently consider: But I must first observe, that setting aside the jests of the Prince and *Poins*, and this censure of *Lancaster*, there is not one [T77] expression uttered by any character in the Drama that can be construed into any impeachment of *Falstaff*'s Courage; —an observation made before as respecting some of the Witnesses; —it is now extended to all: And though this silence be a negative proof only, it cannot, in my opinion, under the circumstances of the case, and whilst uncontradicted by facts, be too much relied on. If *Falstaff* had been intended for the character of a *Miles Gloriosus*, his behaviour ought, and therefore would have been commented upon by others. *Shakespeare* seldom trusts to the apprehensions of his audience; his characters interpret for one another continually, and when we least suspect such artful and secret [T78] management: The conduct of *Shakespeare* in this respect is admirable, and I could point out a thousand passages which might put to shame the advocates of a formal Chorus, and prove that there is as little of necessity as grace in so mechanic a contrivance.*ʄ* But I confine my censure of the Chorus to its supposed use of comment and interpretation only.

all operating to contrast and heighten each other. There is yet another feat in this kind, which *Shakespeare* has performed;—he has personified *malice* in his *Caliban*; a character kneaded up of three distinct natures, the diabolical, the human, and the brute. The rest of his preternatural beings are images of *effects* only, and cannot subsist but in a surrounding atmosphere of those passions, from which they are derived. *Caliban* is the passion itself, or rather a compound of malice, servility, and lust, *substantiated*; and therefore best shewn in contrast with the lightness of [T76n] *Ariel* and the innocence of *Miranda*.— *Witches* are sometimes substantial existences, supposed to be possessed by, or allyed to the unsubstantial; but the Witches in *Macbeth* are a gross sort of shadows, 'bubbles of the earth', as they are finely called by *Banquo*.—*Ghosts* differ from other imaginary beings in this, that they belong to no element, have no specific nature or character, and are effects, however harsh the expression, supposed without a cause; the reason of which is that they are not the creation of the poet, but the servile copies or transcripts of popular imagination, connected with supposed reality and religion. Should the poet assign the true cause, and call them the mere painting or *coinage of the brain*, he would disappoint his own end, and destroy the being he had raised. Should he assign fictitious causes, and add a specific nature, and a local habitation, it would not be endured; or the effect would be lost by the conversion of one being into another. The approach to reality in this case [T77n] defeats all the arts and managements of fiction.—The whole play of the *Tempest* is of so high and superior a nature that *Dryden*, who had attempted to imitate in vain, might well exclaim that

'—*Shakespeare*'s *magic* could not copied be,
Within that circle none durst walk but He.'

[T78n] *ʄ* Aenobarbus, in Anthony and Cleopatra, is in effect the Chorus of the Play; as Menenius Agrippa is of Coriolanus.

Falstaff is, indeed, so far from appearing to my eye in the light of a *Miles Gloriosus*, that in the best of my taste and judgment, he does not discover, except in consequence of the robbery, the least *trait* of such a character. All his boasting speeches are humour, mere humour, and carefully spoken to persons who cannot misapprehend them, who cannot be imposed on: They contain indeed, for the most part, an unreasonable and imprudent ridicule [T79] of himself, the usual subject of his good humoured merriment; but in the company of ignorant people, such as the Justices, or his own followers, he is remarkably reserved, and does not hazard any thing, even in the way of humour, that may be subject to mistake: Indeed he no where seems to suspect that his character is open to censure on this side, or that he needs the arts of imposition.—'*Turk Gregory never did such deeds in arms as I have done this day*' is spoken, whilst he breathes from action, to the Prince in a tone of jolly humour, and contains nothing but a light ridicule of his own inactivity: This is as far from real boasting as his saying before the battle, '*Wou'd it were bed-time, Hal, and all were well*', is from meaness or depression. This articulated wish is not the fearful outcry of a *Coward*, but the frank and honest breathing of a *generous fellow*, who does not expect to be seriously reproached with the character. Instead indeed, of deserving the name of a vain glorious *Coward*, his [T80] modesty perhaps on this head, and whimsical ridicule of himself, have been a principal source of the imputation.

But to come to the very serious reproach thrown upon him by that *cold blooded* boy, as he calls him, *Lancaster*.—*Lancaster* makes a solemn treaty of peace with the *Archbishop of York, Mowbray*, &c. upon the faith of which they disperse their troops; which is no sooner done than *Lancaster* arrests the Principals, and pursues the *scattered stray*:ₐ ⟨A transaction, by the bye, so singularly perfidious, that I wish *Shakespeare*, for his own credit, had not suffered it to pass under his pen without marking it with the blackest strokes of Infamy.⟩—During this transaction, *Falstaff* arrives, joins in the pursuit, and takes Sir *John Coleville* prisoner. Upon being seen by *Lancaster* he is thus addressed:—

[T81] '*Now Falstaff, where have you been all this while?*
        When every thing is over then you come:
        These tardy tricks of yours will, on my life,
        One time or other break some gallows' back.'

T80:3a *stray*:] *LR 8 apparently intended as footnote here; see note to LR 8*
T80:3b A transaction . . . of Infamy] *apparently superseded by LR 8*

This may appear to many a very formidable passage. It is spoken, as we may say, in the hearing of the army, and by one intitled as it were by his station to decide on military conduct; and if no punishment immediately follows, the forbearance may be imputed to a regard for the Prince of Wales, whose favour the delinquent was known so unworthily to possess. But this reasoning will by no means apply to the real circumstances of the case. The effect of this passage will depend on the credit we shall be inclined to give to *Lancaster* for integrity and candour, and still more upon the facts which are the ground of this censure, and which are fairly offered by *Shakespeare* to our notice.

[T82] We will examine the evidence arising from both; and to this end we must in the first place a little unfold the character of this young Commander in chief;—from a review of which we may more clearly discern the general impulses and secret motives of his conduct: And this is a proceeding which I think the peculiar character of *Shakespeare*'s Drama will very well justify.

We are already well prepared what to think of this young man:— We have just seen a very pretty manœuvre of his in a matter of the highest moment, and have therefore the less reason to be surprized if we find him practising a more petty fraud with suitable skill and address. He appears in truth to have been what *Falstaff* calls him, *a cold reserved sober-blooded boy*; a politician, as it should seem, by nature; bred up moreover in the school of *Bolingbroke* his father, and tutored to betray: With sufficient courage and ability perhaps, but with too much of the [T83] knave in his composition, and too little of enthusiasm, ever to be a great and superior character. That such a youth as this should, even from the propensities of character alone, take any plausible occasion to injure a frank unguarded man of wit and pleasure, will not appear unnatural. But he had other inducements. *Falstaff* had given very general scandal by his distinguished wit and noted poverty, insomuch that a little cruelty and injustice towards him was likely to pass, in the eye of the grave and prudent part of mankind, as a very creditable piece of fraud, and to be accounted to *Lancaster* for virtue and good service. But *Lancaster* had motives yet more prevailing; *Falstaff* was a Favourite, without the power which belongs to that character; and the tone of the Court was strongly against him, as the misleader and corrupter of the Prince; who was now at too great a distance to afford him immediate countenance and protection. A scratch then, between jest and earnest as it [T84] were, something that would not too much offend the prince, yet would leave behind a disgraceful scar upon *Falstaff*, was very suitable to the temper and situation of parties and affairs. With these observations in our thought let us return to the passage: It is plainly intended for disgrace, but how artful, how cautious, how insidious is the manner! It may pass for sheer pleasantry and humour: *Lancaster* assumes the familiar phrase and *girding* tone of *Harry*; and the gallows, as he words it, appears to be in the most danger from an encounter with *Falstaff*.—With respect to the matter, 'tis a kind of *miching malicho*; it means mischief indeed, but there is not precision enough in it to intitle it to the appellation of a formal charge, or to give to *Falstaff* any certain and determined ground of defence. *Tardy tricks* may mean, not Cowardice but neglect only, though the *manner* may seem to carry the imputation to both.—The reply of *Falstaff* is exactly suited to the qualities of the speech;—for [T85] *Falstaff* never wants ability but conduct only. He answers the general effect of this speech, by a feeling and serious complaint of injustice; he then goes on to apply his defence to the vindication both of his diligence and courage; but he deserts by degrees his serious tone, and taking the handle of pleasantry which *Lancaster* had held forth to him, he is prudently content, as being sensible of *Lancaster*'s high rank and station, to let the whole pass off in buffoonery and humour. But the question is, however, not concerning the adroitness and management of either party: Our business is, after putting the credit of *Lancaster* out of the question, to discover what there may be of truth and of fact either in the charge of the one, or the defence of the other. From this only, we shall be able to draw our inferences with fairness and with candour. The charge against *Falstaff* is already in the possession of the reader: The defence follows:—

[T86] 'Fals. *I would be sorry, my lord, but it should be thus: I never knew yet but that rebuke and check were the reward of valour. Do you think me a swallow, an arrow, or a bullet? Have I in my poor and old motion the expedition of thought? I speeded hither within the very extremest inch of possibility. I have foundered ninescore and odd posts*, (deserting by degrees his serious tone, for *one* of more address and advantage) *and here, travel-tainted as I am, have I in my pure and immaculate valour taken Sir John Coleville of the dale, a most furious Knight and valorous enemy.*'

Falstaff's answer then is, that he used all possible expedition to join the army; the not doing of which, with an implication of

Cowardice as the cause, is the utmost extent of the charge against him; and to take off this implication he refers to the evidence of a fact present and manifest,—the surrender of *Coleville*; in whose hearing he speaks, and to whom [T87] therefore he is supposed to appeal. Nothing then remains but that we should inquire if *Falstaff*'s answer was really founded in truth; '*I speeded hither*, says he, *within the extremest inch of possibility*': If it be so, he is justified: But I am afraid, for we must not conceal any thing, that *Falstaff* was really detained too long by his debaucheries in London; at least, if we take the Chief Justice's words very strictly.

'*Ch. Just. How now, Sir John? What are you brawling here? Doth this become your* PLACE, *your* TIME, *your* BUSINESS? *You should have been well on your way to York.*'

Here then seems to be a delay worthy perhaps of rebuke; and if we could suppose *Lancaster* to mean nothing more by *tardy tricks* than idleness and debauch, I should not possibly think myself much concerned to vindicate *Falstaff* from the charge; but the words imply, to my apprehension, a designed and deliberate [T88] avoidance of danger. Yet to the contrary of this we are furnished with very full and complete evidence. *Falstaff*, the moment he quits London, discovers the utmost eagerness and impatience to join the army; he gives up his gluttony, his mirth, and his ease. We see him take up in his passage some recruits at *Shallow*'s house; and tho' he has pecuniary views upon *Shallow*, no inducement stops him; he takes no refreshment, he cannot *tarry dinner*, he hurries off; '*I will not*, says he to the Justices, *use many words with you. Fare ye well, Gentlemen both; I thank ye, I must a dozen miles to night.*'—He misuses, it is true, at this time the *King's Press damnably*; but that does not concern me, at least not for the present; it belongs to other parts of his character.—It appears then manifestly that *Shakespeare* meant to shew *Falstaff* as really using the utmost speed in his power; he arrives almost literally *within the extremest inch of possibility*; and if *Lancaster* had not accelerated the event by a stroke of perfidy [T89] much more subject to the imputation of Cowardice than the *Debauch* of *Falstaff*, he would have been time enough to have shared in the danger of a fair and honest decision. But great men have it seems a priviledge; '*that in the* General's *but a choleric word, which in the* Soldier *were flat blasphemy.*' Yet after all, *Falstaff* did really come time enough, as it appears, to join the villainous triumphs of the day, to take prisoner *Coleville of the dale, a most furious Knight and valorous enemy.*—Let us look to the fact. If this incident should be found to contain any striking proof of *Falstaff*'s Courage and Military fame, his defence against *Lancaster* will be stronger than the reader has even a right to demand. *Falstaff* encounters *Coleville* in the field, and having demanded his name, is ready to assail him; but *Coleville* asks him if he is not Sir *John Falstaff*; thereby implying a purpose of surrender. *Falstaff* will not so much as furnish him with a pretence, and answers [T90] only, that *he is as good a man. 'Do you yield Sir, or shall I sweat for you?' 'I think*, says Coleville, *you are Sir John Falstaff, and in that thought yield me.'* This fact, and the incidents with which it is accompanied, speak loudly; it seems to have been contrived by the author on purpose to take off a rebuke so authoritatively made by *Lancaster*. The fact is set before our eyes to confute the censure: *Lancaster* himself seems to give up his charge, tho' not his ill will; for upon *Falstaff*'s asking leave to pass through Glostershire, and artfully desiring that, upon *Lancaster*'s return to Court, *he might stand well in his report, Lancaster* seems in his answer to mingle malice and acquital. *'Fare ye well*, Falstaff, *I in my condition shall better speak of you than you deserve.'* *'I would'*, says *Falstaff*, who is left behind in the scene, *'You had but the wit; 'twere better than your Dukedom.'* He continues on the stage some time chewing the cud of dishonour, which, with all his facility, [T91] he cannot well swallow. *'Good faith,'* says he, accounting to himself as well as he could for the injurious conduct of *Lancaster*; *'this sober-blooded boy does not love me.'* This he might well believe. *'A man*, says he, *cannot make him laugh; there's none of these demure boys come to any proof; but that's no marvel, they drink no sack.'*— *Falstaff* then it seems knew no drinker of sack who was a Coward; at least the instance was not home and familiar to him.—*'They all*, says he, *fall into a kind of Male green sickness, and are generally fools and Cowards.'* Anger has a privilege, and I think *Falstaff* has a right to turn the tables upon *Lancaster* if he can; but *Lancaster* was certainly no fool, and I think upon the whole, no Coward; yet the Male green sickness which *Falstaff* talks of, seems to have infected his manners and aspect, and taken from him all external indication of gallantry and courage. He behaves in the battle of Shrewsbury beyond the promise of his complexion and deportment: [T92] *'By heaven thou hast deceived me Lancaster*, says Harry, *I did not think thee Lord of such a spirit!'* Nor was his father less surprised *'at his holding Lord Percy at the point with lustier maintenance than he did look for from such an unripe warrior'*. But how well and unexpectedly soever he might have behaved upon that occasion, he does not seem to have been of a temper to trust fortune too much or too often with his safety; therefore it is that, in order to keep the event in his own hands, he loads the Die, in the present case, with villainy and deceit: The event however he piously ascribes, like a wise and prudent youth as he is, without paying that worship to himself which he so justly merits, to the special favour and interposition of Heaven.

> *'Strike up your drums, pursue the scattered stray.*
> *Heaven, and not we, have safely fought to-day.'*

But the prophane *Falstaff*, on the contrary, less informed and less studious of supernatural [T93] things, imputes the whole of this conduct to thin potations, and the not drinking largely of good and excellent *sherris*; and so little doubt does he seem to entertain of the Cowardice and ill disposition of this youth, that he stands devising causes, and casting about for an hypothesis on which the whole may be physically explained and accounted for;—but I shall leave him and Doctor *Cadogan* to settle that point as they may.

The only serious charge against *Falstaff*'s Courage, we have now at large examined; it came from great authority, from the Commander in chief, and was meant as chastisement and rebuke; but it appears to have been founded in ill-will, in the particular character of *Lancaster*, and in the wantonness and insolence of power; and the author has placed near, and under our notice, full and ample proofs of its unjustice.—And thus the deeper we look unto *Falstaff*'s character, the stronger is our conviction that he was not in-[T94]tended to be shewn as a Constitutional coward: Censure cannot lay sufficient hold on him,—and even malice turns away, and more than half pronounces his acquittal.ₐ

But as yet we have dealt principally in parole and circumstantial evidence, and have referred to *Fact* only incidentally. But *Facts* have a much more operative influence: They may be produced, not as arguments only, but Records; not to dispute alone, but to decide. —It is time then to behold *Falstaff* in actual service as a soldier, in danger, and in battle. We have already displayed one fact in his defence against the censure of *Lancaster*; a fact extremely unequivocal and decisive. But the reader knows I have others, and doubtless goes before me to the action at *Shrewsbury*. In the midst and in the

---

T94:1 acquittal.] *fol. by* X = *insert LR 9; see LR 9—ED*, app. crit. *to I94:1 and note*

heat of battle we see him come forwards;—what are his words? *'I have led my Rag-o-muffians where they are peppered; there's not three of my hundred and fifty left alive.'* [T95] But to *whom* does he say this? To himself only; he speaks *in soliloquy.* There is no questioning the fact, *he had* led *them*; *they were peppered; there were not* three *left alive.* He was in luck, being in bulk equal to any two of them, to escape unhurt. Let the author answer for that, I have nothing to do with it: He was the Poetic maker of the whole *Corps*, and he might dispose of them as he pleased. Well might the Chief justice, as we now find, acknowledge *Falstaff*'s services in this day's battle; an acknowledgment, which amply confirms the fact. A Modern officer, who had performed a feat of this kind, would expect, not only the praise of having done his duty, but the appellation of a hero. But poor *Falstaff* has too much wit to thrive: In spite of probability, in spite of inference, in spite of fact, he must be a Coward still. He happens unfortunately to have more Wit than Courage, and therefore we are maliciously determined that he shall have no Courage at all. But let us suppose that his modes of expres-[T96]sion, even *in soliloquy*, will admit of some abatement;— how much shall we abate? Say that he brought off *fifty* instead of *three*; yet a Modern captain would be apt to look big after an action with two thirds of his men, as it were, in his belly. Surely *Shakespeare* never meant to exhibit this man as a Constitutional coward; if he did, his means were sadly destructive of his end. We see him, after he had expended his Rag-o-muffians, with sword and target in the midst of battle, in perfect possession of himself, and replete with humour and jocularity. He was, I presume, in some immediate personal danger, in danger also of a general defeat; too corpulent for flight; and to be led a prisoner was probably to be led to execution; yet we see him laughing and easy, offering a bottle of sack to the Prince instead of a pistol, punning, and telling him, *'there was that which would* sack *a city.'*—*'What is it a time,* (says the Prince) *to jest and dally now?'* No, a sober character [T97] would not jest on such an occasion, but a Coward could not; he would neither have the inclination, or the power. And what could support *Falstaff* in such a situation? Not principle; he is not suspected of the Point of honour; he seems indeed fairly to renounce it. *'Honour cannot set a leg or an arm; it has no skill in surgery:—What is it? a word only; meer air. It is insensible to the dead; and detraction will not let it live with the living.'* What then, but a strong natural constitutional

Courage, which nothing could extinguish or dismay?—In the following passages the true character of *Falstaff* as to Courage and Principle is finely touched, and the different colours at once nicely blended and distinguished. '*If Percy be alive, I'll* pierce *him. If he do come in my way,* so:—*If he do not, if I come in his willingly, let him make a Carbonado of me. I like not such grinning honour as Sir Walter hath; give me life; which, if I can save,* so; *if not, honour comes un-look'd for, and there's an end.*' One cannot say which pre-[T98]vails most here, profligacy or courage; they are both tinged alike by the same humour, and mingled in one common mass; yet when we consider the superior force of *Percy,* as we must presently also that of *Douglas,* we shall be apt, I believe, in our secret heart, to forgive him. These passages are spoken in soliloquy and in battle: If every soliloquy made under similar circumstances were as audible as *Falstaff*'s, the imputation might perhaps be found too general for censure. These are among the passages that have ⟨impressed⟩ on the world an idea of Cowardice in *Falstaff*;—yet why? He is resolute to take his fate: If *Percy* do come in his way, *so*;—if not, he will not seek inevitable destruction; he is willing to save his life, but if that cannot be, why,—'honour comes unlook'd for, and there's an end.' This surely is not the language of Cowardice: It contains neither the Bounce or Whine of the character; he derides, it is true, and seems to renounce that grinning idol of Military zealots, *Honour.* But [T99] *Falstaff* was a kind of Military free-thinker, and has accordingly incurred the obloquy of his condition. He stands upon the ground of natural Courage only and common sense, and has, it seems, too much wit for a hero.—But let me be well understood;—I do not justify *Falstaff* for renouncing the point of honour; it pro-ceeded doubtless from a general relaxation of mind, and profligacy of temper. Honour is calculated to aid and strengthen natural courage, and lift it up to heroism; but natural courage, which can act as such without honour, is natural courage still; the very quality I wish to maintain to *Falstaff.* And if, without the aid of honour, he can act with firmness, his portion is only the more eminent and distinguished. In such a character, it is to his actions, not his sentiments, that we are to look for conviction. But it may be still further urged in behalf of *Falstaff,* that there may be false honour as well as false religion. It is true; yet even in that case candour obliges [T100] me to confess, that the best men are most disposed

T98:3 impressed] *underlined to indicate rejection; superseded by* [I98] imposed [SR 12]

to conform, and most likely to become the dupes of their own virtue. But it may however be more reasonably urged, that there are particular tenets both in honour and religion, which it is the grossness of folly not to question. To seek out, to court assured destruction, without leaving a single benefit behind, may be well reckoned in the number: And this is precisely the very folly which *Falstaff* seems to abjure;—nor are we, perhaps intitled to say more, in the way of censure, than that he had not virtue enough to become the dupe of honour, nor prudence enough to hold his tongue. I am willing however, if the reader pleases, to compound this matter, and acknowledge, on my part, that *Falstaff* was in all respects the *old soldier*; that he had put himself under the sober discipline of discretion, and renounced, in a great degree at least, what he might call, the Vanities and Superstitions of honour; if the reader [T101] will, on his part, admit that this might well be, without his renouncing, at the same time, the natural firmness and resolution he was born to.

But there is a formidable objection behind. *Falstaff* counterfeits basely on being attacked by *Douglas*; he assumes, in a cowardly spirit, the appearance of death to avoid the reality. But there was no equality of force; not the least chance for victory, or life. And is it the duty then, *think we still*, of true Courage, to meet, without benefit to society, *certain death*? Or is it only the phantasy of honour? —But such a fiction is highly disgraceful;—true, and a man of nice honour might perhaps have *grinned* for it. But we must remember that *Falstaff* had a double character; he was a *wit* as well as a *soldier*; and his Courage, however eminent, was but the *accessary*; his wit was the *principal*; and the part, which, if they should come in competition, he had the [T102] greatest interest in maintaining. Vain indeed were the licentiousness of his principles, if he should seek death like a bigot, yet without the meed of honour; when he might live by wit, and encrease the reputation of that wit by living. But why do I labour this point? It has been already anticipated, and our improved acquaintance with *Falstaff* will now require no more than a short narrative of the fact.

Whilst in the battle of *Shrewsbury* he is exhorting and encouraging the Prince who is engaged with the *Spirit Percy*—'*Well said Hal, to him Hal*',—he is himself attacked by the *Fiend Douglas*. There was no match; nothing remained but death or stratagem; grinning honour, or laughing life. But an expedient offers, a mirthful one,—

Take your choice *Falstaff*, a point of honour, or a point of drollery.—
It could not be a question;—*Falstaff* falls, *Douglas* is cheated, and
the world laughs. But does he fall like a Coward? [T103] No, like
a buffoon only; the superior principle prevails, and *Falstaff* lives by
a stratagem growing out of his character, to prove himself *no counterfeit*, to jest, to be employed, and to fight again. That *Falstaff*
valued himself, and expected to be valued by others, upon this
piece of saving wit is plain. It was a stratagem, it is true; it argued
presence of mind; but it was moreover, what he most liked, a very
laughable joke; and as such he considers it; for he continues to
counterfeit after the danger is over, that he may also deceive the
Prince, and improve the event into more laughter. He might, for
ought that appears, have concealed the transaction; the Prince was
too earnestly engaged for observation; he might have formed a
thousand excuses for his fall; but he lies still and listens to the
pronouncing of his epitaph by the Prince with all the waggish glee
and levity of his character. The circumstance of his wounding *Percy*
in the thigh, and carrying [T104] the dead body on his back like
luggage, is *indecent* but not cowardly. The declaring, though in jest,
that he killed *Percy*, seems to me *idle*, but it is not meant or calculated for *imposition*; it is spoken to the *Prince himself*, the man in the
world who could not be, or be supposed to be imposed on. But we
must hear, whether to the purpose or not, what it is that *Harry* has
to say over the remains of his old friend.

⟨*P. Hen.* What, old acquaintance! could not all this flesh
Keep in a little life? Poor *Jack*, farewell!
I could have better spared a better man.
Oh! I shou'd have a heavy miss of thee,
If I were much in love with vanity.
Death hath not struck so fat a *deer* to-day,
Tho' many a *dearer* in this bloody fray;
Imbowelled will I see thee by and by;
Till then, in blood by noble *Percy* lye.⟩

[T105] This is wonderfully proper for the occasion; it is affectionate, it is pathetic, yet it remembers his vanities, and, with a
faint gleam of recollected mirth, even his plumpness and corpulency; but it is a pleasantry softned and rendered even vapid by

T104:4 *P. Hen. . . . . Percy* lye] *marked with notation in outer margin:* Ital. = *italicize*
[SR 13]

tenderness, and it goes off in the sickly effort of a miserable pun.ᵍ—
But to our immediate purpose,—why is not his Cowardice remembered too? what, no surprize that *Falstaff* [T106] should lye by the
side of the noble *Percy* in the bed of honour! No reflection that
flight, though unfettered by disease, could not avail; that fear could
not find a subterfuge from death? Shall his corpulency and his
vanities be recorded, and his more characteristic quality of Cowardice, even in the moment that it particularly demanded notice and
reflection, be forgotten? If by sparing a better man be here meant a
better soldier, there is no doubt but there were better Soldiers in the
army, more active, more young, more principled, more knowing; but
none, it seems, taken for all in all, more acceptable. The comparative
better used here leaves to *Falstaff* the praise at least of *good*; and to
be a good soldier, [T107] is to be a great way from Coward. But
Falstaff's goodness, in this sort, appears to have been not only
enough to redeem him from disgrace, but to mark him with reputation; if I was to add with *eminence* and *distinction*, the funeral
honours, which are intended his obsequies, and his being bid, till
then, *to lye in blood by the noble Percy*, would fairly bear me out.

Upon the whole of the passages yet before us, why may I not
reasonably hope that the good natured reader, (and I write to no
other) not offended at the levity of this exercise, may join with me
in thinking that the character of *Falstaff* as to valour, may be fairly
and honestly summed up in the very words which he himself uses to
Harry; and which seem, as to this point, to be intended by *Shakespeare* as a *Compendium* of his character. '*What*, says the Prince, *a
Coward, Sir John Paunch!*' *Falstaff* replies, '*Indeed I am not* John
of Gaunt *your grandfather, but yet* no Coward, *Hal.*'

[T108] The robbery at *Gadshill* comes now to be considered. But
here, after such long argumentation, we may be allowed to breath a little.

[T105n] ᵍ The censure commonly passed on *Shakespeare's* puns, is, I think, not
well founded. I remember but very few, which are undoubtedly his, that may not be
justifyed; and if *so*, a greater instance cannot be given of the art which he so peculiarly
possessed of converting base things into excellence.

> 'For if the Jew do cut but deep enough,
> I'll pay the forfeiture *with all my heart.*'

A play upon words is the most that can be expected from one who affects gaiety
under the pressure of severe misfortunes; but so imperfect, so broken a gleam, [T106n]
can only serve more plainly to disclose the gloom and darkness of the mind; it is an
effort of fortitude, which failing in its operation, becomes the truest, because the most
unaffected *pathos*; and a skilful actor, well managing his tone and action, might with this
miserable pun, steep a whole audience suddenly in tears.

I know not what Impression has been made on the reader; a good deal of evidence has been produced, and much more remains to be offered. But how many sorts of men are there whom no evidence can persuade! How many, who ignorant of *Shakespeare*, or forgetful of the text, may as well read heathen Greek, or the laws of the land, as this unfortunate Commentary? How many, who proud and pedantic, hate all novelty, and damn it without mercy under one compendious word, Paradox? How many more, who not deriving their opinions immediately from the sovereignty of reason, hold at the will of some superior lord, to whom accident or inclination has attached them, and who, true to their vassalage, are resolute not to surrender, without express permission, their base and ill-gotten possessions. These, however habited, are [T109] the mob of mankind, who hoot and holla, hiss or huzza, just as their various leaders may direct. I *challenge* the whole Pannel as not holding by free tenure, and therefore not competent to the purpose either of condemnation or acquittal. But to the men of very nice honour what shall be said? I speak not of your men of good service, but such as Mr. **** '*Souls made of fire*, and *children of the sun*'. These gentlemen, I am sadly afraid, cannot in honour or prudence admit of any composition in the very nice article of Courage; *suspicion* is *disgrace*, and they cannot stay to parley with dishonour. The misfortune in cases of this kind, is, that it is not easy to obtain a fair and impartial Jury: When we censure others with an eye to our own applause, we are as seldom sparing of reproach, as inquisitive into circumstance; and bold is the man, who tenacious of justice, shall venture to weigh circumstances, or draw lines of distinction between Cowardice and any apparently similar or neighbour quality: As well may a lady, [T110] virgin or matron, of immaculate honour, presume to pity or palliate the soft failing of some unguarded friend, and thereby confess, as it were, those sympathetic feelings which it behoves her to conceal under the most contemptuous disdain; a disdain, always proportioned, I believe, to a certain consciousness which we must not explain. I am afraid that poor *Falstaff* has suffered not a little, and may yet suffer by this fastidiousness of temper. But though we may find these classes of men rather unfavourable to our wishes, the Ladies, one may hope, whose smiles are most worth our ambition, may be found more propitious; yet they too, through a generous conformity to the *brave*, are apt to take up the high tone of honour. Heroism is an idea perfectly conformable to the natural delicacy and

elevation of their minds. Should we be fortunate enough therefore
to redeem *Falstaff* from the imputations of Cowardice, yet plain
Courage, I am afraid, will not serve the turn: Even their heroes,
I think, must be for the most part in the [T111] bloom of youth, or
just where youth ends, in manhood's freshest prime; but to be '*Old,
cold, and of intolerable entrails; to be fat and greasy; as poor as Job,
and as slanderous as Satan*';—Take him away, he merits not a fair
trial; he is too offensive to be turned, too odious to be touched. I
grant, indeed, that the subject of our lecture is not without his
infirmity; '*He cuts three inches on the ribs, he was short-winded*,' and
his breath possibly not of the sweetest: '*He had the gout*,' or something worse, '*which played the rogue with his great toe*.'—But these
considerations are not to the point; we shall conceal, as much as may
be, these offences; our business is with his *heart* only, which, as we
shall endeavour to demonstrate, lies in the right place, and is firm
and sound, notwithstanding a few indications to the contrary.—
As for you, *Mrs.* MONTAGUE, I am grieved to find that *you* have
been involved in a Popular error; so much you must allow me to say;
—for the rest, I bow to your genius and your virtues: You have
given to the [T112] world a very elegant composition; and I am told
your manners and your mind are yet more pure, more elegant than
your book. *Falstaff* was too gross, too infirm, for your inspection;
but if you durst have looked nearer, you would not have found
Cowardice in the number of his infirmities.—We will try if we
cannot redeem him from this universal censure.—Let the venal
corporation of authors duck *to the golden fool*, let them shape their
sordid quills to the mercenary ends of unmerited praise, or of baser
detraction;—*old Jack*, though deserted by princes, though censured
by an ungrateful world, and persecuted from age to age by Critic
and Commentator, and though never rich enough to hire one
literary prostitute, shall find a Voluntary defender; and that too at
a time when the whole body of the *Nabobry* demands and requires
defence; whilst their ill-gotten and almost untold gold feels loose in
their unassured grasp, and whilst they are ready to shake off portions
of the enormous heap, that they may the more [T113] securely
clasp the remainder.—But not to digress without end,—to the
candid, to the chearful, to the elegant reader we appeal; our exercise
is much too light for the sour eye of strict severity; it professes
amusement only, but we hope of a kind more rational than the
History of Miss *Betsy*, eked out with the Story of Miss *Lucy*, and

the Tale of Mr. *Twankum*: And so, in a leisure hour, and with the good natured reader, it may be hoped, to friend, we return, with an air as busy and important as if we were engaged in the grave office of measuring the *Pyramids*, or settling the antiquity of *Stonehenge*, to converse with this jovial, this fat, this roguish, this frail, but, I think, *not cowardly* companion.

Though the robbery at *Gads-Hill*, and the supposed Cowardice of *Falstaff* on that occasion, are next to be considered, yet I must previously declare, that I think the discussion of this matter to be *now* unessential to the [T114] re-establishment of *Falstaff*'s reputation as a man of Courage. For suppose we should grant, in form, that *Falstaff* was surprized with fear in this single instance, that he was off his guard, and even acted like a Coward; what will follow, but that *Falstaff*, like greater heroes, had his weak moment, and was not exempted from panic and surprize? If a single exception can destroy a general character, *Hector* was a *Coward*, and *Anthony* a *Poltroon*. But for these seeming contradictions of Character we shall seldom be at a loss to account, if we carefully refer to circumstance and situation.—In the present instance, *Falstaff* had done an illegal act; the exertion was over; and he had unbent his mind in security. The spirit of enterprize, and the animating principle of hope, were withdrawn:—In this situation, he is unexpectedly attacked; he has no time to recall his thoughts, or bend his mind to action. He is not now acting in the Profession and in the Habits of a [T115] Soldier; he is associated with known Cowards; his assailants are vigorous, sudden, and bold; he is conscious of guilt; he has dangers to dread of every form, present and future; prisons and gibbets, as well as sword and fire; he is surrounded with darkness, and the Sheriff, the Hangman, and the whole *Posse Commitatus* may be at his heels:—Without a moment for reflection, is it wonderful that, under these circumstances, '*he should run and roar, and carry his guts away with as much dexterity as possible*'?

But though I might well rest the question on this ground, yet as there remains many good topics of vindication; and as I think a more minute inquiry into this matter will only bring out more evidence in support of *Falstaff*'s constitutional Courage, I will not decline the discussion. I beg permission therefore to state fully, as well as fairly, the [T116] whole of this obnoxious transaction, this unfortunate robbery at *Gads-Hill*.

In the scene wherein we become first acquainted with *Falstaff*, his character is opened in a manner worthy of *Shakespeare*: We see him in a green old age, mellow, frank, gay, easy, corpulent, loose, unprincipled, and luxurious; a *Robber*, as he says, *by his vocation*; yet not altogether so:—There was much, it seems, of mirth and *recreation* in the case: '*The poor abuses of the times*', he wantonly and humourously tells the Prince, '*want countenance; and he hates to see resolution fobbed off, as it is, by the rusty curb of old father antic, the law.*'—When he quits the scene, we are acquainted that he is only passing to the Tavern: '*Farewell*', says he, with an air of careless jollity and gay content, '*You will find me in East-Cheap.*' '*Farewell,*' says the Prince, '*thou latter spring; farewell, all-hallown summer.*' But though all this is excellent for *Shakespeare*'s purposes, we [T117] find, as yet at least, no hint of *Falstaff*'s Cowardice, no appearance of Braggadocio, or any preparation whatever for laughter under this head.—The instant *Falstaff* is withdrawn, *Poins* opens to the Prince his meditated scheme of a double robbery; and here then we may reasonably expect to be let into these parts of *Falstaff*'s character.—We shall see.

'*Poins. Now my good sweet lord, ride with us tomorrow; I have a jest to execute that I cannot manage alone.* Falstaff, Bardolph, Peto, and Gadshill *shall rob those men that we have already waylaid; yourself and I will not be there; and when they have the booty, if you and I do not rob them, cut this head from off my shoulders.*'

This is giving strong surety for his words; perhaps he thought the case required it: '*But how*, says the Prince, *shall we part with them in setting forth?*' *Poins* is ready with his answer; he had matured the thought, and could solve [T118] every difficulty:—'*They could set out before, or after; their horses might be tied in the wood; they could change their visors; and he had already procured cases of* buckram *to inmask their outward garments.*' This was going far; it was doing business in good earnest. But if we look into the Play we shall be better able to account for this activity; we shall find that there was, at least as much malice as jest in *Poins*'s intention. The rival situations of *Poins* and *Falstaff* had produced on both sides much jealousy and ill will, which occasionally appears, in *Shakespeare*'s manner, by side lights, without confounding the main action; and by the little we see of this *Poins*, he appears to be an unamiable, if not a very brutish and bad, character.—But to pass this;—the Prince next says, with a deliberate and wholesome caution, '*I doubt they will be too hard for us.'* *Poins*'s reply is remarkable; '*Well, for two of them, I know them to be as true bred Cowards as ever turned back; and for the* third, *if he fights longer than he* [T119] *sees cause, I will forswear arms.'* There is in this reply a great deal of management: There were *four* persons in all, as *Poins* well knew, and he had himself, but a little before, named them,—*Falstaff, Bardolph, Peto*, and *Gadshill*; but now he omits one of the number, which must be either *Falstaff*, as not subject to any imputation in point of Courage; and in that case *Peto* will be the *third*;—or, as I rather think, in order to diminish the force of the Prince's objection, he artfully drops *Gadshill*, who was then out of town, and might therefore be supposed to be less in the Prince's notice; and upon this supposition *Falstaff* will be the *third, who will not fight longer than he sees reason*. But on either supposition, what evidence is there of a pre-supposed Cowardice in *Falstaff*? On the contrary, what stronger evidence can we require that the Courage of *Falstaff* had to this hour, through various trials, stood wholly unimpeached, than that *Poins*, the ill-disposed *Poins*, [T120] who ventures, for his own purposes, to steal, as it were, *one* of the *four* from the notice and memory of the Prince, and who shews himself, from worse motives, as skilfull in *diminishing* as *Falstaff* appears afterwards to be in *increasing* of numbers, than that this very *Poins* should not venture to put down *Falstaff* in the list of Cowards; though the occasion so strongly required that he should be degraded. What *Poins* dares do however in this sort, he *does*. '*As to the third*,' for so he describes *Falstaff*, (as if the name of this Veteran would have excited too strongly the ideas of Courage and resistance) '*if he fights longer than he sees reason I will forswear arms*.' This is the old trick of cautious and artful malice: The turn of expression, or the tone of voice does all; for as to the words themselves, simply considered, they might be now truly spoken of almost any man who ever lived, except the iron-headed hero of *Sweden*.—But *Poins* however adds something, which may appear more [T121] decisive; '*The virtue of this jest will be, the incomprehensible lyes which this fat rogue will tell when we meet at supper; how thirty at least he fought with; and what wards, what blows, what extremities, he endured: And in the reproof of this lies the jest:*'— Yes, and the *malice* too.—This prediction was unfortunately fulfilled, even beyond the letter of it; a completion more incident, perhaps, to the predictions of malice than of affection. But we shall presently see how far either the prediction, or the event, will go to the impeachment of *Falstaff*'s Courage.—The Prince, who is never duped, comprehends the whole of *Poins*'s views. But let that pass.

In the next scene we behold all the parties at *Gads-Hill* in preparation for the robbery. Let us carefully examine if it contains any intimation of Cowardice in *Falstaff*. He is shewn under a very ridiculous vexation about his horse, which is hid from him; but this is no-[T122]thing to the purpose, or only proves that *Falstaff* knew no terror equal to that of walking *eight yards of uneven ground*. But on occasion of ⟨*Gadshill*'s⟩ being asked concerning the number of the travellers, and having reported that they were eight or ten, *Falstaff* exclaims, '*Zounds! will they not rob us!*' If he had said more seriously, '*I doubt they will be too hard for us*',—he would then have only used the Prince's own words upon a less alarming occasion. This cannot need defence. ⟨But the Prince, in his usual stile of mirth, replies, '*What, a Coward, Sir John Paunch!*' To this one would naturally expect from *Falstaff* some light answer; but we are surprized with a very serious one;—'*I am not indeed* John of Gaunt *your grandfather, but yet no* Coward, Hal.' This is singular: It contains, I think, the true character of *Falstaff*; and it seems to be thrown out *here*, at a very critical conjuncture, as a caution to the audience not to take too sadly what was intended only (to use the Prince's [T123] words,) '*as argument for a week, laughter for a month, and a good jest for ever after*'. The whole of *Falstaff*'s past life could not, it should seem, furnish the Prince with a reply, and he is, therefore, obliged to draw upon the coming hope. '*Well,* (says he, *mysteriously,*) *let the event try*'; meaning the event of the concerted attack on *Falstaff*; an event so probable, that he might indeed venture to rely on it.—But the travellers approach: The Prince hastily proposes a division of strength; that he with *Poins* should take a station seperate from the rest, so that if the travellers should escape one party, they might light on the other: *Falstaff* does not object, though he supposes the travellers to be eight or ten in number. We next see *Falstaff* attack these travellers with alacrity using the accustomed words of threat and terror;—they make no resistance, and he binds and robs them.

T122:2 *Gadshill's*] *requires correction to '*Bardolph*'s*' *to be consistent with LR* 10, I124:2 ff.

T122:5–T124:1 But the . . . in *Falstaff.*] *cancelled; superseded by LR* 10

T122:5 But] *prec. by* X = *insert LR* 10*; corresponding notation in outer margin*: Manu[script] 122 to 134 D°.

[T124] Hitherto I think there has not appeared the least *trait* either of boast or fear in *Falstaff.*⟩ But now comes on the concerted transaction, which has been the source of so much dishonour. *As they are sharing the booty,* (says the stage direction) *the Prince and* Poins *set upon them, they all run away; and* Falstaff *after a blow or two runs away too, leaving the booty behind them.*—'*Got with much ease:*' says the Prince, as an event beyond expectation, '*Now merrily to horse.*'—Poins adds, as they are going off, '*How the rogue roared!*' This observation is afterwards remembered by the Prince, who urging the jest to *Falstaff*, says, doubtless with all the licence of exaggeration,—'*And you,* Falstaff, *carried your guts away as nimbly, with as quick dexterity, and roared for mercy, and still ran and roared, as I ever heard bull-calf.*' If he did roar for mercy, it must have been a very inarticulate sort of roaring; for there is not a single word set down for *Falstaff* from which this roaring may be inferred, or any stage di-[T125]rection to the actor for that purpose: But, in the spirit of mirth and derision, the lightest exclamation might be easily converted into the roar of a bull-calf.

We have now gone through this transaction considered simply on its own circumstances, and without reference to any future boast or imputation. It is upon these circumstances the case must be tried, and every colour subsequently thrown on it, either by wit or folly, ought to be discharged. Take it, then, as it stands hitherto, with reference only to its own preceding and concomitant circumstances, and to the unbounded ability of *Shakespeare* to obtain his own ends, and we must, I think, be compelled to confess that this transaction was never intended by *Shakespear* to detect and expose the false pretences of a real Coward; but, on the contrary, to involve a man of allowed Courage, though in other respects of a very peculiar character, in such circumstances and [T126] suspicions of Cowardice as might, by the operation of those peculiarities, produce afterwards much temporary mirth among his familiar and intimate companions: Of this we cannot require a stronger proof than the great attention which is paid to the decorum and truth of character in the stage direction already quoted: It appears, from thence, that it was not thought *decent* that *Falstaff* should run at all, until he had been deserted by his companions, and had even afterwards exchanged blows with his assailants;—and thus, a just distinction is kept up between the natural Cowardice of the three associates and the accidental Terror of *Falstaff.*

⟨Hitherto, then, I think it is very clear that no laughter either is, or is intended to be, raised upon the score of *Falstaff's* Cowardice. For after all, it is not singularly ridiculous that an old inactive man of no boast, as far as appears, or extraordinary pre-[T127]tensions to valour, should endeavour to save himself by flight from the assault of two bold and vigorous assailants. The very Players, who are, I think, the very worst judges of *Shakespeare*, have been made sensible, I suppose from long experience, that there is nothing in this transaction to excite any extraordinary laughter; but this they take to be a defect in the management of their author, and therefore I imagine it is, that they hold themselves obliged to supply the vacancy, and fill it up with some low buffoonery of their own. Instead of the dispatch necessary on this occasion, they bring *Falstaff*, *stuffing and all*, to the very front of the stage; where with much mummery and grimace, he seats himself down, with a canvass money-bag in his hand, to divide the spoil. In this situation he is attacked by the *Prince* and *Poins*, whose tin swords hang idly in the air and delay to strike till the *Player Falstaff*, who seems more troubled with flatulence than fear, is able to rise; [T128] which is not till after some ineffectual efforts, and with the assistance, (to the best of my memory),ₐ of one of the thieves, who lingers behind, in spite of terror, for this friendly purpose; after which, without any resistance on his part, he is goaded off the stage like a fat ox for slaughter by these *stony-hearted* drivers in *buckram*. I think he does not *roar*;—perhaps the player had never perfected himself in the tones of a bull-calf. This whole transaction should be shewn between the interstices of a back scene: The less we see in such cases, the better we conceive. Something of resistance and afterwards of celerity in flight we should be made witnesses of; the *roar* we should take on the credit of *Poins*. Nor is there any occasion for all that bolstering with which they fill up the figure of *Falstaff*; they do not distinguish betwixt humourous exaggeration and necessary truth.ₐ
ₐThe Prince is called *starveling*, *dried neat's tongue*, *stock fish*, and other names of the same nature. They might [T129] with almost as good reason, search the glass-houses for some exhausted stoker to

T126:2–T129:1 Hitherto, then . . . this picture] *apparently superseded by LR 11*

T128:1 memory] X *in outer margin opposite this word = point at which LR 11b was apparently at first to be subjoined as footnote; see Textual Note to LR 11*

T128:5 truth]*fol. by X with notation in outer margin*: See 136 man[uscript] *to* 138 Dº = *superseded insertion point for ED of part of LR 11a; see Textual Note to LR 11*

T128:6 The] *prec. by as* [SR 14] *see note*

furnish out a Prince of *Wales* of sufficient correspondence to this picture.ₐ⟩

We next come to the scene of *Falstaff*'s braggadocioes. I have already wandered too much into details; yet I must, however, bring *Falstaff* forward to this last scene of trial in all his proper colouring and proportions. The progressive discovery of *Falstaff*'s character is excellently managed.—In the first scene we become acquainted with his figure, which we must in some degree consider as a part of his character; we hear of his gluttony and his debaucheries, and become witnesses of that indistinguishable mixture of humour and licentiousness which runs though his whole character; but what we are principally struck with, is the ease of his manners and deportment, and the unaffected freedom and wonderful pregnancy of his wit and humour. We see him, in the next scene, agi-[T130]tated with vexation: His horse is concealed from him, and he gives on this occasion so striking a description of his distress, and his words so labour and are so loaded with heat and vapour, that, but for laughing, we should pity him; laugh, however, we must at the extreme incongruity of a man at once corpulent and old, associating with youth in an enterprize demanding the utmost extravagance of spirit, and all the wildness of activity: And this it is which makes his complaints so truly ridiculous. '*Give me my horse!*' says he, in another spirit than that of *Richard*; '*Eight yards of uneven ground*', adds this *Forrester of Diana*, this *enterprizing gentleman of the shade*, '*is threescore and ten miles* a-foot *with me.*'—In the heat and agitation of the robbery, out comes more and more extravagant instances of incongruity. Though he is most probably older and much fatter than either of the travellers,ₐ yet he calls them, *Bacons, Bacon-fed, and gorbellied knaves*: '*Hang them,* (says he) *fat chuffs,* [T131] *they hate us youth: What! young men, must live:—You are grand Jurors, are ye? We'll jure ye, i' faith.*' But, as yet, we do not see the whole length and breadth of him: This is reserved for the braggadocio scene. We expect entertainment, but we don't well know of what kind. *Poins*, by his prediction, has given us a hint: But we do not see or feel *Falstaff* to be a Coward, much less a boaster; without which even Cowardice is not sufficiently ridiculous; and therefore

---

129:1 picture.] *fol. by* X *and notation see* 134 man[uscript] *to* 136 Dᵒ. = *superseded insertion point for ED of part of LR 11a; see Textual Note to LR 11*

T130:3 travellers] *fol. by and from the Adventure of the Moment more Exposed to the Danger of hanging [SR 15] see note*

it is, that on the stage, we find them always connected. In this uncertainty on our part, he is, with much artful preparation, produced.—His entrance is delayed to stimulate our expectation; and, at last, to take off the dullness of anticipation, and to add surprize to pleasure, he is called in, as if for another purpose of mirth than what we are furnished with: We now behold him, fluctuating with fiction, and labouring with dissembled passion and chagrin: Too full for utterance, *Poins* provokes him by a few sim-[T132]ple words, containing a fine contrast of affected ease. '*Welcome* Jack, *where hast thou been?*' But when we hear him burst forth, '*A plague on all Cowards! Give me a cup of sack. Is there no virtue extant!*'—We are at once in possession of the whole man, and are ready to hug him, guts, lyes and all, as an inexhaustible fund of pleasantry and humour. ⟨*Cowardice*, I apprehend, is out of our thought; it does not, I think, mingle in our mirth. As to this point, I have presumed to say already, and I repeat it, that we are, in my opinion, the dupes of our own wisdom, of systematic reasoning, of second thought, and after reflection.⟩ The first spectators, I believe, thought of nothing but the laughable scrape which so singular a character was falling into, and were delighted to see a humourous and unprincipled wit so happily taken in his own inventions, precluded from all rational defence, and driven to the necessity of crying out, af-[T133]ter a few ludicrous evasions, '*No more of that, Hal, if thou lov'st me.*'

I do not conceive myself obliged to enter into a consideration of *Falstaff*'s lyes concerning the transaction at *Gad's-Hill*. I have considered his conduct as independent of those lyes; I have examined the whole of it apart, and found it free of Cowardice or fear, except in one instance, which I have endeavoured to account for and excuse. I have therefore a right to infer that those lyes are to be derived, not from Cowardice, but from some other part of his character, which it does not concern me to examine: But I have not contented myself hitherto with this sort of negative defence; and the reader I believe is aware that I am resolute (though I confess not untired) to carry this fat rogue out of the reach of every imputation which ⟨affects, or⟩ may seem to affect, his natural Courage.

[T134] The first observation then which strikes us, as to his braggadocioes, is, that they are braggadocioes *after the fact*. In

T132:4 *Cowardice*, I . . . after reflection.] *requires reformulation; see Intro., p. 54*
T133:4 affects, or] *cancelled* [SR 16]

other cases we see the Coward of the Play bluster and boast for a time, talk of distant wars, and private duels, out of the reach of knowledge and of evidence; of storms and stratagems, and of falling in upon the enemy pell-mell and putting thousands to the sword; till, at length, on the proof of some present and apparent fact, he is brought to open and *lasting* shame; to shame I mean as a *Coward*; for as to what there is of *lyar* in the case, it is considered only as accessory and scarcely reckoned into the account of dishonour.—But in the instance before us, every thing is reversed: The Play opens with the *Fact*; a Fact, from its circumstances as well as from the age and inactivity of the man, very excusable and capable of much apology, if not of defence. This Fact is preceded by no bluster or pretence whatever;—the lies and braggadocioes follow; but [T135] they are not *general*; they are confined, and have reference to this one Fact only; the detection is *immediate*; and after some accompanying mirth and laughter, the shame of that detection ends; it has no *duration*, as in other cases; and, for the rest of the Play, the character stands just where it did before *without any punishment or degradation whatever*.

To account for all this, let us only suppose that *Falstaff* was a man of natural Courage, though in all respects unprincipled; but that he was surprized in one single instance into an act of real terror; which, instead of excusing upon circumstances, he endeavours to cover by lyes and braggadocio; and that these lyes become thereupon the subject, in this place, of detection. Upon these suppositions the whole difficulty will vanish at once, and every thing be natural, common, and plain. The *Fact* itself will be of course *excusable*; that is, it will arise out of a combination of such circum-[T136]stances, as being applicable to one case only, will not destroy the general character: It will not be *preceded* by any braggadocio, containing any fair indication of Cowardice; as real Cowardice is not supposed to exist in the character. But the first act of real or apparent Cowardice would naturally throw a vain unprincipled man into the use of lyes and braggadocio; but these would have reference only to the *Fact in question*, and not apply to other cases or infect his general character, which is not supposed to stand in need of imposition. Again,—the detection of Cowardice as such, is more diverting after a long and various course of Pretence, where the lye of character is preserved, as it were, whole, and brought into sufficient magnitude for a burst of discovery; yet, mere occasional lyes, such as *Falstaff* is hereby supposed to utter, are, for the purpose of sport, best detected in the telling; because, indeed, they cannot be preserved for a future time; the exigence and the [T137] humour will be past: But the *shame* arising to *Falstaff* from the detection of *mere lyes* would be *temporary only*; his character as to this point, being already known, and *tolerated for the humour*. Nothing, therefore, could follow but mirth and laughter, and the temporary triumph of baffling a wit at his own weapons, and reducing him to an absolute surrender: After which, we ought not to be surprized if we see him rise again, like a boy from play, and run another race with as little dishonour as before.

What then can we say, but that it is clearly the lyes only, not the *Cowardice* of *Falstaff* which are here detected: *Lyes*, to which what there may be of Cowardice is incidental only, improving indeed the Jest, but by no means the real Business of the scene.—And now also we may more clearly discern the true force and meaning of *Poins*'s prediction. '*The Jest will be*, says he, *the incomprehensible Lyes that* [T138] *this fat rogue will tell us: How thirty at least he fought with:—and in the reproof of this lyes the jest*'; That is, in the detection of these lyes *simply*; for as to *Courage*, he had never ventured to insinuate more than that *Falstaff* would not fight longer than he saw cause: *Poins* was in expectation indeed that *Falstaff* would fall into some dishonour on this occasion; an event highly probable: But this was not, it seems, to be the principal ground of their mirth, but the detection of those *incomprehensible lyes*, which he boldly predicts, upon his knowledge of *Falstaff*'s character, this *fat rogue*, not *Coward*, would tell them. This prediction therefore, and the completion of it, go only to the impeachment of *Falstaff*'s *veracity* and not of his *Courage*. '*These lyes*, says the Prince, *are like the father of them, gross as a mountain, open, palpable.— Why thou clay-brained gutts, thou knotty-pated fool; how couldst thou know these men in Ken-*[T139]*dal Green, when it was so dark thou couldst not see thy hand? Come, tell us your reason.*'

'*Poins. Come, your reason, Jack, your reason.*'

Again, says the Prince, '*Hear how a plain Tale shall put you down— What trick, what device, what starting hole canst thou now find out to hide thee from this open and apparent shame?*'

'*Poins. Come, let's hear, Jack, what trick hast thou now?*'

All this clearly refers to *Falstaff*'s lyes only *as such*; and the objection seems to be, that he had not told them well, and with sufficient

skill and probability. Indeed nothing seems to have been required
of *Falstaff* at any period of time but a good evasion. The truth is,
that there is so much mirth, and so little of malice or imposition in
his fictions, that they [T140] may for the most part be considered
as mere strains of humour and exercises of wit, impeachable only
for defect, when that happens, of the quality from which they are
principally derived. Upon this occasion *Falstaff*'s evasions fail him;
he is at the end of his invention; and it seems fair that in defect of
wit, the law should pass upon him, and that he should undergo the
temporary censure of that Cowardice which he could not pass off
by any evasion whatever. The best he could think of, was *instinct*:
He was indeed a *Coward upon instinct*; in that respect *like a valiant
lion, who would not touch the true Prince*. It would have been a vain
attempt, the reader will easily perceive, in *Falstaff*, to have gone
upon other ground, and to have aimed at justifying his Courage by
a serious vindication: This would have been to have mistaken the
true point of argument: It was his *lyes*, not his *Courage*, which was
really in question. There was besides no getting out of the toils
[T141] in which he had entangled himself: If he was not, he ought
at least, by his own shewing, to have *been at half-sword with a dozen
of them two hours together*; whereas, it unfortunately appears, and
that too evidently to be evaded, that he had run with singular
celerity from *two*, after the exchange of *a few blows* only. This
precluded *Falstaff* from all rational defence in his own person;—
but it has not precluded me, who am not the advocate of his *lyes* but
of his *Courage*.

But there are other singularities in *Falstaff*'s lyes, which ⟨go more
directly to his vindication⟩.—That they are confined to one scene
and one occasion only, we are not *now* at a loss to account for;—
but what shall we say to their extravagance? The lyes of *Parolles*
and *Bobadill* are brought into some shape; but the fictions of
Falstaff are so preposterous and *incomprehensible*, that one may
fairly doubt if they ever were intended for credit; and [T142] therefore, if they ought to be called *lyes*, and not rather *humour*; or, to
compound the matter, *humourous rhodomontades*. Certain it is,
that they destroy their own purpose, and are ⟨clearly⟩ not the
effect,ₐ in this respect, of a regulated practice, and habit of imposition.
The real truth seems to be, that had *Falstaff*, loose and unprincipled

T141:3 go more . . . his vindication] *superseded by* deserve observation [SR 17]
  T142:2 clearly] *cancelled* [SR 18a]   effect,] *fol. by* one sho^d think [SR 18b]

as he is, been born a Coward and bred a Soldier, he must, naturally, have been a great *Braggadocio*, a true *miles gloriosus*: But in such case he should have been exhibited active and young; for it is plain, that age and corpulency are an excuse for Cowardice, which ought not to be afforded him. In the present case, wherein he was not only involved in suspicious circumstances, but wherein he seems to have felt some conscious touch of infirmity, and having no candid construction to expect from his laughing companions, he bursts at once, and with all his might, into the most unweighed and preposterous fictions, determined, to put to proof [T143] on this occasion his boasted talent of *swearing truth out of England*. He tried it here, to its utmost extent, and was unfortunately routed on his own ground; which indeed, with such a mine beneath his feet, could not be otherwise. But without this, he had mingled in his deceits so much whimsical humour and fantastic exaggeration that he must have been detected; and herein appears the admirable address of *Shakespeare*, who can shew us *Falstaff* in the various light, not only of what he is, but what he would have been under one single variation of character,—the want of natural Courage; whilst with an art not enough understood, he most effectually preserves the real character of *Falstaff* even in the moment he seems to depart from it, by making his lyes too extravagant for practised imposition; by grounding them more upon humour than deceit; and turning them, as we shall next see, into a fair and honest proof of general Courage, by appropriating them to the conceal-[T144]ment only of a single exception. And hence it is, that we see him draw so deeply and so confidently upon his former credit for Courage and atchievment: '*I never dealt better in my life,—thou know'st my old ward, Hal*', are expressions which clearly refer to some known feats and defences of his former life. His exclamations against Cowardice, his reference to his own manhood, '*Die when thou wilt old* Jack, *if manhood, good manhood, be not forgot upon the face of the earth, then am I a shotten herring*': These, and various expressions such as these, would be absurdities not impositions, Farce not Comedy, if not calculated to conceal some defect supposed unknown to the hearers; and these hearers were, in the present case, his constant companions, and the daily witnesses of his conduct. If before this period he had been a known and detected Coward, and was conscious that he had no credit to lose, I see no reason why he should fly so violently from

T142:4 determined] *fol. by* as it sho^d seem [SR 19]

a [T145] familiar ignominy which had often before attached him; or why falshoods, seemingly in such a case, neither calculated for or expecting credit, should be censured, or detected, as lyes or imposition.

That the whole transaction was considered as a mere jest, and as carrying with it no serious imputation on the Courage of *Falstaff* is manifest, not only from his being allowed, when the laugh was past, to call himself, without contradiction in the personated character of *Hal* himself, 'valiant *Jack Falstaff, and the more* valiant *being, as he is*, old Jack Falstaff', but from various other particulars, and, above all, from the declaration, which the Prince makes on that very night of his intention of procuring this *fat rogue a Charge of foot;*— a circumstance, doubtless, contrived by *Shakespeare* to wipe off the seeming dishonour of the day: And from this time forward, we hear of no imputation arising from this transaction; it is [T146] born and dies in a convivial hour; it leaves no trace behind, nor do we see any longer in the character of *Falstaff* the boasting or braggadocio of a Coward.ₐ

Tho' I have considered *Falstaff*'s character as relative only to one single quality, yet so much has been said, that it cannot escape the reader's notice that he is a character made up by *Shakespeare* wholly of incongruities;—a man at once young and old, enter-prizing and fat, a dupe and a wit, harmless and wicked, weak in principle and resolute by constitution, ⟨cowardly in appearance and brave in reality; a knave without malice, a lyar without deceit;⟩ and a knight, a gentleman, and a soldier, without either dignity, decency, or honour: This is a character, which, though it may be de-compounded, could not, I believe, have been formed, nor the ingredients of it duly mingled upon any receipt whatever: It required the hand of *Shakespeare* himself to give to every [T147] particular part a relish of the whole, and of the whole to every particular part;—alike the same incongruous, identical *Falstaff*, whether to the grave Chief Justice he vainly talks of his youth, and offers to *caper for a thousand*; or cries to Mrs. *Doll*, '*I am old, I am old*', though she is seated on his lap, and he is courting her for busses. How *Shakespeare* could furnish out sentiment of so extra-ordinary a composition, and supply it with such appropriated and

T146:1 Coward.] *fol. by* X = *insert LR 12*
T146:2 cowardly in . . . without deceit] *requires reformulation; see Intro., pp. 58 and 92*

characteristic language, humour and wit, I cannot tell; but I may, however, venture to infer, and that confidently, that he who so well understood the uses of incongruity, and that laughter was to be raised by the opposition of qualities in the same man, and not by their agreement or conformity, would never have attempted to raise mirth by showing us Cowardice in a Coward unattended by Pretence, and softened by every excuse of age, corpulence, and infirmity: And of this we cannot have more striking proof than his furnish-[T148]ing this very character, on one instance of real terror, however excusable, with boast, braggadocio, and pretence, exceeding that of all other stage Cowards the whole length of his superior wit, humour, and invention.

What then upon the whole shall be said but that *Shakespeare* has made certain Impressions, or produced certain effects, of which he has thought fit to conceal or obscure the cause? How he has done this, and for what special ends, we shall now presume to guess.— Before the period in which *Shakespeare* wrote, the fools and Zanys of the stage were drawn out of the coarsest and cheapest materials: Some essential folly, with a dash of knave and coxcomb, did the feat. But *Shakespeare*, who delighted in difficulties, was resolved to furnish a richer repast, and to give to one eminent buffoon the high relish of wit, humour, birth, dignity, and Courage. But this was a process which required the nicest hand, and the ut-[T149] most management and address: These enumerated qualities are, in their own nature, productive of *respect*; an Impression the most opposite to laughter that can be. This Impression then, it was, at all adventures, necessary to with-hold; which could not perhaps well be without dressing up these qualities in fantastic forms, and colours not their own; and thereby cheating the eye with shews of baseness and of folly, whilst he stole as it were upon the palate a richer and a fuller *goût*. To this end, what arts, what contrivances, has he not practised! How has he steeped this singular character in bad habits for fifty years together, and brought him forth saturated with every folly and with every vice not destructive of his essential character, or incompatible with his own primary design! For this end, he has deprived *Falstaff* of every good principle; and for another, which will be presently mentioned, he has concealed every bad one. He has given him also every infirmity of body [T150] that is not likely to awaken our compassion, and which is most proper to render both his better qualities and his vices ridiculous: He has associated levity and debauch with *age*, corpulence and inactivity with *courage*, and has roguishly coupled the gout with *Military honours*, and a *pension* with the *pox*. He has likewise involved this character in situations, out of which neither wit or Courage can extricate him with honour. The surprize at *Gads-hill* might have betrayed a hero into flight, and the encounter with *Douglas* left him no choice but death or stratagem. If he plays an after-game, and endeavours to redeem his ill fortune by lyes and braggadocio, his ground fails him; no wit, no evasion will avail: Or is he likely to appear respectable in his person, rank, and demeanor, how is that respect abated or discharged! *Shakespeare* has given him a kind of state indeed; but of what is it composed? Of that fustian cowardly rascal *Pistol*, and his yoke-fellow of few words the [T151] equally deedless *Nym*; of his cup-bearer the fiery *Trigon*, whose zeal burns in his nose, *Bardolph*; and of the boy, who bears the purse with *seven groats and two-pence*;— a boy who was given him on purpose to set him off, and whom he walks *before*, according to his own description, *'like a sow that had overwhelmed all her litter but one.'*

But it was not enough to render *Falstaff* ridiculous in his figure, situations, and equipage; *still* his respectable qualities would have come forth, at least occasionally, to spoil our mirth; or they might have burst the intervention of such slight impediments, and have every where shone through: It was necessary then to go farther, and throw on him that substantial ridicule, which only the incongruities of real vice can furnish; of vice, which was to be so mixed and blended with his frame as to give a durable character and colour to the whole.

[T152] But it may here be necessary to detain the reader a moment in order to apprize him of my further intention; without which, I might hazard that good understanding, which I hope has hitherto been preserved between us.

I have 'till now looked only to the Courage of *Falstaff*, a quality which having been denied, in terms, to belong to his constitution, I have endeavoured to vindicate to the Understandings of my readers; the Impression on their Feelings (in which all Dramatic truth consists) being already, as I have supposed, in favour of the character. In the pursuit of this subject I have taken the general Impression of the whole character pretty much, I suppose, like other men; and, when occasion has required, have so transmitted it to the reader; joining in the common Feeling of *Falstaff*'s pleasantry, his apparent freedom from ill principle, and his companionable wit and good humour: With a stage character, in the arti-[T153]cle of exhibition, we have nothing more to do; for in fact what is it but an Impression; an appearance, which we are to consider as a reality; and which we may venture to applaud or condemn as such, without further inquiry or investigation? But if we would account for our Impressions, or for certain sentiments or actions in a character, not derived from its apparent principles, yet appearing, we know not why, natural, we are then compelled to look farther, and examine if there be not something more in the character than is *shewn*; something inferred, which is not brought under our special notice: In short, we must look to the art of the writer, and to the principles of human nature, to discover the hidden causes of such effects.— Now this is a very different matter—The former considerations respected the Impression only, without regard to the Understanding; but this question relates to the Understanding alone. It is true that there are but few Dramatic characters [T154] which will bear this kind of investigation, as not being drawn in exact conformity to those principles of general nature to which we must refer. But this is not the case with regard to the characters of *Shakespeare*; they are struck ⟨out⟩ *whole*, by some happy art which I cannot clearly comprehend, out of the general mass of things, from the ⟨block⟩ as it were of nature: And it is, I think, an easier thing to give a just draught of man from these Theatric forms, which I cannot help considering as originals, than by drawing from real life, amidst so much intricacy, obliquity, and disguise. If therefore, for further proofs of *Falstaff*'s Courage,ₐ or for the sake of curious speculation, or for ⟨both⟩, I change my position, and look to causes instead of effects, the reader must not be surprized if he finds the former *Falstaff* vanish like a dream, and another, of more disgustful form, presented to his view; one, whose final punishment we shall be so far from regretting, that we ourselves shall be ready to consign him to a severer doom.

[T155] The reader will very easily apprehend that a character, which we might wholly disapprove of, considered as existing in human life, may yet be thrown on the stage into certain peculiar situations, and be compressed by external influences into such temporary appearances, as may render such character for a time

T154:2 out] *cancelled* [SR 20a]   block] *underlined = italicize* [SR 20b]
T154:3 Courage.] *fol. by* or for the better Illustration of Shakespear [SR 21a] both] *cancelled; superseded by* all [SR 21b]

highly acceptable and entertaining, and even more distinguished for qualities, which on this supposition would be accidents only, than another character really possessing those qualities, but which, under the pressure of the same situation and influences, would be distorted into a different form, or totally lost in timidity and weakness. If therefore the character before us will admit of this kind of investigation, our Inquiry will not be without some dignity, considered as extending to the principles of human nature, and to the genius and arts of Him, who has best caught every various form of the human mind, and transmitted them with the greatest happiness and fidelity.

[T156] To return then to the vices of *Falstaff.*—We have frequently referred to them under the name of ill habits;—but perhaps the reader is not fully aware how very vicious he indeed is;—he is a robber, a glutton, a cheat, a drunkard,ₐ and a lyar; lascivious, vain, insolent, profligate, and profane:—A fine infusion this, and such as without very excellent cookery must have thrown into the dish a great deal too much of the *fumet*. It was a nice operation;—these vices were not only to be of a particular sort, but it was also necessary to guard them at both ends; on the *one*, from all appearance of malicious motive, and indeed from the manifestation of any ill principle whatever, which must have produced *disgust*,—a sensation no less opposite to laughter than is *respect*;—and, on the *other*, from the notice, or even apprehension, in the spectators, of *pernicious effect*; which produces *grief* and *terror*, and is the proper province of Tragedy alone.

[T157] *Actions* cannot with strict propriety be said to be either virtuous or vicious. These qualities, or attributes, belong to *agents* only; and are derived, even in respect to *them*, from intention alone. The abstracting of qualities, and considering them as independent of any *subject*, and the applying of them afterwards to actions independent of the agent, is a double operation which I do not pretend, ⟨thro' any part of it,⟩ to understand. All actions may most properly, in their own nature, I think, be calledₐ *neutral*; tho' in common discourse, and in writing where perfection is not ⟨requisite⟩, we often term them *vicious*, transferring on these occasions the attributive from the *agent* to the *action*; and sometimes we call them

T156:2 drunkard] *fol. by* a Parasite [SR 22]

T157:3b thro' any part of it,] *cancelled* [SR 23a]

T157:4 called] *fol. by* indifferent or [SR 23b]   requisite] *cancelled; superseded by* required [SR 23c]

evil, ⟨or of pernicious effect,⟩ by transferring, in like manner, the ⟨injuries incidentally arising from⟩ certain actions ⟨to the life, happiness, or interest of human beings⟩, to the ⟨natural operation, whether moral or physical, of the⟩ *actions* themselves: *One* is a colour [T158] thrown on them by the *intention,* in which I think consists all moral turpitude, and the *other* by effect: If therefore a Dramatic writer will use certain managements to keep vicious intention as much as possible from our notice, and make us sensible that no evil effect follows, he may pass off actions ⟨of very vicious motive, without much ill impression⟩, as mere ⟨*incongruities*⟩, and ⟨the effect of⟩ *humour* only;—*words these,* which, as applied to human conduct, are employed, I believe, to cover a great deal of what may deserve much harder appellation.

The *difference* between suffering an evil effect to take place, and of preventing such effect, from actions precisely of the same nature, is so great, that it is often *all the difference* between Tragedy and Comedy. The Fine gentleman of the Comic scene, who so promptly draws his sword, and wounds, without killing, some other gentleman of the [T159] same sort; and *He* of Tragedy, whose stabs are mortal, differ very frequently in no other point whatever. If our *Falstaff* had really *peppered* (as he calls it) *two rogues in buckram suits,* we must have looked for a very different conclusion, and have expected to have found *Falstaff*'s Essential prose converted into╷ blank verse, and to have seen him move off, in slow and measured paces, like the City Prentice to the toll⟨ing⟩ of a Passing bell;— '*he would have become a cart as well as another, or a plague on his bringing up.*'

Every incongruity in a rational being is a source of laughter, whether it respects manners, sentiments, conduct, or even dress, or situation;—but the greatest of all possible incongruity is vice, whether in the intention itself, or as transferred to, and becoming more manifest in action;—it is inconsistent with moral agency, nay, with rationality itself, and all the ends and purposes of our being.—Our

or of pernicious effect,] *cancelled* [SR 23d]   injuries incidentally arising from] *cancelled; superseded by* incidental effects of [SR 23e]   to the . . . human beings] *cancelled; superseded by* on the Life Happiness or Interest of human Beings [SR 23f] natural operation . . . of the] *cancelled* [SR 23g]

T158:1 of very . . . ill impression] *cancelled; superseded by* produced by vicious motives [*ED:* (R) by (C) ill Motives] and ordinarily productive of ill effects [SR 24a] *incongruities*] *superseded by* incongruity [SR 24b]   the effect of] *cancelled* [SR 24c]

T159:2 into] *fol. by* a sort of [SR 25a]   tolling] ing *cancelled = superseded by* toll [SR 25b]

author [T160] describes the natural ridicule of vice in his MEASURE
for MEASURE in the strongest terms, where, after having made the
angels weep over the vices of men, he adds, that *with* our spleens *they
might laugh themselves quite mortal*. Indeed if we had a perfect discernment of the ends of this life only, and could preserve ourselves
from sympathy, disgust and terror, the vices of mankind would be
a source of perpetual entertainment. The great difference between
Heraclitus and *Democritus* lay, it seems, in their spleen only;—for
a wise and good man must either laugh or cry without ceasing. Nor
indeed is it easy to conceive (to instance in one case only) a more
laughable, or a more melancholy object, than a human being, his
nature and duration considered, earnestly and anxiously exchanging
peace of mind and conscious integrity for gold; and for gold too,
which he has often no occasion for, or dares not employ:—But
[T161] *Voltaire* has by one Publication rendered all ⟨*arguments*⟩
superfluous: He has told us, in his *Candide*, the merriest and most
diverting tale of frauds, murders, massacres, rapes, rapine, desolation, and destruction, that I think it possible on any other plan to
invent; and he has given us *motive* and *effect*, with every possible
aggravation, to improve the sport. One would think it difficult to
preserve the point of ridicule, in such a case, unabated by contrary
emotions; but now that the feat is performed it appears of easy
imitation, and I am amazed that our race of imitators have made no
efforts in this sort: It would answer I should think in the way of
profit, not to mention the moral uses to which it might be applied.
The managements of *Voltaire* consist in this, that he assumes
a gay, easy, and light tone himself; that he never excites the reflections of his readers by making any of his own; that he hurries us on
with such a rapidity of narration as prevents our [T162] emotions
from resting on any particular point; and to gain this end, he has
interwoven the conclusion of one fact so into the commencement
of another, that we find ourselves engaged in new matter before
we are sensible that we had finished the old; he has likewise made
his crimes so enormous, that we do not sadden on any sympathy,
or find ourselves partakers in the guilt.—But what is truly singular
as to this book, is, that it does not appear to have been written for any
moral purpose, but for That only (if I do not err) of satyrising Providence itself; a design so enormously profane, that it may well pass for
the most ridiculous part of the whole composition.

T161:1 *arguments*] *superseded by* argument [SR 26] *see note*

But if vice, divested of disgust and terror, is thus in its own nature ridiculous, we ought not to be surprised if the very same vices which spread horror and desolation thro' the Tragic scene should yet furnish the Comic [T163] with its highest laughter and delight, and that tears, and mirth, and even humour and wit itself, should grow from the same root of incongruity: For what is humour in the humourist, but incongruity, whether of sentiment, conduct, or manners? What in the man of humour, but a quick discernment, and keen sensibility of these incongruities? And what is wit itself, without presuming however to give a complete definition where so many have failed, but a talent, for the most part, of marking with force and vivacity unexpected points of likeness in things supposed incongruous, and points of incongruity in things supposed alike: And hence it is that wit and humour, tho' always distinguished, are so often coupled together; it being very possible, I suppose, to be a man of humour without wit; but I think not a man of wit without humour.

But I have here raised so much new matter, that the reader may be out of hope of see-[T164]ing this argument, any more than the tale of *Tristram*, brought to a conclusion: He may suppose me now prepared to turn my pen to a moral, or to a dramatic Essay, or ready to draw the line between vice and virtue, or Comedy and Tragedy, as fancy shall lead the way;—But he is happily mistaken; I am pressing earnestly, and not without some impatience, to a conclusion. The principles I have now opened are necessary to be considered for the purpose of estimating the character of *Falstaff*, considered as relatively to human nature: I shall then reduce him with all possible dispatch to his Theatric condition, and restore him, I hope, without injury, to the stage.

There is indeed a vein or two of argument running through the matter that now surrounds me, which I might open for my own more peculiar purposes; but which, having resisted much greater temptations, I shall wholly desert. It ought not, however, to be forgotten, [T165] that if *Shakespeare* has used arts to abate our respect of *Falstaff*, it should follow by just inference, that, without such arts, his character would have grown into a *respect* inconsistent with laughter; and that yet, without Courage, he could not have been respectable at all;—that it required nothing less than the union of ability and Courage to support his other more accidental qualities with any tolerable coherence. Courage and Ability are first principles of Character, and not to be destroyed whilst the united frame of body and mind continues whole and unimpaired; they are the pillars on which he stands firm in spight of all his vices and disgraces;—but if we should take Courage away, and reckon Cowardice among his other defects, all the intelligence and wit in the world could not support him through a single Play.

The effect of taking away the influence of this quality upon the manners of a cha-[T166]racter, tho' the quality and the influence be assumed only, is evident in the cases of *Parolles* and *Bobadil*. *Parolles*, at least, did not seem to want wit; but both these characters are reduced almost to non-entity, and after their disgraces, walk only thro' a scene or two, the mere mockery of their former existence. *Parolles* was so changed, that neither the *fool*, nor the old lord *Le-feu*, could readily recollect his person; and his wit seemed to be annihilated with his Courage.

Let it not be here objected that *Falstaff* is universally considered as a Coward;—we do indeed call him so; but that is ⟨nothing⟩, if the character itself does not act from any consciousness of this kind, and if our Feelings take his part, and revolt against our understanding.

As to the arts by which *Shakespeare* has contrived to obscure the vices of *Falstaff*, they [T167] are such, as being subservient only to the mirth of the Play, I do not feel myself obliged to detail.

⟨But it may be well worth our curiosity to inquire into the composition of *Falstaff*'s character.—Every man we may observe, has two characters; that is, every man may be seen externally, and from without;—or a section may be made of him, and he may be illuminated from within.⟩

Of the external character of *Falstaff*, we can scarcely be said to have any steady view. *Jack Falstaff* we are familiar with, but *Sir John* was better known, it seems, *to the rest of Europe*, than to his intimate companions; yet we have so many glimpses of him, and he is opened to us occasionally in such various points of view, that we cannot be mistaken in describing him as a man of birth and fashion, bred up in all the learning and accomplishments of [T168] the times;—of ability and Courage equal to any situation, and capable by nature of the highest affairs; trained to arms, and possessing the tone, the deportment, and the manners of a gentleman;—but

T166:4 nothing] *requires reformulation; see note*
T167:1 detail.] *fol. by* X *see* 167 man[uscript] *to* 168 D°. = *insert LR 13*
T167:2-3 But it . . . from within] *cancelled; superseded by LR 13*

yet these accomplishments and advantages seem to hang loose on him, and to be worn with a slovenly carelessness and inattention: A too great indulgence of the qualities of humour and wit seems to draw him too much one way, and to destroy the grace and orderly arrangement of his other accomplishments;—and hence he becomes strongly marked for one advantage, to the injury, and almost forgetfulness in the beholder, of all the rest. Some of his vices likewise strike through, and stain his Exterior;—his modes of speech betray a certain licentiousness of mind; and that high Aristocratic tone which belonged to his situation was pushed on, and aggravated into unfeeling insolence and oppression. '*It is not a confirmed brow,*' says the Chief [T169] Justice, '*nor the throng of words that come with such more than impudent sauciness from you, can thrust me from a level consideration.*' '*My lord,*' answers *Falstaff,* '*you call honourable boldness impudent sauciness. If a man will court'sie and say nothing, he is virtuous: No my lord, my humble duty remembered, I will not be your suitor. I say to you I desire deliverance from these officers, being upon hasty employment in the King's affairs.*' '*You speak*', replies the Chief Justice, '*as having power to do wrong.*'—His whole behaviour to the Chief Justice, whom he despairs of winning by flattery, is singularly insolent; and the reader will remember many instances of his insolence to others:ᴧ Nor are his manners always free from the taint of vulgar society;— '*This is the right fencing grace, my lord,*' (says he to the Chief Justice, with great impropriety of manners) '⟨*tap*⟩ *for tap, and so part fair.*' '*Now the lord lighten thee,*' ⟨is the reflection of⟩ the Chief Justice,ᴧ '*thou art a* ⟨*very great*⟩ *fool.*'—[T170] Such a character as I have here described, strengthened with that vigour, force, and alacrity of mind, of which he is possessed, must have spread terror and dismay thro' the ignorant, the timid, the modest, and the weak: Yet is he however, when occasion requires, capable of much accomodation and flattery;—and in order to obtain the protection and patronage of the great, so convenient to his vices and his poverty, he was

T169:5 others] *fol. by* [I169] The Hostess is the common subject of his Contempt and oppression and her servants tell the Prince in the simplicity of their Hearts that *He is no proud Jack like Jack Falstaff.* (C) foolish Enough [*ED:* (R) foolish (C) indeed and improper to be said to the Prince] in them but good Proof of impression [*ED:* (R) but (C) excellent (R) Proof of (C) their (R) Impression] [SR 27]   Nor] X *above* N = *insert SR 27; corresponding* X *precedes SR 27 on* I169   tap] *underlined* = *deitalicize* [SR 28a]   is the reflection of] *cancelled; superseded by* says [SR 28b]   Justice,] *fol. by* Mocking if not cutting his Levity [*ED:* (R) Levit(C)ies] [SR 28c]   *very great*] *underlined* = *deitalicize* [SR 28d]

put under the daily necessity of practising and improving these arts; a baseness, which he compensates to himself, like other unprincipled men, by an increase of insolence towards ⟨his inferiors.⟩—There is also a natural activity about *Falstaff*, which for want of proper employment, shews itself in a kind of swell or bustle, which seems to correspond with his bulk, as if his mind had inflated his body, and demanded a habitation of no less circumference: Thus conditioned he rolls (in the language of *Ossian*) like a *Whale of Ocean*, scattering the smaller fry; but afford-[T171]ing, in his turn, noble contention to *Hal* and *Poins*; who, to ⟨keep up⟩ the allusion, I may be allowed↓ on this occasion to ⟨compare to⟩ the ⟨Thresher⟩ and the Sword-fish.

To this part of *Falstaff*'s character, many things which he does and says, and which appear unaccountably natural, are to be referred.

We are next to see him *from within*: And here we shall behold him most villainously unprincipled and debauched; possessing indeed the same Courage and ability, yet stained with numerous vices, unsuited not only to his primary qualities, but to his age, corpulency, rank, and profession;—reduced by these vices to a state of dependence, yet resolutely bent to indulge them at any price. These vices have been already enumerated; they are many, and become still more intolerable by ⟨an ex-[T172] cess of unfeeling insolence on one hand, and of base accommodation on the other.⟩

⟨But what then, after all, is become of *old Jack*? Is this the jovial delightful companion—*Falstaff*, the favourite and the boast of the Stage?—⟩ by no means. But it is, I think however, the *Falstaff* of

T170:1b his inferiors.] *cancelled; superseded by* others. [SR 29]

T171:1 keep up] *cancelled; superseded by* preserve [SR 30a]   allowed] *fol. by* perhaps [SR 30b]   compare to] *cancelled; superseded by* call [SR 30c]   Thresher] *superseded by* Thrasher [SR 30d]

T171:4 an ex-[T172:1]cess . . . the other.] *cancelled except for* (UM) ex-; *superseded by* [T171MS] that [I172:1] Excess of unfeeling Insolence [*fol. by* (C) which belongs to his Nature] on the one Hand and by the Practise of basest Accommodation on the other. [SR 31]

T172:1 cess] *prec. by* ≠ *in upper-outer margin* = *insert SR 31; corresponding* ≠ *above first word of SR 31 in* I172

T172:2 But] *prec. by* X = *insert SR 32b; corresponding* X *above first word of SR 32b on* I172

T172:2-T172:3 But what . . . the Stage?—] *cancelled; superseded by* [I172:2-4] (C) But what then after all is become of old Jack? Is this the jovial delightfull Companion? This disgustfull Being the Falstaff of whom we boast? The Favourite and Delight of the Stage? [SR 32b]

T172:3 the jovial] *prec. by* (C) Is this = *correction of erratum, Intro., p. 133. This correction is superseded by SR 32b.*   companion—] ? *superimposed on* — [SR 32a] =ED *of SR 32b*

Nature; the very stuff out of which the *Stage Falstaff* is composed; nor was it possible, I believe, out of any other materials he could have been formed. From this disagreeable draught we shall be able, I trust, by a proper disposition of light and shade, and from the influence and compression of external things, to produce *plump Jack*, the life of humour, the spirit of pleasantry, and the soul of ⟨mirth.⟩

To this end, *Falstaff* must no longer be considered as a single independent character, but grouped, as we find him shewn to us in the Play;—his ability must be disgraced by [T173] buffoonery, and his Courage by circumstances of imputation; and those qualities be thereupon reduced into subjects of mirth and laughter:—His vices must be concealed at each end from vicious design and evil effect, and must thereupon be turned into incongruities, and assume the name of humour only;—his insolence must be repressed by the superior tone of *Hal* and *Poins*, and take the softer name of spirit ⟨only,⟩ or alacrity of mind;—his state of dependence, his temper of accomodation, and his activity, must fall in precisely with the indulgence of his humours; that is, he must thrive best and flatter most, by being extravagantly incongruous; and his own tendency, impelled by so much activity, will carry him with perfect ease and freedom to all the necessary excesses. But why, it may be asked, should incongruities recommend *Falstaff* to the favour of the Prince?—Because the Prince is supposed to possess a high relish of humour [T174] and to have a temper and a force about him, which, whatever was his pursuit, delighted in excess. This, *Falstaff* is supposed perfectly to comprehend; and thereupon not only to indulge himself in all kinds of incongruity, but to lend out his own superior wit and humour against himself, and to heighten the ridicule by all the tricks and arts of buffoonery for which his corpulence, his age, and situation, furnish such excellent materials. This compleats the Dramatic character of *Falstaff*, and gives him that appearance of perfect good-nature, pleasantry, mellowness, and hilarity of mind, for which we admire and almost love him, tho' we feel certain reserves which forbid our going that length; the true reason of which is, ⟨that there will be always found a difference between mere appearances, and reality: Nor are we, nor can we be,⟩ insensible that whenever the action of external influence upon him

---

T172:5b mirth.] *cancelled; superseded by* Whim. [SR 33]
T173:1 only,] *cancelled* [SR 34]
T174:3 that there ... we be] *cancelled; superseded by* that we are not [SR 35] *see note*

is in whole or in part relaxed, the character restores [T175] itself proportionably to its more unpleasing condition.

A character really possessing the qualities which are on the stage imputed to *Falstaff*, would be best shewn by its own natural energy; the least compression would disorder it, and make us feel for it all the pain of sympathy: It is the artificial condition of *Falstaff* which is the source of our delight; we enjoy his distresses, we *gird at him* ourselves, and urge the sport without the least alloy of compassion; and we give him, when the laugh is over, undeserved credit for the pleasure we enjoyed. If any one thinks that these observations are the effect of too much refinement, and that there was in truth more of chance in the case than of management or design, let him try his own luck;—perhaps he may draw out of the wheel of fortune a *Macbeth*, an *Othello*, a *Benedict*, or a *Falstaff*.

[T176]ᴀ Such, I think, is the true character of this extraordinary buffoon; and from hence we may discern for what special purposes *Shakespeare* has given him talents and qualities, which were to be afterwards obscured, and perverted to ends opposite to their nature; it was clearly to furnish out a Stage buffoon of a peculiar sort; a kind of Game-bull which would stand the baiting thro' a hundred Plays, and produce equal sport, whether he is pinned down occasionally by *Hal* or *Poins*, or tosses such mongrils as *Bardolph*, or the Justices, sprawling in the air. There is in truth no such thing as totally demolishing *Falstaff*; he has so much of the invulnerable in his frame that no ridicule can destroy him; he is safe even in defeat, and seems to rise, like another *Antæus*, with recruited vigour from every fall; in this as in every other respect, unlike *Parolles* or *Bobadil*: They fall by the first shaft of ridicule, but *Falstaff* is a butt on which we may empty the whole quiver, whilst the [T177] substance of his character remains unimpaired. His ill habits, and the accidents of age and corpulence, are no part of his essential constitution; they come forward indeed on our eye, and solicit our notice, but they are second natures, not *first*; mere shadows, we pursue them in vain; *Falstaff* himself has a distinct and separate subsistence; he laughs at the chace, and when the sport is over, gathers them with unruffled feather under his wing: And hence it is that he is made to undergo not one detection only, but a series of detections; that he is not formed for one Play only, but was intended originally at least for two; and the author we are told, was doubtful if he should not

T176:1 Such] *prec. by* X = *insert LR 14*

extend him yet farther, and engage him in the wars with *France*. This he might well have done, for there is nothing perishable in the nature of *Falstaff*: He might have involved him, by the vicious part of his character, in new difficulties and unlucky situations, and have enabled [T178] him, by the better part, to have scrambled through, abiding and retorting the jests and laughter of every beholder.

But whatever we may be told concerning the intention of *Shakespeare* to extend this character farther, there is a manifest preparation near the end of the second part of Henry IV. for his disgrace: The disguise is taken off, and he begins openly to pander to the excesses of the Prince, intitling himself to the character afterwards given him of being *the tutor and the feeder of his riots. 'I will fetch off'*, (says he) *'these Justices.—I will devise matter enough out of this* Shallow *to keep the Prince in continual laughter the wearing out of six fashions.—If the young* dace *be a bait for the old* pike,' (speaking with reference to his own designs upon *Shallow*) *'I see no reason in the law of nature but I may snap at him.'*—This is showing himself abominably dissolute: The laborious arts of fraud, which he prac-[T179]tices on *Shallow* to induce the loan of a thousand pound, create *disgust*; and the more, as we are sensible this money was never likely to be *paid back*, as we are told that *was*, of which the travellers had been robbed. It is true we feel no pain for *Shallow*, he being a very bad character, as would fully appear, if he were unfolded; but *Falstaff*'s deliberation in fraud is not on that account more excusable.—The event of the old King's death draws him out almost into detestation.—*'Master* Robert Shallow, *chuse what office thou wilt in the land,—'tis thine.—I am fortune's steward.—Let us take any man's horses.—The laws of England are at my commandment.—Happy are they who have been my friends;—and woe to my* Lord Chief Justice.'—After this we ought not to complain if we see Poetic justice duly executed upon him, and that he is finally given up to shame and dishonour.

[T180] But it is remarkable that, during this process, we are not acquainted with the success of *Falstaff*'s designs upon *Shallow* 'till the moment of his disgrace. *'If I had had time'*, (says he to *Shallow*, as the King is approaching,) *'to have made new liveries, I would have bestowed the thousand pounds I borrowed of you'*;—and the first word he utters after this period is, *'Master* Shallow, *I owe you a thousand pounds'*: We may from hence very reasonably presume, that *Shakespeare* meant to connect this fraud with the punishment of *Falstaff*, as a more avowed ground of censure and dishonour: Nor ought the consideration that this passage contains the most exquisite comic humour and propriety in another view, to diminish the truth of this observation.

But however just it might be to demolish *Falstaff* in this way, by opening to us his bad principles, it was by no means *convenient*. If we had been to have seen a single repre-[T181]sentation of him only, it might have been proper enough; but as he was to be shewn from night to night, and from age to age, the disgust arising from the *close*, would by degrees have spread itself over the whole character; reference would be had throughout to his bad principles, and he would have become less acceptable as he was more known: And yet it was necessary to bring him, like all other stage characters, to some conclusion. Every play must be wound up by some event, which may shut in the characters and the action. If some *hero* obtains a crown, or a mistress, involving therein the fortune of others, we are satisfied;—we do not desire to be afterwards admitted of his council, or his bed-chamber: Or if through jealousy, causeless or well founded, *another* kills a beloved wife, and himself after,—there is no more to be said;—they are dead, and there an end; Or if in the scenes of Comedy, parties are engaged, and plots formed, for the furthering [T182] or preventing the completion of that great article Cuckoldom, we expect to be satisfied in the point as far as the nature of so nice a case will permit, or at least to see such a manifest *disposition* as will leave us in no doubt of the event. By the bye, I cannot but think that the Comic writers of the last age treated this matter as of more importance, and made more bustle about it, than the temper of the present times will well bear; and it is therefore to be hoped that the Dramatic authors of the present day, some of whom, to the best of my judgment, are deserving of great praise, will consider and treat this business, rather as a common and natural incident arising out of modern manners, than as worthy to be held forth as the great object and sole end of the Play.

But whatever be the question, or whatever the character, the curtain must not only be dropt [T183] before the eyes, but over the minds of the spectators, and nothing left for further examination and curiosity.—But how was this to be done in regard to *Falstaff*? He was not involved in the fortune of the Play; he was engaged in no action which, as to him, was to be compleated; he had reference to no system, he was attracted to no center; he passes thro' the

Play as a lawless meteor, and we wish to know what course he is afterwards likely to take: He is detected and disgraced, it is true; but he lives by detection, and thrives on disgrace; and we are desirous to see him detected and disgraced again. The *Fleet* might be no bad scene of further amusement;—he carries *all* within him, *and what matter* where, *if he be still the same*, possessing the same force of mind, the same wit, and the same incongruity. This, *Shakespeare* was fully sensible of, and knew that this character could not be compleatly dismissed but by death.—'Our author, (says the Epilogue to the Second [T184] Part of Henry IV.) will continue the story with Sir *John* in it, and make you merry with fair *Catherine* of *France*; where, for any thing I know, *Falstaff* shall dye of a sweat, unless already he be killed with your hard opinions.' If it had been prudent in *Shakespeare* to have killed *Falstaff* with *hard opinion*, he had the means in his hand to effect it;—but dye, it seems, he must, in one form or another, and a *sweat* would have been no unsuitable catastrophe. However we have reason to be satisfied as it is;—his death was worthy of his birth and of his life: '*He was born*', he says, '*about three o'clock in the afternoon with a white head, and something a round belly.*' But if he came into the world in the evening with these marks of age, he departs out of it in the morning in all the follies and vanities of youth;—'*He was shaked*' (we are told) '*of a burning quotidian tertian;—the young King had run bad humours on the knight;—his heart was fracted and corroborate;* [T185] *and a' parted just between twelve and one, even at the turning of the tide, yielding the crow a pudding, and passing directly into* Arthur's bosom, *if ever man went into the bosom of* Arthur.'—So ended this singular buffoon; and with him ends an Essay, on which the reader is left to bestow what character he pleases: An Essay professing to treat of the Courage of *Falstaff*, but extending itself to his Whole character; to the arts and genius of his Poetic-Maker, SHAKESPEARE; and thro' him sometimes, with ambitious aim, even to the principles of human nature itself.

THE END.

THE LONGER REVISIONS
(*c.* 1789–1790)
OF
AN ESSAY ON FALSTAFF
(1777)

THE LONGER REVISIONS OF
AN ESSAY ON FALSTAFF

LR 1
REVISION OF *ES.*, T5:2–T6:2

LR 1a: *Main Body of Revision*

[I2] It is of the Nature of Impressions as distinguished from Know- **A1**
ledge to be *latent* To escape the understanding and strike the Sensibility and to produce their Effect without Exciting any special
Notice of their operation. This is the Condition in which we stand
as relative to the World: some Things strike our Judgment and
are known and others touch our Sensibilities and are felt and our
Minds are made up of both. There is a wonderful Analogy between
Phisical & moral Things. The Understanding seems to be the Eye
of the Mind but the mind has other senses by which she can feel
her way thro' the Intricacies of the World. To these Feelings In
other Animals We give the Name of Instinct and we often call it
blind. Man has a Mental Eye but it seems to be superadded only to
these Feelings not substituted in the [I3] Place of them; but in man
these Feelings are perhaps less perfect as they are more various than
in the total Blind.

LONGER REVISIONS. The text consists of the latest versions of the LR, followed
where appropriate by extended ED. The *app. crit.* records (1) significant briefer ED of
either the latest versions or the extended ED (unless otherwise indicated, a briefer ED
is on the same page in the MS. book as the later draft by which it is superseded);
(2) all marks and notations on I and T pages indicating links and insertions; (3) the
MS. readings, unless self-evident, of all emendations; (4) almost all uncancelled MS.
materials not reproduced in the text of the LR or extended ED; and (5) for each
LR or extended ED a listing of whatever punctuation appears in the MS.; all other
punctuation is supplied by the editor.

For further details see Textual Intro. to the Revisions of the Essay. For abbreviations and symbols used in the text and *app. crit.* see pp. xiii–xiv.

LR 1. *For segment designations (A1, E1, E2, etc.) in outer margin see Textual Note
to LR 1–3, pp. 378–80.*

LR 1a. *Punctuation:* I32:2 deceived.

I2:1 It] *prec. by* X = *juncture with T5:1; see app. crit. to T5:2 and note to LR 1–3,
p. 381.* Knowledge] 2 *ED:* (C) observation / (C) the Understanding

I2:2 strike] *ED:* (C) pass I2:5 Instinct] *fol. by false start:* (UM) which

I3:1 Blind] *fol. by* (UM) But a = *beginning of LR 1—ED 1a; a squiggle between*
Blind *and* But *points upward to interlineation above* But: (C) upon this see —?—

Eɪ　[I28:3] If this be the Case as who doubts it we may have a great deal to do with latent Principles if we woᵈ Extricate our Minds from any Errour in which they have been Accidentally involved. It is one Question what the whole Effect of a Play may be as collected from the reading only and free of any preceding Influence and another what [I29] Effect may be produced by an improper & Erroneous Representation on the Stage and yet another if being read withᵗ Prejudice or represented without Errour and if we find notwithstanding our Impressions and understanding at variance with Each other by what Causes such effect is produced and whether We shoᵈ impute it to the Art or Folly of the Writer. The whole Effect [I31] upon a passive auditor is all that the writer looks to. But if this auditor curiously observing in Himself a Disagreement of Judgment and Sensibility shoᵈ Endeavour to investigate the Cause He must Examine the *sources* of his *sensibility* however *latent* as well as the *ground* of his *Judgment* and if He discovers that the Principles of this Disagreement are realy in human Nature and that a mixed Effect was intended to be produced for a special purpose He will then do justice to the art of the Writer tho' He may have thereby defrauded Himself of some Delight [I32] in having united two Things from the apparent opposition of which that Delight was intended to be drawn. The Charm will be dissolved that is I believe in Cases of this Nature the understanding will detect its own Errours for the sensibility is not or at least not much to be deceived. But if

I28:1 If] *prec. by* X = *link with LR 1—ED 1a; cf. last entry and LR 1—ED 1a, app. crit. to 14:1. For subsequent cancellation of LR 1—ED 1a see Textual Note to LR 1, pp. 380-1, and Intro., p. 59*

I29:1 Stage] *fol. by* (C) to which we give all the Force of Truth　　by what ... is produced] *ED*: (C) to which of These we ought to give most Credit　　We shoᵈ ... the Writer] 2 *ED*: (C) corresponding with the condition of human Nature or the Production of mere Errour & Folly / (C) arising out of Nature & Truth or (R) the Production of mere Errour & Folly

I29:2 whole Effect] *fol. by* (UM) upon a Reader

I31:1 a passive ... looks to] *ED*: (C) a passive Reader or Spectators Mind is all that is necessary to his Delight　　the writer looks to] *ED*: (C) is essential to the Author's Design

I31:2 Disagreement] *prec. by afterthought*: (C) suppos[ed]　　tho' He ... thereby defrauded] 2 *ED*: (C) yet He will (R) have thereby defrauded / (C) but (R) He will defraud [ed *added later to* defraud]

I32:1 in] *ED*: (C) by　　was intended to] *ED*: (R) was to

I32:2 The Charm ... own Errours] *ED*: (C) The Charm as to Him will be dissolved and I suspect that the Deceit will be always found in the Understanding　　sensibility ... be deceived] 2 *ED*: (C) Impression (R) is not to be deceived [*full stop added later*] (C) it must and will remain / (R) Impression (C) must I think and will remain the Perplexity sho^d proceed from a false Representation on the Stage then so much as there may be of that sho^d be discharged out of the Question without which it is in vain to reason at all.

This question concerning the Difference between the under- E2 standing [I33] and the sensibility I have been almost afraid to touch least it sho^d draw me beyond My purpose. It has never been fully considered that I know of and might possibly lead us into conclusions by no means Honourable [to] that high Faculty the understanding of which we so largely boast,ʌ but it is Enough for me to remind the Reader that we are all of us conscious of certain Feelings or Sensations of Mind which We do not seem to have passed thro' the understanding etc.

LR 1b: *Footnote to LR 1a, I33:2*

[I39] One sho^d think by the various Epithets of Praise in which G we dress up this Pattern of Perfection human Reason that human Actions were at least under her Conduct and Direction. Nothing however is less true. We cry her up indeed just as if she had run away with all the Wit & Beauty of the Family whilst Passions & Sensibilities & appetites her more homely Sisters do all the work. We love or hate I presume without her Counsel or Interference and we laugh & cry and feast and sing & dance without her Leave. We make Languages so far beyond her ability that she might as well make a world but she comes in with her Boast that after Some Ages she has been able to find out the Principles of the Work. We [I40] form Governments and when it is too late for use she makes grammars perhaps of those too. Not that she has discovered I think much skill of this sort in Europe whatever may have been done in China. We make Peace & War whilst Reason only writes a History of Events. The Sensibilities of England and America were various: it co^d not be otherwise under the Influence of such various situations. If we had not been of one Family we might however have been good Friends but being near Relations this Natural Difference became

I32:3 Perplexity] *fol. by* (C) and Errour of Mind
I33:2 Honourable [to] that] *ED*: (C) to the (R) Honour (UM) of (R) that [able *added to* Honour *in final version*]   so largely boast] X *below and interlineation above these words*: Note on this line see 39 = *subjoin LR 1b*
I33:2b understanding] *interlineation beneath this word*: See print 5 & 6 = *link with T5:4 and T6:4: see Textual Note to LR 1, pp. 381–2*   etc.] = *link with T5:4b*
LR 1b. *Punctuation*: I39:2 work.   I42:3 to do.

the Cause of most unnatural Quarrels. We made furious War to
the Destruction of each other but where was Reason? [141] Oh it
was not her Hour, she does not rise so early. But she has since
discovered we were all in the wrong for that we sho.ᵈ on both
sides have accommodated ourselves as much as might have been
to each others Situation. In short witht knowing the first Principles
of any one Thing in Nature she compares a little finds out a few
Relations and for the rest amuses herself with weaving general
Propositions which will never apply to any particular case whatever.
So little in Fact is there of Reason in the Conduct of Human affairs
that I question if there is a more ridiculous object in the world than
a Council of State. Six or Seven grave dignified Figures sit down with
great grimace to discourse of Peace or War. It is five thousand to
one but that the moment is long past [142] that the operative causes
are gone by without the Knowledge of these grave men and are
at that Instant working Effects out of their Power to Controul.
Even whilst they talk they are borne along mere Pageants on the
Stream of Time and all their mighty Wisdom & Deliberation ends
at last in this that to keep up the Farce of Authority they affect to
give the sanctions of Reason to the foregone Conclusions of Sensibility and whilst to the World they boast of their Power, To Heaven
they confess their weakness and found their best Hopes of Mercy
on their Inability of Controul. In such a Council spies are not
needed: one may venture to swear Months before Hand what it is
that those grave Personages will in their great Wisdom find themselves obliged to do. Shakespeare seldom shows a mere Counsellor
in any other Light than as a better sort of Stage Fool full of saws
& sayings and limping a great way after the Time.

Earlier Drafts

LR 1—ED 1: *Original Continuation of Par. 1, LR 1a*

LR 1—ED 1a: *First Part of Continuation*

Cancelled after Completion of Pars. 2 and 3, LR 1a

A2   [I3:2] (UM) But a (C) Play is intended as a Representation of the
passing world. It sho.ᵈ act therefore upon all the Senses of our Mind

I41:5 the moment is long past] *ED*: (R) the(C)y are 12 months at least behind
[I42:1] the occasion
LR 1— ED 1a. *Punctuation: none*
I3:2 But a] *see LR 1a, I3:1,* app. crit.

and whilst it opens many Things to our Understanding it sho^d
impress others on our Sensibility just as the World itself does. In
general we may say that those different operations sho^d concur in
a common effect but as in the world we find our understanding and
those Feelings frequently at variance with each other—I believe
in general from the Errour of the understanding delighting in [I4]
abstraction and general Propositions whilst the sensibility is excited
by circumstances the most minute and such as the understanding
can frequently neither estimate or indeed ⟨recognize⟩—so in a perfect Imitation of Nature a like opposition may take Place and the
Impression and understanding be sett at variance for any Purposes
worth attainment.

LR 1—ED 1b: *Second Part of Continuation*
Superseded by Par. 2, LR 1a

[I4:2] (C) In such a Case we have much to do with *latent* Principles that we may trace our Impressions and correct the Errour
of our Judgments and thereby unite our Understanding to our
Instinct. If these two Faculties after a full and fair Discussion are
found irreconcielable I shall then confess that we have misemployed
our Time [I5]⟨in commenting upon a wretched Author undeserving
our Notice or regard.⟩ But the author of the Character I am about
to consider is no other than Shakespear Himself and yet I shall
Produce such Instances of Boldness & courage in Falstaffe as are
wholly incompatible with that Idea of Cowardice which other Incidents may seem to suggest. The reader then must accept of my
Explanation or reconcile these apparent contradictions upon some
System of his own or be obliged to own that Shakespear Himself is
an Author undeserving of Notice or Regard.

A3

I4:1 executed . . . minute] *ED*: (C) confined to (UM) minute (R) circumstances
recognize] *scratched out before cancellation of whole passage*   attainment] (C) See
interlined above this word (U) See 28 *written in below it = subsequently rescinded link with
Par. 2, LR 1a: see* app. crit. *to LR 1a, I28:1*
   LR 1—ED 1b. *Punctuation: none*
   I5:1 in commenting . . . or reward] = *original continuation of I4:3; cancelled in
favour of I5:2-3: see note*
   I5:2 Himself] *fol. by false start*: (C) and let the Reader if He dare charge Him as the
Author with Absurdity & Contradiction

LR 1—ED 2: *Cancelled Version of Par. 3, LR 1a*

D1a   [I21:2] (C) The Distinction I have made concerning mental Impressions and the understanding is I think trite Enough and we all readily comprehend it. There are none of us unconscious of certain &c

D1b   But I have nothing to do with the Cause let the —?— Philosopher find it out if He can. It is Enough for us that the Fact is so and that these Feelings and the understanding are often at variance with Each other as Every man's Experience may avouch [I22] and that we often condemn or applaud &c

LR 1—ED 3: *Cancelled LR 2 Materials later Redrafted for LR 1b*
LR 1—ED 3a: *Uncompleted Continuation of T6:3*

D3   [I26:2] (C) The Difference between Sensibility and the understanding has never that I know of been fully discussed and yet a man determined to write might Here find a fair Harvest. But the Choice is made. One might range to be sure on the philosophic shelf but I am destined to perplex the librarian and find I fear no Place whatever: a Novelist a Critic a Polemic an apologist a Biographer— all and Neither.

D2   [I22:2] (C) It is however Whimsical Enough that we sho^d make such a Rout about this superior Faculty the Understanding, of higher Dignity & Beauty forsooth Whilst her more homely sisters do all the work. We often love or Hate at first sight: can the understanding tell why? We judge of Beauty & Deformity: upon what Principle I wonder; our Senses are judicious granted but what has Reason to do in the Matter: does Reason judge of Tones or of Flavour? Does Reason [arouse] our Disgust or provoke our Laughter? We make a Language so reducible to Rules that Reason

LR 1—ED 2. *Punctuation: none*
I21:3 certain &c] = *link with* T5:4
I22:1 applaud &c] = *link with* T6:3
LR 1—ED 3a. *Punctuation*: I23:2 take—   I24:1 Event.   I26:1 what—
I26:2 a man . . . fair Harvest] *ED*: (C) if (R) a man (C) is (R) determined to write (C) it (R) might (C) seem to promise as (R) fair (C) a (R) Harvest (C) as the Courage of Falstaffe
I26:4 perplex the librarian] *ED*: (C) stand alone
I22:2 of higher . . . the work] *ED*: (R) Whilst (C) it seems to have so little Concern in the World
I22:3 tell why] *fol. by 2 false starts*: (C) We look to first Principles of Character: What are they / (C) We take strong Impressions of Character

at length finds it out and boasts long after of her grammar. We form a Government, and Reason [I23] perhaps when it is too late writes a grammar of that too. We make war and we make Peace and what Part does Reason take—she writes a History of Events: the Sensibilities of England & America were various as to certain Points as indeed the Sensibilities of men in various Situations must be. [A]merica & England happened to be of one Family and therefore they quarreled and made War and Reason after a Time found out that they were both in the wrong for that each sho⁴ have accommodated itself as much as might be to the Situation of the other. In the mean Time the world [I24] proceeds; New Sensibilities provoke new Wars, war begets Poverty, Poverty Peace, whilst Reason knows just Nothing of the Matter or comes limping with her Saws & her Sayings a Century or two perhaps behind the Event. ⟨I do not mean however that Reason has not its use in the world but it has not those particular uses I believe which it is supposed to possess. Yet what is very provoking in this Faculty is that it often affects to repeal our Sensibilities and set up a standard of its *own*.⟩ A Council of State is in good Truth the most ridiculous object immaginable. Six or Eight grave Counsellors sit down to talk of Peace or War: [I25] Its a thousand to one but they are a 12 month at least behind the occasion; the operative Causes are gone by with⁴ their Knowledge and are working Effects which they cannot Controul. Whilst they talk they are borne along mere Pageants on the Stream of Time and the Whole of their Wisdom amounts to this that to keep up the Farce of Authority they affect to give the Sanctions of Reason to the foregone Compulsions of Sensibility and whilst to the world they boast of their Power, To Heaven they plead their conscious weakness and Inability of Controul. In [I26] such Council no spy is needed: one may venture to swear Six months at least before Hand what—

I23:3 America] *MS. reads* america   of one Family] *ED:* (C) United Friends
I24:1 provoke new . . . Poverty Peace] *ED:* (C) produce (R) new War [s *added to* War *later*] (C) and new Peace, and Commerce Expands or is contracted
I24:2 I do . . . its *own*] *original conclusion of LR 1—ED 3a: cancelled in favour of incomplete continuation beginning in I24:3*
I24:3 A Council] *begins new line in MS.*
I25:1 Its] *inadvertently indented as if for new par.*
I25:2 Farce] *apparently superimposed on ED:* (C) Face

LR1—ED 3b: *Revision of LR 1—ED 3a*
Originally inserted between T6:3 and LR 2—ED 1

D4 [I27] (C) It is Whimsical Enough What a Fuss we make about this dignified Miss who is supposed to have ingrossed all the Wit & Beauty of the Family. Sensations & appetites & Passions are hardly thank'd for their Labours whilst we pay this drawn up Madam almost divine Honours tho' these her more homely Sisters do all the work. We love or hate I think without her Counsel or Interference and laugh & cry and feast and sing & Dance without her Leave. She Nods sometimes perhaps & condescends to approve of this [I28] Gesture or of that Picture or Song Without knowing a single Principle of the work or indeed the first Principle of any one Thing Moral or Phisical in the whole World. She compares indeed a little and finds out a few Relations and idly weaves general Propositions which will never apply to any particular Case that ever did or ever Will Exist.

LR 2
REVISION OF *ES.*, T6:4–T22:5

F1 [I33:3] A Play in Representation may be considered for the most Part as an Action on our [I34] sensibilities only, the understanding being little more than a mere looker on; for [happier] Sure is that Writer who demanding nothing from us but who treating us as passive Beings excites what Passion He pleases than He who

B2 Wearies us with eternal appeals [I7] to our Judgment and compels us even in the [I8] midst of indolent Relaxation to keep equal Paces with Himself of mental Exertion not worth after all either the Moment or the Toil; but Happier yet is He who referring to both these Faculties knows on some Occasions how to elude the under-

LR 1—ED 3b. *Punctuation: none*
I27:1 make] *fol. by* (UM) so = *part of unreproduced and otherwise duly cancelled ED*
I27:2 drawn up Madam] *ED:* (C) Idol
I28:1 first Principle . . . one Thing] *ED:* (R) first Principle(C)s (R) of any Thing (C) Whatever   Relations] *fol. by* (C) and then sits down
LR 2. *For segment designations (F1, B2, F3, etc.) in outer margin see Textual Note to LR 1–3, pp. 379–80.*
Punctuation: I9:2 attention.   I9:3b Discourse—   T38MS:2 Thread!
I44:1 none.   I46:4 Sport.
I34:1 happier] *MS. reads* happiere   than He] *ED:* (R) than (C) Him   appeals] *fol. by* See 7 m[anuscript] = *link with* I7:1

standing and on others how to challenge and meet its Notice; and happiest of all perhaps who can if he pleases set these Principles at Variance with each other in the Theatre as they often are in real Life and steal such Impressions on his Audience without their Special Notice as shall keep their Hold in spite of any Errour into which He may chuse to lead their understanding [I9] and who may thereupon venture to introduce an apparent Incongruity of Character and Action either for Purposes of Mirth or any other worthy the attainment. This wo.^{d} be such a perfect Draught of human Nature such a nice Imitation as might deserve our utmost Curiosity and attention. [I9b:3] ⟨In this latter case however the writer must be F2 content with that Erroneous Judgment of his Play which He himself has excited for it is the understanding which governs our Discourse—the poor Impression has no Tongue: It is (CM) an imperfect (U) sort of Instinct only and proportionably dumb. Some idle (CM) Critick may explain the Mistery and then we are all right again in our Discourse [I10b:1] (U)—a Rectitude which if it diminishes our pleasure not worth the gaining.

[I34:3] An excellent Play may be considered as a publick stock of F3 rational Pleasure and if those Organs of the writers speech the Players sho.^{d} [I34:2b] so pervert his Designs & excite feelings & Passions opposite to his purpose it may be worth while to redeem such a Play from [Absurdity] and restore to the Public that [I35] Delight of which by the Folly of these men they have been defrauded.⟩ Nor is to be wondered at that the world sho.^{d} be so deceived: we take our amusements just as they are prepared for us with very little Examination of our own and we generally receive our first Impression from the Stage and we seldom in so slight a matter take any Trouble of our own to reform it. A general Concurrence is

I9b:3–I35:1 In this . . . been defrauded] *superseded by LR 3a; see Textual Note to LR 3, p. 388*

I9b:3 an imperfect] *inadvertently cancelled by line drawn through earlier layer (LR 2—ED 2)*

I9b:4 Critick . . . Discourse] *inadvertently cancelled by lines drawn through earlier layer (LR 2—ED 2)*

I10b:1 which if . . . the gaining] *ED*: (C) perhaps not worth the Purchase

I34:3 An Excellent . . . Players sho.^{d}] *passage enclosed by line (see note): supersedes ED*: [I34:2a] (UM) But if those ordgans of the Writers mind [*ED*: (C) thought] the Players shall   sho.^{d}] *fol. by etc. = link with I34:2b*

I34:2b Designs] *ED*: (C) Meaning   Absurdity] *MS. reads* Adsurdity

I35:1 defrauded] *prec. by afterthought*: (C) long

I35:2 the world . . . Examination of our own] *ED*: (C) those persons sho.^{d} possess this Power. They are themselves the Slaves of Established Customs thus obtained and it passes for public opinion and [is] therefore not without Hazzard opposed. There are indeed some very plain Cases wherein the Players cannot impose [I36] their own Folly on others. They cannot convert Mackbeth for example by any Shrugs or Contortions into a Coward or wink down the sweet Desdemona into a venetian Courtezan—tho' I have indeed seen them turn the most sublime Incident in all Shakespeare into Buffoonery and make othello kill Himself only to show How once upon a Time He Himself had kill'd a malignant and a turban'd Turk; but in the case of Falstaffe wherein the Author has designed an Incongruity of Character & Action nothing is so difficult as for them to preserve the Design and at once blend and distinguish the Colours nor any thing so easy as to bring down the Character to the Action and involve them both in the same indistinguishable glare. The Players I suppose mean neither Harm or good; they copy their Predecessers as well as they are able and think no more of the matter but every Copy varying a little for the Worse It becomes at length to bear no Resemblance of the orriginal. Nor are even the Traditions of the Playhouse compleat: the civil War of 1640 produced a Chasm never to be supplied. Cibber I think says that not one of the Players who were [I37] dispersed upon the shutting up of the Playhouse at that Period ever returned to the Stage and consequently all the old Plays upon the opening of the Stage 20 years after were left to the Judgment of men from their Condition the most incompetent of any to the Purpose. Nor were the Plays of Shakespeare in Repute for many years after the Restoration. The Follies of the french Stage, Rhimes & Love & Honour, became all the Vogue for Tragedy and the Manners of a small circle about Court laboriously & artificially profligate & debauched were substituted in Comedy for Wit & Mirth and the little Managements & irregularities of common Life. D'Avenant it is said was the Link which held both Periods together: He had seen the old Stage and had some Direction in the New. [T38MS:1] But this under the Circumstances of the Case does not deserve an Answer. The Play'rs have in Truth no Direction from Tradition concerning the Plays of Shakespear and if they had How diminished

I36:2 Contortions] *ED*: (C) Faces they can make   tho' I . . . turban'd turk] *written longways on inner margin; point of insertion determined by editor*   as for . . . blend and] *ED*: (UM) as to (R) blend and (C) yet

T38MS:1 But this . . . an Answer] *ED*: [I38:1] (C) But D'Avenant never saw the Plays of Shakespear or at least not more than one or two of them revived and indeed does not seem to have used much memory Care or Superintendence in the Matter.

a Thread! Every play'r depends [I38:2] on his immediate predecessor and all lay hold rather on the Errours than Proprieties of those
who have gone before them and as for Judgment it Is a Faculty
which they do not much take upon themselves to use and indeed
durst not use if they were possessed of any.

[I43] These then are the Difficulties which stand in my way. I **H1**
must explain what there realy is of Incongruity and refer it to its
true source and I must discharge all those Errours which the
Ignorance of the Play'rs has mingled with the real Principles of the
Play. To refer to the Book which I might recommend my Reader
to consider as independent of the Stage is not sufficient. He is
already so prejudiced by those very incompetent commentators
and by the common Concurrence & Consent that He will not give
the Text fair Play but make it bend in spite of Himself to so ancient
& general an opinion. The Writer of this wo^d probably have been
precisely in the Same situation if He had not taken his first Impression from the Book and at a Time too when He was Entirely
ignorant of the public opinion concerning this Character; yet had
the Stage afterwards so [I44] powerfull an Influence that tho' very
much astonished to see a Falstaff there so different from his first
Conception that He almost submitted to the general Current and
could scarcely recognize his own Reluctance an accidental Conversation has recalled those Feelings and He finds or thinks He finds
them well founded tho' there is certainly Enough in the Play to
confirm Prejudice once obtained or Even Excuse any careless
Surrender of Judgment where there was none.

[I46:2] ⟨The End proposed is the vindication of Falstaffe from **H3**
the Imputation of Cowardice and this End will be pursued thro'
many a various Proof and many a Page but let not any be therefore
discouraged. The writer knows perfectly that the Chace must be
made to pay itself and Supply its own Delight. The End proposed

---

T38MS:2 Thread] *ED*: (C) sight   T38MS:3 depends] *for continuation see note*
I38:2 Proprieties] *fol. by* (UM) Errours they always seem = *part of otherwise unreproduced and duly cancelled ED*
I43:2 true source] *ED*: (C) Principles   those Errours] *prec. by false start*: (C) that absur[dity]
I43:4 very incompetent commentators] *ED*: (C) popular Comments   an opinion] *ED*: (C) A Comment
I44:1 Excuse . . . none] *ED*: (C) justify submission where there was not some reluctant (R) Surrender
I46:2–I47:1 The End . . . own Defeat] *revised by LR 3c; see Textual Note to LR 3, p. 387*

is almost Nothing and its attainment no otherwise Necessary than as it serves to inhance the Pleasure and Crown the Sport.

The Reader little Expects that this End will be attained; He will even as much as He can resist Conviction. So much the better, the Contention will only be the More interesting. But men cannot resist beyond a certain Point. If Truth be with me she carries [I47] with her so sweet a Compulsion that adversaries as she approaches become converted into Friends and triumph even in their own Defeat.⟩

⟨Just Here we implore the Reader's Patience. When the Play is fairly opened Shakespeare Himself shall reward his attention: the Page will be relieved with borrowed Excellence. His will be the rich Threads; at least however the Tissue may be called my own.⟩

H4   [I47:7] The Drawing of Falstaffe's Character has been often mentioned with Admiration [148] but I do not remember that any nice Investigation has been made of the Draught; the Effect is striking but there seems to be much Incoherence of Parts: old in years & young in Disposition Enterprizing & corpulent Mixing Poverty & Expense Title & Buffoonery A Dupe and a Wit an Humourist and a man of Humour a jester & a jest Without Principle yet acceptable to all and supposed without Courage yet despised by None. This is a singular [I49] Composition and if we trust to our Sensibilities we must add a Natural one; but by what Art those Qualities have been so mingled or what those Principles are in Nature to which under this Mixture they refer we have not enquired. We see a fat jolly lying witty humourous debauched old unprincipled Boy who gets into various scrapes some of which at least seem to imply Cowardice, and We take the Whole as it offers itself satisfied if He jests Himself through and that we laugh (CM) at (U) his Distress & Evasions. When the sport is over [we] Think no more of the Matter: It was not Expected by Shakespeare that we sho^d look further. [I50] He was intitled to have his Peice fairly represented

I47:2-4 Just Here . . . my own] *superseded by LR 12, I145; see note, p. 387*
I47:7 The Drawing] *prec. by 2 false starts*: [I47:6] (C) Often has Falstaffe been mentioned in Books and in Discourse, always with Admiration of his poetic Maker Shakespeare, never that I know of with / [I 47:5] (C) much has been written much has been said
I48:1 Effect] *prec. by* (C) Whole   by None] *fol. by false start*: (C) a glutton
I49:1 what those . . . they refer] *ED*: (R) what (C) that standard is to which they (UM) refer
I49:2 witty] *fol. by* (C) comical
I49:3 Expected] *prec. by false start*: (C) intende[d]   look] *ED*: (C) think

and for the rest whilst the Cause was with Him to his Auditors He never Meant to give more than the Effect.

One single Quality supposed as a Part of this various Character I venture to draw into Question: Is or is not Falstaffe a constitutional Coward?

With respect &c

Earlier Drafts

LR 2—ED 1: *Cancelled Beginning of LR 2*

[16:1a] (UM) If this be so and who is He who doubts it (C) B1
⟨[16:1b] In all dramatic Characters I mean in all worth Notice there are three distinct Relations in which they are to be considered. They must refer in the first Place to the general Principles of human Nature; In the second to the external Influence upon them of their companions of the Drama and of the situations in which they stand; and in the third⟩ [16:3] all Dramatic Characters, I mean all worth Notice, must stand in a double Relation to the Spectators. The optics seeing must be considered as well as the object shewn: the effect arises from the Action and Reaction of both. A [17] dramatic Character acting from and shewn to the understanding alone is imperfectly shewn; it is adjusted to one Part of our Composition only: we see but half a man and with half our Faculties and to say sooth with the worser half; for happier sure is that writer who never allows us to think or reason or judge at all but who treating us not as rational but passive Beings impresses what Images and excites what Passions he pleases and who

wafts us o'er the seas and thro' the air,
to Thebes To Athens when He will and where

(UM) than Him who wearies us with Eternal appeals

I50:2 One single] *prec. by false start*: (C) With respect then to this Character &c see 22 pr[int] = *link with T22:6 superseded by next entry*
I50:3 With respect &c] *fol. by* see 22 pr[int] = *link with T22:6*
LR 2—ED 1. *Punctuation*: 16:3 Characters, Notice, 16:4 both. I7:1 air,
16:1a If] *prec. by* X = *link with T6:3; see T6, app. crit.* doubts it] *fol.*
by false start, partly miscancelled: (C) It is like every other operation of Nature in man a subject of dramatic Imitation *see note*
16:1b-2 In all . . . the third] *false start, partly miscancelled, superseded by I6:3 ff.;*
see note
16:5 A] *fol. by* [I7:1] (UM) a
I7:1 imperfectly] *ED*: (C) but half than Him . . . Eternal appeals] = *overlap*
with LR 2, I34:1

LR 2—ED 2: *Cancelled Continuation of I9:2, Par. 1, LR 2*

B3   [I9a:3] (C) Something perhaps very like this we may discover in the Character of Falstaff. Let not the Reader think that I require his assent in Present. If the Understanding be on purpose Misled It were Vain to Expect it for it is the Understanding not the Impression which forms our opinion and governs our Discourse; the Impression has [I10a:1] (UM) no Tongue: It is an imperfect sort of Instinct and proportionably (C) Dumb. [I10:2] If indeed the Question stood clear of accidental Influences I might venture boldly to demand of Him if He did not find Himself plagued at least with some intrusive Impression on his Mind as if a sort of Courage & Boldness belonged to the Character of Falstaff; and this I might Expect Him to confess as a weakness which being in opposition to his Understanding He co^d not trust; but if even this Impression which I think naturally to arise out of the play has by accident been withheld from Him, If he has taken his first Notices of Falstaff not from the Text but from the comment or the Stage and in a matter so uninteresting has never reconsidered the Point [I11] It were hopeless to demand of Him any thing but a fair and patient Hearing.

B4   ⟨Nor can I hope even this in so desperate a Case without courting his attention by collateral Amusement and at every step compensating his Toil. This if I can accomplish it will be principally by means of those numerous Passages [I12] out of the Play which I must be obliged to produce relieving thereby my Page at every Interval with borrowed Excellence: the rich Threads will indeed be Shakespear's but if they are fairly interwòve I may perhaps be allowed by courtesy at least to call the Tissue in some sort my own.⟩

B5   (C) Every Profession has its Follies but that in which all Professions agree is that Each [has] laid up a kind of Stock Knowledge level to the Capacity of Every Individual and to which Every Individual alike resorts: one wo^d almost swear that Every Member had

---

LR 2—ED 2. *Punctuation*: I13:3 (to ⁗others)

I10:2 intrusive Impression . . . of Falstaff] *ED*: (C) troublesome Impression of Courage as belonging to (R) the Character of Falstaffe (C) which He knew not (UM) how (C) he acquired   Notices] *ED*: (C) Impressions

I11:2–I12:1 Nor can . . . my own.] *superseded in LR 2—ED 4b*

I11:2 Amusement] *ED*: (R) Amusement(C)s

I11:3 Passages] *ED*: (C) quotations

I12:1 but if . . . my own] *ED*: [I11] (C) but I hope by some Art and Care of [*ED*: (R) by (C) no unskillful] interweaving to render the Tissue in some Degree my own

I12:2 has laid up a] has *supplied from ED*: (C) has a

made a vow of Poverty as to Himself and thought it Prophanation
to draw a single Idea from [113] any other source. This produces
a kind of Medium Ability never Exquisitely right or scandalously
wrong and Hence it is that all Professions may be considered as
Stationary: all improvement tending to disarrange and perplex
the common stock and as coming from a Member wo^d be considered and persecuted as the Sin of Ingratitude and of Witchcraft.
In the Profession of the Law I can allow of this and tho' I sho^d
believe that no one Case has ever been in all its Circumstances
exactly like another yet I wo^d rather see them wafted thro' West-
minster Hall in some Authorized Vehicle of established Principle
and Precedent tho' they did not fit exactly in every Point than
whisked about one knows not how or whither in the more phantastical Discretion of a Judge; but I cannot allow of this (to pass
all others) in [114] the Profession if we may call it one of the Player.
He follows the Condition of his Principal and it is a Settled Point
that moderation in a Poet is what Neither Gods or Men or Demons
can Endure. If the scheme of raising Property out of Letters had
been carried into full Execution and a Corporation of Authors with
proper officers—warden & Masters and so forth—had been thereupon created by Letters patent or otherwise [and Laws had been
thereupon made by authority of Parliament ag^t Plagiary, Imitation
and all Hardy Trespass] I sho^d have hoped that the Poets at least
wo^d have been excluded both from the Benefits & Penalties of
these new Laws as too wild for mere material Chains to bind:
better that a thousand free Booters sho^d boldly steal or meanly
imitate.

LR 2—ED 3: *Cancelled Materials later Redrafted*
for Opening of Par. 3, LR 2
Original Continuation of LR 2—ED 4c

[I20] (C) There are two Difficulties which stand at present in my C4
Way. One which I have alread[y] touched I mean the Difference
between Impression and Knowledge a Distinction which tho' it

114:3 and Laws . . . hardy Trespass] *MS. has these words inadvertently careted in
before otherwise instead of after*   better that . . . meanly imitate] *ED*: (C) better to
permit the Crime of Plagiary or what is much worse in my opinion that of Imitation
to pass with^t Loss of Life or Limb
LR 2—ED 3. *Punctuation*: I20:2 for.

looks too Metaphisical for the purpose of *Mere* Amusement yet it is such as I find myself obliged to insist on, for independent of the absurdities of the Stage there is a certain studied Disorder & Dis-arangement as it sho.ᵈ appear in the Character of Falstaffe which must be accounted for. The other arises out of the errours of the stage from whence We have taken Impressions Never intended by the Author. Without remarking on these Things and thereupon accounting for [I21] the Misconception which has as I think pre-vailed respecting this Character it Wo.ᵈ be too presumptuous for a single Man to hold up Even Truth itself against so universal an Errour.

LR 2—ED 4: *Cancelled Versions of Materials*
Incorporated in Pars. 4-6, LR 2

LR 2—ED 4a: *First Version*
Original Continuation of LR 2—ED 2

C1   [I16] (C) I am impatient [to] produce [the] Proofs but I must however open my way. The proposed End indeed is nothing yet I do not mean to trifle with the Reader. Amusement tis true [is] my Principal Aim but I expect no less than to produce full and ample Conviction that Shakespear meant to draw Falstaffe as a man of considerable Courage.

LR 2—ED 4b: *Second Version*
Supersedes First Version

C2   [I16:4] (C) I wo.ᵈ instantly produce my Proofs if I did not think it necessary to open the way. Slight as the Matter is I do not mean to triffle. In addition to the Amusement I hope to furnish the Reader with and which is indeed my principal Aim I Expect to produce the most ample [I17] Conviction that Falstaffe is a Character not of

---

I20:3 intended] *2 ED*: (C) designed / (C) given us
LR 2—ED 4a. *Punctuation*: I16:3 Courage.
I16:1 to produce the] to *and* the *supplied from ED*: (C) to open the
I16:3 Amusement . . . is my] is *supplied from ED*: (R) Amusement (C) . . . which indeed is my   draw] *ED*: (C) show
LR 2—ED 4b. *Punctuation*: I18:1 own.
I16:4 if I . . . to open] *ED*: (C) but (UM) I must however open

a Cowardice but of very considerable Courage. This is what the
Reader I know least Expects and what He will resist to the Utmost
of his Power but I defy Him, and yet not I but she who guides
my Hand beyond a certain Point we cannot resist. There is in Truth
that sweet Compulsion as she grows manifest that stoutest Adversaries drop their Arms and triumph in their own Defeat.

(C) But the Reader must have a little Patience and just Here
when I open [the] Play Shakespeare Himself shall reward his attention: the Page shall be relieved with borrowed Excellence; the
rich [I18] threads at least will be his tho' the Tissue may be called
my own.

LR 2—ED 4c: *Third Version*
Supersedes Second Version

[I18:2] (C) I wo.d instantly proceed to my Proofs if I did not find   C3
it necessary to open the way and I must sollicit just Here the Readers
Patience: when the Play is fairly opened Shakespeare Himself shall
reward his attention; the Page will be relieved with borrowed
Excellence. His will be the rich Threads; at least however the Tissue
may be my own.

(C) My real Purpose is to write a few sheets of (what I think no
irrational) Amusement. [I19] If they do not delight the Hour They
are nothing for what is Falstaffe that we sho.d think or care about
Him? Yet in the Pursuit of this Point I may probably do that which
the Reader I think will least expect: I may fairly prove that this
Character was drawn by Shakespeare not as a Coward but as a man
of considerable and Even distinguished Courage. Universal opinion
is I know against me yet I do not despair. The Reader will resist
me it is true to the utmost of his Power but men cannot resist beyond
a certain Point. If Truth be with me she carries with her so sweet
a Compulsion that Adversaries as she approaches become Friends
and triumph even in their own Defeat.

I17:2 guides] *ED*: (C) directs
I18:1 Tissue] *prec. by* (C) whole   may be called] *ED*: (UM) I may (C) call
  LR 2—ED 4c. *Punctuation*: I18:4 (what irrational)   I19:2 Courage.   I19:5
Defeat.   I18:4 *app. crit.* Aim.
I18:4 My real] *prec. by false start*: (C) Amusement is my real Aim. The End pro-
posed [*ED*: (R) Aim. (UM) The (C) subject itself] is too slight

LR 2—ED 4d: *Fourth Version*
Supersedes Third Version. Original Continuation
of Par. 3, LR 2

H2   [I44:2] (C) The End proposed is to prove that Falstaffe is a Character not of Cowardice but of considerable Courage and— What the Reader little Expects or what the Writer perhaps least cares about—the Point as He firmly believes will be amply and fairly proved. Yet not for this End does He Write a Book of so many Pages, for the [I45] Sole Purpose of proving Falstaffe to be a Character of Courage Might intitle its author to commiseration perhaps or indeed any Thing but a patient Hearing; but this Book will be found singular in many Things and among others in this that the proposed End is realy Nothing, the Means are all. He hopes to furnish Critical Amusement and Well knows that Every page must pay the Trouble of reading by some Novelty. He has started a strange light Question but the Chase over Many a Various Page must furnish its own Delight nor is the final seizing of the [I46] Game of any other Consequence than as it is necessary to the Sport.

LR 3
INCOMPLETE REVISION OF LR 2
LR 3a: *Revision of LR 2, I9:3b–I35:1*

[I156:2] Now Reason I am afraid has very little to do in this Case and had better perhaps take a Nap, least it sho.ᵈ fall as it is very apt to do into great Errours, till the Play is over. In a performance of this Kind if the Player doth his Duty [I157] as the faithfull Organ of the Poet there is no more to be said. The Author must

LR 2—ED 4d. *Punctuation: none*
I45:1 Character of Courage] *fol. by false start*: (C) wo.ᵈ Never prove any Thing Things] *fol. by* (C) So (UM) is = *part of otherwise cancelled* ED   the Means are all] *ED*: (C) and that the pretended Means are in the Truth the real End
I45:2 He hopes . . . Critical Amusement] *2 ED*: (C) Critical Amusement is what the Reader must principally expect / (R) Critical Amusement is (C) his true Pursuit [*ED*: (R) his (C) true object]   Novelty] *fol. by* (UM) or (C) some Delight
I46:1 is necessary to] *ED*: (UM) crowns
LR 3a. *Punctuation*: I 154:3 rejoice,
I156:2–I157:2 Now Reason . . . has made] *ED*: [I150:1] (UM) If the Players wo.ᵈ do justice to their Author and the Audience be content as mere passive Beings to receive the Impressions be they what they might of the Play there co.ᵈ be no further Question. The Author must abide by the Effects he had produced.

abide by the Impressions He has made. [I150:3] We might reason indeed afterwards about the Causes of these Effects but that wo.^d be a Matter of mere curiosity producing indeed great Admiration perhaps of the writer but nothing as to the Force and Influence of the Play; but if the Players will practise Tricks & Tones & Grimaces contrary to the Ends & Designs of the Writer the Whole Work will be disarranged and we shall not be able to understand it with.^t carefully [I151] investigating the Authors Design and the Arts on which it was composed. There are various Arts of impressing but the most general is that of giving Actions & Sentiments a Tone & Colouring which they can derive only from some specific Motive, which Motive however is never Exposed to our special Notice. This Motive however is not lost to us: it operates secretly on our Feelings or if we give ourselves the Trouble we may discover it by Inference & Deduction by which means it operates only on our Sensibilities and escapes the comment of our Understandings. [I152] A dramatic Writer has very seldom occasion to consider his Audience as rational Beings unless it be indeed to keep out of the Way of a very troublesome Faculty. To Him an Audience is only an animated Mass compounded of certain Feelings & Passions which it is his Business to Excite and to play upon for which End He is to exhibit a Fiction so cunningly drawn and so Exactly coresponding to the Laws & Principles of our Nature that we are by the Power of Sympathy to catch the Motion and to sound [I153] in perfect unison with those Organs on the Stage which He has artificially inspired. We become by this Means in the Course of the Pr[o]cess to be in Fact both the Instrument and the Hearers attending with delight to a very interesting Tune skillfully played on our own Sensibilities. This in the Early ages of Greece was so decidedly the Case that the Spectators Mingled as it were in the Peice and Encouraged advised Exhorted & applauded & condemned as their Passions & their

I150:3 Grimaces] *ED*: (C) Attitudes
I151:3 is not . . . our Feelings] *ED*: (C) will operate on our Feelings with.^t the notice of the understand[ing]   Trouble] *fol. by false start*: (C) the under[standing]
I152:1 rational Beings] *fol. by false start*: (C) His Business is with their Feelings and Passions only
I152:2–I153:1 that we are . . . perfect unison] *ED*: (UM) that we are all (C) by the (UM) which playing on our sensibilities to be put into sympathetic motions and to sound in perfect unison
I153:2 in the Course . . . Tune skillfully] *ED*: (C) at once (R) the Instrument and the (C) Audience and perceive with much Delight & Satisfaction a Tune
I153:3 decidedly] *ED*: (UM) openly

Feelings impelled. The more refined Ages of Greece did a very Extraordinary Thing: instead of imitating any certain Action on the Principles of Nature simply, they took it into their [I154] Heads to imitate an Imitation and to bring the History of the heroic Ages, the real Action, and the feigned one, The Spectators of former Times, all at once upon the Stage. A grecian Play was as if an English American sho^d bring on the Stage a Whole Indian Tribe acting with Dance & Song one of their usual Representations: these Spectacles are always an Imitation of some Action in which the Imitators or their immediate Ancestors at least were the orriginal Agents. The Whole Tribe partake: they exhort & they encourage as if the Imitation were a Reality and they join in the Song; they mourn they triumph & rejoice, but what wo^d be the Imitation of this? Not in Fact the Imitation of any certain Action so much [I155] as the Imitation of a certain Age & People in the act of Imitation. This Imitation if it sho^d become a general Custom wo^d be regulated & limitted by Laws of its own that is by Laws arising out of its own Nature. It wo^d be capable of beautifull Accompaniments, but it wo^d always have the Defect of being the Imitation of an Imitation and even so confined that No Act could be represented but what was capable of being thus transmitted thro' two Mediums, and it Wo^d of Course want the Truth the Freedom and the Variety of real Nature. Yet so much are Mankind the slaves of Imitation and the Fools of [I156] Authority that we have Critics at this Day who wish to limit the Spirit of a better Drama by the Laws of a worse or—without hazarding Decisions—by Laws which do not belong to its Nature and who would willingly confine Even Shakespeare Himself to the Precisions of Time & of Place and hang a dangling Chorus like Eo meo & Areo at his Tail.

I153:4 refined Ages of Greece] *fol. by false start*: imitated the whole of this, not only the Action on the Stage

I154:1 the History . . . the Stage] *ED*: (UM) the former Ages (R) History (C) Action Spectators and all upon the Stage

I154:2 the Imitators] *fol. by false start*: (C) were (UM) supposed present

I155:3 Accompaniments] *LR 3b probably to be subjoined here as footnote; see notes, p. 389* 'of an Imitation] *fol. by* (UM) and of wanting the Truth (R) the Freedom and the Variety of real Nature *for last eight words see next entry* the Truth] *fol. by* etc. = *juncture with passage following* an Imitation *see prec. entry*

LR 3b: *Probable Footnote to LR 3a, I 155:3*

[I162:2] The principal Accompanyment of the grecian Drama was music an accompanyment so little in our Power to add to our own Drama that I question if we have any just Idea of the Nature & Use of that Music which the grecians so applyed. I profess neither Learning or Music yet I have known the Bolts of plain Men go sometimes more directly to the Mark than the feathered Arrows of the Wise. Let us try. There grows in every Nation a sort of wild music consonant to the Language Manners & Character of the People Coresponding not only to that Tone in which the Language itself is spoken—for every Language [h]as its own peculiar Tone— but [I163] likewise to the Tones of all the Passions as they are in that particular Society sounded or Expressed; for tho' the Tones of the same Passion are by different Societies variously expressed this Music is capable in every Country alike of being cultivated into Science; but the different Tones must be preserved Every Where pure if men wo^d wish to affect the Passions [I164] for Tones are the Natural and indeed only Language of Sensibility. Now in greece the Natural Music I presume was cultivated with^t foreign Aid into Science. It was therefore as far as Passion and Sensibility were concerned intelligible to all and from Hence it must follow that this Music instead of being a Mere imitation of the Tones it found wo^d become by Degrees a Standard for the Regulation of these Tones. Music was capable of fixedness and having gone the Length of a perfect Imitation was capable of stoping at any given Time and Ever after of driving back the erring Tones of Passion to a steady Conformity to itself. [T164MS] This is an application of Music

LR 3b. *Punctuation*: I166:4 own.

I162:3 profess neither Learning or Music] *ED*: (UM) for (C) my own part have but little (R) Learning (C) & less (R) Music

I162:5 wild music] *fol. by false start*: (C) the genuine Growth and product of the Place

I163:1 are by ... variously expressed] *ED*: (C) among mankind in general are seldom I believe in direct opposition to each other yet who will say that the Tones of Love Hatred Derision Fear and so forth can by People of different Nations be always mutually understood, but the wild music I speak of must of course in every Country imitate the Native (UM) Tones   Music] *ED*: (C) wild (R) Music   cultivated into Science] *fol. by false start*: (C) preserving the Tones as the Elements out of which it is to [be] composed

I164:1 Natural and ... of Sensibility] *ED*: (C) Elementary (R) Language of (C) our Passions

I164:2 foreign Aid] *fol. by* (C) or Imitation

T164MS:1 This is ... private Discourse] *ED*: [I164:4] (UM) which must (C) have given great Force and Beauty to private Conversation and public [I165] Harangues *see note* which every man will feel the Importance of who knows how Passions of Every sort are raised & communicated by Tones and it must have given infinite Force & Beauty not only to public speaking but private Discourse. [I165] But the Drama is in Truth itself little more than an Exercise of Sensibility whilst the Intellect not being offended is almost passive in the Case; but Sensibility is excited by coresponding Tones and the greater Precision they possess the greater & more perfect the Effect. But the Actors of those Times like those of the present might be the most incompetent Judges what Tones to use. It therefore seemed necessary that they sho^d be prompted by the aid of that art which was become the standard of Tone and thus as the Flutes behind the scenes varyed from Love to Rage to jealousy To fear to Derision To Pride to Disdain and [I166] the rest the Actors voice might by coresponding Tones excite Every Passion in conformity to the Author's Design and convey every Impression which the Audience were from the general fixedness of Tones predisposed to take. The flutes were then but Prompters of Passion seldom heard by the Audience because being in accord with the Actors voice they were melted into it or if they were heard they were only Exciters of stronger Feeling. I speak not of the accompanyments of the Chorus which was probably of high and complicated Music such as might please a Modern Conn[o]isseur. If these conjectures be just it will follow that we cannot furnish a musical accompanyment who are without any Native Music or Tones owing [to] the mixture of Inhabitants and all our Science imported from Italy containing Tones utterly discordant to our own.

LR 3c: *Truncated Revision of Pars. 4–5, LR 2*

[I51] The Writer of this Book was conscious that the End held out to the Reader was almost Nothing. He saw therefore that every

I165:1 little more . . . of Sensibility] *ED*: (C) a Tune played (UM) by (C) the Instrumentality of Actors on the Sensibility of the Hearers   not being offended] *ED*: (C) tho' it must (R) not (C) be (R) offended

I165:2 use] *ED*: (C) assume

I166:1 corresponding Tones] *ED*: (C) according Accents

I166:4 these conjectures . . . are without] *ED*: (C) this [these *in final draft is superimposed on* (C) this] Account (UM) be true, where shall England find a Prompter (C) with!

LR 3c. *Punctuation: none*

I51:1 to the Reader] *ED*: (UM) to (C) Himself and (R) to (C) this (R) Reader [the *in final draft superimposed on* (C) this]

I51 2 every Page . . . own Perusal] *ED*: (C) the means of attainment must thro' (R)

Page must compensate by some Entertainment for its own Perusal; critical Amusement became therefore in Truth the sole End tho' regulated & directed by a pretended one of another Sort: thus circumstanced it was indifferent whether the vindication of Falstaffe's Courage was obtained or no Excepting only that it seemed necessary to seize the object of Pursuit not on its own account but to crown the Pleasures of the Chase; [T52MS] but the object might not have been less a Reality for being unimportant and such as it was He had no Doubt in due Time to have possessed it but He doubted however very much whether the Reader wo^d keep equal Pace and hold out to the End of the Chase. He finds however that He has erred both ways: He has been told by many that they have come untired and chearfully through but as for Truth it was what they did not look for or find; that they conceived me no otherwise Employed than in draging a fat Paunch over many a various Page for the sole Purpose of Exercise and sport; that if I held out sometimes a Semblance of Truth it was but looking to the Playhouse and the Illusion instantly vanished. There as in his own Home Falstaffe was to be substantially seen and heard & felt; There He had doffed the Lions skin in which I had phantastically accoutred Him and stood forth once more a wretched Coward & a genuine Poltroon.

> [T53MS] So Proteus hunted in a nobler Shape
> became when seiz'd a Puppy or an Ape.

All this is realy very hard and uncomfortable: just in the Moment when the game seemed as it were in my Hand these cursed Players come accross foil all the ground and disappoint the Sport. [I54] If I wo^d yet succeed I must convert sportfull Hunting it seems into furious War and defy the whole Theatric State to bloody Battle & to bruising Arms. Well, Be it so. Retreat were baseness now.

> To hunt the Deer with Hound & Horn
> Earl Percy took his Way;
> The Child may [rue] which is unborn
> The Hunting of the Day.

every Page compensate by some Entertainment (C) their (R) own Perusal   a pretended one] *ED*: (C) an artificial Pretence   obtained] *ED*: (C) well supported
I54:1 sportfull] *ED*: (C) harmless   and defy . . . Theatric State] *ED*: (C) and wet my grey goose Feather   to bloody . . . bruising Arms] *cancelled; prec. by* stet
   I54:3 Retreat . . . now] *ED*: (UM) it were now inglorious to retreat   now] *fol. by* X = *link with* To hunt . . .
   I54:4 To hunt] *prec. by* X = *link with* now   To hunt . . . the Day] *not stanzaed in MS.; see note*   rue] *see note*

[I55] These are dreadfull Notices and the Theatric Powers tremble no Doubt thro' all their Shadowy Realms and loudly call their departed Heroes their Harrys & their Richards in their now living Forms of former Days to Battle, fearfull at the approach of Truth lest all their Magic structures rear'd so high sho^d tumble into Heaps on their false Heads; but let them lay by their Terrours. Truth is not the Enemy of avowed Deceit; the Magic & Deceits of the Theatre are

Earlier Drafts

LR 3—ED 1: *Materials for Uncompleted Note*
to Es., T70:3
Redrafted in Second Half of LR 3a

A   [I68] (UM) In what is called the heroic and may for variety sake be called the Savage Ages of Greece The Heroes then like the Savages of America now not always droping with Human gore wo^d sometimes with washed Faces recite and pantomime in a circle of their Friends some past Adventure of their own not unaccompanyed perhaps as in American Representations of the like Sort with Dance and Song.—In the Pauses of Recitation & action and whilst the Hero was breathing from his Toils those Friends wo^d comment and applaud adding some Wild Music perhaps, the natural growth of the Country, to flatter and to sooth and sometimes in the very Heat & Bustle of his Action wo^d Encourage Exhort caution and even mingle their own Passions in the Act and thus after five Pauses let us suppose wo^d the Representation be compleatly made.—But it wo^d be a Representation before the Hero's own usual Followers and Kindred who being interested in the Matter wo^d bring real passions and Action [I69] of their own into and thereby become *a component Part of the Act.* But the Act itself wo^d be however a subject of general Curiosity and it wo^d Naturally follow that some

I55:1 Theatric Powers] *ED:* (C) associated Powers of Covent Garden & Drury Lane   Forms] *fol. by* of — &c = *overlap with* of former *written in line above in MS.* lay by] *ED:* (UM) suspend   Terrours] *fol. by false start:* (C) another Time and I may blow them off like Dust. I only mean to rescue Falstaffe that is Shakespear from their oppressions

LR 3—ED 1-3. *For segment designations* (*A, F, D, etc.*) *in outer margin see note to LR 3—ED 1-3*

LR 3—ED 1. *Punctuation:* I68:2 —In   I68:3 —But   I69:3 *Part.* I70:2 *Duration.*   I70:3 *Reward.*   I73:3 it?   I77:2 *Nature.*   I78:1 *Neighbours,*

of those who had been Witnesses of and Partakers in it wo.^d Endeavour to exhibit it to others in all its Parts. But the Accompanying Passions & action and music of the Hero's Friends was according to this Account *a component Part.* Those then who wo.^d Exhibit it at second Hand wo.^d be obliged to procure a competent Number of Persons to represent the Hero's Friends as well as [the] Hero Himself and perhaps other Friends ⟨who Were⟩ engaged with Him in the real Adventure and who possibly sustained their Parts in the First Representation with the Hero Himself. But all this wo.^d be too difficult and complicated a Business to be effected for the Purpose [170] of an occasional Imitation only. A confederacy of this kind co.^d not be made or supported but upon a common Interest and with a view to Duration. They would therefore co[n]vert this imitative Exhibition into a gainfull Trade and travel about in a Cart if Horace pleases and Exhibit this inferiour Interlude for Reward. From this Condition of Things it wo.^d necessarily follow that these Persons wo.^d Endeavour to assume the real Person of the Hero not only as his Face and Figure might be generally known but as it was this or that particular Hero was to be represented and not Heroism itself or general Nature. They wo.^d therefore procure a Masque imitating his Features and such Masques being long preserved might afterwards Enable the Statuary and give that Established Character to ancient statues which was supposed to produce an exact Resemblance of the persons [171] represented. The Hero then and his Companions in the Adventure we may suppose to be represented in Masques of likeness, His domestic Friends in what Masques the Exhibitors thought proper. Here then was a grecian Play in all its essential Parts but We must observe of the Exhibition made by the Hero Himself that it was something more than a mere Representation of Nature for tho' the Action was a bare Imitation yet the Person representing and the Person represented was one and the same; and of the Imitation of this by other Persons that it was something less than Nature because the Person representing

169:4 as well as] *fol. by false start*: (C) a capital Actor   who Were] *apparently cancelled by mistake along with prec. afterthought*: (C) to whom the Story was thus told   and who] *fol. by* (C) living for the most part in Society with Him

170:4 assume the real Person of] 2 *ED*: (C) present (R) the real Person of/(C) give a sort of personal Identity to

170:5 Enable] *ED*: (C) direct

170:5–171:1 Established Character . . . represented] *ED*: [170] (C) Identity of Feature (R) to ancient statues (UM) by which they (C) were so universally [171] distinguished as the perfect Images of different (UM) Persons (C) they represented did not imitate the real action but the Representation of it and affected a real Identity of Person with the first Actor; but thus imitating an Imitation only and assuming a particular Nature He wo.^d be defective in this [I72] whilst He lost that Conformity to general Nature which is the just ground of dramatic Imitation. Every subsequent Copy wo.^d become more and More defective in this particular point which however being a point not worth the Attainment wo.^d as one sho.^d think bring the whole round by Degrees to an Imitation of general Nature. Two Causes however concurred to prevent this: the one that the particular Feature of every ancient Hero was familiarly known—the Masques had instructed the Statues and the Statues were at length able to direct the Masques and thus the particular Hero was always capable of being identifyed; and the other that the public Passions & affections which grew towards this or that Hero compelled the Actors to maintain this personal Identity at whatever Expence of Propriety and general Truth. Hitherto we have [I73] indeed supposed these Representations to have been the favourite Entertainments of greece but yet very imperfect in Dialogue and Decoration but when greece had attained a certain Degree of civilization the whole of these Representations was naturally lifted upon the Public Stage. Nothing co.^d be spared Chorus and Masque and Dance and Song and all to which was added soon after more perfect Dialogue and Music and every other appendage and [Decoration] which the various arts of greece co.^d bestow. Now then the Question arises what was the true Condition of this Exhibition: was it an Imitation of Nature or what else was it? But It was clearly an Imitation only of [I74] the Customs & Manners of the heroic Ages and was no otherwise an Imitation of Nature than as Nature appeared thro' the Medium of those Customs and Manners. It was the Imitation of particular Nature in particular

F Men at a particular Time and in a Particular Country; [I77] and this being the Case the Poets were of Course greatly limitted as to Subjects and action & the Relations of Time & Place &c. Now every distinct Representation has its Laws that is it must be governed by those Ideas of Propriety which necessarily grow out of it. How idle therefore is it to limit our Drama which is an Imitation of general Nature by those Rules of Propriety which grow out of another Drama of a very different and how interesting soever to Greece of a very inferiour Nature. But I am ready [to] believe and

I73:2 every other . . . and Decoration] *ED*: (C) all the (R) Decoration(UM)s indeed suppose that there is something more in this Matter by the Noise which in the last Age was made about it than my understanding goes to. If I was put upon settling Rules of Propriety under distinct Heads for different Dramas I sho.^d realy expect to come thro' with tolerable Effect, without Expecting to be [178] held forth as a great Man or Setting Myself on that account above my Neighbours, but if this or any other Matter involving a supposed Interest of any Kind Even that phantastic Interest or Property which men think they have acquired With much labour & Expence in the opinions of others ⟨or⟩ Critical Dogmas

LR 3—ED 2: *Unintegrated Fragments of LR 3—ED 1*

LR 3—ED 2a: *First Fragment*

[175:2] (UM) If the English in America sho.^d take the whim of D lifting up the Representations common to Every Indian Tribe upon some American Stage It appears to me that they wo^d obtain at once all the Essentials of the grecian Drama but this co^d never grow into popular use because it wo.^d want that popular Interest & Passion upon which alone [176] it co^d thrive. The Indians differ from us in Orrigin & Complexion nor wo.^d the Democracy of Athens have ever diverted the public Revenues to theatric Exhibitions if these Representations had not been considered as connected with public virtue and national Honour.

LR 3—ED 2b: *Second Fragment*

[176:3] (UM) It may be lightly objected that Heroes how heroic E soever were never able to represent or recite the Circumstances of their own Deaths. Events were selected by the Poets as most interesting and grew naturally upon the former and were a kind of last Honour and [apotheosis] of the Hero. I am writing a Note only tho' a long one and must not therefo[re] detail.

178:1 Expence in] *fol. by* (C) matters of mere learning such as   or Critical] or *apparently cancelled by mistake along with prec. ED*: (C) ancient Fable
    LR 3—ED 2a. *Punctuation*: 176:1 thrive.   176:2 Honour.
    176:2 national] *ED*: (UM) public
    LR 3—ED 2b. *Punctuation*: 176:4 Hero.   176:5 detail.
    176:4 Events were . . . the former] *ED*: (UM) but these (C) Exhibitions grew upon the (R) former   apotheosis] *MS. reads* apothoesis

LR 3—ED 3: *Earlier Version of LR 3—ED 1, I77:1-3*

B1 [I74:2b] (UM) and out of this Condition there arose certain
C *Dramatic Laws*, [T74MS] (C) that is in other Words this particular
Condition of the Drama had as Every Thing else has its own particular
Proprieties reducible under certain Heads among which were most
evidently the Unitys of Action Time & Place. The Shifting of Scenes
wo^d have been most singularly absurd. These (UM) Proprieties of
Relation were I presume well Explained by Aristotle and since his
Time well commented on by others but in Reference still to the
grecian Stage. But with great Deference & Consideration towards
such of my Readers as may be supposed by great Labour & Expence
to have acquired a sort of Property or Interest in their Reading which
therefore it may be injurious to invade may it not be considered as
B3 something whimsical to say no more to limit [I75] (C) the Drama
of the present Time which is an imitation of general Nature by
those Rules of Propriety which grew out of another Drama of a very
different and how interesting soever to Greece yet of a Nature
certainly inferiour in a (UM) general view to our own.

LR 3—ED 4: *First Draft of LR 3b, I162:2-I164:3*

[I160] (C) The principal Accompanyment of the grecian Drama
was music, an Accompaniement which it is so far from our Pow[e]r
to add that it does not appear to me that we have any adequate
Idea what it was. The Truth seems to be that no music can be to any
Effect introduced on the Stage or made an Adjunct to the Drama
which has not grown as it Were Naturally in that very Country
where it is to be introduced. Every Country has a kind of wild
music consonant to the Language Manners & Character of the
People. This is the Case Every where but in England. It is the Case
in Scotland and in Wales: the uncommon mixture of People from

---

LR 3—ED 3. *Punctuation: none*
I74:2 *Dramatic Laws] fol. by false start:* (UM) that is there were certain Ideas of
dramatic propriety which necessarily grew out of it
  T74MS:1 the Unitys] *cf. ED:* (C) an (R) Unity [s *added to* Unity]
  T74MS:3 in Reference] *ED:* (UM) with (R) Reference
  T74MS:4 to limit] *fol. by etc. = link with* I75
B2 I75:1 the Drama] *prec. by last two words of unreproduced ED:* (C) to limit = *over-
lap with* T74MS:4
LR 3—ED 4. *Punctuation: none*

various Countreys in England has probably [I161] deprived its music of any specific Character. The music of every Country however various in Character is alike capable of being cultivated into Science but this music being for the most Part an Imitation of the various Tones of various Passions as expressed in any particular Place this Science must conform to the Tone in which every peculiar Language is uttered for every Language has its distinct Tone and the transferring of the Tone of one Language into another is what Marks the Foreigner and distinguishes Him as a german Frenchman Italian etc. Music thus having ascertained its Imitations becomes a fixed Thing and the Inhabitants now begin to look on the music [I162] as a Standard to which they ought to conform, and upon any Deviation, to that Standard they return. Things being in

LR 3—ED 5: *Earlier Continuation of LR 3c, I51:2*
Superseded by LR 3c, T52MS–T53MS

[I52] (UM) But the object might not have been less a Reality for being unimportant. He considered it as a reality and did not doubt but that such as it was He sho.^d be able to possess it but he doubted very much if the Reader wo.^d keep equal Paces and accompany Him over so many & various a Page. He finds however that He erred both ways. He has been told by some Readers at least that they have come untired and chearfully thro' [I53:2] but they have seemed to talk as if they had been amusing themselves with a mere Drag only, a fat Paunch a stuffed Cloak Bag of guts or something

I161:1 deprived . . . Character] *ED*: [I160] (UM) destroyed (C) the [I161] Simplicity of its Music

I161:2 must conform] *fol. by* (UM) to those Tones (C) in which the People of that Country express their Passions (UM) and

LR 3—ED 5. *Text of later layer; see note. Punctuation: none*

I52:1 a Reality] *fol. by* (C) or less difficult to catch

I52:2 reality] *ED*:(R) real (C) Truth [ity *added to* real]   such as . . . possess it] *ED earlier layer*: (C) the Vindication of Falstaffe's Courage was always with[in] his Reach   the Reader . . . a Page] *3 ED*: (R) the Reader wo.^d keep equal (C) Pace and gallop with Him over so many (UM) and (C) various (UM) a (C) Page to the Death / (UM) the Reader (C) hold out over so many a Page and be fairly in at the Death / (R) the Reader (C) keep fairly gayly & chearfully (UM) in   and chearfully thro'] *fol. by overlap*: [I53:2] (UM) & chearfully through

I53:2 a fat . . . of guts] *ED earlier layer*: [I52] (C) a dead Fox or a red Herring   Cloak Bag . . . looked for] *ED earlier layer*: [I52] (UM) Cloak bag of Guts [*fol. by* (C) stinking Herring] or something of the like sort but as for catching a [I53] real Truth it was in sooth nothing which they either looked for or found

of the like sort but as for real Truth It was in good Sooth what they
Neither found or looked for; or if say some we gave ourselves up
momentarily to Illusion It was but looking into the Playhouse and
the Charm was dissolved. There Falstaffe stands forth in his own
shape: an object of all the senses He may be seen and touched and
heard. He has doffed [h]is Lions skin and is become once more
a Coward & Poltroon.

>Thus Proteus hunted in a Nobler shape
>became when seized a Puppy or an ape:

all this is very hard & discomforting.

LR 4

FOOTNOTE TO *ES.*, T41:4

[T41MS:2] The Players conceive very justly that the greatest
Monarchs may be attached with Weariness and therefore they have
prudently provided a well braced Drum in the way of Military
Chair to accommodate his Majesty. The value of artificial Greatness
is best known it seems by its supplying Substitutions for Natural
Infirmity or possibly they imagine that monarchs look more grace-
fully on their Rumps than in the Exercise of all the vigour and
Energies of their Frame; but I ask their pardon—neither the one
or the other: it seems the Drum is intended after all [T42MS]
rather for Corpulence than Royalty. Royalty is curbed and limitted
to the Edge only of Convenience leaving ample Space by a strange
Kind of Prescience for a more ample Possessor. And Lo where
Falstaffe archly steals along and seats Himself back to back with
Royalty. The gallery bursts with Laughter to see fat & lean gravity
& Levity Buffoonery & Dignity thus ingeniously coupled together

LR 4. *Punctuation*: T42MS:6 own.
T41MS:2–T42MS:4 The Players . . . with Laughter] *ED*: [T41MS:1] (UM) The
Players conceiving that (C) Kings (UM) sho⁴ stand as little as possible on their own
Legs [*2 ED* (*false starts*): (R) Kings (UM) Legs (C) are easily attached with / (C)
Crowned Heads (R) are easily attached with] supply his wearied Majesty with a Drum
by way of military stool and yet not altogether out of respect to Royalty but rather to
furnish [*ED*: (C) please] their gallery Friends
T41MS:3 after all] *fol. by* (UM) for *cf. next entry*
T42MS:1 rather for . . . than Royalty] *ED*: [T42MSa:1] (UM) for [*overlap with*
[T41MS:3] (UM) for] (C) the Accommodation of the more corpulent Falstaffe
T42MS:2 Royalty is . . . ample Possessor] *see note*
T42MS:3 steals] *ED*: (C) creeps   seats] *ED*: (C) plants

like a double Headed Janus. The Business of the Play is disaranged
tis true. But what, then, are Players to be always the Slaves of
Propriety and never to discover any good Wit or exhibit any Inter-
ludes altogether their own.

LR 5

DRAFT REVISION OF NOTE C, *ES.*, T49n–T50n

[PT3MS:6] Who writes of a dramatic Poet must speak of the
Drama: this has been the custom of gravest Men. What Books have
not been written—but no Matter careless of Books We will pursue
our own peculiar Course dangerous [PT4MS] to more sober men
but to a rash essayist adventurer Nothing: upon a view of Shakespeares Volumes one is read[y] to cry out with Polonius not with!
Laughter

> [Do not believe his vows; for they are brokers,
> Not of that dye which their investments shew
> But mere implorators of unholy suits,
> Breathing like sanctified and pious bonds,
> The better to beguile.]

[PI4] But let us however give the gentleman a little fair Play.
He can produce a thousand compurgators to swear that He never
wrote ——&——&—— or the taming of the Shrew more than the
Introduction among whom He may venture to rely upon me as a
most determined and vehement Witness. [PI8:3] (CM) Well but are
We to lay then all these Plays aside as not included in Shakespears
Drama? [PI4:3] (U) Who wrote them does not much signify. He con-
descended I am afraid to copy them with his own Hand for want of
an Amanuensis into his Prompter's Book Here and there brightening
them as they past; and the base Editors made use of this Pretext
to cover their Fraud and Swell the Volume. Those who do not believe this May let it alone. They may be very honest Men and yet
not Competent to speak of Shakespeare: but those offences removed

T42MS:4 like a double Headed Janus] *see note*
LR 5. *Punctuation*: PI5:3 Where.   PT8MS:3 Time,   PI8:1 Stages.
PT3MS:6 custom] *ED*: (UM) course
PT4MS:1 Laughter] *fol. by* etc = *Ham. I. iii. 127–31; text supplied by editor from
Johns. 1785*
PI8:3 Well but . . . Shakespear's Drama] *inserted here by editor; see note*

How strangely does he berhime the English Chronicle and with Foot and [PI5] half foot verse fight over York & Lancaster's long wars—a little better however than Mr Benjamin Johnson co.^d have done the Maker as He calls Himself of Many a rough Misshapen Line, Creaking on rusty Latin Hinges and grating in Discords coa[r]se & harsh the pu[b]lic Ear. But even in these Plays Shakespeare had only a very limitted Property. The Execution only was his the Design was no Where. The [Moralities] were succeeded by the Chronicle and the Players like the Priests of old [seem] to have added Poetry as an appendage to their Trade: the Business of the Night being settled the Dialogue was perhaps made up of [unpremeditated] verse and some vagrant Rhime; dumb show was often substituted for Wit [PT5MS] and Noise for Passion; however much tragic Pathos & comic Laugh was recorded in the Prompters Book & grew by Degrees into a Play and Half the Chronicle (CM) was (U) thus reproduced. [PT6MS] Battle & Buffoonery together was the constant Pastime of the good Company who amused their Evening at the Bank Side.

[PI6] (C) Whilst they regaled themselves Within the diligent Shakespear had the Honour of holding their Horses at the Door. He obtained at length the Notice of [the] very Players themselves was admitted into familiar Discourse & advanced by Degrees into the Rank of a Prompter. In this Capacity he furnished great Actors with sweet sounding words and had such a Knack at blank verse and it run so glibly and became their Mouths So Well that He was by common Consent admitted into full Fellowship with the best and being a good natured industrious man and having a Knack He was put to overhawl the old Stock with commission to refit & repair working however upon the old Models and preserving historical Names & Facts and all the popular Incidents of the old Play. Various & great must have been the Labours of our Author [PI7] at this Period. The Horses were wholly resigned to others not I hope without something in the Way of good Will. But He had

PI5:1 rough] *ED*: (UM) rude   Latin] *prec. by* (UM) on   public] *MS. reads* puplic [?]

PI5:3 Moralities] *MS. reads* Moralilities   seem] *MS. reads* seems   unpremeditated] *MS. reads* unpremidated

PT5MS:1 was thus reproduced] *ED*: (R) was (C) fought over

PI6:3 So Well that] *fol. by false start*: (C) the proudest Actor (UM) of them all [*ED*: (R) Actor (C) among them] (C) was not ashamed of his true filed & well turned Lines to Walk the Stage Occasionally and to study Lengths as I think they are called out of the Prompter[']s Book, to Him how base a Toil; and He had to prompt others and to transcribe into the Book old and Whatever new Rubbish was bro[t] & accepted; and He had in a very poor Hand—for I have seen his Handwriting a cause of much future Corruption—to transcribe in imperfect spelling his own Reforms Mingled with a great deal of old Material. He had at the same Time Books such as were then in use to read & Language to obtain. But He had a [PT8MS] Wife & small Children and was as M[r] Johnson attests a very honest Man. To some of those Plays He seems to have given what may be called a thorough Repair that is He new wrote them to the old Names. The two Parts of Hen. IV seems to bid fairest for this Character yet I shall have occasion to remark that there is a mingling of old material even in these. But the reader may Expect that I sho[d] furnish some Proof of the Condition herein described of the Stage before Shakespears Time, beside [PI8] the mere Probability of the Thing. I suppose a very little will do so let the Epilogue to Hen. 5th come forward:

Which oft our Stage has shewn

has been poorly quoted to prove that Hen. 6th was written & acted before Hen. 5th but I trust the Reader will believe it to have Reference to the old Stages.

LR 6

CONTINUATION OF *ES.*, T62n:4

LR 6a: *Main Body of Revision*

[T62MS] To speak of Shakespeare and yet say nothing of his A1 Language and Power [of] Expression may seem strange Especially as the peculiar & forcible Modes [of] Expression which He has given to Falstaffe seems to demand it. [I88] Yet the Question is too B1 large and contains in it too much of Detail for that compendious

PI7:3 Prompter's] *MS. reads* Prompter,s   very poor] *fol. by* (C) & imperfect
PT8MS:1 very honest] *ED*: [PI7] (C) an honest good Natured
PI8:2 Which . . . shewn] *set off as verse by editor; prec. by* X = *to be set off as verse* [?]
    LR 6a. *For segment designation (A1, B1, E etc.) in outer margin see Textual Note to LR 6a*
    Punctuation: T89MS:1 Song. T91MS:2c own. I115:3 *app. crit.* Home. I121:2 learned— I121:3 leave. I107:1 Way.
    T62MS:1–I88:1 it. Yet] *for continuity see Textual Note to LR 6a*

Manner in which to preserve a Proportion of Parts I wish to Touch those incidental Points which I cannot wholly pass: a few observations must however be made mingling Opinion thro' necessity not vanity with Argument. It is my opinion then shall I say that Shakespeare had no other Language than his own tho' perfectly possessed of all the foreign Words which after the revival of Letters was so profusely poured into the Saxon speech; from Hence it followed of Necessity [T88MS] that He must write in the Idioms of his Native Tongue being unable like Milton artificially to build in strange Terms the lofty Rhime—tho' I wish that Milton Himself had been under the like Necessity and [T89MS] instead of Building a Poem of Strange Materials had delivered up his Rhimes to popular Feelings and that fairs & Wakes had resounded with the Song. [B]ut of Shakespeare I think that if this Necessity had not Existed He Wo^d have retained the Saxon Idioms by Choice. Milton not only invited over foreign Troops but formed them under their own Standards. Shakespeare also entered them freely but He entered them as individuals. He mingled them With the National Force and reduced them under the same Discipline & Sway. [T90MS:1] The great Influx at this Time of foreign Words into the Saxon already disaranged by the Norman Invasion must have given the language Even to the men of the Time a very uncouth & irregular appearance like an Army [I90:1] ill dressed Short & Tall close & open foreigners & Natives greek Latin Norman Italian & Saxon unacquainted with Each other and looking Every one a different way. [T90MS:2] This required great Reform & much Time to Effect it and Now that this Reform has been in part made the Language of Harry & Eliz. seems more grotesque by Comparison. We have like the present King of Prussia on the Death of his Father discarded the Giants of the Army and by lowering the former standard [T91MS] have obtained a more orderly

---

188:1 I wish] *prec. by false start*: (C) I find it necessary to touch rather than treat   pass] *ED*: (UM) Neglect   vanity] *ED*: (UM) Arrogance
188:2 shall I] *ED*: (C) let (UM) me
T88MS:1–T92MS:1a that He must . . . wins us all] *supersedes uncancelled ED on 188–191, not reproduced; see note*
T89MS:1 Feelings and . . . the Song] *ED*: (C) Tunes (R) and that (C) Lanes & Alleys (R) had (UM) Ecchoed to the Son[g]
T89MS:2 But] *MS. reads* but   if this Necessity . . . by Choice] *cf. ED*: [188:3] (UM) He co^d not do otherwise [189:1] (C) which is a better security than that of his superiour Taste which probably wo^d not have done otherwise if he co^d
T90MS:1 Army] *fol. by* etc. = *insert I90:1; see note to LR 6a, T88MS-T92MS*

appearance. Many of the admitted words were [I89:2] incapable of Naturalization as Sans Esperance and the like [T91MS:2b] others retained an Alien complexion which co^d not be Well changed others were Duplicates [I90:2] Mere Candidates for selection [T91MS:2c] and to others again it was Exception Enough that we had for the same Uses better of our own. Not but that we have yet too many left as we may well confess when we See strange Authors stalking along upon greek & Latin stilts to the great admiration of the Vulgar; nor shall we be less sensible when we find as find we must in some of Swifts Prose [T92MS:1a] and throughout the odes of Gray a Witchery of speech which charms & wins us all [I111:4] and which seems owing for the Most part to this that they E Every Where keep up as much as possible the Saxon Line of March a little too short and dapper perhaps for a learned Eye but always close and forcible and firm or when kindling most into Rage yet Simply gracefull & correctly strong; foreign Aid however was asked & given but of a Sort to pass for Kindred not allies & seeming of one complexion and Family and Name [I112] and sweet is it to behold the Workings of Nature Where all of one Clan Each word seemed to know the other and to give and to receive unbidden aid with a speed & Effect beyond all the Tricks of Discipline and art. But after all this was a Happiness which seems fairly gone by. It suited only perhaps a little Country or a little Clan. We have Embraced half the World & Sho^d Enlarge our Language into the Condition of our Empire; future Ages may Establish a Standard by which to correct on some larger Scale the incoherent Jumble of our present Speech and Whilst [I113:1a] it allows a Freedom almost commercial It shall yet punish those interlopers [I114:4] Who never once touching the True Points of Practical Life are for ever drawing out of the Clouds some fine spun Samples of Cobweb Truth and carrying

T91MS:2 words were] *fol. by* etc. = *insert I89:2; see note to LR 6a, T88MS–T92MS*
T91MS:2b Duplicates] *fol. by* etc. = *insert I90:2; see note to T88MS–T92MS*
T91MS:3 We may] *fol. by* (UM) We may [*these two words are underlined instead of lined through*]   admiration] *2 ED:* (C) amusement / (C) Terrour
T92MS:1a speech] *ED:* (UM) Words
T92MS:1a–I111:4 us all and which] *for continuity see Textual Note to LR 6a*
I113:1a a Freedom almost commercial] *ED:* (UM) Even a (C) sort of Commercial (R) Freedom
I113:1a–I114:4 interlopers Who] *for continuity see next entry and note*
I113:1a interlopers] *fol. by* (UM) Who daily carry in Three leagued Boots = *overlap with end of I114:4; cf. next entry but one*
I114:4 some fine spun . . . Truth and] *ED:* (C) some cobweb Peices of Universal Truth (UM) and

in three leagued Boots [I113:1b] their Metaphisical Annilizations of brown Bread & small Beer and other pha[ntas]tical Trumpery to Market. I must observe Here that one great Evil of introducing foreign Words is that they furnish Disguises for dull and confused men who come forth occasionally in these phantastic Habits to deceive and Amaze the ignorant & weak. Even Shakespear Himself if some Accidental Cloud passes over Him runs into big Words and Substitutes Noise & bombast for his own Native Sublime. No Man can thus deceive in an unmixed Language but the Misfortune is now that the Native & foreign Languages seem [I114:1] to go thro' a great deal of Business whilst the Meaning is totally asleep.

He stuck adhering and Suspended hung

is a fair See Saw of Saxon & latin Words whilst the poor sense is wholly Neuter betwixt them.

To this mixed Condition of Things in its most confused State Shakespear was born and Every great genius born to an imperfect Language is born to Chains but He is born after a Time to break them. [I115] There was but one Event which Co^d have prevented these Effects. If Shakespear driven out of the Country had taken a more devious Course and instead of holding Horses at the Bank Side had been prefered to a Servitors Plate and Cap at Oxford How fatal w^d have been the Difference. [Cromwell] and others were it seem[s] Embarqued for America in Pursuit of Freedom but restrained they fell to reformation and to make for themselves that Freedom which they co^d not find; and thus of Shakespeare: if He had been infranchised into latian [or] grecian Liberty He might have Expatiated at large and owned No other Home [I116:2] a foreign Classic of No Age or Country and destined to fall before his Time with Classic Lore and in the mean Time an English Barbarian or only with Milton building the lofty Rhime with artifices deep & Spirit bold firm over the void obscure;—a fancifull Essayist we know may say any Thing and I am now in a Course

I11 4:4 Boots] *fol. by* etc. = *link with* I113:1b; *see note*
I113:1b phantastical] *MS. reads* phatasntical [tas *erroneously careted in before instead of after* n]
I114:2 He stuck . . . suspended hung] *set off as verse by editor; cf. below, p.* 257
I114:3 break them] *fol. by false start:* (UM) But there is but one Thing
I115:2 Plate and Cap] *ED:* (C) Gown and Plate
I115:3 Cromwell] *MS reads* Crowmwell   or] *MS reads* of   Home] *ED (false start):* (R) Home (UM). And
I116:2 obscure] *fol. by false start:* (UM) If it depended upon me

[I117] of Danger. If it depended upon me I Wo.^d issue my imperial Edict that No public School or College sho.^d under the severest Penalties presume to teach the greek or latin Language after the year 1800 or perhaps in better Wisdom after 1790. These Things must have an End sure one Time or other. Times long gone by Sho.^d by the Laws of perspective diminish in proportion to their Distance and their Literature be reduced by Degrees to an abstract to a Compendium to a Point to Nothing. We cannot live to any Effect in the past and in the present too and the more we exert ourselves as to the former the less usefull as to the present Time. How strange is it after two or three thousand Years that lost in Admiration of ancient Atchievem.^t we sho.^d ourselves offer no Example to the future [I118] but instead of erecting a Temple to modern glory we sho.^d content ourselves like Children with Making imitative dirt pyes and of Materials not our own. Mars Bacchus & Appollo have had their Day. Their Fanes are deserted and their worship is no more. Why then do we retire to our Closets and there offer up the first Fruits of the present Time to these visionary Idols of the past? Near very Near was the Extinction of the Whole System. It was revived and it Enlightened with sudden Flash the gothic world but it was a Light Shining from afar misleading our Footsteps tho' illuminating the Path. We turned our Faces unhappily from the present & the future to the past and the learned have ever since with reverted Faces deserted the [I119] active World and Whilst coarser men have with Noble Enterprize discovered New Worlds and introduced New Principles of Action commercial & phisical these finer Spirits have been confined within the Pillars of Hercules marking the Ulissean Track Weighing and Measuring departed Things rooting deep the fixed Earth or fighting with immortal Fury before the walls of Heaven Defended Troy. I wo.^d restore them to their Country: They sho.^d assist the active world and tho' hopeless of grecian Excellence they sho.^d shape and polish their own ruder Materials into grace and build a gothic Structure of transient grandeur at least if not of lasting gaze. Chance restored the Classic Ages but there are Causes on the Wing which will as suddenly shut in those ages as they were [I120] suddenly restored

I118:1 erecting a] *fol. by* (UM) a
I118:6 misleading ... Path] *ED*: (R) misleading (UM) as well as conducting our steps
I118:7 reverted Faces] *ED*: (UM) retrograde Motion
I119:1 Weighing and Measuring] *interlined above this phrase appears* (C) fixing the —?— (UM) Earth

and for my single Part let them go. We have Warehoused up their choicest Treasures: let the ancient Vehicles depart and for me return no more: great wo.^{d} be the lamentation however among the learned dreadfull the moan. Not the Demons themselves driven from their Fanes Co^d utter [T120MS:1] deeper Complain[in]gs than their Modern worshippers wo^d in such an Event [I120:3b]—Those Who nightly watch the bright Meonian Star or unsphere the Spirit of Plato or those who love to bathe their gentle Limbs in Soft Illisus [T120MS:2] or court in wanton Lays the [Paphian] Queen [I120:3c] or drink with purest Lips the clear pierian spring of Aganippe's Fount or Walk the Porch with Plato: dreadfull to think, dreadfull, but this is not a world to shut our eyes dream of visions past or fondly chase with invocations quaint in measured Words the fancyed Shadows of Departed Things. But whither have I strayed, into what [I121] Paths of Danger? Spare me ye learned—spare a poor Essayist who pursuing thro' untrod Paths a Winged Child of Nature has midst your lettered Mansions founded deep in Many a loamy Acre lost his way. Shall I be permitted then to return and will you give me leave?

C [I107:2] A Language made by slow Progressions and under the Compulsions of Necessity is always well made and the sounds applied to signify whether Substantives or Qualities or Energetic Power[s] will not only be for the most part uncompounded but have a wonderfull Consonancy & Relation to Each other and as belonging as it were to one Family—an Happiness in which Reason has no Share but to be produced only by the most exquisite sensibility. Yet so produced and so formed they are Capable of runing into one another & of receiving almost infinite Combination the component Parts having distinct Meanings of their own and [I108] [being]

I120:3–T120MS:1 Co^d utter deeper Complainings . . . an Event] *2 ED*: [I120:3] (R) Co^d utter (UM) more despairing groans than their modern Worshippers wo^d in Such an Event [*T120MS:1 overlaps with last 9 words*] / (UM) Ever Murmured More (R) than (C) the learned wo^d in (R) Such an Event *see note*

I120:3b–T120MS:2 Illissus or court] *for continuity see note*

T120MS:2 or court . . . Queen] *ED*: [I120] (UM) or court —?— —?— the paphian Quen Paphian] *MS reads* paplian; *cf. ED in preceding entry*

I120:3c the clear . . . spring] *perhaps an ED of* of Aganippe's Fount

I121:3 leave] *fol. on next line by* a Language etc. = *probable link with* I107:2; *see notes, pp. 394–5.*

I107:2 A] *prec. by* X = *superseded link with* I104:2 *in LR* 6—ED 5 Energetic Powers] *ED*: (UM) Energies (C) of Power uncompounded] *ED*: (C) simple sounds and as . . . one Family] *ED*: (UM) as (C) being all of one Family

capable of Easy Decomposition and thus Language & Ideas wo.^d
keep Equal Pace and by the same Process become complex or
simple or combined or disintangled together. But the Introduction
of one Language upon another makes dreadfull Havoc. [I108:3a]
It introduces two opposite Principles and destroys all analogy:
foreign Words are introduced in a compounded State [T108MS]
and on this account words of different Orrigin will seem to oppose
each [other] Whilst the sense is avowedly the same and hence

He stuck adhering & su[s]pended hung

which is a fair Battle between [T109MS] the latin & saxon Tongue
and thus alien & Native Servants will quarrel whilst their Master
is asleep and thus may the learned author of starvation plead
analogy in vain: He will find to his great wonderation we will fight
the (CM) Saxon (U) ing [against] the latin Ion with the most obstinate Perseverance. [I108:4] Yet tho' [I109] I have spoken thus
rashly of the principles of Language yet I am to confess that the
Saxon how derived I know not seems tho' in many respects much of
a Peice yet not easily to take Composition. Some happy compound
Epithets it has but when Shakespeare has endeavoured to carry it
further He is not successfull: see Macbeths Soliloqui[es]. [I 105:3] B6
But it Wo.^d be out of the Course of Things to Expect that He who
was labouring to break thro' a thousand Impediments and shaking
the incumbent Earth for Freedom Sho.^d come forth at last like a Trim
Journeyman with Brush & paint to burnish [I106] and repair. Yet
is there in his Roughness a grace and in his Force an ease and
agility which future Ages have not even essayed to copy despairing
to obtain. Johnson says

.   .   .   .   .

That is take away that on which the Propriety depends and they
have Propriety no longer.
    This might appear strange to Him who rides a great Horse
galloping at a certain Established particular true Rate two up and

---

I108:3 compounded State] *fol. by* X = *link with* T108MS:1
    T108MS:1 and on . . . Perseverance] *ED*: [I108:3b] (UM) and in that state they
must remain stiffened up for Ever because the Parts of the Composition not being
popularly understood cannot be popularly decompounded and the learned few alas must
conform to the vulgar many *see note*
    T109MS:1 against] *MS reads* aag.^t
    I109:2–I105:3 Soliloquies. But] *for continuity see Textual Note to LR 6a*
    I106:2 Roughness . . . Agility] *ED*: (C) Force a grace (UM) and (C) Even Ease

two down keeping the greensward Way and coming in as He set out with the right Foot foremost and the Sicker Reign dangling in his bridle Hand and maintaining throughout an orderly Cadence & Elevation of Pace. This is a very different Matter M.ʳ Johnson from the Condition of those [I107] who are obliged to ride the wild Mare over Hedge & Ditch and unknown & broken ground and at Their own Hazzard to explore for others the dangerous Path & Mark out a public Way.

LR 6b: *Coda to LR 6a*

[PI3] Yet something ought to have been said concerning the Tone of Shakespeares language. Language ought to speak to our sensibilities as well as our understanding and this it does by Tones according with the sense. It sho.ᵈ swell or sink or lag or fly as the occasion demands and float off as it were in an harmonious vehicle of coresponding Sound. Music alone will thro' its varying Tones Excite the coresponding Passions. How much more ought it [to] do so conveying a coresponding sense. This Accord of Sense & sound is wonderfully preserved by Shakespeare not in little but in the general composition of his whole Works. It is a real lasting legitimate Union throug[h]out and not as in other writer[s] an occasional Intrigue at certain Time[s] and Places between Words & Sense. The sound say the Criticks sho.ᵈ be an Eccho to the sense and thereupon [PT3MS] like school Boys we produce our Exercises in this sort; but how trifling are the Tricks Even of Pope Himself to the Natural Resonance of Shakespeare. Take it in lit[t]le:

The hoarse rough verse sho.ᵈ like the Torrent roar.

This is an Imitation.

I wo.ᵈ *applaud* thee to the very Eccho
Which sho.ᵈ *applaud* again.

I106:4 down] *fol. by* X = *insert* keeping . . . Hand *which follows* Pace *in MS.; cf. next entry* keeping] *prec. by* X = *passage to follow* down *see preceding entry*
LR6b. *Punctuation: none*
PI3:3 occasion demands] *fol. in ED by:* [PI2] (C) and this without a single affectation
PI3:7 writers] *cf. ED:* [PI2] (C) Writers   certain Times] *cf. ED:* (C) a (R) certain Time
PT3MS:1 Tricks Even of Pope Himself] 3 *ED:* [PI2] Tricks of other Men / (C) artificial Resonances (R) of other Men / (C) laboured Ecchoes (R) of other Men
PT3MS:2 The hoarse . . . Torrent roar] *set off as verse by editor; ED:* (C) The line too labours and the words Move slow
PT3MS:4 I wo.ᵈ . . . *applaud* again] *set off as verse by editor*

This is the Thing itself and for that very Reason passes with! Notice; but it is not particular but general Corespondence We sho.ᵈ admire—but I constrain myself and have done.

Earlier Drafts

LR 6—ED 1: *Original Sequel of Opening of LR 6a, T62MS:1*

[T62MS:2] (UM) Yet when I contemplate the Subject I despair A2 of reducing it to that sort of Compendium which may suit the Condition of a Note and to pursue it more at large in the Text wo.ᵈ destroy that Proportion of Parts which it is fit to preserve. It is so copious and so Curious a Subject that on this very account I find myself obliged to decline it. I hold myself well intitled however to consider it in the Text if it Wo.ᵈ admit of any moderate Limitts.

LR 6—ED 2: *Original Version of Second Half of First Par. of LR 6a (I111:4–I114:3)*

[T92MS:1b] (UM) and Which is principally derived from this B2 that they always Maintain as Much as possible the Saxon Line of March some thing short and dapper perhaps but forcible & firm and [throughout] al[l] its motions simply gracefull & correctly strong. [I91] But this is a Happiness which I consider as gone by and to be now a Matter rather of curiosity than use. Yet some Taste for this Purity might keep men from stalking in pollysyllables as we find some do and daily carrying in Three leagued [I92] Boots their Metaphisical analizations and other various Trumpery to Market. The Language of Shakespear then appears to us More grotesque by a comparison With the present reformed State and We find many an uncouth and many a rejected Word which we are

---

PT3MS:5 the Thing itself] *ED*: [PI2] (C) a real Eccho
LR 6—ED 1–5. *For segment designation (A2, B2, D, etc.) in outer margin see Textual Note to LR 6a.*
 LR 6—ED 1. *Punctuation*: T62MS:4 Limitts.
 T62MS:3 that on this very account] *ED*: (UM) that (C) for those very Reasons
LR 6—ED 2. *Punctuation*: I92:3 them.
 T92MS:1b and Which . . . correctly strong] *ED*: (UM) and which is plainly founded in this that they never suffer without strong Necessity any foreign Word to stain the pure Saxon stream   some thing] *fol. by* ir[?]   perhaps] *ED*: (C) to be (UM) Sure   throughout] *MS. reads* thruought
 T92MS:1b–I91:1 strong. But] *for continuity see note.*
 I92:1 various Trumpery] 2 *ED*: (C) learned (R) Trumper(C)ies / sophisticated Erudition

apt to call Barbarism and sometimes justly enough applying the
Word to the Age and not to Shakespeare. Every great genius whatever born to an Imperfect Language is born to Chains but if truly
great He is born to break them. To baser men imperfect Language
[I93] is gain: it induces in appearance at least an Equality of Mind
the finer Soul being unable to display itself under such rude con-
straints; but Shakespeare forced his way thro' all [Impediment]
and bent his rude and ill sorted incumbrances to What Purposes he
pleased. Language must be worn but it is in ourselves Whether
we will wear it as ornament or Chains. Shakespear found Himself
hemed [in] by a Chaos of Words rough heterogeneous and unbend-
ing. He did what Necessity first required. He bent he compressed
He twisted He worked them into use but he left the polishing to
under Workmen and future Time. He broke open new Modes of
Expression. The rough material might be afterwards changed but
the [I100] Mode remained.

LR 6—ED 3: *Continuation of LR 6—ED 2*

Discarded on Completion of Par. 2, LR 6a

D [I109:3] (UM) We know not the obligations we are under to this
wonderfull genius. It is true that We common People cannot put
on the whole Armour of Saul but He has shown us not a single
Suit of armour only but has given us an Armoury. There are
Peices enough which We can find fitting or which with a little skill,
we can fit to our Frames. [I110] He has instructed us how to turn
& wind to contract to expand to glance only or to evade or to draw
if occasion shall require with Collected Strength the feathered
arrow to the Head. Even those who know Him not are profited at
the second Hand: our Books of all kinds nay our very news Papers
teem with Shakespear. We practise in little ⟨his own arts.⟩ We walk
at Ease in his Modes of speech: We grow bold and holding his skirts
walk firmly on the Edge of Danger. [T111MS] This Country has

I93:1 Impediment] *MS. reads* Imdeiment
I93:4 hemed in] in *supplied from earlier of 2 ED:* (C) encircled / (C) bound in
I93:8–I100:1 The Mode] *for continuity see note*
LR 6—ED 3. *Punctuation: none*
I110:3 his own arts] *lined through, perhaps with intention of condemning the whole
sentence as a false start*
T111MS:1–T112MS:1 This Country . . . the occasional] *ED:* [I110:5] (UM) Burke
flouts and even Johnson stalks in Shakespear. We were obliged to take a Rest but we
shoot flying. We form the occasional [*last three words overlap with* T112MS:1]

lately seen a genius of the highest order one to whom Language was necessary as an Instrument of Power and ⟨wh[o]⟩ was capable of bursting his way thro' any Impediment of imperfect Speech but He found the Channels of Freedom already opened by Shakespeare [T112MS] and that He had only to possess ornament to find he knew as well as Shakespeare himself how to hit the sleeping Idea to form the occasional [I110:7] Word which is to be heard no more. We press the unwilling Nay the Awkward into service and give them Grace & Propriety by Position. We know how to Dignify the familiar and familiarize the great. [I111:3] We sleep that we may wake and seem to fall that we may rise the higher. In former Times there was no Want of Dignity
We hit the Instant and boldly break thro' Established Forms to catch it.

LR 6—ED 4: *Original Continuation of LR 6—ED 2*
Subsequently Insertion to LR 6—ED 3, I111:4
Finally Discarded with LR 6—ED 3

[I100:2] (UM) ⟨A great Defect in the old Language [was] that B3 tho' it did not want Dignity⟩ or Force yet the Dignity was Stiff and the Force laborious. It had no Celerity or quickness of adoption. It co^d thunder in long drawn Peals but it co^d not lighten. Shakespear gave it the Electric Snap and co^d hit the flying Idea whilst the Instant remained. ⟨We catch the Instant⟩

T111MS:1 who] *lined through by mistake, apparently before next clause was set down*
T112MS:1 ornament] *fol. by* (UM) not   occasional] *fol. by etc.* = *link with I110:7 ; see also* app. crit. *to T111MS :1–T112MS :1*
I111:3 We sleep that we may wake] *prec. by 2 false starts:* [I111:2] (UM) We slip that we may rise / [I111:1] (UM) We know the use of
I111:4 Dignity] *overlaps with* Dignity *in I100:2 in LR 6—ED 4; blank space following* Dignity *in I111:4 tò end of line in MS.* = *same link*
I111:5 We hit the Instant] *ED:* (R) we (UM) catch (R) the Instant = *overlap with LR 6—ED 4, I 100:6*
LR 6—ED 4. *Punctuation: none*
I100:2 A great . . . want Dignity] *omitted when LR 6—ED 4 was inserted in LR 6—ED 3; see* app. crit. *to I111 :4 and note, p. 395*
I100:6 We catch the Instant] *see* app. crit. *to LR 6—ED 3, I111:5*

LR 6—ED 5: *Original Continuation of LR 6—ED 4*
Discarded on Completion of LR 6—ED 3

B4   [I100:7] (UM) This He did chiefly by turning Effects into Efficient Energies that is by giving to Effects the condition of verbs every verb being either immediately a mental energy or applied by analogy to active and passive Power, (C) for instance:

> (UM) And 'gins (speaking of the glow worm) to pale his ineffectual Fires.

Here by pale is meant to make pale but Shakespeare cuts off the tedious Process and by giving to pale the Condition of an Energy He makes it [I101] at Once both Cause & Effect or in his own Words He makes the Cause to tramel up the Consequence. I begin to pale in Resolution that is I begin to grow Sick or to become as in the Manner of an Infant paling in Resolution but by the making pale Here an active Energy He conveys the Whole in a word. Ye are not Oathable yet I have heard you swear that is ye are not by Law competent Witnesses yet I have heard ye in Discourse profanely Swear Shakespear says with a Boldness which I think too bold but thus converting the Substantive Oath into a Verb To oath and that again into the participle oathable the whole is effected in a single word [I102] and this is a Proceeding so fair and reasonable that I wonder it is not practised at Discretion in the most common Conversation. We use indeed instead of it gives me pain it pains me together with various other established phrases of the same sort but we are surprized to hear a Scotch[man] say it difficults me or I am difficulted or if chance or the Ten shoᵈ introduce a New Phrase tho' it shoᵈ contain no other Excellence than this singularity and shoᵈ say He proses for He talks dull Prose How do We admire at the Novelty or the Wit; [I103] but I am out of my Road. Details tho' I might like to indulge them Here woᵈ lead me I know not where. I Will not however dismiss the Line first quoted without some further Notice:

> and 'gins to pale his ineffectual Fires.

This large word ineffectual with a lattin Negative in its Forehead

---

LR 6—ED 5. *Punctuation*: I100:7 (speaking worm)   I101:1 Consequence.
I101:2 pale] pule [?] *see note*   as in . . . of an] *ED*: (C) like (UM) an
I101:3 but thus converting] *ED*: (UM) but (C) Here by making out of
I102:2 Scotchman] *last three letters uncertain in MS.*
I103:2 Details tho' . . . lead me] *ED*: (R) Details (UM) woᵈ lead Me

agrees but ill with the contracted 'gin & the energetic pale. The cliping of this poor Word seems Wholly unjustifiable. I for [my] Part wo.^d have rejoiced if the Age of Shakespear sparing the pure Saxon had cliped & striped every foreign [I104] Word upon its introduction of all its adjuncts of Every Sort and that We had supplyed those Excisions with our own of and from and to in which case in the words just written We sho.^d not have met with adjoining to and excised of and detracted from and the rest; for not having [introduced] those Adjuncts as English Words the Composition has of course no use and We are still obliged to have recourse to our own and say adjoining to, detract from, and the rest. I Sho.^d undoubtedly prefer conjoined to joined together if con had a seperate Existence in our Language but I hate to see a compound which cannot be decompounded at pleasure. ⟨I believe the Saxon however B5 does not Easily [I105] take Composition. However notwithstanding nevertheless afterwards Heretofore Whatever and even the English of the word con which I suppose was together are all but strange outoftheway roundabout words.⟩

LR 7
RELATED TO *ES.*, T63:3

['This scene is, above any other part of *Shakespeare's* tragedies, and perhaps above any scene of any other poet, tender and pathetick, without gods, or furies, or poisons, or precipices, without the help of romantick circumstances, without improbable sallies of poetical lamentation, and without any throes of tumultuous misery.'— Johnson, note to *Henry VIII*, IV, ii]

[I15] If the Doctor were my near of kin yet there is so much of what I think Imposition in this Note that I wo.^d not let it freely pass. The Character of this scene is dignified *Propriety*. The

I103:6 my] *MS. reads* May
I104:1 in the words . . . and the rest] *ED:* (UM) ad Wo.^d be seperated from junct Pre from position and Ex from cision   introduced] *MS reads* introudced
I104:2 at pleasure] *fol. by* X = *superseded link with LR 6a, I107:2; see notes, p. 394*
I104:3–I105:2 I believe . . . roundabout words] *superseded: see notes, p. 394*
I105:2 con which . . . was together] *ED:* (R) con (UM) together
LR 7. *Punctuation:* I15:1 pass   I15:4 Truth.   I15:12 this?   T15MS:3 World.   T15MS:3 *app. crit.* swig.
'This scene . . . misery.'] *text supplied by editor from Johns. 1785*
I15:1 If the Doctor] *above these words is the notation* Henry 8th 291 *see Intro., p. 39*   near of kin] *ED:* (C) Brother

Sentiment the Language the Characters & — ? — of the speakers and the Subject of their Discourse have all a very exact Corespondence. The Subject gives an interest to the Dialogue and the honest Plainess & Sincerity of Griffith and the holy Resignation of the Queen abstracted now from the sense of Injury & Resentment stamps the Sentiments of both Parties with the Dignity of Truth. In such a Dialogue no ambitious ornaments of speech can be admitted. Figures are for the most Part thrown out by the Tumult of Passion or by a much labouring for the attainment of something beyond its Natural Reach. But this Propriety which is the Basis of all good writing and can never be dispensed with in any composition is taken by itself only the lowest Condition of poetry. All above propriety unviolated may be Exquisite may reach the terrible sublime, all below the dignifyed proper is Dulness and Insip[id]ity and ought not to be borne. But the Doctor has found Here a scene of very correct Propriety and He calls all the world about [Him to admire] Him as if He had found what in vulgar speech is called a Mare's Egg. What is it like Doctor? Why neither like this or that or t'other neither a Pumpion or a Balloon; and so He goes on saying what it is not without ever adverting to what it is. And Why all this? Manifestly for the Purpose of impressing an opinion that He sees further into a Millstone than his neighbours. [T15MS] I despise does he seem to say your hot Madeira and your sparkling Champaign so give me a Draught of good wholesome small Beer without Froth without Bounce without ardent spirits without Fermentation no tumultuous workings no Cholic no Vertigo no gripe. This He wo^d say is the old true and orriginal Taste. Small Beer says [He I uphold] all against the World. But did the Doctor never hear that there are various Modes of Excellence and that we cannot praise the one for no other Reason than it is not the other? The smooth surface of a summer's sea is a pleasing object but it becomes more sublime when it is vexed with storms which [take] the Ruffian Billows by the Top but with the Hurley Death Himself awakes. I do not mean to treat the scene lightly. There is in it

I15:9 Him to admire Him] *MS. has first three words careted in erroneously after second* Him *instead of before*

T15MS:3 Small beer . . . the World] *ED*: (C) I leave to others the sophistication of Poetry and because I have not liked have seemed not to understand but of your genuine small Beer I am always ready to take a heavy swig.   He I uphold] *MS. reads* Her [?] ophuld

T15MS:5 take] *MS. reads* takes

a felt propriety but it is not of the best sort of Excellence and there are
Sentences and half Sentences [T16MS] in Shakespeare which I wo^d
set above a hundred such scenes nor is the Doctor's Tone less high
& peremptory than his opinion if indeed it be his opinion is false.

LR 8

PROBABLE FOOTNOTE TO *ES.*, T80:3a

[180] Shakespear passes this Transaction Without marking it
with Censure. He has trusted it to the Reader but I dont know
whether the Reader is aware that these Toils were spread for Percy.
The Suspicions of Worcester tho' they did not reach the whole
Villainy of the Design prevented at that Time the Effect. The very
same Instruments were then Employed and the same liberal offers
made and doubtless for the same End. But Shakespear does not
allow us to suspect the Prince of any Privity. He takes Care to
inform us that He had no share in his Father's Councils. Thy
Place (says the King) in Council thou has rudely lost which by thy
younger Brother is supplyed that is by this sober Boy now under
our Notice Lancaster. The Frankness & Gallantry of Harry's
Challenge of Percy is another Proof: and thus says the Father We
might trust [181] thee Harry did not considerations infinite forbid.
The most fo[r]cible of those Considerations was I Believe the Hope
of inmeshing the Whole Contrary Party in one great Drag of Perfidy
& Fraud. The Design failed but it was too precious a peice of Mischief it seems to be wholly thrown away. It was treasured up for
another and indeed more proper Period for of their Fraud Machiavel
wo^d say in his way that it was a Resource which ought to be reserved
for the very Close of Life; that it might carry a man successfully
enough thro' the last act but if practised earlier It wo^d be found not

T15MS:7 felt propriety] *ED*: (UM) dignified simplicity

T16MS:1 nor is . . . peremptory] *ED*: (C) and (R) the Doctor's (C) peremptory
(R) Tone (UM) is no (R) less (C) offensive

LR 8. *Punctuation*: 180:7 (says King)   181:4 Sword.

180:1 Shakespeare passes . . . aware that] *ED*: [182:1] (C) Besides the Various traits
of Fraud which strike thro' the Whole Character of Bolingbroke Shakespeare has disposed us to believe that

180:8 The Frankness . . . and thus] *ED*: [182:2–183:1] (C) the Gallantry Warmth
& Frankness of Harry's Challenge to Percy the Day before the Battle to decide the
Quarrel by personal Combat is a further and more compleat Proof of his Innocence
[183] of any intended Perfidy and Fraud: and thus

181:4 in his way] *ED*: [183:2] *fol. by* (C) without referring it at all by [*i.e.* to] he
Test of Moral Honesty

worth the Evil as it wo.^d render all future Resource impracticable and bring every slight Difference to the uncertain Decision of the Sword.

Earlier Drafts

LR 8—ED 1: *Cancelled Continuation of LR 8*

[181:5] (UM) Harry was now in Wales sent there we may say out of the way of this Transaction. I do not look to any other History than the Play. Shakespeare has given us a (C) much better [History] of Man in general than any We can find of particular Men and I confess myself so whimsical (if the Reader pleases) as to give very little Heed or Credit to what is called History beyond the Names of Persons and the Dates of great Events, considering Him who deserting the Trash [T81MS] of curious Anecdote & secret memoir shall best speculate on the general Tendencies of human Nature under the controul of local & temporary Influence to be the best Historian and nearest the Truth of Things.

LR 8—ED 2: *First Draft of LR 8—ED 1*

[184] (C) The Prince was fortunately at this Period in Wales. May we not suppose He was on Purpose sent thither to give the freer Scope to these De[s]igns? I dont consider or care how these things stand in History. Shakespeare has given us a better History of Man in general than any We can find of particular Men. I for my part believe that He had no other materials before Him than the mere Rubbish of the Elder Stage and out of this Dunghill scattering thereon the genuine Principles of human Nature and the seeds of Action He has raised by the sheer Force of Genius a better History of human Nature Discovered as working thro' the various Influences of Character and Situation than [185] any other of hi[g]her & more authentic Pretence but which I consider and do not in this Point stand alone to be at best but the Records of certain noted Facts flourished over with fantastic Lies and splendid Imposition; and indeed so little Heed am I among others inclined [to] give to what is called History beyond the Names of Persons and the

LR 8—ED 1. *Punctuation*: 181:7 (if pleases)   T81MS:1 Things.
181:5-7 Harry was . . . us a] *see note to LR 8*
181:7 History] *cf. LR 8—ED 2, 184:4*
LR 8—ED 2. *Punctuation*: 186:1 remember.

Dates of great Events that I consider Him who deserting the Trash of curious Anecdote & secret Memoir shall speculate best on the general Tendencies of human Nature under the Controul of local & temporary Influence to be the best Historian and as approaching nearest the Truth of Things. Such was Davilla's History of the civil Wars in France which being read to the old Duke D'Epernon by his Sec[r]etary a short Time before his Death this little spirit of Bounce Bustle action & Intrigue was astonished as we are informed by that Secretary in his Life of D'Epernon to find his own Motives & Conduct too various and obscure probably for his own Comprehension rationaly de[ve]loped & laid open by a foreigner with Truth & Precision. I am no litterary [186] Plunderer nor do I now steal from Lord Bolingbroke yet in his Writings as I remember some Reference is had to the foregoing Anecdote contained in the Life of D Espernon written by his secretary but whose Name I do not remember.

LR 9
INCOMPLETE INSERTION TO *ES.*, T94:1

[199] Another Passage remains which seems to deserve a seperate Consideration. It is spoken by a Person of a very different Character from Lancaster and is of a very different Nature from every Passage which I have hitherto discussed. It is an Impression to the Disadvantage of Falstaffe, one of these Things which I dare not combat by Argument. It is one of those seemingly Careless (CM) Touches (U) of Truth & Nature which without challenging Notice drops its Influence secretly on the Mind.

[196:4] That a Man Sho^d have his Head broken under certain Circumstances is Nothing or nothing more than a broken Head. It was the Fate of Pyrrus not only to have his Head broken and by a Woman but to have his Skull fractured into the Bargain. [197] He lost his Life it is true but what then? his Honour was safe & unwounded. But to have one's Head broken merely because another chuses to break it be He who he may is not altogether so pleasant and as to the Effect now upon a Man's Temper if it produces a certain Sobriety of mind reminds a man of marriage and of setling in

LR 9. *Punctuation: none*
199:4 Touches] *ED*: (C) strokes
196:4 is Nothing] *fol. by false start*: (C) He may heal it with the salve of Honour

the World and if He sho^d propose an alliance of that Kind to the
tender hearted [woman] who shall dress the Wound and take up
40^s in advance as part of her Fortune we may indeed Conceive that
there was no Errour in the Case and that his Head was not broken
in Vain but we shall never afterwards I fear be persuaded to think
of Him in the light of a gentleman or a Soldier; after this all Argument and Reflection comes too late; the Impression is Made and
however it may be in real Life from the Impression [I98] in the
Drama there is no appeal. It may be indeed that it was an act of
great Brutality in the Prince to break the Head of a Man of Title
and Rank who was too old or corpulent to resist or who might have
held the Prince's Person as too sacred to assail but if nothing of this
Kind is expressed or insisted on what have we to do with Colours
which are not thrown on the Peice? We might indeed paint differently but in the mean Time we must and will take the Picture as it
is; of as little avail is it to say that a Promise of Marriage to Dame
Quickly may pass among his other Arts of Fraud that his sole object
was the Attainm^t of 40^s and that to this end one Lye considered
simply as such was very little different from another; but that is not
so. He was sworn upon a parcel gilt goblet and if He Wo^d put himself for any

Earlier Draft

LR 9—ED: *First Draft of LR 9*

[I94] (UM) Another Passage remains which appears to me of
Importance enough to deserve a seperate Consideration but it is so
obscured and lies so much out of Notice that if I was not disposed
to seek out and to challenge Difficulty I might Venture perhaps [to]
leave it behind me without any Danger [of] Detection; but having
affirmed that Shakespeare has all along laboured to impress us in
Favour of Falstaffe's Courage whilst He has Ventured to play with

I97:2 if He sho^d propose] *fol. by false start*: (UM) to the woman who dresses the
Wound and if upon the Credit of that Promise the Patient Sho^d (C) Endeavour to
defraud the poor woman of 40^s and Engage Her to beg some Prawns for Him of Neighbour Gossip under the ridiculous Pretence of their being good for a green wound [*see
note to* ridiculous Pretence *LR 9—ED, I95:2*]   woman] *cf. prec. entry*
LR 9—ED. *Punctuation:* I96:2 it.
I94:1 Another] *prec. by* X = *link with T94:1: see* app. crit. *to Es., T94*   Venture
perhaps to leave] to *omitted inadvertently; cf.* ED: (R) perhaps (UM) well (R)
leave   Danger of Detection] of *omitted inadvertently; cf.* ED: (C) Censure or
(R) Detection   play with] *ED*: (C) perplex

our Understandings it seems but honest that I Sho.^d Notice the only Instance which occurs to the Contrary. The Passage which I am now to produce is of a nature very different from the preceding one and is uttered by a very different Person, no other than the very garrulous and nonsensical Mrs Quickly: it is a passage which is thrown out as it were by chance and in the midst of much other Impertinence & Clamour and with.^t other Reference to Falstaffe's Courage than as it may imply Discredit [195] by the aid of logical Inference & Deduction but is yet of a Nature to strike directly on our Feelings and to make Impressions of the utmost Abasement & Dishonour. To hear that a Soldier has had his Head broke for a very light Cause, to find that it produ[c]es no other Effect than a Promise of Marriage to a foolish Prostitute Who dresses his Wound and that upon the Credit of this Promise he shall borrow forty shillings and Employ her to beg Prawns under the ridiculous Pretence that they were good for a green Wound, is certainly as degrading as possible; and to find this Charge uncontradicted by the Party Himself tho' uttered in his Hearing and unaccounted for is to fix indelibly the Impression in our Mind. It is in vain to reflect that it was a brutal Act in the Prince to break the Head of a Man of Rank & Title who was too old or corpulent to resist or who held the Prince's Person too sacred to assail. It is in vain also to say that this Promise was no other than [196] one of his usual arts of Fraud & Imposition, that his object was 40.^s and that one Lye considered as such was very little different from another. That is not so; but if it were yet till these Things are explained which they are not in the Play the Impression Will remain and I doubt if any Explanation Whether found in or out of the Book could erase it. The Reader will doubtless expect that I sho.^d give him some Satisfaction in a Matter which seems so directly to militate against all my Principles & Positions.

I94:2–I95:I and with.^t . . . & Dishonour] *interlined in ED*: (UM) and (C) applies only (UM) to the Discredit of Falstaffe's [195] Courage by Inference & Deduction (C) Yet (UM) strikes directly on our Feelings to his utter abasement & Dishonour
I96:2 That is not so] *ED*: (C) It may be so

LR 10
REVISION OF *ES.*, T122:5–T124:1

[I139] But I beg leave to go over this ground again. The dread of that Tediousness which is apt to grow on Detail has checked me I think too much; some Detail in this Place will open the Arts of Shakespeare as well as authenticate the Courage of Falstaff. I will therefore trust myself to the Patience of the Reader. There is a Propriety in the Prince's Exclamation, What! A Coward, Sir Jn? Paunch? which deserves a full Explanation. Gadshill [who] has sett, as it is called, the Travellers Enters in this scene accompanied with Bardolph whom He is supposed to have accidentally Encountered by the way—but I must transcribe the Whole Dialogue. The Commentators I perceive do not understand it.

Gadshill, entering—Stand!
Fals. So I do, ag^t my will.

The reader will remember the Condition of Falstaff who had not yet recovered his Horse.

[I122:8] Poins *oh! 'tis our Setter I know his voice. Bardolph! What News?*

This is pointed in the Text as if the Question was asked of Bardolph, whereas Bardolph is only recognized upon his Nearer approach by his Person as Gadshill (CM) was before by his voice. (U) This Errour has begot another. The answer is given to Bardolph instead of Gadshill to whom it clearly belongs and I shall correct it accordingly.

LR 10. *Punctuation: All punctuation in quotations from Shakespeare in I122:8–10, I123:1–10, I124:9, I125:3, and I126:5*   I139:1–6 *app. crit.* Dialogue.   I139:5 sett, called,   I139:7–9 *app. crit.* Horse.   I139:7 entering—   I139:9 Fals.   I122:10 Bardolph,   I123:11 Question.   I123:12 Poins,   I124:3–8 *app. crit.* Note   I124:7–8 *app. crit.* Bard.   I124:8 correct—   I124:9 may,   I125:1 Remedy.   I126:2 so, That, short,   I126:3 Imputation. T126MS Honour   I126:5 Play.   I126:6 struck.   I127:1 uttered, Event, Poins. Transaction.   I127:2 (for   Argument)   I128:2 being, are, (as see) mere, idle, scene.   I130:3 *app. crit.* first.   I131:1 subtle, refined, pleases. I131:2 return— Hal.   I132:1 Words, *after.*   I133:1 rely.—   I133:4 them. I134:1 Me.   I134:2 another.

I139:1–6 But I . . . understand it] *ED:* [I122:1–4] (UM) But the . . . whole Dialogue. [*not otherwise reproduced;* But *prec. by* X = *link with* T122:4]
I139:5 who] *MS. reads* what
I139:7–9 Gadshill . . . his Horse] *overlaps virtually word for word with ED:* [I122: 5–7] (UM) Gads . . . his Horse. [*not otherwise reproduced*]
I122:10 This is . . . his Person] *ED:* (C) So it stands in the Text but I beg leave for very obvious reasons [?] to correct it and assign this Question to Bardolph thus: Bard. What News?

[I123] Gads. *Case ye, Case ye. On with your vizzards. There's money of the Kings coming down the Hill, 'tis going to the Kings Exchequer.*
Fals. *You lie you Rogue, 'tis going to the King's Tavern.*
Gadsh. *There is enough to make us all.*
Falst. *To be hanged.*
Prince. H. *You four shall front them in the Narrow Lane. Ned, Poins and I will walk lower. If they escape from your Encounter then they light on us.*
Peto. *But how many be of them?*

The Prince's Direction suggested this very proper Question. It was an Enquiry which *could* not come from the Prince or Poins, *their* high Courage and private Ends forbid it and *Peto* who does not seem to be marked either for Cowardice or Courage is certainly the properest Person to ask such a prudential Question. This Question is [I124] not asked of any particular Person but is thrown out only as a Matter fit to be known and considered. Gadshill is the only Man to give authentic Information. The answer is in the Text assigned to Him but this is I think a third Errour and induced in Part by the preceding two. The answer given is not true and therefore ought not to be assigned to Gadshill. But it seemed fit to the Editors that Gadshill who was best informed sho.ᵈ say something. But Bardolph having been before put in his Place they now put Him in the Place as I think of Bardolph. There appears no Reason why gadshill Shoᵈ falsify contrary to his better Knowledge and the Ends of his Mission but Bardolph who is supposed to have discoursed [with] Him on the way might well avail Himself of that Circumstance for uttering an intrusive Lie suitable to the Condition of his Natural Cowardice and to that extraordinary Tumult of Fear which the Idea of a Seperation had suddenly produced. I will therefore again correct—

Bard. Some Eight or Ten.

But let the Answer belong to whom it may, the Fact seemed to the Persons on the scene incontestible and Falstaff thereupon exclaims:

Fals. *Zounds! Will they not rob us.*

I124:3-8 The answer . . . again correct] *cf. afterthought on T124MS*: The Reply is given to Gadshill. I shall venture to assign it to Bardolph but as it is an Alteration of the Text on which I build no Argument my Reasons will be contained in a Note. *see note*
I124:7-8 had suddenly . . . will therefore] *prec. by last element of ED*: [I124a] (UM) Bard. *Some Eight or Ten my Lord* [*ED otherwise cancelled and unreproduced*]

This Exclamation tho' guarded from Terrour by the humourous Suggestion that the Travellers might rob the Thieves yet conveyed to the Prince the Idea that Falstaff had taken the Alarm of Prudence at least if not of Fear. This was an [I125] Impediment Which had not occured even to Poins nor had either his wit or Malice provided any Remedy. The Seperation of their Strength was now likely to be objected to and the Plott of Course in the utmost Danger of failing. No Expedient therefore which seemed likely to su[c]ceed was too coarse for the Exigence and nothing seemed so proper to stimulate as a Charge of Cowardice:

Prince H. *What a Coward! Sir John Paunch!*

—taking off however the Roughness of the Charge by the Mirth and Humour of the appellative. This is the first instance in the Play of any Suggestion being Made in Falstaff's Hearing at least of his Want of Courage. It is [I126] therefore very material to our Purpose to observe how it was taken. If Falstaff was indeed intended to be shewn as a Notorious Coward and that We are to suppose He had been often called so, nothing sho^d be Expected from Him but a light humourous Evasive answer Wit instead of Dignity: That, in short, which *he had* for that which *He had not*. But if on the Contrary He had hitherto supported the Reputation of a brave Man and a good Soldier we ought to expect that He sho^d value Himself on his Condition and take serious offense at so coarse and [i]njurious an Imputation. [T126MS] But he gets thro' this Test of Character with Honour. [I126:5] *I am not John of Gaunt indeed your grand-father but yet no Coward, Hal*, is almost the only serious sentence which falls from Him thro' the whole Play. The Prince seems struck. He cannot indeed recede but He endeavours as much as possible to reconcile his Policy [I127] With his Justice for at the same Time that He brings his Censure to immediate Use and applies and presses it as a Stimulus to that single Point for the sake of Which it was uttered, The approaching Event, Yet that End obtained He opens a Door for Falstaff to escape the Imputation; at least it must have appeared so to Falstaff tho' the Prince indeed reserves a differ-ent application of the word *Event* for Himself and Poins—*The Event* of the concerted Transaction. The Reader will judge Whether

---

I126:3 injurious] *MS. reads* jnjurious
T126MS:1 But he . . . with Honour] *ED:* [I126:4] (UM) But we have just seen Him abide this Test of Character and come thro' With Honour

the comment I have Here made on the four last speeches in the foregoing Dialogue (for the preceding one's are immaterial as to any Purpose of Argument) be a fair and plain Account of Shakespear's Views & Intention or only the Effect in me of mere Subtlety and false Refinement. If the former then it will be manifest [I128] that Shakespear was so far from intending to Exhibit Falstaff as a Coward that He manages every Thing as towards a Man of known Courage & established Reputation. If the latter then the passages I have transcribed instead of being, as I think they are, a perfect Imitation of Nature and growing necessarily out of Character Motive and Exigence will be (as far as I can see) mere, idle, unmeaning Prattle and such as any Body else might have written as well as Shakespear for there is no Wit or even a splendid Word or Expression in the whole scene. As to Refinement it may be observed Here in passing that Whoever [I129:4b] Will detail the secret Designs & Managements [I130] of Shakespear must deal professedly in Refinement. He must refer the plainest simplest Things and such as co^d not as it sho^d seem be otherwise to latent Artifice and deep Design and investigate with Care that hidden *Art* which not appearing to exist at all we are indolently and ignorantly content to call by the Name of *Nature*. If over Refinement be the Temper of such a writer He will be fortunate at least in this that No Refinement can be too much for the Reach & Artifice of Shakespear; and if in Enquiries & Speculations [I131] of this sort so wholly unimportant to the Concerns of human Life He shall consider Truth only as a secondary Object & Subservient to the Purposes of innocent Dissipation & Amusement He may for any Censure of mine be as ingenious as subtle, as refined, as singular and as Orriginal as He pleases. But to return—

I am not, says Falstaff, John of Gaunt your grandfather but yet no Coward Hal. This is precisely What I take to be the true Character of Falstaff Modestly not Ostentatiously pronounced and it seems to be thrown out at this critical Conjuncture by the Author as Caution to the [I132] Audience not to take too sadly what was intended only, to use the Prince's own Words, *As Argument for*

I128:3 Whoever] *fol. by LR 10—ED.*
I130:1 professedly in Refinement] *ED:* (R) Refinement(C)s false or true
I130:3–I131:1 and if . . . He pleases] *ED:* [I130:3b] (C) nor can Refinement [*ED:* (C) over (R) Refinement] be ever more Excusable than in the Pursuit of a Question Where Truth is but a secondary Consideration and Subservient to critical amusement as the first.

a Week Laughter for a month and *a good jest for Ever after.* The Prince's Reply is suited to the Exigence but We may further infer from it that the Whole of Falstaff's past Life Co^d not furnish a single Fact in support of the Charge of Cowardice which had been before suggested and therefore it is that the Prince seems obliged to draw on the coming Hope. Well, says he mysteriously, let the Event try. The first Event that of a successfull Attack upon the Travellers this very speech was intended to promote. The second Event that of the concerted attack upon Falstaff which is [I133] the reserved Sense the Prince had every Reason to hope wo^d turn out to the Disadvantage of Falstaff and it is upon this Probability he ventures for his own Justification to rely.—But the Travellers approach. Falstaff objects not to the separation but Notwithstanding the Supposed Inequality of Numbers we see Him attack these Travellers with Spirit & alacrity using the Accustomed Words of threat & Terrour. They Make no Resistance and He binds and robs them. The Player Falstaff indeed leaves this Business to the three associates whilst He saws the Air at a [I134] Distance with all the Manifestations of Cowardice & Bragadocioe but it is to be hoped that People of that Sort will make No Difference between the Reader and Me. The Stage and the gallery doubtless understand one another.

Hitherto I think there has not appeared the least Trait either of Boast or Fear in Falstaff but on the Contrary many strong Indications of Courage & Reputation.

Earlier Draft

LR 10—ED: *Cancelled Continuation of I128:3,*
Par. 2, LR 10

[I128:3] (R) Whoever (C) Will comment on Shakespeare in Detail must resolve to set this Censure at Defiance: one knows in [I129:1] general Who these sort of Censures come from: the pedantically learned and the Arrogantly dull. Singularity Caprice false Refinement Paradox & Subtlety are words which afford Men of this Character much Comfort & Consolation. With these Novelty & Orriginality (the most reasonable Apologies for appearing in Print) are Crimes of the blackest Die and well may they anathamize those Actions which they are in no Danger of Committing. Truth is

---

I134:3 Reputation] *fol. by* See Page 124 pr[int] = *link with T124:2*
LR 10—ED. *Punctuation*: I129:3 (the Print)

or ought to be the object of Every Writer and no doubt we may
sometimes overshoot the Mark but of two Conditions I had rather
I confess see a Man break forth in Excess than herd for ever how
ever securely in the Faction of Fools. [I129:4a] But He who

LR 11

REVISION OF *ES.*, T126:2–T129:1

LR 11a: *Main Body of Revision*

[I181] Such are my Ideas of Falstaffe but they are Ideas not F1
Acquired from the Stage and not to be obtained there. Very different
indeed is that Vassal Soul that trembling Coward that greasy slovenly
Compound of Dirt & Meaness Which We Meet occasionally in
Drury Lane & Covent Garden and Whom in spite of real Disgust
We affect to Admire in vicious Conformity to the Supposed Opin-
ions of Each other. I am bold to confess that I never Saw a more
hatefull Character than the Stage Falstaffe: Nor can I join in the
Laugh or [I182] Mingle myself in the common Deception. My Idea
is that of a goodly portly man ifaith and a corpulent of a chearfull
Look a pleasing Eye and a most noble Carriage and when I find
Him depicted as a Trunk of Humours a boulting Hutch of Beast-
liness a grey Iniquity & a Father [Ruffian] I laugh at the Exaggeration and recognize in the Caricature a certain Tendency of Feature,
Not a Woefull likeness of real & subsisting Truth at which I Sho^d
not and could not laugh at all. [I183] Falstaffe is fat indeed but F2
they Make Him bigger than goodman Puff of Barson. The Exaggerations
in the Play go on a Comparison between Him and the Prince

LR 11. *For segment designation (F1, F2, F3, etc.) in outer margin, see Textual Note*
LR 11a. *All differences in phrasing between ED on I136–I138 (= B1) and final text in*
I183:1–I185:1 (= F2) are recorded in app. crit.
   Punctuation: I182:2 Truth.   at all.   I183:1 Barson.   I184:2 P. H.
I137:3 Guts, down.   I184:3 F.   I137:4–5 down. Exchequer.   I185:1
Harry.   I135:5 Condition.   I136:1 Wardrope.   I136:2 *app. crit.*
Injury.   I147:4 Power.   I185:5 others.   I186:4 safety.   I186:5
Prince—   I187:1 Wisdom,   I174:8 replies—   I175:2 you,   I187:2 Books.
   I181:1–2 Such are . . . different indeed] *cf. rejected afterthought:* [I116:1] (C) Such G1
I think is the Impression we sho^d naturally take in the reading [of] the Play [*ED*: (R)
we (C) Wo^d (R) naturally take (C) from the Book] but very different indeed *see note.*
   I181:2 Meaness] *ED*: (C) Servility
   I182:2 Ruffian] *MS. reads* Ruffain   Not a Woefull likeness] *ED*: (C) but (R)
Not a Woefull likeness (C) of Form and not a serious Picture
   I183:1 fat indeed] *ED*: [I136:4] (C) fat and unweildly it is true   B1

Who is represented in History as well as the Play to be remarkably slender but the Players by Endeavouring to bring up the Fact to the [Picture] spoil all the Mirth & Humour of the Peice. The strongest Exaggerations of Falstaffe's Corpulence and inactivity are Made on Occasion of the Robbery but I wonder the Players do not see that this refers to the Disproportion between the Inactivity of the Actor and the Activity which the Action [I184] requires and that they do Not also make some Allowance for the peculiar Temper of Falstaffe who is always ready for any Purpose of Sport to lend out his Wit against Himself.

P. H. Peace [I137:3] [ye] fat Guts, lye down, lay thine Ear close to the ground and list if thou canst not hear the Tread of Travellers.

[I184:3] F. Have ye [I137:4] any Leavers to lift me up again being down. Sblood, I'll not bear my own Flesh so far afoot again for all the Coin in your Fathers Exchequer.

[184:4] The Players take this in sober Sadness and it Was their Custom on occasion of his [being] attacked by the Prince & Poins to furnish Him with an Automaton Leaver in one of his associates.ᴧ It woᵈ be in Vain to ask them How such a Man coᵈ founder a Hundred and odd Posts Within the Extreamest Inch of Possibility or how He who cannot bear his own Flesh coᵈ yet raise both Himself and the dead Percy from the ground in the Battle of Shrewsbury F3 and March [I185] off as a double Man in Pursuit of Harry.ᴧ They have no better answer I suppose to give but that every Place must abide its own Folly; but I am more offended at their Manner of

---

I183:2 as the Play] *ED*: [I136:5] (C) as the Drama   Picture] *MS reads* Piciture [*2 ED*: (C) Description / [I136:5] (C) Description]

I183:2–I184:1 the Mirth . . . Allowance for] *ED*: [I136:5] (C) the Humour and render that a woefull likeness which was intended only as a Whimsical Carracature. There was besides [I137] (UM) a further Occasion in this Place for these Exaggerations. They refer to the Disproportion between the Inactivity of the Actor and the Activity required for such an Enterprise to which we must add

I184:2 Peace] *fol. by* &c = *link with I137:3.*

I137:3 ye] *MS. reads* yet

I184:3 Have ye] *fol. by* &c = *link with I137:4.*

I184:4 The Players . . . Prince & Poins to] *ED*: [I137:6] (UM) This the Players take I suppose in sober sadness and therefore it is that they   Leaver] *ED*: [I137:6] *fol. by* (UM) soon afterwards   associates] *LR 11b to be subjoined here as footnote*

I184:5–I185:1 It woᵈ . . . of Harry] *ED*: [I138:1] (UM) What a Heartbreaking thing it must [*fol. by* (UM) it must] be to them after this to see Him rise from the ground in the Battle of Shrewsbury and carry off the dead Percy on his back *for continuation* (= *B2*) *see LR 11c, app. crit. to I171:4*

I185:1 Harry] *LR 11c to be subjoined here as footnote*

dressing Falstaffe than at any other Injury they do Him. His Habiliments [1135] are not of the same Fashion with those of Cotem- A2 poraries which gives Him a Singularity of appearance altogether improper. Do they imagine that He tricked Himself out like a Holliday Fool on Purpose to draw Notice and make Sport? Nor is his Dress only Singular but Slovenly. He looks like a Captain of Banditti instead of a gentleman fit to be admitted into the Prince's Appartments where we first see Him with all the Ease and Address of a Man of Rank & Fashion. Shakespear and indeed Propriety requires that He sho^d be dressed rather above his Condition. The Hostess had Made Shirts for Him of Holland of Eight Shillings an Ell and He looked that Mr Doubledown the Mercer sho^d have Sent Him two and twenty Yards of Sattin for his Slops and short Cloak. [1136] He was thorough he tells us With the Shop Keepers whom he calls Smooth-Pates in honest taking up and the Poverty of his Purse was likely Enough to be covered by the Splendour of his Wardrope. His Taste for Magnificence was such that if He had had Time He wo^d have laid out the thousand Pound he borrowed of Shallow in new Liveries.

[1147:3] I do not insist upon the Strict Letter of these Quotations. C There is scarcely a Passage relative to Falstaff in the whole Play Which will bear such a Construction but there is always a Spirit to be obtained which tho' it may not be comprehended within any Strait Lines of Precision yet is always to be sufficiently understood; but the Players seem determined as it were Maliciously to degrade this Character by every sort of Injury Within their Power. [1185:4] F4 Something as to the Liveries must be allowed for Exaggeration but it is Wonderfull that the Players will not give Falstaffe credit for anything. They treat Him worse than the Shop Keepers Whilst

I185:3 Habiliments] *fol. by* etc. see 134 = *overlap with I134:6—see next entry*

I135:1 are not] *prec. by* [I134:5-6] (UM) I will add in this Place that the Players A1 discover great want of Judgment in their Manner of dressing Falstaff. His Habiliments [*whole passage prec. by false start:* [I134:4] (C) The Reason why Shakespear insists so much on the Corpulence & Inactivity of Falstaff in this Scene is that He is engaged in an Action] Holliday] *ED:* (C) Lord Mayor(UM)'s

I135:6 Cloak] *fol. by false start:* (C) He had four servants

I136:2 Liveries] *fol. by* (UM) There is scarcely a Passage in the Play which is not A3 too phantastically coloured to be produced as sober Evidence but there is a medium to be obtained Whereas the Players seem determined to degrade this Character by all Kinds of Injury. return to 129 pr[int] *see* app. crit. *to* Es., *T129:1, and Textual Note to LR 11*

I147:3 I do not] *prec. by* 136 = *link with I136:2*

I185:4 as to the Liveries] *ED:* (C) in the last Quotation = *I136:2*

they trust With! Examination every ill Report which is made of Him by others. With respect to [T185MS] Courage if any Reader has during the Perusal of this Book looked to the stage as a Rule of Judgment, If he has given Credit to any one Action or any Emphasis or Tone of voice which He has seen or heard there or has referred to any Thing but his own genuine [T186MS] Taste & Feelings He is already in another Party and I neither sollicit or Wish his Concurrence. If the Players are right this is the most erroneous Book which ever was offered to the Public. In every Scene upon the stage almost in every Speech there is some Intimation of Cowardice in Falstaffe—A Wink a Tone a Shrug or Something or other which indicates the Poltroon: during the Robbery the gallant Nym & Peto & Bardolph do all the work; Falstaffe saws the Air at a Distance with his [I186] broad Sword and Even there covers Himself with his shield and seems frighted at his own Exertion. In the Battle of Shrew[s]bury He comes forth in the Condition of a drowning Man snatching all around at Safety Whilst overwhelming Danger seems pressing Him on all Sides and booming over his Head. Nay on our first Acquaintance with Him in the Princes Chamber Where no Danger of any sort is intimated by the Text but Where on the Contrary He seems to indulge his genius in the Most perfect security and Ease Even there He trembles with the most Vassal Fear. The Prince touches his sword in act to draw & Falstaffe shrinks & shrugs and fawns for safety.

Thou hast the most unsavoury Similes says Falstaffe and art indeed the most comparative rascalliest sweet young Prince—but I prithee Hal trouble me no more with [I187] Vanity, and so goes on in [an] Easy careless way Wishing for a Commodity of good Names and so forth and upon the Prince's repeating something which Falstaffe had said about Wisdom, Falstaffe tells Him that He had a damnable Iteration with the same Freedom as He had before called Him the most comparative rascallest sweet Young Prince after which the conversation goes off to the taking of Purses etc. Wo^d one Expect to see swords near drawn and all the Action of Rage Perturbation & Fear Exhibited on this occasion? Yet so it is that all this is most Exquisitely performed in dumb show. But let us hear the Player:

I185:5 by others] *fol. by false start:* (C) If there realy was such an existing Character so hardly treated   I186:2 all around] *ED:* (UM) He (C) knows not where
I187:1 an] *MS. reads* any

P. Ought I to suffer Myself to be called Rascal with^t some [I188] resentfull Notice?

A. The Question is not about you Sir. If the Prince takes it patiently I don't see how you are concerned.

P. Supposing Sir that I were the Prince of Wales?

A. I sho^d then suppose you Sir to be a Prince of very great ability and Courage and sho^d expect to see you act accordingly.

P. Co^d I bear to be called Rascal?

A. I think if your royal Highness sho^d seek such rude Society that you wo^d have Wisdom enough to submit to the Conditions of it. To attempt Correction wo^d indicate not a Temporary Residence but a Permanent Home.

P. But Who could have Patience?

A. Men of Sense and Dignity. [I173:5] You Wo^d not Much resent **G2** very hard words from a Magpye or Parrot. The offense arises out of the Condition of the Speaker and the construction which others may be supposed to Make but on this Occasion what ill construction Co^d be made of Forbearance? [I189] You Wo^d allow this Man **F5** to be as familiar With you as your Dog and Wo^d you be surprized if He held his Place?

P. But the Prince resents on other Occasions.

A. Where? When?

P. He breaks Falstaffe's Head for likening Him to a singing Man at Windsor and He calls Him else Where fat Paunch and says an He calls Him Coward He'll stab Him.

A. Sir for the first Instance it requires Comment & shall find it; for the last it is most manifestly an Errour. The speech belongs to Poins. No man who will consider a moment can doubt it. Poins indeed is on a level and May be allowed to resent but He is not able to provoke the Prince to do the like how much soever and frequently He attempts it; but how sir [I174] after all if We sho^d **F6** be in an Errour Here and that the word Rascal in the Days of Harry was innocent of offence? You Wo^d then have Cause to regret the Irritability of your Temper.

I188:10 Dignity] *fol. by* X 173 = *link with* I173:5
I173:5 You Wo^d] *prec. by* X = *link with* I188:10
I189:6 requires] *ED:* (UM) deserves
I189:7 The speech] *fol. by* Payne Bookseller Mewsgate | Chapman Stationer K^t Str Ch. side | Nichols Printer Red Lyon Court Fl. Street *see note*
I189:9 but how] *below these words is written* 174 = *link with* I174:1
I174:1 after all] *prec. by* (UM) But how Sir = *overlap with* I189:9

P. It was acted So before my Time.

A. I mean nothing personal Sir. I blame only the general Errour of the stage. Leaness was the Condition I think of What were called rascal Deer and the Epithet 'rascally' thereupon transferred I suppose to other Subjects of the same Quality. It Wo^d be strange then if among so many References to the Leaness of the Prince We had not met with this allusion; but not to carry you Sir out of the Play we meet with this word there on two other Occasions. This oily Rascal, says the Prince of Falstaff, is known as well as Pauls; and in another Place Mrs Doll having called Falstaffe a muddy Rascall He replies—You make fat Rascalls Mrs Doll. [I175] Not I, says She, but gluttony & Diseases Make them. We catch of you, says Falstaffe, We catch of you grant that my poor virtue. It sho^d appear from this that the Condition of a Rascall is to be lean but that there are certain catching Diseases which in their Effects may change this Condition into its contrary, a Disease which seems to be imputed to Falstaffe Under the Description oily Rascall. I am not learned in the Question but there is tis plain some History in the Matter Which if well studied might Discharge this Word rascally from the offence which you have in my Judgment too rashly taken. There does seem however to have been in Shakespear's Time some Equivocation in the Word which is here taken off by the conciliating Addition of sweet young Prince.

P. I cannot think but that to call a Man Rascall was always Matter of offence.

A. I[t] may be so as implying the Whole Condition of the Animal
F7 Taken together Whereas rascally [I86:2] Might in common Discourse refer to the Quality of leaness only. The Reverse of this is the Case when the subject itself implies no Dishonour but is apt to beget some unpleasing or dishonourable Quality. Thus a good Knave a good knave as applied by Shallow to Davy is even Praise but Knavish Wo^d be Dishonour. We are servants to our Mistresses our King or our Country but yet we Wo^d not be thought servile in any Case; or after all the word Rascal might have orriginally signified a lean man and from thence transfered to the Animal in which case the Quality rascally must have held its orriginal Meaning With^t taking [I87] any Taint for a long Time. I am not Antiquarian

I175:3 Under the Description oily Rascall] *ED*: (C) by the Prince in the epithet (R) oily (C) annexed to (R) Rascall
I175:7 rascally] *below this word is written* 86 = *link with* I86:2

Enough to decide the Question and it is too insignificant to deserve
a Reference to Books.

LR 11b: *Footnote to LR 11a, 1184:4*

[1158:3] I have lately seen Falstaff's runing away represented in D
a different Mode: formerly He walked off at least if He did not
run. [1159:2] But now he neither walks or runs but waddles off his
indecent Form wrigling like some Enormous non Descript Animal
equally Strange barbarous and offensive—[1158:5] But this by
the Bye cannot hold for it is a most supprizing Feat of Strength
& Agility and what the first Performer at Sadlers Wells may be
challenged to imitate in vain. This very Falstaffe who has not it
seems Activity enough to rise and run is yet able to raise his Bulk
upon Knees & Elbows and swagging his great Belly on the Floor
to writhe & Hump Himself off with a [Celerity] as We find Sufficient
for all the Purposes of Flight & Safety roaring [1159:1] all the While
as nothing either on Earth or Water ever roared before. [1159:3]
I must confess that I wished on this occasion the very ineffic[i]ent
swords of Hal & Poins had been converted into Excellent Cudgels
and Well placed in the most willing Executive Hands.

LR 11c: *Footnote to LR 11a, 1185:1*

[1170] This Incident is not I think to be imputed to Shakespear E
but to some Earlier Representation of a ruder Falstaffe under the
Name of oldcastle. Shakespear has washed his Hands of it by
manifesting his own better Taste and Judgment on occasion of the
Death of Percy.

LR 11b. *Punctuation*: I159:2 offensive—   I159:1 before.   I159:3 Hands.
   I158:3 I have] *prec. by 2 false starts*: [1158:2] (UM) There has been of late it seems
a different method / [1158:1] (C) The account Here given represents very truly   run]
X *above* n = *link with* I159:2
   I159:2 waddles off] 2 *ED*: (C) paddles (R) off / [1158:4] (C) Crawls off on all
four[s] roaring as Neither Bull Calf or any other Animal I believe ever roared be-
fore   indecent Form] 2 *ED*: (C) beastly odious Form / (C) misshapen Bulk
non Descript Animal] *ED*: (C) Reptile
   I158:5 hold] *ED*: (C) last long   Feat] *ED*: (C) Effort
   I158:6 Celerity] *MS. reads* Cerlerity
   I159:3 very inefficient swords] *ED*: (C) Tin Swords
   LR 11c. *ED on I138* (= *B2: see Textual Note to LR 11*) *is reproduced in* app. crit.
   Punctuation: I171:4 *app. crit.* Indecency. Impropriety.   I173:2 Man.
I173:4 sport.

If thou wert sensible Says Harry [of courtesy,
I should not make so great a show of zeal:—
But let my favours hide thy mangled face;
And, even in thy behalf, I'll thank myself
For doing these fair rites of tenderness.
Adieu, and take thy praise with thee to heaven!
Thy ignomy sleep with thee in the grave,
But not remember'd in thy epitaph!—]

But this Incident coᵈ not Notwithstanding he dispensed With. It was a Sacrifice to the Barbarity of the Age and He left the Players & the groundlings to make the most of it. Thus circumstanced the Manner of representing it does not come Within the Line of my Censure. To the Player & the gallery Where the groundlings are now seated it belongs in full Property and I will not [1171] disturb their Possession. Yet one may venture to hint that there shoᵈ be some Moderation even in absurdity. I Woᵈ not walk I think so often round the Carcass as if it Were to Meditate my prey nor shift or dispose the Limbs of it in such order as if like some great Serpent of Ceylon I were to slaver and swallow it Whole. Nor after it was taken on my Back woᵈ I put both myself and it into such indecent Positions as out of respect to Decency I must not venture to describe. Is there nothing New I wonder to be struck out on such an Occasion ? As the Player we have seen can amble so well upon all fours why may He not take up the dead Body on his Back now Sufficiently stiffened to preserve an upright Posture and so dance off like a Playhouse Hobby? The Spectators Might be pleased With the

I170:3 Harry] *fol. by &c = link with 1H4 V. iv. 94–101; text supplied by editor from Johns. 1785*

I170:4 But this] *prec. by false start*: (UM) Having given this sentiment to Harry [*ED*: (R) Having (C) said this in his own vindication] (C) He next resigns this popular Incident to the groundlings Who demanded it

B2   I171:4 Nor after . . . to describe] *3 ED (which continue from ED recorded in LR 11a, app. crit. to I184:5–I185:1)*: [I138:2] (C) but this Instance of Activity & Strength they take care whether it be in malice or in Kindness I cannot tell not to let pass off with! Marks of infinite Labour accompanyed with the most Enormous [*ED*: (R) Labour (C) and of the most improper and scandalous] Indecency. (UM) Return to 128 pr[int] = *cancelled link with T128:6—see Textual Note to LR 11* / [I138b:2] (UM) but [*prec. by false start*: [I138b:1] (UM) they will not allow it] they have their revenge it shall not pass (C) off with! marks of infinite Labour accompanyed with the most Enormous Indecency return to 128 pr / [I138a:1b] (C) but they take Care however to be even with the Author for this and not to let it pass off with! infinite Impropriety. (R) return to 128 pr

I171:6 like . . . Hobby] *ED*: (UM) in (C) that Fashion

Novelty at least if not the Wit & Humour [1172:6] of the Thing. There is a Difficulty however: Harry on the approach of Falstaffe surprized to see Him alive says, Thou art not What thou seemst. No that's certain, says Falstaffe, I am not a double Man, referring to the dead Body hanging at his Back. But Why may we not alter the Text and say, No that's certain I am Not a Centaur, or indeed why not avail ourselves of the Authority of Dryden who in his indian Emperour makes one of the Princes who had been engaged with the Spanish Cavalry say [1173] that He had killed a double Man only one Part however of Whom as it appeared was dead the other having fairly run away. The only Danger of this Authority wo^d be lest it sho^d prove in such Case what Falstaffe So strenuously denies that He was in Truth what He seemed to be a double Man. I think I co^d find out Many ways of disposing of this Carcase full as much to the Entertainment of the Gallery whose Rights in this Case I do not oppugn as that which is now so exceptionably practised. I dont for my Part see Why the Carcase Might Not be brought to confess that it was in Truth a living Player and not a dead Hero and thereupon become assisting in the sport.

LR 12
INSERTION TO *ES.*, T146:1

[1140] But Here the Reader may perhaps Exclaim What is become after all of the Wit & ability of Falstaff? but a few Pages ago and His Wit was the *principal* His Courage only the *Accessary*. Then it was if his Courage did not come forth into Action that we were desired to look for it behind his Wit and Now it seems We are very clearly to discern it thro' his Folly. If He was not before this Time under the Necessity of covering Cowardice by Lies He was at least in the very full and constant Practise of Lying. [1141] He had the whole Day before Him for Invention and He seems to have Employed the whole Day to this Purpose. Bardolph who affected not Modesty

1173:3 Gallery] *ED*: (C) Spectators
LR 12. *Punctuation*: I140:2 Folly.　　I141:4 *Yea, men.*　　I141:5 Imposition?
I142:2 Imposition?　　I142:5 Errour.　　I143:1–2 *Mountain, pa[l]pable. Fool.*　　I144:2
Way.　　I144:3 *much— two— a month— little month—*　　I144:5 Buckram.
I145:1 *me.*　　I145:3 own.　　I145:4 Fals. speak;　　I146:1 P. H. it?　　I146:2
Fals. (for dark, Hal, Hand)　　I148:4–I149:1 *app. crit.* Fame.
I140:1 But Here . . . may perhaps] *prec. by* X *and written beneath* NB What follows Here is to be inserted in page 146 pr[int] Where Reference will be made to it = *link with T146:1*

*blushed at his Monstrous Devices. He hacked his Dagger and said He
would swear Truth out of England but that He wo.^d make it believed
it was done in fight. Yea, He persuaded his Companions to tickle their
Noses with Spear-Grass to make them bleed and then beslubber their
garments With it and swear it was the Blood of true men.* Were these
things intended for humourous Rhodomontades only or real Imposition? The Charge goes against Shakespear Himself. If the Lies of
Falstaff Were intended for [1142] Imposition How comes it about
that they are so preposterous as to create a Doubt of that Intent?
If for Humour & Rhodomontade only How come they to be detected
as Lies and Imposition? The Charge Says the objector goes against
Shakespear Himself. I agree with Him entirely. If Shakespear has
in fact deserted the ability of Falstaff He has not in my Opinion
behaved like Shakespear and if Shakespear fails us in any Point our
ground becomes Every Where doubtfull & insecure and if He fails
us in the Case before us He is wholly Without Excuse for He has
erred not thro' Neglect or Inadvertance but with his Eyes fully
open on his Errour; [1143] for Many are the Checks and Cautions
He has made the Prince & Poins give to Falstaff Not to Enlarge two
men in Buckram Suits into Eleven and the Prince at last impatient of
this and other absurd Extravagancies cries out *that These Lies are
like the Father who begets them gross as a Mountain, open pa[l]pable.
Why thou clay brained gutts Thou knotty pated Fool.* But the objector
may go further and add that these Lies are not only gross and open
to Detection but that Shakespear may be charged with deserting
on this Occasion Even Nature Herself. The Increase of the Buckram
Men from two to Eleven tho' it makes Excellent Sport is not He
may say strictly [1144] Natural. Men Warmed and kindling with
real Passion will thus indeed increase or diminish as Occasion may
lead the Way. *But two Months dead Nay not so much—Not two—
within a Month—a little Month—* is perfectly Natural. But Falstaff
without any real Impulse from Nature and Passion and watched
and cautioned by the Prince and Poins Sho.^d have been it may be
said more Circumspect and Attentive to that Precision which is the
Character of real or simulated Truth at least when Fact alone is
in Question. But in spite of Probability in spite of Caution How

1142:5 like Shakespear] *fol. by false start*: (C) Yet not for this will I give up one
Iota of Argument in behalf of Falstaff's Courage but the charge however must be
replied to

1143:3 the objector . . . and add] *ED*: (C) I will not rest Here, I will go yet (UM)
further (C) than the objector Himself and declare

strangely does He magnify the Rogues in Buckram. *Two Rogues in Buckram Suits I have paid* and then almost [I145] in a Breath *Four Rogues in Buckram let drive at me*; but I will transcribe the whole Dialogue. I am sure the Reader will not complain of that Art if it is not much abused by which I endeavour to relieve my Page with borrowed Excellence. The rich Threads indeed are borrowed of Shakespear but if they are fairly & honestly interwove The Tissue I may be perhaps allowed to call my own.

Fals. Let them speak; if they speak more or less than Truth They are Villains and the Sons of Darkness.

[I146] P. H. Speak sirs how was it?

[*Gads.* We four set upon some dozen,—

Fal. Sixteen, at least, my lord.

Gads. And bound them.

Peto. No, no, they were not bound.

Fal. You rogue, they were bound, every man of them; or I am a Jew else, an Ebrew Jew.

Gads. As we were sharing, some six or seven fresh men set upon us,—

Fal. And unbound the rest, and then came in the other.

P. Henry. What, fought you with them all?

Fal. All! I know not what you call, all; but if I fought not with fifty of them I am a bunch of radish: if there were not two or three and fifty upon poor old Jack, then I am no two-legg'd creature.

Poins. Pray heaven, you have not murder'd some of them.

Fal. Nay, that's past praying for: I have pepper'd two of them: two, I am sure, I have pay'd; two rogues in buckram suits. I tell thee what, Hal,—if I tell thee a lie, spit in my face, call me horse. Thou know'st my old ward;—here I lay, and thus I bore my point. Four rogues in buckram let drive at me,—

P. Henry. What, four? thou said'st but two, even now.

Fal. Four, Hal; I told thee four.

Poins. Ay, ay, he said four.

Fal. These four came all a-front, and mainly thrust at me. I made me no more ado, but took all their seven points in my target, thus.

P. Henry. Seven? why, there were but four, even now.

Fal. In buckram?

Poins. Ay, four, in buckram suits.

I146:1 was it?] *fol. by* The Dialogue here continued to the following speech of Falstaff's [= *I146:2*] inclusive [*dialogue supplied by editor from Johns. 1785*]

Fal. Seven, by these hilts, or I am a villain else.

P. Henry. I pr'ythee, let him alone; we shall have more anon.

Fal. Dost thou hear me, Hal?

P. Henry. Ay, and mark thee too, Jack.

Fal. Do so, for it is worth the list'ning to. These nine in buckram that I told thee of,—

P. Henry. So, two more already.

Fal. Their points being broken,—

Poins. Down fell their hose.

Fal. Began to give me ground: But I follow'd me close, came in foot and hand; and, with a thought, seven of the eleven I pay'd.

P. Henry. O monstrous! eleven buckram men grown out of two!]

Fals. But as the Devil Wo^d have it three misbegotten Knaves in Kendal green came at my back and let drive at me (for it was so dark, Hal, that thou couldst not see thy Hand).

[1148] The Whole scene is indeed excellent in its Kind and so Whimsically Extravagant that He Who can abstain from Laughter has I believe No Mirth in his Composition; but whilst we laugh we may censure it as Mere Extravagance and as Every Where overstepping the Modesty of Nature. This is a Charge which I feel Myself concerned to Answer. Not that it goes as I conceive Ag^t the Courage of Falstaff but as it bears upon Shakespeare Himself whose genius I have supposed to be greatly above the Necessity of departing from Nature & Propriety in order to produce such farcical Incidents as may make the Groundlings laugh Whi[l]st the judicious grieve. Yet I beg leave to [1149] reserve my Defence till I have opened this Extraordinary Character a little further when the whole Conduct of Shakespeare Will appear Easy Natural & Plain.

I148:1 censure it as Mere Extravagance] *cf. ED*: [1146] (UM) exclaim that this is Mere Extravagance, That it renounces the Ability of Falstaff
I148:4–I149:1 Yet I . . . & Plain] *cf. ED*: [1146–1147] (UM) As yet however we are not wholly prepared but when I have opened this Extraordinary Character a little further (C) We (UM) may perhaps [1147] furnish the Reader with ample Satisfaction. In the Mean Time we will leave Shakespear to the Plaudit[s] of those honest Sensibilities which form his best and surest Fame.
I149:1 & Plain] *fol. lower on I149 by* Fingal and the Fee Fo Fum of Childish Tales & Vulgar Romance *see note*

LR 13
REVISION OF *ES.*, T167:2–3

[I167] And Now then we find Place to inquire into the real Composition of Falstaff's Character considered not as a dramatic Being merely but with Reference to the general Principles of his Frame and to that common Nature to which every dramatic Character ought ultimately to refer; to do this may be worth our Curiosity at least and it may be Necessary for the more perfectly understanding the Arts & justifying the Conduct of Shakespear.

It is a common Observation that every Man has two Characters the ground of Which may be that Every man may be seen externally and from without or a section may be made of Him and He may be illuminated from within and [I168] in these different Views the Characters May take very different appearances but can be perfectly known only from the Consideration & Combination of Both.

LR 14
INSERTION TO *ES.*, T176:1

[I176] Whoever departing from his own Independence Sacrifices his Integrity and lends Himself out to gratify the Vices or unreasonable Passions of another for the End [of] Subsistence and Reward is a Parasite Whether He take the Form of an obsequious Flatterer or that of a Butt a Pimp or a Buffoon. A Butt is acceptable cheefly on this Account that He Enables a Man to flatter Himself just as He likes best and a Buffoon is only a more pleasant & diverting Butt and who furnishes a greater Variety of Gratifications. Some Butts and some Buffoons may have the Merit of not knowing precisely their own Condition and of not acting upon any formed Design or Intention. [I177] But this apology cannot be urged in Behalf of Falstaff. He knew his Condition perfectly and acted

LR 13. *Punctuation*: I167:1 Shakespear.   I168:1 Both.
   I167:1 And Now] *prec. by* X = *insert in place of T167:2–3; see* app. crit. *to Es.,* T167:1.
   I168:1 of Both.] *fol. by circled notation return to* 167 pr[int] = *link with* T167:4.
LR 14. *Punctuation*: I180:4 them.
   I176:1 Whoever] *prec. by false start*: (C) We must now   Himself out] *ED*: (R) out (C) his own separate Portion of Ability   to gratify] *fol. by afterthought*: (C) intentionally   for the End of] *ED*: (C) with a view to   an obsequious . . . that of] *ED*: (R) a [n *added later*] (C) Sycophant
   I176:2 is only] *fol. by* (UM) is only

manifestly upon Plan and under all the arts of Management and Design. His singular Talents will not allow us to conjecture otherwise; but it is beyond Conjecture. We have no Right to call upon Shakespear for Explanations upon Points which He means to obscure. It is Enough if He furnishes the Multitude with proper Impressi[ons.] Let us Suppose that He sho^d open the base Designs of Falstaff and Accompany those Designs with Effects correspondent to the Cause. This might disgust. Let Him then conceal the Design[s] [I180] and permit the Effects to remain in all the Colours which they derive from their Cause. This may impress the Cause on the Multitude with^t Disgust and as to the curious why Let them infer the Cause from the Effect at their Leizure by What logical Process they please. They are not his Subjects. They are for the most part their own Dupes and he does not trouble his Head about them.

I177:3 Talents] *fol. by ED*: (C) & Ability
I177:4 Explanations] *fol. by false start*: (C) It is his Business to impress not to Explain yet

A COMMENTARY ON
THE TEMPEST
(*c.* 1785–1790)

A COMMENTARY ON *THE TEMPEST*

[*Introduction*]

[I2] THE *Tempest*, as Here given, is manifestly a reformed Play, the orriginal of which is *lost*, but of which many *Vestiges* are to be found in the present Play. It is highly probable, almost certain, that the Tempest in its orriginal state was Shakespeare's *first* dramatic Work and in its present state his *last* excepting possibly Henry 8th.. Its over strict adherence to the Laws of Place and Time, by which He has almost strangled the Play, discovers either a Childish Ambition or a peasant-like Acquiescence in the Dictas of some pedantic school, to which, having once released Himself, He was not likely to return. But the Law of *Time* He so little understood, that He has made it run on in unbroken continuity, Without those Intervals between the Acts, in which the Action and Incidents of a Play are prepared for Representation and Effect. Nor has He at all distinguished or seemed to know that there was a Distinction between natural and dramatic [I3] Time, nor does He seem to have known the true meaning of that Rule which prescribes an *Unity of Place*. It is not a very small Island nor Even the two or three hundred yards within which He confines Himself which constitutes that *unity*, but a certain fixed spot represented by a single scene, from which indeed a larger space may be beheld; but there are scenes in the *Tempest* as distinct from Each other as if they were a hundred miles asunder, and are the *worse* for being *nearly right*. The familiar Dialogues also of Sebastian Anthonio and Gonzalo are so unlike the conversation of Men of Rank or of gentlemen that they discover the Author to be ignorant of Manners

A COMMENTARY. The primary text consists of the latest version of each section of Morgann's Commentary found in the MS. book. Each section is preceded by the relevant passage(s) from Theobald's *Shakespeare* (1733) and followed where appropriate by Morgann's ED, including all the Marginal Notes found on TMS pages. The *app. crit.* records (1) all significant briefer ED either in the latest or earlier versions; (2) all symbols on I and on T pages indicating links and cross-references; (3) all MS. readings, unless self-evident, of emendations in the text; and (4) all uncancelled MS. materials not reproduced in the text.

For further details see Textual Intro. to the Commentary on *The Tempest*. For abbreviation and symbols used in the text and *app. crit.* see pp. xiii-xiv.

Introduction. I2:2 excepting ... 8th] *careted in by mistake after a full stop (unreproduced) which originally followed the word last*

how perfect so ever He, [undoubtedly], instinctively, was in the natural Workings of the human mind; to which, in a more advanced Age, He added a [14] Knowledge of the Forms and Manners of the World. The real *Place* of this Play is *Bermoothes* or *Bermuda's*, of which the *Portugueze*, when they deserted it about the year 1550 had spread over Europe an Opinion that it was possessed by Magicians and spirits and Surrounded with magical storms. This they did to prevent other Nations from visiting an Island to which they meant, in the course of Time to return. And these Tales, in a Superstitious age were readily believed, and possessed not only Babes & Nurses but the grave and sober Doctors of the World, and were likely to make great Impressions on the young *Shakespeare* who was *Sensibility* itself. Some Evidences to this Point will be *Noted* in the Course of the Play. Why the true Place of this Play is not avowed is plain. *Bermudas* is so much out of the course of ordinary Navigation and [15] placed so far in the *Atlantic*, that it would not meet that Part of the Tale about the Duke of Milan & King of Naples taken from some *Italian* novel as I suppose. He was therefore obliged to bring *Bermudas* into the *Mediteranean*, where Kings and Dukes were to be found, but without giving to this supposed Island any Name, whilst He Established a Correspondence between it and the *still vexed Bermoothes*, where Ariel was wont to gather *Dew*. The orriginal Play was written, as I think, about 1587[.] In the year 1592 Sir george Summers was wrecked on *Bermudas* and returning by the way of *Newfoundland* made such favourable Reports as that this Island was restored once more and put under the Dominion of Nature, and it was soon afterwards settled & possessed in shares by Subscribers and drew great attention at the Time, which possibly recalled the memory of a Play almost gone into Oblivion for it was probably on its first Representation [16] an unsuccessfull Play as coming from an unknown writer and ill performed[.] In Consequence of all which it was revived, as I think, in 1612 but greatly abridged to make Room for that *Machinery* with which it is now decorated, and which was, at that Time, more valued, as a novelty, than Either Nature or Truth. The first scene that of *a ship at Sea* was evidently, at the Time of its Revival, prefixed to the Play. It only exhibits in advance to the Eye what we afterwards learn more properly from the Play, and this is

I3:3 undoubtedly] *MS. reads* undobctedly
I5:2 *Dew.*] *prec. by* (C) *Wicked*
I5:4 that this Island was restored] *ED*: (UM) to (C) restore (R) this Island

so manifest that I think it proper to separate this Representation from the Play itself, under the Title of *an Induction*, and to call the Entrance of *Prospero* and *Miranda* the *first scene*.

I pass by much learned conjecture of which not having availed myself it does not seem necessary that I sho^d speak[.] [I7] What the plan of this Edition is will best appear from its Execution but it is the Purpose of the editor to say no more in the course of it than need must and in particular to keep the Page, which may be considered as the Poet's Presence Chamber as free as possible from [Brawls] and to refer whatever in that Kind may be found Necessary to an appendix[;] to treat preceding Commentators with all that Respect which is due to Men of much greater Learning and ability than the Editor yet always to remember that this Edition is not theirs but my own.

Marginal Notes

I

[T2MS] (C) It sho^d appear that this Play was written before the Return of Sir Jno Summers after being wrecked at Bermudas but that on the Return of Summers, and the Subscriptions thereupon made for Settling it, this Play was revived with great alterations & much Decoration. The former supposed Magical state of that isle is here represented [T3MS] tho' removed to the Mediteranean, an Island without a Name. *Setebos* however, a transatlantic Idol, is made the Go[d] of Cannibal and the Name Canniba[l] is nothing but a Metastasis of *Caliban* for *Cannibal*.

2

[T75MS] This Play together with that of Har[ry] the 8th seem, by machinery and Show, to be the great Supports of the Play House in the Reign of James. The Court had deserted Truth and Nature for nonsensical Masques, contrived b[y] Ben. & decorated by Inigo, but thes[e] two plays did something to draw the [*whole line cut off*]

I6:4 I think ... this Representation] *ED*: (C) if I were to give an Edition of this Play I would seperate it   Representation] *ED*: (C) scene
I6:5 availed myself ... sho^d speak] *ED*: (C) profited I do not think Myself obliged to retail *fol. by false start*: (C) My Intention being to (*superseded by I7:1*)
I7:1 Brawls] *MS. reads* Brawlgs [= Brawlings?]

I. i. 1

[T3] Scene, *On a Ship at Sea.*
A tempestuous noise of thunder and lightning heard:
Enter a Ship-master, and a Boatswain.

*Scene, On a Ship at Sea] [PI1:1] I wo^d call What is now SCENE IST
an Induction, being no part of the Play, but a speaking *spectacle*,
introductory, and prefixed, on the Revival of the Tempest, in the
year 1614 or thereabouts, Being the *first* Time, as I believe, that the
multitudinous Sea, together with a ship sailing thereon, was ever
brought upon the English Stage, to usher in which spectacle, this
Induction was devised. The word *Induction* is of doubtfull meaning,
but seems to be used by *Shakespeare* as Equivalent to *Introduction*,
and as containing something *inducing* the action of the Play. But as
this Induction *speaks*, we must attend to what it says.

Marginal Note
[T3MS:3] (C) This is an *Induction* merely & composed in the
Reign of James, when the Play was revived with much Machinery
& Decoratio[n.]

I. i. 10–11

[T3] *Alon.* Good Boatswain, have care: where's the master? play
the men.

[PI1:4] (C) *good Boatswain, have Care. Where's the master? play
the men.*]* Shakespeare cannot help drawing Characters, tho' in so
short a scene[.] This Boatswain is at once tyrannical and base. His
Power is in a Storm and He abuses it, tho' in the Article of Death.
The words *play the men* Mr. *Steevens* interprets [PI2] to mean[:]
Act with spirit—behave like men, but I am persuaded, by the Tone
and Manner, that the Reference is to *chess*[:] *employ your Men to
the most advantage.*

I. i. 1. T3 Enter] *prec. by* X = *ref. to* T3MS:3; *see next entry*
T3MS:3 This] *prec. by* X = *ref. to* I. i. 1, T3; *see prec. entry*
I. i. 10. T3 *Alon.* Good . . . the men] *circled a in outer margin opposite this speech* =
ref. to PI1:4; *see next entry*
PI1:4 good] *prec. by a.* page 3 = *ref. to* I. i. 10, T3; *see prec. entry*   good
boatswain . . . the men] ED: (C) *Hence what Care these Roarers for the Name of King.*
[= *I. i. 17*, T3]
PI1:5 scene.] *MS. reads* scene,
PI2:1 mean:] *MS. reads* mean.   chess:] *MS. reads* chess.

I. i. 24–5

[T4] [*Boats.*] You are a counsellor; if you can command these elements to silence, and work the peace o' the present, we will not hand a rope more; use your authority.

Marginal Note
 **work the peace o' the present*] [*Line drawn through Theobald's note:* [T4n] i.e. on the present, at this Instant.]

I. i. 51

[T5] *Gonz.* I'll warrant him from drowning, tho' the ship were no stronger than a nut-shell, and as leaky as an unstanch'd wench.
[PI2:2] (C) *unstanched wench*] *an incontinent wench. Steevens.*

I. i. 63, 64–6 and I. ii. 1

[T5] *Gonz.* He'll be hang'd yet,
Though every drop of water swear against it,
And gape at wid'st to glut him.
A confused noise within.] Mercy on us!
We split, we split! Farewel, my Wife and Children!
Brother, farewel! we split! we split! we split!

. . . .

SCENE *changes to a Part of the Inchanted Island* . . .

[PI2:4] (C) *To glut Him*] *Steevens* thinks that it sho.^d be *inglut* or ingulph. After these words there is a *Stage Direction*, that a confused Noise sho.^d be heard from within, of *Mercy on us* &c which Direction is printed as part of the *Text*, instead of being marked as a *Direction to the Players*. Those words, to the Conclusion, *We split, We split*, sho.^d be printed in *Italics*, as seperated from the Text. The Induction being finished the Play begins, and what is called *Scene the 2.^d* or *Scene Continued* sho.^d be marked as *Scene 1st.*

I. i. 51 T5 unstanch'd] *blot above this word perhaps* = *ref. to* PI2:2; *see next entry*
PI2:2 *unstanched*] *prec. by a* p. 5 = *ref. to I. i. 51*, T5; *see prec. entry*
I. i. 63 &c.] T5 swear against it,] *circled* b *in outer margin opposite these words and referring to entire speech* = *ref. to* PI2:4; *see next entry but two*   *noise within*] *fol. by enclosed a corresponding to circled a above* Mercy on us! = *ref. to* T5MS:1   SCENE]
X *below this word* = *ref. to* T5MS:2; *see next entry but two*
PI2:4 *To glut*] *prec. by* b. page 5 = *ref. to* T5, *I. i. 63 &c.; see last entry but two*
PI2:5 ingulph] *fol. by* (C) *but it may mean only to* glut *his throat with water.*

(C) The proper Delineation of this scene to the Eye is so interesting, that I shall consider it in the [PI3] *Appendix*, to which I refer under *N.° 1.*

Marginal Notes
*A *confused noise*] [T5MS: 1] It sho.^d be a confu[sed] Noise withi[n] of Merc[y] &c whic[h] word[s] sho.^d be mark[ed] in Ital[ics.]
SCENE changes] [T5MS: 2] this is the proper Beginning of the Play [.]

I. ii. 3

[T5]   [*Mira.*] The sky, it seems, would pour down stinking pitch,
              But that the sea, mounting to th' welkin's cheek,
              Dashes the fire out.

[PI3: 2] (C) *stinking Pitch*] But the Lady co.^d not surely *see* the stink, but the words following *dashes the Fire out* require that we should read *flaming.* The word was probably wholly blotted and the Transcriber could think of no word to fill up the Line with but *stinking*[.]

I. ii. 15

[T6]   [*Pro.*]   tell your piteous heart,
              There's no harm done.
              Mira. O wo the day!
              Pro. No harm.
              I have done nothing but in care of thee.

[PI3: 5] (C) oh, Woe the Day] D. Johnson wo.^d take the words which begin the next speech, *no Harm!* from *Prospero*, and give them to *Miranda*, but the Exclamation of *Woe the Day*, sufficiently indicates her *unbelief*, and if she had added, *queriulously, no Harm*, she wo.^d not have been Shakespeare's *Miranda*, but D. Johnson's. Even as it is, and tho' she had seen the wreck with her own Dove's Eyes, the severe *Prospero* says harshly *No Harm*, and she is silent, and He then takes up a softer Tone.

T5MS:2 this is] *prec. by* X = *ref. to* T5, *I. ii. 1; see last entry but two*
I. ii. 3 T5 stinking pitch,] *fol. by circled* a *in margin* = *ref. to* PI3:2; *see next entry*
PI3:2 stinking Pitch] *prec. by* c. [= a] p. 5 = *ref. to* T5, *I. ii. 3; see prec. entry*
I. ii. 15 T6 Mira.] *prec. by circled* a = *ref. to* PI3:5; *see next entry*
PI3:5 oh, Woe] *prec. by* a. p. 6 = *ref. to* T6, *I. ii. 15; see prec. entry*

I. ii. 22 and 37

[T6]   *Pro.* 'Tis time,
         I should inform thee farther.

·   ·   ·   ·

[T7]   The hour's now come,
         The very minute bids thee ope thine ear.

[PI3:8] (C) *'Tis time I sho*ᵈ *inform thee further*] after this He says
the Hour is come The very minute. Never was magic brought to such
[PI4] profitable use. *Miranda* is now near *15,* Not quite *three* when
she was Exiled, and it is now *12* years *since* that Period, and her
Father had by his Instructions *made her more Profit than other
Princes who have Tutors not so carefull,* and yet she was never once
informed *Who* she was or *Where* she came from till it became
necessary to acquaint the Audience, thro' the medium of Miranda,
With the Knowledge of these interesting Facts. But this Play is built
upon *Magic* and we must admit it as *a Principle. The Time,* the *Hour
was not come,* but now the *very Minute* bids her ope her Ear. It is in
vain to ask for Reasons. If Reasons could be given, It would be
Magic no longer. Magic is an Effect without any known cause; and
we have nothing to do, but with *Miranda,* to obey and be attentive.

Marginal Note
  *The very minute] [T7MS:2] (C) Magic˙depends on the *Minu*[*te.*]

I. ii. 23–4

[T6]   [*Pro.*]   Lend thy hand,
         And pluck my magick garment from me: so!
                                      [*Lays down his mantle.*

[PI4:8] (C) *Lend me* [*thy*] *Hand and pluck my magic garment from
me*] In this place *Prospero* [PI5] puts *Miranda* under a *sleepy spel,*
but which was not to operate 'till He resumed his garment. The
actor shoᵈ, on this occasion, use some misterious Action, indicating
the Imposition of some Spel.

I. ii. 22 T6 *Pro.*] *prec. by circled* a = *ref. to PI3:8; see next entry but one*
I. ii. 37 T7 *now come,*] *fol. by circled* a = *ref. to PI3:9*
PI3:8 *Tis time*] *prec. by* a p 6 = *ref. to T6, I. ii. 22; see prec. entry but one*
  I. ii. 23–4 T6 *And pluck*] *prec. by circled* b = *ref. to PI4:8, and by* X = *ref. to
T6MS:1 ; see next entry and next entry but two*
  PI4:8 *Lend me*] *prec. by* b. p. 6. = *ref. to T6, I. ii. 23–4; see prec. entry*   *thy*]
MS. *reads they*

Marginal Note

[T6MS:1] Here He puts a spel on Miranda to operate in a short Time afterwards, which operation He watches heedfully.

I. ii. 27

[T6] [*Pro.*] The direful spectacle of the wrack, which touch'd
The very virtue of compassion in thee.

[PI5:3] (C) *The very virtue of compassion*] The *Energetic Quality.*
Johnson. 'Tis common to say that one is not only patient but *patience itself.*

I. ii. 29

[T6] [*Pro.*] The direful spectacle of the wrack

. . . .

I have with such provision in mine art
[T7] So safely order'd, that there is no foyle,
No not so much perdition as an hair,
Betid to any creature in the vessel.

[PI5:6] (C) *no Foyle*] *Shakespeare* beyond Question wrote *Soyle,* not *Foile,* for such was *Prospero's* Direction to *Ariel*; as may clearly appear from *his Report* of its Execution, *Not a* HAIR *perished, on their sustaining garments not a* BLEMISH, *but fresher than before.* Why those orders that there sho.ᵈ be no *Soil* were particularly given will be presently seen. But *Prospero* in this Place departs a little from his Integrity, and in order to appease *Miranda*, substitutes *Probability* for *Truth.* He had given *orders*, indeed, but *the Report* of their Execution had not been yet made to Him, and He soothes her further by confessing that she *saw* the [PI6] vessel *sink*, but intimates that it was a *Delusion* produced by his Art, and she, who dares not trust Even her senses against his authority, submits, and is consoled.

Marginal Notes

[T7MS:1] Not Foyle but Soyle.

T6MS:1 Here] *prec. by* X = *ref. to* T6, *I. ii. 23–4; see prec. entry but two*
I. ii. 27 T6 The very] *prec. by circled* c = *ref. to* PI5:3; *see next entry*
PI5:3 *The very*] *prec. by* C. p. 6 = *ref. to* T6, *I. ii. 27; see prec. entry*
PI5:6 *no Foyle*] *prec. by* a p. 7 = *ref. to* T6, *I. ii. 29; same ref. also indicated by notation* [I7:2] Note wanted Here *opposite Theobald's note,* T7n, *on* no foyle *see note*

[T7MS:3] (C) It ought to be Soile. He speaks in the words of his own orders to Ariel whom He presumes has obeyed them. See page 13 [i.e. T13, I. ii. 217]

I. ii. 53

[T8]   *Pro.* 'Tis twelve years since, *Miranda*; twelve years since,
Thy father was the Duke of *Milan*.

[I8:2] *twelve years since*] She is now of course 15.

I. ii. 67, 78, 87, and 106

[T8]   *Pro.* My brother, and thy uncle, call'd *Anthonio*—
I pray thee, mark me;—

.   .   .   .   .

Thy false uncle—
(Dost thou attend me?)

.   .   .   .

[T9] now he was
The ivy, which had hid my princely trunk
And suckt my verdure out on't.—Thou attend'st not.

.   .   .   .   .   .

Hence his ambition growing—
Dost thou hear?

[P16:2] (C) *I pray thee mark me*, and again, *dost thou attend me.*] In the course of this Narrative *Prospero* demands of *Miranda again* and *again*, if she attends, if she hears, from whence it shoᵈ follow that tho' the spel was laid on, not to operate 'till He Shoᵈ arise and resume his garment, yet He was doubtfull, and very heedfully watched the Event. Let no Body ask why, it is *Magic*: but there was also a *Natural* Cause, which the poet wished to conceal. The Narrative is a long one, and, I suspect, was but ill attended to on the first Representation of the play, and these Questions are now put rather to keep the [P17] audience awake than *Miranda*. It is as much as to say, Gentlemen, why don't you attend? You do not mark me. Do you hear me? Pray attend, it is *a Tale* (according to Miranda) *which might cure Deafness.*

I. ii. 78 T8 Dost thou] *prec. by* X = *ref. to T8MS:1*
P16:2 *I pray*] *prec. by* a & b p. 8 = *ref. to T8, I. ii. 67 and 78*

Marginal Notes

*Dost thou attend me?] [T8MS:1] (C) Expects the operation of the Spel[.]

*Thou attend'st not.] [T9MS:1] (C) agai[n.]

*Dost thou hear?] [T9MS:2] (C) again[.]

*I. ii. 78, 87, and 106] [T9MS:3] (C) The spel seems to be suspended in consequence of his laying down his magic garment which He calls his *Art*, but when He resumes it in page 12 [i.e. T12, I. ii. 169] the spel succeeds.

I. ii. 81

[T8]   *Pro.* Being once perfected how to grant suits,
            How to deny them; whom t'advance, and whom
[T9]   To trash for over-topping.

[I9:1] *to trash* for over Topping] *To trash* is to cut away superfluities[.] Warburton.

I. ii. 83

[T9]   [*Pro.*]   having both the key
            Of officer and office, set all hearts i' th' state
            To what tune pleas'd his ear.

[I9:4] Key] This *Key* sets all the Hearts in the state to what Tune He pleases so that we are to consider it as a musical Key[.]

I. ii. 99–103

[T9]   [*Pro.*]   He being thus lorded,
            Not only with what my revenue yielded,
            But what my power might else exact; like one,
            Who having into truth, by telling of it,
            Made such a sinner of his memory,
            To credit his own lie, he did believe
            He was, indeed, the Duke.

I. ii. 81 T9 over-topping] a *in outer margin opposite this line* = *ref. to* I9:1; *see next entry*

I9:1 *to trash*] *prec. by* a: = *ref. to* T9, *I. ii. 81; fol. by* (UM)]

[PI7:7] (C) *like one who having into Truth &c*] *Prospero* certainly
means to say that *Anthonio*, like others who often repeat the same
Lie, became at length his own Dupe and gave credit to the Lie He
told. But this very common observation, *Shakespeare*, not always
exempt from Errour, wishes to raise into Consequence and has
obscured it to make it look great. [PI8] Hence the words *made such
a sinner of his Memory* meaning, that He made it the *Instrument of
Lies*, but besides being obscured, the Text is also depraved and Sho^d
be corrected thus—*like one Who having* UN*to Truth, by telling oft* (not
of it, which would render *Truth the sin* and *not Falshood*) *Made such
a sinner of his memory to credit his own Lie*, that is by telling oft
a Lie made such a sinner of his memory as to believe his own Lie.
Very ill and imperfectly expressed at the best.

I. ii. 118

[T10]   *Mira.* I should sin,
          To think but nobly of my grand-mother.

[I10:1] (C) I sho^d sin] Theobald *right*.

I. ii. 120

[T10] [*Mira.*] Good wombs have bore bad sons.

[I10:3] good wombs have bore bad sons] This Line as Theobald
suggests ought to be given to Prospero.

 I. ii. 99–103 PI7:7 *like one*] *prec. by* From page 20 = *I9, where a cancelled ED facing
I. ii. 99–103 on T9 is prec. by (U) See page 7 of the manuscript [= PI7:7] *Prospero*
certainly . . . He told] *cf. ED:* [I9:6] (C) This is quite ridiculous instead of the common observation that a Man may tell a Lie [till] He believes it to be Truth We have it
here that a man May tell Truth till He gives Credit to a Lie
 I. ii. 118 T10 *Mira.*] *prec. by* a *in outer margin and fol. by circled* a *in inner margin* =
ref. to I. 10:1; see next entry
 I10:1 I sho^d . . . Theobald *right*.] *prec. by* a *and fol. by circled* a = *ref. to T10, I. ii.
118; see prec. entry*
 I. ii. 120 T10 Good wombs . . . bad sons] *prec. by* b *in outer margin and fol. by
circled* a *in inner margin* = *ref. to I10:3; see next two entries*
 I10:3 good] *prec. by* b— = *ref. to T10, I. ii. 120; see prec. entry* bore] *circled*
a *above this word* = *ref. to T10, I. ii. 120; see prec. entry but one*

I. ii. 146–51

[T11] [*Pro.*]   they prepar'd
A rotten carcass of a boat, not rigg'd,
Nor tackle, sail, nor mast; the very rats
Instinctively had quit it: there they hoist us
To cry to th' sea, that roar'd to us; to sigh
To th' winds, whose pity, sighing back again,
Did us but loving wrong.

*A rotten carcass of a boat] [I11:1] (C) They meant Destruction at least if they did not Effect it. The last Lines of this speech are very finical and foolish but I think they must be imputed to Shakespeare.

I. ii. 152–8

[T11] *Pro.* O! a cherubim
Thou wast, that did preserve me: Thou didst smile,
Infused with a fortitude from heav'n,
(When I have deck'd the sea with drops full-salt;
Under my burthen groan'd;) which rais'd in me
An undergoing stomach, to bear up
Against what should ensue.

[PI8:3] (C) Oh a Cherubim thou wast &c] I think these Lines are disaranged and I would correct them thus: *Oh! a Cherubim thou wast that did preserve me.* [PI9] *Thou didst smile When I have drench'd the Sea with Drops full salt (under my Burthen groaning) which raised in me an undergoing stomach (infused by a Fortitude from Heaven) to bear up against what should ensue.*—The words *infused with a Fortitude from Heaven* were, I presume, interlined, and drawn down by the Transcriber in the wrong Place. I have written *drench'd* for *deck'd.* I wish I coᵈ find a better word[:] perhaps *track'd* as if his Tears

I. ii. 146 T11 prepar'd] *fol. by circled* a *in outer margin = ref. to* I11:1; *see next entry*

I11:1 They meant] *prec. by circled* a *and full stop = ref. to* T11, *I. ii. 146; see prec. entry*

I. ii. 154–8 T11 Infused with . . . should ensue] *prec. by* (*and fol. by*) *= ref. to* T11*MS:1*

PI8:3 Oh a . . . wast &c] *above these words is the notation* (C) *From page 22 =* I11, *where a cancelled* ED (*facing I. ii. 152–8 and continuing on* I12) *is prec. by* See page 8 *= PI8:3*   &c] *above this symbol is* &

PI9:4 word:] *MS. reads* word. *What follows* ('perhaps . . . Extravagant') *is apparently an afterthought*

had marked the water with a Chain of Bubbles. But that wo^d be Extravagant.

Earlier Draft—Excerpt

[I12] (C) The poet co^d not mean to call the smiles of an Infant ignorant of Danger Fortitude. I have altered likewise the word *deck'd* to *track'd*, tho' perhaps *drench'd* may do better but any Thing is better than *deck'd* and I have turned *groan'd* into *groaning* but I consider the whole passage as greatly depraved and requiring bold measures to restore it.

Marginal Note

[T11MS:1] (C) The Text wrong. I have not space to correct it[.]

I. ii. 164

[T11] [*Pro.*] Some food we had, and some fresh water, that
          A noble *Neapolitan, Gonzalo*,
          Out of his charity (being then appointed
          Master of this design) did give us, with
          Rich garments, linnens, stuffs, and necessaries,
          Which since have steeded much.

[I12:4] *Did give us rich garments, Linnens, stuffs and Necessaries which since have steeded much.*]* Words I believe inserted on the Revival of the Play and the use of which will presently appear.

Marginal Note

[T11MS:2] (C) Contrivance for giving future Splendour to the Habiliments of Prospero & Miranda[.]

I. ii. 169

[T12] *Pro.* Now, I arise:—
          Sit still, and hear the last of our sea-sorrow.

[I12:6] Now I arise. Sit still.] Here the spel is given to operate.

I12 *Earlier Draft*—Excerpt] *see prec. entry but two*
  I. ii. 164 T11 and necessaries,]*fol. by* X = *ref. to* T11MS:2 (*see next entry but one*) *and by circled* c *with* See next Page *written above and below the circled* c = *ref. to* I12:4 (*see next entry*)
  I12:4 *Did give us*] *prec. by circled* c *and* In the former page marked *C*— we find the following words = *ref. to* T11, *I. ii. 164; see prec. entry*
  T11MS:2 Contrivance] *prec. by* X = *ref. to* T11, *I. ii. 164; see prec. entry but one*
  I. ii. 169 T12 *Pro.* Now I arise—] *prec. by* X = *ref. to* T12MS:2 (*see next entry but one*) *and fol. by circled* D = *ref. to* I12:6 (*see next entry*)
  I12:6 Now I] *prec. by circled* D = *ref. to* T12, *I. ii. 169; see prec. entry*

Marginal Note
[T12MS:2] This is not said for nothing. It aids the operation of the spel.

I. ii. 180

[T12] [*Pro.*]   and, by my prescience
I find, my *Zenith* doth depend upon
A most auspicious star; whose Influence
If now I court not, but omit, my fortunes
Will ever after droop.

[I12:8] and by my Prescience] Not Foreknowledge but skill in Astronomy, and judging on principles of science.

I. ii. 185–6

[T12] [*Pro.*] Thou art inclin'd to sleep. 'Tis a good dulness,
And give it way; I know, thou canst not chuse.—
                                        [Miranda *sleeps.*

Marginal Note
 **Thou art inclin'd to sleep.*] [T12MS:1] [S]pel [ta]kes [pl]ace[.]

I. ii. 188

                                        [T12] [Miranda *sleeps.*
[*Pro.*] Come away, servant, come; I'm ready now:
Approach, my *Ariel.* Come.
                        Enter Ariel.

*Enter *Ariel.*] [I13:1] It may be proper to observe that *Miranda* is kept innocent of Magic and has no Intercourse with spirits, and she is Here laid asleep that *Ariel* may appear, after which *Ariel* becomes invisible to Her. There is indeed a Masque exhibited in the 5.th Act but it is no part of the Play nor originally performed with it and to

T12MS:2 This is] *prec. by* X = *ref. to T12, I. ii. 169; see prec. entry but one*
I. ii. 180 T12 and, by my prescience] *circled* a *in outer margin opposite these words* = *ref. to I12:8; see next entry*
I12:8 and by] *prec. by circled symbol, presumably* a = *ref. to T12, I. ii. 180; see prec. entry*
I. ii. 185–6 T12MS:1 Spel takes place] *written in outer margin opposite I. ii. 184–6*
I. ii. 188 T12 *Enter* Ariel] *prec. by* See next Page *and fol. by circled* a = *ref. to I13:1*

which therefore the cuñing of the Play does not apply. *Miranda* has heard of spirits and on the sight of Ferdinand believes that one for the first Time is presented to her view.

I. ii. 216–18

[T13] [*Pro.*] But was not this nigh shore?
    Ari. Close by, my master.
    Pro. But are they, *Ariel*, safe?
    Ari. Not a hair perish'd:
      On their sustaining garments not a blemish,
      But fresher than before.

[I13:4]—But was not this Nigh shore] intimating that such was the order given[.] To which is added that the garments are not blemished which appears to have been also an Expressed Part of the same orders.

Marginal Note

  **On their sustaining garments not a blemish*] [T13MS:1] (C) Such and i[n] these very words wer[e] the orders given, an[d] given that t[he] splendid dress of the Play might be wel[l] accounted for. They were mad[e] up for t[he] Marri[age] of Clarib[el] and af[ter] a shipwreck are fresher than before. This is applying Magic to use.

I. ii. 229

[T13] *Ari.* Safely in harbour
    Is the King's ship; in the deep nook, where once
    Thou call'dst me up at midnight, to fetch dew
    From the still-vext *Bermudas*, there she's hid.

[I13:7] to fetch Dew from the still-vexed *Bermudas*] It sho^d have been written *Bermoothes*—Theobald mistakes. The art of opening an Intercourse [I14] with Bermoothes must be admired by all who consider the Quality of one Island as transfered to another without a Name. By giving them *one Quality* and *attribute* He makes them *one*.

I. ii. 216–18 T13 nigh shore?] *fol. by circled* a = *ref. to I13:4; see next entry*
I13:4 — But was] *prec. by circled* a = *ref. to T13, I. ii. 216–18; see prec. entry*
   I. ii. 229 T13 *Bermudas*] *beneath this word are circled* a (= *ref. to I13:7; see next entry*) *and* X (= *ref. to T13MS:4; see next entry but one*)
I13:7 to fetch] *prec. by circled* a = *ref. to T13, I. ii. 229; see prec. entry*

Marginal Note

[T13MS:4] Very artfull[.] [T14MS:3] (C) Theobald never suspects that the scenery of this Play is taken from Bermudas tho' placed in the Mediteranean.

I. ii. 233

[T14] [*Ari.*] The mariners all under hatches stow'd,
Who, with a charm join'd to their suffered labour,
I've left asleep; and for the rest o' th' fleet
(Which I dispers'd) they all have met again,
And are upon the *Mediterranean* flote,
Bound sadly home for *Naples*;
Supposing, that they saw the King's ship wrackt,
And his great person perish.

Which I dispers'd] [I14:3] It appears that the magical storm which wholey involved the Kings ship did but barely touch the rest, so that no More Magic is used than was needed. It was too precious a Thing to be thrown away. One great Property of this magical storm was that it deluded the Eye. Not only *Miranda* was deceived but the whole Fleet had supposed that they *saw* the King's ship wrecked and his great person perish[.] But no such Thing. The King indeed and his suite even Stephano the *drunken* [I15] Butler and Trinculo who had in the first Play been the King's Fool and wore a patched Coat, tho' now of no occupation whatever[—]all these were frightened out of the ship but the Mariners were all fast asleep in the Hold and the ship safe and sound in Harbour.

I. ii. 239

[T14] [*Pro.*] What is the time o' th' day?
Ari. Past the mid season.
Pro. At least two glasses.

[I15:2] *What is the Time of the Day? Past the mid season. at least two glasses.*] The mid season is the meridian 12 o' th' clock[.] 2 glasses

T13MS:4 Very] X *below* V = *ref. to T13, I. ii. 229; see prec. entry but one*
I. ii. 233 T14 Which I dispers'd] *circled* a *in outer margin opposite these words* = *ref. to I14:3; see next entry*
I14:3 It appears] *prec. by circled* a = *ref. to T14, I. ii. 233; see prec. entry*
I. ii. 239 T14 What is] *prec. by circled* a = *ref. to I15:2; see next entry*
I15:2 *What is the Time*] *prec. by from page 14 and fol. by circled* a = *ref. to T14, I. ii. 239; see prec. entry*

beyond brings the Time to two o' th' clock but the words at *least* intimates that it is something past two that is it is as much Time past as has been already Expended since the opening of the play which is supposed to have opened precisely at two. This is crying the Time with great Care, indeed!

Marginal Note
   [T14MS:1] [Tw]o o' th' clock. [P]lay [E]nds at [*f*]*ive.*

I. ii. 242

[T14]   *Ari.* Is there more toil? . . .
         Pro. How now? moody?

**Is there more toil?*] [I15:6] The Discontents of Ariel and the Reproaches & severities of Prospero require no comment[:] they [exhibit] the perfection of dramatic Art.

I. ii. 250

[T15]   *Pro.* Dost thou forget
         From what a torment I did free thee?

[I154:1] dost thou forget] D. Johnson has upon this Passage a Note of some Length which on account of his Eminence it is proper I should transcribe but as it will draw after it certain observations of my own which may too much incumber the Poets Page It seems best to place the whole in the Appendix. See *A*.

[Appendix A]

   ['That the Character and Conduct of Prospero may be understood, something must be known of the system of enchantment, which supplied all the marvellous found in the romances of the middle ages. This system seems to be founded on the opinion that the fallen spirits, having different degrees of guilt, had different habitations allotted them at their expulsion, some being confined in hell, *some* (as *Hooker*, who delivers the opinion of our poet's age, expresses it) *dispersed in*

I. ii. 242 I15:6 they exhibit] *ED*: (C) it (R) exhibit(UM)s

I. ii. 250 I154:1-2 dost thou . . . Johnson has] *one line in MS. above which is written* Tempest page 25 = *Johns. 1785, pp. 25–6; see note*

I154:2-3 in the Appendix. See *A*] *one line in MS.; beneath it a line is drawn across the page; beneath this line is written* Transcribe *with a line beneath*

I154:3 Appendix A] *reproduced here rather than separately as proposed in* I154:2 'That the . . . enough.'—Johnson] *supplied by the editor from Johns. 1785, note to I. ii. 250; see prec. entry but one and* I154:2

*Air, some on earth, some in water, others in caves, dens, or minerals
under the earth.* Of these, some were more malignant and mischievous
than others. The earthy spirits seem to have been thought the most
depraved, and the aerial the least vitiated. Thus Prospero observes
of Ariel,

> ——*Thou wast a spirit too delicate*
> *To act her* earthy *and abhorr'd commands.*

Over these spirits a power might be obtained by certain rites performed or charms learned. This power was called *The Black Art*, or
Knowledge of Enchantment. The enchanter being (as king James
observes in his Demonology) one *who commands the devil, whereas the
witch serves him.* Those who thought best of this art, the existence
of which was, I am afraid, believed very seriously, held, that certain
sounds and characters had a physical power over spirits, and compelled their agency; others who condemned the practice, which in
reality surely was never practised, were of opinion, with more reason,
that the power of charms arose *only* from compact, and was no more
than the spirits voluntarily allowed them for the seduction of man.
The art was held by all, though not equally criminal, yet unlawful, and
therefore Casaubon, speaking of one who had commerce with spirits,
blames him, though he imagines him *one of the best kind who dealt
with them by way of command.* Thus Prospero repents of his art in
the last scene. The spirits were always considered as in some measure
enslaved to the enchanter, at least for a time, and as serving with
unwillingness; therefore Ariel so often begs for liberty; and Caliban
observes, that the spirits serve Prospero with no good will, but *hate
him rootedly.*—Of these trifles enough.'—Johnson.]

D. Johnson must have been wonderfully satisfied with his own
Energies when thus stopping Himself in full Carrier He cryed out
of these Trifles Enough from which we are to suppose then that He
could have done much greater Things if He had liked but as it seems
he was not in the Humour. I wish it had been otherwise as He has
not given me that Satisfaction found for Himself for I consider that
if these fallen Spirits are supposed realy to enter into Compacts with
Men [1155] and to lend them for a Time their unknown Powers the
matter is by no means a Trifle for both moral and phisical Evidence
seem to be thereby over Thrown and it will become necessary to
counteract these Evils by every Law or statute we can devize but

I154:4 when thus . . . He cryed] *ED*: (C) that He sho^d thus stop Himself (R) in full
Carrier (UM) and (C) cry

on the other Hand if the Fall of these spirits has produced no other
Effect but that of exciting Imaginations of Magic attended with the
practice perhaps of some Fraud then the Doctor has not made his
Cause and Effect sufficiently commensurate to each other for there
never was a people discovered in Continent or Island without some
Notions of an invisible world and of spirits mixing, sought or un-
sought, in human affairs and of Magic and Witcheries founded thereon but of such nations how few have heard of the Angels Fall or
could derive their Imaginations thence. To consider therefore this
cause partial in its operation as capable of producing an universal
Effect is to [1156] Extend the lining very preposterously far beyond
the Coat[.]

[1158:3] But I must declare that in my Thought there appears to
be no Difficulty in the Case as it appears to me that the Cause of
magic and Inchantment is clearly to be found in the general Nature
of the human mind producing of course a general Effect[.] We exist
in midst of superiour Power[s] ignorant of our Orrigin and [1159]
End composed of Light and Darkness and of Hopes and Fears and
Passions of Every Kind conscious of Responsibility and apparently
designed half to rise and half to fall and impelled and restrained from
within[.] It was Natural to conceive that the good within came from
without and was conducted of some invisible power and thereupon
to practice any phantastical ceremonies the farthest possibly from
common sense for who of any Force wo^d be content with half
measures in so nice a Case. [B]ut many of those spirits being derived
as we may suppose of good Affections are of a gentle sort and are
best seen [in] moonlight or some airy Dream but guilt and murder
and Rapine are crimes surrounded by a Ten fold gloom and no
wonder if in the Tumult of passion air drawn daggers break thro' the
curtain of the Dark and that witches scream forth the [1160] accents
of Fate and the Dead rise with fifty mortal murders on their crowns
and push us from our stools[.] [T]he same Circumstances which

I155:2 consider therefore . . . of producing] *ED*: (C) Make (UM) a Cause only
partially (C) operating to produce
I156:1 the Coat] *fol. in MS. by Appendix A—ED 1*
I156:1-I158:3 Coat. But] *continuity indicated by cancellation of intervening materials
(ED 1)*
I159:2 common sense] *fol. by* 2 *ED*: (UM) the (C) better / (R) the (C) more likely
to avail   Force] 2 *ED*: (C) strength of mind / (C) good temper
I159:3 But] *MS. reads* but
I160:1 accents] *prec. by* (UM) the
I160:2 The] *MS. reads* the

Excite these visions in human Life Sho^d attend them in the Play and it behoves the writer to take Heed that his Atmosphere is sufficiently darkened with Horrour before he ventures to call forth his Inchanters and produce either a Baby phantom or a full grown Ghost[.] [I161:2] But let us suppose that the Doctor had made his Causes & Effects corespond and that He had considered Magic under all its variations and as induced by Climate and [I162] other Circumstances to be nothing else but the wrong side of religious Truth yet still He wo^d have had no Right to cry out Enough for tho' perhaps it might be Enough as applyed to Macbeth Hamlet or the Midsummer Dream yet to the Magic of this Play it would not apply at all for the spirits here are not born of human Passions and have no Reference either to moral good or Ill[.] They are an independent Community[;] they have no Relations but to each other and they neither Love or Hate Mankind[.] They are indeed spel bound for a certain Time and compelled under the severest penalties to obey the imperative Voice of an usurping Power but they hate Him rootedly nor would his urchins fright or pinch even Caliban unless He bid them nor has Ariel Himself the least sympathy with man tho' in one Place He speculates on the [I163] Distraction and grief of the King and his Party and says that his affections were he human might possibly become tender at the sight[.] Of the Rabble of spirits possessing this Island as numerous as rabbits in a warren we know scarcely any Thing but that they appear to be a sort of ground spirits and of very limitted Power but of their Pursuits or Delights in their state of Freedom before the Time of Sycorax and of their Families & Kind we know Nothing[.] We find them assume the Form of Hounds and of Hedge Hogs and Moe and Chatter and pinch and the like but yet as Instruments only and without any Disposition of their own nor does it clearly appear whether they had or had not any share in raising of the magical storm[.] [B]ut in the Judgment I make of this Play as being [I164] written in two different periods of Time and with different views I conceive that in the Second Play their powers have been considerably increased for at the Banquet they make good Imitations of human Life and are able in the Masque to assume the Forms of Juno and Ceres and mock the Dignities of the Olympian Hall[.] There is how-

I160:2 and it behoves] *ED*: (UM) and (C) let   Ghost] *fol. by Appendix 2—ED 2*
I160:2–I161:2 Ghost. But] *continuity indicated by cancellation of intervening materials (ED 2)*
I162:3 imperative] *ED*: (C) harsh
I163:4 But] *MS. reads* but

ever a speech in the Beginning of Act the 5th *Ye Elves of Hills &c*
which tho' very classical and Sublime does not properly belong to
Either play and of which no Appropriate Application can be Made[.]
As for Ariel He is a spirit without any Dimensions and passes from
place to place without touching the intermediate Parts but as for Him
his Family connection & Pursuits I shall speak of them in some
other Place and shall also elsewhere Endeavour to Explain the Principle upon which the [I165] Magic of this play is made to stand[;]
and as for D. Johnson I must observe that He obstinately sticks to
his Enough not as deserting his Chair but as setting Himself up as
a sort of Negative Power whose silence is positive & Emphatic and
who seated in vacuity seems to set up a Throne of his own[.]

Earlier Drafts

Appendix A—ED 1

[I156: 1b] (UM) and I sho^d think it much (C) Easier to find out the
efficient Causes in the general Nature of the human mind composed
as it is of Light and Darkness and trembling Hope and conscious
Fear nor can it be thought surprizing if a Creature feeling Himself
accountable sho^d in the gloom of Guilt and Distractions of Terrour
behold Airdrawn Daggers bursting thro' the Dark and find themselves in the Tumults of passion pushed by Blood boultered Phan-
toms from their stools or that they sho^d hear the voice of Fate
articulated in the wind and hear distinctly the spirits of the storm.
The same Circumstances which Excite these visions in human Life
sho^d attend them in a Play and let the writer take Heed that He
darkens his atmosphere sufficiently with Horrour before He ventures
to [I157] (UM) call forth his Inchanter or produce either an armed
Baby or a full grown ghost[.] (C) [B]ut let us suppose that the Doctor
had taken this Course and had ventured to predict of any new found
people from Information of their state of civilization from their
leading Institutions and their Climate what the Quality of their
magic and spirits were likely to be and had considered that the
Falsehoods of superstition were no other than the wrong side of
Truth and were limitted within all their apparent Irregularities [by
the] Principles from which they were drawn yet all this wo^d not
much assist the Doctor in his Judgment of this Play because thus

I164:2 *Hills &c*] *fol. by* (UM)]
I157:2 But] *MS. reads* but   Irregularities by the]*ED*: (C) wildness by the

in a general view human Passions and human Imaginations are relative Things and Act and react and are to be considered as counterparts of Each other [I158] yet in the present Play we have a very different system[:] Community of Spirits between whom and the human Race there is no other Connection or Simpathy than as these spirits happen to be caught in a spel and brought into subjection by an Inchanter's superiour Power[.] They hate Him rootedly take no Interest in his passions or his views neither love or hate and whilst they submitt to his Power and obey his Behests have no wish but to possess their own seperate & independent state[.]

Appendix A—ED 2

[I160:2b] (C) lest mockery and sun shine may otherwise efface them off the Stage. But let us suppose that D. Johnson had reasoned thus and had even undertaken to say that among any new found People in such and such a Climate [I161] under the Line or near the Pole possessing such and such Institutions and civilized or Savage in such a Degree that among such a People their spirits and their magic wo^d be of such a Sort and that He had further undertaken to prove that Falshood in this particular was nothing but the wrong side of Truth and that tho' the Figures were indefinite and distorted yet that they were not arbitrary but being turned back by the Hand of Science on their Causes the more correct Delineations of true Religion and Morality might clearly appear[.]

I. ii. 269

[T15]   *Pro.* This blue-ey'd hag was hither brought with child.

*blue-eyed] [T15MS:1] blear-ey'd[.] [I16:1] (C) I have corrected the Text *blear-ey'd* for *blue-eyed* but I do not peremptorily insist upon it[.]

I. ii. 301-2

[T16]   *Pro.* Go make thy self like to a nymph o' th' sea.
        Be subject to no sight but mine: invisible
        To every eye-ball else.

I. ii. 269 T15 blue-ey'd] *lined through; see next entry*
T15MS:1 blear-ey'd] *written in above* blue-ey'd *see prec. entry; circled* b *in outer margin on level with emendation* = *ref. to* I16:1; *see next entry*
I16:1 I have] *prec. by* in Page in 15 = *T15; see two prec. entries*
I. ii. 301-2 T16 Pro.] *prec. by circled* a = *ref. to* I16:2   invisible *fol. by* X = *probable ref. to* T16MS:1

[I16:2] *Go make thyself like to a nymph of the Sea*[.] *Be subject to no sight but mine*] This seems very Extraordinary. In the first Place what is a sea nymph? and what is it to be like one? And in the next why sho.^d Ariel, if invisible to every Eye but prospero's take any new Form? How then came the Poet to fall into such an Absurdity? [O]nly on the Principle that of two Evils it was prudent to take the least. There were persons from whom Ariel co.^d not be concealed, the *audience*, and what was Ariel? A mere Electric Spark without any definite Form, and it was necessary to give Him some apparency, and a Sea-Nymph might be a Thing of substance composed into some Shape by the Fancy of the Players. But how young and inexperienced an Author must He have been who prepared for the stage a Character which could not be seen there [I17] in any definite shape, a Character to be presented to the mind's Eye only and not to the organs of sense. But in what shape has Ariel passed the former part of this scene? Why in a very awkard one with Legs and arms and so forth without occasion or use. [O]n Board the ship He was a Flame in two Places at once, an Unity and Diversity too.

Marginal Note
[T16MS] (C) Ariel had no definite Form. A Sea-Nymph seemed something definite, and might, in some sort, be represented [T17MS] to the spectators, tho' invisible to the Dramatis Personae. Miranda is never allowed to see a spirit. She is — ? — — ? —

I. ii. 304-7

[T16] [*Exit* Ariel.
[*Pro.*] Awake, dear heart, awake! thou hast slept well;
    Awake.——
Mira. The strangeness of your story put
    Heaviness in me.

**The strangeness of your story put Heaviness in me.*] [I17:5] When Ariel in his old no Figure is withdrawn, *Miranda* awakes. There is great Delicacy of Conduct in preserving her from the sight or hearing of spirits. She says with great simplicity that the strangeness of Prospero's story put Heaviness in her, and D. Johnson is of her

---

I16:2 Go] *has a* before *and circled a* above = *ref. to* T16, *I. ii. 301-2*
I16:7 Only] *MS. reads* only
I17:4 On] *MS. reads* on   too] *ED:* (C) combined, Exceeding even the Powers of Ariel.
    I. ii. 304-7 I17:5 When Ariel] *prec. by page* 16 = *ref. to* T16, *I. ii. 304*

opinion. But the poor girl only reasoned in the ordinary way that the Effect proceeded from the near and apparent Cause, not knowing that another Cause, that of Magic had intervened.

Marginal Note

[T16MS:1] [I B]elieve [she c]annot [te]ll what [a]iled Her and like — ? — — ? — [has] assigned [a]n Effect [for] a [C]ause.

I. ii. 316

[T17]   *Pro.* Come forth, I say; there's other business for thee.
       Come, thou Tortoise! when?——

[I17:9] *Come forth thou Tortoise*] Caliban was the Inhabitant of a Rock like a tortoise in its Shel, which occasions Prospero to call Him Tortoise to which some Reference to his rude form is added.

I. ii. 318

[T17]   [*Pro.*]   my quaint *Ariel*,
          Hark in thine ear.
       Ari. My lord, it shall be done   [*Exit.*
       Pro. Thou poisonous slave, got by the devil himself
          Upon thy wicked dam; come forth.

Enter Caliban.

[I18:1] *Hark in thine Ear*] We find in the Event that the command now whispered, was to draw Ferdinand into the scene with suggestions that his Father was drowned. (C) There is so much to be said of Caliban that I must reserve it for some other Place.

I. ii. 351

[T18]   *Pro.* Abhorred slave;
          Which any print of goodness will not take, . . .

T16MS: 1 I Believe . . . Cause.] *written in outer margin opposite I. ii. 304–7*
   I. ii. 316 T17 for thee.]*fol. by circled* a = *ref. to* I17:9; *see next two entries*   thou
Tortoise] *these two words circled* = *ref. to* I17:9; *see prec. and next entries*
   I17:9 *Come forth*] *prec. by circled* a = *ref. to* T17, *I. ii. 316; see two prec. entries*
   I. ii. 318 T17 *quaint Ariel,*] *fol. by circled* a = *ref. to* I18:1; *see next entry but*
one   *Enter* Caliban.] *fol. by circled* a = *probable ref. to* I18:3
   I18:1 *Hark in*] *prec. by page* 17. *and circled* a = *ref. to* T17, *I. ii. 318; see prec. entry*
but one
   I. ii. 351 T18 *Pro.*] *prec. by* a = *ref. to* I18:4; *see next entry*

*Abhorred slave] [I18:4] Theobald is right in giving this speech to Prospero. It wo.^d be very unbecoming in Miranda.

I. ii. 373

[T18] [*Cal.*]   his art is of such pow'r,
           [T19] It would controul my dam's god *Setebos*,
           And make a vassal of him.

**my dam's god* Setebos] [I19] (C) *Setebos* was a Patagonian Idol a Proof among a hundred others that the Tale had a transatlantic Source.

I. ii. 376
[T19] *ARIEL*'S SONG.

Come unto these yellow sands,
And then take hands: . . .

**Come unto these yellow sands*] [I19:2] This song is a singular Instance of Shakespeare's wonderfull Art. It is a recollected Song sung by the spirits of Ariel's Condition in their state of Freedom and lets us into the secrets & peculiarities of this Class of beings. Their civilities and affections towards each other are marked and their sports in Mocking the House Dogs and the Crowings of the Cocks in the Hours of night when the Waves and the Winds are still, are fancied with so wild a Charm as Nothing can Exceed.

Marginal Note
   (C) [T19MS:1] an old song among the spirits, very artfull[.]

I. ii. 396
[T19] *ARIEL*'S SONG.

Full fathom five thy father lies,
Of his bones are coral made: . . .

I18:4 Theobald] *prec. by* a = *ref. to T18, I. ii. 351; see prec. entry*
I. ii. 373 I19:1 *Setebos*] *prec. by* a = *ref. to T19, I. ii. 373*   a Patagonian] *ED:*
(C) an American
   I. ii. 376 T19 *sands,*] *fol. by circled* a = *ref. to I19:2; see next entry*
I19:2 This song] *prec. by circled* a = *ref. to T19, I. ii. 376; see prec. entry*
T19MS:1 an old] *prec. by blotted symbol* = *ref. to T19, I. ii. 376*
   I. ii. 396 T19 *father lies,*] *fol. by circled* a = *ref. to I19:5; see next entry*

*Full fathom five] [I19:5] The second Song is made by *Ariel* to suit the occasion, suggesting the Death of the King, yet preserving the Character of this Race of Beings. *Gildon* it seems calls these Songs Senseless Trifling[.] D. Warburton vindicates the latter song very ably, but he seems to desert the first tho' sparkling in my opinion with Fancy and rich with fictitious Truth to this gent[.] Mr Gildon who I know only as a member of the *Dunciad*.

See Appendix A [i.e. comment on I. ii. 250, above]

Marginal Note
(C) [T19MS:2] an occasional Song[.]

I. ii. 408

[T20]   *Pro.* The fringed curtains of thine eyes advance,
          And say, what thou seest yond.

[I20:1] *The fringed Curtains of thine Eyes advance]** This line has been ridiculed in the Art of Sinking in Poetry by Swift and Pope &c, but that work ought to have confined itself to the Absurdities of bad Poets and not have extended to the accidental Failings of real genius. But I hesitate if it ought as it stands Here to be blamed. The solemnity of Prospero's Language throughout and the Dignity He assumes as the Master of spirits and the Father of the subdued Miranda, may well excuse, in Him, the attempt of raising ordinary Actions into importance. Familiar phrases wo.d sink Prospero in our opinions. Why then sho.d we be surprized if He sometimes touches the other Extream.

I. ii. 427

[T20]   [*Fer.*]   my prime request
          (Which I do last pronounce) is, O you wonder!
          If you be made or no?

[I20:7] If you be made or no.] Ferdinand means to ask Her if she was made in the manner of mortal Beings[.] To which she answers with much Simplicity and Humility that she is no wonder but doubt-

I19:5 The second] *prec. by circled* a = *ref. to T19, I. ii. 396; see prec. entry*
I19:7 gent.] *MS. has flourish after* t *to indicate abbreviation*
T19MS:2 an occasional] *prec. by* ≠ = *ref. to T19, I. ii. 396*
I. ii. 408 T20 Pro.] *prec. by circled* a = *ref. to I20:1; see next entry*
I20:1 The fringed] *prec. by* a = *ref. to T20, I. ii. 408; see prec. entry*
I. ii. 427 T20 If you] *prec. by circled* a = *ref. to I20:7; see next entry*
I20:7 If you] *prec. by circled* a = *ref. to T20, I. ii. 427; see prec. entry*   made]
above this word is an X = *ref. to T21, I. ii. 447, and to T21MS:1*

less a maid, as never having had any Corespondence with a Man.
[I21] So little Notion had she of the high Compliment implied in
Ferdinand's Question, but this answer was much to Ferdinand['s]
Purpose and He afterwards avails Himself of it. Oh, says He in the
next page, [i.e. T21, I. ii. 447] *if a virgin,* &c

Marginal Note
[T20MS:1] (C) This mistake between *made* and *maid* is afterwards brought to account.

I. ii. 437–8

[T20]　[*Fer.*]　　　　　　　　　　my self am *Naples,*
　　　　　Who, with mine eyes (ne'er since at ebb) beheld
　　　　　The King my father wrackt.
[T21]　*Mira.* Alack, for mercy!
　　　　　Fer. Yes, faith, and all his lords: the Duke of *Milan,*
　　　　　And his brave son, being twain.

[I21:5] *Yes faith and all his Lords The Duke of Milan and his brave
son being Twain*] This is *very very* curious and opens the History of
this Play. Doubtless this brave son of the Duke of Milan was a
Character and no slight one of a former Tempest now lost, but in
order to make way for Machinery and show, He was Expunged, but
this vestige remains.—A *slight forgetfullness* says Mr. Theobald
that is the Poet forgot according to Him an Event which never
Existed at all, and a Person who never [I22] never had a Being but
the poet and Prospero remember very well these non Entities and
they put Prospero's braver Daughter in competition with this brave
youth, who was born it seems of Forgetfullness and cannot now be
found. Prospero's absence from Milan does not Exceed 12 years and
He co^d therefore well tell whether his Brother Anthonio had or had
not at that Time a son.

Marginal Note
[T21MS:2] (C) The Duke of Milan's son was doubtless one of
the Characters in the orriginal Play.

I21:1 Ferdinand's] *MS. reads* Ferdinands'
I. ii. 437–8 T21 being twain.] *fol. by circled* a = *ref. to* I21:5; *see next entry*
I21:5 *Yes faith*] *prec. by circled* a = *ref. to* T21, *I. ii. 437–8; see prec. entry*

I. ii. 447

[T21]   *Fer.* O, if a Virgin,
         And your Affection not gone forth, I'll make you
         The Queen of *Naples.*

Marginal Note
  **O*, if a Virgin*] [T21:MS:1] (C) this is in Referenc[e] to her
hav[ing] called Herse[lf] a *mai[d.]*

I. ii. 452

[T21]   [*Pro.*]   Sir, one word more; I charge thee,
         That thou attend me:—thou dost here usurp . . .

[I21:3] *One word more, I charge thee that thou attend me*] This is the
fo[u]rth Time that Prospero has called on Ferdinand to attend, but
Ferdinand is so rapt in admiration of Miranda that He hears Him
not.

I. ii. 469–71

[T22]   [*Pro.*]   put thy sword up, traitor,
         Who mak'st a shew, but dar'st not strike; thy conscience
         Is so possesst with guilt.

Marginal Note
  **put thy sword up*] [T22MS] (C) Miranda is kept within the Pale
of Nature, wholly innocent of Magic [a]nd neither knowing or noted
by spirits.

I. ii. 495

[T23]   [*Pro.*] Hark, what thou else shalt do me.   [*To* Ariel.

[I23:1] Hark what Thou else shall do] Here an Order is whispered
which we find to be that He sho^d put the King, Gonzalo &c under
a sleepy spel that Sebastian & Anthonio being left awake they may

I. ii. 447 T21 a Virgin,] *fol. by* X = *ref. to T21MS:1; see next entry*
T21MS:1 this is] *prec. by* X = *ref. to T21, I. ii. 447; see prec. entry*
I. ii. 452 T21 here usurp] *fol. by circled* a = *ref. to I21:3; see next entry*
I21:3 *One*] *above this word is a circled* a = *ref. to T21, I. ii. 452*
I. ii. 469–71 T22MS Miranda is] *for ref. of this comment to I. ii. 469–71 see note*
I. ii. 495 T23 do me] *fol. by circled* a = *ref. to I23:1; see next entry*
I23:1 Hark] *above this word a circled* a = *ref. to T23, I. ii. 495; see prec. entry*

freely confer together and Ariel having listened to their Discourse, He was to report it to Prospero. [B]ut Ariel finding them resolved to kill, and on the Point of Killing the King, &c He instantly dissolves the spel by a crash of music and conveys the whole Tale to Prospero.

II. i. 9–107

[T23]   *Alon.* Pr'ythee, peace.

. . . .

[T26]   *Gon.* Not since widow *Dido*'s time.

. . . . .

Seb. What if he had said, widower *Æneas* too?

. . . .

Alon. You cram these words into mine ears against
The stomach of my sense.

*Pr'ythee, peace . . . my sense] [I24:1] (C) This Dialogue, bad as it is, is I think, reformed, or at least new written. I think, in the first Play, that the Duke of Milan's *brave son* and *Trinculo*, the patched Fool were Speakers in the scene, and that it contained Quibles & Fooleries of all sorts. There is no Excusing of Shakespeare's more Early Dialogues. They are (when no special Interest or Passion intervenes) the mere abortive Sallies of desperate wit, Quibles & puns & obscenity and Every Thing but Common Sense. But the Dialogues of Anthonio and Sebastian in this Play have much more Substance & Firmness than those under the like Conditions in *Romeo and Juliet* and the *Midsummer's Nights Dream*, which were doubtless the next Productions of the Poets dramatic Muse. The great Errour of this Dialogue, as it now stands, is that the Levity of youth in the son of Anthonio and the Professional Nonsense of Trinculo are given in a certain Degree to Sebastian and Anthonio, the Brothers of Naples and [I25] Prospero, whose ages & Condition it so ill becomes, ⟨but the⟩ young brave ⟨son of Milan⟩ and Trinculo, ⟨the Fool,⟩ being withdrawn these more ancient and [one] sho^d expect more reverend gentlemen are put under the necessity of sustaining the former Tone.

I23:3 But] *MS. reads* but
II. i. 9–106 T26 *Seb.* What] *prec. by circled* a = *ref. to* Com. *II. i. 9–107,* I25:2–3
I24:1 This Dialogue . . .] *for ref. to* II. i. 9–107 *see note*
I24:2 Quibles & . . . all sorts] *ED:* (C) more (R) Quibles & Fooleries (C) than it does now
I25:1 but the . . . Fool] *see note*

Gon. furnishes them with Occasions for sport, and among other Temptations calls the Queen of Carthage the *Widow* Dido. This they seize as a precious Morsel for Mockery & Ridicule, upon which Doctor Johnson gravely observes, that the Name of a *widow* brings to their Minds their own shipwreck which they consider as having made many widows in Naples: an observation which proves Him to be an Inhabitant of the Moon and wholly un[con]scious of Every Thing which has passed in this sublunary world.

(C) At length the invisible Ariel Enters and lays the whole party, except Sebastian and Anthonio, asleep, ⟨and like a good Spy listens to, that He may [I26] report, their Discourse, which goes to nothing less than an Immediate assassination of the sleepers, which He prevents by dissolving the spel. But, tho' I confidently affirm⟩ this, I speak however in contradiction to the Text, for we find by the Text, as it now stands, that Ariel was not present at the Conference, but had returned to Prospero, and was sent back again by Prospero (who discovered the Purpose of these assassins by his prescience) to dissolve the spel.

Marginal Note
[T24MS] (C) [W]hat is given to Anthonio in this Dialogue was in part at least given to his son in the former Play. Anthonio is too old to make one in so skipping a Dialogue[.]

II. i. 62

[T25]   *Gon.* . . . our garments being (as they were) drench'd in the sea, hold notwithstanding their freshness and glosses.

Marginal Note
*hold notwithstanding their freshness and glosses] [T25MS:1] (C) artful[l.]

II. i. 68

[T25]   *Gon.* Methinks, our garments are now as fresh as when we put them on first in *Africk*, at the marriage of the King's fair Daughter *Claribel* to the King of *Tunis*.

I25:4–I26:2 and like . . . confidently affirm] *see note*
II. i. 62 T25MS:1 artfull] *written in outer margin beside II. i. 62*
II. i. 68 T25 *Tunis.*] *fol. by circled* a = *ref. to non-extant comment, probably on first part of Gonzalo's speech*

Methinks, our garments are now as fresh] [Intended comment was presumably to extend T25MS:1 and 2; cf. *Com.* I. ii. 29 and I. ii. 216–18.]

Marginal Note
 [T25MS:2] (C) artfu[ll.]

II. i. 184

[T29] *Enter* Ariel, *playing solemn Musick.*
*Enter *Ariel*] [See *Com.* II. i. 297–9, I33:6.]

II. i. 220–1

[T30]   *Ant.* I am more serious than my custom. You
            Must be so too, if heed me; which to do,
            Trebles thee o'er.

Marginal Note
 **if heed me*] [T30MS:1] [Read:] *and* [heed me.]

II. i. 235–6

[T31]   [*Ant.*] Although this lord of weak remembrance, this,
            (Who shall be of as little memory,
            When he is earth'd;) hath here almost persuaded
            (For he's a spirit of persuasion, only
            Professes to persuade) the King, his son's alive;
            'Tis as impossible that he's undrowned,
            As he, that sleeps here, swims.

[I31:1] hath here almost persuaded] I am myself *fully persuaded* that the words *for He's a spirit of Persuasion, only professes to persuade,* are idle Words crept out of the Margin into the Text by some Chance or other.

II. i. 184 T29 *Enter . . . Musick*] *fol. by circled* a = *probable ref. to* Com. *II. i. 297–9, I33:6*
 II. i. 220–1 T30 *if heed*] *if lined through and underlined* = *ref. to T30MS:1; see next entry but one*   Trebles thee o'er] *Theobald's note to this passage, T30n, is lined through; see note*
 T30MS:1 *and*] *underlined in outer margin opposite II. i. 220* = *ref. to* if; *see prec. entry but one*
 II. i. 235:6 T31 hath . . . persuaded] *circled* a *in outer margin opposite these words* = *ref. to I31:1; see next entry*
 I31:1 hath . . . persuaded] *circled* a *above this lemma* = *ref. to T31, II. i. 235–6; see prec. entry*

II. i. 243

[T31]   [*Ant.*]   so high an hope, that even
              Ambition cannot pierce a wink beyond,
              But doubt discovery there.

[I31:3] But doubt discovery there] The word *Doubt* is often used
by the writers of Shakespeare's Time for *do out*, of which it is a
compound. The allusion Here, as I think, is to the Horrizon which
at its Extream Edges closes up our view and *does out* or extinguishes
all further Discovery[.] If such be the meaning the word *Doubt*
sho⁴ be *Doubts* or *does-out.*

II. i. 246–50

[T31]   *Ant.* She that is Queen of *Tunis*; she that dwells
              Ten leagues beyond man's life; she that from *Naples*
              Can have no Note, unless the sun were post,
              (The man i' th' moon's too slow) 'till new-born chins
              Be rough and razorable.

[I31:7] (C) She that is Queen of Tunis] He means and very judiciously to Exaggerate but He Exaggerates too much[.] It might suit
Mexico or Peru[.]

II. i. 250

[T31]   [*Ant.*]   she, from whom
              We were sea-swallowed.

[I31:10] She for whom] if as Theobald says all the Copies read *from
whom* It is proper, as I think, to submit, but if the Question lay now
open, I sho⁴ vote for, *for whom*[.]

II. i. 243 T31 But doubt discovery there] *circled a in outer margin opposite these
words = ref. to I31:3; see next entry*
I31:3 But . . . there] *circled a after this lemma = ref. to T31, II. i. 243; see prec.
entry*
II. i. 246–50 T31 Ten leagues . . . new-born chins] *circled a in outer margin opposite
these lines = ref. to I31:7–9*

II. i. 296

[T33] *Ant.* Draw together:
And when I rear my hand, do you the like
To fall it on *Gonzalo.*
    Seb. O, but one word.———

[I33:1] oh but one Word] This word is I believe an Interpolation in order to give Time for Ariel's interpolated speech.

II. i. 297–9

[T33] *Enter* Ariel, *with Musick and Song.*
  Ari. My master through his art foresees the danger,
That you, his friend, are in; and sends me forth
(For else his project dies) to keep them living.
                  [*Sings in* Gonzalo's *Ear.*
    While you here do snoaring lye
    Open-ey'd conspiracy
    His time doth take. . . .

[I33:5] (C) My master &c] It sho^d appear from this speech that after Ariel had imposed the Sleepy Spel in page 29 [i.e. T29, II. i. 184] He had returned to Prospero and had not witnessed the Conference between Sebastian and Anthonio, but that Prospero having discovered the conspiracy by his Prescience had now sent Ariel back to dissolve the spel. [I26:3] Nothing can be more false & nonsensical than this, and can be accounted for in no way perhaps so well as by supposing that Ariel was represented by some Managers favourite Child, who standing in the scene as a motionless Spy in the ridiculous Habit of a Sea Nymph was laughed at and hissed by some of the groundlings. Whereupon the Manager Himself in high Disdain Withdrew his Boy or his Girl from the scene and composed the Exquisite Lines [I27] now spoken by Ariel, *My master by his Art* &c to account for his absence. There are many Interpolations in Shakespeare

---

II. i. 296 T33 O . . . word.———] *circled a opposite this line in outer margin = ref. to I33:1; see next entry*
    I33:1 oh . . . Word] *circled a above this lemma = ref. to T33, II. i. 296*
    II. i. 297–9 T33 My master . . . them living] *circled a in outer margin opposite these lines = ref. to I33:5*
    I33:6 the spel] *fol. by* Nothing can be more false or nonsensical See Note opposite to Page 26 = *overlap and continuity with I26:3; see next entry*
    I26:3 Nothing can] *prec. by* from page 33 = *continuity from I33:6; see prec. entry*

which betray themselves but there never was one more manifest or more impudent and at the same Time more absurd than this. [I27:4] Prospero had no Prescience in the Sense in which that word is Here used that is He had no Consciousness of passing Events further than as He might be informed of them by his spies and if He had it could not properly be called Art but a supernatural Quality or Talent[.] He suspected that Sebastian & Anthonio were likely Enough to form some dangerous Conspiracy and He sends Ariel to watch their Discourse and report[.] He does the like after this with respect to Caliban and his associates and He is Enabled to save the Kings Life in one Case and his own in the other, but Here Ariel who acts as his organ of Information is Withdrawn just in the moment He was wanted [I28] but He returns with all sorts of Lies and Nonsense in his Mouth instead of instantly breaking the Spel for the swords are drawn for immediate Execution[.] He speaks to a Man who is fast asleep and who cannot nor is He supposed to hear[:] My master through his art foresees the Danger that you his Friend are in and sends me forth or Else his Project dies to keep them living[.] Now if Gonzal[o] co^d have heard might He not have snoringly Exclaimed, Who the Devil is your master and who are you? A sound or a Being or what? And what particular Friendship is there towards *me* in that you are sent to keep *them* living, or Else you say his Project dies, and thus at last it is for the sake of keeping his Project living that you are sent at all. And what a Blab you must be to let us know that there was any Project in the Case. If you have any Thing to do, do it and dont stand prating Here to the Loss of the Project, perhaps, [I29] whatever that is. As for us we are fast asleep and know nothing of you or your Master or his projects[;] you may be the Devil Himself for any Thing we know to the Contrary. However at length Ariel having uttered so much Nonsense and Lying gives us a Crash of music and the spel is undone and the Sleepers are kept as He calls it living. There can be no Doubt but that these Lines are an Interpolation and sho^d be expunged after having Usurped the Page of Shakespeare for near 200 years.

(C) It is remarkable that Gonzalo is called the Friend of Prospero not only in this Place by Ariel but in many Places of the present Play[.] But there is no Pretence for this farther than as He is repre-

---

I27:2 than this] *fol. by* [I27:3] (C) The Writer of it ought to have [been] tied to a whipping Post and to have been lashed without Mercy.
I28:3 Gonzalo] *MS. reads* Gonzales

sented Here as a Man of general Humanity and had furnished for the uses of this Play (for there lies the great Point of Friendship) certain Books and a great profusion of fine Cloaths to a man he had devoted to Destruction[.] He was a Neapolitan officer no subject of Prospero's[.] He commanded a Neapolitan Army with [I30] which he forced the gates of Milan and hurried off Prospero & Miranda in the dead of Darkness in the rotten Carcase of a Boat so leaky that the very Rats had instinctively quitted it and pushed them out to sea that they might perish together. But how came they by their fine Habiliments? oh! There was friendship in that, to be sure, He wished them to be drowned in good Cloaths, and this was the Friendship of Gonzalo so amply acknowledged throughout the present Play, to the uses of which these splendid garments were become Essential. This Conduct is therefore a proof among others that the present Tempest is a reformed Play for in the former there was probably no thought of fine Cloaths nor was Gonzalo *therefore* reckoned as a Friend, nor was there at the Early Period of Shakespeare's Life any variety of rich Dresses to be found either at the Globe or any other Booth.

Marginal Note
[T33MS:1] (C) A vile interpolation. Ariel, tho' invisible, was present as a spy and now interposes with music & a song but some Player chose to be absent, and wrote these three miserable lines as an Excuse[.]

II. i. 306

[T33] [*Ari.*] *If of life you keep a care,*
               Shake off slumber and beware:
               Awake! awake!
Ant. Then let us both be sudden.
Gon. Now, good angels preserve the King!   [*They wake.*

[I33:3] Then let us both be sudden] These words if spoken at all sho^d precede the Musical Charm.

II. i. 317

[T34] *Gon.* Upon my honour, Sir, I hear a humming,
            And that a strange one too, which did awake me.

II. i. 306 T33 Then . . . sudden.] *fol. by circled* a = *ref. to* I33:3; *see next entry*
I33:3 Then] *prec. by circled* a = *ref. to* T33, II. i. 306; *see prec. entry*
II. i. 317 T34 *Gon.* Upon *prec. by circled* a = *ref. to* I34:1; *see next entry*

[I34: 1] Upon my honour &c] So, it appears from hence that Gonzalo did not understand one word of what had been told Him by Ariel. He only heard a Humming.

II. i. 326

[T34]   *Ari. Prospero* my lord shall know what I have done.

[I34:4] Prospero my Lord shall know] Why, what then is become of his Prescience if He is to be told such Things in the ordinary Way?

II. ii. 1

[T34] *Enter* Caliban *with a burden of wood.*

[I34:6] (C) Enter Caliban]* I will not Here speak of Caliban now perhaps — ? — to be held forth as a show. He speaks best for Himself.

II. ii. 14

[T34] *Enter* Trinculo.
[*Cal.*] Here comes a spirit of his.

*Enter *Trinculo*] [I34:9] Trinculo as we shall find wears a patched Coat. If He was not the Kings fool He should not have been thrown ashore for all that belonged properly to the ship and were not of the King's Suite are put under hatches. Stephano was the Butler[.] [I35] But Trinculo if He was not the Kings Fool was Nothing. Shakespeare uses Trinculo & Stephano in the way of Sport only, just as He treats his Mobs[:] Folly without Mischief, or character of any Kind but that of Buffoonery and Sport, a sort of playfull Carricature which no Body [h]as a Right to blame.

II. ii. 21

[T35] [*Trin.*] . . . yond same cloud, yond huge one, looks like a foul bumbard that would shed his liquor.

I34: 1 So, it] *circled* a *above these words* = *ref. to* T34, *II. i. 317 ; see prec. entry*
II. i. 326 T34 *Ari. Prospero] prec. by circled* a = *ref. to* I34:4 ; *see next entry*
I34:4 Prospero . . . know] *circled* a *above this lemma* = *ref. to* T34, *II. i. 326 ; see prec. entry*
II. ii. 14 T34 *Enter Trinculo] prec. by circled* a = *ref. to* I34:8 ; *see next entry*
I34:8 Trinculo] *circled* a *above this word* = *ref. to* T34, *II. ii. 14 ; see prec. entry*
I35:2 Mobs:] *MS. reads* Mobs.
II. ii. 21 T35 like . . . bumbard *circled* a *in outer margin opposite this phrase* = *ref. o* I35:3 ; *see next entry. Theobald's note on the phrase,* T35n, *is lined through; see note*

[I35:3] like a foul Bumbard] Noted by Theobald as a large Vessel to hold Liquor, of *Leather*, I suppose, and such as is now called a black Jack.

II. ii. 83

[T36]   *Cal.* Thou dost me yet but little hurt; thou wilt anon, I know it, by thy trembling: now *Prosper* works upon thee.

[I36:1] By thy trembling] Trinculo it seems was sadly afraid[.]

II. ii. 98

[T37]   [*Ste.*] ... come! *Amen!* I will pour some in thy other mouth.

[I37:1] (C) Amen!]* This humourous *Amen* tells us that Caliban had taken a large and long Draught.

II. ii. 103

[T37]   [*Ste.*] ... this is a devil, and no monster: I will leave him; I have no long spoon.

[I37:3] (C) no long spoon] I do not know the orrigin of this Phrase, but it appears that He who wo.^d give spoon Meat to the Devil should at least keep Him at a Distance.

II. ii. 110

[T37]   [*Ste.*] Thou art very *Trinculo*, indeed: how cams't thou to be the siege of this moon-calf? Can he vent *Trinculo's*?

I35:3 like] *circled* a *above this word* = *ref. to* T35, II. ii. 21; see prec. entry
II. ii. 83 T36 by thy trembling] *circled* a *in outer margin opposite this phrase* = *ref. to* I36:1-2; *see next entry*
I36:2 Trinculo] *circled* a *above this word* = *ref. to* T36, II. ii. 83; *see prec. entry*
II. ii. 98 T37 Amen!] *circled* a *opposite this word in outer margin* = *ref. to* I37:1-2; *see next entry but one*
I37:1 Amen!]] *MS. reads* Amen]!
I37:2 This] *circled* a *above this word* = *ref. to* T37, II. ii. 98; *see prec. entry*
II. ii. 103 T37 no long spoon] *circled* a *in outer margin opposite this phrase* = *ref. to* I37:3
II. ii. 110 T37 the siege of this moon-calf] *circled* a *in outer margin opposite these words* = *ref. to* I37:5; *see next entry*

[I37:5] (C) *The siege of this Moon Calf*] D. Johnson explains this. But it is plain enough and should not be stirred.

II. ii. 134

[T38]   *Ste.* Here, kiss the book. . . .
         Trin. O *Stephano*, hast any more this?
         Ste. The whole butt, man.

[138:1] (C) kiss the Book] Stephano is liberal of his Bottle But He has it seems a whole Butt.

II. ii. 149

[T38]   *Trin.* By this good light, this is a very shallow monster: I afraid of him? a very shallow monster.

[138:3] I afraid of Him!] ['It is to be observ'd, *Trinculo* is not charg'd with any Fear of *Caliban*; and therefore This seems to come in abruptly; but in This consists the true Humour. His own Consciousness, that he had been terribly afraid of him, after the Fright was over, drew out this Bragg. This seems to be one of *Shakespeare*'s fine Touches of Nature: for that *Trinculo* had been horribly frighten'd at the Monster, and shook with Fear of him, while he lay under his Gaberdine, is plain, from What *Caliban* says, while he is lying there[:] *Thou dost me yet but little Harm; thou wilt anon, I know by thy* trembling.'—*Warburton.*]

II. ii. 176

[T39]   [*Cal.*]   sometimes I'll get thee
         Young Shamois from the rock.

I37:5 *The siege] prec. by circled* a = *ref. to T37, II. ii. 110; see prec. entry*
     II. ii. 134 T38 Here, kiss the book] *squiggle in outer margin opposite these words* = *ref. to I38:1–2; see next entry*
     I38:2 Stephano] *squiggle above this word* = *ref. to T38, II. ii. 134; see prec. entry*
     II. ii. 149 T38 I afraid of him] *circled* a *in outer margin opposite these words* = *ref. to I38:3; see next entry*
     I38:3 I . . . Him] *circled* a *above this lemma* = *ref. to T38, II. ii. 149; see prec. entry*   of Him!]] *fol. by* The note upon this Passage sho[d] be transcribed and sign'd *Warburton* by whom it [was] written. *see next entry*   'It is . . . trembling.'— *Warburton] transcribed by editor from Theobald's note, T38n, with addition of Warburton's name; see prec. entry*   lying there:] *T38n reads* lying there?
     II. ii. 176 T39 Young Shamois from the rock] *circled* a *opposite these words in outer margin* = *ref. to I39:1; see next entry. Theobald's note on this phrase, T39n, is lined through*

[I39:1] Young shamois from the Rock] There is much Embroil about these Shamois, but the Shamois is the Name of a goat common in Switzerland & the Alps, and by the young Shamois is Here meant a *Kid*, a prize as acceptable as rare, for the whole Island or Rock does not exceed four or five Furlongs.

Marginal Note
[T39MS:1] (C) a *Shamois* is a goat so called in the alps and Switzerland.

III. i. 21

[T41] [*Mira.*]   my father
          Is hard at study; pray now, rest your self;
          He's safe for these three hours.

[I41:1] three Hours] three Hours is too much according to the March of Time in this Island. Three Hours was the Whole Time of the Play.

III. i. 48

[T42] [*Fer.*]   But you, O you,
          So perfect, and so peerless, are created
          Of every creature's best.

[I42:1] Of every creature's Best] I think that Milton has transcribed this passage into his *Paradise lost*[.]

III. i. 50

[T42] *Mira.* I do not know
          One of my sex; no woman's face remember,
          Save from my glass mine own.

I39:1 Young] *circled* a *above this word* = *ref. to T39, II. ii. 176; see prec. entry*
I39:2 Furlongs] *ED:* (C) Fathoms
III. i. 21 T41 three hours] *circled* a *in outer margin opposite these words* = *ref. to I41:1; see next entry*
I41:1 three Hours] *circled* a *above this lemma* = *ref. to T41, III. i. 21; see prec. entry*
III. i. 48 T42 Of every creature's best] *prec. in outer margin by circled* a = *ref. to I42:1; see next entry*
I42:1 Of . . . Best] *circled* a *above this lemma* = *ref. to T42, III. i. 48; see prec. entry*
III. i. 50 T42 Save from my glass] *circled* a *in outer margin before this phrase* = *ref. to I42:3-4; see next entry*

[I42 : 3] Save from my glass] did Gonzalo put a Looking glass among her Attires ?

III. i. 54

[T42] [*Mira.*]   I would not wish
          Any companion in the world but you.

[I42 : 5] I do not Wish any Companion] In a state of Nature, the first woo[e]r is it seems the Maid.

III. i. 78

[T43] *Fer.* Wherefore weep you ?
          Mira. At mine unworthiness, that dare not offer,
              What I desire to give; and much less take,
              What I shall die to want.

[I43 : 1] and much less take] imperfectly expressed—*and much less dares she take that (so great is her unworthiness) which she must die to want.* (C) The Language of Nature and Truth is very interesting Here.

III. i. 93

[T43] *Pro.* So glad of this as they, I cannot be,
              Who are surpriz'd withal.

[I43 : 4] Who are surpriz'd withall] This I think sho^d be written thus[:] *who are sur-prized with all,* using the word *sur-prized* as we do the word *sur-charged* as for something beyond the just Measure,

I42:4 did] *circled* a *above this word* = *ref. to T42, III. i. 50; see prec. entry*
III. i. 54 T42 Any companion] *circled* a *in outer margin before this phrase* = *ref. to I42:5; see next entry*
I42:5 I . . . Companion] *circled* a *above this lemma* = *ref. to T42, III. i. 54; see prec. entry*
III. i. 78 T43 much less take] *fol. by circled* a *in outer margin* = *ref. to I41:3; see next entry*
I43:1 and . . . take,] *circled* a *above this lemma* = *ref. to T43, III. i. 78; see prec. entry*
III. i. 93 T43 Who are surpriz'd withal] *circled* a *in outer margin opposite these words* = *ref. to I43:4; see next entry*
I43:4 Who . . . withall] *circled* a *above this lemma* = *ref. to T43, III. i. 93; see prec. entry*

and as supposing the Blessings & Joys of Love to be heaped on them in the greatest Abundance[.]

III. ii. 3

[T44]   *Ste.* . . . . when the butt is out, we will drink water, not a drop before; therefore bear up, and board 'em, servant-monster; drink to me.
   Trin. Servant-monster!

[144:1] Servant monster] ['If there be never a *Servant Monster* in the *Fair*, who can help it, (he says,) nor a Nest of *Anticks*? He is loth to make Nature afraid in his Plays, like Those that beget *Tales*, *Tempests*, and such like *Drolleries*, to mix his Head with other Mens Heels.'—Ben Jonson, Induction to *Bartholomew Fair*.]

Bartholomew Fair was written in 1614 and it shoᵈ follow that at this Time the Tempest was in full Run at the Globe and had excited the spleen and drawn the Envy of Ben and we may therefore fairly conclude that it was reformed & revived in this or the foregoing Year which coresponds very well with other grounds of conjecture.

III. ii. 47

[T45] *Enter* Ariel *invisible.*

[145:1] Enter Ariel] We have no other Notice of Ariel's being Employed Here as an invisible Spy than as we may very justly conclude from the event that there was such an order given[.]

III. ii. 71

[T46]   *Cal.* What a py'd ninny's this? thou scurvy patch!

[146:1] What a py'd Ninny's this? Thou scurvy Patch] Tho' Caliban did not know what a professed Fool was, He knew that Trinculo's

III. ii. 3 T44 *Trin.* Servant-monster] *prec. by circled* a *in outer margin = ref. to 144:1; see next entry*
   144:1 Servant monster] *circled* a *above this lemma = ref. to T44, III. ii. 3; see prec. entry*   monster]] *fol. by* Transcribe the Passage from Ben *viz. as found in Theobald's note to* servant-monster, *T44n; Theobald's note is lined through*   If there . . . *Bartholomew Fair] transcribed by editor from Theobald's note (see prec. entry) with addition of last six words*
   III. ii. 47 T45 *invisible.] fol. by circled* a *= ref. to 145:1-2; see next entry*
   145:2 We have] *circled* a *above these words = ref. to T45, III. ii. 47; see prec. entry*
   III. ii. 71 T46 *Cal.* What . . . *scurvy patch!] prec. in outer margin by circled* a = *ref. to 146:1 (see next entry) and by* X = *ref. to T46MS:1 (see next entry but three)*
   146:1 What a py'd Ninny's this] *circled* a *above this lemma = ref. to T46, III. ii. 71; see prec. entry*

Coat was patched and py'd[,] and he knew or believed that He was a great Ninny. We are his Interpreters for the Rest. Here then it is clear that Trinculo was in the Kings service as a professed Fool and was not thrown ashore for the sole Purpose of conversing with Stephano the Butler, but neither before this scene nor in any part of the Play does Trinculo bring his pied and patched Coat to account. We cannot therefore but conclude that He was thrown into this Insignificance in Consequence of some great Reform in a Play in which He once held a conspicuous Part.

Marginal Note

[T46MS:1] It appears from this that Trinculo was a professed Fool in the first Play.

III. ii. 95

[T46]   *Cal.* Why as I told thee, 'tis a custom with him
        I' th'a fternoon to sleep; there thou may'st brain him,
        Having first seized his books: or with a log
        Batter his skull, or paunch him with a stake,
        Or cut his wezand with thy knife.

[I46:6] Why as I told thee &c] this speech is finely brutal. He had before spoken of knocking a Nail into Prospero's Head and now He dwells with great Delight on other Modes of Destruction.

III. ii. 102

[T46]   [*Cal.*]   They all do hate him,
        [T47] As rootedly as I

*They all do hate him] [I47:1] We are told here that the Spirits hate Prospero rootedly and we shall find that the gentle Ariel tho' He does his spiriting cheerfully in the near view of Freedom yet has no tender affection or any Common Sympathy or Feeling with Prospero[.]

I46:2 patched and py'd,] *MS. reads* patched, and py'd *last two words careted in by mistake after instead of before the comma*
I46:4 Butler,] *fol. by* (C) for any swabber from the ship would have done as well
T46MS:1 It appears] *prec. by* X = *ref. to T46, III. ii. 71; see prec. entry but three*
III. ii. 95 T46 *Cal.* Why] *prec. by circled* a= *ref. to I46:5-7; see next entry*
I46:7 this] *circled* a *above this word = ref. to T46, III. ii. 95; see prec. entry*
III. ii. 102 T46 They all do hate him] *circled* a *in outer margin opposite these words =* *ref. to I47:1*

III. ii. 124

[T47]   *Cal.* Within this half hour will he be asleep;
        Wilt thou destroy him then?
        Ste. Ay, on my honour.
        Ari. This will I tell my master.

[I47:2] Tell my master] What is become of Prospero's Prescience?

III. ii. 133

[T47] [Ariel *plays the Tune on a Tabor and Pipe.*

[I47:4] Ariel plays on the Tabor]* It does not appear clearly whether
Ariel is in a Machine or on the ground. When He draws Ferdinand,
Ferdinand says of the music I hear it now above me, and I suppose
the Players on this Occasion would be glad to mount Ariel in a
Machine for whether in the air or on the ground He must be visible
to the Audience[.]

III. iii. 19

[T49] *Solemn and strange musick; and* Prospero *on the top, invisible.*
        Enter several strange shapes, bringing in a banquet; and
        dance about it with gentle actions of salutation; and, in-
        viting the King, &c. to eat, they depart.

*Prospero on the top] [I49:1] So, Prospero Himself becomes a part
of the Show[.] He tips the Pyramid like a Spire and Collects all his
Spirits around[.] I hope He is in his most gorgeous Habiliments and
has fully gratifyed the public Eye.

III. iii. 48

[T50]   [*Gon.*]   When we were boys,
        Who would believe . . .
                                      that there were such men,

---

III. ii. 124 T47 tell my master.] *fol. by circled* a = *ref. to I47:2; see next entry*
I47:2 Tell my master] *circled* a *above this lemma* = *ref. to T47, III. ii. 124; see*
prec. entry
III. ii. 133 T47 *and* Pipe.] *fol. by circled* a *in outer margin* = *ref. to I47:4; see next*
entry
I47:4 Ariel . . . Tabor] *prec. by circled* a = *ref. to T47, III. ii. 133; see prec. entry*
III. iii. 19 T49 Prospero *on the top] circled* a *opposite these words in the outer margin* =
ref. to I49:1; see next entry
I49:1 So, Prospero] *circled* a *above these words* = *ref. to T49, III. iii. 19; see prec.*
entry

Whose heads stood in their breasts? which now we find,
Each putter out on five for one will bring us
Good warrant of.

[I50:1] (C) Putter out on five for one] Theobald confesses Here [i.e. in his note] so much foregone Folly that we may well suppose that He has not yet wholly recovered his Wits. *Now* he thinks that travelling adventurers deposited their Wealth In the Hands of Persons who Engaged to pay on their Return five Times the sum deposited as conceiving that they were not likely to return at all and claim Either the Principal or its Increase, whereas M.ʳ Warburton, from whom He derives his Information, only supposes that those who advanced Money to these Adventurers had on their return for the sums they contributed 20 p C.ᵗ; this is a very different story and surely much more consonant to common sense that those who were fitting themselves out for adventure were the Borrowers upon Promises of large Interest to be paid on their Return loaded as it was Expected with Riches, than that they sho.ᵈ deposit money to be paid them upon such high Terms in the Event of their Return as seemed to indicate Despair whilst yet it depended on their own Choice what Hazzards they might run and for what Time and to what Distance they might go. Doctor Thirlby if Theobald says true was in the same Errour with [I51] Himself but I doubt if any two men were likely to concur in drawing an Inferrence in direct contradiction to Mʳ Warburton's premises as approved of and adopted by them and in direct opposition to common sense. But that this construction is *right past Dispute* will appear, He says, from a Passage in Every Man out of his Humour wherein a Bett is laid that a man his Cat and his Dog will go to Constantinople and return all alive. The Bett is five to one that they will not all return. What this has to do with the adventures undertaken to see undiscovered Lands no man in his senses can I think tell. We have of late Times known Betts full as Extravagant and ridiculous as this. But it follows from this note of Theobalds that He was not only ignorant of Shakespeare but of Johnson too. The Text sho.ᵈ be corrected thus[:] which each Putter out of five for one &c meaning that the adventurer was to return five for one [I52] upon his Return and not as Mʳ Warburton seems to suppose, 20 p C.ᵗ by the year[.]

III. iii. 48 T50 Each putter . . . for one] *prec. by circled* a *in outer margin* = *ref. to I50:1; Theobald's note on the passage, T50n–T51n, is lined through*
　I51:7 Putter out of]*fol. by careted in* or *on see note*

III. iii. 52

[T51]   *Thunder and lightning. Enter* Ariel *like a harpy, claps his wings upon the table, and with a queint device the banquet vanishes.*

Marginal Note
*Thunder and lightning. Enter *Ariel*] [T51MS:1] (C) All the Machinery in this Play added on its Revival[.]

III. iii. 56

[T51]   *Ari.* You are three men of sin, whom destiny
.   .   .   .
                    the never-surfeited sea
    Hath caused to belch up.

**Hath caused to belch up*] [Theobald's note, T51n, cancelled.]

III. iii. 82

[T52]   *He* [*i.e. Ariel*] *vanishes in thunder: then, to soft musick, Enter the shapes again, and dance with mopps and mowes, and carrying out the table.*
    Pro. Bravely the figure of this harpy hast thou
        Performed, my Ariel.

**He vanishes in thunder*] [I52:2] The Stage Direction in the foregoing Page [i.e. T51, III. iii. 52] and in Page 49 [i.e. T49, III. iii. 19] and in this refers to machinery which were doubtless the Admiration of the Time and perhaps beat that of the masques out and out— strange music, a scaffoulding with *Prospero* on the Top invisible to the King &c., Strange Shapes, a Banquet and a Dance; after which Thunder and Lightning and a *Harpy* upon Wings, supposed to be Ariel, and the Table & Banquet vanishing by a *queint Device*. Then more Thunder, more music other and Strange Shapes dancing with Mopps & Mowes and carrying off the Table. What could the *Town* or even the *Quality* require more?

III. iii. 52 T51 *Thunder and . . . banquet vanishes*] X *in outer margin opposite this S.D. = ref. to T51MS:1 in bottom margin; see next entry*
    T51MS:1 *All the*] *prec. by* X = *ref. to T51, III. iii. 52, S.D.; see prec. entry*
    III. iii. 82 T52 *Performed*] *prec. by circled* a *in outer margin = ref. to I52:2b*

IV. i. 3

[T53] [*Pro.*]   for I
        Have giv'n you here a thread of mine own life;
        Or that, for which I live.

[I53:1] *A thread of my own Life*] The Reading of the ancient Copies
was according to Mr Theobald a Third of my own Life and He has
corrected the Text very properly as I think into *a Thread of my own
Life*.

IV. i. 14

[T54] [*Pro.*]   take my Daughter. But
        If thou dost break her virgin-knot, before
        All sanctimonious ceremonies may
        With full and holy Rite be minister'd,
        No sweet aspersions shall the heav'ns let fall
        To make this contract grow.

[I54:8] Her Virgin Knot] There are Times and Seasons wherein the
Plainest and most forcible Expressions are the most becoming. From
the Austere Prospero and for holy Purposes nothing can be considered as obscene. The bridal Zones of the ancients are figurative
things which sho^d not be referred to Here.

Earlier Draft
[I54:1] (C) The latter Commentators speak of the ancient Zone
or girdle which it was the Priviledge of the Bridegroom to unloose.
They had better not explain at all[.] Prospero speaks to the point and
is well understood by Ferdinand[.]

IV. i. 3 T53 a thread of mine own life] *circled* a *in outer margin above level of this
phrase* = *ref. to* I53:1; *see next entry. Theobald's note to the phrase,* T53n, *is lined
through*
    I53:1 A thread . . . Life] *circled* a *above this lemma* = *ref. to* T53, *IV. i. 3; see prec.
entry*
    IV. i. 14 T54 If thou dost] *prec. by circled* a *in outer margin* = *ref. to* I54:8; *see
next entry*
    I54:8 Her Virgin Knot] *circled* a *above this lemma* = *ref. to* T54, *IV. i. 14; see
prec. entry*
    I54:2 at all] *ED:* (C) Truth by a symbol
    I54:3 Prospero] *fol. by* (C) with a Dignity which becomes the occasion

IV. i. 36-7

[T54]   *Pro.* Thou and thy meaner fellows your last service
      Did worthily perform; and I must use you
      In such another trick; go, bring the rabble,
      O'er whom I give thee power.

[I54:4] I must use you in such another Trick] those spirits which Prospero here calls the Rabble have never been well defined[.] Ben. calls them a Nest of Antics[.] They seem to have been Spirits of the Earth who pinched and gave stitches & cramps and were themselves a Kind of Mocks and Moes, but they do very well to personate Juno & Ceres and the gone-by Deities of the Olympian Hall.

IV. i. 55-6

[T55]   [*Fer.*] The white, cold virgin-snow upon my heart
      Abates the ardour of my liver.

[I55:1] *Abates the ardor of my liver*]*—This *heart* & *liver* sentence smacks too much of the Shambles to fit any delicate taste, tho' it may be Shakespear throughout—*Passion* perhaps were better substituted[.]—J. S.—

IV. i. 59

[T55] *A MASQUE. Enter* Iris.

[I55:3] *A Masque*]* This is a very bold & decisive Measure. It is calculated not only to draw the fashionable Spectators from the Masques, which were then all the Mode, but to bring into the Play House the Masques themselves and in point of Composition as far as I know or believe it beats them all. [A]fter this we have Nymphs

IV. i. 36-7 T54 I must . . . another trick] *circled* a *in outer margin opposite this sentence = ref. to I54:4; see next entry*

I54:4 I must . . . another Trick] *circled* a *above this lemma = ref. to T54, IV. i. 36-7; see prec. entry*

IV. i. 55-6 T55 The white . . . liver] *circled* a *in outer margin slightly below this passage apparently marks it as object of the comment by J. S., I55:1-2*

I55:1-2 Abates the . . . J. S.—] *written in John Symmons's hand; see Intro., p. 118*

IV. i. 59 T55 A MASQUE. Enter Iris.] *fol. by circled* a *in outer margin = ref. to I55:3; see next entry*

I55:3 A Masque] *circled* a *above these words, which are centred like a title above the comment = ref. to T55, IV. i. 59, S.D.; see prec. entry*

I55:6 After] *MS. reads* after

and Reapers all properly habited who Encounter each other in Country Footing. [A]nd then the scene changes Suddenly into Horrour.

Marginal Note

[T55MS:1] (C) Added to rival the fashionable Masques followed in the Reign of James.

IV. i. 139–63

[T58]   *Pro.* I had forgot that foul conspiracy
                Of the beast *Caliban*, and his confed'rates,
                Against my life; the minute of their plot
                Is almost come. . . .
        Fer. This is strange; your father's in some passion
                That works him strongly.
        Mir. Never 'till this day
                Saw I him touch'd with anger, so distemper'd.

.   .   .   .

[T59] [*Pro.*]   we are such stuff
                As dreams are made on, and our little life
                Is rounded with a sleep.——Sir, I am vext;
                Bear with my weakness, my old brain is troubled:
                Be not disturb'd with my infirmity;
                If thou be pleas'd, retire into my cell, . . .

**I had forgot that foul conspiracy*]

[156:1] *The passion of Prospero.*

Never was there a Passage so sadly Mistaken by the commentators as this. Even D. Warburton, who seldom fails on great Occasions, is Here as dark and Erroneous as the Rest. We are to remember that this Play was reformed in the Reign of James 1st, when it behoved Shakespeare to look about, lest He, Himself, sho^d be taken up for a Magician, and it was therefore necessary to unveil the Dangers of this unholy Art. The *minute* of Caliban's Plott was almost come, and Prospero had nearly forgot it. He dare not disclose the Cause of his

---

155:7 And] *MS. reads* and   Horrour] 2 *ED*: (C) Horrour / (C) Horrour
156:1 Prospero] *fol. by ED.*: [156:5b] (C) and if it had passed without some magical seizure the effect wo^d probably have been no less than that of being seized by all his spirits who so rootedly hated Him and thrown suddenly into the lowest Hell. *The first word of this ED is prec. by X = possible cross-ref. to T62MS:2; see next entry but one and see note*

Disturbance. He conceals it under passionate Reflexions on the Transiency of Things. He cannot bear even the Question of Eyes, and Earnestly intreats Ferdinand & Miranda to retire into the Cell. *She* is astonished and the whole is passed off in Mistery and Silence. It is in vain then to look to natural Causes. The Cause was in Magic and [I57] indicates that the End of the Magician is Despair; unless, says the Epilogue, He be relieved by Prayer. And accordingly we find Him resolve that when He retires to Milan Every third Thought shall be his grave, and He promises to break his Staff and drown his Books by which the Poet doubtless hoped that the royal James wo.ᵈ be some thing appeased. The spels of Prospero are of a Nature so nice that they depend for the most Part on *Silence* and *the minute.* Be mute says He to his daughter or Else our spel is marred. Prospero is of a very grave, Austere Nature and full of Care and Attention, and it is fitting He should be so if the Crack of a Single Spel sho.ᵈ set his spirits who so rootedly hated Him loose and Destruction & Horrour sho.ᵈ Ensue. He will not say what the cause of his Disturbance was but it must have been something of a dreadfull sort. We respect Prospero as of a very dignified and yet affectionate Character, but one would not like notwithstanding to be in his shoes. [P]lain Nature is the Thing after all.

Marginal Note

[T59MS:1] (C) This is a Passion Excited by some misterious Cause in Magic not in Nature, and is [T60MS] meant to intimate both the unlawfullness [a]nd the Danger of the art. It is in [T61MS] vain to Enquire into the efficient Cause[:] if it co.ᵈ be found it wo.ᵈ be *Nature* no[t] *Magic.* Magic depends on a *minute* or [T62MS] a *word*, and the Danger from which Prospero had just Escaped may have been no less than that his Spirits, [r]eleased from his spels, might have torn Him all to peices. He dare not say what the Danger was, and therefore vents his Perturbations in Reflections on Mortality & Mutability.

IV. i. 186

[T60] [*Pro.*] The trumpery in my house, go bring it hither,
      For stale to catch these thieves.

I57:7 Plain] *MS. reads* plain
T62MS:2 and therefore . . . & Mutability] X *in inner margin opposite this clause =*
possible cross-ref. to I56:5*b; see prec. entry but one*
   IV. i. 186 T60 The trumpery] *prec. by circled* a *in outer margin = ref. to* I60:*I*
see next entry

[160:1] The Trumpery] What He here calls Trumpery was no other than the rich Wardrope of the Play House which is Here brought out to make a show. Gonzalo had been very profuse it seems in his Provision of rich garments which are now to be hung on a Line and the finest of them destined to invest Stephano & Trinculo that the splendour of the last scene may be improved to the utmost.

V. i. 4

[T63]   [*Pro.*]   how's the Day?
    Ari. On the sixth hour, at which time, my lord,
        You said, our work should cease.

[163:1] on the Sixth Hour] The Tempest was raised at the *Mid Season*, that is at *12 o' th' Clock*. On the *sixth* Hour that is on the *commencement* of the sixth Hour from the mid Season, the work was to cease, but the Play does not begin till after *two glasses past* the Mid Season that is till *2 o' th' Clock*, from which it proceeds in continuous Time to the commencement of the Sixth Hour, that is to the Conclusion of the 5th, making the whole Time *three Hours* by the Town Clock, and this is ascertained by more Notes of Time than the occasion requires. How says the King to Prospero hast thou met us Here who *three Hours* since were wracked upon this shore. & again What is this Maid says the King to Ferdinand with whom thou wast at Play? Your Eldest Acquaintance cannot be *three Hours*, after which in the last scene the Boatswain says our Ship which but *three glasses* since we gave out split. Who does not see from such Passages that the young Shakespeare was in this his earliest Play the pupil of some [164] pedant school and that He wod have been glad to have brought *Place* also, if He could have done so into *unity*, but that there was no bringing the outside and the inside of the Cell, and the wood yard, and the filthy mantled Pool and the Lime grove which weatherfended the Cell, all out of Sight & hearing of Each other, into *one* and the *same Place*, and so it passes as *one Island* at least, without any further Ostentation or Boast[.]—I do not object to the *Unities*. They were absolutely necessary under the condition

---

160:1 The Trumpery] *circled a above this lemma = ref. to T60, IV. i. 186; see prec. entry*

V. i. 4 T63 On the sixth hour] *circled a and X in outer margin opposite these words = ref. to 163:1 (see next entry) and ref. to T63MS:1 (see next entry but two)*

163:1 on the Sixth Hour] *circled a above this lemma = ref. to T63, V. i. 4; see prec. entry*

of a Chorus. But Time was never confined by any specious Law to three Hours. The meaning of the Law was that the parties sho.^d finish the Fable between sleep and sleep. But this narrowed the dramatic ground; for the Fable and the Time of its Execution must Mutually embrace each other, or the Time will either hang too loose about the Fable or strangle it as too tight. And that Fable can have but few events or incidents which can be contained in a Natural [I65] Day. I mean a Day of real Time but Dramatic Time runs off much faster, six perhaps for one, and the Events must always govern the Time and not the Time the Events; nor did Shakespeare ever submit to these supposed Laws except in this Play, from whence one may reasonably conclude it to be his first Effort. But He soon found out the Art of making *compendious Time* and *compendious Place*; that is of preserving the Passions and Interests in their full Force and throwing them over huge Chasms of Time and Place unimpaired, as the Crow flies.

Marginal Note
[T63MS:1] (C) Meaning full five o' th' Clock. The Time of the Play is three Hours, accordin[g] I presume with the Time of Representation[.]

V. i. 33 and 48–9

[T64] *Pro.* Ye elves of hills, brooks, standing lakes and groves,

. . . .

[T65] graves at my command
Have wak'd their sleepers; op'd, and let them forth
By my so potent art.

graves at my command] [See *Com.* I. ii. 250, I164:2.]

V. i. 50–1

[T65] [*Pro.*]   But this rough magick
    I here abjure.

I65:3 them] *fol. by afterthought*: (C) *so preserved*
T63MS:1 Meaning] *prec. by* X = *ref. to T63, V. i. 4; see prec. entry but two*
V. i. 33 T64 Pro. Ye] *prec. by circled* a *in outer margin* = *probable ref. to Com. I. ii. 250, I164:2; see note*
T65 graves at . . . their sleepers] B. *in outer margin opposite this sentence* = *possible ref. to Com. I. ii. 250, I164:2. Theobald's note on this sentence, T65n, is cancelled; see note*
V. i. 50–1 T65 rough magick] *fol. by* X *in outer margin* = *ref. to note in bottom margin, T65MS:1; see next entry*

Marginal Note

**But this rough magick I here abjure*] [T65MS:1] (C) He is in the right to abjure or James wo^d have him indicte[d] on the Statute[.]

V. i. 57

[T65] [*Solemn musick.*

Here enters Ariel *before; then* Alonso *with a frantick Gesture, attended by* Gonzalo. Sebastian *and* Anthonio *in like manner, attended by* Adrian *and* Francisco. *They all enter the circle which* Prospero *had made, and there stand charm'd; which* Prospero *observing, speaks.*

[I65:4] Here enters Ariel then Alonzo &c] More show and more music[.]

V. i. 74–75

[T66]   [*Pro.*] Thou'rt pinch'd for't now, *Sebastian,* flesh and blood.
You brother mine, that entertain'd ambition,
Expell'd remorse and nature;

.   .   .   .   .   .

I do forgive thee,
Unnat'ral though thou art.

**flesh and blood . . . I do forgive thee*] [Intended comment uncertain; cf. *Com.* V. i. 130]

V. i. 85

[T66]   [*Pro.*]   *Ariel,*
Fetch me the hat and rapier in my cell;
I will dis-case me, and my self present,
                    [*Exit* Ariel, *and returns immediately.*
As I was sometime *Milan.*

[I66:1] and my self present as I was sometimes Milan] ay there was the great Point. He was not fine Enough for the concluding scene

T65MS:1 He is] *prec. by* X = *ref. to T65, V. i. 50–1; see prec. entry*

V. i. 74–5 T66 Thou'rt . . . and blood] *circled* a *in outer margin opposite this line and slightly above level of next line* = *ref. to non-extant comment*

V. i. 85 T66 my self present,] *fol. by* X *in inner margin* = *ref. to T66MS:1 in bottom margin; see next entry but two*   As I was sometime *Milan*] *prec. by circled* a *in outer margin* = *ref. to T66:1; see next entry*

I66:1 and my . . . sometimes Milan] *circled* a *above this lemma* = *ref. to T66, V. i. 85; see prec. entry*

and yet bating the Magic Mantle which might have been heretofore worn by Old Sycorax and the wooden Rod He must have been in ducal apparel such as He had formerly worn in Milan but He wanted it seems fresher Cloaths to match those which had been made up for the Marriage of Claribel and which after being drenched in the Sea were fresher than before but now He has got his Rapier and Diamond Button perhaps in his Hat—Articles of high Account in a Show. Shakespeare seems to be ashamed of all this and perhaps dressed Stephano and Trinculo in coresponding Finery out of Mockery and sport and to show of how little value He Put upon Things to which He gives in different Places the names of Trumpery and Frippery and Luggage and Trash.

Marginal Note
[T66MS:1] Now we see the use of Gonzalo's provision of fine Cloaths[.]

V. i. 88

[T66] [*Ari.*] *Where the bee sucks, there lurk I.*

*there lurk I] [Intended comment probably on Theobald's note, T66n, emending *suck* to *lurk*: see below, Appendix, p. 354.]

V. i. 130

[T68] [*Pro.*] For you, most wicked Sir, whom to call brother
 Would even infect my mouth, I do forgive
 Thy rankest faults; all of them.

**For you, most wicked Sir*] [Intended comment perhaps on subject of Prospero's forgiving Anthonio; cf. *Com.* V. i. 74-5.]

V. i. 149

[T69] [*Alon.*] O heav'ns! that they were living both in *Naples*,
 The King and Queen there; that they were, I wish,
 My self were mudded in that oozy bed,
 Where my son lies.

T66MS:1 Now we] X *above and to left of these words = ref. to T66, V. i. 85; see prec. entry but two*
 V. i. 88 T66 *Where the*] *prec. by circled* a *in outer margin = ref. to non-extant comment*
 V. i. 130 T68 For you] *prec. by circled* a *in outer margin = ref. to non-extant comment*
 V. i. 149 T69 both in *Naples,*] *fol. by circled* a *= ref. to I69:1; see next entry*

[I69:1] that they were living Both in Naples] This King is a great Hypocrite. He is profuse of good Deeds & wishes 'till he is brought to the Test[.] But when He finds Ferdinand to be living and that He has Chosen Miranda for his Wife He is cold and speaks doubtfully.

V. i. 174

[T70] *Mira.* Sweet lord, you play me false,
  Fer. No, my dear love,
   I would not for the world.
  Mira. Yes, for a score of kingdoms you should wrangle,
   And I would call it fair play.

[I70:1] Yes, for a score of Kingdoms you Sho.^d wrangle and I would call it fair Play] Surely, this is unnatural as coming from the innocent Miranda, who cannot have as yet acquired the Lust of Power.

V. i. 190

[T70] [*Fer.*] I chose her, when I could not ask my father
  For his Advice: nor thought, I had one.

[I70:3] I chose Her &c] Here we see the uses of Ariel's 2.^d song in Act 1.st *Full Fathom five* &c.

V. i. 196

[T70] *Alon.* I am hers.

[I70:5] I am Her's] very cold[.]

I69:1 that they . . . in Naples] *circled* a *above this lemma* = *ref. to* T69, *V. i. 149; see prec. entry*
 V. i. 174 T70 Mira. Yes] *prec. by circled* a *in outer margin* = *ref. to* I70:1; *see next entry*
 I70:1 Yes, for . . . fair Play] *circled* a *above this lemma* = *ref. to* T70, *V. i. 174; see prec. entry*
 I70:2 have as yet acquired] *ED:* (UM) yet (R) have (C) Entertained
 V. i. 190 T70 I chose her] *prec. by circled* a *in outer margin* = *ref. to* I70:3; *see next entry*
 I70:3 I chose her &c] *circled* a *above this lemma* = *ref. to* T70, *V. i. 190; see prec. entry*
 V. i. 196 T70 Alon. I] *prec. by circled* a *in outer margin* = *ref. to* I70:5; *see next entry*
 I70:5 I am Her's] *circled* a *above this lemma* = *ref. to* T70, *V. i. 196; see prec. entry*

V. i. 204

[T71] [*Gon.*]   Look down, you Gods,
And on this couple drop a blessed crown.

.   .   .   .   .   .

Alon. I say, *Amen, Gonzalo!*

[I71:1] I say Amen] Not half in Earnest. He Sho^d have been the speaker not the Clerk.

V. i. 213

[T71] *Alon.* Give me your hands:
Let grief and sorrow still embrace his heart
That doth not wish you joy!
Gon. Be't so, *Amen*!

[I71:4] Give me your Hands] Now He is in Earnest and speaks in Sincerity and Truth, and Gonzalo gives the Amen.

Marginal Note
[T71MS:1] (C) He is now fo[r] the first Tim[e] Sincere[.]

V. i. 215–218

[T71] *Enter* Ariel, *with the Master and Boatswain amazedly following.*

[*Gon.*] O look, Sir, look, Sir, here are more of us!
I prophesy'd, if a gallows were on land,
This fellow could not drown.

[I71:6] I prophecied this Fellow Co^d not drown] This is the only Place where the ship scene is referred to, and is of no other Consequence than as it seems to tack that scene to the Play and must have been written on the Reform.

V. i. 204 T71 *Amen, Gonzalo!*] *circled* a *in outer margin opposite these words* = *ref. to* I71:1–3; *see next entry*
  I71:2 Not half] *circled* a *above these words* = *ref. to* T71, V. i. 204; *see prec. entry*
  V. i. 213 T71 *your hands:*] *fol. by circled* a = *ref. to* I71:4; *see next entry*
  I71:4 give me your Hands] *circled* a *above this lemma* = *ref. to* T71, V. i. 213; *see prec. entry*
  V. i. 215–18 T71 *on land,*] *fol. by circled* a = *ref. to* I71:6; *see next entry*
  I71:6 I prophecied . . . not drown] *circled* a *above this lemma* = *ref. to* T71, V. i. 215–18; *see next entry*

It is a Pity that Ariel had not dropt some Frippery on the Heads of these Sailors, that they might have rivaled Stephano & Trinculo, in the glistering apparel of the scene.

V. i. 223

[T71]   [*Boats.*]   our ship,
            Which but three glasses since we gave out split,
            Is tight and yare.

Marginal Note

*Which but three glasses since we gave out split] [T71MS] The Time of the Play appears from hence to be three Hours precisely. [T72MS] [T]he Time of this Play is so very straight [t]hat nothing is allowed for Intervals [b]etween the Acts. It passes in [T73MS] strict Continuity, the Errour of Inexperience and Bad Advice, given probably by some titled Pedant.

V. i. 236

[T72]   [*Boats.*]   straightway at liberty:
            Where we, in all her trim, freshly beheld
            Our royal, good and gallant ship.

[I72:1] (CM) In all her Trim] [I72:4] (U) Theobald has corrected properly *our Trim* into *Her Trim* but with his usual Impertinence, nor would it have been very Extravagant if in a Play wherein so much Attention is given to garments the Crew had been said to have been in their Neatest Trim.

Earlier Draft

[I72:2] (C) Theobald corrected *our Trim* the ancient Text to *Her Trim*, and I think rightly. But it would not be wonderfull if in a Play wherein garments drenched in Brine were yet fresher than before, that the Sailors after being put under Hatches in all the Confusion of a Storm, should yet appear three Hours afterwards in their neatest Trim.

I71:8 It is a Pity] *prec. by* (C) Enter Ariel with master & Boatsw[ain]
    V. i. 233 T71 out split,] *fol. by* X *in outer margin* = *ref. to T71MS:1; see next entry*
    T71MS:1 The Time] *prec. by blotted* X = *ref. to T71, V. i. 223; see prec. entry*
    V. i. 236 T72 in all her trim] *circled a opposite this phrase in outer margin* = *ref. to I72:4; see next entry*
    I72:4 Theobald has corrected properly] *circled a above this line* = *ref. to T72, V. i. 236; see prec. entry*
    I72:3 three] *prec. by* (UM) in

V. i. 267

[T73]   *Pro.* Mark but the badges of these men, my lords.

*_Mark but the badges_] [Intended comment probably an extension of *Com.* V. i. 85 on dressing Stephano and Trinculo in finery.]

V. i. 277 and 279

[T73]   *Alon.* Is not this *Stephano*, my drunken butler?
        Seb. He's drunk now: where had he wine?
        Alon. And *Trinculo* is reeling ripe.

[I73:1] Is not this Stephano and Trinculo] The King acknowledges both the *Butler* and *Trinculo.* Who then was *Trinculo* that the king Sho^d know Him and call Him by his Name. He does not appear to have been in the Kings Service in any Capacity whatever. But He wore a patched Coat. He must then have been heretofore in the Capacity of a professed Fool, but not Acting in that Quality in this Play He must therefore have belonged to a former now lost tho' this among other Evidence remains[.]

V. i. 280

[T73]   *Alon.*   where should they
        Find this grand 'lixir, that hath gilded 'em?

[I73:7] grand 'lixir] Corrected from Liquor by Warburton [.]

V. i. 311

[T74]   [*Pro.*] And . . . retire me to my *Milan*, where
        Every third thought shall be my grave.

Marginal Note
*_Every third thought_] [T74MS:1] (C) [E]stimating Perhaps that magic was a Crime demanding constant Repentance.

V. i. 267 T73 lords,] *circled* a *above* ds = *probable ref. to non-extant comment on* badges
   V. i. 277 T73 butler?] *fol. by circled* a = *ref. to I73:1; see next entry*
   I73:1 Is not . . . and Trinculo] *circled* a *above this lemma* = *ref. to T73, V. i. 277 see prec. entry*
   V. i. 280 T73 grand 'lixir] *circled* a *in outer margin opposite this phrase* = *ref. to I73:7; see next entry*
   I73:3 grand 'lixir] *circled* a *above this lemma* = *ref. to T73, V. i. 280*
   V. i. 311 T74 grave.] *fol. by* X = *ref. to T74MS:1; see next entry*
   T74MS:1 Estimating] *fragmentary* X *above* E = *ref. to T74, V. i. 311; see prec. entry*

MISCELLANEOUS COMMENTS

MISCELLANEOUS COMMENTS

A Midsummer-Night's Dream

Introductory Comment

Marginal Note

[T79MS:1] I take the Tempest to have been Shakespear[e's] first Play, and either this or Romeo and Juliet to have been his second. [T80MS] The Sensibilities of Love and Fancy Each of which had possessed his Early youth seem most likely to [T81MS] have engaged Him in their Representati[on.] But there is one unerring mark of [T82MS] an Early composition Namely that He mistook the Language of familiar conversation in his [T83MS] first Plays, considering it to be rather a sort of Competition in Points of Wit than what it ought to be, Sentiment [T84MS] Easily and Naturally Expressed which in his further Acquaintance with the world He found and [T85MS] imitated properly. This Play appears to have been Taken from some Novel[.] [T86MS] The scene is Athens but the superstitious English, and the —? — —? — Nature.

II. i. 101

[T93] [*Queen.*] The human mortals want their winter here.

Marginal Note

*here] [T93MS] chear

IV. i. 196

[T131] [*Her.*]   every thing seems double.
        Hel. So, methinks;
        And I have found *Demetrius* like a Gemell,
        Mine own, and not mine own.

*And I have found Demetrius *like a Gemell*] [I132:1] It is singular that this word *Gemel* sho.^d be corrupted in the only two Places wherein it is mentioned into *Jewell*[.] When Falstaffe tells the Page that He will send Him back to his Master for a *Gemel*, He means to say *for such another light Thing as Himself.*

Marginal Note

[T131MS:1] In the Play of Harry 4th Falstaffe tells the Page that He will send Him back to his [T132MS] Master for a Jewell[.] But the text there requires that it sho^d be read as Here Gemel a Twin.

V. i. 118 ff.

[T139]   *Thes.* This fellow doth not stand upon points.
        Lys. He hath rid his prologue like a rough colt; he knows
             not the stop, . . .

Marginal Note

This fellow &c] [T138MS:1] The Dialogue between Theseus Lysander & Demetrius very pert and improper. Shakespeare [T139MS] understand Nature perfectly but the Manners of gentlemen He had never seen.

V. i. 408–29

[T 148] The SONG.

Now, until the break of day
Through this house each Fairy *stray.*

. . . . .

Trip away, make no stay;
Meet me all by break of day

Marginal Note

Now, until the break of day, &c.] [T148MS:1] The Song appears to be lost[.] The Text seems to be here given by way of song.

Two Gentleman of Verona

Introductory Comment

Marginal Note

[T154MS:1] Not written by Shakespeare. Clearly. It wo^d be curious to learn who was the [T154MS] writer of a Play in its Quality very Estimable. Perhaps the writer was at the Time unknown. It appears [T155MS] to be a Novel dramatized with very considerable ability.

APPENDIX

MORGANN'S TREATMENT OF
THEOBALD'S NOTES ON THE TEMPEST

IN his 1733 edition of Shakespeare, Theobald printed thirty-five notes on *The Tempest*. Of these, Morgann adopted ten in whole or in part, rejected eleven (four for reasons which are not clear), and let fourteen stand uncancelled and without comment. In the following list the latter are summarized. For the notes Morgann adopted or rejected, see *Com.* and notes. Four notes in Theobald's edition which were written by Warburton are marked 'W' in the list below.

1.	I. i. 24–5	Morgann rejects (reason unclear).
2.	I. ii. 19	Theobald justifies his restoring of Folio 'more better' in Prospero's speech, and protests against Pope's removing the double comparative.
3.	I. ii. 20	Theobald justifies the hyphen he introduces in 'full-poor'; without it, he claims, 'Nonsense' results.
4.	I. ii. 28	Theobald justifies his restoring First Folio 'provision' to replace the later Folios' dittographic 'compassion', repeated from I. ii. 27.
5.	I. ii. 29	Morgann rejects.
6.	I. ii. 41	Theobald justifies the 'old Reading', 'Out three years old', as obsolete for 'out-right'.
7.	I. ii. 118	Morgann adopts.
8.	I. ii. 120	Morgann adopts.
9.	I. ii. 229	Morgann rejects.
10.	I. ii. 351	Morgann adopts.
11.	I. ii. 437–8	Morgann rejects.
12.	II. i. 9–107	Morgann rejects.
13.	II. i. 184	Theobald explains that he restores the S. D., '*Enter Ariel playing solemn Musick*', 'from the old *Folio's*' because it is necessary to account 'for *Gonzalo, Alonzo,* &c. so suddenly dropping asleep'. (Cf. *Com.* II. i. 297.)
14.	II. i. 221	Morgann rejects (reason unclear).
15.	II. i. 250	Morgann adopts (unwillingly).
16.	II. ii. 22	Morgann adopts.
17.	II. ii. 94	Theobald notes a probable echo in *Hudibras* of Stephano's reference to the monster's 'forward voice' and 'backward voice'.
18. W	II. ii. 149	Morgann adopts.

19.	II. ii. 176	Morgann adopts (in part).
20.	III. i. 15	Theobald justifies his emendation of the reading in the 'two first *Folio*'s', 'Most busy least', to 'Most busie-less' and scouts Pope's reading, 'Least busie'.
21.	III. ii. 3	Morgann adopts (in part).
22.	III. iii. 48	Morgann rejects.
23.	III. iii. 56	Morgann rejects (reason unclear).
24.	IV. i. 3	Morgann adopts.
25.	IV. i. 110	Theobald justifies his assigning the passage beginning 'Earth's increase' to Ceres, though all earlier editions give it to Juno.
26.	IV. i. 121	Theobald justifies Folio 'from their confines' and rejects later editors' 'from all their confines' with 'all' supplied on the erroneous assumption that Shakespeare accented 'confines' on the first syallable.
27. W	IV. i. 139–63	Morgann rejects.
28.	V. i. 24	Theobald complains that Pope mistakenly changes Folio 'Passion' to 'Passion'd' in both his editions.
29.	V. i. 48	Morgann rejects (reason unclear).
30.	V. i. 74	Theobald claims his emendation 'Thou'rt pinch'd for't now, *Sebastian*, flesh and blood' gives Shakespeare's meaning more truly than Folio '. . . now, *Sebastian*. Flesh and blood . . .'.
31.	V. i. 88	Theobald justifies his reading 'Where the bee sucks, there lurk I', instead of Folio 'suck I', on the grounds that ethereal Ariel would not want food and 'the sequent Lines rather countenance *lurk*'. (See *Com.* V. i. 88.)
32.	V. i. 92	Theobald justifies his reading 'On the bat's back I do fly / After Sunset merrily', instead of 'After Summer merrily' on the grounds that bats, which fly after sunset, are merry during the summer, not after it, and it is unlikely that Shakespeare was alluding to 'that mistaken Notion of Bats . . . crossing the Seas in pursuit of hot Weather'.
33.	V. i. 236	Morgann rejects (hesitantly).
34. W	V. i. 280	Morgann adopts.
35. W	Epilogue, l. 15	Theobald notes that the speaker, Prospero, is not only 'applying to the Audience for Favour' but, as magician, alluding 'to the old Stories told of the *Necromancers*' Despair in their last Moments, and the Prayers of their Friends for them'. (Cf. *Com.* IV. i. 139–63.)

NOTES

2. *Editions of Shakespeare and Other Works*

(Unless otherwise specified, the place of publication is London and the date of publication is that of the short title.—In the Notes, unless otherwise specified, the reference is to the page in the work cited which contains the Shakespearian passage under discussion or the comment affixed to the passage.)

Abbott 1870 — Edwin A. Abbott, *A Shakespearian Grammar*. 3rd edn.

Alexander 1951 — Peter Alexander (ed.), *William Shakespeare, The Complete Works*. London and Glasgow.

Babcock 1931 — Robert Witheck Babcock, *Genesis of Shakespeare Idolatry, 1766–1799*. Chapel Hill.

Boorman 1957 — Stanley C. Boorman (ed.), *Shakespeare, The Tempest*.

Bushnell 1932 — N. S. Bushnell, 'Natural Supernaturalism in *The Tempest*', *PMLA* xlvii. 685–98.

Campbell 1838 — Thomas Campbell (ed.), *The Dramatic Works of William Shakespeare*.

Capell 1767 — Edward Capell (ed.), *Mr. William Shakespeare his Comedies, Histories, and Tragedies*. 10 vols., 1767–8.

Capell 1774 — Edward Capell, *Notes and Various Readings to Shakespeare*. Vol. i.

Capell 1783	Vol. ii, Part 4 of the completed edition of Capell 1774 in 3 vols., ed. John Collins. (Printed 1774–80, published 1783.)
Cellini 1964	Benvenuto Cellini (ed.), *William Shakespeare The Tempest*. Biblioteca Italiana di Testi Inglesi, ix. Bari.
Chambers 1925	E. K. Chambers, 'The Integrity of *The Tempest*', *RES* i. 129–50. (Reprinted in Chambers, *Shakespearian Gleanings* [Oxford, 1944], pp. 76–97.)
Chambers 1930	E. K. Chambers, *William Shakespeare*. 2 vols. Oxford.
Clark and Glover 1863	William George Clark and John Glover (eds.), *The Works of William Shakespeare*. 9 vols., Cambridge and London, 1863–66. (Vols. ii–ix, ed. Clark and W. A. Wright.) (The Cambridge Shakespeare.)
Coleridge ed. Raysor	*Coleridge's Shakespearean Criticism*, ed. Thomas Middleton Raysor. 2 vols., 1930.
Coleridge Miscellaneous ed. Raysor	*Coleridge's Miscellaneous Criticism*, ed. Thomas Middleton Raysor. Cambridge, Mass., 1936.
Cowl 1914	R. P. Cowl and A. E. Morgan (eds.), *William Shakespeare The First Part of King Henry the Fourth*. (Arden Edition.)
Conway 1921	R. S. Conway, *New Studies of a Great Inheritance*.
Craig 1951	Hardin Craig (ed.), *The Complete Works of Shakespeare*. Chicago.
Curry 1935	Walter Clyde Curry, 'Sacerdotal science in Shakespeare's "The tempest" ', *Archiv fuer das Stadium der Neueren Sprachen*, clxviii. 25–36 and 185–96. (Reprinted in Curry, *Shakespeare's Philosophical Patterns*, 2nd edn. [Baton Rouge, 1959], pp. 163–99.)
Dryden 1670	John Dryden and William Davenant, *The Tempest or the Enchanted Island* (adaptation of Tp.).
Dryden ed. Watson	*John Dryden, Of Dramatic Poesy* [=complete critical writings], ed. George Watson. 2 vols., 1962.
Dyce 1853	Alexander Dyce, *A Few Notes on Shakespeare*.
Dyce 1857	Alexander Dyce, *The Works of William Shakespeare*. 6 vols.
Edwards 1750	Thomas Edwards, *Canons of Criticism*. 3rd edn.
Farmer 1767	Richard Farmer, *Essay on the Learning of Shakespeare*.
Farmer 1773	Richard Farmer, 'Letter . . . to Mr. Steevens', in Johns. 1773, x, Appendix II, Oo2^v–Qq6^v.
F1	Mr. William Shakespeare *Comedies, Histories, & Tragedies*, 1623. (First Folio.)
F2	Second edition of F1, 1632. (Second Folio.)
F3	Third edition of F1, 1663; reissued, 1664. (Third Folio.)

F4	Fourth edition of F1, 1685. (Fourth Folio.)
Fleay 1876	Frederick Gard Fleay, *Shakespeare Manual.*
Fleay 1877	Frederick Gard Fleay, *Introduction to Shakespearian Study.*
Fleay 1886	Frederick Gard Fleay, *A Chronicle History of the Life and Work of William Shakespeare.*
Frye 1959	Northrop Frye (ed.), *The Tempest* (1959), as included in *William Shakespeare, The Complete Works*, ed. Alfred Harbage (1969), pp. 1369–95. (The Pelican Text.)
Furness 1892	Horace Howard Furness (ed.), *The Tempest.* New Variorum Edition of Shakespeare, vol. ix. Philadelphia.
Garrett 1937	George Garrett, 'That Four-Flusher Prospero', *Shakespeare Survey*, Survey Series, No. 2, pp. 37–62.
Gifford 1813	William Gifford, MS. notes on *The Tempest* in an interleaved copy of vol. iv, *Plays of William Shakespeare* (1813), pp. 1–174, in British Museum (C. 45. f. 13).
Gildon 1710	Charles Gildon, 'Critical Remarks on Shakespeare's Plays', in Rowe 1709, vii (1710).
Globe 1864	William George Clark and William Aldis Wright (eds.), *The Works of William Shakespeare.* Cambridge and London. (The Globe Edition.)
Gray 1920	Henry David Gray, 'The Source of *The Tempest*', *MLN*, xxxv. 321–30.
Gray 1921	Henry David Gray, 'Some Indications that "The Tempest" was Revised', *SP* xviii. 129–40.
Greg 1955	W. W. Greg, *The Shakespeare First Folio.* Oxford.
Halliwell 1851	James Orchard Halliwell (ed.), *The Complete Works of Shakspere.* 3 vols., London and New York.
Halliwell 1853	James Orchard Halliwell (ed.), *The Works of William Shakespeare.* 16 vols., 1853–65.
Halliwell 1868	James Orchard Halliwell, *Selected Notes Upon Shakespeare's Comedy of the Tempest.*
Hanmer 1744	Thomas Hanmer (ed.), *The Works of Shakespear.* 6 vols., Oxford.
Hanmer 1770	Final edition of Hanmer 1744. 6 vols., Oxford, 1770–1.
Hazlitt ed. Howe	William Hazlitt, *Complete Works*, ed. P. P. Howe. 21 vols., 1931.
Heath 1765	Benjamin Heath, *A Revisal of Shakespear's Text.*
Hemingway 1936	Samuel B. Hemingway (ed.), *Henry the Fourth, Part I.* New Variorum Edition of Shakespeare. Philadelphia.
Holt 1749	John Holt, *An Attempte to Rescue . . . Maister Williaume Shakespere.*

Horne 1955	David Hamilton Horne (ed.), *The Tempest*. Rev. edn., New Haven, Conn.
Howarth 1936	R. G. Howarth, *Shakespeare's Tempest*. Sydney.
Howarth 1947	Second edition of Howarth 1936. Sydney.
Howe 1805	John Howe, Lord Chedworth, *Notes upon Some of the Obscure Passages in Shakespeare's Plays*.
Hunter 1857	Joseph Hunter, MS. of 'The Tempest, or Love-Labours Won: A Comedy by Mr. William Shakespeare. With Annotations and a Revision of the Text', in British Museum (Additional MSS. 24, 498).
Hurd 1757	Richard Hurd (ed.), *Q. Horatii, Epistolae ad Pisones et Augustum*, 3rd edn., 2 vols., Cambridge.
Johns. 1765[1]	Samuel Johnson (ed.), *The Plays of William Shakespeare*. 8 vols.
Johns. 1773	Samuel Johnson and George Steevens (eds.), *The Plays of William Shakespeare*. 10 vols.
Johns. 1778	Second edition of Johns. 1773. 10 vols.
Johns. Sup. 1780	Edmund Malone, *Supplement* to Johns. 1778. 2 vols.
Johns. Ap. 1783	Edmond Malone, *A Second Appendix to Mr. Malone's Supplement* to Johns. 1778.
Johns. 1785	Third edition of Johns. 1773, ed. Isaac Reed. 10 vols.
Johns. 1793	Fourth edition of Johns. 1773, ed. George Steevens. 15 vols.
Jones 1913	Frank Jones (ed.), *The Tempest*.
Jourdain 1610	Sylvester Jourdain, *Discovery of the Barmudas*.
Kenrick 1765	William Kenrick, *A Review of Doctor Johnson's New Edition of Shakespeare*.
Kermode 1954	Frank Kermode (ed.), *The Tempest*. ([New] Arden Edition.)
Kermode 1958	Revised edition of Kermode 1954.
Kittredge 1936	George Lyman Kittredge (ed.), *The Complete Works of Shakespeare*. Boston.
Kittredge 1939	George Lyman Kittredge (ed.), *The Tempest*. Boston.
Knight 1841	Charles Knight (ed.), *The Pictorial Edition of the Works of Shakspere*. 8 vols., 1839–42.
Langbaum 1964	Robert Langbaum (ed.), William Shakespeare, *The Tempest*. New York and London. (The Signet Classic Shakespeare.)

[1] Johns. 1765–93 = appears in all editions of Johns. from 1765 up to and including 1793.

Johns. 1765, viii, Appendix–1785, initial note = appears first in the Appendix in vol. viii of Johns. 1765 and thereafter in the initial note to the play concerned in all subsequent editions of Johns. up to and including Johns. 1785.

Johns. 1773, x, Appendix–1793 = appears first in the Appendix in vol. x of Johns. 1773 and thereafter in the notes to the line(s) of the play under discussion in all subsequent editions of Johns. up to and including Johns. 1793.

Law 1921 — Ernest Law, *Shakespeare's 'Tempest' as Originally Produced at Court*. Shakespeare Association Papers, No. 5.

Lawrence 1920 — W. J. Lawrence, 'The Masque in the Tempest', *Fortnightly Review* [o.s.], cxiii (June 1920), 941–6.

Lee 1907 — Sidney Lee (ed.), *The Complete Works of William Shakespeare*. 40 vols., 1906–9. (The Renaissance Edition.)

Lowell 1868 — James Russell Lowell, 'Shakespeare Once More' (1868), in *Among My Books*. Boston, 1870.

Luce 1901 — Morton Luce (ed.), Shakespeare, *The Tempest*. (Arden Edition.)

Malone 1790 — Edmond Malone (ed.), *The Plays and Poems of William Shakspeare*. 10 vols.

Malone MS. — MS. note by Malone in his copy of Morgann's *Essay*, now in the Bodleian (Malone 140).

Mason 1798 — J. Monck Mason, *Comments on the Plays of Beaumont and Fletcher*.

Meurer 1928 — R. Meurer (ed.), William Shakespeare, *The Tempest*. The Hague.

Morris 1744 — Corbyn Morris, *An Essay Towards Fixing the True Standards of Wit, Humour, Raillery, Satire, and Ridicule*.

Munro 1946 — John Munro, 'Shakespeare's "The Tempest" ', *The New English Review*, xii. 61–9.

Munro 1958 — John Munro (ed.), *The London Shakespeare*. 6 vols.

Neilson 1906 — William Allan Neilson (ed.), *The Complete . . . Works of William Shakespeare*. Boston. (The Cambridge Edition.)

Neilson and Hill 1942 — William Allen Neilson and Charles Jarvis Hill (eds.), *The Complete Plays and Poems of William Shakespeare*. Boston. (The New Cambridge Edition.)

Nichols 1817 — Vol. ii of John Nichols (ed.), *Illustrations of the Literary History of the Eighteenth Century*. 9 vols., 1817–54.

Nicholson 1886 — B. Nicholson, ' "The Tempest" Shakespeare's Last Drama', *N & Q*, 7th Ser., i. 151 and 250.

Pope 1725 — Alexander Pope (ed.), *The Works of Shakespear*. 7 vols., 1723–5.

Pope 1728 — Corrected edition of Pope 1723. 10 vols.

Pye 1792 — Henry James Pye, *A Commentary Illustrating the Poetic of Aristotle*.

Q1, Q2, etc. — First Quarto, Second Quarto, etc.

Rann 1786 — Joseph Rann (ed.), *The Dramatic Works of Shakspeare*. 6 vols., Oxford, 1786–91 and (vols. v and vi) no date.

Ritson 1783 — Joseph Ritson, *Remarks, Critical and Illustrative, on . . . the Last Edition of Shakespeare*.

Robertson 1917 J. M. Robertson, *Shakespeare and Chapman.*

Rowe 1709 Nicholas Rowe (ed.), *The Works of Mr. William Shakespear.* 7 vols. (vol. vii appeared in 1710: see Gildon 1710.)

Rowe 1714 Revised edition of Rowe 1709. 9 vols.

Rowe 'Account' 1709 Nicholas Rowe, 'Some Account of the Life &c. of Mr. William Shakespear', in Rowe 1709, vol. i.

S.A.B. *The Shakspere Allusion-Book*, reissued with Preface by E. K. Chambers. 2 vols., Oxford, 1932.

Sill 1797 'Chas. Dirrill' [=Richard Sill], *Remarks on Shakespeare's Tempest.* Cambridge.

Sill 1797 MS. Interleaved copy of Sill 1797 with Sill's annotations, Cambridge University Library (Adv. d. 69. 1).

Singer 1826 Samuel Weller Singer (ed.), William Shakespeare, *Dramatic Works.* 10 vols.

Singer 1853 Samuel Weller Singer, *The Text of Shakespeare Vindicated.*

Singer 1856 Second edition of Singer 1826. 10 vols.

Sisson 1954 Charles Jasper Sisson (ed.), William Shakespeare, *The Complete Works.*

Sisson 1956 Charles Jasper Sisson, *New Readings in Shakespeare.* 2 vols., Cambridge.

Sisson 1958 Charles Jasper Sisson, 'The Magic of Prospero', *Shakespeare Survey*, No. 11, 70–7.

Smith 1903 David Nichol Smith (ed.), *Eighteenth Century Essays on Shakespeare.* Glasgow.

Smith 1916 David Nichol Smith (ed.), *Shakespeare Criticism: A Selection.* Oxford.

Smith 1941 Thomas Warnock Smith (ed.), *Shakespeare: The Tempest.*

Smith 1963 Second edition of Smith 1903. Oxford.

Sprague 1944 Arthur Colby Sprague, *Shakespeare and the Actors.* Cambridge, Mass.

Stack 1789 Richard Stack, 'An Examination of the Essay on the Dramatic Character of Sir John Falstaff', *Transactions of the Royal Irish Academy* [vol. ii] *mdcclxxxviii* (Dublin, [1789]), 'Polite Literature', pp. 3–37.

Staunton 1860 Howard Staunton (ed.), *The Plays of Shakespeare.* 3 vols., 1858–60.

Staunton 1872 Howard Staunton, 'Unsuspected Corruptions of Shakespeare's Text', *Athenaeum*, No. 2351 (16 Nov. 1872), pp. 635–6.

Strachey 1610 'A true reportory of the wracke', 16 July 1610, in *Purchas his Pilgrimes*, ed. Glasgow (1906), xix. 5–72.

Sutherland 1939 J. R. Sutherland (ed.), *The Tempest.* (The New Clarendon Shakespeare.) Oxford.

Theobald 1733	Lewis Theobald (ed.), *The Works of Shakespeare.* 7 vols.
Theobald 1740	Second edition of Theobald 1733. 8 vols.
Theobald 1773	Late edition of Theobald 1733. 8 vols.
Thompson 1928	Edward Thompson (ed.), William Shakespeare, *The Tempest.*
Tillyard 1938	E. M. W. Tillyard, *Shakespeare's Last Plays.*
Upton 1746	John Upton, *Critical Observations on Shakespeare.*
Upton 1748	Second edition of Upton 1746.
Verplanck 1847	Gulian C. Verplanck (ed.), *Shakespeare's Plays.* 3 vols., New York.
Warburton 1734	William Warburton, 'Fifty Emendations', 2 June 1734, in Nichols 1817, pp. 635–44.
Warburton 1747	William Warburton (ed.), *The Works of Shakespear.* 8 vols.
Ward 1962	A. C. Ward (ed.), William Shakespeare, *The Tempest.*
Whalley 1748	Peter Whalley, *An Enquiry into the Learning of Shakespeare.*
Wilson 1921	Arthur Quiller-Couch and J. Dover Wilson (eds.), *The Tempest.* Cambridge. (The Cambridge New Shakespeare.)
Wilson 1923	Richard Wilson (ed.), *Shakespeare's Comedy of The Tempest.*
Wilson 1936	J. Dover Wilson, *The Meaning of The Tempest.* Newcastle upon Tyne.
Winny 1963	James Winny (ed.), William Shakespeare, *The Tempest.*
Wright 1874	William Aldis Wright (ed.), Shakespeare, *The Tempest.* Oxford. (Clarendon Press Series.)
Wright 1891	William Aldis Wright (ed.). Revised edition of Clark and Glover 1863. 9 vols., 1891–3.

AN ESSAY ON FALSTAFF AND THE SHORTER REVISIONS

PT1–PT8. *PREFACE.* In the revised edition Morgann could hardly have reproduced the entire Preface in its original form. He might have retained his opening account of the genesis of the essay, PT1:1–PT3:2, perhaps adding the further details supplied in LR 2, 143–144 (cf. Intro., p. 37). He might also have kept his comment on the cheerful tone he wished to preserve in PT5:2–3 and his concluding observations on the size and nature of the book in PT7:3–PT8:1. But he obviously would have had to change his time references—'three years ago' in PT1:1 and 'of late' in PT3:2—and to withdraw the apologies in PT3:3–PT4:1, PT6:1–2, and PT7:1–2 for defects in the first edition which he would have corrected or no longer faulted in the second: inconsistent characterization of Falstaff, over-solemnity in some passages, excessive levity in others (see Intro., p. 41). He might also have gone beyond the early stylistic corrections of SR 1a and b to reconsider the morning excursion analogy, PT4:2–PT5:1, in the light of the 'pleasures of the Chase' figure in LR 3c (see Intro., p. 47). Finally, it seems likely that in the revised Preface he would have said something about his reasons for bringing out a new edition, taken notice of the public reaction to the first edition (see LR 3c and LR 3—ED 5), and perhaps commented on the changes he had introduced.

T1. *unengaged.* Probably 'not committed to a special view or opinion, unprejudiced' (*OED*, sense 3) rather than 'idle and unemployed', as suggested by J. I. M. Stewart, *Character and Motive in Shakespeare* (1949), p. 116. Morgann does, to be sure, associate the *Essay* with the 'amusement' of a 'leisure hour' on T113, but see the discussion of his literary rationale, Critical Intro., I. iii.

T2. *I know how universally the contrary opinion prevails.* See Intro., p. 12 and n. The following had said or implied that Falstaff was a coward: Richard James, *The Legend . . . of . . . Sir Jhon Oldcastle* (*c.* 1625), in S.A.B. i. 330. Peter Heylin, *The Historie of . . . St. George of Cappadocia* (1631), S.A.B. i. 355. George Daniel of Beswick, *Trinachordia* (1647), in S.A.B. i. 507. Thomas Fuller, *Church History* (1655), bk. IV, xv cent., 168 and *The Worthies of England* (1662), ii. 253. John Dryden, 'Of Dramatic Poesy' (1668), Preface to *An Evening's Love* (1671), and 'The Grounds of Criticism in Tragedy' (1679), in Dryden ed. Watson, i. 71, 150, and 250. William Winstanley, *England's Worthies* (1684), in S.A.B. ii. 306 (copies Fuller's *Worthies*). John Oldmixon, Epilogue to *Measure for Measure* (1700), in S.A.B. ii. 432. Rowe 'Account' 1709, in Smith 1963, p. 10. Gildon 1710, p. 290 (quotes 'Of Dramatic Poesy'). Alexander Smith, *Compleat History of the Lives and Robberies*, 5th edn. (1719), i. 1. William Oldys, in Thomas Birch (ed.), *General Dictionary*, v (1737), in S.A.B. i. 519 (quotes George Daniel). Morris 1744, pp. 25–6. Upton 1746, p. 85. Lewis Theobald (ed.), *A King and No King*, note 1, in *The Works of Beaumont and Fletcher* (1750). Arthur Murphy, *Gray's Inn Journal*, No. 38 (1753), ed. 1756, p. 212, and 'The Theatre', *London Chronicle*, 25–7 January, 1757, p. 96. Johns. 1765, final note to 2H4. Elizabeth Montagu (1769), see note to *Es.*, T111. William Kenrick (1774), see Intro., p. 15 n. Giuseppe Baretti, *Discours sur Shakespeare et sur Monsieur de Voltaire* (London and Paris, 1777), p. 71.

T5. *I distinguish between mental Impressions, and the Understanding.* Cf. David Hume, *A Treatise of Human Nature* (1738), bk. I, pt. i, sec. 1: 'All the perceptions of the human mind resolve themselves into two distinct kinds, which I shall call *impressions* and *ideas.* . . . Those perceptions which enter with most force and violence, we may name *impressions*; and, under this name, I comprehend all our sensations, passions, and emotions, as they make their first appearance in the soul. By *ideas*, I mean the faint images of these in thinking and reasoning . . . I believe it will not be very necessary to employ many words in explaining this distinction. Everyone of himself will readily perceive the difference betwixt feeling and thinking.' Here, as in LR 1a, Morgann adapts this distinction to his purposes.

T7. *not from any idea of abstract good or evil.* Cf. *Es.,* T157.

T9. *ill killed.* Wiv. I. i. 84.
Candide. Chaps. ix and xv.

T16. *different modifications of Shakespeare's thought.* See Intro., p. 34, and cf. Coleridge:
(1) 'Shakespeare's mode of conceiving characters out of his own intellectual and moral faculties, by conceiving any one intellectual or moral faculty in morbid excess and then placing himself, thus mutilated and diseased, under given circumstances'.—Coleridge ed. Raysor, i. 37; cf. ii. 117.
(2) 'Shakespeare shaped his characters out of the nature within, but we cannot so safely say, out of *his own* nature, as an *individual person.* No! this latter is itself but a *natura naturata,* an effect, a product, not a *power.* It was Shakespeare's prerogative to have the *universal* which is potentially in each *particular,* opened out to him in the *homo generalis,* not as an abstraction of observation from a variety of men, but as the substance capable of endless modifications, of which his own personal existence was but one, and to use *this one* as the eye that beheld the other, and as the tongue that could convey the discovery. [There is] no greater or more common vice in dramatic writers than to draw out of themselves.'— Coleridge Miscellaneous ed. Raysor, pp. 43-4.
Cf. also Coleridge as cited in Intro., p. 105, and in notes to *Es.,* T59n and T61n.
general criticism is as uninstructive as it is easy. Smith 1963, p. 331, glosses as follows: 'Cf. Joseph Warton, *Adventurer,* No. 116 [15 Dec. 1753]: "General criticism is on all subjects useless and unentertaining; but it is more than commonly absurd with respect to Shakespeare, who must be accompanied step by step, and scene by scene, in his gradual development of characters and passions", &c.'
a task hitherto unattempted. The Miltonic-Ariostoan boast (*Par. Lost,* i. 16) is not fully justified. Morgann had been preceded in some measure by Joseph Warton's five essays in the *Adventurer* (1753-4) on *The Tempest* and *King Lear* (Nos. 93, 97, 113, 116, and 122, excerpted in Smith 1916, pp. 52-69). More recently, extended and detailed criticism of Shakespeare had been written by William Richardson, *A Philosophical Analysis and Illustration of Some of Shakespeare's Remarkable Characters* (1774) and Thomas Whately, *Remarks on Some of the Characters of Shakespeare* (1770). But Whately's comparison of Richard II and Macbeth was not published till 1785 and Richardson's book seems not to have appeared until after Morgann set down his proud claim in early 1774 (see Intro., p. 38).

T19. *ease.* 'In bad sense, idleness, sloth'—*OED,* sense 4. Cf. *Par. Lost,* ii. 227.

T20. *a humourist and a man of humour.* Cf. note to *Es.,* T16.3

T23. *and not an Eagle's talon.* 1H4 II. iv. 363.
the last war. The Seven Years War.

T25. *Caliban . . . Tortoise.* Cf. *Com.* I. ii. 316.
calipashed. By this nonce-verb Morgann means 'made into calipash', i.e. the edible gelatinous substance next to the tortoise's upper shell.

T26. *It was time to counterfeit.* 1H4 V. iv. 113.
chopfallen. With allusion to the context of Ham. V. i. 212.

T29. *Ruffian in years.* 1H4 II. iv. 500: 'that father ruffian, that vanity in years.'
in proof Impression only. An evident misprint, plausibly emended in the 1820 edition of the *Essay* and in Smith 1963 to 'in proof of *impression* only'. SR 27 confirms both the emendation and Morgann's decision in revisal to eliminate the phrase entirely: see next note.
SR 4. Morgann drew a vertical line down through T29:4, the sentence containing the phrase discussed in the preceding note. He did so, it appears, in order to eliminate his use of the term *impression* to refer to a belief held by a character: see Intro., p. 83. For other attempts in the revisions to restrict the term to the sense of 'lively and central feeling' aroused in the audience, a key concept in his theory, see SR 12, SR 24a, and LR2–ED2, *app. crit.* to I10:2.
to arrest Falstaff. 2H4 II. i.

T30. *The officers cry.* 2H4 II. i. 61 (Fang alone cries out, not both officers).
another scene. 2H4 II. iv. 251–3.
A Rascal bragging slave, etc. 2H4 II. iv. 247–8.
SR 5a. The insertion point of SR 5a is further indicated by the first line of I30:1 being on a level with the line of T30:1 containing '—*Alas*'. The word 'and' may be intended to supersede rather than to precede 'Accordingly' in T30:3.
By eliminating the passages he had too hastily and too innocently quoted from 2H4, Morgann seems to be taking into account the objection in Stack 1789, p. 16, that if they conveyed anything more than 'indecent allusion', they would prove not Falstaff's courage but his lack of scruple at shedding blood and attacking a woman. Morgann presumably deletes the passage in question because, accepting Stack's view that they are autotelic bawdy, he now regards them as irrelevant to his argument. See also SR 5b and 6 and next two notes.
SR 5b. The materials revised by SR 5b are indicated by (1) the contents of the SR, (2) the fact that the SR is written on I30 opposite T30:3, and (3) the obvious overlap of 'B.', the conclusion of the SR, with the '*B*' of *Bardolph* in T30:3. On this evidence, Morgann may have intended SR 5b to supersede not just 'and calls upon *B*' but the eight preceding words as well.
Morgann seems to place Falstaff's appeal to Bardolph, 'Away, varlets', etc., 2H4 II. i. 50–2, after the Hostess's speech, ll. 53–9. In the play, Falstaff's reply to the latter, l. 60, is 'Keep them off, Bardolph'. The error does not, however, affect the argument.
The notation, 'Wilt thou &c', leaves unclear how much of the Hostess's speech Morgann intended to reproduce. The entire speech reads: 'Wilt thou?

wilt thou? thou bastardly rogue! Murder, murder! Ah, thou honey-suckle villain! Wilt thou kill God's officers and the King's? Ah, thou honey-seed rogue! thou art a honey-seed, a man-queller and a woman-queller.' In all probability he would have excluded at least the last two epithets, in order to avoid the kind of indecency which he had eliminated by means of SR 5a.

The new point he makes in SR 5b seems calculated to meet the further objection in Stack 1789, p. 16 (see prec. note), that in calling on Bardolph to draw, Falstaff reveals not his own fighting spirit but rather a lack of sufficient resource to act himself.

SR 6. The materials revised by SR 6 are further indicated by (1) the contents of the SR, and (2) the fact that the SR is written on I30 opposite T30:8.

As in SR 5a and 5b he again appears to have Stack in mind. Stack 1789, p. 17, finds Morgann guilty of 'refinement' in taking Falstaff's account of how he routed Pistol as showing he 'did not value himself on the adventure'. On the contrary, Stack claims, Falstaff's words are an attempt 'to reflect lustre on his own prowess in representing Pistol as impressed with so great terror'. While not meeting this objection head-on, Morgann reinforces his original interpretation by putting Falstaff's speech in the context of the assumption attributed to Doll that fighting 'was much his Practise'.

T31. *man of war.* 2H4 V. i. 31.
remembers him . . . a crack thus high. 2H4 III. ii. 28–34.
SR 7a and 7b. Both SR are interlined on T31 with carets marking their respective points of insertion.

T32. *the Brawn Sir John Falstaff.* 2H4 I. i. 19: 'Harry Monmouth's brawn, the hulk Sir John.'

T33. *take a pride to gird at him.* 2H4 I. ii. 7.
Jack Falstaff with his Familiars, etc. 2H4 II. ii. 143–6.
Plump Jack, and Sir John Paunch. 1H4 II. iv. 527 and II. ii. 69.

T34. *I will procure this fat rogue, etc.* 1H4 II. iv. 596–7.
I will procure thee Jack, etc. 1H4 III. iii. 223–5: 'Jack, meet me tomorrow in the temple hall . . . / There shalt thou know thy charge . . .'

T35. *the evidence of the Chief Justice.* 2H4 I. ii. 62 ff.: 'Your day's service at Shrewsbury hath a little gilded over your night's exploit on Gad's-hill' (ll. 168–70).
his whole character. In the sense of his reputation in its entirety rather than in the more specialized sense he elsewhere gives to the phrase *whole character.*
Coleville of the dale. 2H4 IV. iii. 1–81.

T36. *dozens.* 2H4 II. iv. 387–9 (Peto) and 401–2 (Bardolph).

T37. *Men of merit are sought after,* etc. 2H4 II. iv. 405–7.
the whole passage. 2H4 I. ii. 227–49.

T39. *You may thank the unquiet time.* 2H4 I. ii. 170–1.
Well God be thanked for these Rebels. 1H4 III. iii. 213–15.

T40. *a friend at Court.* 2H4 V. i. 33–4.
Westmorland speaks to him. 1H4 IV. ii. 57–65.
in another place. 2H4 IV. iii. 88–9.
'Go,' says he to the page. 2H4 I. ii. 267–9.

T41. *a Prince indeed.* 1H4 V. ii. 61.
the Prince of Wales . . . Sir John Falstaff. 1H4 V. i, initial S. D.

T42. *If I do grow great,* etc. 1H4 V. iv. 167–9: 'I'll grow less, for I'll purge, and leave sack, and live cleanly as a nobleman should do.'

T45. *familiar with John of Gaunt.* 2H4 III. ii. 348–52.

T47–T51. *Falstaff, then . . . Gartered Craven.* According to Rowe Account 1709 (reprinted in prefatory materials of Johns. 1765–93) Shakespeare had originally called Falstaff Oldcastle, but when the latter's descendants protested, he changed the name to Falstaff, after the historic 'Sir *John Falstaff*' = Fastolphe. See Smith 1963, pp. 5 (Rowe's text) and 285 (Rowe's sources). Following Thomas Fuller, *Worthies of England* (1662), ii. 253, Rowe claims that Falstaff (= Fastolphe) 'was a Name of distinguish'd Merit in the Wars in *France* in *Henry* the Fifth's and *Henry* the Sixth's Times'; Morgann, however, both in his text and in his footnote to T48:2 attributes to him the cowardly character he bears in Shakespeare's 1H6. Cf. next two notes.

T48n. *I believe the stage,* etc. Morgann draws on the two layers of comment accumulated in Johns. 1773 as glosses to 1H4 I. ii. 47–8 ('As the honey of Hybla, my old lad of the castle'). The first, dating back to Johns. 1765, is the work of Theobald and Warburton. Following Pope (see Smith 1963, p. 285) they link the passage in 1H4 with the Epilogue to 2H4 ('Oldcastle died a martyr, and this [i.e. Falstaff] is not the man'), and so confirm the tradition reported by Rowe (see prec. note) that Falstaff had originally been called Oldcastle in Shakespeare's play. The second layer of comment, published for the first time in Johns. 1773, is by Farmer, who observes that the expression *old lad of the castle* means 'roaring boy' and therefore in itself provides 'no argument for Falstaff's appearing first under the name of Oldcastle'.
　　SR 9a. Written on the left-hand side of I48 on a level with the four lined-through words on T48 which it manifestly supersedes, SR 9a is Morgann's first attempt to bring his view up to date in the light of a third layer of comment (for the first two, see prec. note), which Steevens and Malone contributed to later editions of Johns. Steevens (Johns. 1778–93, note to 1H4 I. ii. 47–8 and preliminary note to H5) and Malone (Sup. 1780–Johns. 1793, note to 1H4 I. ii. 47–8) claim in addition that (1) the Epilogue to 2H4 refers exclusively to Shakespeare's source, *The Famous Victories of Henry the fifth*, and (2) although Falstaff probably derives from the Oldcastle of the old play, he never bore that

name in H4. (It seems unlikely that Morgann knew the similar argument presented by P. T., 'Observations on Shakespeare's Falstaff', *Gentleman's Magazine*, xxii (1750), 459–61.)

On the supersession and possible reinstatement of SR 9a see next note.

SR 9b. The repetition in SR 9b of phrases found in both sentences of the corresponding passage in *Es.* suggests that Morgann designed the revision to supersede the entire original footnote as emended by SR 9a. In this second and abortive attempt to align his views with the latest accretion of comment in Johns. (see prec. note), he proposed apparently to work out the implications of Farmer's observation for the position adopted by Steevens and Malone: the fragmentary last sentence of SR 9b was seemingly to be completed by Farmer's idea that *old lad of the castle* is a familiar appellation signifying 'roisterer'.

I48 contains materials for several revisions in the following order:

LR 2, par. 7, I48:1a (up to colon).
LR 2, par. 7, ED of I48:1b (not reproduced except for excerpt in *app. crit.*).
SR 9a.
SR 9b.
LR 2, par. 7, I48:1b–2.

Morgann cancelled SR 9b with a vertical line. At a later stage, he discarded the ED of I48:1b by drawing through it a line which he overlapped with the top of the line cancelling LR 9b. The line through the ED extends down the approximate centre of the page to the right of SR 9a. The fact that Morgann did not mark SR 9a as cancelled may mean that he proposed to reinstate the original footnote as corrected by SR 9a.

T49. *that Drum-and-trumpet Thing.* Admired for almost a century and a half as a capsule description of 1H6—e.g. by Charles Symmons, *Life of Shakespeare* (1826), p. 71, James Orchard Phillips, *On the Character of Sir John Falstaff* (1841), p. 13, and Harold C. Goddard, *The Meaning of Shakespeare* (Chicago, 1951), p. 28—this phrase has become part of the anonymous aura of critical opinion enveloping Shakespeare: cf. M. Bradbrook, *Shakespeare and Elizabethan Poetry* (1951), p. 125.

T51. *a Seal ring.* 1H4 III. iii. 94–8, 117–18, and 162–3.
bonds. 1H4 III. iii. 116–17.

T52. *the only one (as he says).* 2H4 II. ii. 144–5. (Falstaff does not say that John is the *only* name given him by his brothers and sisters.)

four, if not five, followers. Bardolph, Pistol, Peto, and the Page make four; Nym of H5 and Wiv. would make a fifth. *Es.*, T150–T151 describe Falstaff's 'state' as comprising Pistol, Bardolph, the Page, and Nym. Cf. note to LR 11a, T186MS.

invitations of Master Gower. 2H4 II. i. 194–5 and 201.
the Prince's question. 2H4 II. ii. 156–7.

T53. *the circumstances of the arrest.* 2H4 II. i.
'but seven groats', etc. 2H4 I. ii. 263–6.

T54. *a page to Thomas Mowbray.* 2H4 III. ii. 27–9.

He broke Schoggan's head. 2H4 III. ii. 32–4. Morgann is unique is supposing Schoggan, or Skogan, to be a fencer. He is usually taken to be a jester at the court of Edward IV.

backsword. 2H4 III. ii. 70.

scarcely an eagle's talon. 1H4 II. iv. 363–5.

T55. *foundering nine score and odd miles.* 2H4 IV. iii. 39–40: 'I have foundered nine score and odd posts', i.e. post-horses. Morgann gets it right on T86.

had he but a belly. 2H4 IV. iii. 22–4.

T56. *A pox of this gout,* etc. 2H4 I. ii. 272–6.

T59n. *some peculiar of its own.* Here 'peculiar'='a special or exclusive characteristic' (*OED*, sense 5), as also in Morgann's *Considerations on . . . France* (1795), p. 28.

The principal earlier pronouncements on the individuality of Shakespeare's characters, which Morgann could scarcely have ignored, were those of Pope and Johnson in the Prefaces to their respective editions (1725 and 1765; the Prefaces are reprinted in the prefatory materials of Johns. 1773–93) and in Smith 1963, pp. 44–58 and 104–50). According to Pope, who refines on Gildon 1710, p. li, 'every single character in *Shakespear* is as much an Individual as those in Life itself; it is as impossible to find any two alike; and such as from their relation or affinity in any respect appear most to be Twins, will upon comparison be found remarkably distinct' (Smith 1963, p. 45). Johnson takes a different, more complex view. Shakespeare's characters, he finds, 'are not modified by the customs of particular places, unpractised by the rest of the world; by the peculiarities of studies or professions, which can operate but upon small numbers; or by the accidents of transient fashions or temporary opinions: they are the genuine progeny of common humanity, such as the world will always supply, and observation will always find. His persons act and speak by the influence of those general passions and principles by which all minds are agitated, and the whole system of life is continued in motion. In the writings of other poets a character is too often an individual; in those of *Shakespeare* it is commonly a species. . . . Characters thus ample and general were not easily discriminated and preserved, yet perhaps no poet ever kept his personages more distinct from each other.' (Smith 1963, pp. 106–8.)

Each of these views had its adherents in the eighteenth century. Whalley 1748, p. 21 and in the comment quoted below, note to *Es.*, T65, echoes Pope on the subject ; Upton 1748, p. 68, anticipates Johnson in expecting Shakespeare to apply the principle that ''tis the human creature in general should be drawn, not any one in particular'. In the early nineteenth century Hazlitt made Pope's opinion his own and repudiated Johnson's (Preface to *Characters of Shakespeare's Plays* (1817), in ed. Howe, iv. 171 and 175–6). Coleridge develops a subtler position in several scattered passages:

(1) 'The truth is, Shakspeare's characters are all *genera* intensely individualized; the results of meditation, of which observation supplied the drapery and the colours necessary to combine them with each other. He had virtually surveyed

all the great component powers and impulses of human nature,—had seen that their different combinations and subordinations were in fact the individualizers of men, and showed how their harmony was produced by reciprocal disproportions of excess or deficiency.' (Coleridge ed. Raysor, i. 137).

(2) 'I adopt with full faith the principle of Aristotle [*Poetics*, ix], that poetry as poetry is essentially *ideal*, that it avoids and excludes all *accident*; that its apparent individualities of rank, character, or occupation must be *representative* of a class; and that the *persons* of poetry must be clothed with *generic* attributes, with the *common* attributes of the class: not with such as one gifted individual might *possibly* possess, but such as from his situation it is most probable beforehand that he *would* possess. . . . Say not that I am recommending abstractions; for these class-characteristics which constitute the instructiveness of a character, are so modified and particularized in each person of the Shakespearean Drama, that life itself does not excite more distinctly that sense of individuality which belongs to real existence. Paradoxical as it may sound, one of the essential properties of Geometry is not less essential to dramatic excellence; and Aristotle has accordingly required of the poet an involution of the universal in the individual. The chief differences are, that in Geometry it is the universal truth, which is uppermost in the consciousness; in poetry the individual form, in which the truth is clothed.' (Chap. xvii, *Biographia Literaria*, ed. J. Shawcross (Oxford, 1907), ii. 33–4).

(3) 'It is Shakespeare's peculiar excellence, that throughout the whole of his splendid picture gallery (the reader will excuse the confessed inadequacy of this metaphor), we find individuality every where, mere portrait no where. In all his various characters, we still feel ourselves communing with the same human nature, which is everywhere present as the vegetable sap in the branches, sprays, leaves, buds, blossoms, and fruits, their shapes, tastes, and odours. Speaking of the effect, *i.e.* his works themselves, we may define the excellence of *their* method as consisting in that just proportion, that union and interpenetration of the universal and the particular, which must ever pervade all works of decided genius and true science.' (Sec. 2, Essay IV, *ad fin.*, *The Friend*, ed. Barbara E. Rooke [1969], i. 457).

T60n. *Be thus when thou art dead.* Oth. V. ii. 18–19.

T61. *Foreign writer.* Voltaire. On Voltaire's evolving view of Shakespeare as an inspired barbarian, with increasing emphasis upon the pejorative noun, see René Wellek, *History of Modern Criticism*, i (New Haven, 1955), 33–7, and the bibliography, i. 263–4.

T61n. *he must have felt every varied situation.* The idea was adumbrated by Margaret Cavendish, Duchess of Newcastle, Letter CXXIII, *CCXI. Sociable Letters* (1664), reprinted in Smith 1916, p. 14: 'so Well [Shakespeare] hath Expressed in his Playes all Sorts of Persons, as one would think he had been Transformed into every one of those Persons he hath Described. . . . Who would not think he had been such a man as his Sir *John Falstaff*?' Cf. also Coleridge in note to *Es.*, T16, and in *The Friend*, Sec. 2, Essay IV (ed. Rooke,

1. 454), where he applies Themistius' words to Shakespeare: 'He that moulded his own soul, as some incorporeal material, into various forms.' See Intro., p. 103.

T62n. *inferred only*, etc. Cf. Coleridge as cited in Intro., p. 105.

T63. *possessions of their own on Parnassus.* Rowe and Pope.
the ablest and best. For Morgann's generally high opinion of Warburton see Intro., p. 102.
Another. 'D! Johnson'—Malone MS. Cf. the similar view of Johnson in Hazlitt ed. Howe, iv. 175–6. Morgann extends his attack on Johnson in LR 5, PI4 and PI8, LR 6, I113 ff. and I106, LR 7, *Com.* I. ii. 15, 250, 304, 396 (see note), II. i. 9–107, III. ii. 71, and V. i. 174 (see note). See Intro., pp. 101–2.
a man take him for all in all. Ham. I. ii. 187.

T64. *some wretched productions.* See LR 5, comment on TG., p. 352, and notes.
The Latin sentences. Morgann could have come upon Warburton's observation that Shakespeare seldom if ever employs Latin phrases in Theobald 1733 i. xxxii. On this observation, omitted in Theobald 1740 and therefore also in the prefatory materials to Johns., see Smith 1963, p. 295. If Morgann already owned the vol. i of Theobald 1733 in the MS. book of *Com.*, he had at hand a copy of the first edition of Theobald's Preface.
a very conclusive one. 'This "very conclusive one" is a few lines being printed twice in the old copies of that play!!!!'—Malone MS.
the very last Editor. To solve the problem created by the tautology mentioned in the preceding note, Capell 1768, ii. 54–5, silently removed ll. 299–304 and 312–19 from Berowne's speech in LLL. IV. iii.

T65. *the Apalachian mountains*, etc. From Kenrick and his contemporaries (see Intro., p. 15), by way of Nathan Drake (see Intro., p. 24) and J. O. Phillips, *On the Character of Sir John Falstaff* (1841), p. 55, to Stephen Potter, *The Muse in Chains* (1937), p. 69, readers' hearts have leaped up at Morgann's glowing account of how the American mid-West would still resound with Shakespeare's accents when the French language shall be no more. Only T. R. Lounsbury, *Shakespeare and Voltaire* (New York, 1902), p. 405, seems to have winced at the jingo strain in the passage.
nothing perishable about him, except that very learning, etc. Annotating this passage, Smith 1963, p. 331, refers to Edward Young, *Conjectures on Origianl Composition* (1759), p. 81. Young wrote: 'who knows whether *Shakespeare* might mot have thought less, if he had read more? . . . possibly he might not have risen up into that giant . . . at which we now gaze with amazement and delight.' Smith further cites Hurd 1757, i. 213–14 (originally in first edition, 1749, p. 127): 'Our Shakespear was, I think, the first that broke through this bondage of classical superstition. And he owed this felicity, as he did some others, to his want of what is called the advantages of a learned education.' Cf. also LR 6a, I115, and Whalley 1748, p. 78: 'I believe . . . that not only the riches of *Shakespeare's* Genius prevented him from borrowing from the Ancients in many Instances, but that he was prevented as much from doing so by his Judgment likewise. For

marking every Character with Sentiments which cannot possibly be applied to any other, he was under the less Necessity of having recourse to any common-place Topics. . . .'

T69. *Macbeth.* Mac. I. v. 18, 49; V. v. 13; V. iii. 23. 'May of life' is Johnson's conjectural emendation of 'way of life': Johns. 1765, supported by Steevens in Johns. 1773–85.

Rymer. In *A Short View of Tragedy* (1693)—*The Critical Works of Thomas Rymer*, ed. Curt Zimansky (New Haven, 1956), pp. 132–64—Rymer invoked the authority of Aristotle in denouncing *Othello* as a 'Bloody Farce without salt or savour', which violated the unities and presented indecorous and hopelessly improbable characters. With Morgann's reaction cf. Dryden, 'Heads of an Answer to Rymer', ed. Watson, i. 218: '. . . Aristotle drew his models of tragedy from Sophocles and Euripides; and if he had seen ours, might have changed his mind.'

T70. *practicer of arts inhibited.* Oth. I. ii. 78–9.
O supreme of Dramatic excellence. M. W. England, 'Garrick's Stratford Jubilee: Reactions in France and Germany', *Shakespeare Survey*, ix (1956), 93, notes that Le Tourneur, *Shakespeare traduit de l'anglois*, i (Paris, 1776), xcvii–xcviii, also puts into Aristotle's mouth the praises he would have uttered had he seen Shakespeare's plays.

T71. *an effect from causes hidden or unknown.* Cf. *Com.* I. ii. 22.

T73n. *a local habitation and a name.* MND. V. i. 17. Morgann lined through the phrase and the two prec. words in SR 11 presumably because the tag would apply only to the 'local and temporary', not to the 'universal' images produced by passion.

T74n. *where it ought to shudder.* i.e. at the witches.
the magic of the Tempest is lasting and universal. Cf. *Com.* I. ii. 250.

T76n. *bubbles of the earth.* Mac. I. iii. 79.
coinage of the brain. Ham. III. iv. 137.

T77n. *Shakespeare's magic*, etc. Dryden 1670, Prologue, ll. 19–20.

T79. *Turk Gregory*, etc. 1H4 V. iii. 46.
Wou'd it were bed-time, etc. 1H4 V. i. 125.

T80. *cold blooded boy.* 2H4 IV. iii. 94: 'sober-blooded boy'.
scattered stray. 2H4 IV. ii. 120.
strokes of Infamy. Cf. Johns. 1765, note to 1H4 IV. ii. 123: 'It cannot but raise some indignation to find this horrible violation of faith passed over thus slightly by the poet, without any note of censure or detestation.' For a different view see Paul A. Jorgensen, 'The "Dastardly Treachery" of Prince John of Lancaster', *PMLA* lxxvi (1961), 488–92.

T81. *Now Falstaff*, etc. 2H4 IV. iii. 29–32: 'when everything is ended then you come.'

T82. *a cold reserved sober-blooded boy.* 2H4 IV. iii 94 (Falstaff employs only the last epithet: cf. note to *Es.*, T80).

T86. *I would be sorry*, etc. 2H4 IV. iii. 33–43.

T87. *How now, Sir John?* etc. 2H4 II. i. 71–3.
nothing more . . . than idleness and debauch. See H. J. Webb, 'Falstaff's "Tardy Tricks" ', *MLN* lviii (1943), 377–9, for evidence that Shakespeare intended to satirize Elizabethan absentee captains.

T88. *tarry dinner.* 2H4 III. ii. 204.
I will not use, etc. 2H4 III. ii. 308–11.
King's Press damnably. 1H4 IV. ii. 13.

T89. *that in the General's but a choleric word*, etc. Meas. II. ii. 130–1: 'That in the captain's,' etc.
a most furious Knight, etc. 2H4 IV. iii. 42–3.
Let us look to the fact. Morgann's contemporaries would apparently not have had the fact to look to in the threatre. Discussing episodes 'always suppressed' on the stage in 'Observations on the plays altered from Shakespeare', *St James's Chronicle* (March 1779), George Steevens reports: 'The Scene in which Colevile surrenders to Falstaff is likewise lost to the audience'. (Steevens is identified as the author by Malone, 'Shakespeariana', vol. i. [Bodleian, Malone 140], 2nd leaf after p. 346.)

T90. *as good a man*, etc. 2H4 IV. iii. 12 ff.
he might stand well, etc. 2H4 IV. iii. 89 ff

T91. *Anger has a privilege.* Lr. II. ii. 76.

T92. *By heaven thou hast deceived me.* 1H4 V. iv. 17–18.
at his holding Lord Percy , etc. 1H4 V. iv. 21–3.

T93. *thin potations*, etc. 2H4 IV. iii. 134–5.
Cadogan. Dr. William Cadogan (1711–97), Fellow of the College of Physicians, enjoyed a mild, temporary notoriety as a result of certain theses in his *Dissertation on the Gout and all Chronic Diseases* (1771). The half-dozen retorts to his treatise that appeared in 1771 and 1772, some of them in verse, paid special attention to his claim, which Morgann appears to have in mind, that the regular drinking of wine not only causes 'nine in ten of all the gouts in the world' (pp. 77–8) but generally undermines health by leaving 'a crapulary, crude and sour load of yesterday to ferment, fret and irritate the stomach and bowels every day' (p. 53).

T94. *Rag-o-muffians.* 1H4 V. iii. 36–8. So all eighteenth-century editions up to and including Johns. 1765; beginning with Capell 1767 and Hanmer 1770, the reading *ragamuffins* was adopted.

T95. *no questioning the fact.* Cowl 1914, note to 1H4 V. iii. 36, cites Elizabethan sources to show that cowardly, mercenary captains were notorious for *leading* their men into danger and abandoning them there. See also Paul A. Jorgensen, *Shakespeare's Military World* (Berkeley and Los Angeles, 1956), pp. 68–9.

T96. *that which would sack a city*, etc. 1H4 V. iii. 55–8.

T97. *Honour cannot set*, etc. 1H4 V. i. 132–41.
if Percy be alive, etc. 1H4 V. iii. 58–64.

T98. SR 12. The supersession of 'impressed' by 'imposed' is indicated by the latter's being written on the left side of I98 directly opposite 'impressed' on T98. (The redrafting of the second half of LR 9—see note to LR 9—flows around SR 12 on I98.) Morgann introduced the correction, it appears, in order to avoid using the term *impressed* for a dramatic effect upon the reason rather than the sensibility. Cf. SR 4 and 24a.

T102. *Spirit Percy . . . Fiend Douglas.* 1H4 II. iv. 404–5.
Well said Hal, etc. 1H4 V. iv. 75.

T103. *no counterfeit.* 1H4 V. iv. 116.

T104. *What old acquaintance!* etc. 1H4 V. iv. 102–10.

T105 and T106n. *miserable pun.* Cf. Johns. 1765, final note to Rom.: Shakespeare's 'pathetick strains are always polluted with some unexpected depravations. His persons, however distressed, have a *conceit left them in their misery a miserable conceit.*' (The italicized passage cites the allusion to Jonson's *Bartholomew Fair*, I. i, in 'The Preface to the Fables', Dryden ed. Watson, ii. 279.)

T105n. *The censure commonly passed on Shakespeare's puns.* The censure was well-nigh universal in the eighteenth century. So Johns. 1765, Preface, in Smith 1963, pp. 116–17: 'A quibble is to Shakespeare what luminous vapours are to the traveller; he follows it at all adventures, it is sure to lead him out of his way, and sure to engulf him in the mire. . . . A quibble was to him the fatal *Cleopatra* for which he lost the world, and was content to lose it.' Cf. A. C. Bradley, *Scottish Historical Review*, i (1904), 295: 'How excellent, how astonishingly different from Johnson's paragraph on quibbles . . . is Morgann's brief note on the same subject!' The defence of Shakespeare's puns is a recurrent motif in Coleridge: see Coleridge ed. Raysor, I. xxxiii–xxxiv, and II, Index, s.v. Puns.
For if the Jew do cut, etc. Mer. V. IV. i. 280–1.

T107. *What, says the Prince, a Coward*, etc. 1H4 II. ii. 69–71.

T109. *Souls made of fire and children of the sun.* Edward Young, *The Revenge*, V. ii.

T111. *just where youth ends,* etc. Cf. *Par. Lost*, xi. 245–6.

Old, cold, and of intolerable entrails, etc. Wiv. V. v. 161–4. This is the only passage in which Morgann clearly draws on Wiv. to characterize Falstaff. Cf. next note.

fat and greasy. The phrase occurs in AYL. II. i. 55. Falstaff is often called 'fat' in the three plays in which he figures; 'greasy' is applied to him in 1H4 II. iv. 252 and Wiv. II. i. 112.

cuts three inches in the ribs. 1H4 IV. ii. 80.

short-winded. 2H4 II. ii. 136.

He had the gout, etc. 2H4 I. ii. 272–4.

Mrs. Montague. In her frequently reprinted and widely known *Essay on the Writings and Genius of Shakespear* (1769), Mrs. Elizabeth Montagu recognized that 'a man must be ill-natured as well as dull, who does not join in the mirth of the jovial companion' (p. 107). But at the same time she called Hal's association with Falstaff a temporary 'stain upon his character' (p. 104) and referred to the knight himself as a person of 'cowardly and braggart temper' p. 103) and as a man given to 'gluttony, corpulence and cowardice' (p. 107).

T112. *the golden fool.* Tim. IV. iii. 18.

Nabobry. See Intro., p. 38.

T113. *measuring the Pyramids.* For the tone cf. *Spectator* No. 1.

T115. *he should run and roar.* 1H4 II. iv. 285–7.

T116. *vocation.* 1H4 I. ii. 116–17.

recreation. 1H4 I. ii. 173–4.

The poor abuses of the times, etc. 1H4 I. ii. 174–5 and 67–9.

Farewell, etc. 1H4 I. ii. 175–8.

T117. *We shall see.* In the next par. Morgann analyses 1H4 I. ii. 179–214.

T122. *eight yards.* 1H4 II. ii. 26–7.

Zounds! will they not rob us! 1H4 II. ii. 68.

I doubt they will be too hard for us. 1H4 I. ii. 204–5.

T123. *argument for a week,* etc. 1H4 II. ii. 100–2.

let the event try. 1H4 II. ii. 72: 'we leave that to the proof.' See note to LR 10, I127.

T124. *the stage direction.* 1H4 II. ii. 110.

And you, Falstaff, etc. 1H4 II. iv. 284–8.

stony-hearted. 1H4 II. ii. 28.

T127. *stuffing and all.* Cf. 2H4 V. v. 87.

T128. *starveling*, etc. 1H4 II. iv. 270–2.

SR 14. The word 'as' is written in above and slightly before 'The', the first word of T128:6. Morgann presumably intends 'As the' at the start of T128:6 and 'nature, they' instead of 'nature. They' in the sequence T128:6–T128:7. Cf. LR 11a, l183:2. SR 14 is superseded by LR 11a: see below, p. 405.

T130. *Give me my horse! . . . Richard.* 1H4 II. ii. 43–4. R3 V. iv. 13.
Eight yards . . . Forrester of Diana, etc. 1H4 II. ii. 26–7 and I. ii. 29.
Bacons, etc. 1H4 II. ii. 88–97.

SR 15. The insertion point of SR 15 is indicated by an 'X' above and to the right of 'travellers' in T130:4 and by a caret below the 'X': corresponding to these notations is an 'X' above and to the left of 'and', the first word of SR 15 in the lower margin of T130.

T133. SR 16. The revision implies the deletion of the comma after 'affect'.

T134. *after the fact.* Refuting this point, E. E. Stoll, *Shakespeare Studies*, rev. edn. (New York, 1942), p. 438, adduces four stage cowards who brag after the fact.
The Play opens with the Fact. 'I take it that by the *Play*, Morgann means the Falstaff plot; and by the *Fact*, the Gadshill robbery and Falstaff's flight.'— Hemingway 1936, p. 413.

T137. *The Jest will be*, etc. 1H4 I. ii. 209–14.

T138. *These lyes . . . are like the father of them*, etc. 1H4 II. iv. 249–59.

T139. *Hear how a plain Tale*, etc. 1H4 II. iv. 281–94.

T140. *instinct*, etc. 2H4 II. iv. 299–304.

T141. SR 17. The revision is written in above 'go more directly to his' in T141:3, and implies the deletion of these words and the next, 'vindication'.

T141. *at half-sword.* 2H4 II. iv. 182–3.

T143. *swearing truth out of England.* 1H4 II. iv. 337.

T144. *I never dealt better in my life*, etc. 1H4 II. iv. 187–9, 215, 140–2.

T145. *attached.* The edition of 1820 emends to 'attached to', that of Smith 1903 and 1963 to 'attacked'. Neither emendation is necessary. As in his *Letter to the Bishops* (1779), p. 18, and in LR 4, T41MS:2, Morgann uses *attach* in the now obsolete sense of 'to seize' or 'to attack' (*OED* senses 3 and 4.)
valiant Jack Falstaff. 1H4 II. iv. 523–5.
procuring this fat rogue a Charge of foot. 1H4 II. iv. 596–7.

T147. *caper for a thousand . . . I am old.* 2H4 I. ii. 216 and II. iv. 294.

T150. *not likely to awaken our compassion.* Pye 1792, p. 123, cites this passage to illustrate Aristotle's view that comedy 'consists in some blunder or ugliness that does not cause pain or disaster' (*Poetics*, v, trans. W. Hamilton Fyfe [1953], p. 19).

T151. *Trigon.* 2H4 II. iv. 288.
seven groats . . . like a sow. 2H4 I. ii. 263 and 12–14.

T158. SR 24a. See Intro., p. 110.
SR 24b. A 'y' is superimposed on the last three letters of '*incongruities*' in T158:1.

T159. *peppered.* 1H4 II. iv. 212–13.
he would have become a cart, etc. 1H4 II. iv. 545–7.
SR 25a. The revision points the allusion more definitely to George Lillo, *The London Merchant* (1731).

T160. *with our spleens*, etc. Meas. II. ii. 122–3.

T161. SR 26. The last letter of 'arguments' in T161:1 is lined through and a corresponding delete symbol appears in the outer margin.

T163. *humourist . . . man of humour.* Cf. Morris 1744, p. 15:
'A *Man* of HUMOUR is *one, who can happily exhibit a weak and ridiculous* Character *in real Life, either by assuming it himself, or representing another in it, so naturally, that the* Whimsical Oddities, *and* Foibles, *of that* Character, *shall be palpably expos'd.*
Whereas an HUMOURIST *is a* Person *in real Life, obstinately attached to sensible peculiar* Oddities *of his own genuine Growth, which appear in his Temper and* Conduct.
In short, a *Man* of *Humour* is one, who can happily exhibit and expose the Oddities and Foibles of an *Humourist*, or of other *Characters.*'
Samuel Foote, *The Roman and English Comedy* (1747), pp. 11–12, makes a similar distinction.
What is wit itself. Cf. Morris 1744, pp. 1 and 4:
'WIT *is the* LUSTRE *resulting from the* quick ELUCIDATION *of one Subject, by a just and* unexpected ARRANGEMENT *of it with another Subject. . . .*
In WIT, the two Subjects are suddenly confronted with each other, and upon their joint View, the *original* one is *elucidated* by the obvious *Agreement* or *Contrast* of the *auxiliary* Subject.'
As Arthur Murphy noted in his 'Commonplace Book' (Folger MS. M. b. 22, p. 78), Morris here improves on the standard view found in Locke (*Essay concerning the Human Understanding* (1690), bk. II, chap. xi, sec. 2: cf. Hobbes, *Leviathan* (1651), chap. viii) that wit consists in discerning likenesses between ideas rather than in bringing out differences between them. Cf. Addison, who devotes most of *Spectator* 62 to presenting the Lockean view, but says towards the end: 'not only the *Resemblance*, but the *Opposition* of Ideas does very often produce Wit.' Murphy concludes (p. 91): 'In short, whenever a *sudden agreem*'.

between Ideas where none was expected, or a *sudden contrast*, or a just *Union of Thwarting Ideas* is presented to the Mind, there is Wit, according to the Best Definition.——'

T164. *tale of Tristram*. Laurence Sterne's nine-volume *Tale of Tristram Shandy* (1759–67) lacks the formal conclusion of a 'finis' at the end of volume ix.

T166. *Parolles was so changed.* AW. V. ii.
nothing. To align the passage containing this word with the view Morgann presents in revision, it would be necessary to omit 'nothing' and reformulate the thought in some such fashion as the following: 'but that is [because of the actors' misrepresentations. Suppose the play produced as Shakespeare intended and Falstaff's cowardice communicated as part of a mixed effect; the quality would not then outweigh the stronger impression of his courage] if the character', etc. See Critical Intro., *Essay on Falstaff*, sec. v.

T167. *to the rest of Europe*, etc. 2H4 II. ii. 145–6.

T168. *It is not a confirmed brow*, etc. 2H4 II. i. 121–41 ('confident brow').

T169. *This is the right fencing grace*, etc. 2H4 II. i. 205–9.
SR 27. On the cancelled part of the SR cf. SR 4, and note.
He is no proud Jack, etc. 1H4 II. iv. 12.

T170. SR 29. The correction allows for Falstaff's insolence to the Chief Justice, who is not his inferior.

T171. SR 30d. The first 'e' of 'Thresher' in T171:1 is lined through diagonally and 'a/' appears in the outer margin on a level with the line of print containing the word. 'Thrasher' is a variant of 'Thresher'=a large shark.
SR 31. Morgann seemingly intended to restore 'an' in T171:4 and cancel 'that' in T171MS when he cancelled the clause 'Which belongs to his Nature' in I172:1.

T173. SR 34. The correction removes an apparent minor illogicality.
But why . . . should incongruities, etc. Cf. Addison, *Spectator*, 47: 'a Man is not qualified for a *Butt*, who has not a good deal of Wit and Vivacity, even in the ridiculous side of his Character. A stupid *Butt* is only fit for the Conversation of ordinary People: Men of Wit require one that will give them Play, and bestir himself in the absurd Part of his Behaviour. A Butt with these Accomplishments frequently gets the laugh of his side, and turns the Ridicule upon him that attacks him. Sir *John Falstaff* was an Hero of this Species . . .'

T174. SR 35. See Intro., p. 110.

T175. *gird at him.* 2H4 I. ii. 7.

T178. *the tutor and feeder of his riots.* 2H4 V. v. 66.
 I will fetch off . . . snap at him. 2H4 III. ii. 324; V. i. 87–90; III. ii. 355–7.

T179. *we are told that was.* 1H4 III. iii. 200.
 Master Robert Shallow, chuse what office, etc. 2H4 V. iii. 129–44.

T180. *If I had had time,* etc. 2H4 V. v. 11–13.
 Master Shallow, I owe you, etc. 2H4 V. v. 77–8.

T183. *What matter where,* etc. *Par. Lost.* i. 256.

T184. *He was born,* etc. 2H4 I. ii. 210–12.

T184–T185. *He was shaked . . . bosom of Arthur.* H5 II. ii. 123–30; iii. 12–14; ii. 91–2; iii. 9–11.

THE LONGER REVISIONS OF
AN ESSAY ON FALSTAFF

LR 1–3: *Textual Note*

In LR 1–3 Morgann projected but did not quite complete a new introductory section designed to replace the whole of T5:2–T22:5 except for T5:4b. He used over 40 per cent of the I pages in the MS. book in drafting these revisions. Unfortunately, he neither marked most of the superseded pages in the introductory section as deleted nor supplied a comprehensive and lucid set of directions to lead one through the maze of new materials he composed. However, the occasional instructions he jotted down along with such other clues in the MS. book as the position of indicatory 'X's and lines, the relative location of materials, the kinds and varieties of cancellation, and the presence or absence of rhetorical continuity, make up together a body of evidence which establishes the successive drafts of the revisions and determines the corresponding cancellations in *Es.* This evidence is discussed in the individual Textual Notes to LR 1, LR 2, and LR 3, below.

The following conspectus of the pages on which Morgann worked up LR 1 and LR 2 designates as A to H the eight stages through which he arrived at the final texts of the revisions. (The several stages are further subdivided, sometimes splitting up passages which Morgann originally drafted as unities, in order to exhibit the subsequent interrelations between revision segments. Internal strata of revision within segments as recorded in the *app. crit.* to the texts are largely ignored; comment on them, where required, is provided in the separate notes to the LR.)

 [I1: blank]
A1 I2:1–I3:1 (LR 1a, par. 1). Originally a continuation of T4:3; on completion of D1a + D1b, moved ahead to continue from T5:1.

A2 I3:2–I4:1 (LR 1—ED 1a). Continuation of A1. Cancelled after E stage.

A3 I4:2–I5:3 (LR 1—ED 1b). Continuation of A2; fol. by T4:4. Cancelled; superseded by E1.

B1 I6:1–I7:1 (LR 2—ED 1). Originally a continuation of T6:3; subsequently a continuation of D4. Cancelled; superseded by F1.

B2 I7:1–I9:2 (LR 2, par. 1, mid-section). Continuation of B1; subsequently, at F stage, intercalated between F1 and F2.

B3 I9a:3–I10:1a, I10:2–I11:1 (LR 2—ED 2, par. 1, 1st part). Continuation of B2. Cancelled; superseded by F2.

B4 I11:2–I12:1 (LR 2—ED 2, par. 1, 2nd part). Continuation of B3. Cancelled; superseded by C2.

B5 I12:2–I14:3 (LR 2—ED 2, par. 2). Continuation of B4. Cancelled; superseded by F3.
[I15–T16MS: LR 7.]

C1 I16:1–3 (LR 2—ED 4a). Continuation of B5. Cancelled; superseded by C2.

C2 I16:4–I18:1 (LR 2—ED 4b). Incorporates B4; supersedes C1 as continuation of B5. Cancelled; superseded by C3.

C3 I18:2–I19:5 (LR 2—ED 4c). Supersedes C2 as continuation of B5. Cancelled; superseded by H2.

C4 I20:1–I21:1 (LR 2—ED 3). Continuation of C3. Cancelled; superseded by H1.

D1a I21:2–3 (LR 1—ED 2). Continuation of A3; dovetails terminally with T5:4. Cancelled; superseded by E2.

D1b I21:4–I22:1 (LR 1—ED 2). Continuation of T5:4; dovetails terminally with T6:3. Cancelled; superseded by E2.

D2 I22:2–I26:1 (LR 1—ED 3a, par. 2). Originally a continuation of T6:3; subsequently preceded by D3. Incomplete; cancelled; superseded by D4 (and G).

D3 I26:2–4 (LR 1—ED 3a, par. 1). Continuation of T6:3; fol. by D2. Cancelled; superseded by D4; absorbed in part into E2.

D4 I27:1–I28:2 (LR 1—ED 3b). Supersedes D2 (and D3) as continuation of T6:3. Cancelled; superseded by G.

E1 I28:3–I32:3 (LR 1a, par. 2). Supersedes A3 as continuation of A2; subsequently, on cancellation of A2, becomes continuation of A1.
[I30:SR 5–6.]

E2 I32:4–I33:2 (LR 1a, par. 3). Continuation of E1; supersedes D1a+D1b; absorbs part of D3; dovetails with T5:4.

F1 I33:3–I34:1 (LR 2, par. 1, opening). Supersedes B1 as continuation of D4; subsequently, on cancellation of D4, continues from T6:3. (Continues from T5:4 when F2 is superseded by LR 3a.)

F2 I9b:3–I10b:1 (LR 2, par. 1, last two sentences). Supersedes B3 as continuation of B2. (Subsequently superseded by LR3a.)

F3 I34:2–I37:4, T38MS:1–3, I38:2 (LR 2, par. 2). Continuation of F2; supersedes B5. (First sentence subsequently superseded by LR 3a.)

G I39:1–I42:4 (LR 1b). Footnote to E2; supersedes D2 and D4.
[T41MS–T42MS: LR 4.]

H1 I43:1–I44:1 (LR 2, par. 3). Continuation of F3; supersedes C4.

H2   I44:2–I46:1 (LR 2—ED 4d). Continuation of H1; supersedes C3. Cancelled; superseded by H3.

H3   I46:2–I47:4 (LR 2, par. 4, 5, 6). Supersedes H2 as continuation of H1. (Subsequently superseded by LR 3c and LR 12, I145:2–3.)

H4   I47:5–I50:3 (LR 2, par. 7, 8). Continuation of H3; dovetails terminally with T22:6.

[I48, middle third: SR 9.]

LR 1

Textual Note. The following table, based on the foregoing conspectus, shows the four versions through which LR 1 evolved and their respective inner links and connections with other materials printed or manuscript. (A comma indicates continuity with the passage to the right. The symbol → or > points to a segment that descends from and supersedes the preceding segment.)

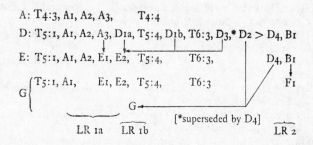

As the table indicates, Morgann arrived at the final versions of LR 1a and LR 1b after considerable casting about. LR 1a is a composite of passages fairly widely separated in the MS. book. For its opening par. he retained A1, which occupies I2:1–I3:1 and is the only early segment to survive unchanged. That he eventually intended A1 to be followed by E1 on I28–I32 can be inferred from the following facts: A2 and A3 are cancelled; beneath 'attainment', the last word of A2, is the notation 'See 28'; a corresponding 'X' is inscribed at the head of E1, which begins on I28 and which recasts A3 (see *app. crit.* to LR 1—ED 1a and LR 1a). Morgann would hardly have marked E1 as a new sequel to A2 in this way unless at the time he intended the sequence of A1, A2, E1, etc. A2 must therefore have been cancelled later. The inference is supported by the fact that the vertical line cancelling all the materials on I4 appears to have been drawn in two sweeps, with a break in the middle at the space between the last line of A2 and the first of A3. This suggests that the upper and lower halves of the vertical line were drawn at different times—the lower, affecting A3, when the latter segment was replaced by E1, and the upper, affecting A2, at a later stage. In the absence of any evidence regarding the time of the subsequent cancellation, the disappearance of A2 is recorded in the above table as a development of the G stage—the last stage represented. When A2 was cancelled, as the table indicates, the sequence that remained was A1, E1, etc. (For the critical significance of the cancellation of A2 see Intro., p. 59.) The continuity from E1 to E2 is evident from the thought flow and from the fact that on I32, E2 follows immediately below E1 as a new par. It is also, of course, implied by the fact that D1a+D1b, the first draft of E2, continues from A3, the first draft of E1.

Morgann marked very plainly the point at which the beginning of LR 1a was to fit into Es. He inscribed an 'X' above 'The', the first word in T5:2 and wrote 'See 2 Man[uscript]' in the outer margin on a level with the 'X' (app. crit., T5). A corresponding 'X' precedes the first word of A1 on I2 (app. crit., LR 1a). These markings clearly require the beginning of LR 1a to be inserted just after T5:1. This plan supersedes an earlier one reflected in the cancelled notation, 'See 2 Manu[script]', on the outer margin between the pars. ending with T4:3 and beginning with T4:4 (app. crit., T4). This notation must refer to the A version of LR 1a, since alone of the four versions it can as required fit in completely between T4:3 and T4:4; the other three mesh terminally with Es. on T5 and T6.

How and where Morgann proposed to link the conclusion of LR 1a with his printed text can best be ascertained by first considering the earlier D version. Despite the facts that D1a comes sixteen I pages later in the MS. book than A3 and that no connection between the two is expressly marked, there is no doubt that D1a is a continuation of A3. D1a manifestly recasts and supersedes T5:2 and 3 and no less manifestly leads into T5:4. Since in addition A3, as we have seen, is the last segment of an earlier written sequence which is marked for insertion at T5:2, there is no point at which D1a can fit in other than immediately after A3. Morgann may have reflected this intention in placing the 'X' on T5 over the last two letters of the 'The' with which T5:2 begins rather than before the word (app. crit., T5). The position of the 'X' seems to suggest not only that the revision as a whole was to follow T5:1 but, as is the case with the D version, that it was to replace the following printed materials, viz. T5:2, 3, and 4 up to the point in the latter sentence with which it dovetails terminally. As for the physical separation of D1a from A3 in the MS., it evidently arises from the fact that Morgann revised his first draft of LR 1 only after he had used all the I pages from I6 to the middle third of I21 (except for I15 which was already occupied with LR 7) for the B and C versions of LR 2. At this stage the first blank space he would have had available for extended writing would have started on the middle third of I21, and it is precisely here that D1a begins.

D1b is clearly designed to follow T5:4, the sentence into which D1a leads, and it no less clearly eliminates T5:5–T6:2. Occurring immediately below D1a in the MS. book, it recasts and absorbs T5:5 and leads into T6:3, thus implying the cancellation not only of T5:5 but also of T5:6–T6:2, the materials of which had earlier been absorbed into A2 and therefore could no longer well stand in the printed text.

In its completed form the D version thus superseded everything in the printed text from T5:2 to T6:3 except for the latter portion of T5:4. When Morgann subsequently worked out the E version of LR 1a, he maintained the same cancellations in Es. Revising A3 as E1 and reworking D1a+D1b and D3 as E2, beneath the last line of the latter he jotted down the instructions 'See print 5 & 6' (app. crit., LR 1a, I33:2b). The concluding words of E2, followed by the indication 'etc.', manifestly mesh with T5:4 ('See print 5') as did the parallel words in

Dıa. As in Dıa, again, the structure of E2 enforces the cancellation of T5:2–3, since it concludes a sequence which is marked for insertion just after T5:1. The preservation in the E version of the cancellation by Dıb of T5:5–T6:2 is established by the following considerations. First, T5:5 cannot well stand in the E version, since it does not flow out of T5:4 as revised by E2. Second, originally at least, the E version retained A2, which contains the substance of T5:6–T6:2 and therefore implies their cancellation as already carried out in Dıb. Third, under these circumstances, the first sentence on T6 to which 'See print . . . 6' can plausibly refer is T6:3; and T5:4 as revised by E2 flows smoothly enough into T6:3. Fourth, the reference to 'print . . . 6' cannot be to any sentence after T6:3 since those which follow had already been lined through and superseded by Bı (see *app. crit.*, T6). Finally, 'See print 5 & 6' cannot mean that T5:4 was to be followed by Bı on I6 which supersedes T6:4ff., since Morgann began revising Bı in the form of Fı immediately below the end of E2 on I33: if he had not intended Fı to be preceded by T6:3, he would not have interlined 'See print . . . 6' between E2 and Fı.

Morgann developed the materials of LR 1b at the D stage as a preamble to LR 2 before disengaging them in the form of G as a footnote to the final text of LR 1a. He began writing D2, the first of the two segments which he would eventually work up into G immediately below Dıb on I22, thus indicating that D2 was to continue as a new par. after T6:3, with which the end of Dıb dovetails. This meant that Bı, the sequel of T6:3 he had already provided, was now pushed forward to follow the newly intercalated D2. After going on for several pages more, however, he stopped short at the top of I26 in the middle of a sentence without providing a junction with Bı, and on the balance of the page he worked up D3, intended to lead into D2. Still dissatisfied, he turned the page and redrafted D3+D2 on I27–I28 in the much shorter form of D4, a complete unit which might readily lead out of T6:3 and into Bı. The solution, however, was temporary. After further labours over LR 1a and LR 2 on I28–I38, among them the assimilation of part of D3 into E2 and the recasting of Bı as Fı which thus became a new sequel to D4, he devoted I39–I42 to conflating the materials of D2 and D4 into a composite unit, G, which he designated as a footnote to LR 1a (see *app. crit.*, LR 1a, I33:2).

LR 1a. I3:1. *app. crit.* —?—. Apparently a philosophical authority for the assertion in the main text about 'the total Blind'.

LR 1b. I40. *such various situations.* Cf. Morgann's earlier view of 'Bodies of Men', Intro., p. 5.

LR 1—ED1b. I5. *But the author*, etc. The vertical line which cancels I5 shows a juncture between the last line of the preceding sentence and the line beginning 'But the author', etc. This implies that Morgann rejected the former before deleting the ED as a whole: cf. the similar situation on I4, discussed above, p. 380.

LR 1—ED 3a. I25 *Farce.* If Morgann first wrote 'Face' (see *app. crit.*), he was moved by the wisdom of hindsight: cf. his earlier advocacy of turning 'the Face of Authority' to American extremists, Intro., p. 5.

LR 2

Textual Note. The following table, based on the conspectus in the Textual Note to LR 1–3, shows the successive versions of LR 2 and their respective inner links and connections with other materials printed or manuscript. (A comma indicates continuity with the passage to the right. The symbol ➤ or > points to a segment that descends from and supersedes the preceding segment. A full stop=no continuation indicated.)

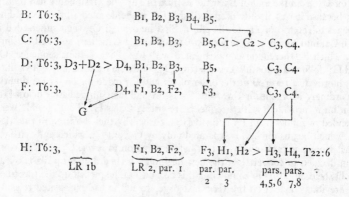

B: T6:3, B1, B2, B3, B4, B5.

C: T6:3, B1, B2, B3, B5, C1 > C2 > C3, C4.

D: T6:3, D3+D2 > D4, B1, B2, B3, B5, C3, C4.

F: T6:3, D4, F1, B2, F2, F3, C3, C4.

  G

H: T6:3, F1, B2, F2, F3, H1, H2 > H3, H4, T22:6
  LR 1b LR 2, par. 1 par. par. pars. pars.
    2   3 4,5,6 7,8

Morgann's design of integrating the seven segments of the final (H) version of LR 2 into a whole can be made out readily enough. The last clause of the first segment, F1, which occurs on I34, overlaps word for word—except for the belated hypercorrection of 'Him' to 'He' (*app. crit.*, LR 2)—with the last clause of B1, which originally led directly into the opening of the second segment, B2, on I7. The juncture of F1 and B2 is further marked by the instructions at the end of F1: 'See 7 m[anuscript]' (*app. crit.*, LR 2). On I9, the conclusion of B2 flows without a break into the third segment, F2, which Morgann wrote on I9–I10 between the individually cancelled lines of B3, the earlier continuation of B2. The sequence F1, B2, F2 is thus clearly established.

F3, the fourth segment, occupies the lower half of I34, beneath F1. Reading forward in the MS. book from F2 on I10, one finds F3, on I34, to be the first uncancelled revision passage not previously assigned to an LR and so available as a sequel. Logically, the succession makes sense, though when examined for rhetorical fluency, the first sentence of F3, which begins par. 2 of LR 2, seems to start a new topic rather than carry on from the preceding one, and at the same time it echoes rather awkwardly the opening sentence of par. 1 (F1). But Morgann introduced the doubly infelicitous sentence in revising F3: the ED (*app. crit.*, LR 2, par. 2) provides a smoother transition. (He would supply a yet better one in LR 3a, which revises F_2 and the opening of F_3: see below, p. 388.) The sequence F_2, F_3 is further indicated by a horizontal line he drew across I34 between F_1 and F_3 below his directions to 'See 7 m': read as a signal to intercalate at that point the uncancelled materials on I7–I10, viz. B_2 and F_2, the line prescribes the sequence F_2, F_3.

The continuity of H_1, the fifth segment, with F_3, is indicated in the first instance by its relation to the corresponding section of the C stage of revision. At this earlier stage, when Morgann first undertook to go on from B_5, it had taken him three tries to arrive at a smoothly integrated continuation. Picking up on I16 from the end of B_5 at the bottom of I14—he presumably had to skip I15 because it was already occupied with LR 7—he devoted all the succeeding I pages to the top of I21 to the effort. First he drafted C_1, then superseded it with C_2, into which he incorporated B_4, and still dissatisfied, polished C_2 into C_3, which he thereupon complemented with C_4. The resultant sequence, C_3 and C_4, followed smoothly enough from B_5. With the transmutation of B_5 into F_3, however, a reversal of the order of C_3 and C_4 made for better continuity. Accordingly Morgann first rewrote C_4 as H_1 and then, immediately below H_1, went on to provide it with a sequel by rewriting C_3 as H_2. That H_1, H_2 were intended to follow from F_3 is further established by their position in the MS. H_1, which begins on I43, is separated only by G from F_3, which ends on I37. What happened, apparently, is that before going on to revise C_3 and C_4 Morgann decided to convert D_4, the new beginning he had drawn up for LR 2 at the D stage, into G. On completing this task on I42, he picked up the thread of his previous concern on the very next page. In F_3 he had completed revising the B stage materials of LR 2; now he went on to recast C_3 and C_4, with the reversal of order mentioned above, as H_1 on I43–I44 and as H_2 on I44–I46. In H_2 he omitted the B_4 materials retained in C_3 from C_2. Dissatisfied with H_2, however, he lined it through, and restoring the B_4 materials, rewrote it as H_3 on I46–I47. Immediately thereafter, still on I47, he began to work up a manifest sequel in the form of H_4, which he finished on I50 with a terminal link with Es. (When he came to I48, he could use only the upper and lower thirds of the page, since the middle section already contained SR 9a and 9b: see T48, *app. crit.* and note.) H_1, H_3, and H_4 thus make up a sequence which continues from F_3 and, by the terminal link of H_4 with Es., concludes the revision as a whole.

The evolution of the revision also throws light on the way it was supposed to affect Es. Morgann marked the place at which he originally proposed to insert B_1, the ED of the opening of the revision, by inscribing an 'X' after the last word of T6:3 (the 'X' may also be described as placed at the par. break between T6:3 and T6:4), and by entering a corresponding 'X' before the first word of B_1 on the facing I page (*app. crit.* to T6 and to LR 2—ED 1). When he later drafted D_4 as a continuation of T6:3, he must have thought of B_1 as moved forward to follow the new revision segment. Still later, on recasting B_1 as F_1, he began the latter on the last two lines of I33 immediately below the instructions 'See print 5 & 6', which, as we have noted, occur at the end of LR 1. This suggests that he intended F_1 to go on from the sequels of LR 1a, which consisted at this stage of T5:4, T6:3, D_4. However, when he subsequently cancelled D_4 in favour of the differently located G, F_1 became the continuation of T6:3.

(The instructions 'See print 5 & 6' would apply perhaps even more clearly to this new sequence of T5:4, T6:3, F1, so he had no need to change them.) The definitive position of F1 in relation to Es. was thus identical with the one he had originally marked out for its ED, B1.

That he intended LR 2 in all its stages to supersede the printed materials following the 'X' after T6:3 rather than be intercalated between T6:3 and 4 is shown by his having drawn a vertical line through the middle of T6:4 and 5, which begin a par. occupying the lower half of T6 and continuing on T7 (*app. crit.*, T6). Further, inasmuch as T6:5 is the first part of a sentence completed by T7:1, he must have thought of the deletion as extending beyond T6. How much beyond is hinted at by his having in varying measure adapted and appropriated T8:2-3 and T14:3 for LR 1a, T7:4 and T15:1 for LR 1b, and T8:1, T9:3-T10:1, and T15:2 for LR 2, thus implying the cancellation of these passages in Es. In addition, by including in H4 an adaptation of T20:1, an expansion of T22:5, and a lead into T22:6, he implicitly cancelled T20:1-T22:5. These scattered indications are brought to a focus and the full and precise extent of the deletion he contemplated is established by examining the initial and terminal points of insertion he assigned to LR 2. The former, as we have seen, ultimately remained what it had been at the start, viz., T6:3. In none of the earlier stages, however, did he indicate the slightest reconnection with Es.; he provided the terminal coupling only in the final H version. Here, after cancelling a too abrupt plunge back into Es., he drafted a more effective transitional par. underneath which he wrote: 'With respect &c see 22 pr[int]' (*app. crit.* to I50:2 and I50:3, LR 2). With this notation he now smoothly dovetailed H4 with the identically phrased opening of T22:6.

Through all their permutations, he consistently designed the parts of LR 2, in so far as he had progressed with them at any given stage, to cohere as a unit which carried on without interruption from T6:3. When, therefore, he eventually designated the point of reconnection with the printed text as T22:6, he thereby recorded his final intention of having LR 2 supplant the fourteen pars. that lie between T6:3 and T22:6. SR3, which implies the retention of T10:2, the sentence it emends, is the sole piece of positive evidence that might be advanced to the contrary. But the stylistic correction of a single word which SR 3 introduces is credibly explained as dating back to an archaic stage of revision (see Intro., p. 38), and so carries no weight against the solid proof of later intentions. When Morgann settled down to revising in good earnest, it may be assumed, he gave no further thought to T10:2, sweeping it away, correction and all, as part and parcel of the inclusive cancellation of T6:4-T22:5.

134. *An excellent Play*, etc. Morgann interrupted I34:2b after the line ending with the word 'redeem' in order to recast I34:2a as I34:3 in the space below. He set the revised draft off from the preceding and following materials by drawing a line above it, below it, and to to its left. The way he intended it to dovetail is clear from its phrasing and final 'etc.' (see *app. crit.*).

136. *the most sublime Incident.* Cf. the extensive modern vogue of the Flathe–Eliot interpretation of Othello's suicide speech as an expression of egocentricity: J. L. F. Flathe, *Shakespeare in seiner Wirklichkeit*, ii (Leipzig, 1864), 340, and

T. S. Eliot, 'Shakespeare and the Stoicism of Seneca' (1927), *Selected Essays* (New York, 1942), p. 130. Flathe's fully developed theory of an 'ignoble' Othello is summarized by A. Ralli, *A History of Shakespeare Criticism* (Oxford, 1932), i. 432–3. Eliot seems to have hit upon the same theory independently.

a malignant and a turban'd Turk. Oth. V. ii. 353.

Cibber. Colley Cibber implies what Morgann here attributes to him in 'A Dialogue on Old Plays and Old Players', in *An Apology for the Life of Mr. Colley Cibber* (1750), p. 530. (But John Downes, *Roscius Anglicanus* (1708), ed. Thomas Davies (1789), pp. 5–8, refers to a 'scattered Remnant' of pre-Civil-War players who at the Restoration revived what later became the Drury Lane company.)

I37. *D'Avenant.* Sir William Davenant (1606–68) composed twenty plays, masques, and other dramatic productions, which began appearing in 1629 After the Restoration he managed 'the Duke's' company of comedians.

T38MS. *But this . . . Player depends.* Written on the lower margin of T38, this passage supersedes the cancelled contents of the upper two-thirds of I38 (reproduced in part in the *app. crit.*) and is by sense and position intended to mesh terminally with the beginning of the uncancelled materials in the middle of I38:2 on the lower third of the I page.

I47. *triumph even in their own Defeat.* Cf. Pye 1792, p. 308: 'though I first took the book [i.e. *Es.*] up . . . with the strongest prejudice against what I thought an indefensible paradox; yet every word led to conviction; and I laid it down with the firmest assurance that the author was perfectly in the right.'

LR 2—ED 1. The text records Morgann's second and third efforts to revise T6: 4 ff. His first try consists of the opening of ED 1 ('If this . . . doubts it') fol. by the false start reproduced in the *app. crit.* On deleting the latter, his hand fell a line too low and he drew his pen through the first line of the new material in his second attempt ('In all dramatic Characters I') instead of the last line of his first ('a subject of dramatic Imitation'). He was again careless at a later stage when, on cancelling the part of his third attempt which occupies the lower third of I6, he overlooked and forgot to cancel the opening it had inherited from his first two tries at the top of the page (I6:1a).

He no doubt rejected his first attempt in part at least because of its ambiguity. It seems to mean that a drama may represent a man torn between head and heart as described in T6:3, whereas what he presumably wished to say was that a drama may legitimately produce such a conflict in the spectator. Both his second and third attempts undertake in different ways to clarify the ambiguity by distinguishing between the dramatic character and the spectator. See next note.

I6. *in the third.* Two considerations suggest that Morgann intended to complete the sentence by some such phrase as 'to the spectator'. First, the idea is called for by his theory of characterization: see Intro., pp. 88–9; cf. p. 103. Second, its presence in his mind explains the state of the MS. As the thought rose before him, it would appear, instead of setting it down, he drew three vertical lines through everything he had so far written on I6, except for I6:1a at the top of the page, and used the remaining lower third of the page to go on from I6:1a in a third attempt which further clarifies his original ambiguity of phrasing (see prec. note) and considers the question in relation to the spectator, as his immediate argument requires, rather than, as in the second attempt, in relation to the character.

17. *excites what Passions he pleases.* For this idea and the following tag in verse see Horace, *Epistles*, II. i. 211–13. Morgann partly misquotes Pope's imitation, ll. 346–7: 'And snatch me, o'er the earth or thro' the air', etc.

LR 2—ED 2. I14. *moderation in a Poet*, etc. Cf. Horace, *Art of Poetry*, ll. 372–3.

LR 3

Textual Note. The three revision segments collected in LR 3 and their ED are distributed as follows in the MS. book:

I51–I55:   LR 3c and LR 3—ED 5. Truncated revision of LR 2, pars. 4–5
[I56–I67:   excised.]
I68–I78:   LR 3—ED 1–3. Incomplete note to T70; subsequently served as
            ED of latter part of LR 3a and (ED 1 only) as source for LR 3b.
[I79–I149: other revisions—see notes to LR 6 and LR 11.]
I150–I157: LR 3a. Revises LR 2, I9b:3–I35:1 (p. 227); implies cancellation
            of T6:3; supersedes LR 3—ED 1–3.
[I158–I159: LR 11b.]
I160–I166: LR 3b and LR 3—ED 4. Probable footnote to LR 3a; develops
            hints in LR 3—ED 1.

As appears from their relative locations in the MS. book, Morgann wrote LR 3c, which begins at the top of I51, before LR 3a and 3b, which are found on much later pages. Ending H4, the conclusion of LR 2, on the upper half of I50, he left the lower half blank, perhaps to take care of any modifications of H4 which the revision of H3 he was about to undertake on I51 might entail. On stylistic grounds alone, some such revision was in order, for the 3 pars. of H3, considered as a piece of continuous prose, lack the concinnity Morgann usually aimed at. He was well on his way to removing this defect in the first four sentences he now wrote, which present more effectively and so supersede the contents of the first two pars. of H3 (LR 2, pars. 4 and 5). The progression from par. 3 of LR 2 to the new material is clearly marked in the otherwise awkward and therefore rejected ED of I51:1: see *app. crit.*, LR 3c. He must also have planned to delete the remainder of H3 (LR 2, par. 6), since he plucked out its concluding threads–tissue image, an object of tireless repolishing in earlier stages (LR 2—ED 2 and ED 4b and c), to lodge it at last in a more appropriate setting provided by LR 12 (I145). He thus intended LR 3c to follow par. 3 of LR 2 and in this position to replace pars. 4–6. But how he proposed to link LR 3c terminally with LR 2 or with *Es.* is an insoluble puzzle. The revision breaks off at the foot of I55 in the middle of a sentence which presumably continued on the next I page, and that page as well as the eleven succeeding ones

(I56–I67) have been removed from the MS. book. Further, he never used the blank lower half of I50 to adjust H4 to the new material now designed to precede it. The conclusion of LR 3c as Morgann composed it and his plan for relating it to LR 2 thus lie beyond recovery.

On I68, the first interleaf extant in the MS. book after I55, Morgann began expounding the theory of Greek drama which he eventually absorbed into LR 3a and drew on for LR 3b. At this earlier stage he intended the revision as a note to the opening clause of T70:3, but though he worked over it from I68 to I78, he failed to complete it or even to articulate all the materials he drafted (for details see below, note to LR 3—ED I–3). Perhaps he left the projected note in this state because it struck him that he could deploy the subject matter more advantageously in a further revision of LR 2. At all events this is what he later did. At a stage when the unused I pages closest to LR 2 were I150 ff., he there began drawing up LR 3a, in the second half of which he digested the earlier account of the Greek drama. He failed to cancel the latter, but obviously intended it to be superseded by his new, more compact treatment of the same material.

Although he did not in any way label LR 3a as a revision of LR 2, he undoubtedly designed it for that purpose. The first four sentences of LR 3a manifestly recast and modify the thought of the last two sentences of LR 2, par. I (i.e. all of F2) and the first sentence of par. 2 (i.e. of F3); and despite an awkward gap in the thought (see Intro., pp. 62–4), LR 3a meshes initially with the third from the last sentence of LR 2, par. I (conclusion of B2). Inserting LR 3a at this point eliminates the ungainly transition from par. I to par. 2 and the inept chime of the first sentence in par. 2 with the first sentence in par. I (see above, p. 383). But if these circumstances suffice to locate the initial link between LR 3a and LR 2, no parallel ones can be found which establish a terminal juncture. To suppose that LR 3a replaces all of par. 2 involves two difficulties. The first is stylistic: the hypothesis assumes that having done away with the lame transition from par. I to par. 2 in LR 2 Morgann was content to introduce a like blemish at another place: insert LR 3a before par. 3, LR 2, and the opening sentence of the latter no longer provides, as it had for par. 2, LR 2, a harmonious transition. The second difficulty has to do with the contents of the revisions. Par. 2 in LR 2 contains an account of actors' distortions which can ill be spared in the revised introductory section (see Intro., pp. 72–3). If, on the other hand, he intended to retain all or a part of par. 2 beyond its first sentence, he failed to provide the requisite suture and as the passage stands it has no phrase into which LR 3a would naturally lead. Perhaps he had not fully worked out his scheme for integrating LR 3a with LR 2. The possibility seems the greater in view of the state of I157. After completing a revised version of the opening of LR 3a on the top of the page, he left the lower five-sixths blank. This suggests that he was reserving space for adjustments which he never got around to setting down. Had he not some further treatment of LR 3a in view, it would seem, he would have begun LR 3b on I157 rather than skipped over I158–I159, presumably already occupied with LR 11b, to start the new revision on I160.

The latter assumption rests on the fact that in LR 3b he was clearly extending LR 3a. Enlarging on the allusions to the music of the Greek theatre scattered through the same incomplete note to T70 which he had just drawn on for LR 3a, he was manifestly still thinking along similar lines. In an ED of one sentence he even fell into almost the same language he had used in LR 3a to describe how the actor affects the audience's sensibility (*app. crit.* to I165:1; cf. LR 3a, I153:2). Although he failed to designate the relation between the two revisions, he apparently conceived of LR 3b as a footnote to LR 3a at the word 'Accompaniments' in I155:3. The three possible alternatives are all less probable. LR 3b neither readily meshes with any part of LR 3a, nor follows it smoothly as a sequel, nor fits in without wrenching elsewhere in *Es*. On the other hand, it falls into place perfectly as a footnote to 'Accompaniments'. Read in this way it does exactly what a comment of this kind should: it elaborates on the passing allusion conveyed by the word to which it is subjoined, and by doubly iterating the same pivotal term in its opening sentence, it effectively brings out the continuity of thought to an eye travelling from main text to small print below.

However, if the intended connection between LR 3a and 3b may be credibly conjectured, the fact remains that as with LR 3c there is no way of determining how the materials were to be integrated into the revised version of LR 2 which they adumbrate. The various parts of LR 3 must therefore be read as a kind of indispensable appendix to LR 2, showing how Morgann proposed to reshape and correct certain passages in the earlier revision (see Intro., pp. 64–5, 74–5, and 80–1). As for the effect on *Es.*, it is clear that the emergent revision was to supplant a trifle more of the original text than does LR 2. The supersession by the first half of LR 3a (I156:2–I153:2) of I9b:3–I35:1 in LR 2 implies both the cancellation of T6:3 (see Intro., p. 75) and, since T5:5–T6:2 have already been cancelled (see above, pp. 381–2), the consequent shifting forward of the initial junction of LR 2 to T5:4. Since there is nothing in any of the passages collected in LR 3 to suggest any other deviations from the earlier plan, the passage in *Es.* superseded by LR 2 as revised by LR 3 would thus extend from T5:5 to T22:5.

LR 3a. I156. *Precisions of Time*, etc. Cf. Babcock 1931, p. 54: 'The uniqueness of the Greek chorus was a stock argument from 1769 [*Monthly Review*, xli. 132] to the end of the century against modern application of the unities.' Cf. LR 3—ED 1, I77: 1–3, and LR 3—ED 3.

Eo meo & Areo. Apparently an allusion to a highly specialized grammatical rule: these three Latin verbs, which might seem to be inflected alike, belong in point of fact to different conjugations.

LR 3b. For further comment on music and feeling see LR 6b.

I163. *the Tones of all the Passions.* Cf. William Cooke, *The Elements of Dramatic Criticism* (1775), pp. 54–5: 'To speak in the language of music, each passion hath a certain tone to which every sentiment proceeding from it, ought to be tuned with the greatest accuracy.'

T164MS. *This is ... private Discourse.* Written on the bottom margin of T164, this sentence clearly supersedes the original continuation of I164:4 (see *app. crit.*) on the facing lower part of I164.

LR 3c. T52MS–T53MS. Morgann rewrote the heavily corrected materials on I52 and I53 (see LR 3—ED 5 and note) on the top, outer, and bottom margins of T52 and on the top margin of T53. This later version of the materials is reproduced in the text in its obvious place between I51:2 and I54:1.

T52MS. *fat Paunch.* 1H4 II. iv. 159.

T53MS. *So Proteus,* etc. Pope, *Dunciad,* ii. 129–30.

I54. *bloody Battle,* etc. 1H4 III. ii. 105.
    To hunt the deer. The second stanza of 'Chevy Chase' (Child 162, Version B), praised by Addison in *Spectator* 74, where he cites it as follows:

> *To drive the Deer with Hound and Horn*
> *Earl* Piercy *took his way;*
> *The Child may rue that was unborn*
> *The Hunting of that Day.*

(See also *English and Scottish Popular Ballads,* ed. H. C. Child and G. L. Kittredge [Boston, 1904], p. 397.) Morgann had earlier adapted the last two lines of the stanza to an argument presented in his *Letter to my Lords the Bishops* (1779), p. 5.

I55. *Truth is not . . . Deceits of the Theatre are. Cetera desunt:* I56–I67 have been removed from the MS. book. Morgann apparently distinguishes between the 'avowed deceits' necessarily and properly involved in dramatic representations and the hidden deceits involved in the misrepresentation of an author's intentions.

LR 3—ED 1–3. Morgann originally wrote up these materials for a footnote to *Es.*, T70:3. This intention is indicated by (1) the symbol ✕ on the outer margin of *Es.*, T70, opposite the line 'confined within the narrow circle of the Chorus'; (2) the description of the revision as a note in LR 3—ED 2b; and (3) the contents of the ED.
    The MS. book contains materials for the note written in six stages, which are designated A . . . F in the following conspectus:

A   I68:1–I74:2a (LR 3—ED 1, opening and main body). Footnote to T70:3. Superseded by LR 3a, I153:3–I155:3.

B1 I74:2b (LR 3—ED 3, opening). Continuation of A. Superseded by F.

B2 I74–I75 (not reproduced except for last two words, *app. crit.* to LR 3—ED 3, I75:1). Continuation of B1. Cancelled; superseded by C.

B3 I75:1 (LR 3—ED 3, conclusion). Continuation of B2, subsequently of C. Cancelled; superseded by F.

C   T74MS:1–4 (LR 3—ED 3, main body). Supersedes B2 as continuation of B1; leads into B3. Partly cancelled; superseded by F.

D   I75:2–I76:2 (LR 3—ED 2a). First unintegrated fragment of LR 3—ED 1.

E   I76:3–5 (LR 3—ED 2b). Second unintegrated fragment of LR 3—ED 1.

F   I77:1–I78:1 (LR 3—ED 1, conclusion). Incomplete continuation of A; supersedes the sequence B1, C, B3. Superseded by LR 3a, I155:4–I156:1.

The intention to have the end of A dovetail with the beginning of F may be inferred from the context and the content of the intervening revisions, but in certain other respects the materials do not form a coherent, rounded whole. Clearly intending D and E as insertions, Morgann failed to integrate them with the main text of his proposed note. Further, he broke off F in the middle of a sentence, and he left the remaining lower half of I78 and all of I79 blank, apparently in order to reserve space for the missing conclusion and perhaps also for the adjustments required for incorporating his floating insertions.

LR 3—ED 1. I68. *washed Faces.* Apparently a comment on Horace's observation, *Art of Poetry*, l. 277, that the first tragic actors smeared their faces with wine lees.

I70. *Horace. Art of Poetry*, l. 276.

LR 3—ED 3. T74MS. *Aristotle.* According to Babcock 1931, p. 55, only with the appearance of Twining's, Tyrwhitt's, and Pye's translations of the *Poetics* in the last decade of the eighteenth century did it come to be generally realized in English literary circles that the unities were not in Aristotle.

LR 3—ED 5. The text of the ED reproduces the second of two earlier versions of the materials which Morgann rewrote in their final form on the margins of T52 and T53 (see note to LR 3c). He failed to cancel the second version. He interlined its first part as a later layer of writing in the largely cancelled first version or earlier layer on I52. He wrote out the remainder on I53 immediately below a few uncancelled lines of the conclusion of the first version, which he had earlier set down on the top of the page (see *app. crit.*).

I53. *stuffed Cloak Bag of guts.* 1H4 II. iv. 497–8.

LR 4

This revision is scrawled on the inner and outer margins of T41 and on the outer, lower, and upper margins of T42. This location in the MS. book as well as the subject-matter of the revision implies that LR 4 was intended as a footnote to T41:4, the logical point for it to be subjoined.

Francis Gentleman, *The Dramatic Censor*, ii (1770), 393 and note to Bell's edition of Shakespeare (1773), iv. 1H4, 64, also denounces the 'contemptible . . . buffoonery' of the drum. He differs slightly from Morgann, however, in claiming that the gallery guffaw was evoked by Falstaff's tumbling off the drum when the king arises rather than by the incongruity of Falstaff's sitting back-to-back with royalty. Sprague 1944, p. 89, calls attention to Gentleman's strictures and notes that the *Monthly Mirror*, xiv (1802), 63, welcomed George Frederick Cooke's refusal to resort to such 'hacknied paltry tricks'. For another early reform of the stage Falstaff by Stephen Kemble see Intro., p. 20 n. 3.

T41MS. *app. crit. The Players*, etc. This uncancelled ED on the bottom margin of T41 is Morgann's first draft of LR 4. It was complete until he replaced 'please' with 'furnish' (third word from last).

T42MS. *Royalty is curbed . . . ample Possessor.* This sentence is written vertically on the bottom margin of T42; its content implies its insertion here. The awkward repetition of the word 'Royalty' with which it begins may have arisen only after Morgann revised the prec. sentence, as indicated in the *app. crit.*

like a double Headed Janus. This phrase is cancelled and then rewritten and left uncancelled immediately below the sentence commented on in the prec. note; its sense suggests its insertion here.

LR 5

Both the contents and some of the phrasing of LR 5 indicate that Morgann designed it to revise footnote c (T49n–T50n). It is not clear why he cancelled the second half of the revision, which duplicates some of the language of the original note. Presumably he used the PI pages of the MS. book rather than the I pages facing the note because the latter were already taken up with LR 2, par. 7.

PI4:1. —— & —— & ——. In addition to the H6 trilogy and Shr. (minus the Induction), Morgann also thought LLL. and TG. spurious: see *Es.*, T50n and T64, and comment on TG., p. 352.

PI8:3. *Well but . . . Drama.* Morgann wrote this sentence as a detached item below the last line of LR 5, and cancelled it, apparently by mistake, with the same line that he drew through the concluding portion of the revision on PI8.

PI4. *not Competent to speak of Shakespeare.* Probably a hit at Johnson. In Johns. 1765–93, initial note to TG. and General Observations on LLL. and 3H6, Johnson argues that the two comedies and the H6 trilogy must be ascribed to Shakespeare, and he rebukes Theobald, Warburton, Upton, and others for pretending to impugn the First Folio canon.

Foot and half foot verse . . . wars. Ben Jonson, Prologue to *Every Man In His Humour*, ll. 10–11, alluding to the 'sesquipedalia verba' of Horace, *Art of Poetry*, l. 97. Upton 1748, p. 64, cites the same lines by Jonson in derogation of the H6 plays, which he earlier describes as inferior and perhaps not 'entirely written by Shakespeare' (pp. 24 and 59).

PI5. *unpremeditated verse.* Milton, *Par. Lost*, ix. 24.

PI6. *holding their Horses at the Door.* Farmer 1767, reprinted Smith 1963, p. 152, had laughed at this legend. As Smith 1963, p. 309, notes, it was first published by Theophilus Cibber, *Lives of the Poets* (1753), i. 130–1, and was subsequently appended to the reprint in Johns. 1765–93 of Rowe 'Account' 1709 as an anecdote related by Rowe to Pope.

PI8. *quoted to prove.* By Johnson, General Observation on 1H6, Johns. 1765–93 (The garbled version in Johns. 1765 was corrected in Johns. 1773.)

LR 6

LR 6a. *Textual Note.* Morgann had ignored Shakespeare's use of language in *Es.*, but in revisal regarded the topic as too important to be passed by. At first he contented himself with a brief apology for not going into the matter, which he began in the blank space following the last word of his long note on Shakespeare's characterization and concluded on the outer margin of the same page. Dissatisfied with this terse comment, however, he presently returned to the subject and wrote out his views at length. The order of materials in the MS. book is as follows:

T62MS:	LR 6a, original version.
[I62–I67:	removed from MS. book, along with I56–I61.]
[I68–I78:	LR 3—ED 1–3 (a note to I70).]
[I79:	blank.]
[I80–I86:	LR 8 (probably a note to T80).]
[I86–I87:	conclusion of LR 11a.]
I88–I93:	LR 6a, first half of initial draft of longer version.
[I94–I99:	LR 9 (revision of T94).]
I100–I107:	LR 6a, concluding half of initial draft of longer version.
I107–I121:	LR 6a, revisions of initial draft of longer version.

From this it appears that he set down his extended observations on Shakespeare's use of language after he had completed LR 3—ED 1–3, LR 8, LR 11a, and LR 9: presumably he started his longer version on I88 because the intervening pages, except for the isolated I79, were already filled in, and he jumped from I93 to I100 for the same reason. The following conspectus designates as A, B, C, D, and E the five stages which may be discerned in the development of LR 6a. (Stage A is subdivided into two units and B into five in order to exhibit their relationship to other segments. Textual problems arising from the inner stratification of stages B–E are dealt with in separate notes to the individual passages concerned.)

A1   T62MS:1 (LR 6a, first sentence). Continuation of T62n:4.

A2   T62MS:2–4 (LR 6—ED 1). Continuation of A1. Superseded by B1.

B1   I88:1–2, T88MS:1–T90MS:1, I90:1, T90MS:2–T91MS:2a, I89:2, T91MS:2b, I90:2, T91MS:2c–T92MS:1a (LR 6a, first half of par. 1, following first sentence). Supersedes A2 as continuation of A1.

B2   T92MS:1b, I91:1–I93:7, I100:1 (LR 6—ED 2). Continuation of B1. Superseded by E.

B3   I100:2–6 (LR 6—ED 4). Continuation of B2; subsequently a continuation (with adjustments) of D. Eliminated in E stage.

B4   I100:7–I104:2 (LR 6—ED 5, except for conclusion). Continuation of B3. Eliminated in D stage.

B5   I104:3–I105:2 (LR 6—ED 5, conclusion). Continuation of B4. Superseded by C.

B6   I105:3–I107:1 (LR 6a, conclusion). Continuation of B5; subsequently a continuation of C.

C   I107:2–I108:3, T108MS:1–T109MS:1, I108:4–I109:2 (LR 6a, par. 3, first half). Supersedes B5; subsequently a continuation of B3 and still later of E.

D   I109:3–I110:4, T111MS:1–T112MS:1, I110:5–I111:5 (LR 6—ED 3). Continuation of B2; leads into B3 (with adjustments). Eliminated in E stage.

E   I111:4–I113:1a, I114:4, I113:1b–I114:3, I115:1–3, I116:2–I120:3a, T120MS:1, I120:3b, T120MS:2, I120:3c–I121:3 (LR 6a, mid-section). Supersedes B2 as continuation of B1.

The conspectus shows that the revision underwent the evolution represented in the following table. (A comma indicates continuity with the passage to the right. An arrow points to a segment that supersedes the segment above, as indicated.)

$$A: A1, A2$$
$$\downarrow$$
$$B: A1, B1, B2, \quad B3, B4, B5, B6$$
$$\downarrow$$
$$C: A1, B1, B2, \quad B3, B4, C, \ B6$$

$$D: A1, B1, B2, D, B3, \quad C, \ B6$$
$$\downarrow$$
$$E: A1, B1, E, \quad\quad\quad C, \ B6$$

Though Morgann did not cancel the latest version of any of these segments, he clearly designated a final order of materials in the E version.

(1) A1 was to be retained and B1 was to supersede A2. This sequence, introduced in the B version and consistently maintained thereafter, is implied by context and phrasing: the opening of B1, which recasts A2, obviously requires some such precedent sentence as A1.

(2) E was to supersede B2. E begins in the middle of a sentence on I111 beneath a horizontal line separating it from the end of D; the half-sentence and its sequel manifestly revise and supersede B2 (except, possibly, for the last four sentences of the latter).

(3) C was to follow E. This is indicated by the notation 'a Language etc.' (=the opening words of C), written immediately below the last line of E on I121 (see *app. crit.* to I121:3).

(4) B6 was to follow C. This sequence is what necessarily remains in the E stage of the earlier C stage arrangement of materials. Set off from what precedes and follows it (B6 and D, respectively) by horizontal lines drawn across I107 and I109, C was originally marked to replace B5. The first word of C in I107:2 is prec. by an 'X' corresponding to an 'X' above the last letter of the word 'pleasure', which concludes B4 (see *app. crit.* to LR 6a and LR 6a—ED 5). The supersession of B5 by C is confirmed by repetition towards the end of C in I108:4–I109:1 of the idea that the Saxon does not easily take composition. (For a similar use of the symbol 'X' on T5 to indicate the start of an insertion designed to delete two sentences which are not otherwise marked for cancellation see p. 381, above.) The new arrangement of materials thus established was B4, C, B6. When Morgann subsequently designated C as the sequel to E, he presumably intended C to continue as before, i.e. with B6.

The text of LR 6a reproduces the E version as thus ascertained. In this form the revision still requires further polishing: see below, notes to T108MS ('He stuck adhering'), I109, and I106. The ED reproduce the five other uncancelled segments which appear in versions A–D. A2 (ED 1), B2 (ED 2), and B5 (conclusion of ED 5) have already been discussed. B4 (ED 5, except for conclusion)

appears to have been eliminated when D (ED 3) was composed. Set off from
C on I109 by the horizontal line mentioned above and from E on I111 by a
similar line, D was clearly intended to mesh terminally with B3 (ED 4) at two
points. (1) 'Want of Dignity', the last phrase of I111:4 (the penultimate sentence
of D), is followed by a blank space to the end of the line, a sign that the phrase
was to dovetail terminally with the similarly worded idea at the beginning of
B3 and that the passage was to continue as in B3. (2) In D, the final sentence,
I111:5, begins 'We hit the Instant . . .', with 'hit' a later revision written in over
an earlier (UM) 'catch'. In B3, immediately after the last word of I100:5,
'remained', and interlined above the first three words of I100:7 (the first sentence in B4), Morgann wrote the words 'We catch the Instant', thus clearly
indicating his intention to insert the last sentence of D at this point. As thus
revised, B3 clearly ceases to mesh as it did earlier with B4: the deliberate break
in continuity implies that Morgann now proposed to delete B4 and jump ahead
from B3 to C.

The apparent fate of D and B3 in the E stage raises a question. As we have
seen, the opening words of C written in immediately below E signal the sequence
E, C, B6, and this, since E unmistakably replaces B2, means the squeezing out
of D and B3. Yet D is as finely felt and eloquent a passage as Morgann wrote,
and one may imagine that he would not willingly have forgone its perceptions
and cadences. Hence a temptation to wonder whether the notation at the end of
E, 'a Language etc.', might not be a slip of the pen. Did he perhaps really mean
to mark E as being continued by D rather than by C? The mistake might have
arisen in part through his confounding the order of composition (C preceded D)
with the order of insertion in B (D precedes C). If so, his final intention in the E
stage was the sequence A1, B1, E, D, B3, C, B6. (To piece this version together,
insert LR 6—ED 3 and 4 at the par. break on p. 256 of LR 6a.) Another speculative way of saving D is to take 'a Language etc.' as an error for 'Language etc.'
On this hypothesis, E would be continued by I93:2 in B2 (ED 2). We would
then get the sequence A1, B1, E, B2 (latter part), D, B3, C, B6. (To construct
this version, insert LR 6—ED 2, I93:2 to end, ED 3, and ED 4 at the par. break
on p. 256 of LR 6a.)

Whatever form Morgann might finally have given to LR 6a, his early comments in LR 6—ED 1 raise the question whether he would have let the revision
stand as a continuation of the already long note on characterization which ends
on T62n. Yet if he proposed to intercalate the revision at some other point in
the *Essay*, he failed to indicate where.

188. *no other Language than his own.* Morgann here accepts the cogently argued
view of Farmer 1767, reprinted Smith 1963, pp. 151–202; summation, p. 201.

T88MS–T92MS. *that He must . . . wins us all.* This passage replaces an uncancelled ED of the same material on I88–I91. The ED is not reproduced except
for an early stratum in *app. crit.* to T89MS:2 and for three brief passages—
I90:1, I89:2, and I90:2—which are incorporated in LR 6a as required in
each instance by the notation 'etc.' after incomplete sentences on T90MS
and T91MS: see *app. crit.* The context in the ED makes clear which passages
are to be thus incorporated. T88MS:1 is on the bottom margin just opposite

the superseded ED materials on I88 and clearly continues from incomplete I88:2.

T88MS. *build in strange Terms the lofty Rhime. Lycidas,* l. 11. Morgann here adopts the standard eighteenth-century view of Milton's style, as found, for example, in Addison, *Spectator* 28, and Johnson, *Life of Milton.*

I114:4. *Who never once . . . three leagued Boots.* Written on the bottom fifth of I114, this passage is separated by a horizontal line from I114:1–3, which is reproduced on p. 254. The 'etc.' after 'Boots' and the thought indicate that the passage was to supersede the uncancelled continuation of I113:1a: see *app. crit.*

three leagued Boots . . . small Beer, etc. Apparently a hit at Johnson. Cf. above, T91MS:3, 'greek & Latin stilts', and LR 7.

I113. *Noise & bombast.* A standard eighteenth-century complaint, given currency by Dryden 'Preface, The Grounds of Criticism in Tragedy' (1679), ed. Watson, i. 239 and 257 ff.; cf. also 'Defense of the Epilogue' (1673), ibid. i. 173, where Dryden ascribes the same criticism of Shakespeare to Ben Jonson.

T120MS. *deeper Complainings . . .Event; or court . . . Queen.* These two sentence elements, the first occupying two lines, the second one line, on the top margin of T120, are manifestly intended to replace uncancelled but much-worked-over ED on I120: see *app. crit.*

T108MS. *and on this account . . . obstinate Perseverance.* The 'X' following the word 'state' at the end of I108:3a marks the point where this passage, begun on the bottom margin of the facing page, T108, and continued on the top and outer margins of T109, was to be inserted. The content of the passage indicates that it was to supersede the corresponding material in I108:3b. See *app. crit.*

He stuck adhering. If Morgann proposed to retain the same illustration in I114:2 (p. 254), he might here have reinstated the ED recorded in the *app. crit.*

I109. *Macbeths Soliloquies.* Cf. Mac. I. vii. 20: 'the deep damnation of his taking off'; II. i. 58: 'The very stones prate of my whereabout'; V. iii. 14 (not a soliloquy): 'over-red thy fear'.

I106. *Johnson says.* I have not found the passage to which Morgann refers. Apparently it shares the presuppositions underlying the comment by Johnson on H8 censured in LR 7.

LR 6b. To judge from the contents and wording of LR 6b, Morgann either wrote it as a coda to LR 6a or let it stand for that purpose after having drafted it as an expanded A version of LR 6a continuing from T62MS:2 or 3, LR 6—ED 1.

A cancelled ED on PI2 of part of LR 6b is not reproduced except for a few phrases recorded in the *app. crit.* The ED appears to be a continuation from another page, but no such page is extant in the MS. book.

PI3. *Eccho to the sense.* Pope, *Essay on Criticism*, l. 365.

PT3MS. *The hoarse rough verse,* etc. Ibid., l. 369.
I would applaud, etc. Mac. V. iii. 53–4.
app. crit. *The line too labours,* etc. Pope, *Essay on Criticism*, l. 371.

LR 6—ED 2. T92MS:1b–I91:1. *strong. But.* The continuity is inferred by the facts that T92MS:1b (1) concludes the revision of the ED on I88–I91 (see note to LR 6a, T88MS–T92MS) and (2) evidently elaborates on the material (unreproduced) in I91 immediately preceding I91:1.

I93. *He broke open new Modes of Expression.* Cf. Walter Whiter, *A Specimen of a Commentary on Shakespeare* (1794), pp. 74–5: 'It was reserved for the knowledge of the present age to discover that Shakspeare has enriched and ennobled our poetry with new forms of language, rythm, fiction and imagery, which we know that he first invented, and believe he has finally completed.'

I93:8–I100:1. *the Mode.* The continuity is inferred from (1) the fact that I94–I99 are occupied by LR 9 and (2) the thought flow.

LR 6—ED 3. T111MS. *a genius of the highest order.* Edmund Burke: cf. ED, I110:5, in *app. crit.*
app. crit. *Burke flouts and even Johnson stalks.* Cf. Dryden 1670, Prologue, of Fletcher and Jonson:

> If they have since out-writ all other Men
> 'Tis with the drops which fell from *Shakespear*'s Pen.

LR 6—ED 5. I100. *And 'gins,* etc. Ham. I. v. 90: 'And 'gins to pale his uneffectual fire.'
by pale is meant to make pale, etc. See Wordsworth and Abbott, as cited in next note but two.

I101. *to tramel up.* Mac. I. vii. 3.
I begin to pale in Resolution. Apparently an emendation of 'I pull in Resolution', Mac. V. v. 42, with 'begin to' brought forward from the sequel, ll. 42–3: 'and begin / To doubt th'equivocation of the fiend.' Johns. 1765 conjectured 'pall'. W. G. Clark and W. A. Wright (eds.), *Macbeth* (Oxford, 1869) in addition suggested 'pale', as does Morgann. (Wright 1891 records 'pale' as an 'anon. conj.'.) (It is barely possible that the MS. reads 'pule' rather than 'pale'. Morgann's minuscule 'a' is here as often so open at the top as to be indistinguishable from his minuscule 'u'. The same holds true for the 'a' in 'paling' and 'pale' (I101:2). The reading 'pule' might explain the reference to growing sick like an infant, perhaps in confused association with 'mewling and puking in the nurse's arms', AYL. II. vii. 144. On the other hand, 'pule' would seem to be an 'active energy' in its own right rather than by conversion.)
converting the Substantive... into a Verb, &c. Hurd 1757, i. 51–3, note on l. 47, Horace's *Art of Poetry* ('callida... junctura'), praises Shakespeare's revitalizing of old words 'by a liberty he takes of converting *substantives* into verbs' and 'by

converting *Adjectives* into Substantives'. Charles Wordsworth, *On Shakespeare's Knowledge and Use of the Bible*, 3rd edn. (1880), p. 249 n, commends Hurd's note, adding that Shakespeare also displays great art in converting adjectives into verbs. Cf. Abbott 1870, par. 290: 'any noun or adjective could be converted into a verb by the Elizabethan authors, generally in an active signification.' Abbott cites Ham. I. v. 90 as an example.

Ye are not Oathable. Tim. IV. iii. 135–6: 'You are not oathable / Although I know you'll swear, terribly swear.'

LR 7

Written in a particularly crabbed hand on I15 and the margins of T15–T16, LR 7 comes between the segments designated as B5 and C1 in the conspectus in the Textual Note to LR 1–3. Morgann apparently interrupted his initial effort at revising the introductory section of *Es.* in order to set down in as little space as possible his violent reaction to Johnson's note on H8. As it stands, the revision reads like a detached observation, but possibly he intended to provide a transition which would convert it into an extension of, or a note to, his reservations, *Es.*, T63, regarding Johnson as a critic of Shakespeare. See note to T63.

With LR 7 as a whole cf. Walter Raleigh, as cited in Intro., p. 102. On Johnson's preference for 'domestic' plays 'in which the tender and pathetic predominate' see Arthur Sherbo, *Samuel Johnson, Editor of Shakespeare*, Illinois Studies in Language and Literature, vol. 42 (Urbana, 1956), pp. 77–80.

LR 8

The first part of a cancelled ED of this revision on I82–I86 is not reproduced except for a few short passages in the *app. crit.*; the latter part of the ED is reproduced in LR 8—ED 2. To judge from its opening sentence (*app. crit.* to LR 8, I80:1), contents, and position in the MS. book, the ED was intended as note to the phrase '*Bolingbroke* his father' in *Es.*, T82:3. In its final, more succinct form, LR 8 is seemingly designed to supersede T80:3b ('A transaction . . . of Infamy') and serve as a footnote to T80:3a. This intention is suggested by the phrasing of LR 8 as finally drafted and by its location on I80–I81. Morgann apparently transferred the revision from *Es.*, T82 to *Es.*, T80 because the discussion of the plot against Percy has more to do with the dramatic impression produced by Lancaster, which is treated on T80–T81, than with the unfolding of his whole character, which begins on T82:1. This consideration may also underlie Morgann's decision to delete his concluding comment on Shakespeare as a historian of general nature, reproduced in LR 8—ED 1. He marked the deletion by tracing a thin line through the centre of the unwanted material, without however including in his cancellation, as he should have, the 2¾ lines of very huddled writing at the start of the discarded passage ('Harry was . . . given us a').

The final version and location of LR 8 may also reflect Morgann's concern to take Stack 1789 into account. Failing to grasp the distinction between the whole and the dramatic character, Stack complained, p. 25, that Morgann erred in discrediting Lancaster because his damning deductions about the prince's whole character, though perhaps logical enough, were 'too philosophical a business for the public understanding'. Morgann would of course have agreed with the latter proposition, since he held the whole character to be concealed from the audience. On the other hand, he also held that Lancaster produces a negative dramatic effect, harmonious with though distinct from the mean motives and tendencies in his whole character, and in LR 8 he elaborates on this effect, which Stack also denied, by implicating the prince in the plot against Percy.

180. *spread for Percy*. Morgann bases his argument not only on Bolingbroke's 'Whole Character' (see *app. crit.*) and 'the Suspicions of Worcester', 1H4 V. ii. 4–23, but also in all probability on the king's ambiguous declaration, 'For on their answer we will set on them', 1H4 V. i. 119.

Shakespear does not allow us to suspect the Prince of any Privity. Cf. M. M. Reese, *The Cease of Majesty* (1961), p. 316: 'It is significant that Hal is not implicated in the treachery committed in Gaultree Forest ([2H4] IV. ii). It is evidently Prince John who inherits the parental notions of statecraft.'

Thy Place . . . in Council, etc. 1H4 III. ii. 32–3.

Harry's Challenge. 1H4 V. i. 85–100; cf. ii. 46–65.

and thus . . . We might trust, etc. 1H4 V. i. 101–3: 'And, Prince of Wales, so dare we venture thee, / Albeit considerations infinite / Do make against it.'

LR 8—ED 1. T81MS. *the best Historian*. Cf. note to *Es.*, T59 n.

LR 8—ED 2. 185. *Davilla.* Enrico Caterino Davila (1576–1631), Italian historian, author of *Historia delle guerre civili di Francia* (Venice, 1630).

the old Duke D'Epernon. Jean-Louis, duc d'Épernon (1554–1642), French general and a favourite of Henri III.

186. *Lord Bolingbroke.* The anecdote is referred to in the fifth of the 'Letters on the Study and Use of History', *Works of Lord Bolingbroke* (1754), ii. 344–5.

Life of D Espernon written by his secretary. Guillaume Girard, *Histoire de la vie du duc d'Espernon* (Paris, 1655).

LR 9

LR 9 is made up of two segments which, as appears from both their content and their position in the MS. book, are designed to supersede the uncancelled ED which immediately precedes them. The first segment, I99:1–4, was written last and revises the opening of the ED, I94:1–I95:1, the second segment, I96:4–I98:5, which was written before the first, revises the remainder of the ED, I95:2–I96:3. The relation of the segments to the ED indicates the intended final structure of the LR. The ED also provides the sole positive indication of how the revision fits into *Es.* The point of juncture is marked by an 'X' written in after T94:1, to which corresponds an 'X' at the head of the ED on the facing I page: see *app. crit.* to *Es.*, T94, and LR 9—ED 1, I94:1.

The ED seems still to require at least a sentence or two to be completed. The second segment, which begins immediately below the end of the ED, is even more obviously incomplete. It cuts off at the right side of the page at the bottom of I98 in the midst of a protasis which has every appearance of heading unerringly towards its apodosis, but the continuation is not to be found in the MS. book. The following page, where one would expect to find it, contains only the first segment. Presumably the missing conclusion of LR 9 and of the ED would have indicated that in the episode under discussion, the Hostess reflects a relaxation in the grouping of Falstaff to show a dramatic character more harmonious with his real personality.

I99. *Another Passage.* 2H4 II. i. 93–112.

I96. *Pyrrus.* Pyrrhus, the martial king of Epirus, was killed in 272 B.C. by a tile an elderly woman threw at him from a house-top.

I97. *40ˢ.* Actually, thirty shillings.

LR 9—ED. I95. *the ridiculous Pretence.* The Hostess says only that on Falstaff's desiring some prawns she told him 'they were ill for a green wound'. Morgann eliminated the error in revision. See *app. crit.* to LR 9, I97:2, where upon taking over the idea from LR 9—ED, the superseded false start stops short a little beyond the middle of a line, the balance of which is blank. This suggests that on repeating the idea Morgann at once reconsidered and revised it out of existence in the new version of the sentence, which begins as an interlineation in the earlier portion of the false start (inadvertently left uncancelled) and goes on just below the partly blank line.

LR 10

Morgann indicated clearly how LR 10 was to revise *Es.* He marked T122:5–T124:1 as cancelled, inserted an 'X' before 'But', the first word of T122:5, and in the outer margin of T122, on a level with the first three lines of the cancelled material, entered the notation 'Manu[script] 122 to 134 D?' (see *app. crit.* to T122:5 and T122:5–T124:1). He entered a corresponding 'X' above and before the first word of the original opening of the revision on I122; and immediately below the conclusion of LR 10 on I134 he wrote, 'See Page 124 pr[int]'. After completing the revision on I134, he composed what is manifestly a new opening for it on I139 (the intervening I pages are taken up with other materials). The uncancelled, superseded opening on I122 is not reproduced except for a few words in the *app. crit.* to I139:1–6.

In drafting LR 10, Morgann seems to have in view certain of the objections to *Es.*, T122, presented by Stack 1789, pp. 9–10. Morgann had defended Falstaff's 'Zounds, will they not rob us?' by comparing it with Hal's earlier 'I doubt they will be too hard for us'. The two cases are not at all alike, says Stack: 'The prince, reflecting that he and Poins were to be opposed to four men in arms, weighed the hazard of the jest with proper discretion', but Falstaff considers only the difference in numbers, not taking into account the fact that his party is armed, the other not. This, Stack declares, shows his mind to be so 'alive to the remotest apprehension of danger . . . that he instantly fancies the characters of the parties interchanged . . .'. Further, when he says, 'I am not indeed John of Gaunt but yet no coward, Hal', he is 'evading a charge, the force of which he had felt; and in this view of it, there appears admirable address, as by indirectly admitting the charge to a certain extent, and flattering the prince with the remembrance of his grandfather's prowess and courage, he has contrived to disarm him of his wit, and prevented him from urging matters to extremity'. Morgann's contrary opinion, Stack concludes, that Falstaff's quip is a mere caution to the audience not to take too seriously what was intended only as a jest, is not the 'natural impression' produced by the speech but 'the very refinement of criticism'. The more elaborate interpretation of the first stage of the Gadshill episode worked out in LR 10 includes replies not only to the two specific points made by Stack but also to his accusation of excessive refinement: see Intro., p. 48.

1139. *Gadshill, who has sett, as it is called.* To 'set' in Elizabethan thieves' cant is to obtain the information and make the arrangements for a robbery. Cf. 1H4 I. ii. 118–19: 'Now shall we know if Gadshill have set a match', and ibid., II. ii. 53 (referring to Gadshill): 'O, 'tis our setter.'

   The Commentators . . . do not understand it. The commentators referred to are Johnson and his predecessors (Rowe, Pope, Theobald, Hanmer, and Warburton) whom Johnson rebukes in his note to 1H4 II. ii. 54–7, Johns. 1765–93. Morgann can say they all misunderstand because he agrees and disagrees with both Johnson and the earlier editors. In reassigning l. 54 to Bardolph (*vice* Poins: see *app. crit.*, and cf. next note) and ll. 55–7 to Gadshill (*vice* Bardolph), he is adopting an emendation which Johnson put forward as a conjecture in Johns. 1765 and which was admitted into the text of Johns. 1778–93, Malone 1790, and many other editions down to the last quarter of the nineteenth century. But if he concurs with Johnson against the line of editors from Rowe to Warburton in his reading of the passage, he sides with the latter against the former regarding a relevant S.D. In his note, Johnson objects to the editors' attempt to support the original reading of the text by having Bardolph enter with Gadshill. This is at variance with the original S.D., which brings Gadshill in alone, and in making the change, Johnson says, the editors forget that Bardolph is already near by, as is shown by Falstaff's calling to him a little earlier (l. 22) for his horse. Morgann holds with the editors, though not for their reasons, that Gadshill enters 'accompanied with Bardolph'. And just as he accepts the altered S.D., though not the uncorrected reading it is designed to support, so he defends the Johnsonian emendation of the text on grounds different from those urged by Johnson. Poins cannot ask Bardolph 'What news?' Johnson claims, because it would be absurd for Poins, who knows that Gadshill is the setter (see prec. note), to request a report from Bardolph. Morgann, who would have Gadshill and Bardolph enter together, offers a different reason, based not on Poins's presumed psychology but on his lack of night vision. This argument, which Morgann presents in compressed form, may be unfolded as follows: If Bardolph comes on with Gadshill, and if Poins is able to recognize Gadshill in the dark only by his voice, how could he at once recognize the silent Bardolph so as to address a question to him? Bardolph would not be recognizable, Morgann explains, until he had come closer and his features could be made out in the obscurity.

The defence by Ritson 1783, pp. 91–2, of the editors against Johnson would range him from Morgann's point of view among the commentators who 'misunderstand'. Holding that Johnson's argument against altering the S.D. falls since 'Falstaff's calling out for Bardolph is not proof that he was within hearing', Ritson also rejects Johnson's emendation in favour of the original reading.

1122. *This is pointed in the Text*, etc. Fully to understand Morgann's argument here, it is necessary to take into account the associated cancelled passage reproduced in the *app. crit.*, which shows that he follows Johnson in taking 'Bardolph' as a speech-prefix rather than as a continuation of Poins's speech. Perhaps Morgann did not reincorporate this idea explicitly in his uncancelled text because the difficulty now dawned on him that if, as he presently argues, Bardolph had an opportunity 'to discourse with Gadshill on the way', it seems odd that of all the people present it should be Bardolph who asks 'What news?' Presumably Bardolph already knows.

1124. *The answer . . . again correct.* Morgann did not carry out his intention of converting the materials of this passage into a footnote to the later-written version of the main text reproduced in the *app. crit.* His proposal to transfer Gadshill's line to Bardolph is original: to be consistent he would have had in his revised edition to adjust *Es.*, T122, where he assigns the speech to Gadshill.

1127. *the word Event.* Here as a little later Morgann builds his interpretation on *Es.*, T123:3, where he quotes the prince as saying 'Well, let the event try'. Actually the words Shakespeare places in his mouth are 'Well, we leave that to the proof' (1H4 II. ii. 72). Morgann could, of course, discover the same double meaning in 'proof' that he finds in 'event'.

LR 11

Textual Note. LR 11 consists of (1) LR 11a, a lengthy revision apparently intended to supersede T126:2–T129:1, and (2) two shorter passages, LR 11b and LR 11c, apparently designed as footnotes to LR 11a. The distribution of the materials for the revision in the MS. book suggests that in its final form LR 11 was the last revision Morgann composed: he wrote most of it on the closing pages of the MS. book, using scattered earlier pages for insertions, redraftings, and a new conclusion. The seven successive stages through which the revision was built up are designated A . . . G in the following conspectus. (Some of the stages are further subdivided in order to exhibit interrelations between revision segments. As thus analysed, LR 11a is made up of ten segments in the sequence F1, F2, F3, A2, C, F4, G2, F5, F6, F7, and LR 11b and 11c are made up respectively of D and E.)

F7   I86:2–I87:2 (LR 11a, 10th segment). Continuation of F6; fol. by T129:2. [I88–I121: LR 6a and LR 9—see Textual Note to LR 6a.]

G1   I116:1 (LR 11a, *app. crit.* to T181:1). Cancelled revision of opening of F1. [I122–I134: LR 10, except for opening.]

A1   I134:4-6 (LR 11a, *app. crit.* to I135:1). Continuation of T129:1. Super-
      seded by F3.

A2   I135:1–I136:2 (LR 11a, 4th segment). Continuation of A1; subsequently
      continuation of F3.

A3   I136:3 (LR 11a, *app. crit.* to I136:2). Continuation of A2; fol. by T129:2.
      Superseded by C.

B1   I136:4–I138 (not reproduced except for I137: 3-5 in LR 11a, 2nd seg-
      ment, and for excerpts in *app. crit.* thereto). Continuation of T128:5;
      fol. by B2, subsequently at E stage by T128:6. Partly cancelled; absorbed
      into and superseded by F2.

B2   I138a:1b, I138b:1–2, I138:2 (LR 11c, *app. crit.* to I171:4). Three
      successive versions of the conclusion of B1; fol. by T128:6. Cancelled;
      superseded by E.
      [I139: LR 10, opening.]
      [I140–I147: LR 12 (insertion to T146) except for final draft of conclusion.

C   I147:3-4 (LR 11a, 5th segment). Continuation of A2; supersedes A3;
      fol. by T129:2, subsequently by F4.
      [I148–I149: LR 12, revised conclusion.]
      [I150–I157: LR 3a.]

D   I158:1–I159:3 (LR 11b). Footnote to T128:1; subsequently footnote to
      LR 11a, F2, I184:4.
      [I160–I166: LR 3—ED 4 and LR 3b.]
      [I167–I168: LR 13 (revision of T167).]
      [I169: SR 27.]

E   I170:1–I171:7, I172:6–I173:4 (LR 11c). Footnote to LR 11a, end of B1;
      supersedes B2; subsequently footnote to LR 11a, F2, I185:1.

G2   I173:5–I173:6 (LR 11a, 7th segment). Continuation of F4; fol. by F5.

F6   I174:1–I175:7 (LR 11a, 9th segment). Continuation of F5; fol. by F7.
      [I176–I180: LR 14 (revision of T176).]
      [I178–I179: removed from MS. book.]

F1   I181:1–I182:2 (LR 11a, 1st segment). Continuation of T126:1; fol. by F2.

F2   I183:1–I184:2, I137:3, I184:3, I137:4-5, I184:4–I185:1 (LR 11a, 2nd
      segment). Continuation of F1; incorporates and supersedes B1.

F3   I185:2-3 (LR 11a, 3rd segment). Continuation of F2; supersedes A1;
      fol. by A2.

F4   I185:4-6, T185MS:1–T186MS:3, I186:1–I188:10 (LR 11a, 6th seg-
      ment). Continuation of C; fol. by F5, subsequently by G2.

F5   I189:1-9 (LR 11a, 8th segment). Continuation of F4, subsequently of G2.

LR 11 evolved through two principal stages—the development of the nucleus
A–E, and the incorporation and expansion of A–E in the final F–G version.
The three main elements of the A–E nucleus are (1) A+C, (2) B+E, and (3) D.
Morgann originally marked A for insertion at the par. break following T129:1.
Presumably because I129 ff. were already occupied with LR 10, he began the
revision on the first subsequent I page space available, on the lower fifth of I134,
below the last line of LR 10. Beneath the conclusion of A, about midway down
I136, he wrote 'return to 129 pr[int]'. This corresponds to the notation 'X see
134 man[uscript] to 136 D?' at the par. break following T129:1. Later, Morgann

expanded A3 into C, again using the first subsequent I page space available at the time, i.e. the lower two-thirds of I147. Though he did not thereupon cancel A3 on I136, he entered the notation '136' at the head of C, and it seems safe to assume that at this stage he intended the instructions at the end of A3 to apply to C, which would provide for the sequence T129:1, A1, A2, C, T129:2.

He also originally designated B as a separate insertion to *Es.* He began the revision on I136 immediately after A3, marked an 'X' above and before its first word, and wrote 'Return to 128 pr[int]' beneath its last line at the bottom of I138. This corresponds to his notation 'See 136 man[uscript] to 138 D?' in the outer margin of T128 opposite an 'X' between T128:5 and 6 just before the beginning of SR 14. Of B1 only the material on I136 is cancelled. In the main, B1 is not reproduced; it may, however, be approximately reconstructed: F2 incorporates B1 with only very minor changes, all recorded in the *app. crit.* to LR 11a, I183:1–I185:1. Morgann later expanded and recast B2 as E (LR 11c). Though he failed to indicate where E was to fit in, it manifestly supersedes B2, and as in this new form the materials no longer dovetail terminally with T128:6 while B1 readily does so, they must have been designed as a note to the conclusion of B1.

To judge from their relative locations in the MS. book, he wrote D (LR 11b) before E. He did not mark D for insertion at any particular point in *Es.*, but the contents of the revision suggest that he designed it as a note to T128:1. This assumption is confirmed by an 'X' entered in the outer margin opposite T128:1 (see *app. crit.*).

After completing A–E, he drew up the more comprehensive revision which includes almost all the earlier materials. He began this final version with F1 on I181–I182 and went on at once to redraft B1 as F2 on I183–I185, without, however, recopying the Shakespeare quotations he had written out in full in the earlier version (I137:3 and 4–5). In the next two sentences, I185:2–3=F3, he provided a link from F2 to A2 and designated the latter as the intended sequel by ending F3 with 'His Habiliments etc. see 134', a manifest overlap with the conclusion of A1 (see LR 11a, *app. crit.* to I185:3 and I135:1). He presumably intended A2 to be followed by C, as before, and picked up from C in F4. He began the latter immediately after F3 with I185:4 and went on without a break to F5 on I189. Later, at the end of F4, on the bottom of I188 he wrote 'X 173' to mark the insertion of G2. A corresponding 'X' precedes G2, which he scrawled on the lower fifth of I173 below the conclusion of E. Obviously, he now intended F5, the original sequel of F4, to continue from the conclusion of G. By writing in '174' beneath the last line of F5 at the bottom of I189, he marked the segment as going on to F6 on I174–I175; and by the notation '86' beneath the last word of F6 at the bottom of I175 he marked that segment as leading into F7 on I86–I87.

In the new, enlarged revision Morgann did not explicitly reassign the notes E and D. However, it seems logical to assume that he maintained E, originally a note to the end of B1, as a note to the end of F2, the segment which recasts B1. It seems equally likely that he now thought of D as another note to F2, to be subjoined at I184:4: this sentence rehandles the material of T128:1, to which D was originally attached as a note. As for LR 11 as a whole, the fact that it absorbed the substance of B1 and the text of A2+C nullified the earlier uncancelled directions for inserting B and A (+C) before the penultimate and after the last sentence, respectively, of the par. that occupies T126:2–T129:1.

He did not provide new directions, but, as the contents of LR 11a shows, he clearly intended the final version for insertion at approximately the same place in *Es*. Stylistically, the only way the revision fits in smoothly is if it supersedes the entire par., and the hypothesis that he had this in mind seems borne out by the following analysis of the materials that would thus be cancelled:

1. T126:2.—Providing a smooth enough transition from what precedes, this leading sentence presents Falstaff's lack of cowardice as the main topic of the par., to which the subsequent discussion of players' distortions is subordinated. The beginning of LR 11a, on the other hand, while affording an equally smooth transition, announces the distortions of the actors as the main theme of the par. This different initial emphasis, which is fully supported by what follows in the revision, accords with the decisive role that Morgann assigns to players' misrepresentations in the revised version of his thesis: see Intro., pp. 75–6.

2. T126:3–T127:4.—This argument that cowardice in an old, infirm man is not funny, though lost in LR 11, is sufficiently brought out in T134:3, T142:3, and, above all, T147:2.

3. T127:2 and 4.—In T127:2 Morgann claims in effect that the players misrepresent Shakespeare out of sheer obtuseness and perversity. In LR 11a, expanding on the hint in T127:4, he damns them more effectively by analysing instead the textual basis for their literal-minded distortions.

4. T127:3.—This description of how Falstaff sat down with the money-bag seems to be the only valuable detail which would be completely lost by having LR 11 supersede T126:2–T129:1.

5. T127:4–T128:1.—LR 11a manifestly revises and so supersedes this account of Falstaff's flight from the disguised Prince and Poins.

6. T128:2–4.—Omitted in LR 11. Retaining what he had said to discredit Falstaff's roaring a few pages earlier (T124:5–T125:1), Morgann may well have felt in revisal that it was impolitic to keep this second attempt, which invokes the dramatic principle that in some situations the less we see, the better we conceive. Though in itself the idea is interesting—it anticipates Lamb: see Intro., p. 22—as applied to Falstaff's roaring it seems particularly vulnerable to the charge by Stack 1789, p. 12, that in refusing to take the word of the Prince and Poins on the subject, Morgann was merely indulging 'a laudable zeal . . . of questioning everything which might reflect on the character of his hero'.

7. T128:6–T129:1+SR 14.—The reference in LR 11a to the historical evidence for Hal's being 'remarkably slender' (I183:2: see note below) obviously supersedes this argument, which both in its original form and as revised by SR 14 might be discounted precisely by the appeal to history.

LR 11a. I181. *app. crit. Such are . . . different indeed.* Written in the relatively capacious top margin of *c*. 47 mm. which Morgann had left on I116 when composing LR 6a and quite unrelated to the other materials on I115 and I116, this cancelled fragment may be inferred from its contents and phrasing to be an attempted revision of the opening of LR 11a. Apparently Morgann thought for a moment it would improve his argument to appeal at this point to the impression 'naturally taken' from the book, and then rejected the afterthought, perhaps because he recalled his more astute earlier statement in LR 2, I43:3–4, that one naturally reads a play under the influence of universally accepted opinion.

I182. *a good portly man*, etc. 1H4 II. iv. 463–5.
Trunk of Humours, etc. 1H4 II. iv. 495–500.

I183. *goodman Puff of Barson*. 2H4 V. iii. 94.
in History. In Johns. 1778–93, note to 1H4 II. iv. 270, Steevens cites Stowe as Shakespeare's 'historical authority for the *leanness* of the Prince of Wales'.

I184. *lend out his Wit against Himself.* Cf. *Es.*, T173.
Peace ye Fat Guts, etc. 1H4 II. ii. 33–9.
a Hundred and odd Posts, etc. 2H4 IV. iii. 38–40: 'nine score and odd posts.' Morgann sometimes takes 'posts' to mean 'miles': cf. *Es.*, T55 and note.

I135. *Singularity of appearance*. Cf. Davies, as cited in Intro., p. 40.
Shirts . . . of Holland, etc. 1H4 III. iii. 77–83.
Mr. Doubledown, etc. 2H4 I. ii. 33–50. Morgann here adopts M. Mason's conjectural emendation of F Dombledon (Q Dommelton) as found in Johns. 1778–93.

I136. *Smooth-Pates in honest taking up*. 2H4 I. ii. 43 and 46. In conflating, Morgann garbles the sense of the second phrase which applies to the customers rather than to the shopkeepers.
the thousand Pound he borrowed of Shallow. 2H4 V. v. 11–13.

T186MS. *the gallant Nym*. A slip for Gadshill? Nym appears only in H5 and Wiv. Cf. note to *Es.*, T52. On the staging of the robbery cf. *Es.*, T124 ff. and LR 10, I133–4.

I186. *Thou hast . . . damnable iteration*. 1H4 I. ii. 89–101.

I189. *He breaks Falstaff's Head*, etc. 2H4 II. i. 97–8.
requires Comment & shall find it. See LR 9.
The speech belongs to Poins. Hemingway 1936 records that except for Capell 1768 all eighteenth-century editions from Rowe 1709 to Johns. 1785 inclusive followed F1–4 and Q 5–8 in assigning the speech in 1H4 II. iv. 159–60 to the Prince. Only with Rann 1786 and Malone 1790 did the earlier Q speech prefix, which Morgann argues for, become established.
app. crit. Payne Bookseller . . . Fl. Street. Morgann jotted down this list of booksellers below the middle of I189 before he used the page for LR 11a, which takes up the rest of the space above and below. Perhaps he was casting about for a publisher of his projected revised edition. Thomas Davies, the original publisher of *Es.*, died in 1785.

I174. *oily Rascal*, etc.; *You make fat Rascalls*, etc. 1H4 II. iv. 575 and 2H4 II. iv. 43–51. Johns. 1765–93 observes of the latter passage that in foresters' language '*Lean* dear are called *rascal* dear'. Morgann uses this information to interpret 'rascalliest' in 1H4 I. ii. 89. Johnson, later abetted *con brio* by Steevens, also expounds the allusions to venereal disease in 1H4 II. iv. 43–51: Morgann applies these glosses to 'oily Rascal' in 1H4 II. iv. 575.

186. *a good Knave*, etc. 2 H4 V. iii. 13 ff.: 'a good varlet', etc. Morgann's argument is not, however, affected by the error.

LR 11 b. Drawing on other contemporary accounts, Sprague 1944, p. 89, describes Falstaff's crawling away after being thrashed by the Prince and Poins as the usual eighteenth-century stage business in the scene (1H4 II. ii. 110).

LR 11 c. The stage episode Morgann here describes in vivid detail was also the subject of comment by others. Francis Gentleman, note to Bell's edition of Shakespeare (1773), 1H4, p. 72, also deplores 'the son of sack's rolling and tumbling' when he raises the dead Hotspur onto his back. So too does Thomas Davies, *Dramatic Miscellanies*, i (1784), 273–5, who reports that 'no joke ever raised such loud and repeated mirth, in the Galleries, as Sir John's labour in getting the body of Hotspur in his back'; but, he adds, the practice was discontinued when John Henderson (who played Falstaff from 1772 to his death in 1785) encountered difficulties 'in getting Smith on his shoulders. So much time was consumed . . . that the spectators grew tired, or rather disgusted. It was thought best, for the future, that some of Falstaff's ragamuffins should bear off the dead body.' It is difficult to determine from this exactly when Henderson discontinued the mummery. Referring apparently to current productions, Morgann's comment suggests that the offensive dumb show may have been restored by Thomas Ryder, Henderson's successor in the role of Falstaff at Covent Garden during the period 1786–90 (Hemingway 1936, p. 485, and Charles Beecher Hogan, *Shakespeare in the Theatre 1701–1800* ii [Oxford, 1957], 258–60).

Davies assigns the 'pick-a-back' business to 1H4 V. iv. 166 ('I'll follow, as they say, for reward') whereas Morgann appears to locate it earlier at ll. 131–2 ('Come you along with me').

I172. *Dryden in his indian Emperour*. Act II, scene iii. The prince is Odmar.

LR 12

In writing LR 12, Morgann seems again to have had Stack 1789 in view. Stack, pp. 12–14, rejects the twin argument on T140 that the tavern scene exhibits not Falstaff the coward but only Falstaff the liar and that on this occasion his wit fails him and he is exposed. Against this Stack declares that Falstaff's lies could have no existence except on the psychological foundation of his cowardice, and that in T140:2, which Stack quotes, Morgann's 'over-strained defence of Falstaff's courage' leads him to sacrifice the knight's 'inimitable wit and humour'. With regard to the latter point, Stack goes on, so far from failing him at the critical moment, Falstaff's wit enables him to triumph over his adversaries, who find no reply to his explanation that he had been a 'coward upon instinct'. In LR 12 Morgann restates his position in such a way as to obviate these objections. As if to forestall the charge that he slights Falstaff's wit, he stresses the hilarity of the scene, and while retaining his argument that not Falstaff's cowardice but only his lies are in question he agrees that their psychological origin poses a question. See Intro., pp. 98–101.

Significantly, LR 12 starts about one-quarter of the way down I140, just opposite the beginning of T140:2, the sentence Stack quotes to prove that Morgann sacrifices Falstaff's wit. The location of the revision reinforces the inference that Morgann was writing with Stack in mind. Originally he may even have designed LR 12 to supersede T140:2 ff. But if he did, he finally decided to insert it on T146, as indicated by the following instructions written in on the top quarter of I140: 'NB What follows Here is to be inserted in page 146 pr[int] Where Reference will be made to it.' Above and below this directive appear single horizontal lines, setting it off from the revision below. An 'X' following T146:1, corresponding to an 'X' at the head of LR 12 (see *app. crit.*), provides the promised 'Reference'.

Morgann subsequently wrote a new conclusion for LR 12 on I148–I149. The uncancelled ED conclusion on I146 (lower half) and I147 (upper third) is not reproduced except for two excerpts in the *app. crit.*

I140. *a few Pages ago. Es.*, T101:7.

I141. *blushed at his Monstrous Devices*, etc. 1H4 II. iv. 336–44. (Morgann re-arranges and conflates two speeches, one by Peto, the other by Bardolph. The former says that Falstaff hacked his sword with his dagger, etc.)

I143. *These lies are like*, etc. 1H4 II. iv. 249–52.

I144. *But two Months dead*, etc. Ham. I. ii. 138, 145, and 147. (Morgann com-presses separate lines into a single speech.)

I148. *overstepping the Modesty of Nature*. Ham. III. ii. 21–2.

I149. *app. crit. Fingal*, etc. It is not clear how, if at all, this jotting is related to the revision of *Es.*

LR 13

LR 13 is clearly marked as superseding T167:2–3: the latter passage is can-celled, the substitution is explicitly required by the notations on T167 and I168, and the 'X' prec. I167:1 corresponds to the 'X' following *Es.*, T167:1.

LR 14

That LR 14 is an insertion at the par. break between T175:3 and T176:1 is indicated by an 'X' on T176 in the outer margin opposite the first word of T176:1 and by the fact that the revision begins on the facing I page. LR 14 occupies I176–I177 and I180. I178–I179 have been removed from the MS. book, but their absence does not disrupt the continuity of the revision.

A COMMENTARY ON *THE TEMPEST*

Introduction. In contending that Tp., as we have it, is a *rifacimento*, with the masque and other spectacular elements among the later additions, Morgann anticipates a controversy which began over a century and a quarter ago and has assumed major proportions in the past fifty years. During the middle decades of the nineteenth century Knight 1841, pp. 398–9, and Verplanck 1847, iii. 5, first suggested that Tp. had been fairly extensively revised, Staunton 1872, p. 636, that it was abridged, and Clark and Glover 1863 (note to Tp. IV. i. 146) that the masque 'can scarcely have come from Shakespeare's pen'. Thus launched, the idea that the play had been altered in one way or another gained adherents among such scholars as Fleay, 1876, p. 54, 1877, p. 29, and 1886, p. 249; Nicholson 1886 (cf. Furness 1892, p. 156); Robertson 1917, pp. 210–15; and Law 1921, pp. 24–7. But not till Gray 1921 and Wilson 1921 was the revision theory elaborated in the detailed and methodical fashion employed long before by Morgann. The debate has since flourished. At one extreme, Kermode 1954, p. xxiv, repudiates all suggestions of later modification, whether by Shakespeare himself or by anyone else. Between his stand and that of the drastic revisionists like Gray and Wilson is a range of opinion which includes Kittredge 1936, p. 3, and 1939, p. viii, who would allow only for retouching, and Chambers 1930, i. 492–3, and Greg 1955, p. 420, both in principle opposed to disintegration (cf. Chambers 1925), yet unable to overcome their uneasiness about 'certain of the spectacular and musical elements' in the play, specifically I. ii. 298–304, 307, II. i. 297–305, and IV. i. 106–11.

Since Morgann scatters his arguments in support of his revision theory through many separate comments, it may be convenient to have his views on the subject brought together and summarized in the following outline.

I. Immaturities, or evidences of professional callowness in the composition of Tp.
   A. Adherence to the Unities: *Com.* Introduction, V. i. 4, and V. i. 223.
   B. The dialogue between Sebastian, Antonio, and Gonzalo: *Com.* Introduction. (But cf. II, C.)
   C. Ariel as an 'Electric Spark': *Com.* I. ii. 301–2.
II. Vestiges, or mutilated survivals of the earlier version.
   A. Trinculo as fool: *Com.* I. ii. 233, II. ii. 14, III. ii. 71, and V. i. 277 and 279.
   B. Antonio's son: *Com.* I. ii. 437–8.
   C. The dialogue between Sebastian, Antonio, and Gonzalo: *Com.* II. i. 9–106.
III. Inconsistencies, or variously inharmonious additions to the earlier version.
   A. Gonzalo's 'kindness' merely the provision of gorgeous raiment: *Com.* II. i. 297–9 (cf. *Com.* I. ii. 146–51 and III. i. 50; cf. also III, D, 3, a).
   B. Miranda's witnessing of the masque: *Com.* I. ii. 188.
   C. The 'meaner' spirits as masquers: *Com.* I. ii. 250.
   D. Spectacular Effects.
      1. The 'Induction': *Com.* Introduction, I. i. 1, and V. i. 215–18.
      2. Show and music, including the masque and other 'machinery': *Com.* Introduction, III. ii. 133, III. iii. 19, III. iii. 52, III. iii. 82, IV. i. 59, and V. i. 57.

3. Sartorial splendour: *Com.* III. iii. 19 and V. i. 215.

   a. Prospero's use of Gonzalo's gifts: *Com.* I. ii. 164, II. i. 297, IV. i. 186, and V. i. 85.

   b. Prospero's orders regarding the shipwreck: *Com.* I. ii. 29, I. ii. 216–18 (cf. *Com.* II. i. 62 and II. i. 68).

IV. Historical Concurrences, or contemporary references, conditions, and events which support the theory.

  A. Those which confirm an early first version.

    1. Limited wardrobe in theatres of the late 1580s: *Com.* II. i. 297.

    2. The earlier history of the Bermudas and their reputation in the late 1580s: *Com.* Introduction.

  B. Those which confirm a late revision.

    1. The vogue of the masque under James I: *Com.* Introduction and IV. i. 59.

    2. Sops to James I's disapproval of magic: *Com.* IV. i. 139 and V. i. 50.

    3. The allusion to Tp. in *Bartholomew Fair*: *Com.* III. ii. 3.

    4. Somers's shipwreck and its consequences: *Com.* Introduction.

Morgann ignores a number of arguments which figure prominently in modern revision theory. Though he regards the masque as evidence of revision, he neither condemns it as bad poetry nor assigns it to a non-Shakespearian hand; he fails to detect the internal rhymes and broken lines which are supposed by some to prove the existence of an earlier version; he regards II. i. 297–9 as a players' interpolation rather than evidence of authorial revision (*Com.* I. ii. 180, II. i. 296, II. i. 297–9, II. i. 306, II. i. 317, and III. ii. 124); and though he appeals to external history, he does not mention the court performance of 1612/13, already cited in his day as significant for dating the play and now often taken (e.g., by Lawrence 1920) as the occasion for which Tp. was altered. On the other hand, as is brought out in the notes to the relevant comments, he anticipates later commentators in certain major points and in others opens a mine of argument still untapped by latter-day revisionists.

In the Introduction, when appealing to Historical Concurrences, he offers unusual views on Bermudan history and makes downright errors regarding Sir George Somers's shipwreck. He probably derived his information about the Bermudas from Sir William Monson's *Naval Tracts*, as published by Awnsham and John Churchill in vol. iii of their *Collection of Voyages and Travels* (1704; later edns., 1745 and 1752)—just the sort of compilation he would have examined in the course of his duties as Shelburne's adviser on American affairs. Monson is the only early source to assert that the Portuguese actually lived on the Bermudas for a while. The more usual view was that the islands were uninhabited till the English came (see Jourdain 1610, p. 8, Adam Anderson, *Historical and Chronological Deduction of Commerce* [1764], i. 486, and William Combe's rev. edn. of Anderson [1787], iii. 254.) Monson, however, declares that the Bermudas were

Discover'd by the *Portuguese* Nation, and inhabited by them, till they found little profit accru'd from it, and then they abandon'd it, . . . and thus it lay waste for many Years, with a general Opinion to be inhabited with Spirits, which made all Men shun the sight of it at their return out of the *Indies*. (iii [1704], 439; iii. 405 in edns. of 1745 and 1752.)

This is pretty much what Morgann says, except for his bit of embroidery that on leaving the island the Portuguese deliberately propagated old wives' tales so as to deter other settlers. In asserting that the Portuguese left the islands 'about the year 1550', he may be echoing another passage in the *Collection of Voyages* (v. 633, edns. of 1732, 1746, and 1752), according to which they obtained the privilege of colonizing the Bermudas in 1552 (an error for 1557 in the source, Herrera, as noted by J. H. Lefroy, *Memorials of the Bermudas* [1877], i. 4 n.), and discounting the claim in the same passage that the plan for settlement 'took no effect'.

Monson misremembered may account for his two errors about Sir George Somers's shipwreck. He incorrectly routes Somers back to England via Newfoundland—in point of fact Somers went on to Virginia—and dates the mishap to 1592 rather than to 1609 when it actually took place. Immediately after the passage quoted in the preceding paragraph Monson mentions two Bermudan shipwrecks, the first by a French captain who returned to Europe by way of Newfoundland, the second in 1592 by the English sailor Henry May, who also 'made shift, as the others did, to get to Newfoundland'. In the next sentence Monson observes without indicating any date that on his passage to Virginia Sir George Somers had a 'like Shipwrack'. Recollecting all this rather hazily, Morgann, it would appear, decided that Somers too escaped by way of Newfoundland, and shifted Monson's date for May's shipwreck to that of Somers's. The likelihood that he was garbling Monson rather than another source is reinforced by the precise wrong date involved, for the other seventeenth- and eighteenth-century accounts of Bermuda concur both in saying that May shipwrecked in 1593—not 1592—and in omitting to mention any shipwreck at all in the latter year (Hackluyt, edn. Glasgow, x. 200, Purchas, edn. Glasgow, xix. 173, Churchill, *Collection of Voyages*, v [1733], 633, ibid., edns. 1746 and 1752). If Morgann had brought his work nearer to publication, he might of course have corrected these inaccuracies. In particular, he could have discovered the true date of Somers's shipwreck by referring to Farmer 1773, repeated in Johns. 1778–93, initial note to Tp., or, even more readily, either by turning back the very pages he was writing on to Theobald's Preface (p. x) or by turning forward to Theobald's note on 'the still-vexed Bermoothes', which he later studied with some care: see *Com.* I. ii. 229 and note. The right date for Somers's shipwreck, as it happens, improves his argument.

In holding that the original Tp. was Shakespeare's first play, written in 1587 (the date commonly accepted in the late eighteenth century for Shakespeare's arrival in London from Stratford), he runs counter to the view already orthodox in his day that the play is late. (So Theobald 1733, p. x, Holt, 1749, pp. 17–18, Capell 1783, ii, pt. 4, pp. 58 and 66, Farmer, Johns. 1773, App. II and 1778–93, initial note to Tp., Malone 'Essay' in Johns. 1778, i. 341, reprinted Johns. 1785–93 and Malone 1790, and Blackstone, Johns. Sup. 1780, i. 79–1793, initial note to Tp.) Today, though briefly revived by Janet Spens, *Elizabethan Drama* (1922), pp. 87–8 and 92, the heresy that Tp. in its original form is one of Shakespeare's earliest works has no adherents. Even exponents of revision, e.g. E. Muir, *Shakespeare's Sources*, i (1957), 243, generally assign the alleged first version of the play to 1611, Morgann's date for the *rifacimento*. The sole exception appears to be Wilson 1921, p. 79, who suggests that Shakespeare 'had an old manuscript to go on, possibly an early play of his own'. In Morgann's own time, James Hurdis, *Cursory Remarks upon the Arrangement of the Plays of Shakespeare* (1792), pp. 6–8, seems to have been the first to claim that Tp. was early. The play, he said, was so ridden by metrical irregularity that it must be the work of a very 'inexperienced poet'. Lacking such obtuseness (Hurdis, p. 40, also finds Ant. 'in almost every scene, dull and laborious'), Morgann has something in common with the early nineteenth-century critics—Coleridge, Knight, and Hunter—who assigned Tp. to an early stage in Shakespeare's career because they found it artistically less mature or profound than many other of his plays (Coleridge ed. Raysor, i. 239–40 and ii. 96; Knight 1841, p. 398; Joseph Hunter, *A Disquisition . . . on Shakespeare's Tempest* (1839), *A Few Words in reply to . . . Mr. Dyce* (1853), and Hunter 1857). Hunter proposed 1596 as the date of Tp., claiming that the Bermudas were generally known in London by that year. Anticipating this claim, Morgann asserts that the Bermudas had been widely heard of even earlier, in 1587. He does not supply in *Com.* the 'evidences to this point' which he declares 'will be *noted* in the Course of the Play'. The promise itself, however, suggests he was aware that his contention ran counter to prevailing opinion in his day. Farmer claimed that the earliest account of the Bermudas dated back to 1593 and was not published till 1600, and Malone and Blackstone expressly said they were not generally known till 1609 (see references at beginning of this par.). Morgann's failure to document his rejection of this view does not, of course, disprove his assertion that as early as 1587 the Bermudas were already known as a place which was supernaturally haunted and surrounded with magical storms. Jourdain 1610 and Strachey 1610 refer to such rumours as having been noised abroad for some time; Sir William Monson, as quoted above, also testifies to such impressions having circulated for many years; and in Sebastian Cabot's Mappa Mundi of 1544, the Bermudas appear, designated as 'De Demonios'.

For Morgann's locating the scene of Tp. in the Bermudas, his idea that the opening scene is an induction, and his opinion of Shakespeare's recourse to the unities see *Com.* I. ii. 229, I. i. 1, and V. i. 4 and the notes thereto, respectively.

His supposition that the play is based on an Italian novel echoes speculation going back to Warburton 1747 and accumulated in Johns. 1765, x, Appendix–1793, initial note to Tp.

With his view, expressed in the Introduction and Marginal Note 2, that Jacobean taste valued the trumpery of masques above truth and nature cf. Ben Jonson's 'Address to the Reader', *The Alchemist*: 'in this age . . . especially in plays . . . the Concupiscence of Daunces, and Antikes so raigneth, as to runne away from nature and be afraid of her, is the onely point of art that tickles the *Spectators*.' See also *Com.* IV. i. 59 and note.

Marginal Note 1. Morgann obviously means to write that Setebos is the god of *Caliban* and that *Caliban* is a metathesis of *Cannibal* into *Caliban*. Setebos is identified as a Patagonian god by Farmer 1773, Oo3ʳ and Johns. 1778–93, note to I. ii. 373; Tollet, Johns. 1778–85 and Malone, Johns. 1785, note to I. ii. 373; and Henley, Johns. Sup. 1780, ii. 683, and 1785, note to I. ii. 229. See also *Com.* I. ii. 373. Farmer (same ref.) and Malone, Johns. 1785–93, note to I. ii. 284, note that 'Caliban' is a metathesis of 'canibal'.

I. i. 1. Gildon 1710, p. 261, had suggested that the storm scene 'has very little to do' in the play. Arriving at the idea independently both here and in *Com. Introduction*, *ad fin.*, Morgann develops the thought along lines that anticipate Coleridge, ed. Raysor, i. 131–2: 'The romance opens with a busy lively scene, admirably appropriate to the *kind* of drama, giving as it were the key-note. . . . It prepares and initiates the excitement required for the entire piece, and yet . . . is purposely restrained from concentering the interest on itself, but used merely as an induction or tuning for what is to follow.'

I. i. 10–11. Morgann again anticipates Coleridge, who remarks, ed. Raysor, ii. 170, on the 'organic regularity' with which Shakespeare shows 'the life and principles' of the boatswain, who grows irreverent in the common danger and reveals his essential vulgarity. As to 'play the men', though Steevens's interpretation, Johns. 1778–93, has for the most part prevailed, Morgann is not alone in balking. The difficulty, as Kermode 1954 points out, is that thus understood, 'Alonso implies a needless and inopportune reproof'. Upton 1746, p. 241, and 1748, p. 249—unrecorded in Johns. 1765–93—suggested that the reading 'should be ply the men:—keep them to their business'. Kermode approves on grounds of sense and Elizabethan pronunciation and usage. Thompson 1928 and Winny 1963 make a similar suggestion. Morgann, through his improbable chess, arrives at pretty much the same meaning.

I. i. 24–5. Steevens, Johns. 1778–93, follows the gloss in Theobald 1733. What Morgann's cancellation signifies is uncertain.

I. i. 51. Steevens's explanation appeared in Johns. 1778–93.

I. i. 63. Not Steevens but Johnson, Johns. 1765–93, thought that 'Shakespeare probably wrote, *t'englut'*, though he at once conceded that 'glut' might stand. To this Steevens appended a further justification of 'glut' in the sense of 'swallow' (Johns. 1778–93), and Morgann, reading inattentively, supposed the notation to be a single one and Steevens the author of the whole. Neither Johnson nor Steevens mentions 'ingulph'.

Modern editors adopt the suggestion about the 'confused noise'. Though Theobald had proposed the emendation in a letter to Warburton, 29 May 1729, in Nichols 1817, p. 243, he ignored the problem in his editions of 1733 and 1740; but Capell 1768 introduced the change in his text and justified it in 1783, p. 55, while Johnson made substantially the same suggestion in a note, doubtless seen by Morgann, in Johns. 1773–93. (In Johns. 1765, Johnson was muddling towards the correction but had not quite seized on it.)

Morgann's 'Appendix No. 1' is not extant.

I. ii. 3. Morgann here anticipates the emendation and reasoning of Singer 1853, p. 1: '. . . we should read *flaming* instead of *stinking*; "dashes the fire out" then follows naturally.' Singer 1856 notes the conjecture, and Hunter 1857, p. 62ᵛ, proposes the same emendation as being 'better suited to the lips of Miranda'. Others who have felt the need for fire in 'stinking pitch' are Verges

('Proposed Emendations to the Text of Shakespeare', *Notes and Queries*, 2nd Ser., vii (1859), 337), who proposed 'kindling', and Craig 1951, who glosses 'suggestion of heat'.

I. ii. 15. Johnson, Johns. 1765–93, proposed the change Morgann objects to on the grounds that Miranda, 'when she speaks the words, *O, woe the day!* supposes, not that the crew had escaped, but that her father thought differently from her, and counted their destruction *no harm*'. Howe 1805, p. 2, thought Johnson's correction 'probable', and Furness 1892 that 'his excellent emendation', which occurred independently to Walker, *Critical Examination* (1859), ii. 13, 'almost carries conviction'; but like Morgann other editors before and since have not been convinced.

I. ii. 22 and 37. Gildon 1710, p. 262, Warburton 1747, Coleridge ed. Raysor, i. 133, and Thomas R. Lounsbury, *Shakespeare as a Dramatic Artist* (1901), pp. 391–2, also admire the art of Prospero's long narration to Miranda, but though they too note the technical need for passing on information to the audience, they differ from Morgann in finding it psychologically probable, natural, and inevitable that Prospero should speak to Miranda on this subject at this moment.

I. ii. 23–4. Cf. *Com.* I. ii. 169. Morgann here differs from Warburton 1747, note to Tp. I. ii. 408 (also Warburton 1734, p. 636), according to which Miranda was put under a spell by the very act of plucking Prospero's magic garment from him. 'The touch communicated the charm', Warburton explained, 'and its efficacy was to lay her asleep.' He further believed that the purpose of the spell was to help break down in Miranda the inhibitions of her Stoical upbringing and so dispose her to fall in love at first sight with Ferdinand. Johns. 1765–93 ignores this view of Warburton's, but see note to *Com.* I. ii. 67.

I. ii. 27. Johnson, Johns. 1765–93, glosses 'virtue' as 'the most efficacious part, the energetic quality'. He is probably reacting to Warburton 1747, who attempted a far-fetched distinction between the true virtue of compassion and the false or inadequate one. Heath 1765, p. 3, in rejecting Warburton's view, claimed that 'the very virtue means no more than the virtue itself'. Morgann appears to fuse Heath and Johnson.

I. ii. 29. In reading 'soil' Morgann follows Johnson, Johns. 1765–93, who invoked the same speech of Ariel's to support the same emendation. Johnson held the Folio reading, 'no soul', to be 'defective' because of the anacoluthon it entails—the very grounds on which Theobald 1733 had emended to 'no foil' in the sense of 'no Damage, Loss, Detriment'. Like Heath 1765, p. 5, and Howe 1805, p. 3, Steevens dissented. As a turn of phrase frequent in conversation, he claimed in Johns. 1773–93, the anacoluthon might well 'be suffered to pass uncensured in the language of the stage'. Wilson 1921, however, renews the Johnson–Morgann reading, 'soil', with added bibliographical arguments.

Com. V. i. 85 explains why the order was given that the clothing should not be soiled. (Cf. *Com.* I. ii. 216, II. i. 62, and II. i. 68.)

Morgann's insistence that Prospero 'departs a little from his Integrity' foreshadows his view that Prospero is not endowed with true prescience: see *Com.* I. ii. 180 and note.

I. ii. 53. Cf. *Com.* I. ii. 22 and 37. Morgann's point in reiterating how old Miranda is may perhaps be supplied by Garrett 1937, p. 38, who observes that she is 'now aged fifteen, and marriageable. This is in keeping with the custom of that period.'

I. ii. 67, etc. In Johns. Morgann could find hints in two places towards his explanation of Prospero's reiterated questions. The first was Johnson's comment, Johns. 1765-93, on I. ii. 185: 'Dr Warburton rightly observes [1747, note to I. ii. 408, and 1734, p. 636], that this sleepiness, which Prospero by his art had brought upon Miranda, and of which he knew not how soon the effect would begin, makes him question her so often whether she is attentive to his story.' The second was the observation by Warner, Johns. 1773-93, appended to Johnson's note on I. ii. 304—and Morgann read the latter with sufficient attention to object pertinently to it: see *Com.* I. ii. 304. 'The poet', according to Warner, 'seems to have been apprehensive that the audience as well as Miranda, would sleep over this long but necessary tale, and therefore strives to break it' by Prospero's questions. Modern editors still puzzle over Prospero's nagging. Quiller-Couch, Wilson 1921, p. li (with Wilson 1936, p. 14, concurring), claims that Prospero keeps after Miranda because she is *fey*, 'absorbed . . . by the sea out of which her fairy prince is surely coming', and Kittredge 1939 that the interruptions 'indicate, not inattention on Miranda's part, but a high-pitched mood of her father's'.

For Morgann's view that Prospero's magic takes effect when he arises and resumes his garment see *Com.* I. ii. 169 and note.

I. ii. 81. Accepted through most of the eighteenth century, this definition of 'to trash' appeared in Johnson's *Dictionary* (1755) and in Johns. 1765-93. In the latter it is credited to Warburton 1747, who had been anticipated by Dryden 1670 ('lop'), Rowe 1710 glossary and 1714 glossary, and Theobald, letter to Warburton, 29 May 1729, in Nichols 1817, p. 245, though not Theobald 1733 and 1740. In Johns. 1773-93 Steevens added to the original note that he had 'met with' the word in this sense in gardening books, but in 1778-93 he went on to describe this interpretation as 'exceedingly disputable' in the light of Warburton's suggestion that in Oth. II. i. 312 F1 'trace' should be read 'trash' with the meaning 'to rate, to check, to stop'. Elaborating on the latter view, 'C' (= 'Wharton' according to Sill 1797 MS., p. 52) in Johns. 1793 proposed the sense preferred by modern editors of 'to weight down a dog who outruns the pack'. As Wright 1874 points out, the difficulty is that there is no evidence for 'trash' as a gardening term and no example of 'overtop' as a hunting term.

I. ii. 83. The musical nature of the key was first tentatively suggested by Johnson, Johns. 1765-85, and then more circumstantially identified by Hawkins, Johns. 1765, x, Appendix-1793, who refers to a 'tuning hammer' for 'the harpsichord, spinnet or virginal'. The idea has won general acceptance.

I. ii. 99–103. Morgann's emended text is that of Warburton 1747, recorded in Johns. 1765–85, and adapted from 'by telling 't oft' proposed by Theobald, 29 May 1729, in Nichols 1817, p. 243. (Theobald 1733 and 1740 reproduces the Folio text.) Steevens, Johns. 1773–93, accepts 'unto' but, like Capell 1783, p. 56, rejects 'oft'. Commentators still find the sense, as Staunton 1860 says, 'hazily expressed', and sometimes emend. Heath 1765, p. 5, Kittredge 1939, Sisson 1954 and 1956, Munro 1958, and Frye 1959 adopt 'unto'. Hunter 1857, pp. 57 and 66ᵛ, proposes 'who loving an untruth, by telling of it oft', as found in Warburton, *A Selection from Unpublished Papers* (1841), p. 343 (and Hanmer 1744). Sill 1797 MS., I53, suggests emending 'telling' to 'tolling'=coaxing, and interprets: 'Like one, who having made such a sinner of his memory, by tolling it into truth, [as] to credit his own lie.'

I. ii. 118. Theobald is 'right', Morgann means, in rejecting the emendation in Pope 1725 and 1728 of Folio 'but nobly' to 'not nobly'. Theobald's reasons are: while the change has no authority, the Folio reading makes sense and is consistent with Shakespeare's usage. Hanmer 1744 is the only editor to have adopted Pope's reading. Steevens, Johns. 1778–93, explains that 'but'='otherwise than'.

I. ii. 120. Theobald 1733, Warburton 1747, and Johns. 1765–73 read 'bore bad sons' instead of Folio 'borne'. Johns. 1778–93 restores 'borne'.

Theobald's reason for giving the line to Prospero is that, having had no experience of the world, Miranda could not 'with any Propriety be furnish'd to make such an Observation'. Warburton 1747 called this reasoning 'idle', and Johns. 1765–93 ignored the suggestion, which had been accepted only by Hanmer 1744. But though never of wide appeal, the idea has since had some interesting devotees. In a copy of Theobald 1773 now in the British Museum Coleridge jotted down, 'I cannot but believe that Tibbald is quite right'. (Coleridge ed. Raysor, i. 132, transcribes 'Theobald', thus eliminating Coleridge's probable echo of Pope's 'piddling Tibbald'.) In a copy of Rann 1786, now in the Folger Library, he wrote in the margin, 'This half-line evidently belongs to Prospero. In the innocent recluse, Miranda, it is inappropriate and unnatural'— reproduced in Coleridge Miscellaneous ed. Raysor, p. 453, More recently, Hunter 1857, p. 67 (cf. p. 66ᵛ), and Hudson and Chambers have (see Munro 1958) reassigned the line, and others, while not offering to modify the text, have been disturbed. Thompson 1928, note to I. ii. 351, refers to the 'things placed in her mouth [which] are out of character', and E. E. Stoll, 'The Tempest', *PMLA* xlvii (1932), 723, complains apropos of the present passage that Miranda's 'familiarity with unmaidenly ideas . . . somewhat grates upon us'.

For a similar emendation which has won far wider approval see *Com.* I. ii 351 and note. Cf. also *Com.* V. i. 174.

I. ii. 146–51. As do all other eighteenth- and many nineteenth-century editions, Theobald 1733 follows F4 in emending F1 'butt' to 'boat'. Reinstated by Knight, the F1 reading is now more usual.

Morgann explains the implications of his first point in *Com.* II. i. 297, *ad fin.* In his second observation he uses the term 'finical' as defined in chapter xii of *The Art of Sinking*: 'The Finical . . . consists of the most curious, affected, mincing Metaphors.' Not till recently, it appears, has the curious turn taken by the last lines of the speech provoked comment. E. M. W. Tillyard, *Shakespeare's Last Plays* (1938), p. 79, regards the lines as belonging to the fairy-tale plane of reality in the play. Kermode 1954 observes that Prospero's imagery suddenly becomes 'almost a parody of Elizabethan conceited writing' in the vein of 'Italianate love poetry'. This change in style, he suggests, marks the entry of the supernatural and miraculous in the story which Prospero has up to this point 'recounted on the level of the probable and the natural'.

I. ii. 152–8. F1 'cherubin' became 'cherubim' in F4, in which form it persisted in Rowe 1709 and subsequent eighteenth-century editions. As for the passage as a whole, other editors have also been moved to take measures, though never such bold ones as Morgann proposes. He is, it seems, alone in doubting that fortitude should be attributed to an infant, or in emending so clumsily as to have to change 'groan'd' into 'groaning'. But most eighteenth-century commentators felt with Johnson, Johns. 1765–93, that 'to deck the sea, if explained, to honour, adorn or dignify, is indeed ridiculous'. Having wondered desperately if the sense might not be 'shed tears into the sea from the deck of the ship' (Letter to Warburton, 29 May 1729, in Nichols 1817, p. 245), Theobald let 'deck'd' stand without comment in his text. Others did not give up so easily. The game of emending, as Johnson records, Johns. 1765–93, began with Hanmer 1744, 'brack'd', and Warburton 1747, 'mock'd'. Though willing to accept 'deck' in the sense of 'cover', as Heath 1765, p. 7, suggested, Johnson himself also hesitantly proposed 'fleck'd', used, he said, 'in rustic language of drops falling upon water'. Morgann's two conjectures reach out semantically towards the view first put forward by 'Eboracensis' and Malone in Johns. 1785–93 that following northern usage 'deck'd' means 'sprinkled'. This interpretation, sometimes with 'Eboracensis's' emendation of 'deck'd' to northern 'degg'd', was largely accepted in the nineteenth century. But recent editors usually maintain, or imply, the minority eighteenth-century view, opposed to Johnson's (and Morgann's), that 'deck'd' can without difficulty be taken as meaning 'adorned'. So argued Holt 1749, p. 24, and Steevens, Johns. 1778–93, and their view was approved by Sill 1797 MS., 157, and Gifford 1813, p. 23. Sill considered that Prospero's 'Royal Tears' might well *adorn* the ocean. Sutherland 1939, Kermode 1954, and Sisson 1954 and 1956 defend 'deck'='adorn', while others like Craig 1951, Alexander 1951, and Frye 1959, who print 'deck'd' or 'decked' without explanation, presumably have the same sense in mind. Boorman 1957 glosses 'adorned (here, sprinkled)', Ward 1962, 'decorated, patterned, spattered, or sprinkled (with tears)'. Only Wilson 1921, approved by Thompson 1928, would still take measures, emending to 'eked', after 'eiked', an anonymous conjecture reported by Thomas White, 'More Notes on Shakespeare' (1793), in J. H. Fennell, *Shakespeare Repository* (1853), p. 14.

I. ii. 164. Folio and modern editions read 'who being then'. Pope 1725 suppressed the 'who' and Theobald 1733 followed suit. Johns. 1773–93 restored 'who'.—Folio and eighteenth-century editions to Johns. 1765 spelt 'steeded'. Johns. 1778–93 introduced the 'steaded' of modern editions.—In both instances Morgann probably noticed no need to change Theobald's text: see Intro., p. 120.

In *Com.* II. i. 297 *ad fin.*, III. i. 50, IV. i. 186, and V. i. 85 Morgann further develops the idea that the rich garments are mentioned in order to account for Prospero's and Miranda's fine wardrobe. Seemingly not noticed till the twentieth century, the same point has since been made by Luce 1901 (note to III. i. 49), who refers to Miranda's dresses, by Kittredge 1939, who explains that the passage 'provides for' the later stealing of Prospero's robes by Stephano and Trinculo, and by Kermode 1954, who observes: 'Possibly this aspect of Gonzalo's kindness is specified to account for the richness of the castaways' costume—Prospero's magic robe here, and his ducal garments in the last act, as well as the clothes to be stolen by Stephano and Trinculo.' No one, however, draws Morgann's conclusion that the passage proves the play is revised and itself forms part of the revision.

I. ii. 169. Morgann here repeats the view of *Com.* I. ii. 23–4 and I. ii. 67 (cf. I. ii. 185), that on saying 'Now I arise', Prospero resumes his mantle and so aids the dormitive spell to operate on Miranda. This suggestion anticipates one of the principal emendations which survive from T. Payne Collier's now discredited copy of the second Folio. Announcing in *Notes and Emendations to the Text of Shakespeare's Plays* (1853), pp. 5–6, that the 'seventeenth-century annotator' had inserted the S.D. 'Put on his robe again' at this point in Tp., Collier triumphantly explained on this basis why, just when she is most absorbed in her father's story, Miranda drops off to sleep—a matter, as he remarked, over which earlier commentators had floundered. Prospero, Collier declared, had had his robe off during the narrative (see I. ii. 24), and now, wishing 'to produce somnolency in Miranda by the exercise of preternatural influence', he resumes his 'magic garment' and puts her to sleep.

Collier's proposal appears to have won immediate acceptance. Halliwell 1853 approved of the suggestion in his notes, while S. W. Singer and A. Dyce, the first to rush books into print which challenged Collier's annotator (Singer 1853 and Dyce 1853) were also the first to follow Collier in incorporating the suggestion in their texts—Singer 1856 and Dyce 1857. (The irony was not lost on Collier: see his *Trilogy* [1874], pp. 6–7.) Since then almost all editions have printed some such S.D. as Dyce's 'Resumes his mantle' or, like Kittredge 1939 and Boorman 1957, have recorded the action in their notes. Sisson 1958, p. 75, typically assumes as a matter of course that 'Prospero's power to induce sleep in Miranda . . . is put in action after he has put on his magic mantle at I. ii. 169 ("Now I arise")'. (Cf. L. Kirschbaum, 'Two Lectures on Shakespeare' [Oxford, 1961], p. 21: 'After long talk, Prospero waves his wand and, lo, his daughter sleeps.') Explicit or implicit dissent has been only occasional, e.g. Staunton 1860, Wright 1874, Furness 1892, Horne 1955, Frye 1959, and Langbaum 1964. Even Luce 1901 and Kittredge 1939, who hold that Prospero's words mean 'now my fortunes begin to rise again', insist that this sense is secondary and subordinate to the allusion to Prospero's resuming his magic garment in order to enforce the magic sleep, and Kermode 1954, who regards the former meaning as primary, agrees that Prospero must put on his cloak again either here or at l. 187.

Collier was right about the inadequacy of earlier critics. For Johnson's view of Miranda's sleepiness see *Com.* I. ii. 304. The sole comment in Johns. before

1793 on 'Now I arise' is by Blackstone, who wished to assign the phrase to
Miranda, with Prospero replying, 'Sit still . . .' (Johns. Sup. 1780, i. 79–80–
1793; adopted by Rann 1786). Earlier, Theobald, letter to Warburton, 29 May
1729, Nichols 1817, p. 246, had suggested emending '*I arise* to *Ariel*', but
Theobald 1733 and 1740 let the text stand without change or comment. Warburton 1747 held that Prospero's words mean 'Now I come to the principal part of
my Story', an interpretation later adopted in different phraseology and without
acknowledgement by Steevens, Johns. 1793. But Heath 1765, p. 8, and Capell
1783, p. 57, had earlier rejected the idea, as Howe 1805, p. 15, and Gifford
1813, p. 25, were to do later, though none of the four proposed anything better
in its place. Heath claimed that Prospero arises in order to give orders to Ariel,
Capell and Howe that Prospero, having finished his story, just happens to get up
at this moment, and for no discernible reason chooses to say that he is doing so.

I. ii. 180. Morgann is laying the groundwork for his theory that II. i. 297–9 is
a 'vile interpolation'. The basis for his contention here is that it is not prescience
as commonly understood, i.e. 'knowledge of events before they happen' (*OED*),
which enables an astrologer to determine his auspicious star, or to know that
ignoring that star will bring him bad fortune.

I. ii. 188. Morgann partly anticipates Coleridge ed. Raysor, i. 134: 'Miranda
is never directly brought into comparison with Ariel, lest the natural and the
human of the one and the supernatural of the other should tend to neutralize
one another.' Cf. S. Butler, 'Note on "The Tempest", Act iii, Scene 1', in
Literary Foundlings (Christchurch, N.Z., 1864), p. 12: 'we can hardly suppose
that she [Miranda] had ever seen Ariel.' See also *Com.* I. ii. 301–2, I. ii. 304, and
I. ii. 469–71.

I. ii. 229. Theobald's mistake was to emend Folio 'Bermoothes' to 'Bermudas'.
In rejecting the emendation, which had been adopted by no other editor,
Morgann was flogging a long-dead horse. The rebuke to Theobald on the
subject administered by Warburton 1747 and reprinted in Johns. 1765–85 was
apparently felt to have done its work so effectively that it was finally dropped
as no longer necessary in Johns. 1793. Morgann broke and still breaks new
ground, however, here and in *Com.* Introduction, with his views on the scene
of the play. To this day (cf. Frye 1959, p. 1371) critics find it puzzling that
Shakespeare should invest Prospero's island with numerous unmistakable
Bermudan attributes, yet locate the island in the Mediterranean and have Ariel
intimate that the Bermudas lie beyond the scene of the play. Morgann's entirely
original solution of the problem is that Shakespeare intends to evoke the specific
glamour of the Bermudas, that to satisfy the needs of the plot he transfers the
island to the Mediterranean, and that by artful recourse to the principle of
association in the present passage he drives home the Bermudan quality of the
scene of the play. For full discussion of his view against the background of
contemporary and subsequent comment on the problem, and for the further
possibility that 'still-vexed' may mean not 'constantly storm-tossed' but
'constantly debated' and so refer to a current controversy over whether the

true Bermudas might not lie to the north of the tempest-swept islands usually so denominated, see ' "The Still-Vex'd Bermoothes" and the Scene of *The Tempest*', in *Romanica et Occidentalia*, ed. Moshé Lazar (Jerusalem, 1963), pp. 246-53.

I. ii. 233. On the magic in Tp. see *Com.* I. ii. 250. On Trinculo see further *Com.* III. ii. 71 and cf. *Com.* II. ii. 14 and V. i. 277 and 279.

I. ii. 239. Morgann calculates the time so carefully in support of his theory about the significance of Shakespeare's adherence to the unities in Tp.: see *Com.* Introduction, V. i. 4 and V. i. 223.

I. ii. 242. On the relation between Ariel and Prospero, see *Com.* I. ii. 250, III. ii. 102, and IV. i. 139 ff.

I. ii. 250. The ref. of 'Tempest page 25' above the first line of the comment (see *app. crit.* to I154:1-2) is clearly to Johns. 1785, i. 25, where the note occurs. (In other editions its location is as follows: Johns. 1765, i. 17; Johns. 1773, i. 19-20; Johns 1778, i. 23; Malone 1790, ii. i, 19; Johns. 1793, iii. 30-1.)

In this comment, which carries further the theory of magic found in *Es.*, note e, T71n-T77n, Morgann fails fully to elucidate his thought. Where in note e he finds the supernatural beings in Tp. to be universal because they are personified 'remote effects' of human passions which have been abstracted from 'particular habits, institutions and climate', here he claims that Ariel and the rabble of spirits 'are not born of human Passions and have no Reference either to moral good or Ill'. His position would no doubt be clearer if he had provided as promised his account of Ariel and of 'his Family connection & Pursuits' (though see *Com.* I. ii. 376 and 396) and his explanation of 'the Principle upon which the Magic of this play is made to stand'.

In the first par. of *Com.* I. ii. 250, Morgann deals with a certain ambivalence in Johnson's attitude—a contempt for superstition accompanied by a belief in spirits which had earlier, on a much lower level of debate, led Kenrick 1765, pp. 4-5, to jibe that Johnson must either give up his belief in apparitions or retract the scepticism in his note. But Morgann's primary objection to Johnson's note is that it roots the play's magic in medieval and Christian belief rather than in human psychology. The most Morgann would concede to contemporary influences is that Prospero's relation to the enchanter's art was in part determined by James I's attitude to magic: see *Com.* IV. i. 139-63 and V. i. 50-1. Taking an otherwise anti-historical stand, he extends the well-known observation by Warburton 1747, reproduced in Johns. 1765-93, note to Tp. I. i. 1, that in in his preternatural beings Shakespeare 'soars above the Bounds of Nature without forsaking Sense: or, more properly, carries Nature along with him beyond her established Limits'. Even more strikingly, his approach anticipates Coleridge ed. Raysor, i. 131: classing Tp. as a 'romantic drama', Coleridge explains that this is a type of play 'the interests of which are independent of all historical facts and associations, and arise from their fitness to that faculty of our nature, the imaginative I mean, which owns no allegiance to time and place'. An anti-historical position of this kind usually underlies the variety of allegorical and symbolical interpretations of Tp. which have flourished in the past hundred years. But side by side with the conception of a universal magic there has run a current of interpretation which has accounted for the system of magic in the play by referring to specific Elizabethan notions on the subject. Shakespeare 'then writ as people then believed', Dryden wrote in the Prologue to his paraphrase. Gildon 1710, pp. 264–5, echoed Dryden, and Johnson in his widely quoted and erudite note consolidated the view, thus laying the foundation for the subsequent scholarly discussion. The modern historical view is, as Curry 1935, p. 27, observes, that Johnson 'would darken counsel by identifying the preternatural of this play' with medieval beliefs. The true source of Prospero's magic, it is now explained, is the white magic or theurgism of the neo-Platonists, interest in which was renewed by a minority in the Renaissance. The theurgist, unlike the diabolically inclined black magician, or goetist, practised a wholly beneficent art through which he prepared himself for union with the gods. The view that Prospero is essentially a virtuous magician of this type prevails among scholarly critics. Referred to favourably by Kittredge 1939, p. xx, and adopted by Hardin Craig, *An Interpretation of Shakespeare* (New York, 1948), pp. 350–1, and Kermode 1954, pp. xlvii–xlviii, it also colours Frye 1959, p. 1370, and the suggestion by Sisson 1958, p. 75, that Prospero's hocus-pocus would have been recognizably imaginary to Elizabethans, since it is distinctly different from that employed by Elizabethan practitioners of the art.

Morgann's psychological explanation of the 'Cause of magic' (1158–1159) alludes to Pope, *Essay on Man*, ii. 15. The succeeding discussion of evil supernatural powers (1159–1160) draws on Mac. I. v. 52 (Morgann probably follows Davenant's influential version of Mac. in referring to 'curtain' rather than 'blanket' of the dark), II. iii. 61–2, III. iv. 62 and 81 (Morgann raises to 'fifty' Shakespeare's 'twenty' mortal murders), and IV. i. 76 and 86. The account of Ariel and the spirits (1162–1164) is based on Tp. I. ii. 196–206, II. ii. 3–14 (Morgann substitutes 'Hounds' for 'apes'), III. ii. 102–3, IV. i. 35–8, and V. i. 17–24.

For Morgann's comment on '*Ye Elves of Hills, &c.*' see *Com.* V. i. 33 and note.

I. ii. 269. Morgann here anticipates Staunton 1860 and G. C. Macauley ('Shakespeare's "Tempest", Act I, Scene ii, l. 269', *MLR* xi [1916], 75), whose emendation, 'blear-eyed', has received 'bibliographical' sanction from Wilson 1921 and is cited by Craig 1951 as an interesting alternative reading. Most editors, however, are content with 'blue-eyed', which has been variously glossed as meaning (1) blue-lidded, a sign of pregnancy (Wright 1874); (2) having bluish 'circles' under the eyes (Luce 1901); and (3) 'tear-stain'd or livid eyes' (Sisson 1956).

I. ii. 301–2. The sole comment on the passage in Johns. before 1793 was Steevens's complaint, Johns. 1778–93, that 'no sufficient cause [appears] why Ariel should assume this new shape, as he was to be invisible to all eyes but those of Prospero'. Closer to Morgann's thought is Gifford 1813, 135, who observes that since the audience was to see Ariel, and 'he was to take some dress, this might serve as well as another'. The idea recurs in Jones 1913.

Morgann clearly does not know the Folio reading, 'Be subject to no sight but
thine, and mine', which furnishes a still stronger argument for crude workmanship. Retained in modern editions, the two words 'thine, and' were silently
suppressed from Rowe 1714 to Johns. 1785. In Johns. 1793 the fact of editorial
tampering was disclosed when Steevens defended the emended text against
Malone 1790 who, like Rann 1786 and following his own correction in 1781 in
his copy of Capell 1768 (now in the British Museum), had restored the original.
According to Steevens, 'the ridiculous precaution that Ariel should not be
invisible to himself plainly proves that the words . . . were the interpolations of
ignorance'. Howe 1805, p. 5, concurred.

Considering the passage as evidence for revision, Morgann finds it to show
the inexperienced hand of the young Shakespeare, in contrast to the modern
commentator, Wilson 1921, pp. 83–4, who characterizes the lines as 'suggestive
of botchery' in a crude late effort at revision. Other commentators who are less
inclined to disintegrate strain to find aptness in Prospero's command. Sill 1797,
p. 61, observes that Ariel can thus be seen in a new costume, Kermode 1954,
pp. xviii–xix, and Winny 1963, that Ariel's garb adds to the 'spectacular element'
in the play, and Kittredge 1939 that since Ariel is to sing the songs of a water-
nymph, 'it is important that the audience should think of him in that character,
to which end his costume serves'. Since Morgann's day, it may be added, his
question, 'What is a sea nymph?' has been answered. Such beings had a literary
existence in Elizabethan times: see Kermode 1954 and his ref. to M. W. Latham,
The Elizabethan Fairies (New York, 1931), p. 60.

On Miranda and the spirits see *Com.* I. ii. 188, 304–7, and 469–71.

I. ii. 304–7. On Ariel's 'no Figure' see *Com.* I. ii. 301–2. On Miranda's sleep
being induced by magic see *Com.* I. ii. 23–4, 67, 169, and 185. On her being
kept totally unaware of spirits see *Com.* I. ii. 188, 301–2, and 469–71. The
remark by Johnson at which Morgann glances had provoked comment on its
first appearance. It reads: 'Why should a wonderful story produce sleep?
I believe experience will prove that any violent agitation of the mind easily
subsides in slumber, especially when, as in Prospero's relation, the last images
are pleasing.' Kenrick 1765, pp. 7–8, objected to this as being bad psychology
and as forgetting that it was Prospero's magic that put Miranda to sleep. James
Barclay, *An Examination of Mr. Kenrick's Review* (1766), pp. 6–7, retorted that
the psychology was sound, while, as Kenrick complained, *Defence of Mr.
Kenrick's Review* (1766), p. 36, the *Gentleman's Magazine*, xxxv (1765), 529,
disingenuously suggested that Johnson had in mind only the plausibility of such
an explanation's coming from Miranda. (In his personal copy of the *Defence*,
p. 31, in 'Shakespeariana', vol. iii [Bodleian, Malone 142], Malone ascribed the
Gentleman's Magazine article to Johnson himself.) Others who have rejected
a magical cause for Miranda's slumber are Bushnell 1932, p. 687, who claims
that Prospero hypnotizes his daughter, and F. Kemble, *Atlantic Monthly* (Sept.
1860), p. 117, who argues that the delicate girl is prostrated after harrowing
experiences and unnerving disclosures.

I. ii. 316. The first to comment on the epithet, 'tortoise', appears to be Brinsley
Nicholson, 'Shakespeare Illustrated by Massinger, No. II', *Notes and Queries*,

4th Ser., i (1868), 219. He has been followed by Luce 1901, Lee 1907, Howarth 1936, p. 12, and Neilson and Hill 1942. All say that the term applies to Caliban's slowness or sloth. Nicholson and Lee add, as does Morgann, that 'tortoise' also refers to Caliban's unwieldy form, but Howarth denies this on the grounds that Caliban is fundamentally not a fish but a variety of man. No one else seems to have associated 'tortoise' with Caliban's rock. Cf. *Es.*, T25.

I. ii. 318. Cf. *Com.* I. ii. 396 (and note) and V. i. 190. Morgann does not provide elsewhere the discussion of Caliban which at a certain stage he had in view; see, however, *Com.* II. ii. 1 and III. ii. 95, and cf. *Es.*, note e, T75n.

I. ii. 351. Morgann here concurs in the almost unanimous endorsement in the eighteenth and nineteenth centuries of Johnson's view, Johns. 1765–93, that Theobald 1733 had 'very judiciously bestowed' the speech on Prospero. Following Dryden 1670, Theobald originally proposed the change in his letter to Warburton, 29 May 1729, in Nichols 1817, p. 246. In 1733 he gave the following reasons for the emendation: 'In the first Place, 'tis probable, *Prospero* taught *Caliban* to speak, rather than left that Office to his Daughter; in the next Place, as Prospero was here rating *Caliban*, it would be a great Impropriety for her to take the Discipline out of his hands; and, indeed, in some sort, an Indecency in her to reply to what *Caliban* last was speaking of [i.e. his attempted rape of her].' In all fairness, Johnson, Johns. 1765 Appendix–1785, reproduced under Holt's name a protest to the effect that the speech was not indelicate and that further it explained how Caliban had been in a position to make 'the attempt complained of'. But the argument convinced no one. So idle did it appear that in Johns. 1793 Steevens dropped the protest, and according to Furness 1892 all editions from Theobald 1733 to Wright 1891 gave the speech to Prospero. Significantly, though Staunton 1872, p. 636, argued that the speech should be restored to Miranda, he did not do so in his editions of 1860, 1879, 1882, and 1894 and reproduced in the latter his 1860 note that the speech 'plainly belongs to Prospero'. Only in the present century has Theobald's decision in the matter been reversed. Most modern editors agree, in the words of Sisson 1956, that 'the speech was "bestowed" on Miranda by Shakespeare and that the Folio is not in error here'. Insistence on the earlier view, still found in Luce 1901, Neilson 1906, Kittredge 1936 and 1939, Sutherland 1939, Neilson and Hill 1942, and Winny 1963, is diminishing. The trend, as well as the hold of tradition, is shown by Jones 1913, who assigns the speech to Prospero hesitantly, claiming it could as well be given to Miranda, by Howarth, who in 1947 omits his reproof in 1936, p. 52, of Wilson 1921 for returning the speech to Miranda, by Craig 1951, who gives the speech to Prospero but restores it to Miranda in a note, and by Frye 1959, Ward 1962, and Langbaum 1964, who give it to Miranda but observe in a note that other editors give the speech to Prospero.

I. ii. 373. See note to *Com.* Introduction, Marginal Note 1.

I. ii. 396. Morgann apparently knew Gildon's opinion only as attributed to him by Warburton 1747 in a lengthy note reproduced in Johns. 1765–85 (originally communicated to Theobald in Warburton 1734, pp. 635–6).

Remarking that Gildon's view of the song—'an insufferable and senseless piece of trifling'—is 'the general opinion', Warburton defends Shakespeare by pointing out that Ariel uses his song to persuade Ferdinand of his father's death. The measure is necessary, Warburton goes on, because otherwise the admirable young man's 'pious temper and disposition . . . would prevent his contracting himself without his father's knowledge', and Prospero could not count on Alonso's friendliness to the match he was determined to arrange between Ferdinand and Miranda. (Cf. *Com.* I. ii. 318 and V. i. 149, 190, 196, 204, and 213.) Where Morgann praises this vindication of Shakespeare, Johnson condemns it in the following note subjoined, Johns. 1765–85, to Warburton's comment:

> I know not whether Dr. Warburton has very successfully defended these songs from Gildon's accusation. Ariel's lays, however seasonable and efficacious, must be allowed to be of no supernatural dignity or elegance, they express nothing great, nor reveal anything above mortal discovery.
> The reason for which Ariel is introduced thus trifling is, that he and his companions are evidently of the fairy kind, an order of beings to which tradition has always ascribed a sort of diminutive agency, powerful but ludicrous, a humorous and frolick controlment of nature, well expressed by the songs of Ariel.

Johns. 1793 eliminated Warburton's note and abbreviated Johnson's.

I. ii. 408. Morgann refers to chap. xii of *The Art of Sinking*, which seems to aim at Dryden 1670 rather than at Shakespeare: see E. L. Steevens, ed. *Martinus Scriblerus* [='Swift and Pope &c'], *The Art of Sinking in Poetry* (New York, 1952), p. 169. Pope 1725 and 1728 does not mark the line as bad poetry. The passage in *The Art of Sinking* (ed. cit., p. 69) holds up Prospero's imagery as a specimen of the mixed 'Cumbrous' and 'Buskin' style, i.e. lofty metaphors, in themselves too heavy, applied to artificially raising the commonplace. Although unmentioned in Johns. 1765–93 or Malone 1790, this observation was seemingly well known. Capell 1783, ii, pt. 4, p. 61, had it in mind, for example, when, forgetting the competition his own prose style might offer, he wrote that the line 'has not its parallel anywhere for stiffness and quaintness'.

The sense of Prospero's dignity as a 'Master of spirits' had earlier been noted by Warton, *Adventurer* 97 (9 Oct. 1753), who refers to 'the awful solemnity of his character, as a skilful magician'. Coleridge ed. Raysor, ii. 179–80, evokes the same image in what is apparently the first public rejection of the judgement offered in *The Art of Sinking*. Employing an argument strikingly similar to the one which had occurred to Morgann, Coleridge disagrees with 'the very severe, but inconsiderate, censure of Pope and Arbuthnot'. On the contrary, Coleridge claims, Prospero's words are most appropriate, for he 'sees Ferdinand, and wishes to point him out to his daughter, not only with great, but with scenic solemnity, he standing before her, and before the spectator, in the dignified character of a great magician'. Therefore, Coleridge proceeds, 'the solemnity of the phraseology assigned to Prospero is completely in character, recollecting his preternatural capacity, in which the most familiar objects in nature present themselves in a mysterious point of view'. Luce 1901, Sutherland, 1939, and Kermode 1954 concur. In a similar vein Boorman 1957 observes: 'This sudden touch of rather over-elaborate poetry suggests that Shakespeare wanted a deliberately "theatrical" ("masque") effect for the moment when Miranda first sees Ferdinand (perhaps with a background of music . . .).' Winny 1963 says the artificiality has 'special significance': Prospero 'is showing Miranda her husband'.

I. ii. 427. Morgann here falls in with the dominant eighteenth-century view that Shakespeare intended F4 'made' rather than the 'maid' or 'mayd' of the earlier Folios. The standard explanation of the F4 reading was in Warburton 1747, originally in Warburton 1734, p. 637, and reprinted in Johns. 1765–93. 'Miranda', Warburton observed, 'was an utter stranger to the flattery invented by vicious and designing Men to corrupt the other sex'; hence she could not even imagine that the worthy 'desire of appearing amiable . . . could ever degenerate into such excess, as that any one should be willing to have his fellow creature believe he thought her a Goddess, or an Immortal'. Johnson, it is true, reproduced this note only in order to knock it down with his own opinion that Warburton had 'found a beauty' which Shakespeare 'never intended'; and he restored 'maid' to his text, claiming that Ferdinand is merely asking Miranda if she is unmarried (see Tp. I. ii. 447). But it was Johnson himself who was knocked down, and in his own edition. Johns. 1773, x, Appendix, contained a note by Tollet defending 'maid' (X, L13ʳ) and another by Farmer favouring 'made' (Oo3ʳ–3ᵛ), but 1778–93 kept only Farmer's note, dropping Tollet's, and App. 1783–93 added one by Malone (also in Malone 1790) and 1793 one by Warton, both defending 'made' as understood by Warburton. Further, in Johns. 1793 the long-rebuked 'maid' disappeared from the text, to be replaced by the seemingly irresistible F4 reading. Others who like Johnson unavailingly sought to stem the tide were Holt 1749, pp. 33–4, Capell 1768 and 1783, p. 61, Sill 1797, pp. 67–9, Mason 1798, pp. 5–6, and Howe 1805, p. 7. But by and large to reject 'made' seemed to the eighteenth century 'chimerical', to use the epithet applied to dissent in 'Remarks on the Tempest', *Gentleman's Magazine*, xlii (1772), 574. According to the anonymous author, since Ferdinand at this stage still thinks Miranda a goddess, it is premature for him to ask her if she is a virgin, i.e. marriageable.

The tide turned when Gifford 1813 and Singer 1826 re-established 'maid' in their texts: Singer set the precedent for most subsequent editors, who explicitly or implicitly accept Johnson's view. The present attitude may be gauged from the facts that Kermode 1954 follows Luce 1901 in barely recording 'made' as a historical curiosity not worth a comment, while Munro 1958 does not even mention it in his usually wide-ranging critical apparatus.
See also *Com.* I. ii. 447.

I. ii. 437–8. Theobald 1733 comments as follows on the passage: 'Here seems a slight Forgetfulness in our Poet: No Body was lost in this Wreck, as is manifest from several Passages: and yet we have no such Character introduc'd in the Fable, as the Duke of *Milan*'s son.' In 1740, as if aware that this left him open to the point of ridicule seized upon by Morgann, Theobald departed from his usual practice of shortening his earlier notes to add: 'No doubt, in his Plan, he had mark'd out such a Character; but, on second Thought, found it unnecessary.' Morgann, of course, had the edition of 1733 before him, and Johns. 1765–93, which abbreviates Theobald's note as its only comment on the passage, omits the added sentence, as does Theobald 1773 and Malone 1790. (Coleridge, ed. Raysor, i. 133, is commenting on the note as found in Theobald 1773 when he writes: 'Must not Ferdinand have believed so—in the fleet that the tempest scattered?')

Morgann anticipates by almost a century the earliest use of Antonio's missing son as evidence for the revision of Tp. Staunton 1872, p. 636, suggested that either the young man was Francisco (cf. Hunter 1857, p. 77^v, who proposes Francisco or Adrian) or, to shorten the representation, the character was 'struck out by the actors, while the allusion to it was inadvertently retained'. Fleay 1876, p. 54, mentioned a theory by Staunton which accounts for the lost character by supposing 'that each player had a property in his own part, and that sometimes all the parts could not be bought up by the publishers'. Fleay ibid. and 1877, p. 29, also presents the view finalized in 1886, p. 249, that in the 'evidently abridged' play, either Antonio's son was dropped by the actors, or Francisco is the remaining '*débris*' of the part. More recently, Gray 1921, p. 249, has accepted Staunton's suggestion that the actors cut the role, and Wilson 1921, p. 94 (cf. p. 79), has claimed that Antonio's son 'must have been one of the Alonso group in the earlier version'. Boorman 1957 suggests that Milan's lost son 'may be (as Quiller-Couch suggested) a remnant from an earlier version of the play, kept in so that Prospero can make his effective retort'. Among non-disintegrators, Holt 1749, p. 35, claims that Ferdinand refers to himself; Halliwell 1851 and 1868, Wright 1874, Luce 1901, Lee 1907, and Thompson 1928 attribute the anomaly to Shakespeare's still-undiscovered source; Kermode 1954, note to I. ii. 437–8 and p. xix, recalls Shakespeare's propensity for committing such howlers; and Winny 1963 suggests that 'Shakespeare may have decided to drop the character when he came to write Act II, Scene I'.

In *Com*. II. i. 9–107 Morgann attempts a partial reconstruction of the missing character's part.

I. ii. 447. See *Com*. I. ii. 427.

I. ii. 469–71. The MS. does not refer this note, which occurs on the bottom margin of T22, to a particular passage. Of the lines printed on T22—ll. 464–93—the most relevant appear to be those in which Prospero offers a 'naturalistic' explanation of what is really a magic charm he has thrown over Ferdinand.

Miranda neither knows nor is noted by Ariel, who is constantly on the stage from l. 375 to the end of the scene. See also on this point *Com*. I. ii. 188 and 301–2.

I. ii. 495. For Morgann's critical objective in thus rewriting the play see *Com*. II. i. 297 and cf. *Com*. II. i. 9–107, *ad fin.*

II. i. 9–107. Three degrees of cancellation appear in the comment. I24 has one line down its centre, I25 has three, and I26:1–2 is criss-crossed diagonally. The inner cancellations on I25 ('but the', 'son of Milan', and 'the Fool') appear to be part of an incomplete effort at revision. So too does the inner cancellation in I25:4–I26:2a ('and like . . . confidently affirm').

The comment deals with three questions. The first is that of the literary quality of the passage and its significance. Morgann had before him the reaction of Theobald 1733 to the view in Pope 1725 that the passage 'seems to have been interpolated, (perhaps by the *Players*) . . . [it] not only being very impertinent stuff, but most improper and ill-plac'd Drollery in the mouths of the unhappy shipwreckt people'. Agreeing that the 'Matter of the Dialogue' was 'very poor and trivial', Theobald nevertheless thought the interpolation theory 'injudicious and unweigh'd'. Take out this dialogue and, he asked,

what would become of these Words of the King?

—— —— *Would I had never*
Married my Daughter there!

What Daughter? and, *where* married? For it is from this intermediate part of the Scene only, that we are told, the King had a Daughter nam'd *Claribel*, whom he had married unto *Tunis*. . . . Besides, poor and jejune as the Matter of the Dialogue is, it was certainly design'd to be of a ridiculous Stamp; to divert and unsettle the King's Thoughts from reflecting too deeply on his Son's suppos'd Drowning.

Reproduced as the only comment on the passage in Johns. 1765–85 (1793 has no comment at all), this note of Theobald's reflects the common eighteenth-century tendency, found also in Morgann's comment, simultaneously to share Pope's view that the passage is 'low' and to reject his charge of psychological inappropriateness. Echoing Theobald's argument, Holt 1749, p. 40, justifies the 'Lowness of the Dialogue, . . . which has been so often lamented and condemn'd' as a deliberate satire 'on the vicious Prevalence of . . . snip-snap Wit'. Heath 1765, pp. 14–15, merely repeats in substance what Theobald had said. Expanding Theobald's view, Capell 1783, p. 62, nevertheless holds Pope's charges to be 'almost beyond palliating'. The first fully to emancipate himself from Pope's judgement was Coleridge. Pope, Coleridge declared (ed. Raysor, ii. 178–9; cf. ii. 323), 'objected to this conspiracy; but in my mind, if it could be omitted, the play would lose a charm which nothing could supply'. In their dialogue, he explained, Antonio and Sebastian reveal the villain's tendency to listen to his betters not for possible profit but in order to gratify a sense of superiority; characteristically, the sight of Alonso and Gonzalo asleep suggests to them the thought of murder.

Morgann modifies the position adopted in his Introduction. There he claimed that the dialogue is silly and clearly exposes the painful ignorance of gentlemen's familiar discourse which characterizes Shakespeare's early work. Here, though still holding that Shakespeare was at first deficient in this respect, he denies that the generalization applies to Antonio and Sebastian. This revaluation undermines one of his arguments for the original play's early date. Accordingly, even while he concedes this bit of evidence, he makes a special point of affirming anew his belief that Tp. is Shakespeare's first play. His revised view, moreover, comes as a further proof of his complementary thesis that the extant play is a *rifacimento*. With this line of thought he in some measure anticipates Gray, who also claims that the dialogue attests to the play's being revised. Reverting to Pope's interpolation theory, however, Gray 1921, p. 137, suggests that the passage was inserted in the revised Tp. in order to 'lighten the play'.

Morgann's second topic (on I25) is the widow Dido joke in ll. 76–82 and 100–1. The rather humourless remark of Johnson's (Johns. 1765–93) at which he bridles is this: 'The name of a widow brings to mind their own shipwreck, which they consider as having made many widows in Naples [see ll. 132–3].'

Apart from this comment Morgann could find in Johns. 1778–93 only inconclusive stabs at the meaning, not all surviving their initial appearance, by Steevens, Malone, and Ritson. Scholars still do not agree on an explanation as simple and direct as the allusion seems to be in the play.

For Morgann's third point, in which he rewrites Ariel's part (I26), see *Com.* II. i. 297 and I. ii. 495.

II. i. 62. Cf. next note.

II. i. 68. Cf. *Com.* II. i. 62, I. ii. 216, and V. i. 85.

II. i. 220–1. Morgann's emendation is original. Rowe 1709 and 1714, Pope 1725 and 1728, and Hanmer 1744 fussed over the seeming awkwardness of Folio 'if heed', emending 'if' to 'you' or 'ye', but most other editors, like Theobald 1733 and 1740 and Johnson, Johns. 1765–93, have retained the original reading. Perhaps Morgann's emendation is related to whatever he had in mind in cancelling Theobald's note on 'Trebles thee o'er' (see *app. crit.*). Theobald was concerned to justify his restoration of Folio 'Trebles', which Pope 1725, following Rowe 1714, had changed to 'Troubles'. The Folio reading is adopted by virtually all modern editors. (Wilson 1921 revives the Rowe–Pope reading.)

II. i. 235–66. Repunctuating the text in Johns. 1765–73, Johnson subjoined the following note (Johns. 1765–93); 'Of this entangled sentence I can draw no sense from the present reading', and went on to propose minor surgery. Johns. 1778–85 restored the Folio punctuation and added a suggestion by Steevens that the text, though 'perplexed and irregular', might make some sense if one takes 'only professes to persuade' as meaning 'he is content to be plausible, and has no further aim'. But by Johns. 1793 Steevens himself was no longer persuaded. Taking up the approach anticipated by Morgann and invoking Porson as authority for believing that marginal notes have crept into texts 'not merely in *hundreds* or *thousands*, but in *millions* of places', he excluded the phrase 'professes to persuade' as 'a mere gloss . . . written in the margin . . . [which] was afterwards injudiciously incorporated'. Staunton 1860 cites and approves of Steevens's later view, and other nineteenth-century editors, agreeing with Halliwell 1851 that 'the sentence is rather obscure', continue worrying at the text in other ways. More recent editors usually accept the text more or less as it stands, taking 'only professes to persuade' to mean, as Capell 1783, p. 64, and Howe 1805, p. 7, suggested, 'persuading is his only profession'.

II. i. 243. The form *dout* (='do out', 'extinguish')' occurs nowhere in the Shakespeare Quartos and Folios. It was first revealed as an item in Shakespeare's lexicon by Rowe 1709 and 1714, who read 'dout' instead of F1–4 'doubt' in H5 IV. ii. 11. Widely adopted in the nineteenth and twentieth centuries, Rowe's emendation was forgotten in favour of 'daunt' in Pope 1725 and all subsequent editions until Malone 1790 and Steevens in Johns. 1793 (the latter with a credit to 'the late Rev. Henry Homer' as of *c.* 1789) brought 'dout' into view again both as the proper reading of the H5 passage and as a far less widely accepted emendation of Ham. I. iv. 37. Morgann's proposal for Tp.

II. i. 243 anticipates by a century the same suggestion by Furness 1892 and by Brinsley Nicholson in Wright 1891. Unlike Morgann, Furness and Nicholson had accessible models not only in Rowe's now well-known emendation and the Malone-Steevens treatment of Ham. I. iv. 37 but also in the reading 'douts' for F1 'doubts' in Ham. IV. vii. 192, proposed by T. Caldecott (ed.), *Hamlet and As You Like It* (1819), p. 70, and accepted as preferable to Q1-2 and F2-4 'drowns' in Knight 1841 and a line of major editions including Clark and Glover 1863, Globe 1865, Furness (ed.), New Variorum *Hamlet* (Philadelphia, 1877), and Clark and Wright (eds.), Clarendon *Hamlet* (Oxford, 1872). The Nicholson-Furness proposal anticipated by Morgann to emend Tp. II. i. 243 has won recent converts: Wilson 1921 approves, Kermode 1954, finding it 'attractive', has suggested a pun on 'doubts-douts', and Winny 1963 prints 'douts' in his text. However, most modern editors seem to reason with Sisson 1956 that the compositor would not have had 'a critical preference for the *durior lectio*'. The easier reading, 'doubts', is still usually interpreted in the light of Johnson's explanation, the sole comment in Johns. 1765-93: 'That this is the utmost extent of the prospect of ambition, the point where the eye can pass no further, and where objects lose their distinctness, so that what is there discovered, is faint, obscure and doubtful.' Morgann adapts this gloss of Johnson's to his emended reading.

II. i. 246-50. Morgann here casually discovers what modern historical scholarship finds in the passage—a would-be 'judicious' attempt by Antonio to use the devices of rhetoric. Kermode 1954 illustrates by quoting Puttenham's characterization of hyperbole as 'by incredible comparisons giving credit'. The only comment on the passage available to Morgann was by Steevens, who in Johns. 1773-93 solemnly wagged his head over the 'great ignorance of geography' Shakespeare displayed in supposing 'Tunis and Naples to have been at such an immeasurable distance from one another'. In Johns. 1778-93, still solemn as ever, Steevens mitigated the censure by adding the consoling thought that Apollonius Rhodius and Aeschylus were also rather hopeless at geography. It took almost a hundred years for this view to be replaced by the modern one, anticipated by Morgann. Wright 1874 seems to be the first to state clearly 'that Antonio's language is intentionally exaggerated and that Sebastian is fully aware of it'.

II. i. 250. The reading 'for whom' is an emendation by Pope 1725 which Theobald 1733 repudiates as without authority and unreasonable. (Theobald 1740 drops the note.) Theobald misleads in implying that the Folio reads 'she from whom'. Actually, the reading is 'She that from whom', a construction to this day conducive to editorial woe. Morgann was apparently unaware of the problem. Not till 1793 did Johns. indicate, with a note by Malone (also in Malone 1790), that 'she from whom' in the text of Johns. 1765-93 involved an emendation.

II. i. 296. See *Com.* II. i. 9-107 and II. i. 297-9 and notes.

II. i. 297-9. Whereas Wilson 1921, p. 80, would include Ariel's speech as a significant link in the chain of evidence showing Tp. to be a *rifacimento*,

Morgann finds in the awkward lines only an isolated interpolation, unconnected with the alleged revision of the play. This view he buttresses with *Com.* II. i. 306, his sketch in *Com.* I. ii. 495 and II. i. 9–107 of how Ariel originally functioned in this scene, and his reiteration that Prospero was not endowed with prescience: see also *Com.* I. ii. 180, II. i. 326, and III. ii. 124. Sill 1797, p. 61, appears to be the only other critic who has wondered about Prospero's prescience. If so endowed, Sill asks, why must Prospero inquire of Ariel in I. ii. 218 whether the voyagers are all safe? To pass on information to the audience?

Morgann was neither the first nor the last to find Ariel's lines absurd. In Johns. 1765–93 the baffled comment swelled from edition to edition, with most of the critics seeing no way out but emendation—a device finally adopted in 1793. Less eager to emend, modern editors are often not much happier about the situation. Greg and Chambers would prefer to dissociate Shakespeare from the lines: see above, p. 409. Noting 'some confusion' in the passage, Kermode 1954 agrees with Wright 1874 that 'Ariel is half apostrophising the sleeping Gonzalo, half talking to himself', but adds that in the third line of his speech Ariel speaks only to the audience.

If Morgann misses a modern argument for revision in Ariel's lines, he compensates by finding another, never proposed by anyone else, in the nature of Gonzalo's gift of books and fine clothes and its relation to his fame as Prospero's friend. In *Com.* I. ii. 164, IV. i. 186, and V. i. 85, Morgann sees the gift of fine clothes as an innovation of the revised spectacular version of the play. Here, noting that the gift is the sole concrete manifestation of Gonzalo's much-vaunted friendship for Prospero, he claims that the anomaly furnishes further proof of revision. In the original version, he reasons, there must have been better, more convincing grounds for Gonzalo's reputation for kindness to Prospero, which were obliterated when the gift of fine clothes was introduced in the revision. That there is a lack of more convincing grounds seems not to have been noticed by others. The old courtier is almost universally accepted as 'Holy Gonzalo, honourable man', who has been the 'true preserver' of Prospero while remaining loyal to his own master (V. i. 62 and 69–70). Pope 1725, vi, Index, twice notes his honesty, and Johnson, Johns. 1765–93, note to I. i. 26, voices the common view that Gonzalo is 'the only good man that appears with the king'. Yet such praise fails to take into account, as Morgann does, the actual reported facts of Gonzalo's participation in the crime against Prospero and his baby daughter. The only critic apart from Morgann who seems to have remarked the difficulty is Hunter 1857. Noting how Gonzalo commits Prospero and Miranda in a frail vessel to the mercy of the open sea, Hunter writes in a first draft that the old counsellor hoped 'that thus the guilt of murder might not rest upon his head' (p. 8), and in a later version that he behaved as he did 'so that he might not be accessory to such a murder' (pp. 33–4). But even the latter account hardly squares with the idea of 'Holy Gonzalo'. It suggests rather a man paltering with and bribing his conscience, a conception like the one implied by Morgann but without his explanation that Gonzalo appears so unworthy of his good name because the character has been blurred and distorted in the revision of the play.

II. i. 317. See *Com.* II. i. 297–9.

II. i. 326. See *Com.* II. i. 297–9 and note.

II. ii. 14. For Morgann's inference from Trinculo's patched coat see *Com.* III. ii. 71, and cf. *Com.* I. ii. 233, and V. i. 277 and 279.

Gildon 1710, p. 263, had referred to the Stephano–Trinculo plot as 'the Attempts of the Mob-Characters'. Like Morgann, Coleridge, ed. Raysor, i. 136–7 (cf. i. 233, 89, and 89 n.), was stimulated by Stephano and Trinculo to reflect on the 'good nature' with which Shakespeare 'seems always to make sport with the passions and follies of a mob, as with an irrational animal. He is never angry with it, but hugely content with holding up its absurdities to its face; and sometimes you may trace a tone of almost affectionate superiority, something like that in which a father speaks of the rogueries of a child. See the good-humoured way in which he describes Stephano passing from the most licentious freedom to absolute despotism over Trinculo and Caliban.'

II. ii. 21. Basing himself on letters to Warburton, 29 May 1729 and 3 Feb. 1729/30 (Nichols 1817, pp. 246 and 469), Theobald 1733 deduced from the context that 'bumbard' must mean 'a large Vessel for holding Drink'. To this note, reproduced in Johns. 1765–93, Steevens subjoined in 1773–93 information which linked 'bumbard' with 'black-jack'.

II. ii. 83. The available comment on the line was that of Steevens, Johns. 1778–93: 'This tremor is always represented as the effect of being possessed by devils.' Morgann's point is that of Kittredge 1939: 'Trinculo is shaking with fear, but Caliban thinks it is the effect of Prospero's magic working on the evil spirit.'

II. ii. 98. Cf. Steevens in Johns 1773–93: 'Amen! . . . .means stop your draught, come to a conclusion.' Most commentators, e.g. Wright 1874 and Kittredge 1939, concur.

II. ii. 103. Cf. Steevens in Johns. 1773–93: the phrase alludes 'to the proverb, *A long spoon to eat with the devil*'.

II. ii. 110. Morgann has in view a comment not by Johnson but by Tollet, Johns. 1773, as elaborated on, adopted, and signed by Steevens, Johns. 1778–93: 'Siege signifies *stool* in every sense of the word, and is here used in the dirtiest.' No other comment appears in Johns. Holt 1749, p. 55, had made the same point more decorously, and Heath 1765, p. 21, had concurred, as do most modern editors, though not all: Lee 1907 takes 'siege' as 'seat'.

II. ii. 149. Theobald presumably received the note from Warburton in reply to his puzzled observation in his letter of 29 May 1729 (Nichols 1817, p. 247), that Trinculo 'is not charged with any such fear'. Theobald did not, however, acknowledge his source in 1733, and withdrew the note in 1740. Morgann could have discovered the true author by consulting the concise version in Warburton 1747, Johns. 1765–93, or Malone 1790.

II. ii. 176. In his note Theobald explains that he has removed 'Scamels', found in all earlier editions, from his text because he 'can no where else meet with such a Word'. He has, he explains, substituted '*Shamois* (as Mr. *Warburton* and I have both conjectur'd) i.e. young Kids', though Shakespeare may have intended '*Sea-malls*' or 'another Bird, call'd the *Stannel*'. He concludes: 'It is no Matter which of the three Readings we embrace, so we take a Word signifying the Name of something in Nature.' Morgann lines through this note (see *app. crit.*), replacing it with his briefer comment in which he accepts 'shamois' and adds on his own that the goats are Swiss. Warburton 1747 also proposed 'shamois' in a note, and Capell 1774, glossary, concurred, though both Holt 1749, pp. 56–7 and Heath 1765, p. 21, objected on the grounds that shamois would be too swift-footed for Caliban to catch. Johns. 1765–85 retained Folio 'scamels' in the text, but each successive edition adds to the controversial annotation below, where 'scamel' is now an animal, now a fish, now a bird. The 'embroil' has since seethed and expanded vastly, with 'shamois' long ago sunk and forgotten, except by Hunter 1857, p. 92ᵛ, who dredges it up because shamois are found on Lampedusa, the island which he claims is the true scene of the play. Since the late eighteenth century, 'sea-mels' or 'sea-mews' have been the preferred emendation of the emenders. The trend is illustrated in Johns. 1793, where 'sea-mells', clearly the annotators' favourite in prec. editions, appears in the text. But modern editors usually print 'scamels'. Reflecting that William Strachey refers to 'sea-mews', but that in certain parts of Norfolk, at any rate, a 'scamel' is a godwit, they no doubt share the hope of Kermode 1954 and Sisson 1956 that the word in the Folio may yet turn out to mean something.

III. i. 21. The concern with time-references in the play is explained in *Com.* V. i. 4.

III. i. 48. Cf. the invocation to Eve in *Par. Lost*, ix. 896–9:

> O fairest of Creation, last and best
> Of all God's Works, Creature in whom excell'd
> Whatever can to sight or thought be form'd,
> Holy, divine, good, amiable or sweet!

The specific parallel appears not to have been noted by others, and the more general similarity between Eve and Miranda has been observed by only a few, among them Lowell 1868, pp. 191–2, and Verplanck 1847, p. 3, who remarks that Miranda is 'paralleled only by the Eve of Milton, who, I cannot but think, was indirectly indebted for some of her most fascinating attributes to the solitary daughter of Prospero'. To Johnson, Ferdinand's speech suggested not Milton's Eve but Apelles' picture of Venus (Johns. 1765–93), a gloss approved by Sill 1797, p. 79, Sutherland 1939 (by implication), and more recently by Kermode 1954, who follows Wright 1874 in citing AYL. III. ii. 157–60 as analogue. Steevens rejected the idea of a reference to Apelles on the grounds that 'every creature's best' includes much more than every woman's best; he preferred to illustrate instead in Johns. 1773–93 with a passage from Sidney's *Arcadia* (1598), p. 386, which presents man as a summing-up of the best qualities in the lesser animal creation. Sill 1797 MS., I79, seems to have had a similar idea in mind in suggesting an allusion to the freighting of Noah's ark. The

Miltonic apostrophe to Eve also evokes the microcosmic concept and the hierarchic scheme associated with the Great Chain of Being.

III. i. 50. Cf. the view of Gonzalo presented in *Com.* II. i. 297–9.

III. i. 54. Miranda's natural candour in her courtship, regarded as implying a rebuke to the coy subterfuges of sophistication, had been praised by Holt 1749, p. 59, and is still admired, e.g. by Meurer 1928, p. 30, and Smith 1941, p. 17. Cf. the cancelled sentence in *Com.* III. i. 78.

III. i. 78. Unravelling the grammatical knot which troubles Morgann, Wright 1874 refers to Abbot 1870, par. 218, to explain that the subject of 'dare' must be supplied from the prec. possessive pronoun, 'mine', and 'dare' itself must be understood as being repeated before 'much less take'.

III. i. 93. Morgann's conjecture is unsupported by the *OED*. It seems to reflect the same dissatisfaction with 'surprised' = 'taken unawares' that leads Sutherland 1939 to propose 'surprised' = 'seized with', and 'overpowered', 'overwhelmed' (*OED*, *surprise*, v., senses 1a and 1b). The Folio reading 'with all' seems to agree better with Morgann's view than Theobald's silent emendation 'withal', a change adopted by Warburton 1747, Johns. 1765–73, and many modern editions. Since Morgann says nothing on the matter, it seems likely that his own 'with all' is not an attempt to return to the Folio reading as in Johns. 1778–92 but merely another instance of careless copying out from Theobald's text.

III. ii. 3. The lengthy note in Theobald 1733 on 'servant-monster', which Morgann lines through (see *app. crit.*), admires Shakespeare's 'Genius, in creating [in Caliban] a Person which was not in Nature', notes Jonson's 'Virulence' in attacking Caliban and the entire Tp. (in the quoted passage transcribed in Morgann's comment), claims that this was rank ingratitude since Shakespeare had 'first brought *Jonson* upon the Stage' and was now 'retreated from the Scene', further claims that when Jonson found 'the Publick . . . out of Humour at his Performances' he would often revenge himself 'by being out of Humour with those Pieces which had best pleas'd them', and concludes that Jonson knew better in cooler moments since he spoke of 'the *Impossibility* of any Man's being the *good Poet*, without first being a *good Man*'. Theobald seems to be the first to make the assertion, which is still often repeated, though Gifford 1813 and Furness 1892 object, that the quoted passage is an attempt by Jonson 'to throw Dirt' on Tp. as a whole. Holt 1749, p. 62, Capell 1783, p. 66, and Blackstone, Johns. Sup. 1780, i–1793, initial note to Tp., use this allusion to date the play. Like them, Morgann seems unaware that, though *Bartholomew Fair* was first staged in 1614, the Induction did not appear till the edition of 1616. He is, of course, marshalling the alleged evidence to support his own special theory of revision.

III. ii. 71. Morgann here takes a side-thrust at Johnson, without mentioning his name. Johnson, Johns. 1765–85, asserted dogmatically that 'this line should certainly be given to Stephano. "Pied" alludes to the striped coat worn by fools, of which Caliban could have no knowledge.' Steevens withdrew this note in Johns. 1793, substituting Malone's suggestion that Caliban's reference to 'the striped coat worn by fools' is merely a quite forgivable lapse on Shakespeare's part. Recent editors agree with Morgann that there is nothing questionable in Caliban's exclamation.

Morgann repeats elsewhere that Trinculo's apparent loss of his profession proves the play to have been revised: see *Com.* I. ii. 233, II. ii. 14, and V. i. 277 and 279. The same argument figures in the arsenal of recent disintegrators. As part of his case for revision, Wilson 1921, p. 79, remarks that 'Trinculo . . . though styled a "jester" in the Folio "names of the actors", does very little to support this title, except to be called "patch" and "pied ninny" at one point'.

III. ii. 95. Warton, *Adventurer* 97, 9 Oct. 1753, had admired the 'brutal barbarity and unfailing savageness' of this speech.]

III. ii. 102 On Ariel's relation to Prospero cf. *Com.* I. ii. 250 and IV. i. 139 ff.

III. ii. 124. See *Com.* II. i. 297–9 and note.

III. iii. 19. Here as elsewhere (see above, pp. 409–10), Morgann pokes fun at the spectacular effects, which he believes are extraneous additions to the original play intended to satisfy the Jacobean taste for spectacle. On the different ground that only the rationally explicable supernatural belongs in Tp. (cf. note to *Com.* I. ii. 304) Bushnell 1932, p. 687, has held that the 'supernatural displays' in Tp.—the masque, the banquet, etc.— 'are not in the least essential to the action'.

III. iii. 48. Morgann draws a line through Theobald's long note on 'putter out', T50n–T51n. In its place he offers an interpretation advanced by no one else except Samuel Henley, the translator of *Vathek* (see Johns. 1785, i. 87), who in an unnoticed note, which appeared only in Johns. Sup 1780, i. 82 and Johns 1785, claimed that 'considerable sums were borrowed at the rate here mentioned, and squandered in making discoveries, and pursuing adventures with the hopes of acquiring immense treasures'. The Henley–Morgann interpretation is the only one which makes straightforward sense out of the Folio reading, 'putter out of five for one', and at the same time satisfies Johnson's generally accepted condition, Johns. 1765–85, that 'the *putter out* must be a traveller, else how could he give this account?'

The standard view, originating with Thirlby, and almost universally repeated since Theobald published it in his note, is that the 'putter out' is a travelling investor (or gambler) who on setting forth deposits a sum of money, which he forfeits if he fails to return, but receives again with manifold increase, if he comes back alive. This practice, which Morgann erroneously tries to reason out of existence, is attested to by abundant documentary evidence, collected in Halliwell 1853 and in part available to Morgann in Theobald's note and in Johns. 1778–93. Theobald noted Thirlby's highly relevant reference to Fynes '*Morison's* Itinerary [1617], Part I, p. 198, &c.' and quoted the following speech by Puntarvolo in Ben Jonson's *Every Man Out of His Humour*, which since

Johnson's allusion to it, Johns. 1765–85, and Steevens's requotation of it, Johns. 1773–93, has become a *locus classicus* on the subject:

> I do intend, this Year of *Jubilee* coming on, to travel: And (because I will not altogether go upon Expence,) I am determin'd to put forth some *five* thousand pound, to be paid me *five* for *one*, upon the Return of my self, my Wife, and my Dog, from the *Turk's* Court in *Constantinople*. If All, or Either of Us miscarry in the Journey, 'tis gone; if We be successful, why, there will be *five* and *twenty* thousand Pounds to entertain Time withal.

Theobald adds, as does Morgann, that because Puntarvolo's wife refuses to accompany him, the knight is eventually forced to make his venture on the return of himself, his dog, and his cat. Morgann is of course wide of the mark when he argues that Theobald is wrong to cite the passage as reflecting the practice by Elizabethan underwriters of repaying returned travellers' deposits at rates as high as five to one. Perhaps he cancelled his note when he discovered that Theobald's contention was amply confirmed by evidence assembled in Johns. 1778–93.

But proof that the practice existed does not necessarily establish a reference to it in Tp. In order to substantiate the allusion, editors have had to go to extremes. Kermode 1954, ignoring Johnson's condition to the contrary, suggests that the putter out is the underwriter, not the traveller. Other editors resort to emendation or semantic legerdemain. Most emenders, including Johns. 1765–93, adopt Theobald's 'putter out *on* five for one'; a few, including Halliwell 1853, prefer Thirlby's and Malone's 'putter out of one for five' (Thirlby to Theobald, 7 May 1729 (Nichols 1817, p. 224): cf. Theobald to Warburton, 29 May and 11 Nov. 1729 (Nichols 1817, pp. 244 and 259); Malone, unaware of Thirlby, in his corrected copy of Capell 1768 now in the British Museum and in Johns. 1785–93 and Malone 1790). The non-emenders, from Knight 1841 and Furness 1892 to J. C. Maxwell in Kermode 1958, p. 169, achieve the same end by insisting that the Folio reading means exactly what the emended texts of Theobald and Thirlby convey, i.e. 'he who puts out one in the hope of receiving five', even though, as Dyce 1857 points out, this is to reverse what the words would normally signify.

The interpretation put forward by Morgann avoids these unhappy alternatives and can lay claim to historical support. There is evidence to show that if Elizabethan travellers invested money in the life-insurance-in-reverse scheme referred to by Puntarvolo, they also borrowed money at exorbitant rates for their ventures abroad: see *Second Part of the Young Clerk's Guide* (1652), pp. 108–9, reproduced in Halliwell 1853. Thus documented, Morgann's understanding of the matter, although he eventually cancelled it, deserves consideration.

Morgann also raises a still-unresolved question about the rationale of the inverted life-insurance practice. Why should an underwriter have agreed to repay from three to five for one on a safe return from Venice or Edinburgh—places mentioned in the contemporary references and documents? In calling the practice 'reckless speculation' rather than 'honest enterprise', George Unwin, *Shakespeare's England*, ed. Sidney Lee (Oxford, 1916), i. 334, seems to beg rather than clarify the question. Thompson 1928 argues that 'the fact that such a system was found profitable by the bankers shows us how great were the risks in travelling then'. But was travel *that* hazardous? Were the odds even two to

one against a traveller returning safely from Edinburgh to London? Bothered
by this point, Lee 1907, Jones 1913, and Boorman 1957 suggest that the traveller
may have wagered five to one on his chance of returning safely, but their conjecture runs counter to the evidence that it was the underwriters who paid
five for one. In an effort to make the underwriters' behaviour plausible, Hanmer
1744 observed that 'the increase bore a proportion to the length and danger of
the voyages', Knight 1841 that '*Five for one* appears to have been the rate for
a very distant voyage', and Hunter 1857, p. 102ᵛ, that the sum deposited was
'doubled, trebled, quadrupled and quintupled . . . according to distance,
length of time and hazard'. More recent scholars have claimed that the traveller
had to fulfil other conditions over and above returning alive. Mentioning such
conditions in general, Kermode 1954 exemplifies with the only one which is
documented (see William West, *Symboloeography* [1544], I. ii, secs. 120 and
121), the fairly obvious stipulation that the traveller had to produce proof of
having been where he was supposed to go. Also wishing, it appears, to meet
the sort of objection raised by Morgann, Kittredge 1939 and Alexander 1951,
glossary, say that the traveller, in addition to returning safely, had to come back
within a specified time limit, while Winny 1963 says that he had further to
prove 'he had accomplished some set task'. Such hypotheses, which are not
borne out by the known contemporary evidence, underline the difficulty to
which Morgann draws attention.

Morgann's positive interpretation grows out of his baffled encounter with
Theobald's note. The 'foregone Folly' to which he alludes is Theobald's con-
fession that, until set right by Thirlby and Warburton, he 'understood the
Passage thus: that every *five* Travellers (or *Putters out*) did bring authentick
Confirmation of these Stories, for *one* that pretended to dispute the Truth of
them'. Theobald goes on to trace his education on the point as follows:

Mr. Warburton observ'd to me . . . That, particularly, by *Each Putter out of Five
for One*, was meant the Adventurers in the Discovery of the *West Indies*, who had for the
Money they advanc'd, and contributed, 20 *per Cent.*—Dr. Thirlby did not a little assist
this Explanation by his Concurrence, and by instructing me, that it was usual in those
Times for Travellers to put out Money, to receive a greater Sum if they liv'd to return.

Morgann is clearly puzzled by this reference to Thirlby's and Warburton's
explanations, which are quite different, as being one and the same. Theobald
appears to be unintentionally guilty of the confusion for two reasons, both tied
up with the special point of view from which he writes. First, since he at one
time took 'putter out' to mean 'traveller', Warburton and Thirlby have the
common denominator, important for him but for no one else, of understanding
a 'putter out' to be in the first instance an investor. Second, he is absorbed in
puffing what he rightly regards as his personal contribution, the emending of
Folio 'putter out of five for one' to 'putter out on five for one'; and this change
will indifferently make Thirlby's or Warburton's interpretation more intelligible. Thus, compounding the confusion, Theobald goes on to produce the
quotation from Ben Jonson reproduced above, which he asserts, still referring
to the two quite divergent interpretations as if they were a single one, 'will
put both their Explanation, and my Correction of the Text, past dispute'. In
point of fact, the quotation supports only Thirlby's explanation and justifies
Theobald's correction only as applied to Thirlby's view. Small wonder that

Morgann, trying to make sense out of all this, should be provoked by Theobald's 'right past dispute', and erroneously conclude that Thirlby based his view on Warburton and that Theobald misunderstood Thirlby—and misapplied Jonson.

Warburton 1747 adopted Theobald's emendation, and saying never a word about 20 per cent interest explained non-committally that the travellers' 'ventures' on their expeditions 'are alluded to in the title given them of putters out on five for one'. In dealing with the 20 per cent interest theory, therefore, Morgann is discussing an idea later abandoned by Warburton and seemingly taken up by no one else except Wilson 1923; but he rephrases the proposal accurately, even though he applies the term 'Adventurers' to the travelling borrowers, whereas Warburton as cited in Theobald's note uses the term for the stay-at-home lenders.

Morgann's final conjecture about the true original reading is somewhat obscured. Having re-established the Folio reading, he then careted in 'or on' between the two words 'of five' in the phrase 'putter out of five for one'. In the context 'or on' makes no sense. Possibly he intended to write 'for on', i.e. 'putter out *of*—for [Theobald's] *on*—five for one'.

III. iii. 56. Theobald's note, which Morgann cancels, observes that 'the whole Set of Editions' reads 'Hath caused to belch you up'—obviously faulty grammar, which he has 'cur'd . . . by throwing out *you*'. The correction occurs in all subsequent eighteenth-century editions, and several later ones.

In point of fact, the first three Folios read 'belch up you'; F4 introduced 'belch you up', adopted by Rowe 1709 and Pope 1725, and rebuked by Theobald.

The significance of Morgann's cancellation is not clear. Since Theobald's note comes immediately below the conclusion of his longer one on III. iii. 48 on T51n, it may be that in lining through the latter, Morgann carelessly let his pen sweep down through the second note as well.

IV. i. 3. Theobald, in the justificatory note which Morgann cancels, explains his correction on the grounds earlier set forth in his letter to Concanen, 13 Mar. 1728 (Nichols 1817, pp. 201–2), that Prospero, as a widower with no other child, would if thinking mathematically regard Miranda as half of his life, 'nor could he intend that he lov'd himself twice as much as he did her; for he immediately subjoins that it was *She for whom he liv'd*'. Theobald cites Oth. I. i. 87 as a parallel for Prospero's regarding Miranda as half his life and quotes H5 III. vi. 49, 1H6 I. i. 34, 2H6 IV. ii. 31, and Oth. V. ii. 207 to illustrate Shakespeare's fondness for the phrase 'thread of life'. In approving Theobald's emendation, Morgann joins the dominant trend, as illustrated in Johns. Earlier editions carried a protest by Johnson against Theobald's 'ratiocination' (1765–78) and restored the Folio reading (1765–85); but Johnson's protest was first swamped under new notes by others vindicating Theobald (1778–93), then dropped (1785–93); and finally 'thread' appeared in the text (1793). The meaning 'thread', spelled *thread, thrid,* or *third,* has since had a continuous history of scholarly acceptance (e.g. Globe 1864, E. Dowden, *Shakspere* [1874], p. 425, Alexander 1951), except for arithmetical interpreters, who hold Prospero's three thirds to be Miranda, himself, and (*a*) his realm, Milan (Capell 1783, pp. 67–8, Rann 1786, Furness 1892, Lee 1907, Neilson and Hill 1942, Kermode

1954), or (*b*) his wife (Wilson 1921, Craig 1951), or (*c*) Ferdinand (Holt 1749, p. 66). Frye 1959 proposes 'Prospero's love, his knowledge and his power . . . ?'

IV. i. 14. The 'latter commentators' Morgann refers to in his ED and still bears in mind in his final version may include Warburton 1747, who notes simply that 'virgin-knot' alludes 'to the Latin phrase of Zonam solvere'. Almost certainly, however, Morgann is thinking of the following comment by Henley in Johns. Sup. 1780, ii. 85–1793:

> This, and the passage in *Pericles Prince of Tyre* [IV. ii. 160]
>
> Untide I still my *virgin-knot* will keepe

are manifest allusions to the zones of the antients, which were worn as guardians of chastity by marriageable young women. Puellae, contra, nondum viripotentes, hujusmodi zonis non utebantur: quod videlicet immaturis virgunculis nullum, aut certe minimum, a corruptoribus periculum immineret: quas propterea vocabant ἀμίτρους, nempe *discinctas*. There is a passage in NONNUS [*Dionysiaca*, xvi. 267–9], which will sufficiently illustrate Prospero's expression.

> Κούρης δ' ἐγγὺς ἵκανε· καὶ ἀτρέμας ἄκρον ἐρύσσας
> Δεσμὸν ἀσυλήτοιο φυλάκτορα λύσατο μίτρης
> Φειδομένῃ παλάμῃ, μὴ παρθένον ὕπνος ἐάσσῃ.

Thomas Edwards, *Canons of Criticism* (1750), pp. 134–5, ridiculed Warburton's note on the subject as one of those 'which either explane things which do not want explanation, or such as do not explane matters at all, but merely fill up so much paper'. Gifford 1813 cancels the Henley note. Modern editors and critics, when they offer a comment, usually take the words in the literal sense understood by Morgann. Exceptions: Luce 1901 and Kermode 1954, who continue to invoke the zones.

IV. i. 36–7. On 'Ben' and the 'Nest of antics' see *Com.* III. ii. 3. The only comment on Johns. 1765–93 is by Johnson, who identifies 'the rabble' as 'the crew of meaner spirits' in l. 35. Furness 1892 says the term is not a slighting one. Curry 1935, p. 192, takes the 'meaner fellows' to be lesser spirits in the neo-Platonic hierarchy: see above, note to *Com.* I. ii. 250.

IV. i. 59. Capell 1787, p. 68, declares that the masque in Tp. was 'written in compliance with fashion, the time swarming with them; (witness the works of Jonson, which in manner are sunk by them) and against the grain seemingly, being weak throughout, faulty in rimes, and faulty in it's mythology'. Morgann goes further, regarding the masque as a foreign element in the play as originally conceived (cf. *Com.* I. ii. 188) and so anticipating a spectrum of later criticism ranging from those who look upon the masque as an interpolation in an otherwise little-changed play to those who, like Gray 1921, p. 131, and Wilson 1921, p. 80, regard it as primary evidence for the play's having been considerably revised. Morgann differs from many of these critics, however—e.g. from Clark and Glover 1863, note to Tp. IV. i. 146, Fleay 1886, p. 249, and Law 1921, pp. 26–7—in avoiding the suggestion or hope that someone other than Shakespeare wrote the masque.

IV. i. 139–63. It is not clear what commentators other than Warburton Morgann was thinking of. In Johns. 1765–85, as in Theobald 1733, he could find, duly credited, only the same note by Warburton which also appeared in Warburton 1747. (In Johns. 1793 Warburton's note was dropped, allowing more space for the discussion of two points which in earlier editions of Johns. had been attracting increasing attention—the meaning of the word 'rack' and the relation of the passage to an analogue in Sir William Alexander, Earl of Stirling's *Tragedy of Darius*.) In his note Warburton inquired how Prospero could be angry for the reason he alleges—'the Plot of a contemptible *Savage*, and two drunken Sailors, whom he has absolutely in his Power'. The answer, Warburton explained, is that Prospero is not moved by any 'Apprehension of Danger', but by 'the Resentment of Ingratitude'. Caliban's conspiracy reminded him of his brother's, and 'that these Two, who had receiv'd at his hands the two best Gifts that mortals are capable of, when rightly apply'd, *Regal Power* and the *Use of Reason*; that These, in return, should conspire against the Life of the Donor, would certainly afflict a generous Mind to its utmost bearing.'

Virtually all subsequent comment has followed Warburton's lead in discovering something more than the mere imminence of Caliban's conspiracy behind Prospero's distemper. According to Phillpotts, Rugby edition of Shakespeare (1876)—the only critic other than Warburton cited in Furness 1892 on the passage—Prospero is overwrought by 'a sense of all injuries past and present surging in his mind at once' and wishes to clear his thoughts of the desire for revenge on his enemies. Tillyard 1938, p. 54, follows Phillpotts, while the original Arden editor and his successor follow Warburton, each with a supplement of his own. Luce 1901, p. lix, believes that Prospero's philosophizing also reveals Shakespeare pondering his own dramatic career as it draws to a close—a common enough idea till recently: cf. Conway 1921, p. 186, Howarth 1936, p. 45, and see note to *Com.* V. i. 33–57. Kermode 1954, p. lxxxv, suggests that Prospero's 'apparently unnecessary perturbation' may also be caused by a crudely applied neo-Terentian principle of comic structure. Garrett 1937, p. 60, claims that Prospero is outraged because he regards the revolt of a slave against his master as a peculiarly monstrous crime. More recently, Clifford Leech, 'The Structure of the Last Plays', *Shakespeare Survey*, xi (1958), 27 and 30, traces Prospero's perturbation to his sense of responsibility for Caliban and finds in his philosophizing 'a commentary' on his 'assertions of power'.

Modern exponents of the theory that Tp. is revised find support for their view in Prospero's seemingly unmotivated perturbation. Calling the episode 'dramatically inappropriate', Wilson 1921, pp. 81–2, says that Prospero's philosophizing is 'irrelevant' at a moment when 'he is evidently in great haste "to prepare to meet with Caliban" '. The 'absurd' pause in the action, he asserts, is one more proof that the play has been revised. Gray 1921, pp. 135–6 (cf. Gray 1920, p. 328), argues that Prospero's behaviour in the extant play is inexplicable because, in the process of revision, his passion has been severed from its rational causes. In the earlier play, he explains, Prospero was quite understandably perturbed over a temporarily successful plot to steal his books and powers. Morgann rejects by implication all such arguments.

Wilson 1921, note to Epilogue, regards the Epilogue as an apology to James I 'for dabbling in magic', but does not connect the utterance with his revision theory. Morgann, on the other hand, treats the present passage, which he connects with the Epilogue, as evidence of revision only in so far as he finds that Prospero's relation to magic takes into account James I's disapproval of the practice. Otherwise he emphasizes the original and striking idea that Prospero's passion arises from his sense of the precarious position in which his practice of magic places him (cf. ED recorded in *app. crit.* to I56:5). The only critic to interpret even approximately along similar lines seems to be Howarth 1936, p. 43, who touches on the 'element of uncertainty' created by the chance that the spirits may revolt against Prospero.

The connection Morgann notes between magic and silence was also remarked by Johnson, Johns. 1765–93, note to IV. i. 58 and by Steevens, Johns. 1778–93, note to Epilogue, l. 10.

IV. i. 186. For the place in Morgann's revision theory of his view that the effects of sartorial splendour are spectacular irrelevancies added to the play see above, pp. 409–10. Johns. 1765–93 lets the passage go by in silence, but other commentators, both in the eighteenth century and more recently, have found various subtleties. Warburton 1747 thought that the trumpery was necessary because, in order to have power over his subject, the conjurer had to have him at the disadvantage of committing some such sin as theft. Edwards 1750, pp. 66–7, and Holt 1749, p. 78, laughed at this notion, the latter holding the true explanation to be that the trumpery diverts the assassins from entering the cave and perpetrating their villainy, a possibility which, if not forestalled, would leave the stage painfully empty of actors and action. Agreeing with Holt, Luce 1901 (cf. p. xlvii) and Kermode 1954 add that the episode further reveals the characters of Caliban and his confederates.

V. i. 4. Morgann is original in his conception of dramatic time as running off perhaps six times faster than real time. The usual view in his day was that indefinite periods might elapse between the scenes and acts, but that within each scene, as Johnson, Johns. 1765–93, Preface, put it, 'of so much action as is represented, the real and poetical duration is the same' (cf. Dryden ed. Watson, i. 28). On the other hand, in deprecating the unities, here and in *Com.*, Introduction, Morgann writes in a quite common eighteenth-century vein. Equally common is his notion, still generally accepted despite the demurrer by Johnson (Johns. 1765, viii, Appendix–1793, final note to Tp.), that in Tp. Shakespeare went out of his way to write a play according to the rules. Gildon 1710, p. 261, especially admired Shakespeare's limiting the action to three and a half hours, thus making the play 'far more Regular in that Particular, than any that I know of on the Stage'. Steevens, Johns. 1778–93, note to V. i. 136, noted how 'rigidly' the unity of time is observed, the fable scarcely taking up more time than is employed in the representation, and with what 'very particular care' Shakespeare points out 'this circumstance in so many other passages, as well as here'. In the matter of interpreting this fact, Morgann is unique. Steevens thought that Shakespeare desired to show the Jonsonians that 'he too could write a play within all the strictest laws of regularity, when he chose to load himself with the critick's fetters'. This persists, by and large, as the standard explanation, e.g. in Kittredge 1939, p. xvi, though Munro 1946, p. 68, sees rather the influence of an unknown dramatic source. No one else has ever drawn Morgann's inference, as expounded here, and in *Com.* Introduction, and V. i. 223 (Marginal Note) that Shakespeare was submitting to a pedantry which he did not fully grasp and from which he quickly emancipated himself. In his strictures on Shakespeare's mishandling of the unity of place, Morgann was preceded by Gildon 1710, p. 261, who objected to the storm scene as extraneous to a set of scenes which might otherwise be 'reasonably supposed pretty contiguous', and by Warton, *Adventurer*, 97 (9 Oct. 1753), in Smith 1916, p. 59, who observed that 'it would have been more artful and regular' for Shakespeare to confine the action to the 'single spot' of Prospero's cave.

Morgann also discusses the unities in *Es.*, T70, LR 3a, and LR 3—ED 1.

V. i. 33 ff. *Com.* I. ii. 250, I164:2, seems to be the earliest notice of the present-day commonplace that, for all its sublimity, Prospero's invocation of the elves, etc., seems to be irrelevant to the play. Entirely ignoring this point, comment on the passage in Johns. 1773–85 was largely concerned with the discovery in Warburton 1747 that the lines were taken from Ovid's *Medea* and with Farmer's opinion that for his version of Ovid Shakespeare depended entirely on Golding's translation. When in Johns. 1793 Steevens observed of the elves, etc., 'to what purpose they were invoked does not very distinctly appear', he had in mind only the anacoluthon in relation to the conclusion of the speech, 'But this rough magic', etc. The note on V. i. 48–50 in Theobald 1733, which Morgann cancels, cites *Bonduca* and Virgil to justify the apparent oddity 'of *Graves waking their Dead* instead of the Dead waking in their Graves'. Perhaps Morgann lines through Theobald's comment because he feels that his own, that 'no appropriate application can be Made' of Prospero's speech (*Com.* I. ii. 250), is far more relevant to these lines which speak of resurrecting the dead. Not till the Victorian period does it appear to have been remarked that this claim of Prospero's is inharmonious with the powers he actually displays in Tp. The observation apparently emerged as a concomitant of the view, unknown in Morgann's day, that Prospero's speech here, like his earlier philosophizing after his 'passion' (see note to *Com.* IV. i. 139–63), is part of Shakespeare's personal valedictory to his dramatic art. This theory appears first to have been advanced by Campbell 1838, p. lxiii (after hints by Coleridge ed. Raysor, i. 131 and 133, and the *Retrospective Review*, vii [1823], 381), and it soon became established critical dogma. Conway 1921, p. 182, could say that the passage under consideration 'is so disproportioned, so out of relation to its setting, that an allegorical, that is an extra-dramatic, interpretation seems forced upon us, and has been adopted by such eminently sane writers as James Russell Lowell and George Brandes, who are followed, I believe, by all later critics'. The inference which Conway found inevitable, that Shakespeare rends the veil of dramatic objectivity to reveal his own feelings, could still be described as generally acceptable to 'latter-day scholars' by Munro 1946, p. 61 (including himself, p. 68), but as Cellini 1964, p. 1, reports, it is 'oggi caduta un po' in disgrazia'. However, it is still recognized that the speech is not readily applicable to Prospero. Noting the apparent inappropriateness of Prospero's claim to have brought back the dead, Kermode 1954 explains that 'the function of the speech is not . . . informative . . .; its object is the general one of using every possible resource to enforce the potency of his powers, immediately before he abjures them'. Sisson 1958, p. 76, declares more roundly: 'It is difficult to reconcile ourselves . . . to his claim to have opened graves and to have resurrected the dead. . . . The invocation, in fact, conflicts with our conception of Prospero as a white magician.'

V. i. 50–1. The statute prescribing the death penalty for black magic was conveniently reproduced in Johnson's initial note to Mac., Johns. 1765–93.

V. i. 85. Cf. *Com.* V. i. 267.

V. i. 149. See *Com.* V. i. 196, 204, and 213.

V. i. 174. This suggestion of Morgann's, which appears to have occurred to no one else, is a consistent if refined extension of the kind of reasoning involved in *Com.* I. ii. 120 and I. ii. 351. Morgann may also be reacting to Johnson's elaborate paraphrase of the passage, which rejects the suggestion by Warburton 1747 that 'score'=the 'stake' of the bet or wrangle. Johnson's gloss, Johns. 1765–93, is: 'Ferdinand would not, he says, play her false for the *world*: yes, answers she, I would allow you to do it for something less than the world, for *twenty kingdoms*, and I wish you well enough to allow you, after a little wrangle, that your play was fair.'

V. i. 190. Morgann's observation derives from Warburton: see note to *Com.* I. ii. 396 and cf. *Com.* I. ii. 318.

V. i. 196. Cf. *Com.* V. i. 149, 204, and 213.

V. i. 215–18. For Morgann's view that the first scene of the play is an added Induction see *Com.* I. i. 1 and note.

V. i. 236. Morgann here hesitantly anticipates a still sporadic and unvictorious rebellion against an emendation originally suggested to Theobald by Thirlby (7 May 1729, Nichols 1817, p. 234). Theobald's 'impertinence' is his sarcastic remark, refuted by Morgann, that by 'our trim' his predecessors in editing Shakespeare could only have understood, if they understood anything, 'the Fright' which the sailors 'had been put into by the Diversity of Noises'. Agreeing with Theobald, all subsequent eighteenth-century editors accepted the emendation. According to Furness 1892, Theobald was not challenged on this point till Knight 1841 restored Folio 'our trim'. Furness overlooked Sill 1797, p. 95, who defended the Folio reading on the grounds that a sailor 'speaking of his vessel, generally includes himself as a part of it' and hence, thinking of the ship, would say 'our'. Knight argues for 'our trim' because it 'expresses what Ariel had mentioned in the First Act, "On their sustaining garments not a blemish" '— i.e., in essence, Morgann's reasoning. But Knight failed to convince. Though Hunter 1857, p. 119, reads, 'our trim', all the editions collated by Furness 1892, from Collier 1842 to Wright 1891, retained 'her trim', which to this day is the usual reading. Exceptions are: Chambers 1904, Kermode 1954, Boorman 1957, Langbaum 1964, and Cellini 1964. Kermode justifies his decision in the

Morgann–Knight vein: 'They themselves being unscathed, saw their ship to be equally unharmed.'

V. i. 277 and 279. On Trinculo as a supposed vestige of the hypothetical earlier Tp. see *Com.* III. ii. 71, and cf. *Com.* I. ii. 233 and II. ii. 14.

V. i. 280. Theobald 1733 emended Folio 'liquor' to ''lixir', and was followed by Hanmer 1744 and Warburton 1747. The latter was only claiming his own, and accordingly reprinted the justificatory note which, duly acknowledged, had already appeared in Theobald 1733. By insinuating that 'Sack was the only Restorer of Youth and Bestower of Immortality', Warburton argued, Shakespeare was mocking the alchemists' grandiose claims for their 'gilded' *aurum potabile.* Though sufficiently impressed to reproduce Warburton's lengthy note without comment, Johnson none the less restored 'liquor' to the text (Johns. 1765–93), a reading which, except for Capell 1766 and 1783, ii. pt. 4, pp. 72–3, and Morgann, has since remained unchallenged. In Johns. 1773–93, Steevens subjoined a further note explaining Johnson's decision: 'As the Elixir was a liquour, the old reading may stand, and the allusion holds good without any alteration.' Holt 1749, p. 94, and Heath 1765, p. 40, had already made this observation, with which modern editors agree.

V. i. 311. See *Com.* IV. i. 139–63 and note, and *Com.* V. i. 50–1.

MISCELLANEOUS COMMENTS

MND. Introductory Comment. On Morgann's dating of Tp. see *Com.*, Introduction and note. As to Rom. and MND., it was generally agreed that they were early. In a note added to Rowe's 'Account of Shakespeare's Life' and reproduced in Johns. 1765–93, Pope 1725 had observed that 'the highest date' of any of Shakespeare's plays he could find was that of Rom. in 1597. Malone held that both plays were early because of the high frequency of rhyme in them. The earliness of MND., Malone thought, was further substantiated by the insignificance of its principal personages and its meagre and uninteresting fable.

Shakespeare's deficiency in the conversation of gentlemen had been a commonplace of criticism ever since Dryden ed. Watson, i. 68, 'Eassy of Dramatic Poesy' (1668), had pronounced Beaumont and Fletcher to be superior in imitating the 'wild debaucheries, and quickness of wit in repartees'. Morgann's standards for such conversation reflect, of course, later, post-Restoration taste. He perhaps innovates in trying to use the quality of polite conversation as a criterion for dating the plays, though Blackstone, Johns. Sup. 1880, i. 79–1793, initial note to MND., suggested that the relative absence in a play of 'pun and quibble' in general might indicate lateness. Morgann applied the criterion in *Com.*, Introduction and II. i. 9–107. Cf. also *Es.*, T49n–T50n.

MND. II. i. 101. Like most editors, including those of Johns. 1765–93, Morgann here follows Hanmer 1743 in accepting the conjecture 'cheer', which

Theobald 1733 mentioned only to let it be out-dazzled by what he called War-burton's 'more refin'd Emendation', 'heried' = 'praised', 'celebrated'. The stimulus to emend, as Theobald points out, is the fact that the concluding word in the line, as it stands, is 'a very dragging Expletive'.

MND. IV. i. 196. Morgann here follows the text and note of Theobald 1733, who takes over Warburton's suggested emendation of Folio 'jewell' to 'Gemell'. Subjoining Warburton's explanation that the sense calls for 'something that has the Property of *appearing* the same, and yet not *being* the same', Theobald adds that his friend's 'fine Conjecture' is a *hapax legomenon* in Shakespeare consistent with his general linguistic practice and habits of thought. Heath 1765, p. 57, scoffed at Warburton's inventiveness, but Johnson was unconvinced and pro-voked Ritson 1783, p. 46, to rebuke him for reprinting the note on the subject in Warburton 1747 with the observation: 'This emendation is ingenious enough to deserve to be true' (Johns. 1765–93). Morgann would have it not only true but also a *dis legomenon* applicable to 2H4 I. ii. 22. as well.

MND. V. i. 118. See Introductory Note to MND. and note.

MND. V. i. 408–9. Morgann here follows Johnson, Johns. 1765–93, who re-stored the lines to Oberon on the authority of the Quartos and claimed that the song itself was lost. This view was generally accepted in the eighteenth and nineteenth centuries. More recently, Richard Noble, *Shakespeare's Use of Song* (1923), p. 55, has suggested that the text as it stands is correct, with Oberon beginning to sing solo and then being joined by the fairies. Accepted by some editors, e.g. Wilson 1921 and Alexander 1951, Noble's proposal has, however, been rejected by others, e.g. Sisson 1956, who, like Johnson and Morgann, hold the song to be lost.

TG. Introductory Comment. Others who claim that TG. is not Shake-speare's include Hanmer 1744, initial note, Upton 1746, pp. 274–5 (also rejects LLL.), Pye 1792, p. 333, and Coleridge ed. Raysor, ii. 308 (letter postmarked 19 May 1818, 'apparently in Green's hand', according to Raysor, but catalogued at Shakespeare Folger Library as an autograph letter by Coleridge). Theobald 1733, initial note to play, regards TG. as one of Shakespeare's 'very worst' productions, and Malone, Johns. 1785, i. 285, describes it as 'hasty, undigested and uninteresting'. Johnson, Johns. 1765–93, initial note to TG., quotes Hanmer on the subject disapprovingly, rebukes Upton for pretending to unwarranted certainty in denying the play to Shakespeare, and goes on to praise the gnomic lines and beautiful verses in the play. In the final note to TG., Johns. 1773–93, Johnson inquires: 'If the play be taken from Shakespeare, to whom shall it be assigned?' Morgann is unusual in esteeming the play despite his conviction that Shakespeare is not the author.